3D STUD
PROFESSIONAL ANIMATION

ANGIE JONES

SEAN BONNEY

BRANDON DAVIS

SEAN MILLER

SHANE OLSEN

COVER ART BY ANGIE JONES

New Riders

201 West 103rd Street, Indianapolis, Indiana 46290

CHAPTER 1 • Sean Bonney

CHAPTER 11 • Brandon Davis

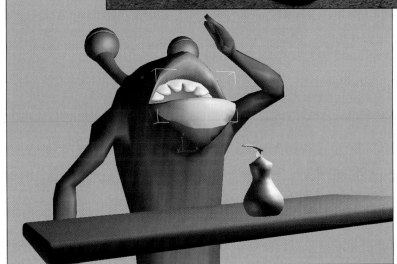

CHAPTER 1 • Sean Bonney

CHAPTER 4 • Mouth Mite by Nermin Bajagilovic (a.k.a. Cosmo) and Angie Jones

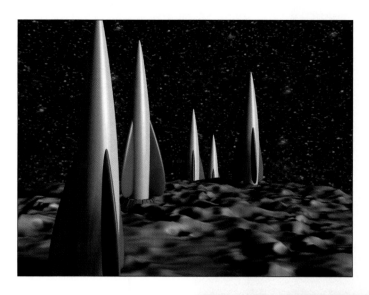

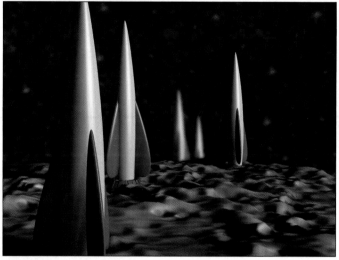

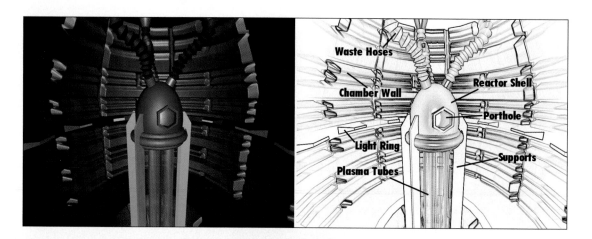

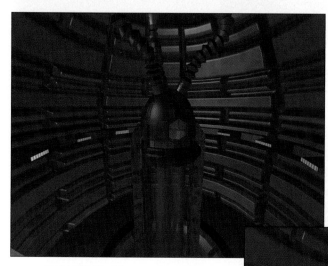

CHAPTER 10   •   Sean Bonney

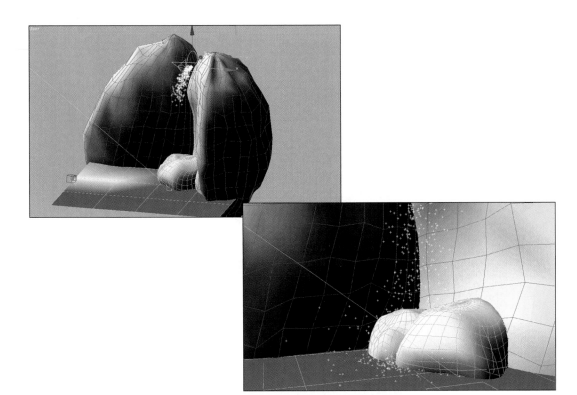

CHAPTER 11 • Brandon Davis

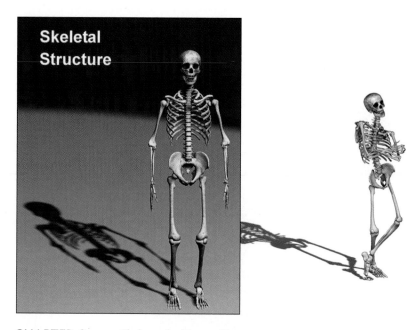

Skeletal
Structure

CHAPTER 3 • Skeleton by Troyan Turner
and Angie Jones

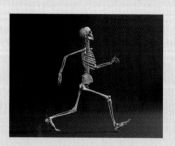
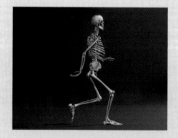
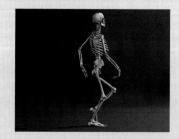

CHAPTER 3 • Skeleton by Troyan Turner and Angie Jones

 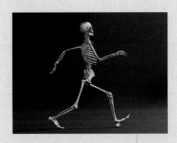

CHAPTER 4 • Angie Jones

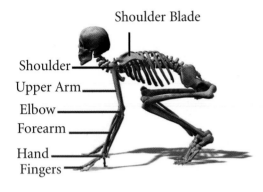

Shoulder Blade

Shoulder
Upper Arm
Elbow
Forearm

Hand
Fingers

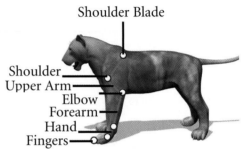

Shoulder Blade

Shoulder
Upper Arm
Elbow
Forearm
Hand
Fingers

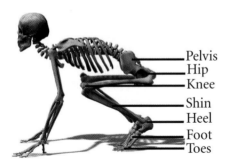

Pelvis
Hip
Knee
Shin
Heel
Foot
Toes

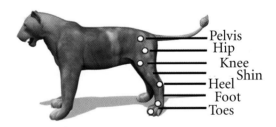

Pelvis
Hip
Knee
Shin
Heel
Foot
Toes

CHAPTER 3 • Lion by Zygote and Angie Jones
Skeleton by Troyan Turner and Angie Jones

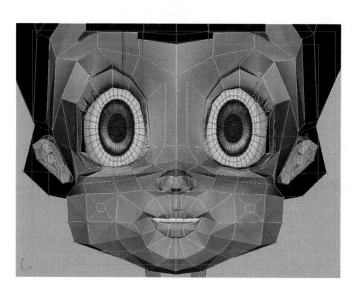

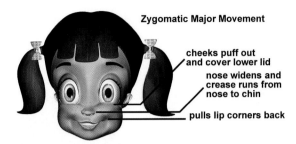

Zygomatic Major Movement

cheeks puff out
and cover lower lid

nose widens and
crease runs from
nose to chin

pulls lip corners back

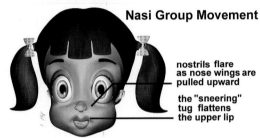

Nasi Group Movement

nostrils flare
as nose wings are
pulled upward

the "sneering"
tug flattens
the upper lip

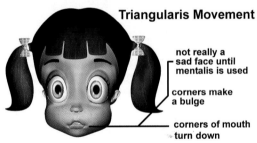

Triangularis Movement

not really a
sad face until
mentalis is used

corners make
a bulge

corners of mouth
turn down

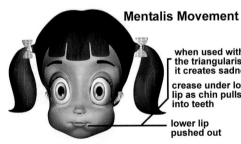

Mentalis Movement

when used with
the triangularis,
it creates sadness

crease under lower
lip as chin pulls
into teeth

lower lip
pushed out

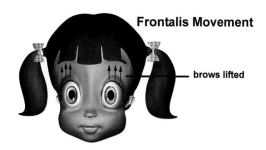

Frontalis Movement

— brows lifted

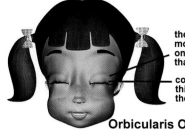

the lower lid
moves higher up
on the eye
than in a blink

compression of
this muscle creates
the eye squint

Orbicularis Oculi Movement

Orbicularis Oris Movement

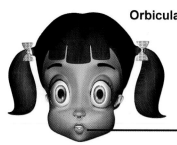

"oo" mouth pose;

this muscle can take on
many shapes

brows try to meet,
causing wrinkles

brow lowers
and protrudes out
like a shelf

Corrugator Group Movement

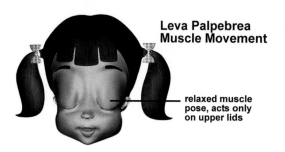

**Leva Palpebrea
Muscle Movement**

relaxed muscle
pose, acts only
on upper lids

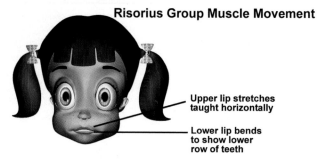

Risorius Group Muscle Movement

Upper lip stretches
taught horizontally

Lower lip bends
to show lower
row of teeth

3D STUDIO MAX® 3
PROFESSIONAL ANIMATION

ANGIE JONES

SEAN BONNEY

BRANDON DAVIS

SEAN MILLER

SHANE OLSEN

COVER ART BY ANGIE JONES

New Riders

201 West 103rd Street, Indianapolis, Indiana 46290

3D Studio MAX 3
Professional Animation

Copyright © 2000 by New Riders Publishing

International Standard Book Number: 0-7357-0945-9

Library of Congress Catalog Card Number: 99-068971

Printed in the United States of America

First Printing: February 2000

04 03 02 01 00   7 6 5 4 3 2

Interpretation of the printing code: The rightmost double-digit number is the year of the book's printing; the rightmost single-digit number is the number of the book's printing. For example, the printing code 00-1 shows that the first printing of the book occurred in 2000.

Trademarks

Warning and Disclaimer

Publisher
David Dwyer

Associate Publisher
Brad Koch

Executive Editor
Steve Weiss

Acquisitions Editor
Laura Frey

Development Editors
Linda Laflamme
Barb Terry

Managing Editor
Jennifer Eberhardt

Project Editor
John Rahm

Copy Editor
Audra McFarland

Technical Editors
Mark Gerhard
Jeff Solenberg

Compositors
Kim Scott
Wil Cruz

Proofreaders
Bob LaRoche
Debra Neel
Linda Seifert

Indexer
Lisa Stumpf

Software Development Specialist
Jay Payne

Contents at a Glance

Table of Contents

Introduction

Part III Animating the Environment

About the Authors

Angie Jones is a 3D animator with over six years' experience with 3D Studio MAX and specializing in character animation. She is currently an animator at Oddworld Inhabitants (www.oddworld.com), creators of the Sony PlayStation games Abe's Oddysee and Abe's Exoddus and currently producing Munch's Oddysee. Prior to joining Oddworld Inhabitants in May of 1998, she was a Senior 3D Animator at The Lightspan Partnership Inc. At Lightspan, Angie worked on over 25 of the 60+ character driven educational software products released for the PC and Sony PlayStation. In 1995, Jones also worked on the children's educational TV show *Reality Check* for Mindflex, Inc., New Line Home Video, and Conduit Communications. This production aired on both NBC and CBS affiliates in the Summer and Fall of 1995. She also worked as a successful freelance and animator in Atlanta, Georgia after graduating from the Atlanta College of Art in 1994. Other credits to her freelance career include: Coca-Cola USA, McDonald's Worldwide, and Majority Stock Presentations; AT&T True Experience On-line Interface; Castleway Entertainment Film Trailer; and the "Cyberdillo" 3DO Game by Panasonic. Finally, Angie was introduced to the field of technical writing by George Maestri with whom she co-authored another New Riders book, *Inside 3D Studio Max R2 Volume III Animation*. In addition, Angie was Artist and Tech Editor for George Maestri's *Digital Character Animation 2: Essential Techniques*. Her freelance work and her drive to help others learn about computer animation continues under the identity of Spicy Cricket Animation at http://www.spicycricket.com who you see on the cover of this book.

Seán Bonney is a 3D animator, fine artist, and designer who lives in historic Fredericksburg, Virginia. His effects career began at age 10 with the careful construction, pyrotechnic rigging, and fiery destruction of a model B-17 bomber. After considering the vast influence George Lucas holds in the computer graphics industry, Seán has refused to reveal the final fate of his Star Wars action figures. Seán graduated from Virginia Commonwealth University in Richmond, VA, in 1991, with a B.F.A. in Illustration and Design. He has been employed as Graphic Designer for the Central Rappahannock Regional Library system for eight years. He has worked for Rainbow Studios in Phoenix, AZ, on a variety of game and broadcast projects. Sean is currently the principal of Anvil Studios, and specializes in freelance animation and game design. For more information about Seán Bonney or Anvil Studio, visit the website at anvil-studio.com or email sbonney@anvil-studio.com.

Brandon Davis is an effects animator at visual effects studio Computer Café on the California central coast. Though his background covers many facets of 3D animation, including AEC, design visualization, and game development, he specializes in procedural animation, particle and volumetric effects for broadcast, cinematics, and film. He has made a name for himself in the 3D industry by consistently annoying people and telling bad jokes about his former days as a paratrooper.

Sean Miller, who has a background in fine arts, theater, and computer graphics, is a character animator at Oddworld Inhabitants. The head of the real-time animation team for the 3D adventure game Oddworld: Munch's Oddysee, he has also worked on the in-game character animations and the award-winning cinematics for the game Oddworld: Abe's Exoddus.

Shane Olsen is an artist with the gaming company Saffire, which creates games for Nintendo, Electronic Arts, G.T. Interactive, and Midway. Recently he worked on several characters for Titus's new Xena Warrior Princess: The Talisman of Fate game for Nintendo 64.

Dedications

Angie Jones:

For Tuong, who has taught me patience and passion

Sean Bonney:

To Brigid and Bonnie, two amazing grandmothers

Acknowledgments

Angie Jones

This book belongs to the people listed below, for if I had not had their help, encouragement, creative and technical input, this book would not exist.

Special thanks to Javier Solsona for his assistance with the MAXScript sections of this book. Truly a technical genius and a very patient man with my demanding insistence on specific CG tools for the animator.

A "shout out" to Mike Brown and Michael Comet for their technical support and encouragement with 3D Studio MAX IK systems.

An extra big thank you to Hal Hickel and Andrew Gordon for their critical animator's eyes and Kyle Clark and Michael Ford for a most excellent and informative website (www.animfound.com).

The dialog voice-over for the Facial chapter was provided by the gracious Lani Minella (http://www.spicycricket.com/audiogodz.html), and I thank her for her undying enthusiasm and support.

Thank you to Eric Pinkel for being the "cool daddy-o" he is and Jo-ann Panchak at Autodesk for always coming through.

Thanks to everyone on the CG-Char mailing list for inspiration and support.

I was very fortunate to have 3 very generous modelers create some great models for this book. The beautiful skeleton was provided by Troyan Turner, the mouth mite creature was provided by Nermin Bajagilovic a.k.a. Cosmo, and Shane Olson was very gracious in creating the Dorothy character used throughout this book.

Also, thanks to Zygote for providing the Lioness model.

Without the organizational and editing skills of Linda Laflamme and Laura Frey I just do not know where my head would be. Thanks for your significant contribution!

Thanks to Tuong Nguyen for just being there and for your constant love and support.

Sean Bonney

I would like to thank Chad Carter for his valuable research assistance with the Animating Cameras chapter.

A Message from New Riders

Just a note of welcome if you're new to New Riders's MAX publishing line, and a friendly salutation if you're already familiar with our MAX books. New Riders is the industry leader in 3D CG publishing and in MAX publishing in particular. Whatever your needs, we probably have at least one title—if not several—that belong nearby your computer in your daily work: from *3D Studio MAX 3 Fundamentals* to *Inside 3D Studio MAX 3* (the BIG book) to *Inside 3D Studio MAX 3: Modeling, Materials and Rendering;* from the specialized breakout hit *3D Studio MAX 3 Media Animation* to the book you're reading now, New Riders is dedicated to creating the MAX resources you truly need. We think we're on the right track: more and more educational programs are picking up New Riders graphics titles for use in the classroom and in corporate education…

A quick but important message of thanks, as well, to each of the amazingly talented artists/teachers who wrote this book:

Angie Jones, we're awed by your talents and thrilled to make you and Spicy a member of the New Riders family!

Sean Bonney, it's been a distinct pleasure to discover a new talent. This kind of thrill never gets old, and we look forward to many more adventures together.

Brandon Davis, Sean Miller, and Shane Olsen: Each of you has made this book immeasurably richer for your unique contributions; thanks for your expertise and your insight.

And on behalf of everyone who made this book happen, we hope you'll let us know how *3D Studio Max 3 Professional Animation* works for you and how we can make all of our books ever-better. Thanks, and please keep in touch!

How to Contact Us

As the reader of this book, you are our most important critic and commentator. We value your opinion and want to know what we're doing right, what we could do better, in what areas you'd like to see us publish, and any other words of wisdom you're willing to pass our way.

As the Executive Editor for the Graphics team at New Riders, I welcome your comments. You can fax, email, or write me directly to let me know what you did or didn't like about this book—as well as what we can do to make our books better. When you write, please be sure to include this book's title, ISBN, and author, as well as your name and phone or fax number. I will carefully review your comments and share them with the authors and editors who worked on the book. For any issues directly related to this or other titles:

Email: steve.weiss@newriders.com

Mail: Steve Weiss
            Executive Editor
            Professional Graphics & Design Publishing
            New Riders Publishing
            201 West 103rd Street
            Indianapolis, IN 46290 USA

Visit Our Website: www.newriders.com

On our website you'll find information about our other books, the authors we partner with, book updates and file downloads, promotions, discussion boards for online interaction with other users and with technology experts, and a calendar of trade shows and other professional events with which we'll be involved. We hope to see you around.

Email Us from Our Website

Go to www.newriders.com and click on the Contact link if you

- Have comments or questions about this book
- Want to report errors that you have found in this book
- Have a book proposal or are otherwise interested in writing with New Riders
- Would like us to send you one of our author kits
- Are an expert in a computer topic or technology and are interested in being a reviewer or technical editor

- Want to find a distributor for our titles in your area
- Are an educator/instructor who wishes to preview New Riders books for classroom use. (Include your name, school, department, address, phone number, office days/hours, text currently in use, and enrollment in your department in the body/comments area, along with your request for desk/examination copies, or for additional information.

Call Us or Fax Us

You can reach us toll-free at (800) 571-5840 + 9+ 3567. Ask for New Riders. If outside the USA, please call 1-317-581-3500 and ask for New Riders.

If you prefer, you can fax us at 1-317-581-4663, Attention: New Riders.

Technical Support/Customer Support Issues

Call 1-317-581-3833, from 10:00 a.m. to 3 p.m. US EST (CST from April through October of each year—unlike most of the rest of the United States, Indiana doesn't change to Daylight Savings Time each April).

You can also email our tech support team at userservices@macmillanusa.com, and you can access our tech support website at http://www.mcp.com/product_support/mail_support.cfm.

Introduction

In the tradition of the previous 3D Studio
MAX books brought to you by New Riders, *3D
Studio MAX 3 Professional Animation* brings
you all you would expect from an insider professional animation book and more! Real
workflow applications are described in detail

using the features and functions provided in 3D Studio MAX Release 3. This book provides tutorials written by real working professionals, so you can be sure the information is applicable to any studio pipeline. In addition, line-by-line explanations of how to create scripts with the newly implemented MAXScript in R3 will take your controls and animation to the next level of computer graphics.

Organization of the Book

3D Studio MAX 3 Professional Animation is organized in three sections:

- Part I, "Animation Techniques," includes Chapter 1.
- Part II, "Character Animation," includes Chapters 2 through 8.
- Part III, "Animating the Environment," includes Chapters 9 through 12.

Part I covers animation techniques in MAX 3. This section does not describe the tools; instead, it describes the techniques that are best served by MAX R3's tools and plug-ins. Animation tutorials take you through the steps needed to animate with transforms, controllers, expressions, and multiple modifiers. By learning how to mix tools, you will expand your animation toolkit and improve your ability to achieve desired animation results.

Part II takes you through the unique world of character animation. From creating a character to animating it with MAX tools and plug-ins, this section teaches the best methods of animating for a variety of situations.

Part III explores animating the environment. These chapters cover how to animate cameras, light, and atmosphere to achieve the feel you are looking for in your animation. You'll also learn how to animate with particles and space warps to generate a number of effects.

How to Read the Exercises

Unlike most tutorials you read, this book's exercises do not rigidly dictate every step that you perform to achieve the desired result. These exercises are designed to be flexible and to work in a wide range of situations. This approach provides you with the following benefits:

- *A better understanding of the concepts.* You must think through the example rather than blindly follow the minutiae of many steps.

- *The opportunity to apply the examples to your own work.* The flexibility built into the exercises enables you to experiment with the effects until you achieve the results you want.

Most exercises begin with some explanatory text, as shown in the following sample exercise. The text tells you what the exercise should accomplish and sets the context for the exercise.

Because this book is designed for people who already have some experience with 3D Studio MAX 3, some exercise steps are implied rather than explicitly stated. You might, for example, find yourself instructed to "Create a smooth, 20-segment sphere with a radius of 100 units," rather than reading all the steps required to create the object.

Similarly, you will not always be given exact measurements for the scale and position of objects you create. In cases where the relationship between a newly created object and the rest of the scene is more important than numerically precise placement, you may be instructed to follow figures illustrating how the scene should be set up.

Part I

Animation Techniques

C h a p t e r 1

Animating with Multiple Modifiers

By Sean Bonney

Modifiers in 3D Studio MAX enable you to shape, tweak, sculpt, and otherwise deform geometry without committing to any changes. At any time, the animator can tweak the parameters of, deactivate, delete, add, or change the order of modifiers to the selected geometry. You can even copy modifiers from one object to another, easing the duplication of modifier-based effects.

This chapter explores the following topics:

- Animating object modifier parameters
- Interactive feedback within Edit Mesh, Editable Mesh, Mesh Select, and Volume Select operations
- Layering multiple modifiers
- Animation on the Object/Sub-Object level

Animating Object Modifier Parameters

Every object in 3D Studio MAX R3 has a *modifier stack* associated with it that contains the sum history of that object. This history includes the creation parameters of the object and the modifiers assigned to the object. Almost every entry in the modifier stack has animatable parameters.

The modifier stack is organized chronologically: The modifiers that were first assigned to a model are at the bottom of the stack, and the modifiers assigned to the model last are placed at the top of the stack. MAX uses the stack's order as an order of operations. As you add standard modifiers on top of an object's creation parameters, you may choose to animate different parameters of those modifiers. The gizmos that control the placement of such effects as Bend, Skew, Twist, and Taper can be animated over time. Furthermore, the strength and angles, as well as other attributes, can be animated. Many of the modifiers you use to model your scenes are also excellent tools for achieving beautiful animation. By layering multiple modifiers, you can achieve very complicated and sophisticated animation with minimal work.

Take, for example, the case of a simple tube morphing into a delicate vase. This sort of transformation can be created by animating the parameters of only a few modifiers (see Figure 1.1).

First, the tube in Figure 1.1 had the Spherify modifier applied. This modifier, new to R3, deforms an object toward a spherical volume. Taper was then applied to stretch the volume and curvature of the tube (see Figure 1.2).

Figure 1.1 The effect of cumulative modifiers: a standard tube primitive, with Spherify applied, and with both Spherify and Taper.

Figure 1.2 The modifier stack for the shape-changing vase, as shown in the Edit Modifier Stack dialog box.

If you would like to experiment with the results of changing the order of modifiers in the stack will have, you can do this easily within the Edit Modifier Stack dialog box. To reverse the order of the two modifiers, select the Spherify modifier and click on Cut. Then select the Taper modifier and click on Paste. The Paste button inserts the modifiers that have been copied or cut after the currently selected modifier.

These two modifiers' shape changes can be easily animated by simply turning the Animate button on and changing parameters in the Modifier panel at different frames. To see the effects of animating the vase, see the AVI file 01max00.avi.

Figure 1.3 shows the different shapes that would be created over time if you were to animate the Spherify and Taper parameters. The vase with the flower represents the final form.

Figure 1.3   The changes in the vase's form over time. The vase has been snapshot over the length of the animation, and the copies are arranged in a spiral to show various stages of the animation.

New Modifiers in R3

Among the many improvements in R3 are the addition of new modifiers, which will be of great aid to animators. Here are some highlights of new modifiers and exciting upgrades to existing ones:

- **Edit Mesh: Show End Result.** This toggle button passes Sub-Object editing changes to later modifiers in the stack, without requiring you to leave Sub-Object mode. This makes it very easy to see the effect that, for example, tweaking the position of a few vertices will have after MeshSmooth is applied. You will use this function in a later exercise to interactively view a smoothed version of a character animated on the sub-object level.

- **Edit Mesh: Soft Selection.** This feature, available in Vertex, Sub-Object mode, will revolutionize the way modifiers are used to animate mesh, patch, or NURMS objects. No longer are you restricted to applying modifiers to hard sub-object selections. Any modifier effect or control linkage can be applied in a gradated fashion. Imagine controlling a muscle bulge with a linked dummy object. If you link the dummy to a soft selection, muscle bulges will be smoothly spread out over the area you choose. Throughout this chapter, you will see how you can use soft selections to improve your animation in a variety of tasks.

- **Free Form Deformation.** This modifier has been improved to offer a Set Volume mode, which allows you to adjust control points without affecting the modified object. This gives you greater control over FFDs because you can position control points where they will be most effective. FFDs will be used in several exercises in this chapter to animate large, organic movements, often to a sub-object selection.

- **Flex.** An easy-to-use but very powerful tool, this modifier enables you to add natural secondary motion to animated objects. Flex causes an object's vertices to respond to simulated momentum, lagging behind the movement of a fast-moving object, for example. After a character has been animated, Flex is a great tool to use for adding the natural jiggle and recovery expected from organic objects. Later in this chapter, you will apply Flex on top of a completed character animation to add dynamic soft-body effects to the entire character.

- **Morpher.** This modifier offers fast and flexible object morphing with 100 morph channels, sub-object morph targets, and compound target creation on-the-fly. Morpher will be especially useful in pose-to-pose type animation, such as facial expressions. An exercise has been provided to show you how to use Morpher to provide facial animation to a character whose body is animated with other tools. Morpher can also be linked to the new Morpher Material, so that an object's materials will change in conjunction with its morph channels' settings.

- **Skin.** This skeletal deformation modifier is similar to the Physique portion of Character Studio. It lets you deform an object with another object, using envelopes to apply the deformation. Many options and techniques are available within the modifier to specify how movement is transferred to the deformed object. Later, you will deform a character using a hierarchy of pre-animated bones, tweaking bone envelopes to ensure that you're using anatomically proper deformation.

- **Editable Patch: Bind.** This command allows you to connect patch edges with unequal numbers of vertices. This makes it quite simple to connect a low detail area (such as an arm) to a high detail area (such as a hand) without leaving any obvious seams.

- **MeshSmooth.** In R3, this modifier offers a new output option, called NURMS, that enables you to weight vertices and edges to control the final shape of the object.

- **Push.** This modifier inflates or deflates an object along averaged vertex normals. This is a great aid for when you need a breathing or shrinking effect.

- **Melt.** This modifier, previously available as part of the Ishani MAX: Form free-ware plug-in from Harry Denholm and Ishani Graphics, is now built into MAX R3. Melt simulates the effect of melting an object. It offers several animatable options, such as degree of spread and simulated object solidity.

- **Squeeze.** This modifier moves an object's vertices inward, dependent on their proximity to the object's pivot point. This is similar to a Squash transformation, except that Squeeze applies influence on a curved basis rather than a linear basis.

- **Volume Select.** This modifier now allows you to use mesh objects, patches, NURBS, and even splines or particle systems to define the selection.

- **CrossSection and Surface.** Once part of the Surface Tools add-on, these two modifiers are now included in R3. They facilitate the creation of patch surfaces based upon splines. For organic shapes, such as character heads, these modifiers can be extremely helpful.

- **Displace Approx.** This modifier brings displacement mapping to modified meshes. Previously, only meshes that had been collapsed to editable meshes could be displaced.

- **Transform Gizmo.** This viewport icon appears whenever you select an object with a transform button active. This gizmo allows you to constrain transformation to an axis or plane, without having to select transform axes from the toolbar.

In addition, many of the modifiers present in previous versions of MAX have undergone subtle but very helpful changes. For example, the addition of a Center, Sub-Object mode to the Bend modifier allows for exact placement of the center of a bend effect, regardless of the position or scale of the Bend Gizmo.

Character Animation Using Multiple Modifiers

Your test subject for this chapter will be an alien figure nicknamed "Wormy" (see Figure 1.4). You will use Wormy to explore the possibilities afforded by modifier animation—especially the modifiers new to R3, which ease the creation and animation of organic models. You will make this character jump, wave, contort his face, and grab and toss objects. You will use a wide variety of techniques, from Free Form Deformation to Skin, to breathe life into a simple mesh creature. Throughout this chapter, you will familiarize yourself with tools that will prove useful not only in similar character animation, but in most any object animation.

Figure 1.4   Wormy says hello.

Edit Mesh and MeshSmooth for Sub-Object Animation

R3 boasts some substantial improvements to the Edit Mesh modifier. The primary change in terms of animation is in the functionality of the Show Results button. You can now view the effect of an Edit Mesh operation on subsequent modifiers while you're still in Sub-Object mode. In other words, you can use this feature to animate your base model, viewing the changes to its modified state interactively. In the first exercise, you will try this feature on Wormy.

Specifically, to make Wormy's tail curl, you will animate him as an editable mesh. When you're using sub-object animation, your object must be an editable mesh object. Sub-objects within an Edit Mesh modifier are not animatable. To animate sub-objects, you have to collapse to an editable mesh.

Sub-object animation allows you to animate the vertices, faces, and so on, of your object directly, transforming them over time to create your animation. The vertices of an object animated in this fashion show up in Track View with the default Bezier controller applied. You can perform key and curve edits, and you can assign individual controllers to vertices. When complex setups are not desirable, sub-object animation is a quick and simple animation method.

Note

The Edit Mesh modifier in MAX R3 duplicates almost all the functionality of the Editable Mesh base object (for example, the ability to Select Open Edges). However, direct Sub-Object level animation is still supported only in the base object.

1. Load the scene 01max01.max from the accompanying CD-ROM (see Figure 1.5). Wormy is supported by a pair of bars so he can perform some tail curls. To see the effects of animating the tail, see the AVI file 01max01.avi. For most exercises in this chapter, you will use a continuous mesh version of this figure. For this exercise, the tail has been detached as a separate object.

2. Open the Time Configuration dialog box. Set Start Time to 0 and End Time to 90. Assuming that Frame Rate is set to NTSC, or 30 frames per second, this will create an animation sequence lasting 3 seconds.

3. Select the tail object in the active viewport.

4. Apply a MeshSmooth modifier and note that the MeshSmooth Type is set to NURMS by default. This produces a Non-Uniform Rational MeshSmooth object, which is similar to a NURBS object in that control vertices and edges can be weighted to determine their influence on the NURMS shape. Under Surface

Parameters, check Smooth Result if it's not already checked, and check Separate by Smoothing Groups. This will help the tail blend into the upper body by preserving the edges where the tail and body meet.

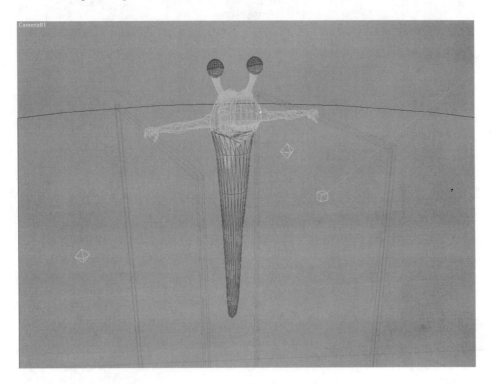

Figure 1.5   Wormy posed to perform some tail lifts.

5. Return to the Editable Mesh modifier. Note that the model returns to its original state, not reflecting the MeshSmooth modifier. Turn on the Show End Results button. Your model should now reflect all the modifiers in the stack.

6. Go into Vertex Sub-Object mode. You should now see two iterations of the model. The orange model represents the model at the level you are currently editing (Editable Mesh). In Wireframe viewing mode, the white model represents the model after all modifiers have been applied. In Smooth and Highlight viewing mode, this version of the model will be shaded normally.

It will probably be easier to edit the original in Shaded mode, unless the surface of the shaded model encompasses vertices of the original. Try dragging a couple of vertices around to get a feel for how they affect the final model (see Figure 1.6).

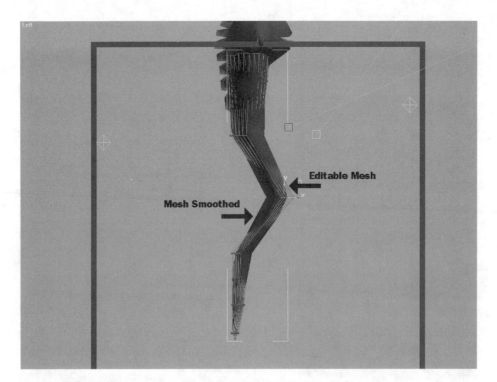

Figure 1.6   Changes to vertices in the Editable Mesh are reflected in real time in the MeshSmoothed version.

7. Turn the Animate button on. Go to frame 12. Change to a Left view window.

8. Select Move, and then confirm that you are working in the View coordinate system. Select the row of vertices third from the top, constrain to the x-axis by moving your mouse over the x-axis in the Transform gizmo until it turns yellow, and move the selection to the left. Note that the MeshSmoothed model "lags" behind the movement of the original model; that's because the MeshSmooth modifier is interactively applied to your editing changes.

9. Go to frame 16 and select all the vertices below the previously selected row. Constrain to the XY plane by moving your mouse over the small right angle in the upper corner of the Transform gizmo, and then move the selection up and to the right. Select Rotate, constrain to the z-axis by moving your mouse over the Z in the Transform gizmo, and rotate the selection counterclockwise. Select the bottom two rows and the bottom vertex, and then move and rotate as before until the tail tip has a nice curl (see Figure 1.7).

Figure 1.7   Wormy begins to curl the end of his tail.

10. Go to frame 25 and move and rotate vertices as before to intensify the curl. Then go to frame 45 and move and rotate vertices until the tail is curled tightly as shown in Figure 1.8. If the end of the tail seems to lose volume at any point, vertices are being interpolated directly between keyframes. To correct this, go to the frame where the effect is most pronounced and move the vertices at the end of the tail to compensate.

11. Now you will uncurl the tail. Go to frame 55 and select all the vertices to which you have applied animation, including the row you animated in step 8. Rotate clockwise and move downward to slightly uncurl the tail.

12. Go to frame 70 and move and rotate vertices to uncurl the tail (see Figure 1.9). Then play your animation.

13. Go to frame 80. At this point, the tail should be mostly straight. New to R3 is the addition of the Track Bar, which displays a selected object's Animation track under the Time slider. Copy the original model position to the current frame by selecting the key at frame 0 and Shift-dragging it to frame 80.

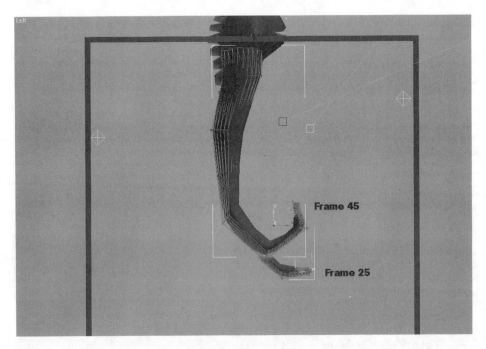

Figure 1.8   The curve of the tail intensifies over two keyframes.

Figure 1.9   Wormy's tail begins to uncurl.

14. Now you will add secondary motion to this animation. Move and rotate vertices at the bottom of the tail to curl the tail to the left. Add some reaction by moving the vertices in the third and fourth rows to the right, as shown in Figure 1.10.

Figure 1.10   Secondary motion adds an important touch of realism.

15. To make this animation loop smoothly, copy the key from frame 0 to the last frame (frame 90).

16. Change to the Camera view and play your animation. Wormy's tail should curl forward and back. If you render this sequence to an AVI, consider increasing the Iterations value in the MeshSmooth modifier to smooth the model further.

Either render this animation to an AVI, or view the AVI file 01max01.avi on the accompanying CD-ROM.

Although you may not be called upon to animate exercising aliens often, sub-object animation is useful anytime you want to add simple animation to an editable mesh. With the addition of the Show End Result feature, you can now see the final results of your sub-object animations as you are keying them. Using this technique for animating facial expressions when using morph targets is inadvisable (if your mesh is very dense, for example).

Using Free Form Deformation

The Free Form Deformation (FFD) modifier is a powerful tool for smoothly deforming geometry. It surrounds an object with a lattice that allows you to abstract the desired deformations over a number of control points. With FFD, instead of trying to control every vertex in an object or group of objects, you animate a simpler control structure, and your animations are applied smoothly to the affected object. The FFD is available in three pre-set control point resolutions: 2×2, 3×3, and 4×4. In addition, you can customize the number of control points in the FFD Box and FFD Cylinder variations.

FFDs have been improved in R3 to allow for a more customized fit of the lattice to complex objects. When you use the Conform To Shape button of the FFD modifier panel, the lattice is automatically adjusted to place control points along the surface of a selected object. Note that this feature is available with single objects only, not with a selection or group of objects. Because the adjusted position of the control points is determined by a straight-line intersection from the object center to the original position of the control point, this feature works best with simple convex objects such as primitives.

For exact control of the FFD lattice, the Set Volume Sub-Object mode allows you to move control points without affecting the modified object. This is the recommended method for customizing the lattice for multiple or complex objects.

Another significant upgrade to FFD is the ability to automatically apply a Point3 controller to each control point via the Animate All button. This displays your control points in Track View and allows you to perform key editing operations.

An FFD is useful for adding a soft deformation to an object, such as breathing motion to a character's chest or gentle swaying to a tree's foliage. FFDs can also be used to smooth problem areas that result from other control systems. For example, you can reduce polygon tearing, which can occur when a mesh object is twisted or deformed, by using FFD to add a counter-deformation to the affected sub-objects.

Basic Free Form Deformation

If you closely examine the results of the preceding tutorial (or view the AVI file 01max01.avi), you will note that when Wormy performs his exercise, he looks very stiff-armed. His body does not react to the motion of his tail as you would expect it to. This animation could be greatly improved by adding some realistic flexing. Of course, you wouldn't want his hands to flex; they need to remain firmly affixed to the supports.

By modifying the default gizmo and center associated with FFDs, you can deform all or part of an object. In this exercise, you will add body flex to most of this character by using the FFD 3×3×3 modifier, while leaving part of the character firmly anchored.

1. Load the scene 01max02.max from the accompanying CD-ROM or continue from the file you created in the preceding tutorial. If you want to see the final result of this tutorial, view the AVI file 01max02.avi.

2. Select "body," "tail," and all six eyeball objects. Apply an FFD 3×3×3 modifier (see Figure 1.11).

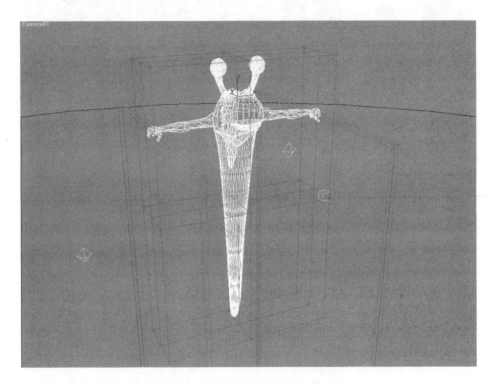

Figure 1.11   A Free Form Deformation 3×3×3 is applied to Wormy.

3. Go to a Top viewport. Then go to Control Points, Sub-Object mode and select the nine control points that run vertically through the center of Wormy's body. Turn the Animate button on and go to frame 30. Go to the Camera viewport and move the selected points 30 units on the z-axis. To measure this movement,

watch the prompt area while you move the selection. Note that this measurement is approximate. If you desire greater precision, you can enter exact units using Type In-Transform (Ctrl+T).

You can constrain this transformation to the z-axis by using the Transform gizmo. Move your mouse over the z-axis to highlight it, and then click and drag to constrain to the z-axis (see Figure 1.12).

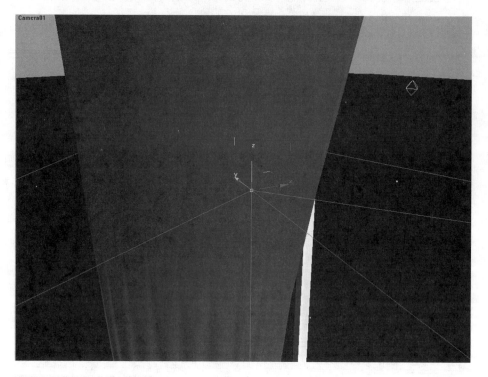

Figure 1.12   The camera has been zoomed in to show the Transform gizmo, currently in z-axis mode.

4. Go to frame 40 (near the most extreme point of Wormy's tail curl) and move the selected points 10 units on the z-axis and 10 units on the y-axis.

5. Go to frame 60 and move the selection –65 units on the z-axis and –10 units on the y-axis.

6. Go to the end of the animation, at frame 90, and move the selection 25 units on the z-axis. This should return Wormy to his original position. To force Wormy's position to exactly duplicate his position at frame 0, select the key at frame 0 on the Track Bar and copy it by Shift-dragging to frame 90.

Either render this animation to an AVI, or view the AVI file 01max02.avi on the accompanying CD-ROM.

In this exercise, you added subtle deformations to a previously animated character. Because you are able to control which parts of a modified object are included in the FFD, you can quickly add realistic flexing, bending, and volume changes to all or parts of an animated object. You could, of course, animate an object directly with Free Form Deformation.

In some cases, it will be more straightforward to apply the FFD to a sub-object selection. In the next tutorial, you will use FFD to animate the movement of one specific piece of a character's anatomy.

Sub-Object Free Form Deformation

As you learned in the last exercise, FFDs can add a valuable sense of realism to an animation through the addition of subtle deformations. In some cases, however, you might animate an object directly with Free Form Deformation. In this exercise, you will make Wormy jump up and down excitedly using FFD to control the curl and extension of his tail.

One frustration animators typically experience is unwanted motion that often accompanies float controllers at their default settings. Setting keys intended to maintain an object's position relative to a ground plane, for example, will often cause that object to "wander" between two identical keys. When you use FFDs, it is important for you to realize exactly what motion curve is being created for each control point. In some cases, it will be necessary to change the tangents of the curve to prevent undesired movement.

1. Load the scene 01max04.max from the accompanying CD-ROM or continue from the file you created in the preceding tutorial. For the purposes of this exercise, Wormy has been merged into one mesh. He is sitting on the tip of his curled tail and is ready to push off from the ground. If you would like to see the final results of this tutorial, view the AVI file 01max03.avi.

2. Open the Time Configuration dialog box and set Start Time to 0 and End Time to 100. Assuming that Frame Rate is set to NTSC (30 frames per second), the animation sequence will last 3.33 seconds.

3. First, you will add an FFD Box modifier to control the spring in Wormy's tail as he launches himself into space. Then go to a Left viewport, select "Wormy," apply a Mesh Select modifier, and go into Face, Sub-Object mode. Select the faces in Wormy's tail, from his waist on down.

4. Without leaving Face, Sub-Object mode apply an FFD Box modifier. The asterisk next to the stack entry shows that you have applied a modifier to a Sub-Object selection. Click the Set Number of Points button and set the following control point resolution: Length = 2, Width = 2, Height = 3. Go into Set Volume, Sub-Object mode and move your control points to more closely match the curve of the tail (see Figure 1.13). Exit Sub-Object mode.

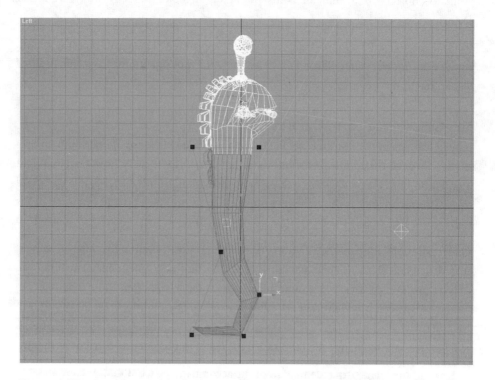

Figure 1.13   Set Volume mode allows you to fine-tune the placement of control points before you deform the object.

5. Now, you will animate the motions of Wormy's body as he attempts to launch himself into space. Turn the Animate button on and go to frame 0 (if you're not there already). Go to the Camera viewport. Wormy's arms and torso look a little stiff; let's put him in a more natural "ready" pose.

6. Go to frame 12 and select the FFD modifier. Then go to Control Point, Sub-Object mode and marquee-select the bottom three control points (you are actually selecting six points because you are including the ones behind the visible points in your marquee box). Move those points 35 units on the y-axis.

7. Now that you've compressed the spring in Wormy's tail, you must drop him down to the floor. Go back to the top of the stack and move Wormy –32 units on the y-axis. Note that a dummy has been positioned on the ground plane to help you align Wormy with the ground.

8. Wormy will push off from the ground at frame 20. Go to frame 20 and select the FFD modifier. Then go to Control Point, Sub-Object mode. The same control points should be selected from the last edit. Move them –50 units on the y-axis. Then go back to the top of the stack and move Wormy 50 units on the y-axis.

9. Go to frame 26, which will be the highest point in Wormy's leap (see Figure 1.14). Select the FFD modifier and the same control points from the last edit. Rotate them 20 degrees on the z-axis, and then move them 10 units on the x-axis and 35 units on the y-axis. Select the control points at the very tip of the tail and move them one grid division up on the y-axis.

Figure 1.14   The high point of Wormy's first jump.

10. Go to frame 37. Wormy will land in this frame, as shown in Figure 1.15. Select the FFD modifier and the same three control points. Rotate them –20 degrees on the z-axis and 30 units on the y-axis.

Figure 1.15 Wormy lands on his tail after jumping.

11. Now, you will copy keys to add another jump. Right-click on Wormy and select Track View Selected from the pop-up menu. In the Track View Filter dialog box, check Selected Objects and Animated Tracks. Right-click on "Wormy" in the left pane and select Expand All. This displays all the keys set for Wormy.

12. Extend the time that Wormy is on the ground by copying the keys from frames 37–44. Copy the push-off from frames 20–53. Copy the high point of Wormy's jump from frames 26–62. Then copy the end of Wormy's jump from frames 37–80.

13. Go to the Camera viewport and play your animation back. You will see that Wormy's tail passes through the floor when he is on the ground—in frames 12–20 and 37–53. This is due to the default In and Out tangents created by the Bezier Position controller. The usual method for changing these In/Out tangents is to use either the Key Info area of the Motion panel or the right-click properties of keys in Track View. New to R3, the Track Bar allows you to access key properties as well.

14. Right-click on the key at frame 0, select Key Properties, and choose Wormy:Position. Change the Out tangent to Linear (the second one in the drop-down list) as shown in Figure 1.16.

15. Increment the Key Number to 2, which brings up the properties of the key at frame 12. Change both the In and Out tangents to Linear.

16. Increment the Key Number to 3, which brings up the properties of the key at frame 20. Change the In tangent to Linear.

17. Increment the Key Number 5, which brings up the properties of the key at frame 37. Change the Out tangent to Linear.

Figure 1.16
Editing In and Out tangents to minimize excess movement using the Bezier Float controller.

18. Increment the Key Number to 6, which brings up the properties of the key at frame 44. Change both the In and Out tangents to Linear.

19. Increment the Key Number to 7, which brings up the properties of the key at frame 53. Change the In tangent to Linear.

In these last six steps, you flattened the curve of Wormy's trajectory while he's supposed to be on the ground. To get a better feel for the effects of changing these tangents, try changing them in Track View while viewing your keys in Function Curve mode (see Figure 1.17).

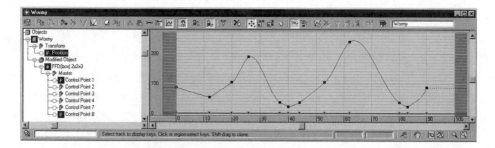

Figure 1.17 Wormy's jumping trajectory is displayed in Function Curve mode after you've flattened the tangents during Wormy's landing.

20. If you zoom in on Wormy's tail in a Left viewport, you will see that his tail still doesn't rest flat against the ground when he's readying his push-off (frames 0–12). This is because the default controller, Bezier Point3, is applied to FFD control points. To fix that, open Track View, and then open the Filters dialog

box. Check Animated Tracks and Selected Object. Expand the list to view the controllers applied to your control points. You should see six control points listed (the only ones that have had animation applied).

21. Select the Control Point 1 channel and turn on Function Curves if you haven't already. The blue curve displays the z-axis transformations applied to this control point. Right-click on the key at frame 0 on the curve, and then change the Out tangent to Linear. Right-click on the key at frame 12 on the curve, and then change both the In and Out tangents to Linear. This flattens the Z transform curve between frames 0 and 12.

22. Repeat step 19 for the remaining five channels. This should prevent Wormy's tail from intersecting the ground plane.

Note

If you would like to access controllers for the unanimated control points, use the Animate All button in the FFD modifier panel. This function adds a Point3 controller to all the control points that are still unanimated. (Of course, you will have to deselect Animated Tracks in the Filters dialog box or they won't show up in Track View.)

23. Wormy's tail will still intersect the floor during the end of his push-off, but you can easily fix that. Go to frame 18, select the FFD control points, and move them four units on the y-axis. Repeat this operation at frame 50 to duplicate the effect for the second jump.

24. Now let's add a little character. You may have noticed from playing this animation back (or from the keys in Track Bar) that the second jump is slower. It would stand to reason that Wormy should jump higher if he is going to be aloft longer. So, go to frame 62 and move Wormy another 50 units on the y-axis.

25. Pay close attention to the way Wormy's tail contracts as he approaches his landing at frame 37. As the FFD control points are interpolating directly from the apex of his jump at frame 26 to his landing, his tail contracts evenly throughout instead of reacting to contact with the ground plane. To fix this, open Track View, expand to the FFD control points, and copy the FFD keys from frames 26–34.

26. The same thing happens prior to his landing at frame 80, so copy the FFD keys from frames 62–76.

27. Between his jumps (from frame 37 to frame 44), Wormy is frozen stiff. He should be squashing in reaction to having just landed. Go to a Left viewport, go to frame 40, and move Wormy –15 units on the y-axis. Select the FFD modifier and the bottom three control points. Move them 8 units on the y-axis.

28. Now that you have created a nice reaction pose for Wormy, copy this key to frame 83 to duplicate the effect for the end of his second jump.

29. To keep Wormy from intersecting the ground plane between jumps, you must change some of his tangents to Linear, as you did in step 10. Right-click on the key at frame 40, select Key Properties, Wormy:Position, and change both the In and Out tangents to Linear. Likewise, the tangents must be changed for the newly created FFD keys. Open Track View, edit the properties of the control point keys at frame 40, and change their In and Out tangents to Linear. Edit the key properties of the keys at frame 37 and change their Out tangents to Linear.

Either render this animation to an AVI, or view the AVI file 01max03.avi, on the accompanying CD-ROM.

As you have seen, in some cases Free Form Deformation is a powerful tool for animating organic objects. The ability to apply FFDs to a specific part of a body enables you to add deformation where it's needed while simultaneously animating the object as a whole. It is important to keep in mind what the effect of various controllers and key angents will be, even for control points. Viewing these curves in Track View gives you complete control over the way FFDs enhance your animation.

Applying FFDs to a sub-object selection can be useful in a variety of situations when part of an object either needs to remain rigid or will be deformed with another modifier. You might need to deform a character's floppy ears, for example, without affecting the more rigid head.

If you play back the animation you just created, you should see nice smooth deformations in Wormy's tail as he pushes himself off the ground. This flexing contrasts with the rigid pose of Wormy's upper body. In the next exercise, you will add flex to Wormy's arms and torso with a series of Bend modifiers.

Sub-Object Bends

The Bend modifier lets you bend an object or sub-object selection around the center and axes you specify. New to R3 is the ability to move the center of the bend effect independently from the Bend gizmo or the modified object's pivot point. Bend can be used to easily flex an object part around an arbitrary center, making it a good choice for creating flapping motions with limbs or extruded body parts.

In this tutorial, you will build upon the jumping animation from the preceding exercise. Some balance-checking and anticipating motions are needed in Wormy's upper body.

You will flail Wormy's arms and flex his torso by applying Bend modifiers to sub-object selections.

1. Load the scene 01max05.max from the accompanying CD-ROM or continue from the file you created in the preceding tutorial. If you would like to see the final results of this tutorial, view the AVI file 01max04.avi. Play the animation back. Wormy jumps twice, his tail flexing via Free Form Deformation.

2. Wormy needs a Bend modifier applied to his upper body to help him bend at the waist. Go to a Front viewport, select Wormy, and then apply a Mesh Select modifier. Do *not* go into Sub-Object mode. Applying Mesh Select resets the selection to the entire mesh. Apply a Bend modifier and set Angle to –25.

3. Note that the default Direction setting causes Wormy to bend to the side. Set Direction to –90 to align the Bend effect with Wormy's y-axis. Do not change the Bend Axis from the default. Go to Sub-Object, Center mode and move the center of the bend effect to the row of vertices directly between the chin and the tail. Now, Wormy bends forward from the waist (see Figure 1.18). Return the Angle setting to 0.

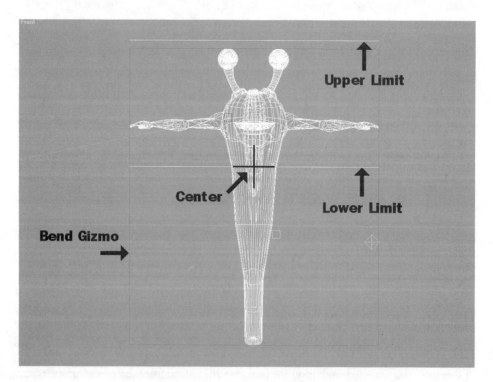

Figure 1.18   A Bend modifier will be used to flex the upper body.

4. To keep the Bend modifier from affecting the lower body, check the Limit Effect box and set Upper Limit to 110. If you drag the Angle spinner, the upper body will bend smoothly without affecting the lower body. Exit Sub-Object mode, open the Edit Modifier Stack dialog box, and select the Bend modifier. In the Modifier Name box, rename it to "Bend:Torso." You will be applying several Bend modifiers in this stack, and renaming them helps you keep them organized.

5. Two additional Bend modifiers will be used to control the movement of Wormy's arms. Now that you can precisely place the bend center, it will be a simple matter to bend the arms around the shoulder joint.

6. Apply a MeshSelect modifier and go to Face, Sub-Object mode. Select the faces that define Wormy's right arm. Apply a Bend modifier, go to Center, Sub-Object mode, and move the center of the bend effect to the center of the shoulder joint. Set the Bend Axis to X to align the effect along the long axis of the arm. Open the Edit Modifier Stack dialog box and select this Bend modifier. In the Modifier Name box, rename it to "Bend:Right Arm." If you drag the Angle spinner, you will see that the arm bends smoothly from the shoulder (see Figure 1.19). Change the Bend Angle and watch the result.

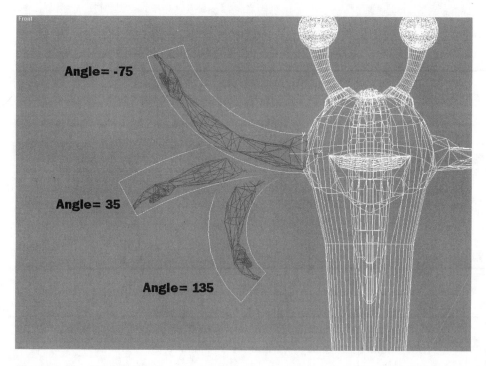

Figure 1.19   The Bend Angle can be used to animate arm position in a smooth, rubbery-style movement.

7. Repeat step 5 for Wormy's left arm, renaming that Bend modifier to "Bend:Left Arm."

8. Go to frame 0, select the "Bend:Torso" modifier, and set Angle to 25. Select the "Bend:Right Arm" modifier and set Angle to 80. Select the "Bend:Left Arm" modifier and set Angle to 80.

9. Go to frame 12 where Wormy is preparing to jump. Select the "Bend:Torso" modifier and set Angle to 60. Select the "Bend:Right Arm" modifier, set Angle to 135, and set Direction to 45. Select the "Bend:Left Arm" modifier, set Angle to 115, and set Direction to 45. Wormy is now hunched down and ready to spring, as you can see in Figure 1.20.

Figure 1.20   Wormy is ready to launch into the air.

10. At frame 26, go to the top of the stack. Move Wormy 85 units on the Y axis. Select the "Bend:Torso" modifier and set Angle to –60. Select the "Bend:Right Arm" modifier, set Angle to 85, and set Direction to –150. Select the "Bend:Left Arm" modifier, set Angle to 85, and set Direction to –150. This is the apex of Wormy's jump, shown in Figure 1.21.

Figure 1.21   The highest point of Wormy's jump.

11. At frame 37, go to the top of the stack. Move Wormy −200 units on the y-axis. Select the "Bend:Torso" modifier and set Angle to 80. Select the "Bend:Right Arm" modifier, set Angle to −115, and set Direction to 210. Select the "Bend:Left Arm" modifier, set Angle to −115, and set Direction to 12. This is the bottom of Wormy's jump.

12. Go to frame 40. Select the "Bend:Torso" modifier and set Angle to −30. Select the "Bend:Right Arm" modifier and set Angle to −30. Select the "Bend:Left Arm" modifier and set Angle to −30.

13. To finish this sequence, copy the key from frame 0 to frame 90 so that Wormy will return to a resting pose. At frame 90, select the "Bend:Torso" modifier and set Angle to 45.

14. Go to frame 100 and select the "Bend:Torso" modifier. Set Angle to −10. Select the "Bend:Right Arm" modifier and set Angle to 145. Select the "Bend:Left Arm" modifier and set Angle to 145.

Play your animation back. By adding reaction and anticipation gestures to Wormy's arms and torso, you have greatly enhanced the realism of this animation. Either render this animation to an AVI, or view the AVI file 01max04.avi on the accompanying CD-ROM.

Applying Bend modifiers to sub-object selections is a great way to focus on creating specific movements for the parts of your object that need them. Consider this technique the next time you need to bend tree limbs around a trunk, cables around a piece of machinery, or a radio antenna in a strong gust of wind.

Soft Selections and Linked Xform

The smooth deformation of organic objects is enhanced in R3 with the addition of the *Soft Selection* feature. The Soft Selection control option is available on a vertex Sub-Object level in Edit Mesh and Mesh Select modifiers, as well as in the Editable Mesh base object.

The Soft Selection feature is similar to the Affect Region option in the Edit Mesh modifier in R2. Soft Selection is a big improvement, however. With this new feature, vertices are colored according to the influence that will be applied, making it much easier to tweak the affected area. The vertices near the selected vertices will change color to indicate the degree of influence. Yellow vertices, which should be nearest the selected vertices, will be most affected; vertices approaching the default blue color are the least affected. The Pinch and Bubble values function as they do in the Affect Region control, changing the Soft Selection Curve to adjust which vertices are affected and to what degree.

The Soft Selection option is also much more powerful than Mesh Selection modifiers because the vertex selections are passed to subsequent modifiers, allowing soft deformation through a variety of methods.

Soft Selections can improve nearly any animation technique that employs sub-object selections being either passed to subsequent modifiers or linked to external controls, such as bones. Sub-object modifiers can now be thought of as *influences*, rather than one-to-one transformations.

In this exercise, you will use Soft Selections to animate the blinking of Wormy's eyelids by linking the rotation of selected vertices to a dummy. Although the basic technique may be familiar to you, this tutorial will put a new spin on the setup by employing Soft Selections to gradate the influence of the controlling dummy over just the portion of the eyelids that need to be deformed. In addition, you will learn a simple trick that will enable you to rotate Wormy's upper as well as lower eyelids in *opposite* directions using a single controller.

1. Load the scene 01max07.max from the accompanying CD-ROM. This time Wormy is one continuous mesh, divided by Material IDs, with the exception of the eyes (see Figure 1.22). You will create the lower eyelids as part of the setup. If you would like to preview the final results of this tutorial, view the AVI file 01max05.avi.

Figure 1.22   Wormy is sitting on his tail, ready to be animated.

2. First, you will set up the controls for the eye blink. Go to a Left viewport and zoom in on the eyes. Select the "eyelid_upper_right" object. The upper eyelids are simple spheres, with Hemisphere set to 0.5 in the creation parameters to yield a half-sphere.

3. Create a dummy in roughly the same position and size as the eyeballs. Name the dummy "dummy_eyelids." Align it to an eyeball, select Align Position, X Position, and Y Position, and align the center of each object. Go to the Camera viewport and note where MAX created the dummy: It is directly between Wormy's eyes. When you create objects in an orthogonal viewport, the value for the non-represented axis (World X for a Left viewport) is set to 0. Therefore, the newly created dummy is centered on Wormy's x-axis because Wormy is centered on the World X axis.

4. Select the "eyelid_upper_right" object. Apply a Mesh Select modifier and go into Vertex Sub-Object mode. Select the 12 vertices in the lower-right corner of the hemisphere. Open the Soft Selection panel and check Use Soft Selection. Drag the Falloff spinner up toward 40 and down to 0, noting that the affected vertices are indicated by color change as you change the value. Set Falloff to 15, and set both Pinch and Bubble to 0. This allows you to affect the vertices along the front half of the eyelid and leave the back half unaffected (see Figure 1.23).

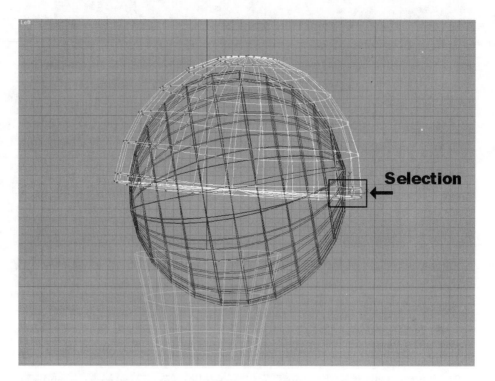

Figure 1.23   Selecting a few vertices along the front of the eyelid and using Soft Selection allows you to deform the eyelid without affecting the entire object.

5. While still in Vertex Sub-Object mode, apply a Linked XForm modifier. Pick "dummy_eyelids" as the Control Object. Then select the dummy and rotate it around the View Z axis. Note that the dummy rotation is passed to the dependent object and the rotational influence varies according to the Falloff settings you specified in the Mesh Select modifier.

6. Repeat steps 4 and 5 for the "eyelid_upper_left" object.

7. Go to the Camera viewport. Select both eyelids, and select Mirror. Choose Z as the Mirror Axis, and choose Copy as the Clone Selection. Move the newly created lower eyelids –7 units on the z-axis. Rename them "eyelid_lower_left" and "eyelid_lower_right."

Note

Cloning objects after they have been linked to a controller allows you to modify the cloned object's position and Xform without changing the local orientation of the linked transforms. For example, a tree branch waving in the breeze via Linked Xform can become a dangling root with precisely the same—if inverted—motions; simply clone and mirror the branch *after* applying Linked Xform.

8. Select the dummy and rotate it in the negative direction around the x-axis. Note that the upper lids rotate in a direction opposite the lower lids. This gives the appearance of the eyelids opening and closing, all with a single control (see Figure 1.24).

Figure 1.24   Rotating the dummy around the x-axis allows you to move the upper and lower eyelids away from each other, creating an effective blink control.

9. Go to the Motion Panel, open the Assign Controller panel, and select the Rotational channel. Click the Assign Controller button and assign a Euler XYZ controller. Click on the plus symbol next to the Euler XYZ listing and assign a

Linear Float controller to each of the X, Y, and Z channels, respectively. This controller assignment makes the rotational interpolations linear, with no ease in and out. This will make the eye blinks look more mechanical, but it reduces any extraneous fluttering. You could get the same effect by keeping the default Bezier Float controllers that initially appeared under the Euler XYZ controller and editing the Key Info manually, but this would require a lot more work, without much advantage.

10. Now you will create some eye blinks. Turn the Animate button on, select the "dummy_eyelids" object, and confirm that you are still in Rotate mode and constrained to the x-axis. Turn on Angle Snap and right-click on the Angle Snap toggle to set Angle to 5 degrees.

11. Go to frame 0 and rotate the dummy –35 degrees on the View X axis. Go to frame 7 and create a rotational keyframe either by right-clicking on the Time slider and checking only the Rotation box, or by clicking the Create Key, Rotation button in the Motion panel. This keyframe will lock down the eyelids up to frame 7, making the next motion abrupt, rather than easing it over the preceding frames.

12. Go to frame 10 and rotate the dummy 35 degrees on the x-axis. Then go to frame 12 and rotate the dummy –45 degrees on the x-axis.

13. Go to frame 20 and create a rotational keyframe as you did in step 5. Next, go to frame 22 and rotate the dummy 35 degrees on the x-axis. Then go to frame 24 and rotate the dummy 45 degrees on the x-axis. Wormy has just blinked. Make this single blink a double blink by copying the keys at frames 12, 20, and 22 to frames 28, 36, and 38. Note that the Track Bar supports only one key copy at a time. If you want to copy multiple keys in a single operation, you will need to open Track View.

14. Go ahead and open Track View, open the Filters, and check Show Only: Animated Tracks and Selected Objects. Expand the list in the left pane until you are viewing all three rotation keys for the selected dummy. A shortcut to this would be to right-click on the Objects item and select Expand All. Select the keys in all three rotational tracks at frames 28, 36, and 38. Copy them several times, creating eye blinks beginning at frames 43, 63, and 78. To have Wormy open his eyes at the end, go to frame 91 and rotate the dummy –40 degrees on the x-axis If you want to add some variation to these blinks, move the keys around a frame or two.

15. Play your animation back. Wormy will blink throughout this sequence, 1 to 2 times each second.

Either render this animation to an AVI, or view the AVI file 01max05.avi on the accompanying CD-ROM.

By using Soft Selection, you have transformed what might have been a mechanical-appearing blinking motion into a smooth deformation. The possibilities for this technique are endless. For example, you might use it to apply soft undulations to terrain, warp objects in response to a simulated impact, or bulge muscles.

Linked Xform for Anatomical Deformation

Linked Xform allows you to pass a controlling object's transforms to another object or sub-object selection. For example, suppose you need to rotate a single-mesh character's head. By using Linked Xform to control the vertices that make up the head, you could animate a turning head with a dummy. Likewise, several objects could be linked to a single Control Object. As you will see in this exercise, you can also link Control Objects to parent objects to create a hierarchy.

In the previous tutorial, you learned how to rotate eyelids using a single controller. Now, you will use a series of linked dummies to create a fairly complex set of movements for Wormy's arm.

You will link anatomically specific selections to one of several dummies, link those dummies into a hierarchy, and create a nice arm wave using those control objects.

1. Load the scene 01max08.max from the accompanying CD-ROM or continue from the file you created in the preceding tutorial. Wormy has been posed in a sitting position, ready for the upper body animation you will be applying. If you would like to preview the final results of this tutorial, view the AVI file 01max06.avi.

2. Now you will set Wormy's pose in preparation for a friendly wave. Turn the Animate button off, go to a Front viewport, and zoom in on Wormy's right arm. Select the "body" object and apply an Edit Mesh modifier. You could perform the following edits within the Editable Mesh base object, but using a separate modifier will make it easier to remove the edits or to change their locations with the stack should that become necessary. Go into Face, Sub-Object mode, select all the faces of the right arm (including the shoulder area), and enter the name "right arm" in the Named Selection Set drop-down list box. This selection set will come in handy later—after this arm has been posed—when you need to recall the faces of the arm. Figure 1.25 shows the selection set you just created.

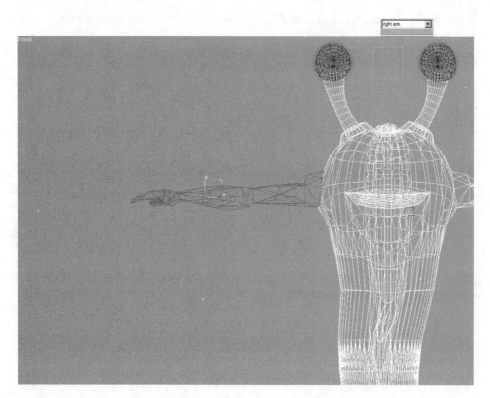

Figure 1.25   The named (sub-object) selection set called "right arm."

3. Go into Vertex Sub-Object mode. Select all the vertices of the arm and rotate 65 degrees around the z-axis. This will cause the shoulder area to stretch terribly. Move the selection back into position until the shoulder looks natural. Then deselect the vertices above the elbow. Rotate the remaining selection 60 degrees around the z-axis. Again, move the selection back into position until the elbow joint looks correct. The hand should be intersecting the body at this point. Deselect the vertices above the wrist and rotate the remaining selection –35 degrees around the z-axis and 20 degrees on the y-axis. Move the selection until the wrist looks correct. Your goal is to create a natural "hand-on-hip" pose for this arm, as shown in Figure 1.26. It may be helpful to switch to the Camera viewport for final positioning of Wormy's hand.

4. Now you will set up the animation controls for the other arm. In the Front viewport, pan over to Wormy's left arm. Exit Sub-Object mode and deselect Wormy.

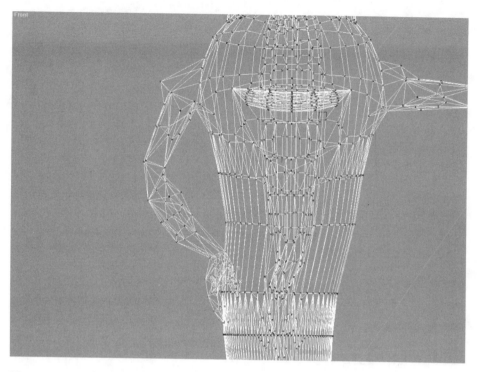

Figure 1.26   Wormy's right arm is at rest on his hip.

5. Create three dummies, one at each arm joint. At the shoulder joint, place "dummy_leftarm_shoulder." At the elbow joint, place "dummy_leftarm_elbow." At the wrist joint, place "dummy_leftarm_wrist." Be sure to center the dummies on the joints correctly because the dummy axes will determine the pivot points of the arm deformation (see Figure 1.27).

6. Select the "body" object and apply a Mesh Select modifier. Go to Vertex Sub-Object mode and select the vertices in the hand and wrist. Apply a Linked Xform modifier and pick "dummy_leftarm_wrist" as the Control Object.

7. Apply another Mesh Select modifier. Go to Vertex Sub-Object mode and select the vertices in the forearm and elbow. Apply a Linked Xform modifier and pick "dummy_leftarm_elbow" as the Control Object.

8. Apply another Mesh Select modifier. Go to Vertex Sub-Object mode and select the vertices in the upper arm and shoulder. Apply a Linked Xform modifier and pick "dummy_leftarm_shoulder" as the Control Object.

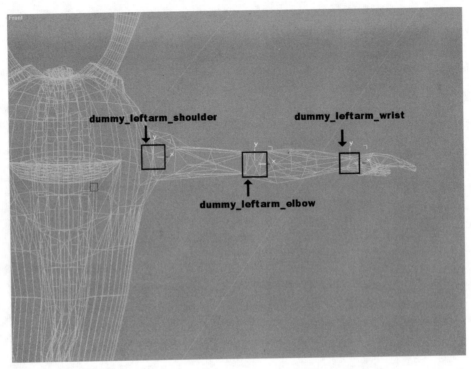

Figure 1.27   Dummies are set up to control the movement of Wormy's left arm.

Caution

Be certain that no vertex is selected in more than one Mesh Select modifier. That would cause that vertex to be influenced by more than one controller, which would result in exaggerated deformation when the controllers are animated.

9. Now you will smooth out the result of these Linked Xform deformations. Go back in the stack to the Edit Mesh modifier. Go into Face, Sub-Object mode, select the "right arm" selection set from the drop-down list, and select Copy from the Named Selection Sets area of the Modifier panel. When the Copy Named Selection list appears, select "right arm."

10. To avoid resetting the Sub-Object selections you used to link the arm to the dummies, go to the next modifier in the stack (Mesh Select) and allow that vertex selection to come up. Then you can jump to the last modifier in the stack (Linked Xform) without losing your Mesh Select settings.

11. Apply another Mesh Select modifier, go to Face, Sub-Object mode, and select Paste under the Named Selection Sets area. Add the faces of Wormy's left arm to

the selection (see Figure 1.28). Apply a MeshSmooth modifier. Keep the default settings, but clear Apply to Whole Mesh because you need to smooth only the selected polygons. You may want to set the MeshSmooth to Inactive in Viewport to avoid slow screen refreshes during animation.

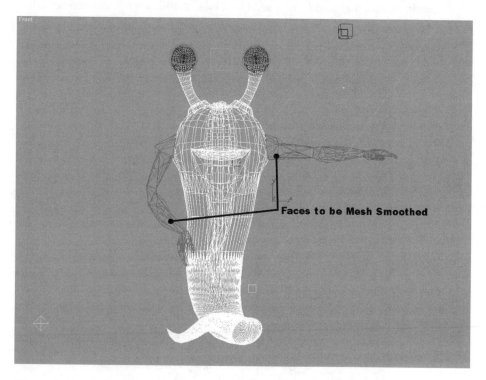

Figure 1.28   Applying MeshSmooth to these low-resolution arms will minimize polygon tearing.

12. The final step in setting up the arm control is to link the dummies. Select "dummy_leftarm_wrist" and link it to "dummy_leftarm_elbow" using the Select and Link button. Similarly, link "dummy_leftarm_elbow" to "dummy_leftarm_shoulder."

Note

If you try to link a dummy to the "body" object, you'll get the following error message: "Cannot link, would cause dependency loop." Because Wormy's body is partially controlled by the arm dummies, the dummies cannot, in turn, be controlled by the "body." You can use the Select Objects list to select a parent if necessary, but this dialog box will be named Select Parent while the Select and Link button is active.

13. Experiment with these controls. Use the PageUp/PageDown keys to automatically select the parent/child of the current object. You should be able to rotate the shoulder control around the View Z axis and cause the entire arm to rotate. The elbow dummy should control the lower half of the arm, and the wrist dummy should control the hand (see Figure 1.29). Note that this is not a complete skeletal deformation solution. Extreme movements will cause some tearing and pinching at the joints.

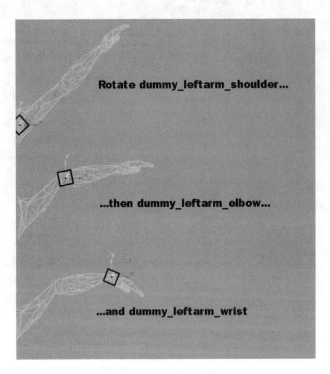

Figure 1.29   The arm control dummies in practice: Each dummy is controlled by the one above it and in turn controls the arm below it.

14. Turn the Animate button on, turn Angle Snap on, and go to frame 0. Set your Reference Coordinate System to Local. Select the "dummy_leftarm_shoulder" and rotate –55 degrees on the z-axis. Select "dummy_leftarm_elbow" and rotate –80 degrees on the z-axis. Select "dummy_leftarm_wrist" and rotate 30 degrees on the z-axis and 15 degrees on the x-axis. This will be Wormy's starting position, which is shown in Figure 1.30.

15. Go to frame 10, rotate "dummy_leftarm_shoulder" –20 degrees on the x-axis and 10 degrees on the z-axis, rotate "dummy_leftarm_elbow" 15 degrees on the

z-axis, and rotate "dummy_leftarm_wrist" –15 degrees on the z-axis. Wormy is getting ready to raise his arm.

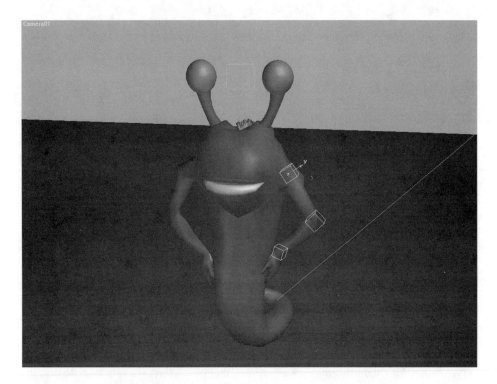

Figure 1.30   The left arm is posed in a resting position via dummy controls.

16. Go to frame 15, rotate "dummy_leftarm_shoulder" –35 degrees on the x-axis, –40 degrees on the y-axis, and 25 degrees on the z-axis. Rotate "dummy_leftarm_elbow" 10 degrees on the x-axis and –40 degrees on the zaxis. Rotate "dummy_leftarm_wrist" –15 degrees on the z-axis.

17. Go to frame 18 and rotate "dummy_leftarm_shoulder" –10 degrees on the y-axis. Rotate "dummy_leftarm_elbow" 35 degrees on the x-axis, –10 degrees on the z-axis, and –105 degrees on the y-axis. Rotate "dummy_leftarm_wrist" 60 degrees on the x-axis. This is the first extreme of Wormy's wave (see Figure 1.31).

18. Go to frame 23 and rotate "dummy_leftarm_shoulder" 25 degrees on the y-axis. Rotate "dummy_leftarm_elbow" 40 degrees on the z-axis. Rotate "dummy_leftarm_wrist" 25 degrees on the y-axis. This is the second extreme of Wormy's wave.

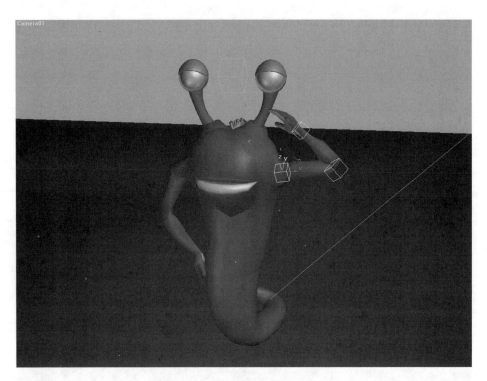

Figure 1.31   The inside extreme pose of Wormy's wave.

19. Now, you will duplicate this wave a few times by copying the appropriate keys in the Track Bar. Select all three arm control dummies. Copy the key from frame 18 (the first extreme wave pose) to frames 28, 42, and 60. Copy the key from frame 23 (the second extreme wave pose) to frames 34, 50, and 73. If you want to find out at what frame a particular key is set, click on the key in the Track Bar and hold the mouse button down. The status bar will change to indicate the frame number of the selected key (or the frame number of the earliest occurring key if several are selected). You can easily see in the Track Bar (and in Figure 1.32) that the keys are getting farther apart, essentially slowing down the velocity of the wave motion.

Figure 1.32   The increasing distance between keys indicates that the velocity of the motion is decreasing.

20. Starting at frame 73, you will end the wave motion and return Wormy's arm to his hip.

21. Go to frame 80 and rotate "dummy_leftarm_shoulder" 55 degrees on the x-axis and –25 degrees on the z-axis. Rotate "dummy_leftarm_elbow" 70 degrees on the x-axis. Rotate "dummy_leftarm_wrist" 30 degrees on the x-axis. Then turn the Animate button off.

22. Select all three dummies. Copy the key from frame 0 to frame 95 to return Wormy to his initial pose.

23. Play your animation back. Wormy waves a couple of times as he blinks and then relaxes.

24. If you think that Wormy looks a little stiff after animating his waving arm, try adding some elasticity to his movement by using the Bend modifier. Apply Bend to his body and all six eye objects, being sure to reset the selections of the objects currently operating at a Sub-Object level by applying Mesh Select first. Bend must be applied to all six eye objects to force them to follow the bending motion. Otherwise, they will be left behind when the body bends.

25. The most realistic effect will be to balance the waving of his arm with an opposite body motion. Try to key the Bend a frame or two after the arm motion keys to avoid an overly mechanical look. Because the body supposedly has more mass than the arm, it should move more slowly and in reaction to the smaller, quicker motion of the waving arm (see Figure 1.33).

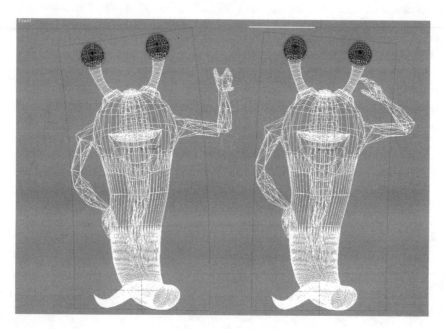

Figure 1.33   The body sways in a direction opposite from the waving arm, creating a compensating force.

Either render this animation to an AVI, or view the AVI file 01max06.avi on the accompanying CD-ROM.

As you have seen, Linked Xform can be used in a hierarchy to apply complex animations. You could even link the top-level dummy ("dummy_leftarm_shoulder") and the objects that make up this character to a parent dummy and then animate the position of that parent to move Wormy about in the scene. Anytime you need to animate objects or sub-object selections in which the transforms of one part build upon another, consider a hierarchy of linked control objects.

Adding Secondary Motion

One of the elements of animation that helps lend a sense of mass and velocity to organic objects is the secondary motion caused by inertia. A classic example of this is a bouncing rubber ball. Imagine a ball bouncing vertically on a hard surface. If the ball never changes its shape from a perfect sphere, it gives the impression of an impossibly rigid object. If, however, the ball squashes against the floor on impact, and stretches along the trajectory at the height of its bounce, it appears to be elastic and much more dynamic.

In cases when you want simple, large-scale reactions, using a modifier like Twist or Bend can be the easiest method. As these modifiers apply smooth deformations over an object or sub-object selection, you can quickly key in reactions to the overall animation.

Using Twist and Bend

So far in the animation, Wormy blinks and waves. But to whom is he waving? Note also that his eyestalks, which should be fairly flexible, do not respond to his bending upper body. You can turn Wormy's upper body toward the camera by using the Twist modifier, and you can add secondary motion to his eyestalks by using Bend. Give it a try.

1. Load the scene 01max09.max from the accompanying CD-ROM, or continue from the file you created in the preceding tutorial. If you would like to preview the final results of this tutorial, view the AVI file 01max07.avi. Play this animation back.

2. Select the "body," the four eyelids, and the eyeballs. Go to a Front viewport and apply a Twist modifier. Go into Center, Sub-Object mode and move the Center down on the y-axis until it is lined up horizontally with Wormy's right hand. This determines the center of the Twist effect, or the area that will be affected the least.

3. To limit the effect to Wormy's upper body, check Limit Effect. Increase Upper Limit to 125, until the upper part of Wormy's body is encompassed (see Figure 1.34). Which areas are being affected will be especially apparent if you change the Angle value before changing the limit values. Exit Sub-Object mode and return to the Camera viewport.

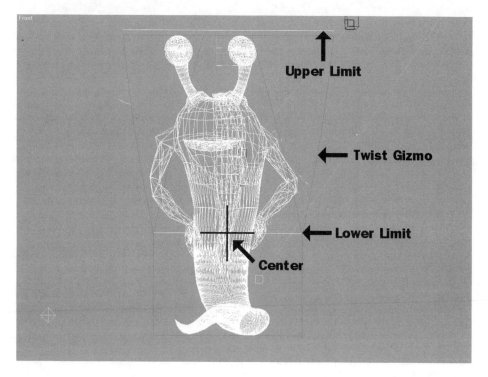

Figure 1.34   A Twist modifier will be used to angle Wormy's upper body and arms.

4. Turn the Animate button on. Go to frame 8 and set Angle to 5. Go to frame 20 and set Angle to –25. Go to frame 35 and set Angle to –35. Go to frame 60 and set Angle to –30. Go to frame 93 and set Angle to 5. Go to frame 100 and set Angle to 0. Then turn the Animate button off.

5. Play your animation back. Wormy now twists toward the camera for his waves and then twists back. His eyestalks, however, remain rigid; they do not flex with his movement. You will add secondary motion to his eyestalks with a Bend modifier.

6. Select the "body," the four eyelids, and the eyeballs. Go to a Front viewport and apply a Bend modifier. Go into Center, Sub-Object mode and move the Center up on the y-axis until it is at the base of Wormy's eyestalks.

7. To limit the effect to the eyestalks, check Limit Effect. Increase Upper Limit to 40 until the eyestalks and eyes are encompassed. Exit Sub-Object mode and return to the Camera viewport (see Figure 1.35).

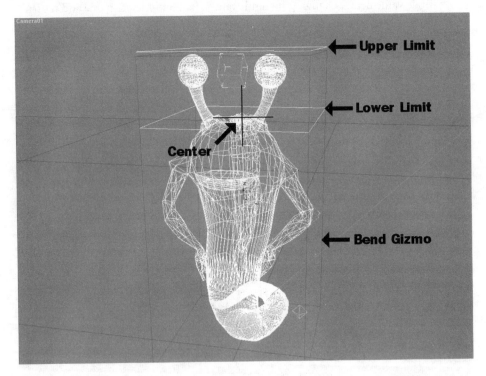

Figure 1.35   A Bend modifier limited to the eyestalks will be used to add secondary motion so the eyes will move in reaction to Wormy's larger movements.

8. Turn the Animate button on and set the Angle parameter for the keyframes as shown below:

Frame 10: Angle = −15
Frame 20: Angle = −15
Frame 26: Angle = −10
Frame 31: Angle = 12
Frame 38: Angle = −10
Frame 46: Angle = 10
Frame 54: Angle = −10
Frame 63: Angle = 8
Frame 83: Angle = −10
Frame 93: Angle = 0

9. Play your animation back. Wormy's eyestalks now twist back and forth, reacting to the overall twist of his body.

Either render this animation to an AVI, or view the AVI file 01max07.avi on the accompanying CD-ROM. To see a completed version of this MAX file, load the scene 01max10.max from the accompanying CD-ROM.

When you need specific secondary motion, Twist and Bend can be used to enhance your animation. You might also consider using Free Form Deformation or Xform, applied using the same technique, to deform portions of an animated object.

Flex for Soft-Body Dynamics

In some cases, you may need to apply secondary motion to a more complex object. Instead of creating an intricate set of Bend, Twist, or similar modifiers, you can use a new modifier called Flex.

The Flex modifier simulates soft-body dynamics by causing the vertices of an object to lag behind as the object moves. The amount of bend that's applied is determined by the Flex value in the Modifier panel; rigidity is set with the Strength value; and the delay until a flexed object comes to rest is set with the Sway value. The degree to which the Flex effect will be applied can be set either interactively by painting the vertex weight with the Paint tool or manually by specifying a value in the Vertex Weight area. Flex is a very versatile tool: It can be applied to NURBS, patches, shapes, and FFD space warps in addition to meshes. Forces such as Wind, Motor, and Push can also be linked to Flex.

 Note

If you're network rendering using Flex, you'll need MAX 3.1 instead of MAX 3.0.

Earlier in this chapter, you animated Wormy jumping on the end of his tail and then added bends to his arms and torso to make the action more lifelike. In this tutorial, you will use Flex to add the sort of jiggling you would expect from a soft creature such as Wormy.

1. Load the scene 01max06.max from the accompanying CD-ROM, or continue from the file you created in the earlier tutorial. If you would like to see the final results of this tutorial, view the AVI file 01max04.avi.

2. Open the Time Configuration dialog box and set the Start Time to 0 and the End Time to 150. Assuming that Frame Rate is set to NTSC or 30 frames per second, this will create an animation sequence lasting 5 seconds. Adding time after Wormy lands will allow his body to finish jiggling after he stops jumping.

3. Turn off the Animate button and go to a Front viewport. Apply a Mesh Select modifier to reset the selection to the entire object. Then apply a Flex modifier and go to Center, Sub-Object mode. Move the Center gizmo to the bottom of Wormy's tail. Note that the vertices change color to indicate that those closest to the center are going to be affected less than those farther away (see Figure 1.36). The Flex Center creates the first determination of which vertices will be affected most strongly. Here, the Center is near the bottom of the object, meaning that vertices near the top will be deformed most strongly.

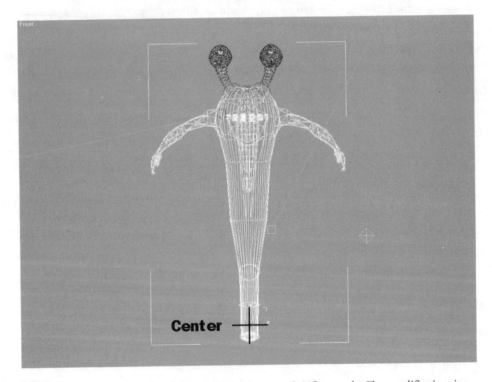

Figure 1.36   Vertices change color to indicate how much influence the Flex modifier is going to impart. Vertices farthest from the Center gizmo are most strongly affected.

4. Turn off Sub-Object mode and set Flex to 0.1. This minimizes the Flex effect. Set the Strength value to 30. This increases the simulated rigidity of Wormy's body and makes him wobble like gelatin instead of stretching like a rubber band.

5. You need to apply Flex most during the parts of the animation where Wormy is on the ground. Turn the Animate button on and go to frame 33, where Wormy is approaching his first landing. Set Flex to 0.2. You want Flex to ramp up to the next key by the time Wormy touches the ground, so go to frame 37 and set Flex to 0.5.

6. To get immediate feedback on how Flex will be changing Wormy, go to a Left viewport. Note that when the Flex setting is increased to 0.5, the vertices in Wormy's upper body—those farthest from the center of the Flex effect—are deformed in the direction of Wormy's simulated momentum. Because he has just stopped a movement toward the ground plane, that is the direction in which his Flexed vertices are still moving (see Figure 1.37).

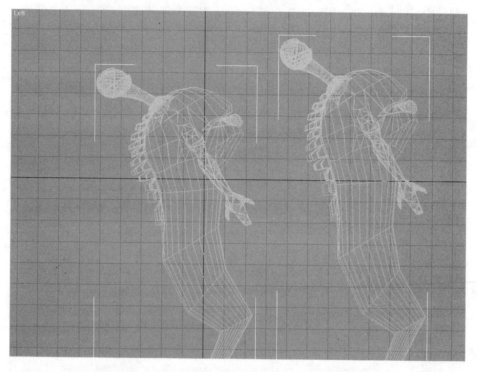

Figure 1.37   Wormy has just landed. Applying Flex [the figure on the left] causes affected parts of his body to deform in the direction in which they were most recently moving.

7. Go to frame 48, where Wormy is about to leave the ground, and set Flex to 0.2.

8. At frame 77, Wormy is approaching his second landing. Set another 0.2 key at that frame. Wormy touches the ground at frame 80, so set Flex to 1 at frame 80. Because no movement keys are set after frame 90, the primary use of Flex at the end of your animation will be to add some wobble as he recovers from his landing.

9. Open Track View and expand to the Flex track. If you turn on Function Curve mode, you will see that, with the default Bezier Float controller applied, the curve swings both higher and lower than key values. Values less than 0 are not significant because they are taken as 0, but values higher than your keys will

increase the effect significantly. Select the Flex track and assign a Linear Float controller.

10. Play your animation. After Wormy makes that final landing, his body wobbles and sways. But you don't want him to wobble forever, so you'll have to dampen the effect. Go to frame 150 and set Flex to 0. This gradually reduces the Flex effect toward the end of your animation.

11. The final step before you render your animation is to smooth over the deformation of Wormy's tail. Turn the Animate button off. You will need to retrieve the face selection for Wormy's tail. Mesh Select allows you to pass Sub-Object selections between modifiers.

12. Go to the first Mesh Select modifier, the one immediately before the FFD. Go into Face, Sub-Object mode. In the Named Selection Set drop-down box, name this face selection "Tail." Then select Copy from the Selection Sets area of the Modifier panel and select "Tail" from the list of selections that appears.

13. Go to the top of the stack (the Flex modifier), apply another Mesh Select modifier, and go into Face, Sub-Object mode. Select Paste under the Selection Sets area of the Modifier panel. This will paste the face selection from the first Mesh Select modifier to the current one.

14. Without exiting from Sub-Object mode, apply a MeshSmooth modifier. Clear the Apply to Whole Mesh setting so that only the selected faces will be smoothed. You might want to set the MeshSmooth option to Inactive in Viewport to prevent slow screen refreshes during animation.

Caution

It is important that you not apply MeshSmooth prior to Flex in the modifier stack. That will greatly increase the computational demands of your animation, without offering much visual benefit.

Note

If you do render this animation to an AVI, be prepared for a much longer render. Flex is a computationally intensive modifier, and adding it to a complex mesh in your scene may increase render time several-fold.

15. To get a feel for what the effects of Flex will be, try out the View Ghosting feature. New to R3, this feature enables you to display several frames of animation simultaneously. To set the number of frames that will be ghosted, go to Customize/Preferences/Viewports. Set the number of Ghosting Frames to 1, and set Display Nth Frame to 2. This will display one image two frames before and

one image two frames after the current frame. You can also determine whether frames will be displayed from before, after, or both before and after the current frame. By default, both are displayed.

Note

Each frame is calculated separately, so displaying a large number of ghosted frames will slow your screen refresh rate.

16. Go to frame 86 and go to the Camera viewport. View Ghosting applies to the current selection only, so select Wormy. To turn Ghosting on, select View, Show Ghosting. You will need to refresh your screen or change frames to see the ghosted frames. To refresh, select Views, Redraw All Views (or press the 1 key). If you are in Wireframe mode, the blue mesh represents the past frame, and the green one represents the future frame. If you check Ghost in Wireframe in your Preferences, shaded viewports will display only the current frame's mesh as shaded. The past and future meshes will be rendered in Wireframe mode (see Figure 1.38).

Figure 1.38   View Ghosting reveals several frames of Wormy's landing.

Either render this animation to an AVI, or view the AVI file 01max04.avi on the accompanying CD-ROM.

Flex greatly eases the task of adding soft-body dynamics to an existing animation. For cartoonish characters, strong amounts of flex will add expressive qualities of movement. More realistic characters and objects can benefit from the subtle applications of lower flex values. Try applying Flex to projects you've completed, even in conjunction with forces like Wind and Push. The results may allow you to explore new aspects of your animations.

Using Morpher and Skin

The Morpher modifier works on meshes, patches, and NURBS models to alter an object's shape. Morphing is typically used in instances when the goal is a series of sequential changes between several reference versions of an original model. For example, consider facial animation, such as a character that's going to be speaking and going through a series of facial expressions. Morphing allows you to create several poses of your character's face and morph the original toward these variations throughout the course of your animation.

The Morpher modifier in MAX supports 100 *channels*, or variations of a model. Channel influences are additive, meaning that the results of several channels can be added together in the same frame.

The Skin modifier is a skeletal deformation modifier that deforms an object based on the movement of another object, typically called a *bone*. The vertex-deforming influence, or *envelope*, of a particular bone is created by default along its longest axis, but these envelopes can be easily reshaped. Cross sections that define bone envelopes can be added along a bone's length to further define specific envelope shapes. Specific vertices can be excluded from deformation, and bone influence can be interactively "painted" on an object's surface.

Although Skin does not offer all the advanced skeletal deformation controls that the Physique portion of Character Studio does (such as tendons or bulges), it is a powerful tool for effecting smooth deformations.

In the following exercises, you will use these two modifiers together to deform Wormy's body and face. You will use Skin to attach Wormy's mesh to a hierarchy of pre-animated bones, and you will use Morpher to animate the expressions of his face. The final animation will have Wormy snatching up a piece of fruit, popping it into his mouth, and chomping away.

Setting Up Morpher

To get the most out of this powerful modifier, you must take care to set up useful and accurate morph targets that will give you the expressive range necessary for your animation. In this tutorial, you will create morph targets and set up the Morpher modifier to prepare for a facial animation.

1. Load the scene 01max11.max from the accompanying CD-ROM. If you would like to see the final results of this tutorial, view the AVI file 01max09.avi.

2. Go to the Camera viewport. Note that Wormy is in his default "ready" pose. This model is a little different from the version used in previous exercises. In order to support a wide range of mouth expressions, Wormy's mouth interior has been enlarged and tesselated, and his chin area has been tesselated (see Figure 1.39). You will note that Wormy has also been outfitted with a set of teeth. These teeth have been retained as a separate object so you can morph them separately from the lips and mouth.

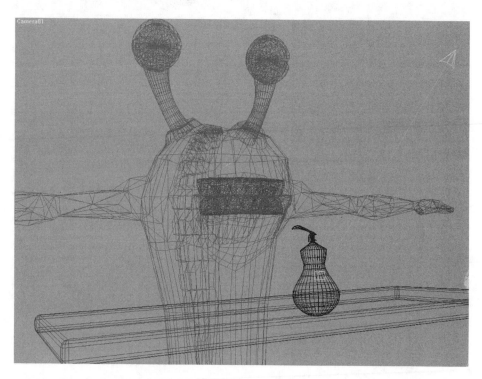

Figure 1.39   The details in Wormy's face and mouth area have been increased to support facial animation.

3. Go to the Front viewport. You will see several variations on Wormy's head and one of his left hand off to the side (see Figure 1.40). These morph targets have been created by simple vertex editing of the original model. The missing parts of the morph targets have not been deleted, neither has the vertex count; the order has not been changed in any way. This is a requirement for morphing between mesh objects. In this case, the missing faces have been hidden to allow you to focus on the area to be animated. If you want to unhide these faces, select a target, go to Face, Sub-Object mode, and select Unhide All. Moreover, the prepared morph targets have been set to non-rendering, so you will not have to hide them for test renders. To access this setting, select an object, right-click on it, select Properties from the submenu, and check the Renderable setting under Rendering Control.

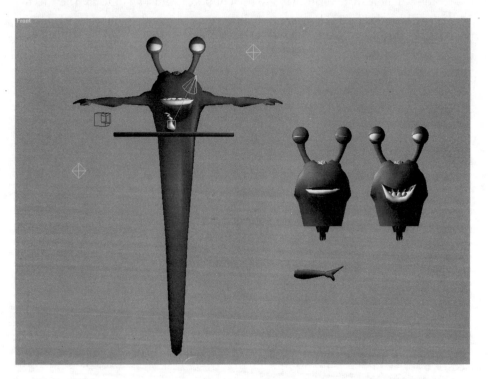

Figure 1.40   Morph targets, to the right of the original, have been provided for blinking, smiling, and open-hand poses.

4. You will now create two morph targets to support Wormy's biting pose. Two objects have been set aside: "open" and "teeth_open." Select both. These two targets represent Wormy's open mouth pose. To make it easier to work on just these two objects, go to the Display panel and select Hide Unselected.

5. Apply an Edit Mesh modifier, go to a Left viewport, and zoom in on Wormy's profile.

6. Select "open." Go to Vertex, Sub-Object mode and fence select the outermost vertices of the lower lip and chin as shown in Figure 1.41. Turn on Soft Selection, set Fall Off to 15, and confirm that Affect Backfacing is turned on. Turn on Edge Distance and set the spinner to 8. The Edge Distance control keeps vertices that are separated from the selected vertices by more than the set number of edges from being included in the soft selection influence. This will help you to edit Wormy's lower jaw without influencing his upper jaw as well.

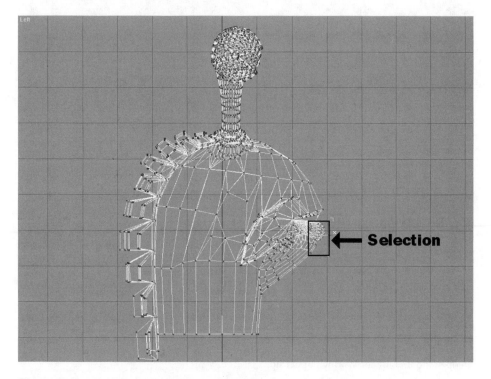

Figure 1.41   Vertex selection to support creation of open mouth pose morph target.

7. Go to Rotate mode and select Use Transform Coordinate Center under the Use Center flyout. Choose Parent as the Reference Coordinate System. This allows you to rotate the selection around the pivot point of the main object. Turn on Angle Snap and rotate the selection 30 degrees on the Parent's x-axis.

8. Select the lower-most vertex on the inside curve of the neck and move it down and to the right on the View XY Plane to smooth out the underside of the jaw.

This particular vertex is number 261. To confirm that you have the correct vertex selected, check the bottom of the Selection area just above Soft Selection. This area lists the number of vertices selected, or the number assigned to a single vertex if only one is selected.

9. Select the vertex on the tip of the upper lip (number 344), set Fall Off to 30, and move up and to the right to stretch the upper jaw. You should now have a nice wide open pose for Wormy's mouth (see Figure 1.42).

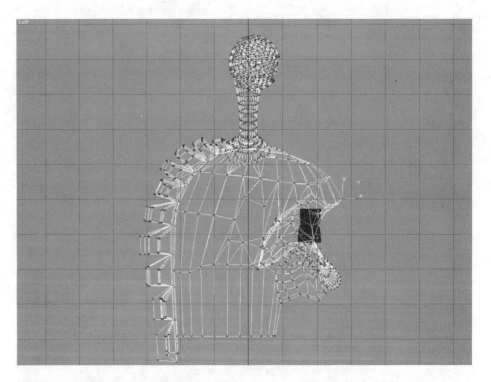

Figure 1.42   Moving just one vertex and deforming many others with Soft Selection creates an open mouth pose for Wormy's upper lip.

10. Now, you will create a morph target for the teeth in the open mouth position. Select the "teeth_open" object, apply an Edit Mesh modifier, go to Element, Sub-Object mode, and select the top row of teeth. Go to Rotate mode, choose Parent under the Reference Coordinate system flyout, and choose Use Transform Coordinate Center under the Use Center flyout. Rotate the selection –10 degrees on the x-axis.

11. Select the bottom row of teeth and rotate 15 degrees on the x-axis.

12. Because the lower jaw is stretched in this position, the extreme ends of the bottom row of teeth will poke through the skin. To repair this, apply a Bend modifier to the sub-object selection, set Angle to 50, set Direction to –200, and choose X as the Bend Axis. Your mileage may differ, so adjust accordingly.

13. Apply a Mesh Select modifier, go to Element, Sub-Object mode, and select the top row of teeth. Apply a Bend modifier to the sub-object selection, set Angle to 50, set Direction to 15, and choose X as the Bend Axis. Figure 1.43 shows the result.

Figure 1.43 Wormy's teeth are also edited to complement the open-mouth pose.

Note

When creating morph targets, feel free to apply whatever modifiers or space warps you want. As long as you do not change the number of vertices, you will be able to use the target. Also, note that the actual position of the teeth morph target in your scene is meaningless. Morpher takes into account only transformations relative to the object's pivot point. Placing the mouth-open target for the teeth with the target for the body simply makes it easier to see how the two morphed objects will interact.

14. Before you can add the Morpher modifier to your original objects, you must unhide them. Moreover, hidden objects cannot be assigned to morph channels,

so you must unhide all your target objects as well. Go to the Display panel, select Unhide by Name, and choose the following objects to unhide: "blink," "smile," "teeth_smile," "teeth_closed," "hand_open," and "Wormy."

15. Go to the Camera viewport, select the original "Wormy" object, and apply a Morpher modifier.

Note

Morpher consists of several panels. The Channel Color Legend panel displays a key explaining the significance of the color codes displayed next to each channel in the Channel List. The Global Parameters panel provides controls for affecting all channels in the Morpher modifier. You will use the Channel List and Channel Parameters panels most often; these areas provide controls for picking targets, setting up morph channels, and reloading targets should you modify them after creating a channel. Finally, the Advanced Parameters panel controls a few aspects of the Morpher interface, as well as offering an estimate of the memory cost determined by channel usage (see Figure 1.44).

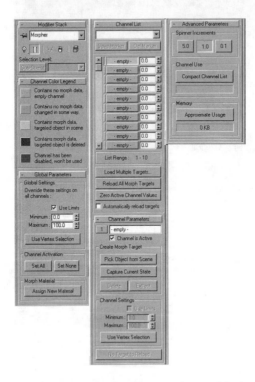

Figure 1.44   Details of the Morpher modifier's panels.

16. You can choose from several methods of assigning morph channels. Right-click on the first empty channel in the Channel List, choose Pick from Scene from the pop-up menu, and press the H key to bring up the Selection List. Choose the "blink" object from the list and click OK.

17. Click on the next empty slot to choose that channel. Go to the Channel Parameters rollout and click on the Pick from Scene button. Use the Selection List to assign the "smile" object to this channel.

18. Go to a Front viewport. Activate the next empty slot, click on Pick from Scene, and click on the "open" object.

19. Assign the "hand_open" object to the fourth channel. Note that only compatible objects with the same number of vertices can be selected via the Select Objects list or by direct selection.

Note

When you have assigned your morph targets, you are no longer required to keep them in your scene. The requisite vertex deformations are stored in the modifier, not in your scene. You may hide them or even delete them entirely. Of course, if you remove them from your scene, you will not be able to reload them into your Morpher modifier should you need to edit your targets.

20. Go to the Camera viewport. Turn on Smooth + Highlights and play with the channel Percentage sliders. Note that as you drag a slider toward 100, the original object's vertices move toward the state they have been edited to in the morph target. Try mixing the "blink" and "open" channels. Because these channels do not share edited vertices in their respective targets, you can freely change one channel's percentage without affecting the other. Now try mixing the "open" and "smile" channels. These two channels influence many of the same vertices, so their effect is cumulative.

21. Go to the Global Parameters panel and clear Use Limits. This allows you to drag your sliders beyond the specified minimum and maximum. Channel percentages outside this range will cause affected vertices to be interpolated. For example, set the "blink" channel percentage to –100. The eyelids will then move in the direction opposite from the morph target, giving Wormy a very suprised expression.

22. Wormy's teeth did not, of course, move with his jaw when you changed those channel percentages. You will need to apply a Morpher modifier to the "teeth_closed" object to do so. Assign "teeth_open" to channel 1 and "teeth_smile" to channel 2. If you set the "teeth_open" slider to 100 and the "open" slider in Wormy's main Morpher modifier to 100 as well, you should see a nice open-mouth pose.

23. Reset all channel percentages to 0 using the Zero Active Channel Values button at the bottom of the Channel List of each object's Morpher modifier, and you are finished with the Morpher setup for this animation.

To see a completed version of this MAX file, or to ensure that your morph channels are set up properly, load the scene 01max12.max from the accompanying CD-ROM.

Now that you have prepared for the morphing portion of this animation, the next step is setting up the Skin modifier. These two modifiers will work in conjunction to create the final animation.

Setting Up Skin

One of the most important steps in using the Skin modifier is ensuring that the envelopes being used to deform the modified object are properly shaped. Envelopes that are too large will deform areas that should be beyond that particular bone's influence. A prime example of this occurs when the rotation of a character's upper arm causes movement in the rib area. Envelopes that are too small to encompass the modified object leave vertices behind when the object is deformed.

1. Load the scene 01max12.max from the accompanying CD-ROM, or continue from the file you created in the preceding tutorial.

2. Go to the Camera viewport. Go to frame 0.

3. A pre-animated skeleton has been provided for this exercise. Hide all objects with the exception of "Wormy," "teeth_closed," "table," and "fruit." To unhide the 16 bones, select "bones" from the Named Selection Set list. At the prompt that asks if you want to unhide the objects, click Yes. Figure 1.45 shows the standard MAX bones, joined in a simple hierarchy and positioned to control Wormy's head, torso, and arms. The Skin modifier does not require that bone objects be in a hierarchy, which makes Skin particularly useful for high-detail facial animation.

4. Scrub the Time slider; you will see that these bones have already been animated. Beginning at frame 1, the character implied by the bones seems to swipe at the fruit, gesture towards its face, and then resume an unright pose. At frame 0, however, this skeleton has been keyed into its initialization pose. Skin requires a frame to initialize its influence over the modified mesh. This frame defaults to 0, but you can specify another frame. Select "Wormy" and go to frame 0 to apply the Skin modifier.

Note

The fruit is linked to Wormy's right hand during the frames in which he is holding it, and it is unlinked from his hand to fall into his mouth by use of the Link Controller. This controller allows you to animate the link between a child and various parents. The link of the "fruit" object is passed from the table to Wormy's hand and then to Wormy. To examine these keys, go to the Link Parameters area of the Motion panel.

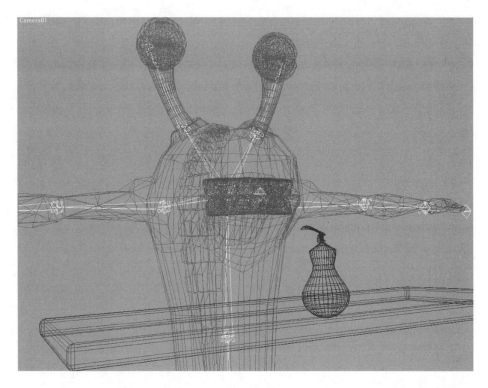

Figure 1.45   Pre-animated bones for use with the Skin modifier.

5. Select the "Wormy" and "teeth_closed" objects and apply a Skin modifier. Bones are listed in the List window and are added or removed using the buttons below the window. Select Add Bone, select all 16 "bone_" objects in the Select Bones dialog box, and click Select. (You can also type "bo" in the selection field, which will select for you all objects in the scene beginning with those two letters.) If you scrub the time slider, you will see that Wormy follows the bones' movement, but with some unsettling distortions. The bone envelopes need to be edited to fit Wormy's mesh.

6. To edit the radius and strength of an envelope, go into Envelope, Sub-Object mode. You can select specific envelopes either by selecting the gray boxes positioned near the ends of each bone or by selecting a specific bone from the List window. Select the "bone_head" envelope, for example. The envelope's primary area of influence is drawn in bright red, and the outer limits are drawn in dark red. Vertices are shaded, ranging from red to green to blue, according to the degree by which the selected envelope will influence those vertices. Note that the

vertices defining the lower end of Wormy's ruffle are shaded blue, which means those vertices will not be deformed.

7. Each cross section is delineated by four red handles. Select the lower cross section by clicking one of its handles. To scale a cross section, click and drag the handle. While a cross section is selected, you can also enter radius values directly using the entry box in the Envelope Properties area of the Skin modifier.

8. First, you will examine the envelope settings for the main part of Wormy's body to make sure he will deform smoothly. Start with the "bone_neck" envelope. Go to a User viewport and zoom to the selected envelope. The vertices shaded blue will cause some trouble when bending this joint, so select the upper cross section and scale both the inner and outer radii to 30.

9. Moving up the body, select the "bone_head" envelope. Note that its radii will need to be increased as well, to encompass the vertices in the neck area. Scale the inner radius of the lower cross section to 25 and the outer radius to 30. Scale the inner radius of the upper cross section to 30 and the outer radius to 38. The goal here is to encompass the entire head without affecting the eyestalks, as this will conflict with the bones used to animate the eyestalks (see Figure 1.46).

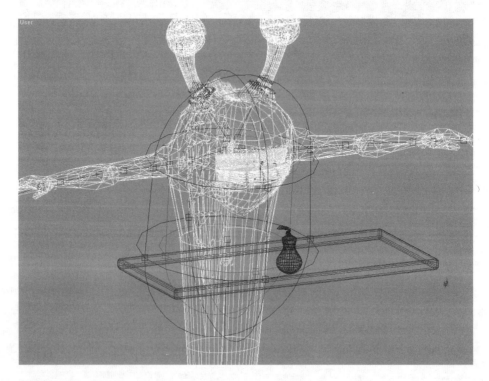

Figure 1.46   Tweaking envelope cross section settings.

10. Select the "bone_mouth" envelope. Select the outer radius of the cross section closest to the center of the head and scale to 30. Scale the inner radius to 29. Select the outer radius of the cross section farthest from the head center and scale to 30. Scale the inner radius to 29.

Note

Using a cross section radius greater than that which is required to contain Wormy's "at rest" pose gives you some extra room to accommodate morph targets that will be applied earlier in the stack. If you recall the "open" morph target you created, parts of Wormy's mouth and lips were moved away from his head. If the Skin envelopes encompassed Wormy's basic mesh only, and Morpher caused some vertices to move beyond those envelopes, then tearing can occur where those vertices cease being deformed by Skin.

11. Scrub the Time slider to show how much more smoothly Wormy is being deformed, especially in the face area, now that some of the Skin envelopes have been expanded.

12. Now let's examine some of the areas that traditionally require extra attention when animating characters. Select the "bone_right_elbow" envelope. To prevent the vertices under the arm from pinching toward the center of the torso when Wormy's hand bends down, scale the outer radius of the cross section closest to the body to 14 and the inner radius to 7.

13. The elbow is another area to watch. To keep the elbow area from collapsing or appearing to decrease in volume, scale the outer radius of the cross section closest to the elbow to 10 and the inner radius to 4. Repeat this step for the "bone_left_elbow" envelope.

14. Select the "bone_right_wrist" envelope. Select the cross section closest to the elbow and scale the inner radius to 7 and the outer radius to 8. Select the other cross section and scale the inner radius to 4 and the outer radius to 5. If you go to frame 60, where Wormy's elbow joint is flexed, you can see how these edits improve the appearance of the bent arm. Repeat this step for the "bone_left_wrist" envelope.

15. Select the "bone_right_hand" envelope. Select the cross section closest to the wrist and scale the outer radius to 8. Repeat this step for the "bone_left_hand" envelope.

16. Finally, after completing the setup, you are ready to animate this character with Skin and Morpher. Hide the bones in your scene, leaving just the following objects visible: "Wormy," "teeth_closed," "table," and "fruit."

17. Open the Time Configuration dialog box and set the Start Time to 1 and the End Time to 90. Assuming that Frame Rate is set to NTSC or 30 frames per second, this will create an animation sequence lasting nearly 3 seconds. Starting your animation at frame 1 will prevent conflict with the Skin modifier's initialization at frame 0.

To see a completed version of this MAX file or to ensure that your envelopes are set correctly, load the scene 01max12.max from the accompanying CD-ROM.

Now that you have completed the setup of the Skin modifier, Wormy should follow the bone motions without distortions. Because Skin works according to envelope settings as opposed to specific vertex selections, it is especially effective when combined with Morpher. When morphing causes vertices to change position (even moving from the influence of one bone to another), Skin will simply include those vertices in the appropriate envelope.

Morpher and Skin for Character Animation

With Morpher and Skin properly set up for this character, you can animate using both modifiers. Note that the parameters of Skin are not animatable; it is solely through the bone animations that Skin deforms the modified object.

Note

In most cases, you won't want to animate your character from a Camera viewport; but because Wormy's morph targets are all pre-set and his expressions will be playing to the camera, feel free to follow the next steps using Morpher in the Camera viewport.

1. Load the scene 01max13.max from the accompanying CD-ROM, or continue from the file you created in the preceding tutorial. If you would like to preview the final results of this tutorial, view the AVI file 01max09.avi. Select "Wormy" and go to the Morpher modifier in the stack.

2. Turn the Animate button on and go to frame 1. Select Wormy and choose Morpher from the Modifier stack. Start by "softening" Wormy's expression. Set the "blink" channel to 20 and the "smile" channel to 10.

3. At frame 10, increase Wormy's smile of anticipation by setting the "smile" channel to 60. His right hand should be opening wide in preparation for the snatch, so set "hand_open" to 50. You will need to maintain his teeth in a similar pose, so select "teeth_closed," go to the Morpher modifier, and set "teeth_smile" to 60 as well.

4. Select Wormy again. At frame 23, Wormy makes his grab and is getting serious, so set both "smile" and "teeth_smile" to 10. His gaze should intensify, as well, so set "blink" to 40. As his hand makes contact with the fruit, set "hand_open" to −50. You will be using Wormy's "open" pose at the next keyframe, so set an empty key now to keep him from slowly opening his mouth over frames 1–23. The quickest way to set an empty key is to increment the "open" channel percentage and then decrement back to 0.

5. At frame 35, Wormy is about to pop that fruit into his mouth (see Figure 1.47). Set "open" to 80 and "smile" to 0. Set "hand_open" to −30. He'll close his eyes for the bite, so set "blink" to 100. For his teeth, set "teeth_open" to 100 and "teeth_smile" to 0.

Figure 1.47   Wormy's mouth is wide open to accept his lunch.

6. At frame 39, the fruit disappears down his gullet. Set "open" to 100, "teeth_open" to 130, and "hand_open" to 0. To set values higher than 100, you will need to clear Use Limits in the Global Parameters panel.

7. Wormy will bite down fairly quickly, so go to frame 42 and set both "open" and "teeth_open" to 0.

8. At frame 50, Wormy is ready to start chewing. Open his eyes by setting "blink" to 20. Use the open mouth morph target to close his mouth tightly by setting "open" to –25.

9. Now you will add a couple of blinks to the last half of this sequence. At frame 60, set "blink" to 0. At frame 65, set "blink" to 100. At frame 72, set "blink" to 10. This creates a nice slow blink in frames 60–72.

10. The second blink will be a bit quicker. At frame 80, set "blink" to 0. At frame 83, set "blink" to 100. At frame 86, set "blink" to 10.

11. Play your animation back. You may notice some strange effects from the morphing process. Wormy's eyelids close tightly around frame 10 when they're supposed to be ramping from 20% to 40%. By default, morph channels are assigned the default Float controller. This can cause channel values to vary greatly between keys, especially if Use Limits is turned off. When Use Limits is turned on, channel percentages may still range beyond the specified limits, but the actual morph effect is limited to only the range you specify.

12. In the case of this animation, you will get better results by editing the In/Out tangents of the morph channel function curves. Open Track View and expand Objects, Wormy, Modified Object, Morpher until the morph channels are visible. Checking Show Only: Animated Tracks in the Track View Filter dialog box removes extraneous information. A shortcut to expanding multiple levels in Track View is to right-click in the viewport and select Track View Selected from the pop-up menu.

13. Select the "blink" channel and turn on Function Curves. Note how the curve swings up between frames 1 and 23. Fence select those two keys on the function curve and right-click to bring up Key Properties. Change both tangent types to Linear (the second item in the pop-up menu). This will flatten the curve as the "blink" channel ramps up. Feel free to correct the curve during the two blinks at the end of the animation, although you might want to allow the exaggerated motion—as long as it doesn't distort the eyelids excessively.

14. The "open" channel actually curves into a negative value between frames 0 and 23 and frames 42 and 50. Select those keys and set their tangents to Linear.

15. Examine the "smile" and "hand_open" channels. The tangents for these curves don't seem to be creating excessive changes, so leave them at their defaults.

16. The chewing motion, which will be the main focus of this animation, is between frames 50 and 91 and will be created by a sub-object Xform. This is a fairly

simple modifier, but it's powerful when it comes to animating sub-object transformations and transforming objects at a specific point in the stack.

17. Select Wormy, go the top of the stack (the Skin modifier), and apply a Mesh
    Select modifier. The actual vertex selection has been prepared for you. Go to
    Editable Mesh, Vertex Sub-Object, and select Copy from the Named Selections
    list. Select "Chewing" from the list. Close Sub-Object mode and return to Mesh
    Select. Go to Vertex, Sub-Object mode and select Paste from the Named
    Selections list. The vertices that make up the center and underside of Wormy's
    lower lip should be selected.

18. Turn on Soft Selection, set Fall Off to 18, and set Bubble to 0.25. This is the selec-
    tion to which you will apply the chewing motion.

19. Without leaving Sub-Object mode, apply an Xform modifier. A gizmo will
    appear, surrounding the selected vertices. Confirm that the Animate button is on,
    and then select the Squash variant of Scale mode.

20. Go to frame 50 and squash the gizmo on the z-axis 95%. This will cause the
    gizmo to increase in scaling 105% on both the x- and y-axes.

21. Wormy will chew approximately twice per second. So go to frame 57 and squash
    on the z-axis 125%. Then go to frame 64 and squash to 75%. For the second
    chewing motion, squash to 125% at frame 70 and squash to 75% at frame 77.
    For the third and final chewing motion, squash to 125% at frame 82 and to 90%
    at frame 88.

22. Go to an early frame (around 20) and note that Xform is creating a severe distor-
    tion. To correct this, open Track View and examine the Xform gizmo's Scale
    track. Select the keys at frames 1 and 50 and set their tangent types to Linear.

23. Play your animation back. Note that Wormy's teeth protrude through his skin at
    certain points during his chewing motions. You could animate the scaling of his
    teeth to make them stay within his head, but because his teeth aren't visible after
    frame 50, animating the visibility of his teeth will be more straightforward.

24. Exit Sub-Object mode and select "teeth_closed." Open Track View, expand
    Objects, and select the "teeth_closed" track. Select Add Visibility Track from the
    Track View toolbar. Note that this tool is available in Edit Keys mode only. If you
    have checked Show Only: Animated Tracks in the Filters dialog box, you will
    need to clear it for your Visibility track to be displayed. Select the visibility track,
    select Add Key, and add keys at frames 50 and 51. Right-click on the key at frame
    51 and change its value to 0. This will cause Wormy's teeth to completely disap-
    pear at frame 51 and remain invisible for the remainder of the animation.

As you have learned in the preceding tutorials, Skin and Morpher work well together for creating character animation. Skin works best when applied to limbs and body parts that need to move in conjunction with other parts. Morpher should be considered for animating objects or sub-object selections that need to move from one pose (or combination of poses) to another. You could even use Skin to deform a morphed portion of a character, such as the lower jaw. In such a case, the transforms created by Skin and Morpher would be added together to determine the final deformation.

In Practice: Animating with Multiple Modifiers

- **Modifying geometry.** Modifiers are the primary tool for manipulating geometry. Each deforms geometry in a different manner. A single modifier can also be applied to multiple objects to create a unified effect.

- **Animating with modifiers.** Every modifier provides you with a different animation option. For almost any animation need, a modifier or combination of modifiers can create the desired geometric manipulation.

- **Layering modifiers.** The order that modifiers appear in the stack can completely alter the resulting geometry. Pay careful attention to the chronological order of the Stack History.

- **Selection methods.** You have several different techniques to choose from in passing selections to subsequent modifiers. Sub-object selections can restrict modifiers to specific portions of an object. The placement of a modifier's gizmo or center can drastically alter the effect.

- **Soft Selections.** This option added to the Edit Mesh and Mesh Select modifiers can turn straightforward modifier effects into organic transformations. Any sub-object animation can be turned into a gradual effect by adding a Soft Selection.

- **Free Form Deformation.** A powerful tool for organic manipulation of objects or a selection of objects, an FFD applies a gradated influence on object geometry according to the position of Control Points.

- **Flex.** This modifier greatly eases the addition of natural secondary motion to your animations. Reaction and inertia are automatically calculated according to object movement. Flex can even take into account sub-object movement, such as that caused by morphing.

- **Morpher.** Morpher is a great tool for animating a series of specific, sequential changes to an object. Facial animation, lip synch, and muscle bulges are just a few examples of the kinds of effects this modifier can help you achieve.

- **Skin.** The Skin modifier enables you to quickly and easily achieve skeletal deformations. Envelopes used to define bone influences can be tweaked in a number of ways to allow for a variety of deformations.

Part II

Character Animation

Chapter 2

Basic Character and Creature Setup

By Angie Jones

The *setup* or *skeleton rig* of your character is literally and figuratively its backbone. To create a stable setup, you'll need a technical and creative eye, as well as a comprehensive understanding of 3D Studio MAX R3's character tools, such as bones, Forward Kinematics, and Inverse Kinematics. A clean skeleton will save you much heartache and frustration when you animate. Planning and flexibility are the two most important elements of your character setup. This chapter will help you plan the best route to a stable yet versatile skeleton.

The tutorials included in this chapter should clear up many of the problematic and difficult areas of creating a basic skeletal framework in 3D Studio MAX. For example, a stable skeleton in 3D Studio MAX has always been beyond reach for most users. The bones in MAX R3 have many settings that are *not* hardwired into the default parameters and will lead you down a path of frustration. Follow the tutorials here and you should learn much about MAX R3 character tools, how they work, and how to create a solid skeleton in MAX. If you already have a good understanding of how to build skeletal structures in MAX, move on to the next chapter, which covers advanced skeletal setup in MAX.

This chapter explores the following topics:

- Basic anatomy structures
- Basics of character setup in 3D Studio MAX R3
- Planning a skeleton rig
- Forward Kinematics (FK)
- Inverse Kinematics (IK)
- Use of dummy constraints and expressions to drive the skeleton

Skeletons and Anatomical Structures

Before beginning any task, you should educate yourself on the subject matter at hand. The human skeleton is a complex structure. Even though your character might be some sort of creature (see Figure 2.1), you will need an understanding of a human skeleton to build it. All creature and human skeletons share these basic frameworks:

- Leg tree
- Spine, neck, and head
- Pelvis
- Arm tree
- Scapula, clavicle complex shoulder
- Phalanx (finger, toe joints)

Figure 2.1 Skeleton rigging can be fun!

These six skeletal structures are in all creatures. So why does a human look so different from a mountain lion? The answer is *proportion*. All living things are built with basically the same framework but have different proportions on that very framework (see Figure 2.2).

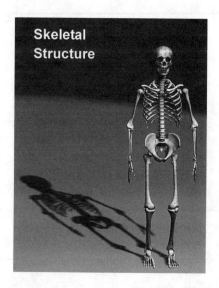

Figure 2.2 Skeleton structure for an upright bipedal character.

For example, the phalanx or finger and nail bones of a chimpanzee are very similar to those of a man; however, these bones are proportionately longer than a human's. The proportion changes also affect how the character moves. For example, a chimpanzee's longer fingers enable it to use its hands to move on all fours. Humans would have a more difficult time propelling motion on all fours because their finger joints are smaller and would have difficulty supporting the weight of a human. There are anatomy book references in the back of this book. I suggest you use them as supplemental reading to help you understand how the skeleton is designed and how the joints work together to create motion.

Planning and Flexibility

Advance planning is important for a successful character animation. Knowing the proportions of your character's skeleton is a good first step. Next, you must decide which type of skeletal structure to rig for the setup. Skeleton *rigging* is the process of creating the basic framework you will use to produce motion for a character. MAX offers several types of skeletal structures or *hierarchies* with which you can rig this framework. The main types are listed here:

- Forward Kinematics (FK)
- Inverse Kinematics (IK)
- Broken hierarchies
- FK using expressions
- Mix of IK and FK

Note

If you're new to character animation, some of the terminology might be confusing. To be sure we're all speaking the same language, you need to know a few definitions:

Hierarchy. A MAX R3 term, a hierarchy is the arrangement of all parent and children objects linked in a single structure.

Skeleton. This is any structure designed for use in animation that is created by linking hierarchies. In a general sense, it stands for the supporting structure or framework for the body. In any CG package, the skeleton serves the same purpose it does in real-life anatomy: It holds up the rest of the body and permits motion.

Structure. Any specific hierarchy of objects that represents the skeleton.

Framework. Any specific structure that represents the skeleton.

Skeleton rig. The complex linking of additional constraints to create a setup for the character that will deliver the motion demanded by the scene.

If you really want to get the most out of your skeleton rig, you will use all these hierarchies at one time or another, depending on the demands of your animation, such as the complexity of the character mesh and the motion needed. This means you will have to use more than one rig to animate the character. The transition between hierarchies will be easy once you understand the tools and possible combinations for the setup. Simply by linking a structure and its constraints in different ways, you can change a rig to suit your needs. Planning and a complete understanding of the tools and skeletal structures will help eliminate the frustration you would experience with an improperly built setup.

In the sections that follow, you will learn how to create a structure that is extremely light and easy to use but that doesn't give up important functionality. As you approach a project, be open to various setups. The demands of one scene might require a different skeletal setup than those of another. When you learn how to use the tools provided in MAX R3, you can create most any skeleton rig to meet the demands of your character animation.

Forward Kinematics

Forward Kinematics is the most basic of all hierarchy structures. When you create a tree of linked objects or bones, you have created an FK hierarchy. As you go down the links of a hierarchy, FK bones are children to the previous bone in the tree and take on the rotation, translation, and scale properties of the previous bone. See Figure 2.3 for an example FK tree.

 Note

You can make any arbitrary objects and link them into a hierarchy. Or, if you create MAX Bones, they are already linked into a chain.

Figure 2.3   A Forward Kinematic hierarchy tree.

FK is a great introduction to basic tree framework and how it functions. However, there are limitations to this type of tree because of its simplicity. FK makes animation difficult because you will always have to work your way down the tree to create poses.

In other words, if you rotate the shoulder joint, the elbow, wrist, and finger joints will all follow that initial rotation of the parent. You must always compensate for each parent bone's rotation when you pose each joint. FK is a good skeleton rig to choose if you need to create poses of the character for still images only. This is because you will never depend upon the previous pose to create motion. An FK rig could be very cumbersome if you needed to animate the character.

For example, it's very difficult to create a walk cycle with an FK setup because every time you move the hips, the leg trees follow as children to the hip bone. The legs and feet need to stay in place as the hips compensate for weight shifts when you animate a walk. Therefore, with an FK setup, you always have to compensate for the motion as it moves down the tree, which can be very frustrating.

One advantage to using FK is that this constant compensation guarantees the use of arcs in your animation and provides more control of the breaks in the joint motion. By arcs, I am referring to the basic motion any joint has when moving. When you turn your head it does not move directly to the left like a machine. The head arcs down and then up to complete the turn. Every joint in the body follows these arcs. FK forces you to create arcs because every bone is rotated on its individual axis. These rotations force the skeleton to move in arcs. This is one reason why many animators prefer to have FK on the arms of their skeleton when working on pantomime or dialogue sequences. This power to rotate each bone is also bittersweet control because it requires you to keep up with more keys in the Track View. This can make adjusting the animation very difficult. Choose your character tools wisely.

One more tool that can help with FK trees is Link Info. The Link Info rollout under the Hierarchy panel is helpful for locking or limiting the motion of FK hierarchies. An example of this is used in the exercises on the neck and head tree. The human head rotates on its vertical axis only, while the neck handles the rotations for both a side-to-side rock and a nodding action. To limit this movement, you can use Link Info to lock axes that should not move for that bone. Whatever axes you lock will not receive any animation information, nor will the bone be able to rotate on those locked axes. One other function under Link Info is Link Inheritance, which limits the bones or objects in the tree so they rotate only on their local axes and do not inherit the rotations of their parents. This function is not used in this chapter, and it is commonly used for mechanical machine motion more than for a character's organic movements.

Note

If you were to use IK on your skeleton, you could translate the hand to move in a straight line. However, this motion would look very mechanical and puppet-like. This is why you have to check your arcs with IK and be sure you have used linear translations only where they are needed (like if the character was hit by something).

Another advantage to using FK is that you can decide which part of the tree rotates first. This is where "breaking" joints comes in. For example, to point at something, you tend to move from the shoulder first and then the elbow joint makes a quicker rotation than the rest of the joints in the arm's tree to point. This breaking of the joint action is what will give your animation snap. With the other main structure, Inverse Kinematics, the IK solution decides the order and rotation of the bones in that chain for you. You cannot achieve the same snap you would get if you were rotating the bones individually. So, if your character has some really active motion going on, you might opt for FK on the arms to get more control over arcs and breaking joints.

When to Use FK

A segmented mesh is a good choice for applying FK because you can create the tree without a hierarchy of bones at all. Appropriate for stiff items, such as wooden puppets, plastic toys, suits of armor, and armature, the segmented mesh structure is a bunch of pieces linked at the joints. The skeleton file on the CD, called Skeleton_SEG_OK.max, is an example of a segmented mesh linked as one whole FK tree. All the mesh parts have been linked to create this hierarchy. If you rotate the upper leg bone, you will see that the rest of the tree follows (see Figure 2.4).

It is important to note that when a segmented skeleton is created, you must move the pivot points of all the pieces from the default center of the object to the joint rotation axis area. For example, you must move the pivot point of a shin bone/object to the top of the knee joint where it will bend so that it will rotate correctly. In Figure 2.3, you can see that the axis of the thigh bone has been moved to the hip area so it rotates at the hip joint.

FK skeletons are best used in scenes for narrative pantomime in which the character will simply be talking and not moving about much. The choice of FK and IK structures is a creative and personal choice for many animators. For example, I prefer IK on the legs and feet to make them stick to the ground, but I like to use FK everywhere else so I have complete control of the skeleton. I will, however, provide an explanation of an IK setup for the arms, as well as its uses, in specific animations later in this chapter.

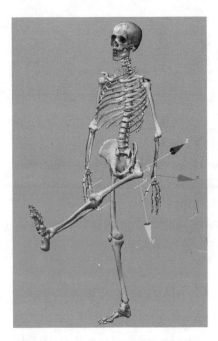

Figure 2.4   When you move the parent in an FK tree, the children follow. As the hip rotates, so do the knee and ankle joints, which follow the axis of the parent hip bone.

Inverse Kinematics

Inverse Kinematics is essentially the reverse of an FK tree. The last bone in an IK tree is the "parent" of the previous bones. With IK, a foot bone in a leg tree can be translated, and the IK solution will solve how the knee and hip bones should rotate and position themselves to create convincing motion. If animating an FK tree is like individually moving each part of a solid armature, working with an IK rig is like moving a puppet around with strings attached to the limbs.

Inverse Kinematics is possibly the most difficult setup of the choices you can make for the skeleton rig. However, the payback for this painful process can be enormous when a rig is created correctly. Many people shy from IK rigs, but if you ever want to create a walk cycle, IK is necessary to keep those feet stuck to the floor. Therefore, IK makes the animator's job easier.

You need to know about the following MAX R3 tools before you begin creating an IK setup:

- **IK controller (Create/Systems/Bones/Bone Parameters).** This is one of the many controllers you can use in MAX to animate. The IK controller applies an end effector to either the root or the child of the bones tree you create, depending on the settings you choose. In turn, the end effector will solve the rest of the tree's motion for you through Inverse Kinematics.

- **End effector (Motion Panel/IK Controller Parameters).** This is the node that controls the IK chain. The position and rotation of the end effector determine the solution for the rest of the tree. Both a Position end effector and a Rotation end effector are available in MAX. The Position end effector tells the IK chain to follow its *position* in space, and the Rotation end effector tells the IK chain to follow its *orientation* in space. Dummies are used in MAX R3 to constrain the motion of the end effector. Both the Position and Rotation end effectors have important uses, so pay attention to how they are used in the tutorials.

- **Applied IK (Customize/Preferences/Inverse Kinematics).** This command enables you to "pin" a bone in your IK structure to follow another object. Applied IK is useful for when you want an object to match exactly to the motion of another object. Beware: Using Applied IK places a key on every frame for your animation, so don't overuse this tool.

- **Show/Lock Initial State (Motion Panel/IK Controller Parameters).** This setting will show or lock the position in which your bones were initially created. It operates much like Figure mode in Biped. You can use this setting to reorient your bones outside of the IK solution and create limits for the joints. Remember: You must have Show/Lock Initial State turned on to "interactively" adjust the bones limits with the spinners. In other words, if you want to see how much of an angle in rotation you are assigning to each bone while dragging the spinner, Show/Lock Initial State must be turned on.

- **Weight (Hierarchy Panel/Object Parameters).** Very important to solid IK in MAX, this setting for Position and Orientation tells the IK rig the relative importance of the joints in the chain. This is a fairly complex concept, but it's vital to the success of your skeleton.

If you have two effectors in the same tree, the one with the highest Weight value will be solved first. This means if you had a value of 35 on the knee effector and a value of 300 on the foot effector, the foot position would be solved before the knee. Therefore, the foot would more accurately follow your Position end effector first, and the knee's rotation would be solved relative to the foot position. In other words, the Weight value determines how closely the end effector follows the IK solution. If you weight the IK to follow one end effector more than the other, it will do so. The Weight values are relative to one another through the tree, so a little experimentation might be needed to find the right value for this setting. This value is important to a separate end effector for a knee. By making the knee controller less important than the end effector controlling the foot position, you can command the foot end effector to solve its position first and then solve the rotation of the knee second. This is one of the more confusing parameters in MAX's IK, but it's very important when you're creating a skeleton that follows an IK solution correctly.

- **IK Thresholds (Motion Panel/IK Controller Parameters).** This MAX setting is what tells the IK solver how closely to match what the end effector is doing. The lower the number, the more closely the solver will match the end effector's position and rotation; however, on a machine with a CPU slower than 300MHz, it could affect display performance, so be aware of the value you select for this setting and its impact on display. The default value is 1.0, which instructs the IK solution to follow about half of what the end effector does. This parameter was added to help with display problems on slower machines, but the default value becomes a hindrance to solid IK. A value of 0.0 will ensure your IK solution always follows the end effector exactly.

- **IK Solution Iterations (Motion Panel/IK Controller Parameters).** This setting also controls how closely the IK solution follows the end effector. The Iteration is a recursive value that will be used to test the solution over and over again. The higher the value, the more times the solution will be tested to create the most exact result. This also could affect performance on machines with a CPU slower than 300MHz. Always use the most flexible value to enable the best performance without slowing the display. I recommend a value of 500 for this setting; it's a solid value that won't tax most machines. It means every time you move the end effector, the placement of the IK solution for the rest of the tree will be recursively tested 500 times to ensure it is exactly where it should be.

- **IK Solution Start and End Time (Motion Panel/IK Controller Parameters).** The IK solution Start and End Time also affects how accurately the IK is solved. The value here should be at least the length of your animation. This setting will affect performance on any machine if it is set too high. Set the Start and End Time to match the animation you are animating. A value of 500 for the End Time should be sufficient for most animations; anything higher might affect performance.

Again, the default value of 100 for this setting will not cover most animations. If your animation is longer than 100 frames, you will have to change the value to include all the frames in your scene. I choose 500 as a good round number for most scenes because many times a scene gets longer or shorter as I work on it, and this way I don't have to remember to always change the value. 500 covers most clip lengths I work on. Your value might need to be higher or lower, or you might prefer to keep this value at exactly the frame range at all times. The preceeding tools are very important to creating a stable IK rig. Even if you carefully apply them all, however, you could run into a problem depending on the controller you choose.

Gimbal Lock

When using the Euler XYZ controller, you could run into the dreaded *gimbal lock*, a very frustrating reality that occurs with all CG software today in most all kinds of hierarchy trees that use the Euler rotational matrix calculation. Gimbal lock is the annoying popping you see in IK solutions as they reach their limits and when joints use the Euler calculation to assess the joint orientation.

When you use the Euler XYZ controller, MAX uses a Euler rotation calculation to determine the rotational value of an object/bone. When you rotate a bone to which the Euler rotational matrix is attached, the Euler controller calculates the three axes in a set order (first x, then y, and then z). You can control the order of these axes manually by selecting the Rotation PRS Parameter in the Motion panel and clicking on the Euler Parameters rollout. However, a better way to ensure control over the up-vector axis of a joint such as the hip (Z-up in MAX R3) is to create an extra bone in the hierarchy that controls the z-axis. By creating the extra bone in the tree, you separate that axis from the next bone in the chain, which you will assign to control the x- and y-axes. This way you have the first bone solving the z-axis and the next bone solving the x- and y-axes together using Euler rotational calculations. You get the best of both worlds with this framework.

By creating this extra bone for your skeletal framework you are telling the Euler axis to be calculated always on z first and then to calculate x and y together on the next bone. The best way to eliminate gimbal lock is to have all three axes calculated together like Quaternion does, but Euler does not allow for this. Therefore, you must create the extra bone to designate your own up-vector and eliminate gimbal lock.

Euler Versus TCB

To avoid gimbal lock entirely, you could use MAX R3's default controller, the TCB Rotation controller. The Quaternion-type of rotational calculation TCB uses is not widely implemented in 3D software, but it is the most solid solution that does not encounter gimbal lock. MAX R3 assigns this as your default rotational controller, but you can change that when you assign a Euler controller.

Although the TCB controller is more stable because it evaluates all three axes at the same time, it has its own drawback: MAX can't easily represent the TCB controller as a two-dimensional Bezier spline (a function curve) in the Track View. Animating without the benefit of function curves to adjust timing, arcs, and paths of motion can be difficult. This is why most 3D packages use the Euler rotational calculation for orientation values in space. The following tutorial is written in accordance with the use of Local Euler controllers to enable the curves needed in the Track View to assess motion.

Skeleton Rig Part I: Leg, Ankle, and Toe Tree with IK

The series of exercises in this first tutorial explain the process of creating a stable IK leg chain. Before you begin, remember that the order of these steps and the type of end effector you use on the IK chain are very important when it comes to creating a tight skeleton. Do not skip steps!

Create and Name the Bones

The first step in building a skeleton is to create the bones for your tree and to name them. Remember what you have already learned regarding the IK panel; this tutorial will go by easily if you understand how the IK panel and IK controllers function.

1. Open the file called Skeleton_IK_WORK.max on the accompanying CD. This file contains a realistic skeleton mesh for which you will be building your leg chain.

2. Select Create Panel/Systems/Bones/Bones Parameters.

3. Under IK Controller Parameters, make sure the default settings for Assign to Children and Assign to Root haven't been inadvertently changed. Assign to Children should be on, and Assign to Root should be off. If Assign to Children is turned off when you build your bone structure, the bones will have absolutely no IK controllers assigned to them and, therefore, will operate like regular PRS bones. If Assign to Root is turned on for the root bone as well as the children bones, the tree will receive an IK controller. You want the root bone to be stable and a PRS bone, so you want this setting to be turned off.

4. Click the Create End Effector check box to turn it off (see Figure 2.5).

Figure 2.5
IK controller interface.

Tip

You want an IK controller to be attached to the chain, but you also want to be the one to determine what kind of end effector is created and where. If Create End Effector is left turned on, the
end effector, by default, will be set as a position effector and created on the last bone in the chain.
If this happens, delete that default end effector in the Motion Panel.

5. In the Right view, create four bones in a tree following the skeletal structure of
   the mesh. The first bone should be near the hip area, and the last should end at
   the ankle. An original leg tree is in the file for you to use as a template. The bones
   are frozen, so you can simply click on top of their placement to build the leg tree.
   Do not worry too much about the bone's initial placement because you will
   adjust the placement later.

6. While a bone in the tree is still selected, go to the Motion panel and click Show
   Initial State and Lock Initial State on.

Note

Show Initial State is the IK solution's rest position when created. If you keep this state locked, you
will always be able to return to the initial rest pose for the IK setup. This state enables you to
restructure bones without affecting the IK solution. *Never* scale your bones! Scale and rotation are
intrinsically connected, and you should never scale your bones. Instead, transform them to place
them where they should be.

7. Move the bones around so they follow the skeleton mesh and look as much like
   Figure 2.6 as possible.

8. Press the H key to get the Select by Name editor, and then select each bone and
   name them the following:

   Bone01: Bone_HIPZ_LEFT

   Bone02: Bone_HIP_LEFT

   Bone03: Bone_KNEE_LEFT

   Bone04: Bone_FOOT_LEFT

Note

You can also move up and down a tree with your Page Down and Page Up buttons and select the
bones this way.

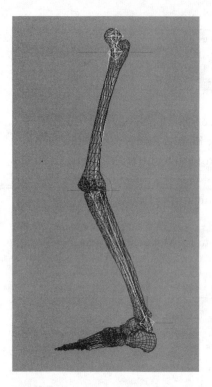

Figure 2.6   Position of IK leg tree within the skeleton mesh.

Adjust the IK Settings

The next step is to adjust the IK settings. In most other packages, these setting are hardwired or invisible to you. The defaults on these settings are designed to give you a better refresh and display, but they are also a path to demise with MAX's IK. Pay close attention to the values entered into these parameters.

1. Select any IK bone in the tree. Remember the first bone in the tree is a PRS FK Bone, so you will not see the IK parameters if you select that bone. Go to the Motion Panel/IK Controller Parameters and change your Threshold Position and Rotation settings for the IK threshold to 0.0 (see Figure 2.7).

2. Next, change the IK Solution Iteration parameter to 500 (see Figure 2.7).

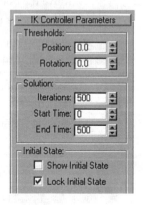

Figure 2.7
In the IK Controller Parameters rollout, the defaults will create a very unstable IK tree; make sure you understand what these settings do.

Tip

The Threshold Position and Rotation settings will make the IK solution follow at its most accurate precision. If you are using a 300MHz or faster computer, this setting should not affect performance. These settings are now also available under the Customize/Preferences/Inverse Kinematics dialog box as global settings for all IK solutions in your scene. Only use this global function if you have more than one IK tree in your scene and you want all the IK trees in your scene to follow the same settings.

Tip

The IK Solution Iteration parameter is a recursive value that will try as many times as you specify to meet the IK solution accurately. The higher the value, the more accurate the solution will be. Again, on most 300MHz or better computers, this will not affect performance.

3. Change the Start and End Time of the IK solution to 0 and 500, respectively (see Figure 2.7).

Tip

The Start and End Time settings *will* eventually affect performance if they are set high enough. If you do not have a 10,000 frame animation, do *not* make this setting that high. The end time of 500 should be plenty for most animation lengths. You can set this to be exactly the amount of frames you are using at the time, but I find that it is easier to use 500. This way you do not have to go back and change it as you work. A value of 500 should cover most animations. If your animation is longer than 500 frames, you probably should break it up into clips. I rarely have worked on a scene that stays exactly the length production asks for, so it is my personal choice to use a value of 500 to keep from having to remember to change the value.

Adjust the IK Limits for Joints

The IK limits for the joints are very important. These limits prevent the skeleton from hyperextending at the joints and rotating in wacky directions.

1. Open the Select by Name editor and select the bone called Bone_HIPZ_LEFT.

2. Activate the rotational axis of this bone in the Hierarchy/IK Panel/Rotational Joints dialog box to be active on only the rotational joint in z (check Active under Z Axis). Uncheck the Active options under Y Axis and X Axis so they are *not* active. This hip bone will separate the z-axis from x and y for the hip rotation, thereby preventing the dreaded gimbal lock associated with the Euler controller and IK pops.

3. Press the Page Down key to select the next bone, called Bone_HIP_LEFT.

4. Now, activate the rotational axis of this bone in the Hierarchy/IK Panel/ Rotational Joints dialog box to be active on only the rotational joints in x and y.

The z-axis is *not* active. This hip bone will control the x- and y-axes of the hip as a child under the HIPZ bone. Again, this step prevents gimbal lock on the hip.

5. Call up the Select by Name editor and select the bone called Bone_KNEE_LEFT.

6. By default, the rotational x-axis of this bone in the Hierarchy/IK Panel/Rotational Joints dialog box should be activated. The Y Axis and Z Axis options are not active by default. Make sure this is true for your skeleton.

7. Page down to select the bone called Bone_FOOT_LEFT.

8. Also by default, the rotational axis of this bone should be activated on x-axis, as in step 6. So, make sure that the x-axis is active and y and z are not.

9. Page up to select the bone called Bone_KNEE_LEFT.

10. Next, you must set a limit for the knee joint so it cannot penetrate itself or turn itself inside out. Click on Limited in the Hierarchy/IK Panel/Rotational Joints/X Axis dialog box.

11. The limit value for the knee bone should be approximately −20 for the From spinner. The value for the To spinner should be approximately 137 (see Figure 2.8).

Figure 2.8
The IK Rotational Joints Limit Settings panel.

Caution

The values in step 11 are totally dependent on how flexible you want the joint to be and on the joint's location in space. This means your values might be a few digits off depending on how you created your bones in the world space.

Adjust Spring Back Values for Joints

The Spring Back values help prevent your IK tree from locking up when it meets the limits. So it makes sense to set these values next. Spring Back is one setting that will make or break your skeleton as far as a clean motion when animating. The Spring Back value is an angle that will soften the ease between the limits of the joint in question. When the joint comes close to its limit in MAX R3, it tends to want to pop back to its resting position. The Spring Back value pulls the joint back into the position it should be in when it reaches its limit. If the joint reaches its limit, the value you apply to spring back the action will begin to ease into its limit, preventing a locking or popping action.

In addition, when you set the Spring Tension value, the spring back action pulls harder as the joint moves farther away from its resting position. A low limit is all you need to calculate an ease for the Spring Back on a joint.

1. Click on Spring Back in the Rotational Joints panel to turn it on. To set the Spring Back value, click on the From spinner and drag it up and down. When the value in the Spring Back box changes, the knee bone rotates.

Tip

The interactive spinner click-and-drag function is possible only if you are in Show Initial State mode. This way you can drag each rotational axis spinner to see the limit of that joint's flexion. When you are happy with the flex limit of a bone, stop dragging, and the appropriate value appears in the spinner box. You need to turn off Show Initial State mode when you want to test your IK solution and animate the character. It is common to forget this and then wonder why things aren't working. Turn off Initial State now.

2. Next, you need to click the Spring Back option to activate it. This puts tension on the bone, making it spring back and keeping the knee from locking.

Tip

To keep knees from locking, always create your IK leg trees with a slight bend in the knee. If you create them with a straight leg bone, they will lock when you try to animate the tree.

3. Next, you need to set a limit value for the spring back tension to calculate the neutral angle position of the knee. Click on the value to the right of the Spring Back check box and drag the slider to be a value close to the neutral position of the knee. In this case, it should be around 10, because 10 is a relatively short distance from the knee angle.

4. The Spring Back Tension value must be assigned also. A low value of 0.2 is best because you do not need a lot of tension, just enough to keep the knee from locking.

Create Dummy Constraints

In this next phase of the tutorial, you will be using the dummies and not the actual end effectors. To work efficiently while assigning the dummy constraints, you will need to recognize the dummies quickly. In the Customize/Preferences/Colors/Objects/Dummy Object panel, you can change the dummy's color from the default light blue. Make the color darker and a color that contrasts to the default gray background so that you can see the dummies. Dark red is a good color to use.

1. Press T on the keyboard to change to a Top view. Do not worry that the leg bone tree is not placed within the mesh at this time. You will move the tree later in the chapter.

Tip

Always create your dummies in the Top view. This will create the dummy with an axis of 0,0,0, matching the World axis. Otherwise, you will be constantly countering the axis rotation of the dummy as you link it to your end effectors.

2. Go to Create/Helpers/Dummy panel and create a dummy for the foot and knee anywhere in the viewport. You will align these later to the bone they will be controlling. Make the knee dummy largest and the foot dummy a little smaller than the knee.

Caution

Never scale your dummies! Because scale and rotation are interdependent, you will get unpredictable results.

3. In the Select by Name editor, select the smaller dummy created for the foot and name it C_LTFOOT, which stands for Constraint Left Foot. This dummy will be the constraint controlling the IK end effector on the foot bone.

4. In the Select by Name editor, select the largest dummy you created for the knee and name it C_LTKNEE (Constraint Left Knee). This dummy will be the constraint controlling the IK end effector on the knee bone.

5. Press R to change to a Right view. Click Zoom Extents to see all the objects.

6. With the largest dummy (C_LTKNEE) still selected, click the Align Selection button on the Main toolbar.

7. Click on the top hip bone (Bone_HIPZ_LEFT). Use the Align Selection/ Align/Position/Pivot Point X, Y, and Z options for both Current and Target under Align Position (Screen). Click OK. This will align the dummy to have the same position as the bone you selected (see Figure 2.9).

8. In the Select by Name dialog box, select the Bone_HIPZ_LEFT bone. Click the Main Toolbar's Select and Link tool again. Then pick the Select by Name icon again and link the HIPZ_Left bone to the C_LTKNEE dummy constraint. This constraint will control the rotation of the hip and knee.

9. Deselect the Select and Link mode. In the Select by Name editor, select the smaller dummy (C_LTFOOT). With C_LTFOOT still selected, click Align

Selection. Press the H key again to open Select by Name, and then click
Bone_FOOT_LEFT. Align the dummy to the same position as the bone (refer
to Figure 2.8).

Figure 2.9   The Align Position (Screen) dialog box and its settings.

Assign the End Effectors

The end effectors are not the best representation for the animator to use. They are hard
to select, and it is bad form to use these directly to animate a character. It is much cleaner
to create dummy constraints that drive the IK setup. This will make selecting the IK
handles, handling the Track View, and assigning additional constraints or controllers
possible. When using end effectors directly, you cannot apply any other controllers to an

IK handle, but you can apply several controllers to a dummy with
no problem. So, this next step will assign the end effectors to
follow the dummies.

1. In the Select by Name editor, select the bone called
   Bone_FOOT_LEFT.

2. Go to the Motion Panel and scroll down to the End
   Effectors group in the IK Controllers rollout. Click
   Position: Create to create an IK Position End Effector for
   that bone.

3. Under End Effector Parent, link that effector to the dummy
   called C_LTFOOT (see Figure 2.10).

4. With the end effector for the foot still selected, go to the
   Hierarchy Panel.

5. Under Object Parameters, change the Position Weight to be
   300.0 on all three axes (as shown in Figure 2.11).

Figure 2.10
In the End Effector
Parent box, link the
effector to the
C_LTFOOT dummy.

Note

The Weight setting gives you the power to control the influence of the end effectors in the chain. You will want the knee to control more of the leg chain rotation through its end effector. In turn, you will want the foot to have even more influence over the end effector's position in the IK chain. Do not be concerned with the Bind check box; leave it turned off (the default). This box is connected to the Bind to Follow function, and this exercise does not use the Bind to Follow for any of the steps.

6. Deselect the Select and Link Mode. In the Select by Name dialog box, select the Bone called Bone_KNEE_LEFT.

7. With the end effector for the knee selected, go to the Hierarchy panel.

8. Under Object Parameters, change the Orientation Weight to be 35.0 on all three axes (see Figure 2.12).

9. With Bone_KNEE_LEFT still selected, go to the Motion panel and create an IK rotation end effector for that bone.

10. Make sure Bone_KNEE_LEFT is still selected and turn Show Initial State off (in the same IK Controller Parameters panel). This ensures that the bones will follow the IK solution and leave their resting pose.

11. Now, you will test your IK setup and make sure the steps you followed so far have created a working tree. In the Select by Name dialog box, select the constraint called C_LTFOOT and translate it along the *local* z-axis.

If all went well, your skeleton should be moving with the C_LTFOOT dummy leading the rest of the tree as children. If not, retrace your steps to be sure you did everything in order.

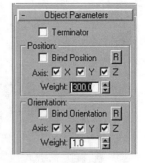

Figure 2.11
A weight of 300 is applied to the Foot end effector so that MAX will solve the IK solution for the position of the foot first.

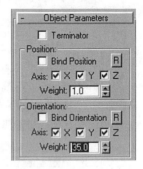

Figure 2.12
A weight of 35 is applied to the Knee end effector so that MAX will solve the IK solution for the orientation of the knee second.

FK Foot and Toe Setup

You will want to create a low-resolution box skeleton to represent the mesh. This will make animation easier because you will be able to quickly pose the low-resolution skeleton without waiting for the high-resolution mesh to update. In this exercise, the boxes are already created for you, but observe how they are reshaped to fit the mesh.

Also, because the foot and toes will be animated with FK, the exercises will use boxes instead of bones. I recommend that you use boxes whenever possible because they are easier to view and orient in space than bones are. Always create your boxes from the Top view so they will have the same orientation (0,0,0) as the World axis. Try to shape the boxes to emulate the size and shape of your mesh for easy posing. Do *not* use Scale to reshape your boxes, however; instead, readjust the height/length and width. Scale is related to rotational values. Either use Edit Mesh/Vertex to reshape your boxes or collapse them to Editable meshes. If you reshape the boxes to be as close to the mesh as possible, it will be easier to pose the box skeleton.

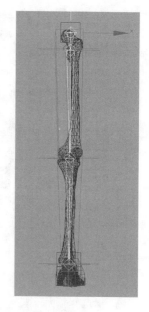

Figure 2.13
Frontal placement of IK bones structure within skeletal meshes.

1. Go to the Display panel and click on the Unhide by Name button.

2. Unhide all the boxes. The boxes listed should be Ankle, Toe, Shin, and Thigh. These boxes will be the Forward Kinematic feet bones for the skeleton rig and the low-resolution representations of the mesh.

3. Go to the Top view.

4. By default, your bone chain was created at 0,0,0, but the left leg of the mesh is actually located to the left of 0,0,0. Select the two dummy constraints (C_LTFOOT and C_LTKNEE) and the entire tree of bones, and then slide them to the right. They should now be placed inside of the mesh. Verify from the Front view that the placement is correct. Figure 2.13 shows frontal placement.

5. Still in the Top view, use the Select by Name editor and select the box called Box_Ankle_Left.

6. Go to the Main toolbar and click the Select and Link tool.

7. Using the Select by Name list with the H hotkey, click on the box you selected (Box_Ankle_Left) and link the ankle to the foot constraint dummy (C_LTFOOT).

8. From the Main toolbar, choose the Select Object tool and deselect the Select and Link mode.

9. Select the five boxes that represent the first row of toe bones (see Figure 2.14).

10. Go to the Main toolbar and click the Select and Link tool again.

11. Click on the five selected toes and drag the link icon to link the toe bones to the ankle box, called Box_Ankle_Left.

12. Go to the Main toolbar and choose the Select Object tool.

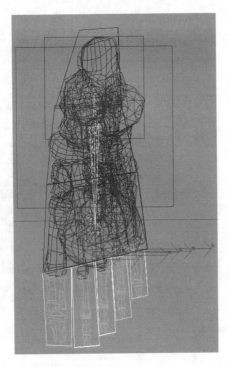

Figure 2.14 FK toe placement and linking.

13. Individually select the five boxes that represent the second row of toe bones and link them to their preceding toe bones one at a time so they will follow the ankle.

14. In the Display/Unfreeze All section, unfreeze all the objects in the scene.

15. Go to the Hide box on the same panel and choose Unhide All.

16. In the Select by Name editor, select the bones that are called Tutorial Bones. These are the bones that were frozen that you used as a template to build your tree. Delete them.

17. Carefully select all the skeleton mesh bones (all these mesh objects start with an "S" for skeleton) and link them to their corresponding bones so they follow the IK/FK trees. For example, the S_LFEMUR Bone should be linked to the Bone_HIP_LEFT. When you finish, the tree should look like the one in Figure 2.15.

That is it! You built a solid IK leg in MAX R3! Make sure Show Initial State is turned off so you can test your work. Grab the dummy constraint C_LTFOOT and move it around. The leg should move with it. Rotate the same dummy constraint on the local x-axis, and you will see the ankle rotation. Grab the dummy constraint called C_LTKNEE and rotate it on the local z-axis, and you have control over the knee rotation. To see a completed version of this tutorial, open the file on the CD called Skeleton_LEGONLY_OK.max.

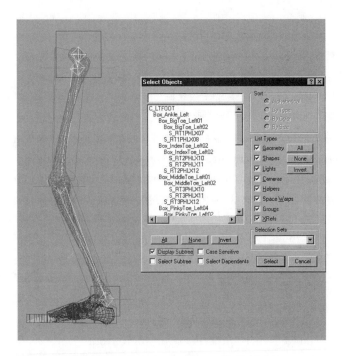

Figure 2.15   The IK leg tree, complete with linking.

Create a Second Leg

Now that you have built a single working IK leg, you will need a second one to complete the skeleton for a human. The best way to create a second leg tree is to go through the same process you used for the first leg. This may seem cumbersome, but it is the best way to ensure that the rotation and scale of all bones and boxes are set to (0,0,0). You may be tempted to mirror a copy of the first leg to create the second. Don't even think about it. Do it the hard way, and you won't have problems later.

Skeleton Rig Part II: Spine with Expressions

The spine is a tricky framework because it has so many joints. The spine is also very important to describing the action line of your character's poses. Choosing the best spine solution for your skeleton rig is critical. I prefer FK on the spine. Most animators do not like IK as a solution for any spine because when you apply IK to trees with more than two bones, they tend to have *severe* gimbal lock problems. To construct a stable spine for our example character, you will use Forward Kinematics and add two dummy constraints that control the spine's bend and arc through mathematical expressions.

Creating a Constraint Expression Controller

A mathematical expression applied to a dummy constraint gives you the power to animate more than one FK bone at a time, using one controller. This streamlines your setup and makes it easier to get that quick pose. This setup also gives you more power and control and provides for fewer keyframes to keep up with in the Track View.

To apply the dummy constraint, you will use the Local Euler rotational constraint. You will align the dummy constraint to the general area of the spine and apply an expression to tell the bones in the spine to rotate when the dummy constraint is rotated. Then you can assign multiple bones to move when you orient the dummy constraint. Because this realistic spine has 22 bones, two constraints will be used. If you used only one constraint to control the whole spine, it would be very heavy in the viewport for interactive display and also would hinder many poses that have a counter arc through the spine. Mathematical expressions can make your rig very heavy, so be sure to use them where they will apply most effectively to the efficiency of a quick pose tool.

Mathematical expressions are great for some solutions, but at other times they can paint you into a corner. The disadvantage is that if you choose to control your FK trees with expressions, you cannot rotate individual bones outside of the expression. For the purposes of the example character's spine, this should not be an issue. If your character is simpler than this skeleton—say with only two or three bones in its trees—you might opt to use the FK bones themselves to create the pose you need.

In the series of exercises in this spine tutorial, you will create two controllers to bend more than spine bones. Two dummy constraints are needed to break the arc in the spine between the lumbar and thoracic sections. One controller will rotate the upper part of the spine, and another will rotate the lower part to keep it light and allow you to create all spine poses. By rotating both controls in the same direction, you can create a complex C-shaped arc in the spine when the character bends over. By rotating the two controllers in opposite directions, you can create an S-shaped arc in the spine when the character is in a tip-toe pose.

Remember, always have a low-resolution version of your mesh to work with interactively. Boxes are best to use for a low-resolution skeleton. When you open the exercise file, you will find a box in the same area as each skeleton mesh of the spine. These boxes will help you get quick poses during animation without having to work directly with the high-resolution mesh. All the mesh parts (ribs and spine) have been linked to the boxes to save time.

Create Dummy Constraints

Before you begin the exercises, open Skeleton_SPINE_WORK.max from the CD and take a moment to observe a few things about the spine. The spine has three colors assigned to its mesh objects.

The lower spine bones (Box_Spine01 through Box_Spine06, in red) represent the lumbar section. The lumbar section is the main pivot for the lower spine, and for extreme sitting or bent-over poses, it is usually rotated first, before the second level of the spine. The larger middle group of bones (Box_Spine07 through Box_Spine18, in purple) represent the spine's thoracic section. The thoracic section controls the compression of the spine during shifts in weight throughout the body. Finally, the top few bones are the cervical bones (Box_Spine19 through Box_Spine–22, in green), which attribute to the neck motion. The neck controls almost all the head motion. The skull actually pivots and rotates about the vertical axis only, creating the shaking of the head "no." The cervical section of the neck and spine are what create the head's side-to-side and nodding actions. With these different sections of the spine in mind, you're ready to get to work.

1. With Skeleton_SPINE_WORK.max open, go to the Named Selection Sets box on the Main toolbar and choose the pre-made set SKELETON MESH. Then choose Freeze Selected from the Display panel.

2. Go to the Top view and click Zoom Extents to see the mesh. In the Create/Helpers/Dummy box, create two dummies anywhere in the viewport for the spine, making one dummy just a little larger than the other.

3. Name the larger dummy C_SPINE and the smaller one C_SPINEUPPER.

4. Open the Select by Name editor and select the larger constraint dummy (C_SPINE). Click on the Align button, press the H key, and select the spine bone called Box_Spine04 from the list. As you did in the previous tutorial, align the dummy to the general area of the lower spine.

5. Open the Select by Name editor and select the smaller constraint dummy (C_SPINEUPPER). Click on the Align button, press the H key, and select the spine bone called Box_Spine13 from the list. As you did in the previous tutorial, align the dummy to the general area of the lower spine.

Assign the Mathematical FK Expression

Mathematical expressions can help streamline a complicated FK tree. By using a mathematical expression you can control multiple bones with one dummy constraint.

Figure 2.16
The Assign Rotation
Controller dialog box.

1. With the dummy constraint for the lower spine (C_SPINE) still selected, go to the Motion panel and open the Assign Controller window.

2. Under Transform, choose the Rotation: TCB Rotation controller, and then click the green Assign controller button to open the dialog box that displays the many controllers you can assign to the transform.

3. Choose the Local Euler XYZ Rotational controller from the list (see Figure 2.16).

4. Select the spine box of the lower lumbar section, called Box_Spine01, and open the Track View.

5. Assign the same Local Euler rotation to the Box Spine01 bone that you placed on the dummy constraint; to do so, copy the Local Euler XYZ Rotational controller from the dummy constraint and paste it onto this bone using the Copy and Paste controller buttons in the Track View and holding down the Shift key to paste the controller to all the bones.

Tip

You can access the controllers and their properties from the Motion panel/Assign Controller box or the Track View. Right-click on the controller in either panel to get to the Properties dialog box.

6. In the Select by Name editor, select Box_Spine01.

7. Right-click on Box_Spine01 and click Track View Selected to open a Track View for the selected object.

8. In the Track View, expand the Box_Spine01's transform tree to reveal the Local Euler Rotational controller and its X, Y, and Z transforms.

9. Hold the Shift key and select the X, Y, and Z transforms.

10. Assign a Float Expression controller to all three axes using the green arrow Assign Controller button on the Track View toolbar (see Figure 2.17).

Tip

New to R3 is the Local Euler Rotation controller, which is based on the object's local axis. The older Euler Rotation controller was based only on the World axis. Local Euler is much easier to apply to objects that are not oriented according to the World axis.

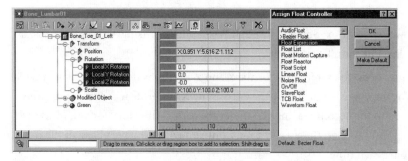

Figure 2.17   Apply Float Expression to a Local Euler controller.

11. Select the Local Euler X Rotation in the Track View, and then right-click and select Properties.

12. Here, you will assign a simple expression to tell the spine box to orient itself exactly like the dummy constraint is in space. Make sure Scalar is checked for the type of variable. Then, in the Name box under Create variables, type **Xrot**. Click Create.

13. Under the Scalars box, select Xrot, and then click on the Assign to Controller button.

14. Next, you tell the Xrot of the spine box to follow the X rotation of the dummy constraint. Under the Track View Pick box, select the corresponding X rotation controller for the dummy constraint called C_SPINE (see Figure 2.18).

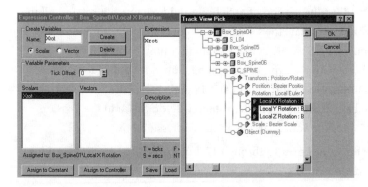

Figure 2.18   The Local Euler controller x-axis.

Open the file Skeleton_SPINE_WORK1a.max to see this much of the exercise completed.

15. Repeat steps 1 through 14 for the other five spine boxes that complete the lumbar/lower spine (Box_Spine02 through Box_Spine06), using Xrot as your Scalar variable name for all X rotations.

16. Continue to do the same steps for the Y and Z rotations using the Scalar variable Yrot for the y-axis and Zrot for the z-axis. The Xrot, Yrot, and Zrot expressions are saved to the accompanying CD under the scripts directory for you to use as a guide. You can load these expressions, but you will still have to assign the controller each time.

Tip

You can save out the expressions to make this process easier and then load them for each spine bone; however, you will have to assign the controller for each expression manually.

17. Now test your expressions. Select the dummy constraint called C_SPINE and rotate it on the x-, y-, and z-axes. You now control all six lower spine boxes at once with one dummy in x, y, and z.

   If the box bones are not moving like you expected them to, open the file Skeleton_SPINE_WORK1b.max to see this part of the exercise completed.

18. Repeat steps 1 through 6 for the rest of the spine (Box_Spine07 through Box_Spine18), assigning the Local Euler controller to each. Then, assign the float expressions and set their controllers in x, y, and z to be the other dummy you created (C_SPINEUPPER).

19. Next, you must adjust the tension of each bone and how much it rotates. All the spine joints should not rotate the same: Some joints in the tree should be less flexible than others. Because FK in MAX cannot set limits, you will adjust the limits of each bone with the expressions you have already applied to the spine bones. Select spine boxes 12 through 14 and 18 and change the Xrot, Yrot, and Zrot of each to be half of the controller rotation. To do this, add the division symbol and 0.5 after the Scalar variable in the Expression box.

20. Repeat step 19 for spine boxes 15 through 17, but divide these by 80%, making the expression divided by 0.8.

You now have an operational spine. To study the completed spine you created with this tutorial, open the file Skeleton_SPINEONLY_OK.max. Hide the skeleton mesh selection set and rotate the C_SPINE and C_SPINEUPPER dummies to observe the effect of the expressions.

Skeleton Rig Part III: Neck, Head, and Jaw

You also create the example character's head, neck, and jaw with FK. IK offers no advantage here. As for the spine, you'll work with boxes for the neck mesh, making it easier to recognize the FK tree's orientation. It is more difficult to represent the orientation of the skull and control where the eyes are looking at with a box, so a low-resolution polygonal model is provided for the head. This lo-res mesh for the skull and jaw will help you create quick animation poses and see where the skull is looking. To create an easy-to-pose rig for the head, neck, and jaw, you will use an approach similar to that of the spine tutorial: You use dummy constraints that drive the FK boxes and expressions that connect the bones to the constraints.

Before you begin working on the exercises, open Skeleton_NECKHEAD_WORK.max from the CD and take a moment to observe a few things about this file. The high-resolution mesh of the skull, jaw, and cervical neck bones are all visible, as are the low-resolution skull and jaw and five boxes for the neck.

You will use the five cervical neck boxes with FK to create motion in the neck. Note that two other bones look similar to the neck bones. Called the Atlas and the Axis, these two bones work with the head to create the shaking "no" motion. The skull moves only on the vertical axis to create this motion. The cervical bones of the neck create the rest of the side-to-side and nodding motions.

In addition to the boxes and low-resolution mesh, there are three bones for the head and jaw motion. You will use these for facial animation, which is discussed in more depth in Chapter 5, "Facial Animation."

Create Bones for the Head and Jaw

The head and jaw will also be controlled by dummy constraints to keep the setup streamlined and easy to use. Mathematical expressions used in the spine tutorial are also applied here to drive the bones of the head and jaw.

1. With Skeleton_NECKHEAD_WORK.max open, go to the Right Side view and click Zoom Extents to see the mesh and bones.

2. Select Create Panel/Systems/Bones/Bones Parameters. Under IK Controller Parameters, clear the Assign to Children check box. Assign to Root will become unavailable. You want to create simple PRS controller bones here with *no* IK. The Create End Effector option is also unavailable now (see Figure 2.19).

3. In the Right view, create five bones in a tree following the skeletal structure of the mesh. The first bone should start at the base of the skull and go to the top of the skull. Continue back down to the cheek (where the jaw connects to the skull) and follow down through the jaw mesh. An original head and jaw tree is there for you to use as a template. The supplied bones are frozen, so you can simply click on top of their placement to build the head and jaw tree. Do not worry about their initial placement because you will adjust the placement later (see Figure 2.20).

4. Press the H key to open the Select by Name editor, and then select each bone and name it according to the following list:

Bone_Head
Bone_Skull_End
Bone_Jaw
Bone_Jaw02
Bone_Jawend

Leave the bottom two bones as they are.

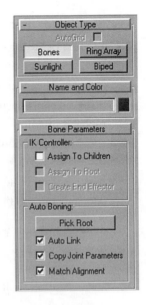

Figure 2.19
Clear the Assign To Children check box

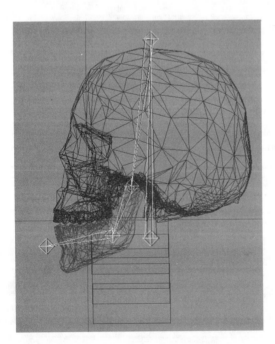

Figure 2.20   Head, jaw, and neck placement.

Create Dummy Constraints

As discussed before, dummy constraints assist in streamlining the setup. It doesn't matter where you create the dummies because you will realign their positions to the bones they are controlling.

1. Go to the Top view.

2. Go to the Named Selection Sets box on the Main toolbar and choose the pre-made set SKELETON MESH. This will select the entire skeleton mesh in this file.

3. Go to the Display panel and choose Freeze Selected. This will freeze the mesh so you do not accidentally select it in the following steps. You can also press the 6 key to freeze selected objects.

4. Go to Create/Helpers/Dummy and create three dummies for the neck, head, and jaw. Make each just a little larger than the next.

5. Name the largest dummy C_HEAD. The middle-sized dummy should be called C_NECK, and the smallest dummy should be C_JAW.

6. Click Align Selection on the Main toolbar. In the Select by Name editor, select the largest constraint dummy (C_HEAD). Click Align button, press H, and select the mesh called LOWREZ_LOWPOLY_Skull from the list. Align the dummy to the general area of the skull.

7. Repeat step 6 twice. First, use the middle-sized constraint dummy (C_NECK) and the box called Box_Spine21, aligning the dummy to the general area of the neck. Second, use the smallest constraint dummy (C_JAW) and the box called Bone_Jaw, aligning the dummy to the joint area of the jaw where it connects to the skull.

Assign the Mathematical FK Expression

The same mathematical expressions used for x, y, and z on the spine will be used here to control the head and jaw motion.

1. In the Select by Name editor, select C_HEAD.

2. Go to the Motion panel and Open the Assign Controller window.

3. Repeat steps 6 through 20 from the "Assign the Mathematical FK Expression" exercise in the Spine tutorial. You will use the dummy constraints to drive the motion of your FK bones. This time, however, you must assign the Local Euler controllers to both the C_HEAD dummy and the bone called Bone_HEAD. After assigning the controllers and Float Expressions to make the bone follow the head

constraint, do the same for the neck and the jaw. Finally, unfreeze the high-resolution mesh parts and link all the corresponding meshes to their boxes and bones.

4. Now test your expressions. Select the dummy constraint called C_NECK and rotate it on the x, y, and z-axes. You now control all five cervical/neck spine boxes at once with one dummy in x, y, and z. The C_Head dummy should do the same for the head bone, and the C_JAW should rotate the jaw bone in all three axes.

Lock Axes

The final step for this tree structure is to lock the x- and y-axes of the dummy constraint for the head. Because the neck should provide these rotations, you will lock the x and y on that dummy.

1. In the Select by Name editor, select C_HEAD.

2. Go to the Hierarchy/Link Info panel and check the X Axis and Y Axis settings under the Locks/Rotate Box.

3. In the Select by Name editor, select C_NECK.

4. Go to the Hierarchy/Link Info panel and check the Z Axis setting under the Locks/Rotate Box.

You have completed the FK head, neck, and jaw structure with dummy constraints used as controllers. To study the completed neck, head, and jaw created from this tutorial, open the file Skeleton_NECKHEADONLY_OK.max.

Skeleton Rig Part IV: Pelvis Broken Hierarchy

When you tested the skeleton leg setup, you probably noticed that the ankle and leg are not attached. If you select the C_PELVIS dummy constraint and pull it upward far enough, the ankles will stay on the ground and break apart from the rest of the tree when they reach their limit. This is called a *broken hierarchy*. With the current IK in MAX R3 bones, broken hierarchies are needed to get a solid setup.

Broken hierarchies are a great way to get the most control out of your skeleton. Before R3 of MAX, broken hierarchies limited you to using only the BonesPro as your deformation plug-in because it was the only skinning feature that could handle more than one hierarchy in the tree. When you use R3's new Skin modifier, a broken hierarchy and a complete tree linked to one root node will deform the mesh with no problems.

Broken hierarchies have another purpose besides assisting in a clean setup with MAX bones. They help with squash and stretch animation, which is a handy way to solve scaling problems on a "cartoony" character. If your character has an exaggerated design with short legs and really long feet, for example, how do you get those big feet under the body for a walk cycle? With a broken hierarchy, you can create the squash and stretch that 2D traditional animators use to pull it off. You can also create crazy animations, such as the ones in the movie the *Mask* where Jim Carrey's arm stretches across an entire room.

A broken hierarchy would also be helpful for a sci-fi cyborg character that had an organic body hooked into mechanical/robot legs. If you need the character to be blown-away out of the leg apparatus, it is much easier to do it with a broken hierarchy. Break the hierarchy at the hips, and you can separate the organic body from the mechanical leg apparatus. Break the hierarchy at the arms and legs, too, and you can blow the character to bits like the Battle Droids in *The Phantom Menace*. Depending on your character and the demands of the animation, broken hierarchies might even be considered a feature instead of a workaround.

Broken hierarchies are difficult to get used to at first for realistic characters because you always have to be sure the ankle or wrist is attached for your pose. But what you gain in return—a stable IK setup—is worth that little flaw. Our example skeleton has a broken hierarchy at the wrists, ankles, and hips with IK on the arms. The bottom line is that the broken hierarchy will provide the most simple, stable, and flexible setup to meet the demands of any animation.

Link the Pelvis Boxes for FK

Now that you clearly understand what a broken hierarchy is, the exercise below will explain how to link your IK leg trees to the pelvis. The extra C_HIPS dummy enables you to rotate the hips independently of the spine, or you can rotate the whole tree with the dummy constraint C_PELVIS.

1. Open Skeleton_PELVISLEG_WORK.max from the CD. This file contains a realistic skeleton mesh that you will use to build your pelvis hierarchy.

2. Go to the Top view.

3. Go to Create/Helpers/Dummy and create two dummies for the pelvis and hips. Make one dummy just a little larger than the other.

4. Name the largest dummy C_PELVIS and the smaller dummy C_HIPS.

5. Click Align Selection on the Main toolbar. Press the H key to open the Select by Name editor, and then select the largest constraint dummy (C_PELVIS). Click

the Align button, press H, and select the mesh called S_Pelvis from the list. Align the dummy to the general area of the pelvis.

6. Repeat step 5, this time aligning the smaller constraint dummy (C_HIPS) to the absolute center of the larger dummy (C_PELVIS).

Link the Legs and Dummy Constraints

You will now link the legs to the pelvis to complete the lower portion of this two-legged tree.

1. In the Select by Name editor, select the C_LTKNEE constraint dummy. Click the Select and Link tool in the Main toolbar. Click on the C_LTKNEE dummy and drag the Link icon to link the left leg tree to C_HIPS. Then click the Select icon on the Main toolbar.

2. Repeat step 1, but this time link the C_RTKNEE constraint dummy (and the right leg tree) to C_HIPS.

3. Repeat step 1, but this time link C_HIPS (the hips dummy constraint) to the dummy constraint C_PELVIS.

4. In the Select by Name editor, select the box called Box_Pelvis. Click the Select and Link tool. Click on the Box_Pelvis dummy you selected and drag the Link icon to link the low-resolution box for the pelvis to the dummy constraint C_HIPS. Now you have a pelvis and leg tree.

Select the dummy constraint C_HIPS and rotate that constraint on any axis. Notice that you can rotate the hip angle independently of the spine. Next, select the dummy constraint called C_PELVIS and rotate it on any axis. It does the same thing as C_HIPS. However, when you link the spine tree you created earlier to this dummy constraint, you can rotate the spine with the body to make the whole body bend over. Flexibility is so important!

Skeleton Rig Part V: Arm, Wrist, and Finger Tree

You can create the wrist and arm tree of your skeleton with FK, IK, or a combination of the two. Most animators prefer FK on the arms because FK forces the use of arcs. Therefore, no frustrating IK popping or gimbal lock will appear in the animation, and most importantly, you can break joints to create that real snap in an animation. As you will see, however, IK has some advantages of its own.

One of the big advantages to using FK for the arms is that it enables you to use a technique called *progressive breaking*. Progressive breaking enables you to animate the bones of a tree independently and can adjust timing of the animation independently to offset the motion. For example, if FK is applied to an arm tree, you can animate the forearm on a different timing than the upper arm. When creating a pointing motion, for example, you can add a real snap to the animation by moving the forearm faster than the upper arm. IK disables the progressive breaking function because the IK solution figures out how the entire arm will resolve itself once the wrist is placed in space.

This progressive breaking of joints will breathe life into your animations and prevent them from looking mechanical. You can create the same motion with IK, but you will spend more time fussing over timing and keys in the Track View.

At times, however, you might want to use IK on arms (for example, if your character is going to shake the bars in a jail cell, ride a bike, or hang from a tree). In each of these instances, IK is necessary to constrain the arms to the objects with which the character is interacting. The IK solution will solve the rest of the arm for you as you move the body around, and the hands will stick to the cell bars, handlebars, or branch.

Remember that both IK and FK can be helpful, but which you choose depends on the demands of your scene. Make the educated decision on which setup you will need. Many times you will need to set up the character both ways. For instance, your character night need FK for a dramatic pantomime clip that has great gestures with dialogue, but in the next scene, that same character might have to hang from a tree limb and pull himself up. This is where planning and flexibility will be your best friends. Be open to creating several rigs and reconstructing their functions through different linking of dummy constraints. To help you make an informed choice, I've included an exercise to illustrate each method.

Building the Arm Tree with FK

FK is a good place to start with the arms because it is the simplest setup. Open Skeleton_ARMFK_WORK.max from the CD and observe a few things about realistic skeleton mesh for which you will be building your arm chain. The first thing that may strike you is that this file has no MAX bones in it. Boxes are much easier to view and judge, and they are perfect for creating FK trees. The boxes in this file will be the bones you rotate to get the pose you need. In this exercise, the boxes are already created for you, but observe how they are reshaped to fit the mesh.

Link the Boxes for FK

As you remember from the previous exercises, the meshes must be linked to the boxes so they will follow the boxes' motion. You need to create two dummies for this file. You do not have to use dummies with FK, but the dummy constraints help keep the file clean and make it easier to transfer animation information from one file to another.

1. Go to the Display panel and click on the Unhide by Name button.

2. Unhide all the boxes by clicking on Selection Sets and choosing the set called BOX BONES. These boxes will be the Forward Kinematic arm bones for the skeleton rig and the low-resolution representations of the mesh.

3. Go to the Front view, if you are not already there, and select the box called Box_Forearm_Left in the Select by Name dialog box. Click the Select and Link tool in the Main toolbar. Click on Box_Forearm_Left and press the H key again. Then choose Box_Bicep_Left and click Link. Click the Select icon.

4. Go to the Right view and select the box called Box_Hand_Left. As in step 3, link Box_Hand_Left to Box_Forearm_Left. Then click the Select icon.

5. In the Select by Name editor, select each finger box and link it to its parent in the tree. For example, Box_ThumbLeft03 should be linked to Box_ThumbLeft02, and then Box_ThumbLeft02 should be linked to Box_ThumbLeft01 (see Figure 2.21).

Figure 2.21   The finger hierarchy.

6. Select the box called Box_Bicep_Left and link it to Box_Shoulder_Left.

To see the linkage as it is completed up to this point, open the file Skeleton_ ARMFK_ WORK1a.max.

Relocate the Pivots

Now you have the entire arm tree linked through the boxes. However, if you try to rotate the boxes, you will see that they are not rotating like they should. This is because their pivots have not been moved to where the joints are.

1. In the Select by Name editor, select the box called Box_Bicep_Left.

2. Go to the Hierarchy/Pivot panel and click on Affect Pivot Only (see Figure 2.22).

3. Move the pivot for that box upward on the local z-axis to align it to the shoulder joint, as shown in Figure 2.23.

4. Next, change the pivots on every box in the file to be at the joint area and not the center of the box.

5. Test your skeleton and rotate the individual boxes to see if they rotate correctly at the joints. If they do not, go through the pivot placement again and relocate the pivot to be at the joints.

Figure 2.22
The Adjust Pivot dialog box.

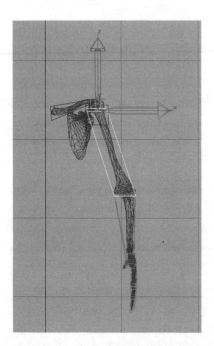

Figure 2.23   Adjusting pivot locations.

In the file, all the meshes are linked to the boxes for you. Because you learned how to do this earlier in the FK Toe setup, I omitted this linking step from the exercise but completed it for you in the file. When you create your own skeletons, however, you must remember to link the meshes to the boxes also.

Link the Dummy Constraints

Because you are using FK on this skeleton and have no need for MAX bones for this tree, you do not need to use Local Euler controllers to link the boxes to follow the dummy constraints. You are simply going to link the dummy constraints into the hierarchy of the tree.

1. Go to the Display/Unhide/Unhide By Name panel and unhide the last two objects in this file—the dummy constraints C_LTSHOULDER and C_LTCLAV.

2. Following the same procedure you used in the "Link the Boxes for FK" exercise, select and link the box Box_Shoulder_Left to the dummy constraint C_LTSHOULDER. Click the Select icon when you finish.

3. Select the dummy constraint called C_LTSHOULDER and link it to the Box_Clavicle_Left. Click the Select icon.

4. Select the Box Bone called Box_Clavicle_Left and link it to the dummy constraint C_CLAV_LEFT.

5. Verify your linkage by clicking the Select icon, then Select By Name, and then Display Subtree.

You now have built a complete FK ARM TREE with the clavicle and scapula movement connected to drive the shoulder rotation. To test your setup, rotate the dummy constraint called C_LTCLAV on its local y-axis. This moves the entire arm tree from the shoulder down.

Unfortunately, you cannot set limits on FK trees in MAX. So you will have to watch the motion of this tree and try to keep from taking it outside of a natural range (approximately −10 to 10 degrees in x, y, and z) The IK tree will enable more motion controls than the FK tree. To see a completed version of these exercises, open the file called Skeleton_ARMFKONLY.max on the CD.

Building the Arm Tree with IK

Before you begin the IK arm exercises, remember the order of these steps and that the type of end effector you use on the IK chain is very important when it comes to creating a tight skeleton.

Create and Name the Bones

To create an IK tree, you will use MAX bones. This exercise will take you through the steps of creating an IK tree of bones for the arm.

1. Open the file Skeleton_ARMIK_WORK.max from the CD.

2. Select Create Panel/Systems/Bones/Bones Parameters.

3. Under IK Controller Parameters, click Assign to Children and make sure Assign to Root is not checked.

4. Clear the Create End Effector check box.

5. In the Right view, create four bones in a tree following the skeletal structure of the mesh. The first bone should be near the shoulder area, and the last should end at the wrist. The second bone should be right on top of the first. As in the leg tree, the first bone here will control only the z-axis of the shoulder, and the second bone will control the x- and y-axes. An original arm tree is included in the file for you to use as a template. The bones are frozen, so you can simply click on top of their placement to build the arm tree. Do not worry too much about their initial placement; you will adjust the placement later.

6. With a bone in the tree still selected, go to the Motion panel and click on Show Initial State and Lock Initial State.

7. Move the bones around so they follow the skeleton mesh and look as much like Figure 2.24 as possible.

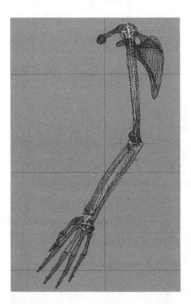

Figure 2.24   The IK arm tree.

8. Press the H key to open the Select by Name editor. Then select each bone and name it according to this list:

Bone01	Bone_SHOULDERZ_LEFT
Bone02	Bone_SHOULDER_LEFT
Bone03	Bone_ELBOW_LEFT
Bone04	Bone_WRIST_LEFT

Leave the bottom two bones as they are.

Adjust the IK Settings

As you did for the leg, you must not adjust the arm tree's IK settings in the Motion panel's IK Controller Parameters rollout. The necessary values are shown here:

Threshold Position and Rotation = 0.0
IK Solution Iteration = 500
Start Time = 0
End Time = 500

Adjust the Limits for Joints

Gimbal lock can afflict your character's arms as easily as its legs. To prevent this, select each of the following bones in the Select by Name editor, and then activate the specified axes as each bone's rotational axis:

Bone_SHOULDERZ_LEFT	z-axis
Bone_SHOULDER_LEFT	x- and y-axes
Bone_ELBOW_LEFT	x-axis
Bone_WRIST_LEFT	x-axis

Note

Bone_SHOULDER_LEFT controls the x-axis and y-axis of the shoulder as a child under the SHOULDERZ bone.

Like you did for the knee, you must set a limit for the elbow joint so it cannot penetrate itself or turn itself inside out. Select Bone_ELBOW_LEFT and click on Limited in Hierarchy/IK Panel/Rotational Joints/X Axis. Set the From spinner to approximately 26 and the To spinner to about –142 (see Figure 2.25). Remember, these values might be a few digits off depending on where you created the bones in World space.

Adjust Spring Back Values for Joints

The process of adjusting Spring Back values for the elbow is almost identical to that for adjusting them for the knee (which you learned in an earlier tutorial). Again, clicking on the From spinner and dragging it up and down changes the Spring Back value. Turn on Spring Back to cause tension on the bone to "spring back" and keep the elbow from locking. Click on the value to the right of the Spring Back check box, and then drag the slider to be a value close to the neutral position of the elbow. In this case, it should be around 10 because 10 is a relatively short distance from the elbow angle. Finally, set the Spring Back Tension to 0.2, applying just enough tension to keep the elbow from locking.

Figure 2.25
IK arm limits for the elbow.

Create Dummy Constraints

Again, you will be using dummy constraints to manipulate your IK tree. The dummy constraints make for a cleaner, more flexible setup and enable you to add controllers to the dummies if needed. In this exercise, you create a dummy constraint to control the elbow rotation and the hand translation.

1. Go to the Top view. Do not worry that the arm bone tree is not placed within the mesh at this time. The tree will be moved later in the chapter.

2. Go to Create/Helpers/Dummy. Create one dummy for the elbow and a slightly smaller one for the hand. In the Select by Name editor, name the smaller dummy C_LTHAND and the other one C_LTELBOW. C_LTHAND will be the constraint controlling the IK end effector on the hand bone, and C_LTELBOW will be the constraint controlling the IK end effector on the elbow bone.

3. Go to the Right view. With the largest dummy (C_LTELBOW) selected, click Align Selection on the Main toolbar. Click on the top shoulder bone (Bone_SHOULDERZ_LEFT) and align the dummy to have the same position as this bone.

4. In the Select by Name editor, select the Bone_SHOULDERZ_LEFT bone. Click the Select and Link tool in the Main toolbar. Link the SHOULDERZ_Left bone to the C_LTELBOW dummy constraint. This constraint will control the rotation of the shoulder and elbow.

5. Align C_LTHAND with the hand bone called Bone_HAND_LEFT.

Assign the End Effectors

Assigning end effectors for the arm is very similar to the procedure you used for assigning the leg's end effectors. You must select the various bones in the Select by Name editor, create end effectors for them in the Motion panel, and then change their weights in the Hierarchy panel's Object Parameters rollout.

1. Select Bone_HAND_LEFT and create an IK Position End Effector for it. Under End Effector Parent, link that effector to the dummy called C_LTHAND (see Figure 2.26). Under Object Parameters, change the Position Weight to 300 for all three axes.

2. Select Bone_ELBOW_LEFT. Create an IK rotation end effector for it. Select the end effector, and change the Orientation Weight to be 35 for all three axes.

3. With Bone_ELBOW_LEFT still selected, turn off Show Initial State (in the same IK Controller Parameters panel) to make sure the bones will follow the IK solution and leave their resting pose.

Figure 2.26
The end effector for IK arm is linked to follow the dummy constraint C_LTHAND.

4. Finally, test your IK setup to make sure you have created a working tree. In the Select by Name editor, select the constraint called C_LTHAND and translate it along the *local* z-axis.

If all went well, your skeleton should be moving with the C_LTHAND dummy leading the rest of the tree as children. If not, retrace your steps to be sure you did everything in order.

FK Hand and Finger Setup

An arm isn't complete without a hand, so the next exercises will concentrate on our character's hands and fingers. While working with the hands' FK setup, you will use low-resolution boxes to represent the skeleton mesh. Chapter 3, "Advanced Character and Creature Setup," will take this basic FK setup one step further with MAXScript and create a way to animate all these bones with sliders. For now, however, you just need to create the basic structure and linkage.

1. Go to the Display panel and click on the Unhide by Name button.

2. Unhide all the boxes—Hand, Finger, Bicep, Forearm, Shoulder, and Clavicle. These boxes will be the Forward Kinematic (FK) bones for the skeleton rig and the low-resolution representations of the mesh.

3. Go to the Top view.

4. By default, your bone chain was created at 0,0,0, but the left leg of the mesh is actually located to the left of 0,0,0. Select the C_LTHAND and C_LTELBOW

dummy constraints and the entire tree of bones. Slide them to the left. They should now be placed inside of the mesh. Verify from the Front view that the placement is correct (see Figure 2.27).

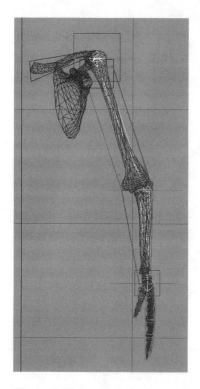

Figure 2.27   Frontal placement of bones in the arm tree.

5. Go to the Right view and select the Box called Box_Hand_Left. Click the Select and Link tool. Click on Box_hand_Left, and then drag the Link icon to link the hand to the hand constraint dummy called C_LTHAND.

6. Choose the Select Object tool from the Main toolbar. Select the five boxes that represent the first row of finger bones (see Figure 2.28). Link the finger bones to the hand box called Box_Hand_Left.

7. Repeat step 6 for the five boxes that represent the second row of finger bones, linking them to their preceding finger bone one at a time so they will follow the hand. Do the same for the final row of finger bones.

8. Go to Display/Unfreeze All and unfreeze all the objects in the scene.

9. Go to the Hide box in the same panel and check Unhide All.

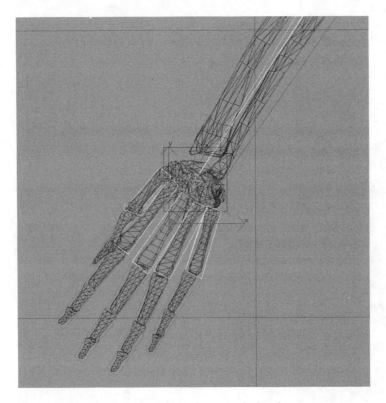

Figure 2.28   The first row of finger bones in the hand.

10. In the Select by Name editor, select the bones called Tutorial Bones. These are the frozen bones that you used as a template to build your tree. Delete them.

11. Carefully select all the skeleton mesh bones (all these mesh objects start with an S for skeleton) and link them to their corresponding bones so they follow the IK/FK trees. For example, the S_LHUMOR Bone should be linked to the Bone_SHOULDER_LEFT. When you are finished, the tree should look like the one in Figure 2.29.

Tip

You will most likely want the hands to move with the character and not be left behind, so link the dummy constraints C_LTHAND and C_RTHAND to the root constraint called C_PELVIS when you link all the trees together.

With one arm finished, give it a try. Grab the dummy constraint C_LTHAND and move it around. The arm should move with it. Rotate the same dummy constraint on the local x–axis, and you will see the wrist rotate. Grab the dummy constraint called C_LTELBOW and rotate it on the local z–axis, and you have control over the Elbow rotation. To see a completed version of the IK exercise series, open the file on the CD called Skeleton_ARMIKONLY.max. For more complex arm, hand, and finger control, move on to Chapter 3.

As you did for the second leg, you can build a second arm by repeating the whole process. Simply use the same principles you used in the section "Create a Second Leg."

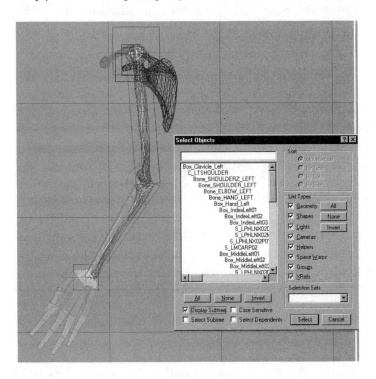

Figure 2.29   The IK arm tree and hierarchy.

Skeleton Rig Part VI: Clavicle, Scapula Complex Shoulder

The last step toward creating a skeleton rig is the complex shoulder chain that many forget. The shoulders, clavicle, and scapula all work together to create the motion of the entire shoulder area, as well as the rest of the arm. You can use the same setup for this on an FK or IK skeleton because it will be an FK structure. This structure is very important to many different kinds of movements, from a chuckle to a shrug. This complex structure enables the clavicle, scapula, and shoulder to all move when the shoulder rotates upwards. The exercises in the following tutorial use the IK arm to illustrate the complex setup, but the same principles can be used on an FK tree. (Open Skeleton_FK_OK.max from the CD to view the clavicle setup on FK arms.)

Create Dummy Constraints

The first phase of the process should be very familiar by now: creating a dummy constraint, specifically one that will control the FK rotation of the clavicle. You do not have to create this constraint, but it makes for much easier selection and a cleaner setup. Working in the Skeleton_ARMIK_WORK.max file and the Top view, create a dummy for the clavicle that's about the same size as the one you created for the feet. Name it C_LTCLAV and align it to the same position as the topmost shoulder bone, Bone_SHOULDERZ_LEFT.

Link Boxes and Bones

Just as you did in previous tutorials, you must link the boxes and meshes together. You should link the dummy constraint C_LTELBOW to the box called Box_Clavicle_Left. Finally, link the Box_Clavicle_Left to the dummy constraint called C_LTCLAV.

To test the setup, rotate the dummy constraint called C_LTCLAV on its local z-axis. The whole arm/shoulder tree should compensate. Unfortunately, MAX does not enable limits for FK, so you will need to watch the scapula to judge how far you can rotate this bone. The shoulder/elbow rotation can also be adjusted independently of the clavicle.

See the file Skeleton_ARMIK_ONLY.max for a complete IK arm/clavicle setup.

In Practice

- **Plan skeleton rigs ahead.** Flexibility, an understanding of anatomy, and a solid grasp of MAX's bones tools are all very important to creating a solid skeleton. Keep your setup open to different rigs that accommodate the demands of the animation.

- **Inverse Kinematics.** IK is the only way for animators to solve the leg tree of any skeleton. The IK solution will keep the feet stuck to the floor as you create a walk cycle. This tool has many settings in MAX R3 that can make or break your skeletal set-up. The default settings for many of these tools will not create the most stable setup, so know your tools. Also, for complex scenes where the character must interact with other objects or characters, a solid IK arm rig is described in this chapter.

- **Forward Kinematics.** FK is also a very stable choice and the preferred method among most animators for the upper tree of a skeleton. FK advantages are forced arcs in animation, the ability to progressively break joints, and overall power and control over each individual joint.

- **Dummy constraint controllers.** Dummy constraints enable you to create a clean, easy-to-use skeleton. In many studios, more than one animator uses the skeleton setup, so it is very important to create skeletons that are easy to use. Dummy constraints make it clear what is to be moved to create a pose.

- **Expression controllers.** Using mathematical expression controllers gives you the tools to create a pose for several bones with one controller. The 20+-bone spine in this chapter is controlled with two expression controller dummy constraints. These constraints are used to create the arc in the spine by setting only one key for the constraint instead of having to rotate all the bones individually to get a pose.

- **Broken hierarchies.** Max's current bones need broken hierarchies to create a stable skeleton. This is a great way to control the trees individually. The hips can be animated separately of the pelvis tree with this setup.

Chapter 3

Advanced Character and Creature Setup

By Angie Jones

By learning the connections that exist in a real-life skeleton, you will be able to make your skeleton rigs more realistic. The advanced skeleton rigging techniques discussed in this chapter will help you take your character setups to the next level. Two keys to these techniques are using scripts and expressions.

Scripts are especially useful for building multi-legged creatures, which require even more demanding setups than those described in the previous chapter. With MAX R3's new scripting capacity and more open architecture, you can hack the software to cooperate with the special demands of your animations. In addition, the provided quadruped and multiped skeleton tutorials should help eliminate the confusion creators often experience when adding limbs.

The tutorials in this chapter will introduce you to creating scriptable interfaces, using more complex expressions, and automating your animation through both. It's crucial that you embrace the more technical side of your character setup. When you do, you will open more avenues to a stable skeleton and enable easier animation of the skeleton.

Note

You need a solid understanding of all the basic setup tools and techniques described in Chapter 2, "Basic Character and Creature Setup," before you proceed through the following advanced tutorials.

This chapter explores the following topics:

- MAX script and how to build rollout menus
- Using MAXScript to create a Gripper function
- Building front and rear three-bone leg setups
- Creating a four-legged skeleton
- Using MAXScript to create a tail motion
- Designing a multiped six-legged setup

Using MaxScript to Create a Gripper Function

One of the best ways to learn about MAXScript, and scripting in general, is to examine an existing script line by line. The script called gripper.ms on the CD-ROM serves double duty: Not only can it animate the skeletal hands you made in Chapter 2, but it will also teach you some basic syntax used in MAX scripting and some simple commands you'll need to create a rollout interface. To access the script, follow these steps:

1. Click on Utilities, MAXScript, and then choose Open Script.
2. Open gripper.ms.
3. Click on Run Script to see how it works.

The script creates five sliders for the left hand and five for the right. Each slider moves one finger to create a pose. To accomplish this, the script performs 12 operations:

- Defines the interface
- Defines the floater and rollout
- Defines the groups for the rollout
- Defines the right and left hand sliders
- Defines the right and left hand slider function
- Opens and checks for the floater
- Defines the floater's name and size
- Defines the rollouts for the floater
- Defines the axis for the Local Euler and slider update function
- Defines the MAXScript Utility buttons and functions
- Defines the function that opens the Floater when the script is run
- Defines the `Slider Update Time` routine

Figure 3.1   Advanced techniques with MAX R3 are here!

As the next sections explain each stage of the script, follow along line by line in the gripper.ms file.

Define the Interface

First, you must create an interface to manipulate the finger bones. This is done with the following line:

```
displayFloaterRun=true
```

MAXScript lets you create dialog box windows, or *floaters*, that can roll out and "float" above the regular interface. The `displayFloater` global variable is used to open the floater automatically when the script runs. This is not necessary for the script to run, but it is nice to have the floater window open by itself.

Define the Floater and Rollout

This is the point where the action really starts in the script. The next two lines create the floater, name it, create the rollout that will contain the sliders, and name it:

```
GripperFloater
rollout mvGripper "Gripper"
```

Define Groups for Rollout

Groups enable you to create sets, similar to selection sets in MAX. By naming and placing multiple buttons or sliders into a *group* you will create a more tidy script. Commands can be executed upon all the buttons or sliders in your named group, as well, so you will not have to individually place the command on each slider.

The next line establishes a *group*. Although using groups is not essential, it's better to keep things in groups because groups keep things tidy and easy to find. In this case, you have two groups (Right Hand and Left Hand) for the skeleton. If you had a lot of other sliders and buttons, managing them without groups would be very complicated. An example would be to add a spread of the fingers so they open wide as if to catch a ball. When you put the sliders in groups, things are neat, and it's easy to locate the different controls. By using the group names in the script, you can reference the group over and over again and use commands on that whole named group. The `Left Hand` group line comes after the `Right Hand` sliders are established.

```
(
    -- Defining Groups -- Right Hand
      group "Right Hand"
```

Define the Sliders

The next line establishes the first slider, which is named `rPinkyFinger` and has the caption "Pinky."

```
    (
      slider rPinkyFinger "Pinky" range:[0,100,0] type:#integer ticks:0
➥across:5 orient:#vertical
```

```
    slider rRingFinger "Ring" range:[0,100,0] type:#integer ticks:0
➥orient:#vertical
  slider rMiddleFinger "Middle" range:[0,100,0] type:#integer ticks:0
➥orient:#vertical
    slider rIndexFinger "Index" range:[0,100,0] type:#integer ticks:0
➥orient:#vertical
      slider rThumbFinger "Thumb" range:[0,60,0] type:#integer ticks:0
➥orient:#vertical
  )
```

The range `[X,Y,Z]` is defined in this way:

- *X* is the lowest number (all the way to the left)

- *Y* is the maximum number (all the way to the right)

- *Z* is the default value (the value with which you start)

The type says that you'll be using integers to describe the position and orientation of the finger bones. Ticks establish little ticks on the slider so it clicks between the values. Orient explains which way the slider will move: vertical or horizontal. For this example, vertical is used. Each finger is given a slider, so there are five entries under this part of the script, and they are named after the five fingers.

The preceding lines control the right hand. The left hand lines in this script are exactly the same, except the names of the sliders start with an "l" for left instead of an "r" for right. Before you describe the sliders, remember that you must define the group, just as you did for the right hand. Here are the lines for the left hand:

```
-- Defining Groups -- Left Hand
  group "Left Hand"
(
  slider lPinkyFinger "Pinky" range:[0,100,0]  across:5 orient:
➥#vertical ticks:0 type:#integer
  slider lRingFinger "Ring" range:[0,100,0] ticks:0 orient:#vertical
    slider lMiddleFinger "Middle" range:[0,100,0] ticks:0 orient:
➥#vertical
    slider lIndexFinger "Index" range:[0,100,0] ticks:0 orient:
➥#vertical
      slider lThumbFinger "Thumb" range:[0,60,0] ticks:0 orient:#vertical
  )
```

The values of 0 to 60 on the thumb describe the amount of curl each slider will output to the finger bones. For instance, on the left thumb, when the slider is all the way at the top, the thumb is completely flexed at 60 degrees of rotation. In turn, when the slider is at the bottom, the finger is in its neutral relaxed state of 0 rotation.

Define the Slider Functions

The following lines tell the slider to rotate each finger bone on the z-axis by val, which is the value input from the slider. For example, you can move the right thumb slider from

0 to 60 degrees so each of the bones moves 60 degrees when the slider is at the maximum setting. If the slider is halfway up, the gripping action will be 30 degrees. If the slider is dead on 0 in the center, the finger will be in its neutral centered straight pose. This is a big section of the script because each finger bone must have a value to look for so the slider input will be applied. Only the thumb segment is shown, but all ten fingers are listed in this section of the script and are separated by hand groups.

```
------Right Hand------
    -- Moving Thumb Finger in Right Hand
          on rThumbFinger changed val do
    (
    in coordsys parent $Box_ThumbRight03.rotation.z_rotation = val
        in coordsys parent $Box_ThumbRight02.rotation.z_rotation = val
    )
```

Open and Check for the Floater

Next, the `fn GripperFloater` local function initializes (opens) the floater that you see when you run the script. This means you are declaring a local function and referencing the Gripper floater variable you set previously.

```
)
fn createGripperFloater =
(
```

The next line is a `try` expression that checks to see if there is a floater opened already. If there is a floater open, the script closes it and opens a new one. (This is so you don't end up with 20 floaters that look exactly the same on the screen.) The `try` expression is a simplified form of the C++ exception handling scheme, which lets you bracket a piece of code to catch any runtime errors. In this case, we are checking to see if the gripper floater is already open. The `try` expression lets you take corrective action, instead of MAXScript halting your script and giving you an error message. Each line of the script is physically bracketed in the script with parentheses.

```
        try
        (
                    closeRolloutFloater GripperFloater
        )
        catch
        (
        )
```

The `try-catch` function tries to close a floater if there is one open. If there was not a floater and the script tried to close one, MAXScript would normally give an error; but with the `try-catch` function, no error is displayed. If the `try-catch` function finds a floater, it closes that floater.

Define Name and Size of Floater

This next line tells Max to open a new floater named `GripperFloater` with the caption "Gripper." The script specifies a size of 230 by 322 pixels, but you can use any dimensions you want.

```
GripperFloater = newRolloutFloater "Gripper" 230 322
```

Define Rollouts for Floater

Next, the rollouts called `mvGripper` to `GripperFloater` are added. A good way to explain the process is with an analogy: You buy some sweets in a shop, but you have too many sweets to hold. You want to put them all together in one place so it's not so difficult to carry them around. You ask for a bag. When you get the bag, you can put all the sweets inside. Let's compare that with the following line:

```
addRollout mvGripper GripperFloater
    )
```

This script gets the bag (which is the rollout called `mvGripper`) to hold the sweets (which are the groups Right Hand and Left Hand).

You can think of the rollout `GripperFloater` as a shopping cart that can hold multiple bags. So, the script creates a cart (`GripperFloater`) to put your bags into, and then the script creates a bag (`mvGripper`) into which you can put all your sweets (Right Hand and Left Hand).

Define Axis for Local Euler and Update Slider

The next section is also big, but it's easy to explain. The `Update Slider` function moves the sliders in the floater in time. You'll notice that as you move the `Time Slider` up and down, the fingers grip with the animation, and the sliders in the floater also move in time.

```
fn Slide_Update =
(
    ------Right Hand------
    -- Update Thumb Slider
    mvGripper.rThumbFinger.value = in coordsys parent -
➥($Box_ThumbRight02.rotation.z_rotation)
```

The `Update` function looks at the value of the first bone in the tree. You need to check only one angle to update. Then it puts that value on the slider. For instance, a bone rotates from 0 degrees at frame 0 to 100 degrees at frame 30. When you move the `Time Slider` to frame 15, the slider in the floater will be in the center (50) because you are rotating the bone at a 50-degree angle at that frame.

Basically, the whole thing would still work if you didn't have this function, but the sliders in the floater (the Pinky, Ring, and other finger sliders) wouldn't move up and down when you move your Time Slider around. You must apply the Update function to each finger on both hands so that as you move the slider, the script knows to move the finger and on what axis.

Define MAXScript Utility Buttons and Functions

The next few lines create the buttons you see under the Max Utility panel in the MAXScript drop-down menu. This MAX Utility rollout is the body of the program; it's what appears on the right-hand side under the MAXScript Utilities.

```
Utility utlGripper "Gripper"
(
```

The next line creates a button that you can click on to open the floater. This button ensures that if you close down your floater, you can always get it back.

```
button floatGripper "Open Floater" width:140 offset:[-1,0]
```

The following line tells the button you just established what to do when pressed: Create the floater and the sliders needed to manipulate the finger bones.

```
    on floatGripper pressed do createGripperFloater()
    on GripperAvars pressed do createGripperAvars()
)
```

Open Floater When Script Is Run Function

This next line is not absolutely necessary, but it's a nice little addition. It opens the floater when you run the script. To do this, you need the code that is on the top of the script

```
(displayfloaterrun = true).
```

```
if displayFloaterRun == true then createGripperFloater()
```

Slider Update Time Routine

The last line in the script is a Time routine that is always called when you move the U around. The Time routine ensures the function of Slide_Update. Time calls Slide_Update, which moves the Right Hand and Left Hand groups of sliders so that you know the exact position of the fingers in relation to the sliders.

```
registerTimeCallback Slide_Update
```

That's it! You now know how this script opens itself when it's run or clicked on in the MAXScript Utility menu, you know that the script has ten sliders to make the fingers on the hand grip, and you know how these sliders update when you move the Time Slider—and it took only 185 lines to do it!

This particular script can be use to create a fist or gripping action on any character. If your character is more cartoony (maybe it has only three fingers), you will hack the script accordingly by dumping one of the reference fingers throughout. To push the script even further, try to create a slider that will spread all the fingers out as if the character is catching a ball. Many of the tools you have learned about here are referenced in a script used later in this chapter that will animate a lion's tail. As you can see, MAXScript is very useful for handling complex skeletal data and multiple-boned trees, which the lion's tail further illustrates.

Skeleton Rig Part I: Three-Bone Rear Leg Tree

The best way to understand animal anatomy is to compare it to what you already know about human anatomy. The main difference between an upright human skeleton and that of a four-legged creature is the part of the foot the character walks on. Humans walk on the heel and toes. Four-legged creatures walk on their toes only, but they can sit back on their feet much like a sphinx posture. This complex structure means the skeleton will have to compensate for placing the weight of a character on both the toes and feet intermittently.

The human skeleton discussed in Chapter 2 is set up to handle a stable IK leg. You can follow it closely with a few simple adjustments to compensate for the mainly toe-driven walk. Two adjustments are needed: the use of both rotational and position end effector on the IK tree ankle, and the placement of the FK bones for the foot and toes so the creature is walking on its toes. In other words, the foot becomes the third bone in the tree because the creature walks on its toes most of the time unless it is crouched down ready to pounce on its prey. So, the foot must be rotated to point down at the ground and the toes rotated up to be parallel with the ground. Because the heel/ankle joint becomes the third bone in the leg and the toes are what the creature balances on, the back legs are built just like the human leg where they bend at the knee. The front legs work just as if the human skeleton were bent over on all fours, and they bend the opposite direction at the elbow (see Figure 3.2).

Another difference between the human limbs and those of a four-legged creature is proportion. The rear legs on a four-legged creature are shorter, making them more even with the front and compensating for the additional bone structure of the foot as part of the leg tree. The foot bone tends to be slightly longer because it becomes a third bone in the leg tree. The legs hinge up into the body just like a human's, and the scapula shoulder blades slide freely over the rib cage. The setup for a three-bone leg is similar to the basic bipedal leg tree, but because of the additional bone in the tree, it has some different end effectors regarding the IK solver.

The main facet to recognize with a four-legged framework is that the hind legs bend in the opposite direction of the front (with the exception of elephant legs). Figure 3.3 illustrates this point.

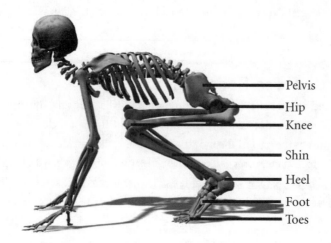

Pelvis
Hip
Knee
Shin
Heel
Foot
Toes

Figure 3.2   Breakdown of the rear leg on a human.

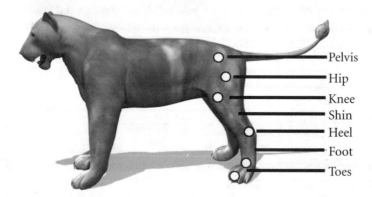

Pelvis
Hip
Knee
Shin
Heel
Foot
Toes

Figure 3.3   Breakdown of the rear leg on a lioness.

The same framework used on the rear legs is applied to the front legs. The only difference with the front leg structure in comparison to the human skeleton is that the creature is walking on its fingers; therefore, the hand becomes an additional bone in the fore leg tree.

The following exercise explains how to set-up the rear three-bone leg tree for a lioness. To create this tree, you will reuse many of the steps described in the previous chapter regarding building an IK leg. If you are lost, refer to Chapter 2's section "Skeleton Rig Part I." The process of creating a three-bone leg tree is divided into several phases:

- Creating and naming the bones
- Adjusting the IK settings
- Adjusting the IK limits for joints
- Adjusting Spring Back values for joints
- Creating dummy constraints
- Assigning the end effectors
- FK paw/foot setup

Before you begin, remember that the order of these steps and the type of end effector you use on the IK chain are very important to creating a tight skeleton. Do not skip steps!

Create and Name the Bones

To create a three-bone rear leg tree, you should place the first bone near the hip area and the last at the ankle. You will name the bones accordingly so you do not get confused later as to which is the right and which is the left rear leg tree.

1. Open the file on the accompanying CD called Lion_IKRear_WORK.max. This file contains a lion mesh for which you will be building your leg chain.

2. Create an IK leg tree following the skeletal structure of the mesh using three bones in the Right view. The first bone should be near the hip area, and the last should end at the ankle. An original leg tree is included for you to use as a template. The bones in this template are frozen, so you can simply click on top of their placement to build the leg tree. Just like in the previous tutorials, don't worry too much about their initial placement because you will adjust the placement later.

3. In the Motion panel under the IK Controller Parameters rollout, turn on Show Initial State and Lock Initial State.

4. Move the bones around so they follow the skeleton mesh and look as much like Figure 3.4 as possible.

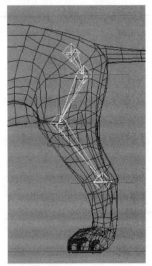

Figure 3.4
Placement of three-bone leg tree.

5. Select and name each bone according to the following list:

Bone01   Bone_REAR_HIPZ_LEFT

Bone02   Bone_REAR_HIP_LEFT

Bone03   Bone_REAR_KNEE_LEFT

Bone04   Bone_REAR_FOOT_LEFT

Adjust the IK and Spring Back Settings

As you learned in Chapter 2, the Spring Back setting must be applied to keep the joints from popping back to their 0 values when they near their limits. Using the Threshold setting of 0.0 ensures that the IK follows the end effector placement as closely as possible. The IK solution Iteration parameter also ensures the correct IK solution for the leg tree by recursively checking it 500 times before moving the bones. Finally, the Start Time and End Time can be set to be exactly the length of your animation. However, I prefer to keep it at 500 so I don't have to remember to change if the length of the animation ever changes.

1. Change your Threshold Position and Rotation settings for the IK Threshold to 0.0

2. Change the IK Solution Iteration Parameter setting to 500.

3. Change the Start Time and End Time for the IK solution to 0 and 500, respectively.

4. Next, you must adjust the IK limits for each joint. To start, select the bone called Bone_REAR_HIPZ_LEFT. Select the IK button from the Hierarchy command panel. On the Rotational Joints rollout, activate the rotational axis of this bone to be active on only the rotational joint in z. The y- and x-axes are *not* active.

5. Select the bone called Bone_REAR_HIP_LEFT. Activate the rotational axis of this bone to be active on only the rotational joints in x and y. The z-axis is *not* active.

6. Select the bone called Bone_REAR_KNEE_LEFT. Activate the rotational x-axis of this bone. The y- and z-axes are not active.

7. Select the bone called Bone_REAR_FOOT_LEFT. Activate the rotational axis of this bone as in step 6. The x-axis is active; y and z are not.

 Tip

Most four-legged animals, such as the lioness used here, have very little rotational range on the ankle and wrist joints. These joints are hinge joints that rotate only when the shoulder/hip and knee/elbow twist. This is because the quadruped walks on its toes and needs the foot bone to work as an additional leg bone. Therefore, the ankle/wrist joints are free to rotate on the x-axis only. The toes of a quadruped orient themselves much more like a human ankle for handling the rotational impact of the body and carry rotation on all axes.

8. Select the bone called Bone_REAR_KNEE_LEFT. Limit the knee joint by checking Limited under the Y Axis parameters. The limit value for the knee bone should be approximately 100 for the From spinner. In addition, the value for the To spinner should be approximately –60 (see Figure 3.5).

9. For realism, you must also set the joint's Spring Back value. Turn on the Spring Back option.

10. Set the limit value for the Spring Back tension to 90.

11. Set the Spring Tension value to 0.2 (as in Figure 3.5).

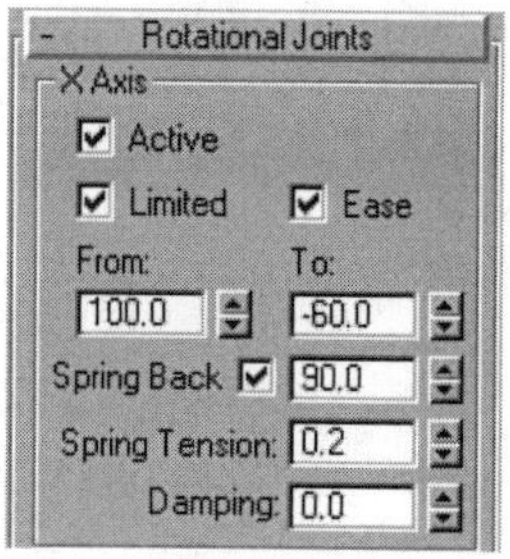

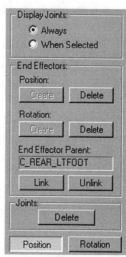

Figure 3.5
Knee values for the three-bone leg tree.

Create Dummy Constraints

After all the practice you had creating dummy constraints in Chapter 2, this phase of the tutorial should be very familiar. Go to the Top view and create a foot dummy and a knee dummy to use as constraint controllers for the leg tree. Name your dummies C_REAR_LTFOOT and C_LTKNEE. Because the lioness has four legs and four feet, this will help avoid confusion in naming conventions. Use the Align tool to align the C_LTKNEE dummy to the topmost hip bone (Bone_REAR_HIPZ_LEFT), and then link them using the Select and Link tool. Next, align the C_REAR_LTFOOT dummy to the foot bone called Bone_REAR_FOOT_LEFT.

Assign the End Effectors

Assigning end effectors might also seem like a repeat from Chapter 2, but this exercise has one very important difference. The end effector used on the ankle is both a Position and Rotation end effector. This compensates for the third bone, which is really a foot bone that becomes part of the leg tree in a multiple-legged creature.

1. Select the bone called Bone_REAR_FOOT_LEFT.

2. Create an IK Position End Effector *and* a Rotation End Effector for that bone.

3. Link that effector to the dummy called C_REAR_LTFOOT (see Figure 3.6).

4. Change the Position Weight to be 300.0 on all three axes.

Figure 3.6
Position and Rotation end effector parent.

5. Select the bone called Bone_REAR_KNEE_LEFT.

6. Change the Orientation Weight to be 35.0 on all three axes.

7. Create an IK Rotation end effector for Bone_REAR_KNEE_LEFT.

8. Turn off Show Initial State.

9. Test your IK setup and make sure the steps you followed so far have created a working tree.

FK PAW/FOOT Setup

You will want to create a low-resolution box skeleton to represent the mesh. This will make animation easier because you will be able to quickly pose the low-resolution skeleton without waiting for the high-resolution mesh to update. The third leg bone is actually an FK box bone representing the foot. You will link the paw to the foot and the foot to the foot dummy constraint. In this tutorial, the boxes are already created for you, but observe how they use Edit Mesh to reshape to fit the lion mesh.

1. Open the file called Lion_IKRear_WORKa.max on the accompanying CD.

2. Unhide all the boxes: Foot, Paw, Shin, Thigh, and Hip. These five boxes will be the Forward Kinematic feet (FK) bones for the skeleton rig and the low-resolution representations of the mesh.

3. Go to the Top view and select the two dummy constraints (C_REAR_LTFOOT and C_REAR_LTKNEE) and the entire tree of bones and slide them to the right. They should now be placed inside the mesh. Verify from the Front view that the placement is correct. You might have to turn on Show Initial State to get the actual placement correct because the leg tree is angled a bit throughout the mesh around the shoulder area. Figure 3.7 shows the correct frontal placement.

4. When you have placed all the bones within the mesh correctly, select the box called Box_Rear_Paw_Left and click the Select and Link tool.

5. Click on Box_Rear_Paw_Left and drag the Link icon to link the ankle to the bone called Box_Rear_Foot_Left.

6. Select and link each of the boxes to its corresponding bone.

Test your rear three-bone leg tree to be sure the box mesh linking you chose is correct. You can now set a limit for the ankle bone just as you did for the knee bone, because you have the box called Box_Rear_Paw_Left to gauge the orientation. To create a second leg, go through the steps again.

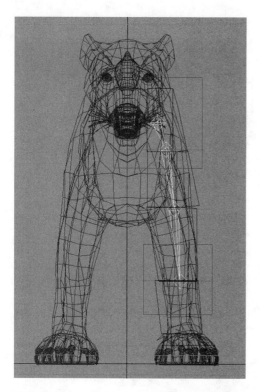

Figure 3.7   Frontal placement of rear leg bones in lioness.

The file LION_3boneREAR_LEG_OK.max shows a leg tree that was created using the steps from this tutorial.

Skeleton Rig Part II: Three-Bone Front Leg Tree

All four limbs will be IK here to ensure that they stay on the ground while animating the torso. This will make animating a multi-legged creature easier than using FK on the limbs.

Understanding anatomy is important to building a clean four-legged skeleton. The front legs of four-legged animals vary in proportion, so it is important to get animal anatomy books to help visualize how the bones work together as a framework for that specific animal. The front legs of a lion are similar to a human's arms in basic framework (see Figure 3.8).

The lion's front leg joints, like those of a human's arm, are the reverse of the lion's (and the human's) rear legs. One big difference between the front legs and back legs on a lion is that the proportion of the hand bone is much shorter than the foot bone (see

Figure 3.9). In a horse, the hand bone is equal to the foot bone. This shows how important it is to study the anatomy of the animal you are animating.

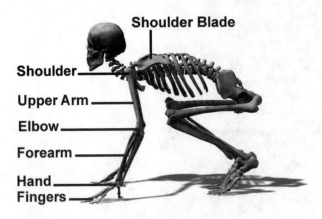

Figure 3.8   Breakdown of the front leg on a human.

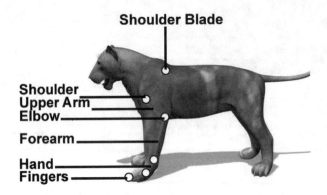

Figure 3.9   Breakdown of the front leg of a lioness.

The following exercise set explains how to set up the front three-bone leg tree for a
lioness. To create this tree, you will reuse many of the steps from the rear leg exercise. If
you get lost, refer to the "Skeleton Rig I" tutorial.

As before, the order of the steps and the type of end effector you use on the IK chain are
vital to creating a tight skeleton. Do not skip steps!

Create and Name the Bones

As you did for the rear leg, you will start this tutorial by putting together your bone tree.
Open Lion_IKFront_WORK.max on the accompanying CD. An original arm tree is

there for you to use as a template. The bones are frozen, so you can simply click on top of their placement to build your new four-bone arm tree.

In the Right view, create four bones in a tree following the skeletal structure of the mesh. The first bone should be near the shoulder area, and the last should end at the wrist. The second bone should be right on top of the first. Again, like in the previous leg tree, the first bone will control only the z-axis of the shoulder, and the second bone will control the x- and y-axes.

Turn on Show Initial State and Lock Initial State, and then move the bones around so they follow the skeleton mesh and look as much like Figure 3.10 as possible.

Figure 3.10 Frontal placement of the front leg bones of a lioness.

Finally, select and name each bone as listed here:

Bone01	Bone_SHOULDERZ_LEFT
Bone02	Bone_SHOULDER_LEFT
Bone03	Bone_ELBOW_LEFT
Bone04	Bone_FRONT_FOOT_LEFT

Adjust Settings and Limits

Once again, you need to adjust the IK settings, the limits for joints, and the Spring Back values.

For the IK settings, change the Threshold Position and Rotation settings for the IK Threshold to 0.0, the IK Solution Iteration Parameter setting to 500, and the Start Time and End Time of the IK solution to be 0 and 500, respectively.

To adjust the limits for joints, activate the rotational axes of the four bones as listed here:

Bone_SHOULDERZ_LEFT	rotational joint in z only
Bone_SHOULDER_LEFT	rotational joints in x and y only
Bone_ELBOW_LEFT	rotational joint in x only
Bone_FRONT_FOOT_LEFT	rotational joint in x only

Figure 3.11
Elbow values for the three-bone leg tree.

You will also need to set a limit for the front leg elbow. Because the front elbow joint on the lioness moves in the reverse direction of the rear leg knee, the limits for this joint are different. Select the bone called Bone_ELBOW_LEFT and make the elbow joint Limited with a Limit value of approximately –93 for the From spinner. In addition, make the value for the To spinner approximately 83 (see Figure 3.11).

To set the Spring Back values for the elbow joint, turn on the Spring Back value and set the limit value for the Spring Back option to –83. Finally, set the Spring Tension value to 0.2.

Create Dummy Constraints

This exercise is exactly the same as the one for the rear leg setup. In the Top view, create a foot dummy and an elbow dummy to use as constraint controllers for the leg tree. Name your dummies C_FRONT_LTFOOT and C_LTELBOW. Align the C_LTELBOW dummy to the topmost shoulder bone called Bone_SHOULDERZ_LEFT and align the C_FRONT_LTFOOT dummy to the foot bone called Bone_FRONT_FOOT_LEFT. Finally, link Bone_SHOULDERZ_LEFT to C_LTELBOW.

Assign the End Effectors

Assigning front leg end effectors is exactly the same as assigning them for the rear leg (which you learned earlier). You need to create both a rotational and position end effector for the last bone in the chain.

To create the end effectors, select the bone called Bone_FRONT_FOOT_LEFT and create an IK Position end effector *and* a Rotation end effector for that bone. Link that effector to the dummy called C_FRONT_LTFOOT. Next, change the Position Weight to 300.0 on all three axes. Select the bone called Bone_ ELBOW_LEFT and change the Orientation Weight to 35.0 on all three axes. Finally, create an IK Rotation end effector for Bone_SHOULDER_LEFT, and then turn off Show Initial State. Test your IK setup and make sure the steps you followed so far have created a working tree.

FK Front Paw/Foot Setup

To complete the front leg setup, repeat the steps from the rear leg tutorial's "FK Rear Paw/Foot Setup" section. Use the file Lion_IKFRONT_WORKa.max in place of Lion_IKRear_WORKa.max. For dummy constraints, use C_FRONT_LTFOOT and C_LTELBOW. Instead of linking a paw to the rear foot, you will link Box_FRONT_Paw_Left to the bone called Bone_FRONT_FOOT_LEFT. As for the rear leg, finish by linking each of the boxes to their corresponding bones. Figure 3.12 shows the placement of rear leg bones, while Lion_IKFront_WORKb.max is a completed front leg tree.

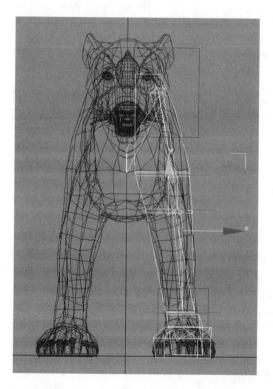

Figure 3.12 Frontal placement of front leg bones in the lioness.

Skeleton Rig Part III: Clavicle and Scapula Complex Shoulder

The last step of creating a front leg on a four-legged skeleton rig is the complex scapula, or shoulder blade. The shoulders, clavicle, and scapula all work together to create the motion of the entire shoulder area as well as the rest of the arm—or in this case, the front leg. You see this motion of bones very clearly in any kind of cat, so it is very important to the lioness structure. This complex structure enables the clavicle, scapula, and shoulder to all move when the shoulder rotates upwards.

To create this tree, you will reuse many of the earlier steps, so these steps will only be covered briefly. If you are lost, refer to the rear leg section. To begin, you will need to open the file Lion_IKFront_WORKb.max, which contains the lioness mesh from which you will be building the complex shoulder chain.

Create Dummy Constraints

The first step is to create dummy constraints. In the Top view, create a single dummy constraint and name it C_LTCLAV. This constraint will be used to control the clavicle.

Align C_LTCLAV to the box that represents a clavicle bone called Box_CLAV_Left. Be sure to align the constraint to the box's pivot point instead of its center. The pivot is at the end of the box where the rotation should be. The constraint will drive the clavicle box bone, which is an FK bone, and this FK bone will drive the IK tree below it.

Link Boxes and Bones

Just as you have done in previous tutorials, you must link the boxes and meshes together. Link the dummy constraint C_LTELBOW to the box called Box_CLAV_Left, and then link Box_CLAV_Left to C_LTCLAV.

To test the setup, rotate C_LTCLAV on the local z-axis. The whole arm and shoulder tree should compensate. Unfortunately, MAX does not enable limits for FK, so you will need to watch the scapula to judge how far you can rotate this bone. The shoulder and elbow rotation can also be adjusted independently of the clavicle.

See the accompanying file Lion_IKFront_OK.max for a complete IK arm/clavicle setup.

Skeleton Rig Part IV: FK Spine

As stated in Chapter 2, the spine is very important for describing the action line of your poses. This is why it is critical to choose the best spine solution for your skeleton rig and creature. As I do for a bipedal structure, I prefer FK on a four-legged creature's spine. Most animators do not like IK as a solution for any spine because when IK is applied to a tree with more than two bones, severe gimbal lock problems are common. To construct a stable spine for the example character, you will use Forward Kinematics and add two dummy constraints that control the spine's bend and arc through mathematical expressions.

Using Constraint Expression Controllers

To manipulate the spine, you will apply a mathematical expression to a dummy constraint. This gives you the power to animate multiple FK bones at the same time using one controller. This streamlines your setup and makes it easier to get a quick pose. This setup also gives you more power and control during animation and leaves fewer keyframes to keep up with in the Track View. To apply a constraint expression controller, you create the dummy constraint as usual and then apply mathematical expressions to each bone telling the bones how to act when the dummy is transformed.

The lioness has a much simpler spine structure than Chapter 2's realistic human skeleton. For this reason, the tutorial uses only one controller for the spine boxes. Boxes are the best choice to use for a low-resolution skeleton because they are so easy to position and orient in space. When you open the file below, you will find a box placed in the same area as the back of the lioness mesh.

Create the Spine

If you already went through Chapter 2's "Spine with Expressions" tutorial as recommended, this section should be very easy. The steps are the same, but there are fewer spine bones to control.

One other major difference is that the Local Euler controller has already been assigned to all the boxes in this file. It is best to make Local Euler your default rotation controller for any objects you create in MAX R3. This new controller will enable a local x-, y-, and z-axis function curve in the Track View, making animation much easier. You can set the Local controller to be your default by assigning a Local Euler controller to any object and then clicking on it to make it the default. All objects you create from then on will have a Euler rotational controller instead of the default Quaternion controller. The dummy constraint for this exercise has also been created for you because you probably know what the steps are for creating an operative dummy with a (0,0,0) axis by now.

To create the spine tree, you will reuse many of the earlier steps. Those steps have been included in the working file to give you a jump start. If you are lost, refer to the previous exercises.

1. Open the file on the accompanying CD called Lion_IKFront_WORKb.max if you do not already have it open from the last tutorial. This file contains a lioness mesh from which you will be building your complex shoulder chain.

2. Select the first box spine bone called Box_Spine01.

3. In the Track View, expand the Box_Spine01's transform tree to reveal the Local Euler Rotational controller and its x, y, and z transforms.

4. Hold the Shift key and select the x, y, and z transforms.

5. Assign a Float Expression controller to all three axes using the green arrow Assign Controller button on the Track View toolbar.

6. Select the Local Euler X Rotation in the Track View, and then right-click and select Properties.

7. Here, you will assign a simple expression to tell the spine box to orient itself exactly like the dummy constraint is in space. Make sure Scalar is selected for the type of variable. Then, type **Xrot** in the Name box under Create Variables and click Create.

8. Under the Scalars box, select Xrot, and then click on the Assign to Controller button. This brings up the Track View Pick dialog box.

9. Now, you will tell the Xrot of the spine box to follow the X rotation of the dummy constraint. Under the Track View Pick box, select the corresponding X rotation controller for the dummy constraint called C_SPINE.

10. Repeat steps 2 through 9 for the other four spine boxes that complete the spine (Box_Spine01 through Box_Spine04) using Xrot as your Scalar Variable Name for all X rotations.

11. Repeat these steps for the Y and Z rotations using the Scalar variable Yrot for the y-axis and Zrot for the z-axis. The Xrot, Yrot, and Zrot expressions are saved to the accompanying CD under the scripts directory for you to use as a guide. You can load these expressions, but you will still have to assign the controller each time.

To test your expressions, select the dummy constraint called C_SPINE and rotate it on the x-, y-, and z-axes. You now control all the spine boxes at once with one dummy in x, y, and z and have an operational spine. To study the completed spine created from this tutorial, open the file Lion_SPINE_OK.max.

Skeleton Rig Part V: Neck, Head, and Jaw

In the following tutorial, three individual controllers will be used to transform the jaw, head, and neck. Mathematical expressions will be applied to the Local Euler controllers so that the boxes will follow the constraints. The head, neck, and jaw of the lioness are also created with FK; IK offers no advantage here. As for the neck, you'll work with boxes for the neck mesh, which will make it easier to recognize the FK tree's orientation. It is more difficult to represent the orientation of the skull and where the eyes are looking with a box, so a low-resolution polygonal model is provided for the head. This low-resolution mesh for the skull and jaw will help you create quick animation poses and see where the skull is looking. Before you begin working on the exercises, open Lion_NECKHEAD_OK.max from the CD and take a moment to observe a few things about this file.

In addition to the low-resolution polygonal meshes for the head and jaw, the dummy constraints are already created for you in the file and aligned to the bones and/or boxes they will be manipulating. You will use the two neck boxes with FK to create motion in the neck using the dummy constraint called C_NECK. There is also a head and jaw bone tree that will be used to rotate the jaw and head. The only difference between this tree and the one used for the human in Chapter 2 is the proportion. A lioness jaw is much higher on the skull, providing a wider range for the jaw to open and flex. Remember, the skull moves on only the vertical axis to create a shaking "no" motion. The bones of the neck create the rest of the side-to-side or nodding motion. So, the x- and y-axes of the bone called Bone_Head are locked under the Link Info panel. Only the neck can create motion on these axes.

Many of the steps used in this exercise to create the head, neck, and jaw structure are familiar to you. Most of the things you have already learned—creating dummy constraints, locking axes on the head bone, and assigning Local Euler Rotation controllers—have already been applied to the working file. Therefore, you can move quickly into the more advanced part of the setup. There is only one phase to this tutorial: applying the mathematical expression controllers to the boxes, bones, and low-resolution meshes so they follow their constraints. Try this on your own since you have done this several times by now. If you are lost, refer to the "Neck, Head, and Jaw" tutorial in Chapter 2. To check your work, view the completed neck, head, and jaw created from this tutorial in the file Skeleton_NECKHEADONLY_OK.max.

Skeleton Rig Part VI: Pelvis Broken Hierarchy

As you did for the two-legged skeleton, you need a broken hierarchy to link the rear legs and front legs to the four-legged creature's hips and shoulders and to link the neck to the shoulders. (Refer to Chapter 2 for more information on broken hierarchies.) To create this tree, you will reuse many of the steps you've already learned, including those for creating and aligning dummy constraints. The file for this tutorial jumps directly to the linking of the tree structures to make one whole skeleton. Linking the trees is the final phase, as well as one of the most important phases, so follow each step closely.

1. Open the file on the accompanying CD called Lion_PELVISLEG_WORK.max.

2. In the Right view, select the constraint dummies called C_RTKNEE and C_LTKNEE.

3. Click the Select and Link tool in the Main toolbar.

4. Click on the C_RTKNEE and C_LTKNEE dummies, and then drag the Link icon to link the left and right rear leg trees to the dummy constraint called C_HIPS. Deselect Link mode by clicking on the Select tool.

5. Select the constraint dummy called C_HIPS.

6. Click the Select and Link tool.

7. Click on C_HIPS and drag the Link icon to link the hips dummy constraint to the spine dummy constraint called C_SPINE. Deselect Link mode.

8. Select the constraint dummies called C_LTELBOW and C_RTELBOW.

9. Click the Select and Link tool.

10. Click on the dummies you selected called C_LTELBOW and C_RTELBOW, and then drag the Link icon to link the right and left front leg trees to the dummy constraint C_SHOULDERS. Deselect Link mode.

11. Select the constraint dummy called C_SHOULDERS.

12. Click the Select and Link tool.

13. Click on C_SHOULDERS and drag the Link icon to link the shoulders dummy constraint to the dummy constraint C_SPINE. Deselect Link mode.

14. Select the dummy constraint called C_NECK.

15. Click the Select and Link tool.

16. Click on the dummy you selected called C_NECK and drag the Link icon to link the neck dummy constraint to the dummy constraint C_SHOULDERS. Deselect Link mode.

To test your linking, select the dummy constraint C_SPINE. Rotate that constraint on any axis. The whole tree should be moving to compensate for the spine rotation. You can also rotate the hip and shoulder angle independently of the spine using C_HIPS or C_SHOULDERS. Flexibility is so important!

To study a completed lioness skeleton created from this tutorial, open the file Lion_IK_OK.max.

Skeleton Rig Part VII: MAXScript for the Tail

There is another way to control a tree of bones instead of using the FK dummy constraint controllers. The newly improved MAXScript in R3 can help automate some of the animation functions of a tree like the lioness tail. This is a more advanced approach because it involves scripting, but if you understand the basics of MAXScript, the options are endless.

Use MAXScript to Create Tail Motion

To look at the script that will be used to animate the lion's tail, click on Utilities, MAXScript and click Open Script. Open the script called liontail.ms from the accompanying disc. Click on Run Script to see how it works.

There are two sliders for the tail. Each slider will move each bone in the tail in a curling or swinging action to create a pose. The Curl slider curls the tail up or down, and the Swing slider swings the tail back and forth. This script was built in a fashion similar to the gripper script described at the start of the chapter. Each line of the script that was not already explained in the gripper exercise is explained in detail here. This script is more complex than the gripper script even though it has fewer sliders. There are two reasons for this: This script is designed to create specific motion, and AVAR controls are created for the Track View enabling one curve for all of the bones in the tail. The AVAR controls are a powerful function of this script. They create a track in the Track View for the swing and the curl functions. This means you will be able to control the swing and curl of the eight bones of the tail with *one* function curve! The AVARs represent the motion path of all eight bones according to the sliders.

Caution

Very important: This Lion Tail script was written for the Local Euler Rotational controller to be applied to the bones in question (the tail bones). I prefer to apply a Local Euler to any bones I use because it enables an x, y, and z function curve that the regular MAX PRS quaternion rotational controller does not. So, if you are going to adjust this script for use on any skeleton other than the lion provided in this chapter, make sure you apply Local Euler Rotational controllers to those bones on which the script will execute its functions.

Follow each line in the script so you can understand what it is doing. The 15 main parts of this script are listed here:

- Define interface
- Check for previous interface
- Check for multiple copies
- Define rollout
- Define group for rollout
- Define `Curl` and `Swing` sliders
- Define `Curl` and `Swing` slider function
- Define AVARs for the Track View
- Define `Slider Update` function
- Open and check for the floater
- Define name and size of floater
- Define rollouts for floater
- Define MAXScript utility buttons and functions
- Open Floater when script is run function
- Define `Slider Update Time` routine

Define Interface

First, you must create an interface to manipulate the tail bones. This is done with the following line:

```
displayTailFloaterRun = true
```

Check for Previous Interface

Next, you simply check the tail and verify that a script has not already manipulated it. This global variable is used to see whether the AVAR controllers for the tail have been created before:

```
TailAvarsCreated = false
```

Check for Multiple Copies

This line is necessary to confirm that you don't open multiple copies of the same floater:

```
TailFloater
```

Define Rollout

Next, you create the floater—with the sliders—and tell it how to behave.

```
rollout mvTail "Lion's Tail"
```

Define Group for Rollout

The next line establishes a group. In this case, you have two objects (swing and curl) for the tail group.

```
(
-- Defining Groups --
        group "Tail"
```

Define Swing Slider

The next line establishes the first slider, named swing, which has the caption "Swing." The range [X,Y,Z] works as described previously in the gripper script breakdown.

The type used to describe the position and orientation of the tail bones is integer. Ticks show you little ticks at the bottom. Orient explains that the slider will move horizontally.

```
(
    slider swing "Swing" range:[-10,10,0] type:#integer ticks:1
➥orient:#horizontal
```

The values of –10 to 10 describe the amount of swing each bone will have when the lion is swinging its tail. So, when the slider is at 10 (the right-hand side), the tail is swinging to the right, as shown in Figure 3.13.

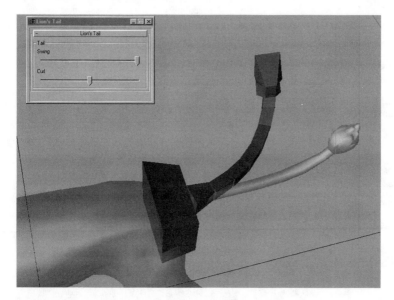

Figure 3.13   Lion's tail swinging to the right.

When the slider is at −10, the lion looks like Figure 3.14.

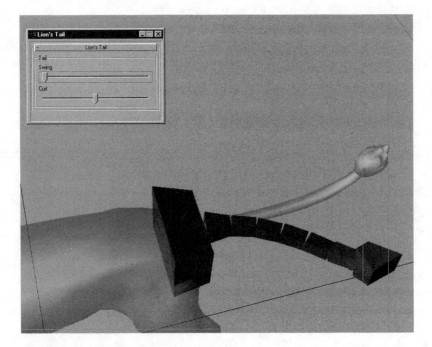

Figure 3.14   Lion's tail swinging to the left.

Define `Curl` Slider

The setup for the curling action of the tail is very similar, but the range used is −1 to 1. This is because percentages will be used later, and it's easier to work with single integers when referencing percentages. Because all the numbers between −1 and 1 will be used to define the motion of the curl, floaters will be used in this line instead of integers.

```
slider curl "Curl" range:[-1,1,0] type:#float ticks:1 orient:
➥#horizontal
)
```

Define `Swing` Slider Function

As in the gripper script, these lines tell the `Swing` slider to rotate each tail bone in the z-axis by `val`, which is the value input from the slider. Because the slider moves from −10 to 10 degrees, each of the bones moves (when at a maximum) 10 degrees. If the slider is half way to the right, the swing will be at 5 degrees. If the slider is dead on 0 in the center, the tail will be in its neutral, centered, straight pose.

```
-- Swinging
on swing changed val do
```

Whenever you move the Swing slider, a function is called. The following lines tell each of the bones to rotate on its local z-axis according to the slider's output value.

```
(
   in coordsys parent $Box_Tail01.rotation.z_rotation = val
   in coordsys parent $Box_Tail02.rotation.z_rotation = val
   in coordsys parent $Box_Tail03.rotation.z_rotation = val
   in coordsys parent $Box_Tail04.rotation.z_rotation = val
   in coordsys parent $Box_Tail05.rotation.z_rotation = val
   in coordsys parent $Box_Tail06.rotation.z_rotation = val
   in coordsys parent $Box_Tail07.rotation.z_rotation = val
   in coordsys parent $Box_Tail08.rotation.z_rotation = val
)
```

Define Curl Slider Function

Next the Curl slider is defined. Curl is similar to Swing but is a little bit more sophisticated.

```
-- Curling
on curl changed val do
```

To break the symmetry of the curling tail, the bones were rotated differently than the even swing back and forth. For example, when the tail is up, it looks like Figure 3.15.

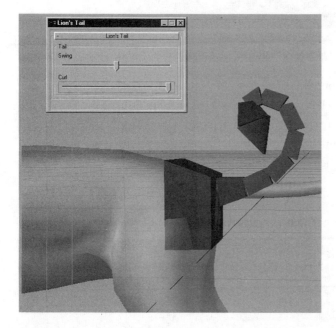

Figure 3.15 Lion's tail curling up.

But when the tail is down, it looks like Figure 3.16.

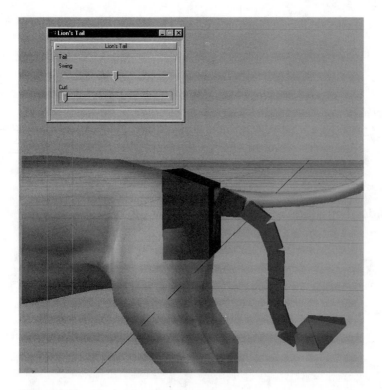

Figure 3.16   Lion's tail curling down.

The demands of this motion necessitate two different scenarios, so an `if, then` statement must be used. One is when the slider (or tail) is above 0 (above the body). This will rotate and behave differently than when the value is below 0 (when the tail rotates down). The line below shows how an `if, then` statement uses the greater than sign to tell the script what to do when the slider is above the value 0.

```
(
   if val > 0 then
```

If the tail curls up (the value is above 0), it will rotate with the following values:

```
(
in coordsys parent $Tail01.rotation.y_rotation = -(7.5*val)
in coordsys parent $Tail02.rotation.y_rotation = -(15*val)
in coordsys parent $Tail03.rotation.y_rotation = -(20*val)
in coordsys parent $Tail04.rotation.y_rotation = -(25*val)
in coordsys parent $Tail05.rotation.y_rotation = -(35*val)
in coordsys parent $Tail06.rotation.y_rotation = -(42.5*val)
in coordsys parent $Tail07.rotation.y_rotation = -(50*val)
in coordsys parent $Tail08.rotation.y_rotation = -(62.5*val)
```

These values were determined by rotating each bone of the tail and writing down the angle of rotation as it was created.

In this case, it is helpful to use the −1 to 1 floater instead of the −10 to 10 integer. The first bone should rotate a maximum of 7.5. If 7.5 is multiplied by 1 (1 being the value of the slider when it's at the far-right side), the input value is 7.5. However, when the slider is closer to 0 (for example, halfway from 0), val will be 0.5. If you multiply 0.5 by 7.5, you get 3.75, which is halfway on the slider between 0 and 7.5.

The negative values are there because of the axis orientation. The axes could have been rotated around from their original creation positions instead, but why do all that when the code can adapt with a simple minus sign?

Next is the final definition for the if, then statement introduced earlier. Remember, the script has only established what happens when the slider is above 0. Now, it must declare what will happen when the slider drops below 0.

```
    )
      else
```

According to this example, if the value of the slider is below 0, it should behave differently; the following values determine what happens then:

```
    (
    in coordsys parent $Tail01.rotation.y_rotation = -(16*val)
    in coordsys parent $Tail02.rotation.y_rotation = -(23*val)
    in coordsys parent $Tail03.rotation.y_rotation = -(33*val)
    in coordsys parent $Tail04.rotation.y_rotation = -(24.5*val)
    in coordsys parent $Tail05.rotation.y_rotation = -(8.5*val)
    in coordsys parent $Tail06.rotation.y_rotation = (19.5*val)
    in coordsys parent $Tail07.rotation.y_rotation = (32*val)
    in coordsys parent $Tail08.rotation.y_rotation = (42.5*val)
                    )
        )
    )
```

Again, these values were determined by rotating each bone and taking down the values.

Define AVARs for the Track View

The next step of this script is not required, but it *is* a valuable addition. This part of the code will enable an AVAR track in the Track View for both the swing and the curl of the tail. The AVAR will give you one function curve for all eight bones so you have fewer keys to keep up with. At the same time, you can still adjust the timing and animation of each individual bone! How is that for control *and* flexibility? The AVARs will appear in the track View below the Global Tracks and the Video Post Tracks (see Figure 3.17).

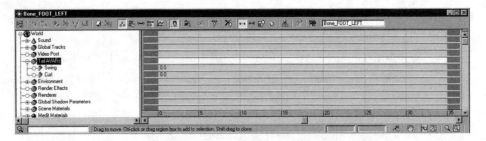

Figure 3.17   Lion's tail Swing and Curl MAXScript AVARs in the Track View.

```
-- Creates all the AVARs
fn createTailAvars =
```

The TailAVARs global variable was set at the beginning of this script and is now being called out. This ensures that the script creates only one set of AVAR tracks.

```
(
    if TailAvarsCreated == false then
```

Here we define the AVAR node. This line creates the Tail AVARs nodes that appear below Video Post in the Track View when you click on Create AVARs.

```
(
-- Defines the Node
        tail_Avars = newTrackViewNode "Tail AVARs"
```

When you open the TailAVARs node in the Track View, you see two controllers: Swing and Curl. The following lines establish those two nodes:

```
Right Hand AVARs
addTrackViewController tail_Avars
$Tail01.rotation.z_rotation.controller "Swing"
                addTrackViewController tail_Avars $Tail01.rotation.y_rotation.
                ➥controller "Curl"
```

The next line tells the script that the global variable has been turned on. This means the next time the script tries to create the AVARs, it will know that they already exist and won't keep creating new ones.

```
TailAvarsCreated = true
        )
)
```

Define Slider Update Function

This next function is used to update the sliders. This means when you move the Swing and Curl slider back and forth, you'll see the actual value of your curl and swing changes in the Track View and vice versa.

```
fn AVAR_Update =
(
```

What's happening here is that the value of the Swing slider (`mvTail.swing.value`) is being updated with the value of the Z rotation of the tail bone.

```
-- Updates the swinging slider
mvTail.swing.value = in coordsys parent $Tail01.rotation.z_rotation
```

Again, the same update values must be set for the curling action. The script will have to cater to the fact that your curling was a little bit more complicated.

Once again, the script must recognize what should happen when the tail is below 0 and when it's above 0. The first bone's value was multiplied by 7.5 before in this script, and now the value must be divided by the same number (7.5) to find the value the slider should be on.

```
-- Updates the Curling slider
if (in coordsys parent $Tail01.rotation.y_rotation < 0) then
        mvTail.curl.value = in coordsys parent -
        ➥($Tail01.rotation.y_rotation/7.5)
else
        mvTail.curl.value = in coordsys parent -
        ➥($Tail01.rotation.y_rotation/16)
```

All the script needs is the value of *one* of the bones to figure out where the slider would be. The script bases everything in relation to the first bone, but you could choose any one you'd like to get the slider.

Open and Check for the Floater

The `fn createfloater` initializes (opens) the floater you see when you run the script.

```
fn createTailFloater =
```

As described earlier in relation to the gripper script, the next line checks to see if a floater is already open. If a floater is open, the script closes it and opens a new one.

```
(
try
(
        closeRolloutFloater TailFloater
)
catch
(
)
```

Define Name and Size of Floater

This next line tells MAX to open a new floater named `tailfloater` with the caption "Lion's Tail" and that it should be 300 by 200 pixels in size.

```
TailFloater = newRolloutFloater "Lion's Tail" 300 200
```

Define Rollouts for Floater

Next, the rollouts `mvTail` through `TailFloater` are added (the floater that you just created). Refer to the gripper script's detailed explanation for more information regarding what this part of the script is doing.

```
    addRollout mvTail TailFloater
)
```

Define MAXScript Utility Buttons and Functions

The next few lines create the buttons you see when you click on Lion's Tail in the drop-down menu on the right side under the MAXScript Utilities.

```
Utility utlTail "Lion's Tail"
(
```

The next line creates a button you can click on to open the floater.

```
button OpenTailFloater "Open Control Floater" width:140
```

This line creates a button that will be used to close the floater.

```
    button CloseTailFloater "Close Control Floater" width:140
)
    button TailAvars "Create AVARs"
```

The line below specifies what happens when you click on the newly created button when it's provided in the same Utility menu. When you click on it, you go to the `createfloater` function, which is the code just discussed.

```
on OpenTailFloater pressed do createTailFloater()
```

The following code is executed when you click the Close Control Floater button; it does just that.

```
on CloseTailFloater pressed do closeRolloutFloater TailFloater
```

The function `createTailAvars` is called when the TailAvars button is clicked.

```
    on TailAvars pressed do createTailAvars()
)
```

Open Floater When Script Is Run Function

This next line opens the floater when you run the script. If you did not offer this as a feature of opening itself, you could still open it using the Lion's Tail buttons in the right side of the MAXScript panel.

```
    -- opens the floater when the script is run.
    if displayTailFloaterRun == true then createTailFloater()
```

Slider Update Time Routine

The `Slider Update Time` routine ensures that the function `AVAR_Updates` updates the sliders when the curves in the Track View are adjusted. (Remember the function that updated the sliders in the floater from the position of the bones?)

The `Slider Update Time` routine is called here, and it moves the `Curl` and `Swing` sliders so that you know exactly what the position of the tail is in relation to the AVARs and the keys set in the Track View and function curves. This basically makes sure that no matter how you change the animation for the tail, everything updates accordingly.

```
registerTimeCallback AVAR_Update
```

That's it! You now know how this script opens itself, creates two sliders to curl and swing the lion's tail, enables these sliders to update when you move the `Time` slider, and creates AVARs in the Track View that make adjusting function curves easier. And on top of all that functionality, it took only 138 lines to do it!

Multiped Six-Legged Setup

Keeping track of four legs is a challenge, but keyframing six legs can be quite tedious and time consuming. The simple linking of dummy constraints can speed up this process. As you have seen before in their use with the complex skeletal rigging, dummy constraints allow you to create relationships between objects. In the case of an insect, translating one leg can easily automate the action of the two other legs through the use of dummy constraint connections.

The key to making constraint-driven insect work is that insect motion follows a very predictable pattern. As described earlier, the transforms on each leg tree mirror the transforms of the leg tree in front of it. Every other leg follows the opposite leg's motion on an insect. For example, the front left leg can drive the middle right and back left legs. These simple rules make it quite easy to set up a series of connections that can make one leg drive the others.

For the following exercise, load the file Mite_WORK.max. This file contains a very simple bug mesh. Boxes will represent the mesh in low resolutions as they have in all the previous tutorials. The whole setup for this mite has been completed using all the tasks you learned in the previous exercises. The legs for this insect were built exactly as described before—with IK using dummy constraints to control the foot and knee on each leg. The only difference is the Limit settings because of the different angle of the legs. The process for creating the additional constraint setup beyond this multiple leg rig is simple: Link the constraints to a Master Dummy controller.

1. Open Mite_WORK.max on the accompanying CD.

2. Select the dummy constraints called C_LTFRONTFOOT, C_RTMIDFOOT, and C_LTBACKFOOT.

3. Click the Select and Link tool in the Main toolbar.

4. Click on the dummies you selected (C_LTFRONTFOOT, C_RTMIDFOOT, and C_LTBACKFOOT), and then drag the Link icon to link those leg constraints to the dummy constraint called C_LEGS01. Deselect Link mode by clicking on the Select tool.

5. Select the dummy constraints called C_RTFRONTFOOT, C_LTMIDFOOT, and C_RTBACKFOOT.

6. Click the Select and Link tool.

7. Click on C_RTFRONTFOOT, C_LTMIDFOOT, and C_RTBACKFOOT, and then drag the Link icon to link the leg constraints to the dummy constraint called C_LEGS02. Deselect Link mode.

8. Test your linking. If you select C_LEGS01, you should be able to move the left-front, right-middle, and left-back legs together. The opposite should happen if you move C_LEGS02. Because an insect has a rhythm to the movement of its legs, you can move them together like this.

You could have made these connections with expressions. However, expressions would paint you into a corner, disabling your access to each leg individually for tweaking other kinds of motions. With this setup, you get the most flexibility and control. You can control the legs with the master dummy controls, or you can control each leg individually with its own dummy constraint.

In Practice

- **Using MAXScript.** The introduction of more accessible MAXScript functions enables you to hack the software to do what you need it to do—create hands-on interfaces and provide more control over your characters.

- **A three-bone leg setup.** One bone must be added to a normal leg tree for most creatures. This setup also demands an extra end effector that's not used in a human leg setup. The front three-bone leg is the reverse of the rear, except in elephants.

- **Linking the trees together.** By linking dummy constraints and bones, you attain the most control over your rig and create flexibility for the demands of your scene.

- **Multiped six-legged setup.** Complex linking of the dummy constraints gives you the power, flexibility, and control you need to animate a complex six-legged creature.

Chapter 4

Animating a Walk

By Angie Jones

Animating a walk is one of the most diffi-cult things you can attempt. There are many different weight shifts throughout the body as a person walks, and the body is constantly compensating for these weight shifts. This means you need to mimic weight shifts with timing and offset keyframing. In addition, everyone has a signature walk. Each of us walks differently, and our walks contribute to the descriptions of who we are. A person's body structure, personality, mood, psychological state, and health all affect the way he walks. Some people drag their feet, and others bounce as they walk. Watch people the next time you are out and see how differently they all move.

In this chapter, you will learn about the general mechanics of walking, as well as how to do the following:

- Add personality to a walk
- Animate two-, four-, and six-legged walks
- Use straight-ahead and pose-to-pose methods to layer motion

The Mechanics of Walking

Walking has been described as controlled falling. Every time you take a step, you actually catch yourself with the outstretched foot. After that foot plants on the ground, the knee bends and the body lowers to absorb the shock of the impact. The body then lifts up and propels forward, pulling the opposite foot up and forward to catch up with the rest of the body and plant itself (See Figure 4.1).

Figure 4.1   Illustration of shifts in weight during a walk cycle.

While the body is propelling the feet forward with weight shifts, the hips, shoulders, and spine compensate for the force through the body. Because this is a lot of motion to keep track of, layering is key to creating a good walk. Take the complex motion one step at a time. When you have the lower body motion paced out, for example, you can continue to create the weight shifts throughout the body one layer at a time.

The point where the heel touches the ground is the most stable pose of an entire walk. This is the phase right before the planted pose. At this point, the body weight is most evenly divided. This pose also provides for the stride length and is the best pose from which to start your walk animation.

You will need to understand three poses before beginning a walk cycle:

- **Planted.** This pose comes right after the foot is extended to take a step. The planted foot is fully in contact with the ground, and the other foot is preparing to pass underneath the body, driving the momentum of the step. The arm on the same side of the weight-bearing foot is fully extended at its back swing for balance, and the other arm is swinging forward slightly in front of the body.

- **Passing.** The planted foot bears all the weight of the body, and the passing foot is directly under the body. The arms have crossed at this pose to prepare their swing to the pose opposite of their first planted positions.

- **Lifted.** The lifted pose is right before the foot prepares to plant. The foot that was bearing all of the weight is now lifted and the other foot is up on its toes preparing to shift weight back to that lifted foot. The arms have crossed at the passing phase and are now preparing for their fully extended swing.

The Feet and Legs

The feet and legs propel the body forward. To keep your character looking natural, you should always keep the joints bent slightly, even at full leg extension. The walk usually starts with the feet at the *extended position*—where the feet are farthest apart. This is the point where the character's weight shifts to the forward foot (see Figure 4.2).

As the weight of the body is transferred to the forward foot, the knee bends to absorb the shock. This is called the *recoiled* or *planted pose* and is the lowest point in the walk (see Figure 4.3).

The planted pose is halfway through the first step. As the character moves forward, the knee straightens and lifts the body to its highest point. This is called the *passing pose* because this is where the free foot passes the supporting leg (see Figure 4.4).

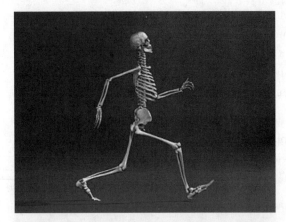

Figure 4.2   Extended position: This is where the walk starts. Legs are extended, with "soft" knees.

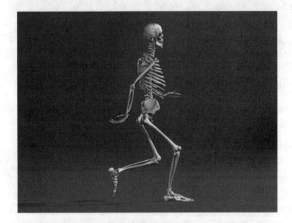

Figure 4.3   Planted pose: The planted leg recoils from the weight of the body, and the knee bends to absorb the shock.

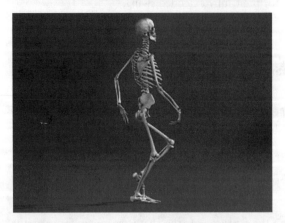

Figure 4.4   Passing pose: As one foot passes the other, the knee straightens, lifting the body. The one foot is still planted, but the body now lifts to bring the passing foot under the body.

Note

In a cartoony double-bounce walk, the passing pose has the body lowered again to create the double bounce effect.

As the character moves forward, the weight-bearing foot lifts off the ground at the heel, transferring the force to the ball of the foot. The body now starts to fall forward. The free foot swings forward like a pendulum to meet the ground. This is the *lifted pose* and is shown in Figure 4.5.

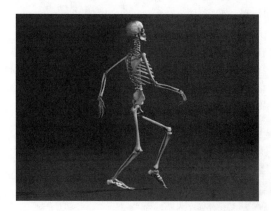

Figure 4.5   **Lifted pose:** As the weight is transferred from one foot to the other, the passing leg swings forward and lifts to catch the body as it moves forward.

Next, the free leg makes contact as shown in Figure 4.6. Half the cycle has been completed. The second half is an exact mirror of the first. If it differs, the character might appear to limp.

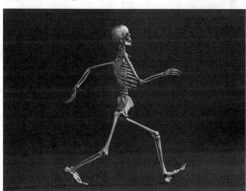

Figure 4.6   As the weight is transferred from one foot to the other, the passing foot is extended with a soft knee and is preparing to plant again.

The Hips, Spine, and Shoulders

The body's center of gravity is at the hips; all balance starts there, as does the rest of the body's motion. During a walk, it is best to think of the hips' motion as two separate, overlapping rotations. First, the hips rotate along the axis of the spine, forward and back with the legs. If the right leg is forward, the right hip is rotated forward as well. Second, at the passing position, the free leg pulls the hip out of center, forcing the hips to rock from side to side. These two motions are then transmitted through the spine to the shoulders, which mirror the hips to maintain balance.

When the feet are fully extended, the hips must rotate along the axis of the spine. To keep balance, the shoulders swing in the opposite direction. From the front, the spine is relatively straight (see Figure 4.7). From the top, however, you can see how the hips and shoulders twist in opposite directions to maintain balance (see Figure 4.8). The motion is very complex because every part of the body affects another part as the body compensates for weight shifts.

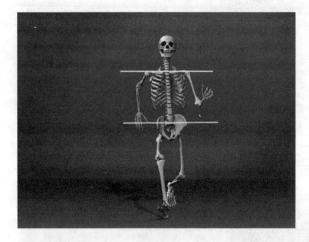

Figure 4.7   Extended position: Rotation is less apparent here, but it's still easy to see in the pelvis, which is turned out to compensate for the extended leg.

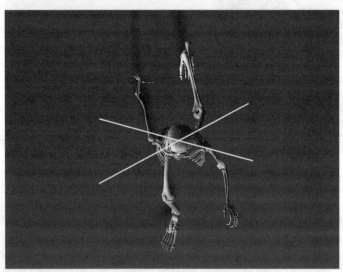

Figure 4.8   Extended position: The rotation of the hips and shoulders is apparent from the Top view, with opposite rotation occurring in the shoulders and the hips.

At the passing pose, the Front view shows the hip being pulled over the planted leg and the spine curving to keep the weight balanced throughout the body (see Figure 4.9). A counter-rotation occurs in the shoulders to counter the rotation of the hips and curve of the spine in addition to rotating forward to compensate for the passing arm that is coming forward. From the top, the hips are at nearly equal angles, and the shoulders are turned out to compensate for the extended arm (see Figure 4.10).

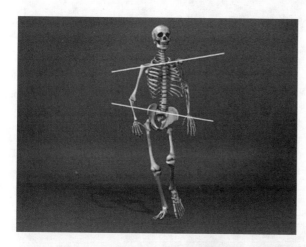

Figure 4.9   Passing position: The rotation and translation of the hips is obvious from the top. The hips move over the planted foot to compensate for weight shifts, while the shoulders are turned out to compensate for the passing arm preparing to extend to full swing.

Figure 4.10   Passing position: The rotation of the hips on the spine axis is nearly neutral, whereas the shoulders are turned out to compensate for the passing arm preparing to extend to full swing.

At the extension of the second leg, the hips and shoulders again are flat when viewed from the front (see Figure 4.11). Looking from above, however, you can see that the hips and shoulders have completed their rotation (see Figure 4.12).

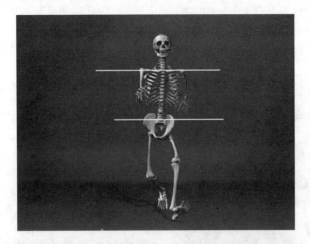

Figure 4.11   Extended position: You can also see the twisting of the hips with the large pelvis bone from the front, complementing the twisting of the previous extended foot pose.

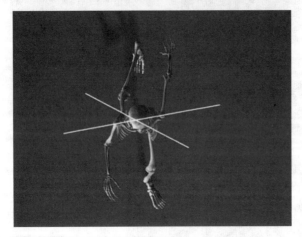

Figure 4.12   Extended position: When the weight shifts from one foot to the other, the hips are again twisted when viewed from above.

The Arms

Unless the character is using his arms, they generally hang loose at the sides, swinging back and forth to compensate for the rest of the body's movement. In this case, they tend to act like pendulums, dragging a few frames behind the hips and shoulders. Even at full extension, the arms should be slightly bent at the elbows. This keeps them looking natural.

The arms follow a path of motion that is similar to the shape of a figure eight (see Figure 4.13). When the arm swing follows this motion path, the arm provides a clean extension as it passes the body and a bending of the elbow as the arm reaches the end of both the forward and back swing.

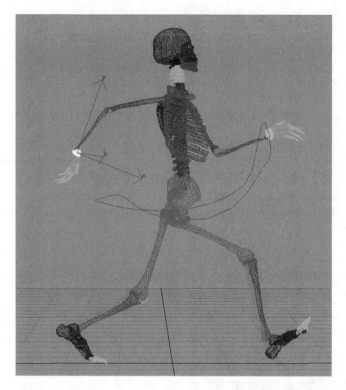

Figure 4.13   The motion path of the arm swing for a walk follows a kind of figure eight shape. Turn your trajectories on to create the motion path, and use your function curves in the track view to shape this motion.

An arm swing consists of three phases:

- **Passing.** The hand is at its lowest point in the swing.
- **Forward swing.** The hand is fully extended to its forward swing pose.
- **Back swing.** The hand is fully extended to its backward swing pose.

During the forward and back swings the arm is slightly bent but close to a full extension at the elbow. As the arm reaches the apex of the swing forward, the elbow begins to break or bend. The arm continues its arc upward as it bends back toward the body. This motion path starts the first breaking of joints as the arm swings backward. Keeping the arms extended with a soft elbow on the forward and backward positions helps sell the breaking of the elbow as the arm moves in the opposite direction.

The Head

In a standard walk, the head generally tries to stay level, with the eyes focused on where the character is going. The head then bobs around slightly to stay balanced. If a character is excited, this bobbing is more pronounced. The head might also hang low for a sad character or might look around if the scene requires it.

Body Posture and Emotion

The character's body posture changes depending on the character's mood. Power centers are also great clues to the demeanor of your character. A *power center* is where the gravity is concentrated and is usually connected with the body part that is leading the action. A second clue is the line of action through the character. A line of action determines where the energy is coming from and its direction of thrust through the body. Even a character standing still has a line of action because of the shifts of weight in the body. All movement is driven by some force, and the line of action describes the thrust of weight through the character. For example, a happy or proud character arches his back, puts his chest out proudly, and swings his arms in wide arcs exhibiting the nature of how he feels inside. Football players and superheros are great examples of characters that would walk like this (see Figure 4.14).

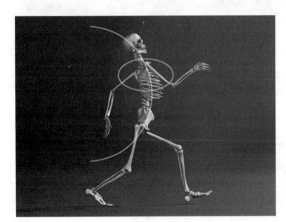

Figure 4.14   A proud or happy character has a line of action that is highest at the chest. The power center of gravity is in the chest, and the character leads with the chest area when walking.

In contrast, a sad or intellectual character keeps all the energy in its head. This character might slump over, barely swing his arms, and hang his head low in concentration or distress. You might have seen a professor in school or a friend who is troubled walk like this (see Figure 4.15).

If a character is "from the streets" and has an attitude like a hoodlum (or even if it is a sexy character), the line of action and power center are concentrated in the pelvis. Mick Jagger has a great pelvis-driven walk (see Figure 4.16).

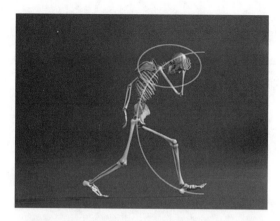

Figure 4.15 A sad or intellectual character has a line of action that is highest in the head. The power center of gravity is cerebral, and the character leads with the head area when walking.

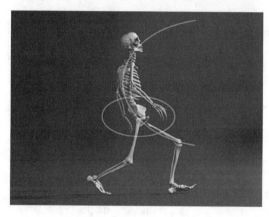

Figure 4.16 The pelvis-driven walk occurs with a sexy figure or a strut for a punk from the wrong side of the tracks. The power center of gravity is located in the pelvic area, and the character leads with the hips when walking.

Another posture occurs when a character leads with his stomach. Characters with this type of walk tend to be tubby or overweight. A great example of a tubby walker is John Goodman. With a tubby walk, the arm swing tends to stop around the most outer edge of the stomach; the arm swings only that far before returning to the back swing motion (see Figure 4.17).

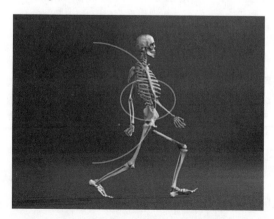

Figure 4.17 An overweight or tubby character holds all his energies in his stomach. Observe the line of action and power center in the abdominal area.

These postures translate beyond walking and should also be used as examples for portraying emotion in non-locomotive scenes. Try experimenting with different power centers and lines of action after you get the basic walking motion down.

Pose to Pose or Straight Ahead

You should understand one more concept before animating. There are three ways to animate a character. The first two come from traditional animation styles.

- Pose-to-pose
- Straight ahead
- Combination of the two

The pose-to-pose method is a planned structure approach to animating. Every pose is well thought out before the animation is created. All the extremes are created from one to another. This approach is used for scenes requiring heavy acting abilities and readable poses. The advantage to this animation approach is the clarity and strength of the motion. The disadvantage is lack of spontaneity, flow, invention, and naturalness.

The other option to animating is the straight-ahead approach. This method means you just start animating frame by frame, getting new ideas as you go along, and you see where you end up. This approach is great for wild, crazy motion, such as in a fight sequence. The pros to this approach are the flow, spontaneity, and inventiveness imparted to the motion. The disadvantages to the straight-ahead method are mushy, unclear motion and that it takes longer to animate this way.

Finally, the third option, and the one I prefer, is a combination of pose-to-pose and straight-ahead animation. This is easy to do in CG because you have a hierarchy you can work down in layers. You can first plan out the extreme poses—working down the body parts in layers—and then refine the action with straight-ahead animating for the in-between keys. Planning is very important to keep the poses clear and defined. Instead of animating in strictly the pose-to-pose method, you create layers of animation throughout the tree. In the mixed method, the keys to in-betweens are offset on the layers to create a more natural motion. Some parts of the tree get more animation than others. The in-between frames begin to have more emphasis than the extreme keys. By layering, you also use the spontaneous efforts of the straight-ahead method by adding elements throughout the animation to each layer.

Stride Length

The best place to start a walk is with the pelvis. Here, you will map out how far the character will step and how high and low the body will move up and down through the arcs of the walk. Think of a bouncing ball when you animate the pelvis for a walk (see Figure 4.18).

The first step to decide is how long the stride will be. This determination will tell you where the bouncing ball motion of the hips should be placed. An average stride is usually four feet wide, meaning the stride length is the size of the foot plus three more of the character's feet in front of the planted foot. If your character has

Figure 4.18
Bouncing ball action describes the arcing motion used for a walk.

unusually large proportioned feet with stumpy little legs, this obviously will not apply. For that kind of character, the foot steps might overlap a little, and the character might waddle more than take a full step. The upcoming tutorial assumes a more realistic stride equaling four of the character's feet lengths. The best way to determine a natural stride for your character is to extend the legs so they have a soft knee and are not fully extended; at that same time, define a full stride.

Timing

You also need to establish the timing of your animation. You can animate at 24 fps (frames per second) for film or 30 fps for video. 30 fps will be used for this chapter; however, it is very easy to scale all keys to equal whatever timing you need, in case you change your mind. Using 30 fps for the timing, the first stride should be taken by frame 15, halfway through the first second of animation. Therefore, by frame 15, the character will have a stride of 4 units in place. This means the second stride will fill the remaining 15 frames.

Animating a Two-Legged Walk

This tutorial uses the IK setup described in Chapter 2, "Basic Character and Creature Setup," to animate a simple walk, and it relies heavily on the use of end effectors on the legs to keep the feet locked to the ground. The exercise also uses the FK arm and IK leg skeleton from Chapter 2. You will use a pose-to-pose method to block out the main stages of a walk and then refine the animation using the straight-ahead approach to adjust in-between keys. While you're working through your animation, refer to the poses described earlier and try to match them closely. Watch your arcs on the arms, and remember the figure eight when creating their motion paths.

> **Note**
>
> For walks, the arms are probably best animated by using forward rather than Inverse Kinematics. This is because the arms usually swing freely instead of aiming for specific targets (such as when the character is lifting an object). The skeletal hierarchy used for this series of exercises is the FK structure, but if you prefer, you can use the IK structure later after you understand the basic steps of animating a walk.

Animating the Legs

The legs are usually the best place to start when animating a walk. The positions of the legs and hips drive the position of the upper body. The process can be divided into four phases:

- Blocking out the main keys of the stride
- Adjusting the hips to be centered over the weight-bearing legs
- Adjusting the ankle and toes to rotate as they lift off the ground
- Blocking out the second step

Block Out and Adjust the First Stride

To block out your animation, you will create key poses for your timing. After you block out the initial timing of the animation, you will adjust the poses to give them a more natural motion. You will be using the Motion panel, Select and Move tool, Select and Rotate tool, Transform Type-In tool, and Local Reference Axis Coordinate field to animate the skeleton in this tutorial, so you should become familiar with these tools.

1. Open the file WALK_CYCLE_WORK.max from the CD-ROM. This scene contains a simple skeleton with the legs controlled by IK, the arms controlled by Forward Kinematics, and the spine controlled via a set of expressions.

2. Move the Time Slider to frame 0. Toggle the Animate button to On.

3. Go to the left side Camera view provided for you in the file. The walk starts with the right leg, which is manipulated at the ankle.

4. Open the Motion panel and select the dummy constraint C_RTFOOT. Change the Reference Coordinate System to Local so you will be moving the constraints on their local axes. In the Transform Type-In tool under Offset Local, enter the value –20 on the y-axis. To set a key on this frame, click on the Position button under Create Key in the Motion panel (see Figure 4.19).

5. Continue to sketch out the remaining foot positions. Select the dummy constraint C_LTFOOT and enter a value of 20 on the y-axis under Offset Local. Set a

key on this frame by clicking on the Position button under Create Key in the Motion panel.

You will notice that the ankle becomes detached when you place the back foot this far behind the body. This is because the foot has hit a limit. Compensate for this by adjusting the hips to be centered better over the feet.

6. Select the dummy constraint C_PELVIS and in the Transform Type-In box, enter –9 on the local z-axis and enter 2 on the local y-axis under Offset Local. The back leg should bend slightly at the knee, and the leg should be in contact with the ankle now (see Figure 4.20). Set a key on this frame by clicking on the Position button under Create Key in the Motion panel.

7. The walk takes 15 frames per step. Scrub the Time Slider to frame 15, which is the start of the right step. Move the C_LTFOOT dummy constraint 40 units forward by entering –40 in the local y-axis of the Transform Type-In box under Offset Local.

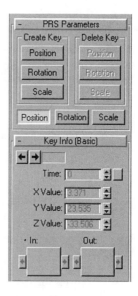

Figure 4.19
In the Motion panel's PRS Parameters, click Position under Create Key to set keys in the animation as you create poses.

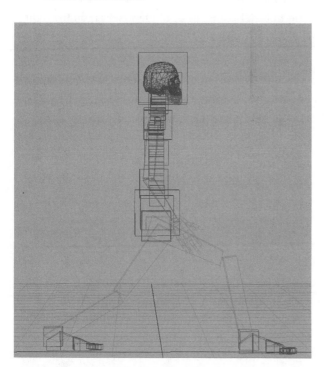

Figure 4.20   The placement of the feet and hips for the first step of a walk.

Note

After you set the first key frame, you do not have to manually set the key frames in the Motion panel if you have the Animate button turned on. The Animate button will set a key every time you move an object on the frame. You are moving the object, so you will only use the Set Keyframe function for refining actions or setting a key that is the same as a previous one.

8. Move the C_RTFOOT effector 40 units backward by entering 40 into the local y-axis of the Transform Type-In box. Select the C_PELVIS constraint, and then click the Position button under Create Key in the Motion panel so its placement is set.

   Scrub the animation, and the legs appear to slide across the floor. If your character were ice skating, this might be acceptable. But for this walk, you want the leg to lift off the ground.

9. Move the Time Slider to frame 7, halfway through the first step. Select the dummy constraint C_LTFOOT and move it up approximately 8 units by entering 8 into the local z-axis of the Transform Type-In box.

10. At the halfway point of the step, the hips are also at their highest point (refer to Figure 4.3). Move the C_PELVIS dummy constraint up and forward to stabilize the body over the legs by entering 7 into the local z-axis and –3 into the local y-axis of the Transform Type-In box. Because most of the weight is on the right foot for this pose, the hips should be somewhat centered over that foot or the character will fall over.

    Scrubbing the animation now gives a very basic step that looks pretty funny, but you will fix that in the next phase by adjusting the ankle and toes. Open the file called WALK_CYCLE_WORK1a.max to see the file completed up to this point in the exercise.

11. Go to frame 0, select the C_LTFOOT dummy constraint, and move it up by entering 4 on the local z-axis of the Transform Type-In box. Click on Select and Rotate and check to see if you are operating on the local axis in the Reference Coordinate system. Then, rotate the foot on the local x-axis 37 degrees of the Transform Type-In box. Click the Rotation button under Create Key in the Motion Panel.

12. Adjust the toe joints so they are level with the ground by selecting them with the preset Named Selection sets Left Toes01 and Left Toes02. Rotate them on their local x-axis –37 degrees in the Transform Type-In box under Offset Local (see Figure 4.21).

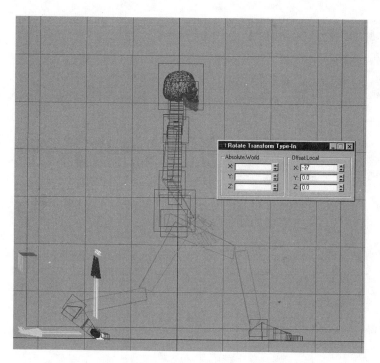

Figure 4.21   Refine the step by rotating the toes. This will make the character push off for each step, giving the walk weight.

13. Still at frame 0, select the C_RTFOOT dummy constraint and rotate it on the local x-axis –35 degrees in the Transform Type-In box. Then, you'll want to create some drag in the right foot by curling the toes back on this pose. To do so, select the Named Selection sets Right Toes01 and Right Toes02 and rotate them backward –35 degrees on the local x-axis.

14. At frame 7, select the C_LTFOOT dummy constraint and rotate it on the local x-axis 45 degrees.

15. Still at frame 7, select and move the C_LTFOOT dummy constraint –4 on the local z-axis. Straighten the toes out at this frame by entering 35 on the local x-axis of the Right Toes01 Selection set in the Transform Type-In box.

16. Go to frame 4, select the C_RTFOOT, and rotate it on its local x-axis 35 degrees. Select the Named Selection set Right Toes01 and rotate it down 35 degrees on the local x-axis.

17. Create some drag in the left foot by curling the toes back on this pose. Select the Named Selection set Left Toes01 and rotate it backward 50 degrees on the local x-axis. The pose at frame 4 should look like Figure 4.22.

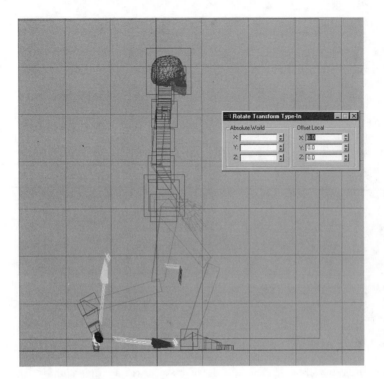

Figure 4.22   Create drag in the toes as the foot passes under the body. This will give the walk a more fluid, natural motion.

18. Go to frame 15. Select and rotate the C_LTFOOT dummy –120 degrees on the local x-axis. Bend the left toes to be parallel to the floor at this frame by entering –35 on the local x-axis of the Right Toes01 Selection set. Select and move the C_RTFOOT dummy constraint 4 on the local z-axis and 2 on the local y-axis. Select and rotate the dummy 45 degrees on the local x-axis. Bend the right toes to be parallel to the floor at this frame by entering –35 on the local x-axis of the Right Toes01 Selection set (see Figure 4.23).

Open the file called WALK_CYCLE_WORK1b.max to see the file completed up to this point in the exercise.

The Second Step

With the basics of this first step complete, you're ready to start repeating yourself. Specifically, repeat steps 3 through 18 for the left leg, creating a second step that starts on frame 15 and ends on frame 30. The top of this step should occur at frame 23 and the recoil, or planted, pose should occur at frame 19.

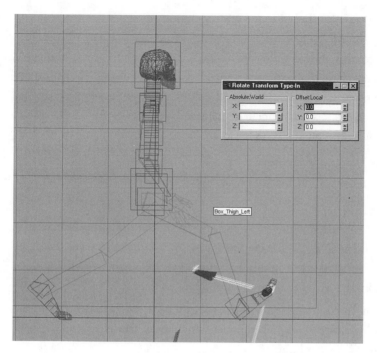

Figure 4.23   Continue to adjust the ankle and toes so the character is using the foot to push off from the previous step and is bent in anticipation of the next step.

During this exercise and those that follow, remember that you can continue to refine the motion. These exercises are intended to provide the most basic blocking of a walk. It is up to you to infuse life and personality into that walk using timing, adjustment of curves, line of action, and power centers. In addition, resist the temptation to skip ahead. Each exercise layers the important motion of a specific body part on the project, helping refine your animation as you progress. As you have already seen, all the body parts and their movements are closely related.

To see the walk completed up to this point, open WALK_CYCLE_WORKa.max on the accompanying CD, or run the movie called First steps.avi.

Animating the Hips

You can further modify the walk by adding the proper rotation to the hips. The hips rotate forward with the legs on the vertical axis and also rock side to side as the free leg pulls to the side of the weight-bearing foot.

The skeleton setup from Chapter 2 gives you power and flexibility in manipulating the hips for this exercise. I prefer to use the C_PELVIS dummy constraint for most of my pelvis animation because it is linked to the spine and forces me to deal with the line of action. The rotation of the C_PELVIS constraint causes the spine to rotate with the hips and forces you to counter this action by arcing the spine. However, there is also pelvic control outside of the spine in the form of another constraint called C_HIPS. You can rotate this constraint outside of the pelvis to get certain poses you desire. C_HIPS will not rotate the spine tree and is independent of that tree's motion. This kind of constraint can be used to refine a motion and gives the animator more flexibility in how to create motion.

Use the file you completed in the previous exercise, or you can open WALK_ CYCLE_ WORKa.max from the CD-ROM.

1. Go to frame 0 of the animation. With the Animate button still on, select the dummy constraint C_PELVIS. From the Top viewport, rotate the hips 20 degrees around the vertical, or z, axis in the Transform Type-In box under Offset Local. This should make the right side of the hips rotate forward.

2. Move the Time Slider to frame 15. Rotate the hips back –30 degrees on the local z-axis in the Transform Type-In box under Offset Local. The left side of the hips should be rotated forward now.

3. Move the Time Slider to frame 30. Rotate the hips forward 40 degrees on the local z-axis in the Transform Type-In box to match the pose on frame 0 (see Figure 4.24).

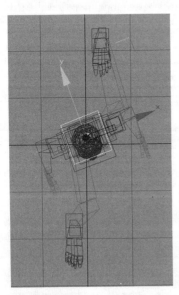

Figure 4.24   As the leg moves forward to take a step, the hips also rotate out to help the leg take that wide stance and plant the foot.

Tip

Another way to accomplish step 3 is to click on the key at frame 0 to highlight it and then hold the Shift key down as you drag the highlighted key to frame 30. This copies the key exactly, as does duplicating anything in the viewport with Shift-Drag.

4. Now get the side-to-side motion of the hips. Move the Time Slider to frame 7. This is the top of the left step, where the left leg is off the ground. The weight of this leg pulls the hip out and above the weight-bearing foot. From the Front viewport, rotate the dummy constraint C_PELVIS along the local y-axis 16 degrees in the Transform Type-In box. Notice that the spine follows this rotation; you now need to compensate for that rotation by arcing the spine back.

5. Select the dummy constraints C_SPINE and C_SPINEUPPER and rotate them individually to arc the spine to compensate for this weight shift and bring the head upright again. Use approximately –3 for C_SPINE and –1 degree for C_SPINEUPPER on the local y-axis (see Figure 4.25).

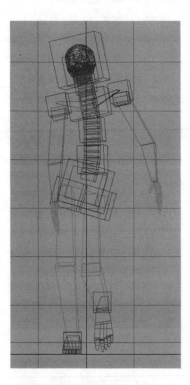

Figure 4.25   When the hips are rotated to favor the weight-bearing leg, the spine absorbs the shock of the shifts in weight on that leg by arcing back to neutralize the rest of the body into an upright position.

Tip

Another great way to set keys for your constraints is to have the Motion panel open at all times so you can work from there with the spinners. To set a key, click on either Rotation or Position under the Create Key panel. From there, under Key Info Basic, you can adjust the time and value of the key, as well as the curve. Using the spinners can be helpful for minute rotations of one degree on the dummy constraints because it is difficult to make that tight of a rotation visually with the mouse in the viewport.

6. Move the Time Slider to frame 23, which is the top of the right step. Rotate the dummy constraint C_PELVIS –20 degrees on the local y-axis.

7. Select the dummy constraints C_SPINE and C_SPINEUPPER and rotate them individually to arc the spine to compensate for this weight shift and bring the head upright again. Rotate approximately 6 degrees for C_SPINE and 2 degrees for C_SPINEUPPER on the local y-axis.

8. Zero out the rotations of the two spine dummy constraints (C_SPINE and C_SPINEUPPER) at frames 0, 15, and 30 so the spine is straight using the Motion panel. To do this, set the keys under the Create Rotation Key panel, and then under Euler Parameters/X axis zero out the constraints on those keys.

   Copy frame 0 for the pelvis dummy C_PELVIS to frame 30 to complete the cycle. To see what the file should look like at this point in the exercise, open the file called WALK_CYCLE_WORK1c.max. Finally, you need to push the hips over the weight-bearing leg.

9. Go to frame 0 and select the dummy constraint C_PELVIS. Drag C_PELVIS to the right 3 units on the local x-axis. This will move the hips over the legs.

10. Go to frame 7 and with the pelvis dummy still selected, drag it –3 units to the left on the local x-axis so it is more centered over the right foot (see Figure 4.26).

11. Go to frame 15 and center the pelvis dummy once more by dragging it 3 units to the right on the local x-axis in the Transform Type-In box under Offset Local.

12. Repeat steps 9 through 12 to complete the second step and to center the hips over the weight-bearing foot.

Scrub the Time Slider to see how the hip rotation adds a more natural motion to the walk. The motion might seem a little extreme right now, but it will be adjusted as you work through the body parts. Later, you can play with the amount of hip rotation in your curves to increase or tone down the motion and to create personality in the walk.

To see the walk at this point in the tutorial, open Hips.avi or WALK_CYCLE_WORKb .max from the CD-ROM.

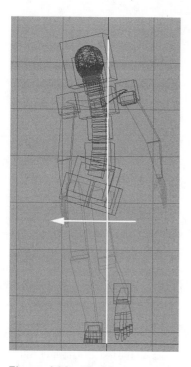

Figure 4.26   The hips must move over and rotate up over the weight-bearing foot.

Animating the Knees and Adjusting Foot Positions

The character setup has knee controls that can help you point the knees outward or inward. The next exercise will place the knees in a neutral position, but later you can easily change a walk to be more pigeon-toed or bow-legged. Either continue with the file you have created from the previous exercises or open the file called WALK_ CYCLE_ WORKb.max.

1. Still in the Front view, select the dummy constraint C_RTKNEE and rotate it on its local z-axis –35 degrees in the Transform Type-In box under Offset Local.

2. Select the dummy constraint C_RTFOOT and enter a value of 4 units for the local x-axis so it is centered under the spine in the Transform Type-In box under Offset Local.

3. Go to frame 7, select the dummy constraint C_RTKNEE, and rotate it on its local z-axis 44 degrees in the Transform Type-In box. The knee should be facing the front (see Figure 4.27).

4. Go to frame 15, select the dummy constraint C_LTKNEE, and rotate it on its local z-axis 35 degrees.

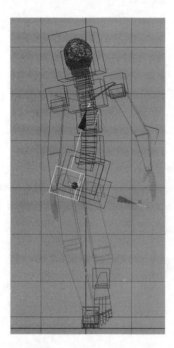

Figure 4.27   The knee rotates out slightly as the hips rotate out and the foot extends to plant position.

5. Select the dummy constraint C_LTFOOT and move it to the right −2 units so it is centered under the spine in the Transform Type-In box.

6. Repeat steps 1 through 6 to complete the second step and center the weight-bearing foot under the hips.

The reference files on CD-ROM for this stage in the tutorial are Knees.avi and WALK_CYCLE_WORKc.max.

Animating the Shoulders

The next motion to animate is the shoulders. The shoulder motion mirrors that of the hips but lags by a frame or two because it takes a bit of time for the force generated by the hips to traverse the spine and reach the shoulders. The spine also compresses and arches forward as the hips move up, and then it straightens out as the hips move down.

You have already created the side-to-side and front-to-back spine motion because the pelvis constraint forced you to when you used to set the hip rotation. However, you could have used the dummy constraint C_HIPS and rotated the hips independently of the spine. In that case, this would be the tie to counter that hip rotation by compressing the spine into an arc when the foot is planted. Flexibility is key when building a setup, and the ability to counter rotations made with the C_PELVIS constraint or to create the motion independently using the C_HIPS constraint illustrates how flexible this skeletal setup is for posing.

Consult the CD-ROM file Shoulders.avi and the shoulder motion that occurs with the spine rotations.

Animating the Arms

The next portion of the body you will animate is the arms. The arms of the example skeleton are animated with Forward Kinematics. They are controlled at the shoulder and clavicle by dummy constraints. The clavicle will drive much of the motion as well as the shoulder. As you work, remember that the arms follow a path of motion that is similar to the shape of a figure eight (refer to Figure 4.13).

To animate the arms you will do the following:

- Create basic right and left arm swing
- Adjust the swing to make a figure eight
- Follow through with the wrists and fingers
- Refine the motion and start over for the second step

Create the Arm Swing

When you animate the arm swing, remember that the arm that swings out compensates for the opposite extended leg. In other words, if the left leg is extended forward to take a step, the right arm is in front of the body compensating for the right leg that is trailing behind.

1. Open the file called WALK_CYCLE_WORKc.max or continue with the file you have been creating. Go to the Side view camera provided in the file and move the Time Slider to frame 0. At this frame, the left leg is trailing behind. This means that the right arm is forward to counter it. Select the dummy object C_LTEL-BOW and rotate it forward –25 degrees in the Transform Type-In box under Offset Local.

2. Notice how the arm does not rotate at the elbow. This is because you are using FK on the arms. Select the box bone named Box_Forearm_Left and rotate it approximately –48 degrees on the local x–axis in the Transform Type-In box under Offset Local.

3. Select the dummy constraint C_RTELBOW and rotate it back 66 degrees on the local x-axis in the Transform Type-In box.

4. Again, the arm does not rotate at the elbow because of FK. Select the box bone Box_Forearm_Right and rotate it 22 degrees on the local x-axis in the Transform Type-In box.

5. Move the Time Slider to frame 15 and mirror rotations, using steps 1 through 4 as a guide (see Figure 4.28).

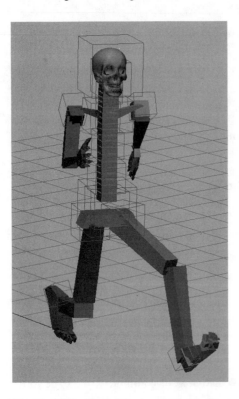

Figure 4.28   The left leg is extended in front of the body in this stride, so the right arm is also extended in front of the body.

6. Move the Time Slider to frame 30. Create the forward rotations of the arms to match those on frame 0. This is easily accomplished from within the Track View by selecting the keyframes and cloning them. Hold down the Shift key and drag them to the right, positioning the cloned keys on frame 30.

The reference files on CD-ROM for this stage of the tutorial are Arms.avi and WALK_CYCLE_WORKd.max.

Adjusting to Make a Figure Eight

You have blocked out the arm swing, but now you must refine it to give it a more natural motion. The swing looks very mechanical, and you need to give it a motion path that will dictate lag and overshoot as the arm swings back and forth. Using the trajectory and function curves, you will "sculpt" the motion path of the arms to resemble a figure eight shape. Use the file you created in the previous exercises, or open the file on the accompanying CD called WALK_CYCLE_WORKd.max.

1. Select the box bone Box_Hand_Left01. Then go to the Display panel and under the Display Properties rollout, turn on Trajectory. The trajectory represents the object's motion through space according to the timing and keys you provided. The trajectory will help you refine the elliptical path the hand follows (see Figure 4.29).

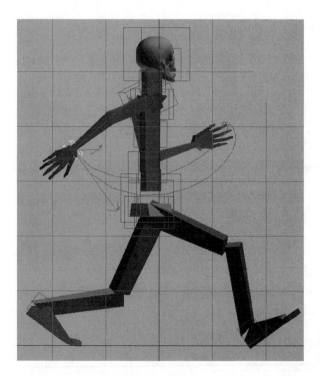

Figure 4.29   The trajectory will help you sculpt the motion path of the arms. Right now, the arms have a very mechanical swing back and forth. Using a more elliptical figure eight path will force the arm swing to have drag and overshoot.

2. If you scrub through the animation as it is, you will notice that the arm swing is very mechanical with little drag through the arm as it swings back and forth. Go

to frame 4 and select the dummy constraint C_RTELBOW. Rotate C_RTELBOW back 37 degrees on the local x-axis in the Transform Type-In box under Offset Local. The trajectory interactively changes, and you can already see the figure eight coming to life.

3. Still on frame 4, select the box bone Box_Forearm_Right and rotate it 9 degrees on the local x-axis in the Transform Type-In box under Offset Local.

4. Still on frame 4, adjust the arm's position from the front view. Select the dummy constraint C_RTELBOW and rotate it on the z-axis 28 degrees in the Transform Type-In box.

5. Go to frame 15 and adjust the arm's position from the front view. Select the dummy constraint C_RTELBOW and rotate it on the y-axis 15 degrees in the Transform Type-In box (see Figure 4.30).

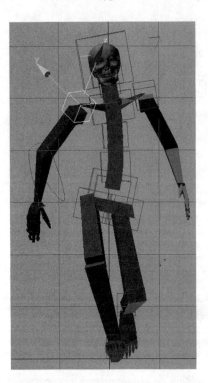

Figure 4.30   The arm should also swing out a little on the back swing. In the Front view you will rotate it out and around on the y- and z-axes.

6. Now you will adjust the back swing. Change views to the Camera called side Cam and go to frame 23. With C_RTELBOW still selected, rotate it backward 10 degrees on the local x–axis.

7. Select the box bone Box_Forearm_Right and rotate it backwards 28 degrees on the local x-axis.

8. Finally, create a little drag in the back swing. Go to frame 19 and rotate Box_Forearm_Right up –22 degrees on the local x-axis. The figure eight for this arm is complete, and you will see a more natural swing in the arm as shown in Figure 4.31.

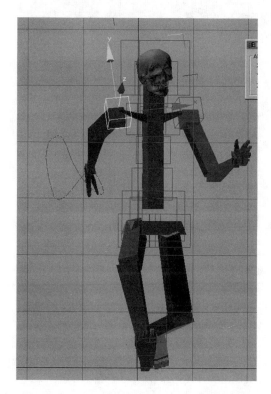

Figure 4.31   The Front view of the figure-eight trajectory.

Tip

If you are having difficulty adjusting the figure eight shape with the rotations in the viewport only, you can fine-tune your adjustment in the Track View. Simply open the Track View for the bone in question and observe the function curve. Select a key at the point that needs sculpting, and slide it vertically or horizontally to adjust the value of rotation of that bone. Keep the viewport in view while you do this so you can watch the trajectory interactively change with your adjustments. This way you can really fine-tune your motion path. Understanding your curves and how they relate to your motion paths is very important when it comes to creating natural motion (see Figure 4.32).

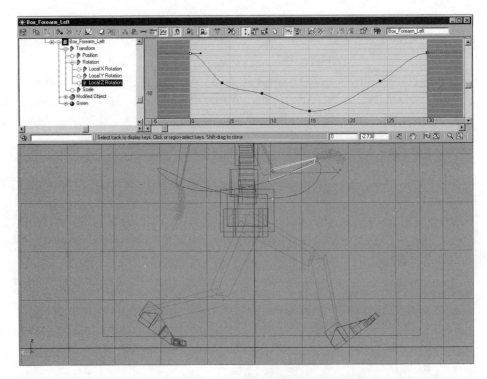

Figure 4.32   Fine-tuning the trajectory with the Track View using the function curves is the best way to adjust the motion path of your animation.

9. Move the Time Slider to frame 0 and mirror the rotations, using steps 1 through 8 as a guide for the other arm. Remember to turn on the trajectory so you can see how the swing turns out.

The reference files on CD-ROM for this stage in the tutorial are figure8.avi and WALK_CYCLE_WORKf.max.

Follow Through with Wrists and Fingers

As you create the arm swing, the wrists need to break the motion by moving at a slightly different rate. When the arm swings completely in front of the body and then begins its swing behind the body, the wrist rotates with that motion but drags behind a few frames because it is limp and follows the motion driven by the arm.

1. Go to frame 0, select the box bone Box_Forearm_Left, and rotate it –100 degrees on the local z-axis in the Transform Type-In box under Offset Local so the palm faces the ground. Copy the same key frame to frame 30 using the Shift-drag function in the Time Slider.

2. Still at frame 0, select the wrist bone called Box_Forearm_Left and rotate it –28 degrees on the local y-axis in the Transform Type-In box. Copy the same key frame to frame 30 using the Shift-drag function.

3. Go to frame 4, select the box bone Box_Hand_Left, and rotate it –70 degrees on the local y-axis in the Transform Type-In box under Offset Local so the palm faces the ground. In addition, rotate the same bone 25 degrees up on the local z-axis in the Transform Type-In box.

4. Go to frame 10 and rotate the same box bone –40 degrees backward on the local z-axis so the palm faces the back.

5. Go to frame 15 and rotate the same box bone –30 degrees backward on the local z-axis so the palm faces the back.

6. Go to frame 23 and rotate the same box bone –30 degrees backward on the local z-axis so the palm breaks the joint and causes drag through the line of the arm as it moves into the forward swing.

7. Now you will continue this subtle drag through the fingers. These subtle tweaks really begin to add life to the motion. Open the gripper.ms file on the accompanying CD. Use this script to animate the fingers. You should already be familiar with the script and its functions, but for more info on how to load and run a script, refer to Chapter 3, "Advanced Character and Creature Setup." Go to frame 0 and curl the fingers of the left hand into a more relaxed pose. Move the sliders for the left hand about a third of the way up. As long as the Animate button is on, the keys for all these FK bones will be automatically set for you.

8. At frame 4 and frame 10, straighten all the fingers on the left hand by pulling all the sliders in the Gripper rollout down to the bottom.

9. Go to frame 17 and curl all the fingers on the left hand again by pulling all the sliders in the Gripper rollout halfway up the slider.

10. Move the Time Slider to frame 0 and mirror the rotations, using steps 1 through 6 as a guide for the other arm.

11. Now scrub through the animation, and you should see the wrist and fingers dragging behind the rest of the animation in a very natural motion.

To see a movie of the walk at this point in the tutorial, open the file HandsFingers.avi; to open a MAX file that is completed using the exercises above, open the file WALK_CYCLE_WORKg.max.

Finalizing the Walk

The basic walk is complete, but it still seems a little stiff. You can tweak the walk by adding a bit of drag to more of the joints, just as you did for the fingers. It takes a bit of time, for example, to transfer the force and rotation of the hips through the spine to the shoulders, which in turn take some time to transfer the rotation to the elbows. In other words, the further the joint is from the hips, the more it lags behind the motion of the hips.

Normally, this drag is slight, typically on the order of only a few frames. It can be accomplished by selecting the keys for the joints and moving them forward in time by a frame or two. Also, if you look at the animation from the front view, you will see one of the arms is going through the body. You can continue to tweak this by adjusting its rotation.

Offsetting Keys

The first phase of refinement is to offset the keyframes and is very simple. From within Track View, select the "inner" keys for the dummy constraints C_SPINE and C_SPINEUPPER. Do not touch the first and last keys of the cycle because these keys must remain the same so they will hook up at the beginning and end of the animation. Move the selected keys to the right by one frame. Select the keys for C_RTELBOW and C_LTELBOW and move them two frames to the right.

Touching Up from All Views

Many times as you animate, you might forget to check all the views. After you have the basic motion and timing down, it is a good practice to check the animation from all views. Most game houses, for example, insist that the animation look great from multiple views. Thorough checking can also help you find mistakes in weight distribution. For example, in the tutorial file, the right arm goes through the right leg as it moves forward. At frame 12, adjust the right arm so it doesn't go through the leg by rotating the arm's z- and y-axes.

Function Curves and Custom Tangents

You can also add head motion to the animation by adjusting the rotation of the head and neck to keep it level. Approach the head rotations just as you did all the other counter rotations in the body. Remember how the force in the body begins at the hips and works its way throughout the body. Create drag and overshoot using your understanding of these forces throughout the body. In other words, because the head is the last bone in a very long tree beginning at the hips, its movement will be offset a few frames later than the hip and spine motion.

Finally, you will need to play with the curve's ease in and out and the spline tangents to really imbue even more life into the walk (see Figure 4.33). This will take much time and patience. I prefer to apply the custom tangent type to most of my curves at this point because, again, I can sculpt the curve I want for the motion. Scrub the animation and continue adjusting it to suit your tastes.

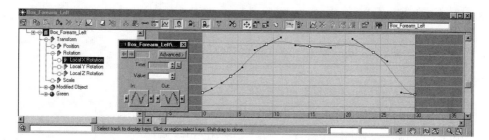

Figure 4.33   The function curve for a bone with the Custom Tangents type applied to all the keys. Adjust the spline tangent handles to create the function curve you desire. It is helpful to turn Trajectory on for the bone you are adjusting and to interactively sculpt the timing and curves from there.

Moving the Walk Cycle Through Space

When you have tweaked the walk cycle until you are pleased with the motion, you can move it through space. The walk cycle enables you to create only 30 frames and use them over and over again for your animation. For this exercise, you will just deal with the 30 frames of time and move the character for the two steps. However, you will need to turn all your beginning and ending frames of the cycle to loop if you want the cycle to continue through more than just 30 frames of time.

1. In case you were wondering what that huge dummy constraint is for in the scene, you will be using that to move the skeleton through space. Select the dummy constraint called Skelly_Root. Then go to frame 30, turn the Animate button on, and go to the left-side view.

2. Slide Skelly_Root –80 units forward on the local y–axis in the Transform Type-In box under Absolute World.

3. Go to frame 0 and, in the Motion panel, set Skelly_Root to be 0 on the local x–axis under the Position XYZ and Key Info boxes (see Figure 4.34). Now the character is moving 80 units forward through space, but if you play the animation back, the feet slide.

4. When people walk, the motion is not constant like a machine. You will have to generate a few more keys to create the natural slowing and pick-up in speed. Go

to frame 7 and slide the Skelly_Root dummy constraint to –13 on the local y-axis in the Transform Type-In box under Offset Local.

5. Go to frame 15 and slide Skelly_Root to –25 on the local y-axis in the Transform Type-In box under Offset Local.

6. Go to frame 18 and slide Skelly_Root to –2 on the local y-axis in the Transform Type-In box under Offset Local. You are slowing the forward motion as the character takes a step.

7. Go to frame 20 and slide Skelly_Root to –9 on the local y-axis in the Transform Type-In box under Offset Local.

8. Go to frame 24 and slide Skelly_Root to –7 on the local y-axis.

Figure 4.34
Using the Motion Panel/Position XYZ/Key Info box, you will set a key that is at 0 for the beginning placement of the character in the World space.

Play the animation. The character now walks as if you created the cycle moving through space. The only difference is that you can continue to loop the cycle by copying keys or looping the animation. To continue the translation through space beyond these 30 frames, simply select the keys you made for Skelly_Root and Shift-drag them in the Track View to loop. Then slide them up or down in the Track View to create a continuous line (see Figure 4.35), and the character will continue to move through space.

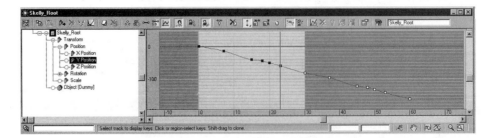

Figure 4.35   Shift-drag to copy the translation keys you created to move the character forward, and them drag them down in the Track View so they continue the line of translation forward.

A final version of this animation is on the CD-ROM. It is called WALK_CYCLE_ OKmove.max. There is also a movie on the CD called FinalTut.avi, which is what all the work from these exercises should produce. Finally, three QuickTime movies are provided with the front, side, and perspective views of a final render of the walk cycle. Use these as guides also.

Creating a Four-Legged Walk

A four-legged walk is very similar to the two-legged variety, but multiplied by two. The creature's legs still rock back and forth at the hips, but the upper body motion happens parallel to the ground instead of perpendicular to it. Whereas human shoulders rock back and forth in the vertical axis, a lion's shoulders rock back and forth horizontal to the ground as the front paws walk. The hips and shoulders have rotations that mirror one another. When the right hip is forward, the left shoulder is back, and vice versa. This action usually varies a bit in that the front and back legs might be offset by a few frames. Notice how the spine curves much like a human and that the left shoulder and leg are back, mirroring the hip pose. This means that the left front leg, too, is about to plant (see Figure 4.36).

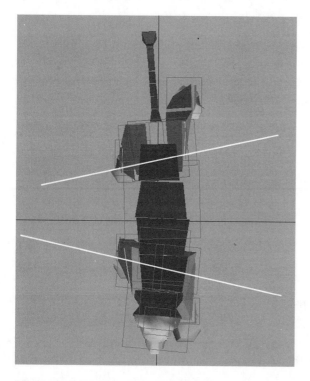

Figure 4.36 The four-legged creature has the same arc through the spine to compensate for weight shift that a human or bipedal character does. The only difference is that the arc in the spine of a four-legged creature is seen from the Top view instead of the Front view.

As the legs move forward through the step, the legs that are not currently planted on the ground (the free legs) move forward. The rear legs are fairly similar to a human's, bending at the knee in much the same fashion. The front legs, however, are actually jointed so that they bend forward much like a bird's. This dictates a slightly different lift motion for the front legs. At this point, the spine is straight when viewed from the top, but it might bow or arch a bit more when viewed from the side. This is character dependent; a dilapidated horse's back, for instance, might sag quite a bit.

The legs then move through the step and plant the free feet, repeating the first step. In addition to this, a four-legged animal can have several different gaits: the walk, the trot, the canter, and the gallop. The animal varies the timing and rhythm of its steps as it moves faster and faster. In the walk, the animal's legs behave very much like the arms and legs of a human: If the right rear leg is back, the right front leg is forward, with the opposite happening on the left. This changes as the strides change, however. By the time the creature has reached full gallop, the front legs are in sync—going forward and back nearly in unison, with the back legs mirroring the front.

The legs for this tutorial are manipulated at the feet, which stay locked in place. The spine is animated by using simple rotations using dummy constraints, which you should be quite familiar with by now. Finally, the head and tail are animated with additional dummy constraints to give the shot a final polish.

Animating the Legs

The best way to start a four-legged walk is to block out the motion of the feet. When the feet are moving properly, the rest of the body can be animated quite easily.

The process can be divided into several phases:

- Blocking out the stride
- Adjusting the hips
- Following through with paws
- Refining the motion and blocking out the second step

The scene you'll be working on in this exercise contains a simple four-legged skeleton in which the legs are controlled by IK and the spine is controlled by a set of expressions and dummy constraints.

1. Open the file Lion_WALK_WORK.max from the CD-ROM. This scene contains a simple four-legged skeleton in which the legs are controlled by IK and the spine is controlled by a set of expressions and dummy constraints.

2. Move the Time Slider to frame 0. Toggle the Animate button to On.

3. Go to the Left view provided for you in the file. The walk starts with the left leg, which is manipulated at the ankle. Select the dummy constraints C_FRONTLT-FOOT and C_REARRTFOOT using the Ctrl key and enter a value of –1 on the local y-axis in the Transform Type-In box under Offset Local.

4. Continue to sketch out the remaining foot position. Select the dummy constraint C_FRONTRTFOOT and C_REARLTFOOT and enter a value of 1 on the local y-axis in the Transform Type-In box under Offset Local (see Figure 4.37.)

Figure 4.37 Starting position for the four-legged walk.

5. Next, you will create the second step. Go to frame 15 and create an exact mirror of the first step. Select the forward paws (C_FRONTLTFOOT and C_REARRT-FOOT) and enter a value of 2 on the local y-axis in the Transform Type-In box.

6. Select the other two feet (C_FRONTRTFOOT and C_REARLTFOOT) and enter a value of –2 on the local y-axis in the Transform Type-In box (see Figure 4.38).

You see why it is helpful to color code the legs: Determining which ones you're selecting and animating can be pretty confusing. When you view this file from the left side view, red represents the inside of the left legs, and green is the outside of the right legs. The opposite holds true when the lion is viewed from the right side.

Figure 4.38   Second step for the four-legged walk.

So, if you scrub through the animation at this point, you will see the feet slide in an ice skating fashion—the same problem you had on the two-legged skeleton. To fix this, you will create the lifting position for the feet that are passing and preparing to plant for the second step. These two feet are easiest to determine from the first step's frame 0. The two paws farthest back will be passing.

7. Move the Time Slider to frame 7, halfway through the first step. Select the dummy constraints C_REARLTFOOT and C_FRONTRTFOOT and move it up 0.5 units on the local z-axis and forward –0.5 units on the local y-axis.

8. At the frame 7 halfway point of the step, the hips are also at their highest point. Move the C_HIPS dummy constraint up approximately 0.2 units on the local z-axis and forward –0.2 units on the local y-axis to stabilize the body over the legs.

9. Move the Time Slider to frame 15 again, and you will see that the hips are now following the key you set for the passing pose. They are too high. Copy the placement of the hips from frame 0 to frame 15 so they move back down. Scrubbing the animation now gives a very basic step that looks pretty mechanical, but we will fix that. To open a MAX file that is completed using the preceding exercises, open the file Lion_WALK_WORK1a.max.

10. Go to frame 0, select the C_REARLTFOOT dummy constraint, enter a value of –0.8 units on the local y-axis, and then rotate it on the local x-axis 40 degrees in the Transform Type-In box.

11. Adjust the paw called Box_REAR_Paw_Left so it is lagging behind the leg action and pointing at the ground by rotating it on the local z-axis –85 degrees.

12. Rotate the ankle and paw for the complementary paw called C_FRONTRTFOOT (see Figure 4.39).

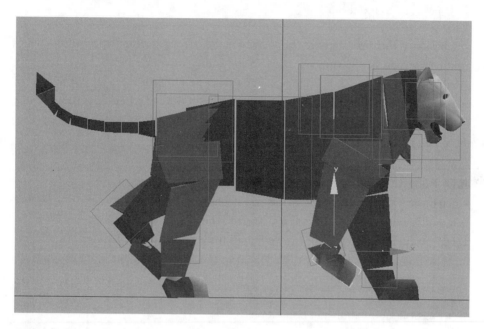

Figure 4.39   Adjust the paws so the creature uses the foot to push off from the previous step and bends in anticipation of the next step.

13. If you scrub ahead, you will see the two paws you rotated hold that rotation in anticipation of the next step. This is good, but by frame 15, they need to be parallel with the ground again. To change this, rotate these two paws back to their flat pose like at frame 0.

Tip

An easy way to transfer a rotation key from one pose to another leaving the translation behind is to use the MAX R3 filters in the Time Slider. Right-click on the key and filter out everything but the Current transform and make sure you are in the Rotational Transform mode. Then just Shift-drag the rotation.

14. To copy the rotational keys from frame 0 to frame 15, right-click on the key at frame 0 and click on Filter/Current Transform. This will place a hold on only the current transform. Make sure your transform mode is on Rotation, and then Shift-drag that key from frame 0 to 15. Do the same for the paw (Box_REAR_

Paw_Left) and the other foot and paw(C_FRONTRTFOOT and Box_FRONT_ Paw_Right).

15. Select all four dummy constraints for the feet and go to frame 0. Right-click on the key there and change the filter to All Keys. Shift-drag to copy the first key pose at 0 to frame 30.

The basics of this first step are complete. For the left leg, repeat steps 3 through 14, creating a second step starting on frame 15 and ending on frame 30. The top of this step should occur at frame 23, and the recoil position should be at frame 19. For reference, take a look at the file called Lion_WALK_CYCLE_WORKa.max on the accompanying CD. There is also a movie on the disc that illustrates what the cycle should look like at this point; it's called Lionsteps.avi.

Animating the Spine, Hips, and Shoulders

When the feet are moving properly, the next step is to nail down the motion of the spine, hips, and shoulders. Just like in a two-legged walk, the hips and shoulders of a four-legged creature rotate to mirror the motion of the legs. The body of a four-legged creature also bounces up and down as the weight is transferred from one foot to another.

There are four phases to this exercise. You must create the following:

- Vertical hip rotation and translation
- Side-to-side hip rotation
- The spine arcing motion
- The same motions for the second step

Scrub the animation as it stands so far. Notice how the body moves in a relatively straight line. This might be good for an incredibly sneaky creature, but in a normal walk, the body tends to bounce up and down and swagger side to side more. Use the file you have been building with the previous tutorial exercises, or open the file on the accompanying CD called Lion_WALK_CYCLE_WORKa.max.

1. Move the Time Slider to frame 4. This is where the planted legs fully absorb the weight of the body. Select the dummy constraint C_HIPS and move it down –0.3 units on its local z-axis in the Transform Type-In box under Offset Local.

2. Move the Time Slider to frame 19. This is where the planted legs again fully absorb the weight of the body. Select the dummy constraint C_HIPS and move it down –0.3 units on its local z-axis in the Transform Type-In box under Offset

Local. (You could also copy the keyframe as previously shown from frame 4 to frame 19.)

Scrub the animation. The body should have a more natural bounce and sense of weight. It's all happening on the same frames and still looks mechanical, but you can fix that later.

3. Next, work on the rotation of the spine and shoulders. Go to frame 0 of the animation. Select the dummy constraint called C_SHOULDERS. From the Top viewport, rotate it along the vertical axis –5 degrees clockwise on its local z-axis in the Transform Type-In box.

4. Select C_HIPS and, from the Top viewport, rotate it 5 degrees counterclockwise on its local z-axis in the Transform Type-In box. This will move the rest of the spine just like on the two-legged setup. Compensate for this by rotating the spine dummy constraint C_SPINE back –3.5 degrees so the head faces forward.

5. Move the Time Slider to frame 15. Select the dummy constraint called C_SHOULDERS. From the Top viewport, rotate it along the vertical axis –20 degrees counterclockwise on the local z-axis.

6. Select C_HIPS and, from the Top viewport, rotate it along the vertical axis 10 degrees clockwise. This will move the rest of the spine just like on the two-legged setup. Compensate for this by rotating the spine dummy constraint C_SPINE back –7 degrees on the local z-axis so the head faces forward.

7. Copy the keys from 0 to 30 for the C_SPINE, C_SHOULDERS, and C_HIPS constraints so the cycle is complete.

Scrub the animation. The spine now has a more natural motion. To open a MAX file that is completed using the preceding exercises, open the file Lion_WALK_WORK1b.max.

The spine can be given another extra motion, however, to add to the sense of weight. As the creature walks, the spine acts much like a taut cable stretched between the hips and shoulders. The weight of the abdomen causes the spine to sag slightly as the weight of the body is lifted. Conversely, as the body moves downward, the weight of the body causes the spine to arch up slightly. Try adding this to your lion.

8. Activate the Left viewport and scrub the Time Slider to frame 6, two frames after the lowest point of the walk.

9. Select C_SHOULDERS and rotate it approximately –5 degrees on the local x-axis so the front of the spine arches up in an arc.

10. Scrub the Time Slider to frame 12, two frames after the top of the first step. This is where the spine arches down. Select C_SHOULDERS and rotate it 8 degrees on the local x-axis. This compensates for the original 5-degree rotation and adds 3 degrees of arch in the opposite direction.

To create the same motions for the second step, you simply repeat steps 8 and 10 for frames 22 and 28, respectively. This adds the same motion to the second step. Scrub the animation to see your results, if you want. To open a MAX file that was completed using the preceding exercises, open the file Lion_WALK_WORK1c.max.

Animating the Head and Tail

The final steps in this exercise series add a bit of secondary motion in the tail and straighten the head so the character looks forward. If the head stayed as it was and you put a small camera on the lioness' head, it would be bobbing around all over the place. Animals' heads remain stable while they're moving.

To start the exercise, you need the MAXScript file called LionTail.ms from the accompanying CD-ROM. The script's Swing and Curling sliders enable you to easily and quickly manipulate all eight bones of the Lion's tail.

1. Move the Time Slider to frame 0. Go to the Top view and open the MAX script LionTail.ms. Drag the Swing slider halfway to the right from dead center. This makes the lion's tail swing to the left, curling with the spine action of the lioness.

2. The motion of the tail tends to drag behind that of the spine. Move the Time Slider to frame 4. With the Swing slider still selected, drag it all the way to the right to get the maximum leftward motion of the tail.

3. Move the Time Slider to frame 15. Slide the Swing slider all the way to the left from center so the tail is to the right of the body.

4. Move the Time Slider to frame 23. Drag the Swing slider all the way to the right to place it to the left of the body. When you scrub the animation, you'll see the tail now has a natural left-to-right sway.

5. The tail also needs to bounce up and down ever so slightly as the character walks. This motion drags behind the up and down motion of the body by a few frames. Move the Time Slider to frame 0. From the Left viewport, slightly arch the tail down with the Curling slider in the LionTail rollout.

6. Move the Time Slider to frame 10. Arch the tail so it is arched slightly upward when viewed from the side.

7. Repeat the poses in steps 5 and 6 for frames 16 and 26, respectively.

Not only does the MAX script on the CD-ROM help you animate the eight bones in the tail, it also creates a track in the Track View with which you can manage all those keys. The tail AVARs enable you to manage one curve for the swing and curl functions, and at the same time, you can individually animate the bones in the tail yourself and adjust the individual keys to get additional breaking of joints. Now that is flexibility! To see the tail AVARs, open the Track View and click on the Lion's Tail script in the MAX Utilities box. This opens the additional functionality of the script. Click on the button that says Create AVARs, and open Global tracks the Track View. A Swing and Curl track has been created for the tail here (see Figure 4.40).

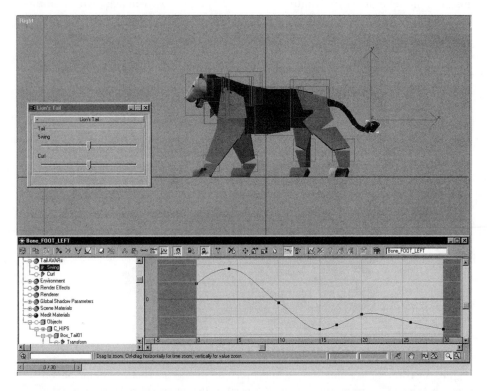

Figure 4.40   Track View provides AVARs for managing the eight bones of the tail through the MAX script. You have swing and curl curves to manage the tail now, but you can still manipulate the individual bones if you desire.

Animating the Head Action

Animating the head is relatively simple. Move through the animation and correct the motion of the head so that it points forward throughout the walk. When you do this, the walk is complete. Go back through the animation and tweak the keyframes to suit your taste. A copy of this animation is saved on the CD-ROM as Lion_WALK_OK.max. A movie of the animation called Lionwalk.avi is also on the disk.

Six-Legged Walks

If four-legged walks seem complex, six legs might seem intolerably difficult. This, fortunately, is not the case. An insect walk actually follows a definite, repeatable pattern that can be animated on a cycle. A six-legged walk is very similar to the four-legged walk: The front two legs move back and forth, and the second set of legs mirror this motion. The insect's third set of legs simply mirrors the second again, closely matching the motion of the front legs. Generally, insects keep at least three legs on the ground, forming a stable tripod at all times.

Animating a Six-Legged Walk

The animation of this particular insect, the Mouth Mite (shown in Figure 4.41), is accomplished strictly by manipulating the abdomen and legs through the dummy constraints. To begin, you need to know how fast the legs will move and how far each step will move the mite.

Figure 4.41 For the Mouth Mite used in this exercise, the legs are controlled with dummy constraints set up to control multiple leg movements with one controller. It's streamlined for success!

The rate of an insect's walk depends on the species of bug and the bug's demeanor. Generally, bugs move pretty fast compared to mammals, and a quarter- or eighth-second per step is not out of the question. For walks this fast, the frame rate of the animation becomes a limiting factor. At 24 fps, an eighth-second stride takes only three frames per step. This is about as fast as a walk can be animated, with one frame each for the forward, middle, and back portions of the step. For this animation, six frames per step gives you a good pace for the insect walk.

The distance is determined by the size of the insect and the length of the legs. Longer-legged insects naturally take longer steps. Additional dummy constraints have been created to make creating this complex motion even easier.

1. Load the file Mite_WALK_WORK.max from the CD-ROM.

2. Move the Time Slider to frame 0 and toggle the Animation button on.

3. On frame 0, move the dummy constraint called C_LEGS01 60 units on the local y-axis in the Transform Type-In box under Offset Local. This constraint controls the front-left, middle-right, and rear-left legs all together.

4. Move the dummy constraint called C_LEGS02 60 units on the local y-axis in the Transform Type-In box under Offset Local. Again, this will pull the front-right, middle-left, and rear-right legs backward all together.

5. Go to frame 6 and select C_LEGS01. Translate it 120 units on the local y-axis in the Transform Type-In box.

6. Select C_LEGS02 and set a keyframe for these legs.

7. Now for the middle of the step, move the Time Slider to frame 3. Select C_LEGS01. These legs are moving forward, so they need to lift off the ground. Move them 40 units on the local z-axis in the Transform Type-In box (see Figure 4.42).

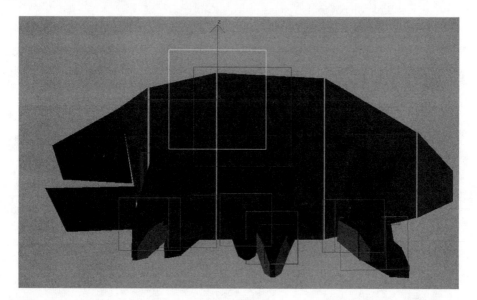

Figure 4.42   Use the additional dummy constraints to control multiple legs and raise them as they move forward.

8. The body also lifts during the middle of the step. Select the Box_Spine03 and move it 30 units on the local z-axis in the Transform Type-In box.

This completes the first step. The second step is simply a mirror of the first. Repeat the steps to create the second step (and a third, fourth, and fifth, if desired). The file on the CD-ROM is named Mite_WALK_OK.max.

In Practice

- **Walks.** The two-legged walk is an ever-changing event that constantly compensates for weight shifts throughout the body. The arc of the arms run in a figure-eight shape, and the spine constantly arcs to absorb the shock of the weight-bearing foot.

- **Walk cycles.** Walk cycles are a great learning tool for understanding weight shifts. They also make creating a walk through space much easier because you create a sequence of frames and then loop them over and over as the character moves through space and time.

- **Four-legged walks.** The key to a four-legged walk is the spine, which moves much like the spine of a two-legged walk—with the hips and shoulders of the character following a set of complementary rotations. In addition to the basic walk, four-legged creatures also can trot, canter, and gallop, which involve differing combinations of footsteps.

- **Six-legged walks.** The number of legs and joints involved with these creatures makes keyframing a bit bothersome. A simple dummy constraint setup can make your life much easier.

Chapter 5

Facial Animation

By Angie Jones

Facial animation involves close observation of life and a clear understanding of MAX's tools. We are all experts in facial expression, but you must be a precise observer to create living breathing expression in your

characters. If you can work with MAX R3's new MeshSmooth NURMS, Edit Mesh, and the Nurms control mesh, as well as the Soft Selection and Morpher modifier tools, you will hold the power to creating natural and life-like facial animation.

The best way to create life-like facial animation is to look at life itself. We see facial expressions every day in observing conversations, lecturers, actors, and more. For the most natural animation, the facial setup must emulate life. The lightest way to create facial animation in CG today is to use morph targets. The underlying structure of muscles in the face is a great starting point for creating your poses for the morphing process. Just as the anatomy of the body is so important to the skeletal setup, the anatomy of the face is equally important in creating a solid facial rig. Animating the face requires these skills:

- A good eye for catching the *visual cues* we see when someone is speaking or expressing herself
- A strong knowledge of acting and emotion
- An understanding of the underlying anatomy of the human head and face

The face is driven by a dozen or so muscles that connect the skin to the skull. As with muscles in the body, these muscles affect the shape of the skin by bulging, stretching, and pulling it in a number of directions. This chapter will describe what the muscles of a real face are, where they are located, and how they move. Using your newfound knowledge of facial anatomy as a foundation, you will then learn how to set up a character in MAX for facial animation, mimicking these muscle structures and their movements with MAX's morphing and bones tools to mimic the jaw bone movement.

Specifically, this chapter explores these topics:

- Creation of target poses for expression and lip sync
- Using the Morpher modifier for facial animation
- Breaking down a dialog track
- Animating eyes
- The four keys to successful facial animation

The Facial Muscle Framework

Although your emotions fuel your expressions, your facial muscles are in charge of contracting to display them. Knowing which muscles contract in which direction and where they're located will help you better mimic their effects in your animations, making your characters more natural and emotive (see Figure 5.1).

Figure 5.1   If you build your facial setup based on muscles, there is not a facial pose you can't create!

Of the 26 muscles in the face, 11 are involved in facial expression (see Figure 5.2). The others contribute to different actions, such as eating. The 11 relevant muscles are listed here and are described in detail in the following sections:

- Zygomatic major
- Nasi group
- Triangularis
- Mentalis
- Frontalis
- Orbicularis oculi
- Obicularis oris
- Corrugator group
- Levator palpebrea
- Risorius and platysma group
- Depressor labii inferiors

Figure 5.2
Muscles of the face.

Each muscle has a left and right component, which allows the face to move asymmetrically. Let's look more closely at how each muscle, as well as its individual left and right components, contributes to displaying emotion. You should try to create abbreviated names for each of these muscles to make them easy to select in the Morpher modifier. Long names are more difficult to discern because they will be truncated in the spaces provided. For example, zygomatic major left could be called "ZygM_L."

Each of these muscles influences the many expressions of the face. Six universal expressions cross all cultural and racial boundaries:

- Anger
- Sadness
- Fear
- Joy
- Disgust
- Surprise

Each of these emotions can be changed into other emotions through the intensity of the muscle contractions. For example, a sly, debauched smiled is less intense and symmetrical than a laughing expression. Use Table 5.1 to figure out which muscles affect what emotional state. Even a quick look at the table reveals that the workhorses of the facial expression are the nasi group, triangularis, and mentalis.

Note

It is important to get as much reference material as you can regarding your character's facial structure and the skeletal framework under the muscles, as well. How the skull is designed has much to do with how thick, how many, and even if there are any muscles in certain areas of the face.

Zygomatic Major

The zygomatic major is the muscle used for smiling. One end is attached to the side of the head, halfway back to the ear on the cheek bone root, and the other end of this thick muscle body is attached to the mouth in the corner crease (see Figure 5.3.)

The zygomatic major muscle pulls the lips into the face, widening the base of the nose and creating a fold on either side of the mouth (see Figure 5.4). Another visual cue that the zyg major creates is that this muscle pulls into the face the excess fat, and the overlying skin on the cheeks puffs out. The cheeks also push up beyond the lower lid line. The zygomatic major muscle is dedicated to smiling, and it is quite large, which proves that although frowning may take more muscles than smiling, a smile is more work. This is why your zygomatic major muscle hurts when you laugh or grin for along time. To see which expressions this muscle influences, refer to Table 5.1.

Figures 5.3   Zygomatic major muscle location.

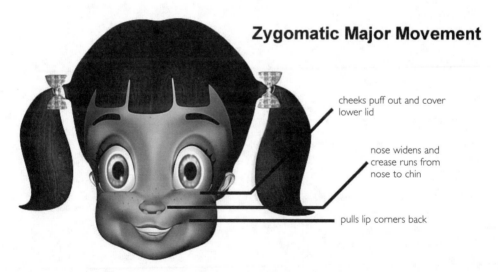

Zygomatic Major Movement

cheeks puff out and cover lower lid

nose widens and crease runs from nose to chin

pulls lip corners back

Figure 5.4   Zygomatic major muscle movement.

Table 5.1   Facial Muscles and the Expressions They Influence

Six Universal Expressions	Zyg major	Nasi	Triang	Ment	Front
Joy	X				
Anger		X	X	X	
Surprise		X	X	X	X
Disgust					
Fear		X	X	X	
Sadness			X	X	
Intensity Controls					
Laugh	X				
Hate		X	X	X	
Rage		X	X	X	
Scorn		X	X	X	
Indignation		X	X	X	
Astonishment		X	X	X	X
Suspense		X	X	X	X
Awe		X	X	X	X
Contempt	X	X	X	X	X
Sneering	X	X			
Impatience	X	X	X	X	X
Cynicism	X	X	X	X	X
Haughtiness	X		X	X	X
Terror		X			
Fright		X			
Horror		X			
Suffering		X		X	X
Pleading			X	X	X
Worry		X	X	X	X
Sorrow		X	X	X	X
Pain		X	X	X	X
Shame		X	X	X	X
Anxiety		X	X	X	
Questioning	X			X	X
Jealousy	X	X	X	X	X
Mistrust	X	X	X	X	X
Questioning	X	X	X	X	
Skepticism	X	X	X		X
Suspicion	X	X	X		X

Orb-oculi	Orb-oris	Corrugtr	LevatorP	Risorius	DepressorL
X	X				
X	X	X	X	X	X
	X		X	X	X
		X	X		
X	X				
X	X	X		X	X
	X	X		X	X
X	X	X		X	X
X	X	X		X	X
			X	X	
			X	X	X
			X	X	X
X	X		X	X	X
X	X	X	X	X	X
X	X	X	X	X	X
X	X	X	X	X	X
		X	X		
		X	X		
		X	X		
X	X	X		X	X
X	X	X		X	X
X		X		X	X
X	X	X		X	X
X	X	X		X	X
X	X	X		X	X
			X		
X	X	X	X	X	X
X	X	X	X	X	X
X	X	X	X	X	X
X	X	X	X	X	X
X	X	X	X	X	X

Nasi Group

The next muscle group can be called many things: the levetor labii, the Nasalis, the sneering, or the "something stinks" muscles. To keep things simple, I'll call this group of muscles the nasi group.

Three branches encompass this area of muscle. All three insert at the lips just under the wings of the nose. The inner branch originates on the base of the nose and follows alongside the nose. The middle branch starts on the bottom edge of the eye socket (orbit), and the outer branch begins on the cheekbone (zygomatic arch). (Figure 5.5 shows the location of these muscles.) The outer branch is also called the zygomatic minor.

Figure 5.5   Nasi muscle group location.

Overall, the three nasi muscle branches pull the upper lip back into the face and upwards, making for a squared-off lip shape that looks as if you pushed the upper lip flat against wall (see Figure 5.6). The zygomatic minor involuntarily contributes to the face with the nasi muscles in the expression of sadness by squaring the upper lip without a sneer. In addition, the nose wings are pulled upward to create flared nostrils.

In addition to an "Elvis" sneering motion, the nasi group is used for many expressions. One or both sides of the nasi group can contribute to all of them, depending on the level of intensity of the emotion. To see which expressions this muscle influences, refer to Table 5.1.

Triangularis

You cannot have facial expression without the triangularis, which might be called the "had a bad day" muscle. The triangularis begins on the lower edge of the chin and inserts into the mouth corner at the same place as the zygomatic major, sort of like a chin strap (see Figure 5.7).

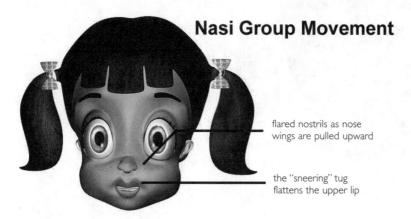

Nasi Group Movement

flared nostrils as nose wings are pulled upward

the "sneering" tug flattens the upper lip

Figure 5.6 Nasi group muscle movement.

Figure 5.7 Triangularis muscle location.

The triangularis pulls down on the mouth corners, creating a kind of upside-down smile. The visual cues to this muscle's action are the curved bulges below each mouth corner as it lowers (see Figure 5.8). Many older people have a crease that suggests the traingularis is being contracted. Look closely: If the corners of the mouth are actually turned down, the triangularis is at work. If not the crease is caused by a relaxed wrinkle. The triangularis rarely moves without the mentalis as part of a sad expression, pout, or "facial shrug." This is the muscle we use to hold back or stifle a smile. To see which expressions this muscle influences, refer to Table 5.1.

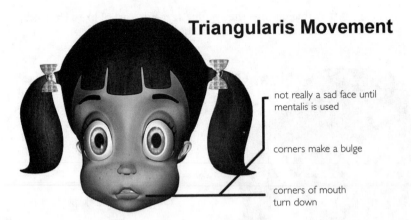

Figure 5.8   Triangularis group muscle movement.

Mentalis

The levator menti, also called the mentalis, can be thought of as the pouting muscle. The mentalis originates below the teeth on the lower jaw and connects at the ball of the chin (see Figure 5.9).

Figure 5.9   Mentalis muscle location.

The mentalis pushes the lower lip up and out further than the upper lip. The skin on the chin is pulled toward the base of the teeth and is flattened. This flattening creates another visual cue under the bottom lip: A crease and shadow appear under the bottom lip, and the chin pulls into the teeth. The lips lift and project out like a shelf. This muscle creates a sad mouth by indirectly pushing the center of the lips up as shown in Figure 5.10.

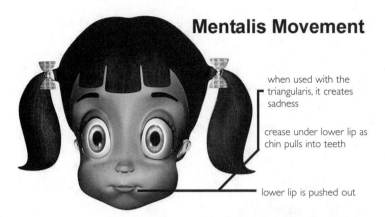

Mentalis Movement

when used with the triangularis, it creates sadness

crease under lower lip as chin pulls into teeth

lower lip is pushed out

Figure 5.10   Mentalis muscle movement.

The mentalis muscle contributes to many expressions, usually those requiring restraint (restrained anger, sadness, or smiling) and conveys the facial shrug by simply pushing up on the center of the lips. To see which expressions this muscle influences, refer to Table 5.1.

Frontalis

The frontalis, or brow-lifter muscle, originates at the hairline and runs vertically until it floats freely under the eyebrows. It's a broad flat muscle that lies across the forehead about where the bill of a baseball cap covers (see Figure 5.11).

Figure 5.11   Frontalis muscle location.

When it contracts, the frontalis muscle pulls the skin above the eyes, nose, and forehead upward. As the forehead rises, the skin above creates "worry lines." These creases usually have a long dip in the middle and are arched with the eyebrow. The skin around the eyes and nose is stretched so tightly that you can see the bone structure underneath (see Figure 5.12).

The eyes, however, do not necessarily open wider with this motion. The opening of the eyes is a separate function of another muscle. In fact, more of the upper lid is exposed instead of lifted. The raised eyebrow has a similar meaning as a hand gesture, and we use it often when speaking. Raising one eyebrow is a skill only some people have; they can contract one half of the frontalis while leaving the other half relaxed.

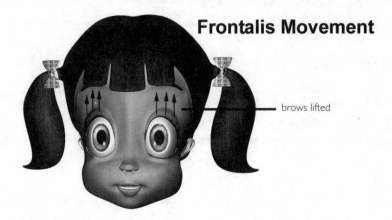

Figures 5.12   Frontalis muscle movement.

To see which expressions this muscle influences, refer to Table 5.1.

Orbicularis Oculi

The orbicularis oculi, or orb OC for short, is the muscle for squinting. Its motion should be independent of the brow motion.

The orbicularis oculi is a ring of muscles that encircle the eye and spread into the cheek (see Figure 5.13.) When this muscle contracts, the skin around the eye pulls in toward the nasal bridge. The eyes begin to close, and crows feet appear.

The orb OC muscles create a squint by narrowing the lower lid. The orb OC motion is the key to a smile: It creates the smile-shaped crease below the eye, crows feet, and an additional narrowing of the eye (see Figure 5.14). This narrowing of the eye is the visual cue that signals when a smile is genuine and heartfelt. In addition, when you blink, your top lid covers more of the eye than the bottom, but when you squint, your bottom lid comes up much higher, covering the iris. The most important cue about our eyes is the shape of the eye and its relationship to the iris. The orbicularis oculi muscle has the most influence on that eye shape. To see which expressions this muscle influences, refer to Table 5.1.

Figure 5.13   Obicularis oculi muscle location.

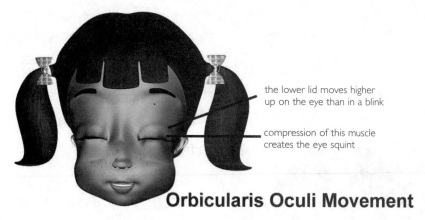

the lower lid moves higher
up on the eye than in a blink

compression of this muscle
creates the eye squint

Orbicularis Oculi Movement

Figure 5.14   Obicularis oculi muscle movement.

Orbicularis Oris

Similar in shape to the orbicularis oculi, the orbicularis oris can be thought of as the lip-compressor muscle. It is the most important muscle for talking, eating, and creating the phoneme "OOO." These responsibilities, coupled with its influence on expressions, make the orbicularis oris possibly the hardest working of the 11 facial expression muscles.

The orbicularis oris runs in a circle around the lips (see Figure 5.15.) The muscle is sort of "suspended" and is held onto the facial muscle structure at the corners of the mouth with a knot (connecting the zygomatic major, triangularis, and risorius) that surfaces when you smile.

Figure 5.15   Obicularis oris muscle location.

Because the orbicularis oris is attached to other muscles instead of the skull, it can take on an enormous number of shapes. When both lips tighten with the mouth closed, there is also a bulging-out around the lips, as though the person is trying to hold in a mouthful of air (see Figure 5.16). This is important to note for a "B" or "P" phoneme pose for dialog and also for a restrained anger pose. To see which expressions this muscle influences, refer to Table 5.1.

Orbicularis Oris Movement

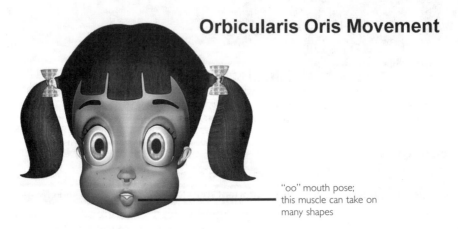

"oo" mouth pose; this muscle can take on many shapes

Figure 5.16   Obicularis oris muscle movement.

Corrugator Group

The muscles for an angry brow or frowning, the corrugator group includes another muscle called the *procerus*, which always contracts with the corrugator. The procerus is attached at the bone on the top of the nose and connects to the skin between the eyebrows. The two corrugator muscles stretch diagonally from the inner corners of the eyes and insert above the middle of the eyebrow (see Figure 5.17).

Figure 5.17   Corrugator muscle group location.

To get the most out of your brow shapes, it is best to create three controllers for each brow: inner, middle, and outer. In Figure 5.18a the inner brow controller is being used. Both muscles pull brows down and together. The corrugator also pulls the brows forward like a shelf projecting outwards. The inner third of the eyebrow lowers and drops below the top of the upper lid, creating a wrinkle or *corrugation* around the inner brow.

The downward pressure of the brow shoves the upper lid lower and hiding more of the iris. This is the visual cue that the character is angry or perplexed. For the facial setup in the later tutorials, this upper lid motion will be created with a separate muscle target called the *leva palpebrea*. It is important to note this involuntary action here because it is caused by the corrugator group. To see the upper lid poses forced by the corrugator group, go to the section "Leva Palpebrea," later in this chapter.

Because these two muscles have such a complex motion, you should make animation controls for the outer, inner, and middle of the brow. This way the animator can sculpt the brow in many different ways. Remember, isolation is key to the brow movements. Figures 5.18a, b, and c show the inner, middle, and outer corrugator target controls..

To see which expressions this muscle influences, refer to Table 5.1.

Levator Palpebrea

The levator palpebrea is the muscle that contracts the upper lid to widen the eye in a more alert pose. This muscle is attached to the skin of the upper lid on one end and to the roof of the eye socket on the other end (see Figure 5.19). We are the only species with such an obvious eye structure. Our eyes translate our emotions quickly because of the shape of the lid and its relation to the pupil and iris. So the shape of the eye and how the lid lies on the iris are incredible visual cues to a face's expression.

brows try to meet, causing wrinkles

brow lowers and protrudes like a shelf

Corrugator Group Movement

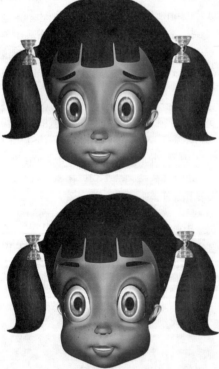

Figures 5.18a, b, and c   Corrugator inner (a), middle (b), and outer (c) control group muscle movement for brows.

Figure 5.19   Levator palpebrea muscle location.

The levator palpebrea muscle raises the upper eyelid as in a surprised, wide-eyed look. Although this motion is independent of the brows, the muscle can be involuntary contracted by the brows. (Involuntary action will have to be generated later.) The most important factor to a muscle drive rig is isolation of the muscle actions, so double deformations are not used when the targets are in place. See Figure 5.20 for images of the isolated involuntary poses of the levator palpebrea muscle. The muscle also works with the orbicularis oculi to create additional eye shapes that reinforce the brow (see Figure 5.21).

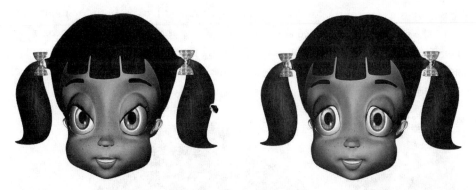

Figure 5.20   Levator palpebrea provide additional controls for eyelid shapes.

For an awake, neutral state of the eye, this muscle is always a little contracted. When you sleep this muscle is completely relaxed. The levator palpebrea acts as an intensity control for all expressions. In other words, the more it contracts, the more vivid anger, fear, or surprise seems. To see which expressions this muscle influences, refer to Table 5.1.

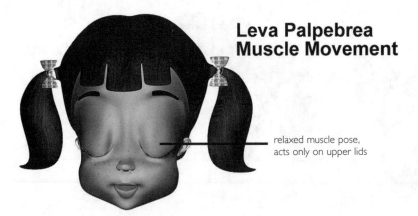

**Leva Palpebrea
Muscle Movement**

relaxed muscle pose,
acts only on upper lids

Figure 5.21   Levator palpebrea muscle movement.

Risorius and Platysma Group

The risorius muscle is used only in the most intense expressions. It shows itself in extreme circumstances, for example to express anguish, but not for basic sadness.

The risorius originates at the same knot as the zygomatic muscles and triangularis. Instead of pulling up, back, or down, however, this muscle pulls towards itself. The platysma originates in the neck and connects to the mouth corners. (See Figure 5.22.) These two muscles contract together to create a strained look in both the mouth and neck. The platysma is connected at the mouth corners, and when the risorius contracts, the platysma involuntarily contracts as well, flexing the muscles in the neck. Depending on your character and the detail between the head and neck, you might not need all of this action. But if your character is realistic, that contraction will add life to it.

Figure 5.22   Risorius and platysma muscle group location.

The neck muscles tend to tighten when the risorius flexes. Use this only if your character is very detailed and realistic. This neck tightening might look extreme on more cartoony characters like the one used in the later tutorials. Moving in the opposite motion of the zygomatic major (smiling muscle), the risorius stretches the upper lip and bends the lower lip, exposing the lower row of teeth (see Figure 5.23). To see which expressions this muscle influences, refer to Table 5.1.

Risorius Group Muscle Movement

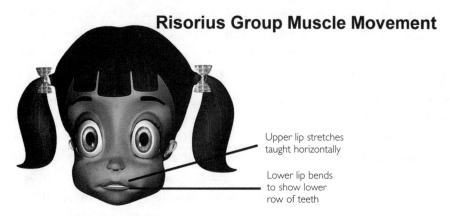

Upper lip stretches taught horizontally

Lower lip bends to show lower row of teeth

Figure 5.23   Risorius and platysma group muscle movement.

Depressor Labii Inferiors

The depressor labii inferiors muscles assist the risorius in creating that anguished expression, specializing in curling the lower lip. The depressor starts at the middle of the lower lip and extends to the bottom of the chin (see Figure 5.24). The two depressor muscles together "curl" the lip down, exposing teeth and gum. Note that this muscle bares the teeth *and* the gum, but the risorius exposes only the bottom teeth. To see which expressions this muscle influences, refer to Table 5.1.

Figure 5.24   Depressor labii inferiors muscle location.

Morphing Techniques for Facial Animation

Using morphing, you can create complex facial animation yet keep the Track View manageable. Morphing changes the shape of the *base object* into the shape of other *target objects*. MAX R3 offers a more powerful way to morph in the new Morpher modifier. This new modifier combines the same mixing of multiple targets available in previous releases of MAX with the power to manipulate them more easily in a more streamlined interface. Morph target animation requires that your target meshes have the same number of vertices in the exact same order as the base object. This is accomplished by creating one stock face that is expressionless and neutral, copying it, and reworking the stock face into as many expressions and facial poses as necessary.

The target morphing method for facial animation relies on the creation of individual models that represent the major muscle poses of the face. Because poses can be mixed, all you need to model are the extremes of the individual muscles. If you model an extreme for each muscle, you can achieve high-quality animation with minimum spinners. Because ease of use and a light setup are very important, you might want to minimize even further. If you can mix two muscles together for your character and not lose subtleties, do so. The fewer spinners you have, the less information you have to deal with and the easier it is to change your animation. If your character has less geography in one area of the mesh, such as thin cheeks, do not use all the muscles in that area because they will be wasted.

Choosing the Relevant Muscles

How do you decide which muscles need target poses to mimic actions? As when you created your skeletal character setup, keep in mind your main objectives:

- Power
- Flexibility
- Speed in use

Look at your character and size up which targets are most needed and will most influence facial expression. Because the character you will be using in the tutorial is a cartoon-style character, you will omit or combine many of the muscles to keep the setup light. For example, the platysma neck muscle that contracts with the risorius will not be used on this character because of her cartoon-ish style and also because her neck is so small this action would be lost on her model. When more realism is needed, a heavier setup may be desired.

In addition, some single muscle movements might be isolated into several additional targets for a more cartoon-ish character. A creature does not need inner and outer brow controls like the characters used in this chapter. Creatures have a less obvious eye display and reveal less emotion through their brows than a cartoony or human character does. If you consider the face of a creature that has a less-pronounced brow and eyelid movement, you might find you don't need all 11 muscle controls. Because the eye region of the character in the upcoming tutorial is so large and open to expression, however, you will add even more controls to the one or two muscle that control this area.

Of the 11 muscles detailed earlier, you will use 10 in the upcoming tutorial and combine the other one with muscles in the same region. The tutorial character's face will use these muscles:

- Orbicularis oculi
- Levator palpebrea
- Nasi (combined with the zygomatic minor)
- Zygomatic major
- Risorius
- Frontalis
- Orbicularis oris
- Corrugator
- Triangularis
- Mentalis (combined with the depressor)

When preparing for other projects, remember that the choices you make will greatly affect the facial animation—so make them wisely. Make sure you keep the power, but also keep the setup light and easy to use.

Morpher Modifier Interface

The interface for the Morpher modifier is broken down into five sections:

- Channel Color Legend
- Global Parameters
- Channel List
- Channel Parameters
- Advanced Parameters

You will mostly be concerned with the Channel List and parameters sections. The important tools in this modifier are covered briefly in the sections that follow.

Global Parameters

The Global Parameters rollout gives you the power to influence the targets on a global level.

- **Use Limits.** The limits are probably the most important tool in this section. Each acts as a "clamp" of sorts to be sure that your targets do not go to extremes that might break the mesh. If you open them wide enough, the limits will still enable you to get an extreme negative or positive target pose for that perfect facial expression. You can turn off the limits altogether, but I think it's best to use these so your curves do not get out of control and are around 400% of the target. A good range is –150 for your minimum and 150 for your maximum, but you might find that you need to widen or narrow this envelope for your character and its controls.

- **Use Vertex Selection.** The Use Vertex Selection tool enables the Morpher modifier to affect only those vertex selections made in a previous Edit Mesh in the stack. This tool could be useful for affecting motion in only one area, but because the option is set at the global level, you probably will not use it very much.

Channel List

The Channel List rollout is where you enter your targets' shapes into the channel list. A great new tool called the Marker allows for quick navigation through the list of targets you are using.

- **Channel List.** One hundred channel slots are provided for your targets. When a target is entered into a channel, its name appears in the channel list. You can change the channel name in the Channel Parameters rollout. By adjusting the percentage value with the spinner, you change the target's influence. If you right-click on any channel in the list, you will get additional menu options for manipulating that channel.

Note

These same 100 channels can also morph materials, but for this tutorial, we are only concerned with the shape animation. The type of Float controllers assigned to the targets is up to you. I prefer the Bezier controller, which is the default, because it provides curves in the Track View with which you can manipulate the timing of your animation.

- **Save Marker.** To help you keep track of your targets' channels, MAX R3 enables you to set markers for single channels and channel ranges. To save a marker, move the channel list's scroll bar to include a single channel or a set of up to 10 channels. Type a name in the marker list's text field, and then click Save Marker to store the marker for the range.

- **Marker list.** A drop-down list of currently set markers. Click on the name of a previously saved marker in the list to select that channel or range.

- **Delete Marker.** To delete a marker, you must display the marker name in the text field in the Marker list and then click Delete Marker.

- **Zero Active Channel Values.** This is a powerful tool that you should use often to keep your curves under control and prevent distortion. When the Animate button is on, this sets a key of zero value on every channel to zero-out your pose so it will return to the neutral resting pose.

Channel Parameters

The next section of the Morpher modifier is the Channel Parameters rollout. Here you choose your channels and targets, as well as ways to manipulate them.

- **Channel Number.** Each channel has an integer assigned to it relative to its placement in the channel list. When you right-click on it, you see a quick editing menu for reorganizing your targets in the channel list.

- **Channel Name field.** Displays the name of the current target's channel. You can change the name of the target in the text field.

- **Channel Is Active.** Toggles a single channel on and off. This affects the channel designated in the Channel Name field. Inactive channels do not affect the Morpher result. This is a powerful tool for layering because it enables you to concentrate on fine-tuning or animating certain channels by turning the others off.

- **Pick Object from Scene.** Click this button to choose a target from the scene and place it in the current selected channel. If you use this tool, the targets must not be hidden. You cannot select hidden targets.

- **Capture Current State.** Although you should keep your setup light in use by using strategically placed targets, this tool enables you to create even more targets quickly. To do this, you select an empty channel to activate this function and then click to create a target using the current channel values.

- **Delete.** Deletes the target assignment for the current channel.

- **Extract.** If you accidentally lose or delete a target and want it back, you can still get it if the geometry reference is stored in the Channel Editor. The blue-colored channel lets you know that the original geometry created for that pose is no longer available. The data has been saved into the Morpher modifier so the morphing mechanism still works, but you cannot refer to the original target. When a target is deleted, the color next to the channel name turns blue in the channel list. Select a blue channel and click Extract to create an object from the data. Using Extract in conjunction with the Capture Current State tool can enable you to create even more targets. Capture the current state of a group of channel values, and then use Extract to make a new target object. Finally, pick the new object as the channel's target and then start editing.

- **Use Limits.** This is a limit control on the local level. If some of your targets have very small envelopes of values before distortion occurs and others have larger ranges, it is best to manipulate the limits on a local target level. This works only if the global limits are not activated.

- **Use Vertex Selection.** When this option is checked, a target acts on only the selected vertices in the current channel. These selected vertices are created in the previous Edit Mesh. Use Vertex Selection is helpful for isolating muscle poses and creating the left and right offsets of each pose. You will use this function more often than you will the global vertex selection option.

Advanced Parameters

This rollout provides even more functionality for the Morpher modifier, including adjusting spinner increments, cleaning up the channel list, and viewing memory usage.

- **Spinner Increments.** Here you can adjust the spinner increments. The default is 1.0. This is purely the user's choice. If you prefer to use increments tighter than whole integers, this is where you can change it.

- **Compact Channel List.** This very neat little tool helps you organize your channels. If you have empty spaces where channels have been deleted or you just decided they did not work, you can move those channels so they appear all in a row with the Compact Channel List function. The status window then displays how many channels were moved.

- **Approximate Usage.** Click here to display current memory usage. This function can help you decide if the target you created is really worth its memory usage for the setup.

Tutorial: Creating Morph Targets for Facial Expression

With a firm grasp of the tools required and a solid foundation of facial anatomy, you are ready to create the morph target poses necessary for animating facial expression. To create these poses, you'll rely on MAX R3's new NURMS option in the MeshSmooth modifier, the Morpher modifier, and the Soft Selection in the Edit Mesh modifier. The NURMS option in MeshSmooth creates a control mesh that encompasses the mesh and simplifies the mesh to a small number of control points. You use these control points to manipulate the mesh and create the contractions of the muscles on the face.

The process of creating target poses can be divided into five phases:

- Applying the MeshSmooth NURMS control mesh

- Adjusting the control mesh points to create the pose

- Creating a snapshot of the pose and naming it

- Creating an asymmetrical pose with the Morpher modifier

- Entering each pose into the Morpher modifier for animation

Caution

Remember that the order of the modifiers in the stack is very important for a successful target pose. Think of it like building a sandwich. If you place the tomato on top of the ham and Swiss, it might taste different than if you placed it between the cheese and meat. The same goes for MAX's modifier stack, the final output is greatly affected by the order of the modifiers in the stack because they act on each other procedurally according to their order.

The tutorial that follows will get you started on modeling muscle poses for the facial setup of a little girl. In it, you will create the zygomatic major muscle movement only, but all the other poses are created with the same steps. To begin the tutorial, open the file called Facial_WORK_OK.max from the accompanying CD. Select the head in the viewport by pressing the H key, and then go to the Modify panel for the first phase of the process.

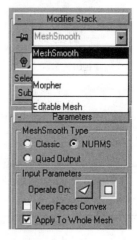

Apply the NURMS Control Mesh

Under Modifier Stack (see Figure 5.25), you will see the Editable Mesh, Morpher, and MeshSmooth modifiers applied to the little girl's head. You will use the Editable Mesh modifier and MeshSmooth's NURMS control mesh to create the different poses.

Figure 5.25
The modifier stack.

1. To turn the NURMS control mesh on, add an Edit Mesh modifier on top of the existing one but below the Morpher modifier. The smooth NURMS surface reveals the low-resolution polygonal mesh underneath.

2. Turn the control mesh on by selecting Sub-Object mode and turning vertices on. The MeshSmooth is applied, and the mesh is smooth and at a high resolution.

3. Turn on Sub-Object mode. A control mesh appears, and you can manipulate the vertices to get the pose you desire (see Figure 5.26). Only MAX R3 NURMS give you this functionality.

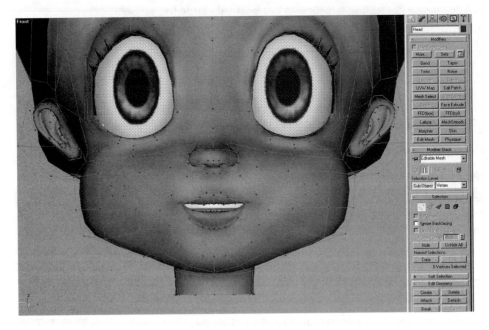

Figure 5.26   The NURMS control mesh.

Create the Pose

In this exercise, you will create a smile with the zygomatic major action pose.

1. Go to the Side view and select all the control mesh points that encompass the back of the head. Hide these with the Hide function in Editable Mesh. This will ensure that you do not accidentally select any points on the back of the head and move them for a pose.

2. Select the vertices on either side of the mouth. Pull them upward and back so they create a pose for the zygomatic major muscle. Do the same for the nose wings, which are the two sides of the nose where you breath in air. Remember

that the cheeks rise into the bottom lid as they puff out; so you will need to create this action by pulling on control points around the cheek area also. You will need to tweak the individual control points to get the additional muscle movement and mimic the visual cues that indicate the zygomatic major is being used.

3. Adjust the vertices until you get a contracted zygomatic muscle pose (see Figure 5.27). You can refer to the mesh called Head_targets in the file you are using. This mesh has a history of every single morph target needed for the facial created for you in Edit Mesh modifiers. Study these poses in their Edit Mesh states to see exactly how each muscle is created.

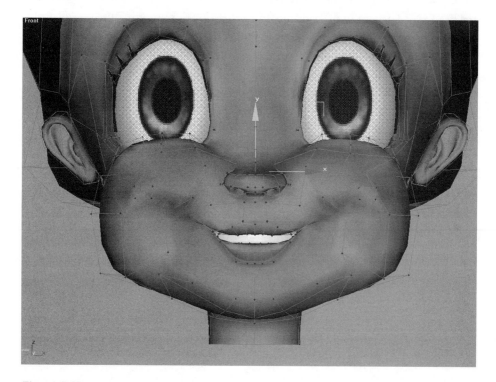

Figure 5.27   Zygomatic muscle pose.

Tip

Check your poses with a render to be sure that the mesh deforms cleanly. *Always* check this render with no lights in the scene, whether you have to delete the lights you have created or turn them off. The default lighting will reveal creases and dimples you might not want, but a lighting setup might hide these flaws in shadowing. Nothing is worse than working hours on a few poses only to find problems later when you use different lighting.

4. Click on the Edit Stack button to open the modifier stack. You will name this modifier to avoid confusion. Select the Editable Mesh you use to manipulate the head and enter **Zyg** in the Name box.

Create and Name a Snapshot

Next, you will create a snapshot of this pose to use as a final morph target. To keep your animation setup light, you will need to create the morph target without the NURMS MeshSmooth modifier. This way the mesh will be at its lowest resolution. After you create all the targets this way, you will reapply the NURMS MeshSmooth to the master/neutral head to add detail and make it smooth again. Using this procedural setup will enable you to keep the animation light, quick, and interactive and will provide the power to act on either the high-resolution mesh or the low-resolution one by adjusting the MeshSmooth modifier.

1. Click on the Show End Result On/Off toggle icon again in the Zyg Edit Mesh. This will return the mesh to its low-resolution state but keep the Edit Mesh manipulation you used to create the Zyg pose.

2. Go to the Main toolbar and select the Snapshot icon. (This icon is a flyout from the Array button next to the Mirror function.)

3. Create a new Editable Mesh with the settings Single and Mesh selected.

4. Select and name the new mesh Zyg.

5. Select the master head called "Head."

6. Go to the Edit Mesh you used to manipulate Head and turn the Sub-Object mode off.

7. Turn the Active/Inactive modifier (the little light bulb icon) off so that the manipulation of the mesh is turned off and the head is back to its neutral state.

Create an Asymmetrical Pose

An asymmetrical pose will give your facial rig even more power and flexibility. It is important to create a right and left pose for each muscle contraction because they can contract independently of one another.

1. Go to the first Editable Mesh below the Zyg modifier and turn Sub-Object vertices on. Select the left half of the head.

2. Under the same Editable Mesh, go to the Soft Selection rollout. Turn on Use Soft Selection and change Falloff to 25 (see Figure 5.28).

Note

Another tool new to MAX R3, Soft Selection enables you to ease out the modifier that comes next in the stack. Using Soft Selection will make the next modifier in the stack (the Morpher modifier) less abrupt in creating half the zygomatic pose. The Soft Selection tool is represented by colored vertices that ease from the warm red color of being 100% active down to a cold blue of 0% manipulation (being inactive). You can also use the Soft Selection function on the control points for tighter control over your target creation.

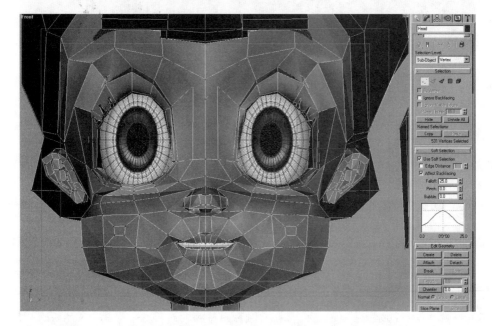

Figure 5.28   Use the Soft Selection tool to create half of your muscle poses

3. Go to the Morpher modifier in the stack above the Zyg Editable Mesh.

4. The channel list is currently empty and ready for you to place your targets in. Click on the Load Multiple Targets button and select the mesh you named Zyg. This file is only temporary and will be used to create a left and right pose for asymmetry.

5. The Zyg Head should now be in the first slot of the channel list in the Morpher. Change the spinner next to it to read 100.

6. Half the head should be smiling and the smile pose should ease out on the right side making for a smooth transition. (See Figure 5.29.)

7. Go to Create Snapshot again and create a snapshot of this pose. You have now created the left zyg major pose at the low-resolution.

8. Select the pose and name it Zyg_L for zygomatic major left.

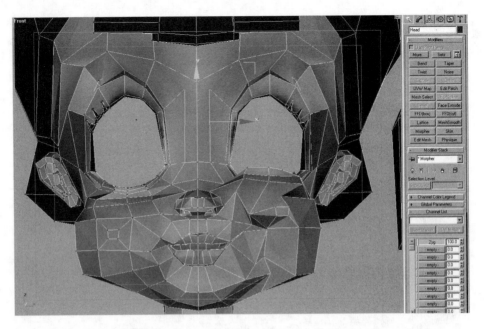

Figure 5.29   Morpher modifier.

9. Repeat these nine steps, selecting the right half of the head in your first Editable Mesh to create the other pose.

Tip

A quick way to select the other half of the head is to go to the Main toolbar and click Edit/Select Invert. If you selected exactly half of the head before, this function will inverse that selection to be the other half.

Enter Each Pose for Animation

You will now assign each target into the Morpher modifier channel list.

1. Go to the Morpher modifier and delete the existing Zyg Head from the top slot.

2. Insert the Zyg_L and Zyg_R poses into the first and second slots.

3. Move the spinners to test them. The change will be visible in the viewport.

You have created your first facial muscle target. Simply follow the same steps to complete the other muscle poses. When you create them, be sure to maintain the proper volume in the face. Remember all the visual cues discussed earlier. For example, if the jaw drops, the corners of the mouth stretch, and if the zygomatic major muscle is animated, the cheeks puff up. If the individual meshes are solid and correct, the animation will follow along and look terrific.

At the same time, be sure you isolate each muscle's movement, so that if another muscle is close to it, the two will not create an additive distortion. In other words, if you make the zygomatic major muscle puff the cheeks up above the lower lids, make sure you don't move any of the lower lid vertices. If you do move them, you will get an additive effect that distorts the eyelids because the two targets move the lids double the amount. The more you isolate the muscle targets, the more flexibility you will get from your setup.

Tip

It is best to divide the face into two parts when creating the final targets for the animation setup. The lower face is everything from the nose down, and the upper face involves the eyes and brows.

To see a completed version of the tutorial head with all the muscle targets, open the file Facial_OK.max on the accompanying CD.

Facial Lip Sync Breakdown

Until now, you've concentrated on animating facial expressions. The other half of facial animation is successful lip syncing. Both types of animation use many of the same muscles, but you need two types of muscle extreme targets that are created in very different ways to get the best animation. Expression poses are strictly muscle contractions all over the face to create expressions. Lip-sync poses are muscle contractions isolated to the mouth and cheek areas to create sound for dialog. These lip-sync poses are called *phoneme* poses.

Basic Phoneme Poses

Phonemes are the most basic phonetic building blocks of words. Phoneme poses are the facial positions that represent the sounds used to form words. These poses should be created only with the lips and cheeks. Only the "AH" and "LA" poses use the jaw bone to drop the jaw. This might be difficult to get used to because many poses, such as "F," "V," and "EE," require the mouth to truly be open . However, if you create the phoneme poses independent of the jaw, you can create a clenched mouth talking or a screaming mouth yelling the same line, in turn providing a much more life-like animation.

The most basic phonemes needed to create dialog and their poses are listed here:

- **"MMM" sound.** The relaxed closed mouth pose is specifically used for the "M" sounds (see Figure 5.30). In this position, the lips are closed and pursed slightly using the orbicularis oris muscle.

Figure 5.30   "MM" phoneme.

- **"B" and "P" sounds.** The rolled, taut, and closed mouth pose is specifically used for the "B" and "P" sounds (see Figure 5.31). In this position, the lips are closed like "MMM" but also roll inward and puff up a little as if the mouth is going to blow out air. This pose uses the mentalis, orbicularis oris, and depressor muscles.

Figure 5.31   "B" and "P" phoneme.

- **"EEE" sound.** The mouth is open, and the teeth are almost touching (see Figure 5.32). The "EEE" phoneme is used often in dialog for the consonants "E," "C," "D," "G," "K," "N," "R," "S," "TH," "Y," and "Z." A little of "EE" mixed with the "AH" phoneme pose creates the "I" pose. This pose uses the zygomatic major muscle.

Figure 5.32 "EE" phoneme.

- **"OOO" sound.** The mouth is pushed out in a pursed "O" shape (see Figure 5.33). It is used for the "OOO" sound, as in "boot." This pose can be mixed with a slight "EEE" pose to simulate the vowel "U" as in the word "muddy." Also, "OOO" is mixed with "AH" to drop the jaw in order to create the "OH" sound. This is another good example of how using multiple morphs reduces the number of poses required.

Figure 5.33 "OO" phoneme.

- **"FF" and "VV" sounds.** A very important pose for all speech, this gives the crispness dialog needs. The pose has the bottom lip tucked under the teeth to make the sound of the letters "F" and "V" (see Figure 5.34).

Figure 5.34   "F" and "V" phoneme.

- **"AH" sound.** This is used for the wide-open vowels, such as "A" and "I." The tongue should be visible at the bottom of the mouth, and the jaw is relatively slack (see Figure 5.35). A bone structure is used to create this phoneme because the lips do not change shape for "AH." Only the jaw is dropped for the "AH" pose. For the "I" pose, a little "EE" is mixed with "AH." Always look for ways to streamline your setup by mixing muscles and phonemes.

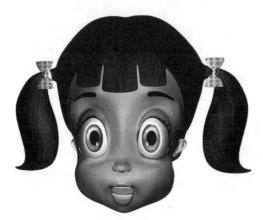

Figure 5.35   "AH" phoneme.

- **"LA" sound.** This is basically the "AH" pose with the tongue up against the roof of the mouth. Because this pose will be created mostly from the jaw bone motion, only the tongue should move (see Figure 5.36). A morph target for the tongue is created to get this motion. The tongue movement is very subtle, how-ever; remember that the eye follows movement, and any movement will draw attention to the object. The "LA" pose will give snap to your dialogue. If you are going to animate a character who licks and smacks his lips with more complex tongue movements, you might consider creating a bone structure to animate that motion.

Figure 5.36   "LA" phoneme.

Blended together, these basic phoneme poses can create almost any facial dialogue animation through the use of weighted multi-target morph tools and techniques. By using the muscle morph targets with these phonetic poses and asymmetrical animation in the brows and eyelids, you can create very believable motion.

Because the muscle-based targets provide almost any pose you might require for facial and lip-sync animation together, the phoneme poses needed for this setup are few and very specific. These poses are chosen because they are the most widely used and because it would take too many spinners to create them with individual muscle targets. This is the best way to draw a line in the sand to determine what targets you'll make for your setup. Even though you could mix several targets to get one pose, if you are using a pose often—say for dialogue—it's better to create it as an individual target. Weighing ease versus heavier setup, the payoff of ease is worth it.

Tutorial: Creating the "AH"

The following tutorial explains how to create the "AH" phoneme pose with the jaw bone. You could just rotate the vertices on the NURMS control mesh downward to open the jaw and then use that as a target, but an actual bone will give you the sliding and rotation that a real jaw bone has, as well as more asymmetry in your poses. The process can be divided into three phases:

- Create the head/jaw skeleton rig
- Create a dummy constraint for the jaw
- Use the Skin modifier to assign vertices to follow the bone

This process produces a jaw that can be oriented on all three axes, enabling more flexibility for the animator. The steps that follow will walk you through the three phases.

1. To begin creating the head and jaw skeleton rig, open the file on the accompanying CD called Jaw_WORK.max.

2. The head mesh is frozen so you can concentrate on the bone structure. Choose IK from the Command panel. Create PRS (Position, Rotate, Scale) FK bones by turning off the Assign to Children controller in the Bone Parameters rollout.

3. Go to System/Bones and change to the Side viewport.

4. Create five bones: two head bones and three jaw bones. Use Figure 5.37 for placement reference. (For tips on creating bones, see Chapter 2, "Basic Character and Creature Setup.")

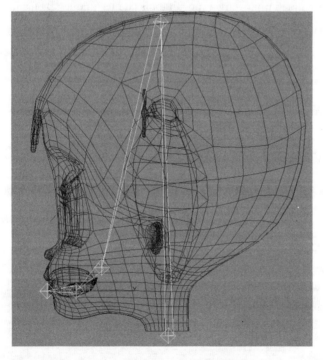

Figure 5.37   Placement of the jaw and head bones.

5. Rename the bones as outlined here:

   Bone01 to Bone_Head

   Bone02 to Bone_Head02

   Bone03 to Bone_Jaw

   Bone04 to Bone_Jaw02

   Bone05 to Bone_Jaw_end

6. Now get ready to create a dummy constraint for the jaw. Go to the Top view and create a dummy. Name the Dummy **C_JAW**. Align this dummy to the bone called Bone_Jaw so it is centered on its pivot.

7. Select the bone called Bone_Jaw and assign a Local Euler controller to it if it is not already set as a default.

8. Assign a float expression to the x-, y-, and z-axis of the Local Euler controller. (See Chapter 2 for more information on Euler controllers and assigning expressions.)

9. Right-click on each float expression and, under Properties, assign the Xrot, Yrot, and Zrot expressions provided on the accompanying CD.

10. Link the bottom teeth and the tongue to the jaw bone.

11. Now test the setup. Click the Select icon to deselect the Link mode, and then select and rotate the C_Jaw dummy. The jaw bone tree with bottom teeth and tongue should follow the rotation of the jaw.

12. Unfreeze the head mesh for the final phase of applying the Skin modifier to the mesh.

13. In the modifier stack, click on the Editable Mesh below the MeshSmooth modifier. You will place the Skin modifier above the Editable Mesh and below MeshSmooth so you have to assign fewer vertices to the bones.

14. Go to the Modify panel and click on the Skin modifier to assign it to the mesh. Make sure the Show End Result toggle is off so the MeshSmooth modifier is not applied at this level.

15. In the Skin modifier rollout, click on Add Bone and add the jaw bone tree only. If you were skinning the whole character, you could assign the whole tree including the head bones; however, for demonstration purposes, you will skin only the jaw.

16. Click the Envelope Sub-Object level to activate it and assign the vertices to the correct jaw bone. Adjust the envelopes first, and then manually assign the vertices to the jaw bones. (Refer to Chapter 8, "Mesh Deformation," for help on this.)

> **Tip**
>
> Use the Weight Vertex options with the Skin modifier. It is much easier to assign vertices when you turn the vertices filter on and manually assign the vertices to the bones and weight them.

You now have an operational jaw that can be oriented on all three axes. This will enable even more flexibility in offsets and power in getting that great pose. In addition, you can use the Audio controller discussed later in this chapter on the jaw constraint to animate the opening and closing of the jaw by using the amplitude of the sound wave. This kind of jaw setup might be a little advanced, but the strides it allows you to make in facial animation are worth the work of setting it up.

To see a completed version of this head/jaw setup, open the file Facial_HEADJAW _OK.max on the accompanying CD.

Tutorial: Creating the "LA" Pose

This tutorial explains how to create the "LA" sound with a tongue morph. You will create a morph target just like you did for the facial expression animation, but it's for the tongue this time. If your tongue animation needs to be more complex, like licking the lips, you will want to build a bone structure and apply skin to animate it just as you did for the jaw previously. For a simple phoneme position however, you can use target shape animation and morphing to do the trick.

The easiest way to build a tongue is by squashing a sphere and putting a dent down its length. Texture and bump maps can be used to create a more detailed surface. It's a good idea to fade this texture to black at the back of the tongue so it remains hidden.

The tongue and teeth are particularly important in animated speech. The tongue is a very flexible object. Here are the steps for producing a natural "LA" pose:

1. Open the file Facial_WORK_OK.max, apply a lattice to the tongue, and rotate the end control points until it curls upward as if the tip will lie against the upper teeth. Remember that the upper teeth are locked down to the skull and do not move, so you can unhide them to gauge your lattice manipulation.

2. Create a snapshot of this pose and name it T_LA.

3. Turn the Lattice modifier off for your master tongue and keep it for reference.

4. Apply a Morpher modifier and insert the T_LA pose into a channel. Now you can animate the tongue from the resting pose to a "LA" pose.

For some variation, experiment with different tongue positions, such as making a twist for an "RR" sound. To see a final example of a working tongue morph target, open the file FACIAL_OK.max on the accompanying CD. Select the tongue and choose Hide Unselected under the Display Panel so you can see what the spinner does. Move the spinner on the tongue Morpher modifier and see how it moves back and forth between a neutral position and the "TH" and "LA" pose.

Track Reading

Now that you are familiar with the basic mouth position poses and how to create them, you're ready to break down the dialogue track into individual phonemes, a process called *track reading*. This is best done on good traditional animator's exposure sheet paper. An exposure sheet is a great tool for production because after you have track read the dialogue, you can always refer to that sheet. The sheet also has places where you can create thumb-nail poses for the body gestures as you become more familiar with the line.

There is an example exposure sheet on the CD-ROM in the Microsoft Word file CGXsheet.doc. Print this exposure sheet and use it to read your track. In case you do not have Word, the CD-ROM also contains an HTML version of the page that you can print from any Web browser. The HTML page is slightly different because of the limitation of the HTML code and tables. The provided example has 30 rows dedicated to 30 frames of animation per sheet. To get really tight clean animation, I advise you not to tackle more than 30 frames at a time.

The example exposure sheet also has columns dedicated to the camera and lights if you choose to represent their movement on the sheet. The other numbered columns are used for planning details ranging from eye blinks to hand gestures to even entry of other characters into the scene. For these purposes, you should be concerned with only the first three columns.

Analyzing the Sound File

The first step to track reading is to listen to your sound file and figure out what the character will be doing with his body for the scene. The body gestures will direct what the face should be doing, so it is best to figure out the silhouette of the body for the line of dialogue first, and then think about the facial expression. Just keep in mind that if you do the facial movements first, you might become a little more familiar with your sound file, because you have to break it down with the track reading process. This, in turn, can make blocking out the body motion a little easier, because you will know every inflection in the voice and where it is in the track. At this time, you can decide if you need a little dead air before the sound file starts in which you can animate the character walking into the scene or looking around before it speaks.

To insert silence and make your sound file the proper length, you will need to use a sound-editing program. Then you can load the adjusted sound file into MAX and use it as reference. Available sound editing programs can help you insert the silence, cut the sound together, and even track read. A good choice is CoolEdit, a shareware program available on the Internet at **www.syntrillium.com/cool96.htm**.

Track Reading with Max R3

To read a track, you can load the sound file into MAX R3. MAX R3 has the capability to load sound directly into the Track View, which makes it excellent for lip-sync applications. Right-click the Sound Track object and select Properties from the menu that appears. MAX then displays the audio waveform from within the Track View. Simply sliding the Time Slider audibly scrubs the audio, allowing you to read the phonemes of the dialogue frame by frame. It's best to do this before animation begins because a properly read track serves as a good reference for use when you're animating.

Also, reading the track after animation has been added to the shot can prove troublesome due to machine speed, length of animation, and animation complexity issues. If high-resolution morph-target animation is being used, the calculations required to perform this job can tax even the most powerful systems, so real-time playback might not be possible. This is why you want to keep your facial setup as light as possible. The files provided for the book's tutorials should be very light. You should be able to scrub the Time Slider and hear the sound as you work because the new MeshSmooth NURMS surface enables you to interactively adjust the level of detail of the mesh to be very low or very high.

When the sound file is loaded into MAX R3, match your sound editing program's frame rate to the frame rate you are animating. For example, if you are animating for NTSC video, you should set the frame rate to 30 frames per second. Also, you will not be able to hear the sound in MAX R3 unless you turn on the Playback Real Time setting in the Time Configuration box at the bottom of the interface.

You can start reading the track and writing down the phonemes as you drag the Time Slider in MAX and listen to the sounds. You should work in small pieces, for example, 30 frames at a time, maybe less. This will break down the sounds into syllables and make it easier for you to discern what phonemes will be needed.

The visual readout or wave form of the sound file gives you clues as to where the words start and end and how loud the character's voice gets as it speaks. Move the Time Slider back and forth across the track one frame at a time and write down each sound as it occurs on your exposure. It is a tedious but necessary chore, but it will save you time and energy down the line because you will have a written reference that shows the timing of each line of dialogue.

Tip

It is best to create a lower resolution sampled version of your sound file for use in MAX. This way, when you do scrub through the dialogue, the sound file is small and won't bog down the interface as much. A good low-end sample setting is 22MHz. Use your higher frequency sampling for the final render and test renders.

Using Magpie

As discussed above, 3D Studio MAX R3 enables you to play back audio in sync with your animation. This can work only if your system offers at least a benchmark speed of 300MHz and your model is light. Otherwise, you will not be able to scrub your animation interactively. Third-party sound editors can provide flexibility when reading a track, but there is no immediate feedback as to how your character will animate. Many animators have turned to third-party lip sync applications to help, particularly if they cannot scrub audio interactively within MAX because of system limits.

A good example of one of these third-party packages is Magpie, a shareware program available on the Internet at **http://thirdwish.simplenet.com/magpie.html**. Magpie enables you to load a series of bitmap files that represent the key mouth poses found in your library of poses. These bitmaps can then be timed to the track on a frame-by-frame basis; the final result output is a text file that looks very much like an animator's dope sheet.

Track Reading and Accuracy

When you're reading a track, be sure to represent the sounds accurately. To get the cleanest dialogue, place your phonemes two frames before they happen in the sound file. In human speech, most consonants are short and usually do not take up many frames, but you must have at least two frames to show that they read. If you must, take some time off the preceding sound to get the two frames for the consonant. Always hit a mouth's apex of a sound on the vowel. All vowels need two poses in order to come across to the viewer. These two poses fill an *accent* pose and a *cushion* pose. To use these two poses, snap the mouth open for the accent pose and immediately ease into a cushion pose.

Unless your character is shouting, do not hold the mouth in the same position for very long—it would look unnatural. Instead, adjust the Morph spinner for the jaw so that it relaxes slightly through the vowel. This keeps the mouth positions and the mouth moving between them so the character looks alive. Also, never use in-between frames on the tongue motion. Always snap the tongue from one position to the next. Be aware of your curves, and watch how they dive in and out of one another. The visual cues you get from the curves in the Track View will help you tighten up your lip sync and make holds more interesting by adjusting their placement.

Finally, try to choose a sound file that has a character arc. In other words, a sound file that changes from sad to happy or angry to amazed will really tax your facial setup and reveal it's weaknesses.

Tutorial: Reading a Track

The following exercise explains how to read a track with the exposure sheet provided on the accompanying CD. You can use a sheet of lined paper to read the track if you do not have access to Microsoft Word or a Web browser.

1. Load dorothy_speaks.wav from the accompanying CD-ROM into your favorite editing program. The dialogue says "Ahhh uh Haaaaa, ooooeeeewwww I ought'da, oooowww, Wow! Giggles, I'm tired." At 30 fps, the dialogue measures 310 frames.

2. Open the Track View and click on Sound to expand the waveform. As you watch the waveform, scrub through time slowly in the Time Slider to find out where the phonemes go, keeping an eye out for the peaks and valleys.

3. Highlight the first 30 frames of the sound file. This is the word "ahhh uh heaaah." Play this section back, highlighting smaller sections to get the individual phonemes. Keep in mind that because most of this first part is using the "ah" sound, you can get quite a bit of this area timed out with simple jaw bone open and closing keys.

4. The next sound, from frames 30 to 60, is the final cry, an inhale and the beginnings of the word "wwwoooo." Usually you don't worry about inhales, but because this one is so prominent, mark it down.

5. Work through the entire track examining 30 frames or fewer at a time and writing the positions of each phoneme in the exposure sheet.

You might want to open the file call trackread.doc on the accompanying disk, which has the entire sound file mapped out.

As a final note, be careful about reading the track too literally. Concentrate on the sounds, not the script. Listen to the track over and over again until you no longer hear the words, but instead hear syllables and simple sounds. In this track, the character doesn't pronounce the "T" in the word "ought." Instead she slurs that "T" with the "T" in "to," making the whole phrase sound more like "awdah" instead of "ought to."

Using Audio Controllers

One of the easier ways to map out the basic timing of your lip sync is to use MAX's Audio controllers. These controllers enable you to translate, rotate, and scale objects based on the volume of a standard Windows WAV file. The lip sync produced by this method is not exceptionally accurate; it produces a simple lip-flapping effect, which is not particularly convincing because of its automated and mechanical qualities. However, for more stylized characters, such as a mouth resembling a duck bill, the method can prove more than adequate. You could use this to block out the jaw motion on the head initially and fine tune it as you work on the phonemes.

The AudioRotation controller is the one chosen most often for sound applications because it can be used to rotate and flap the lower jaw (although the Translate and Scale controllers can also be put to similar use). These controllers can be applied from the Motion/Parameters/Assign Controller panel or the Track View/Assign Controller button.

After it's applied, the AudioRotation controller is accessed from the Track View/Controller/Properties dialog box to be edited. The controller's dialog box has a number of parameters. First is the name of the sound file to be loaded. Note that each controller can have its own sound file, and the sound file does not have to match the sound track in Track View. This enables you to use multiple sound files as controllers—perhaps to flap the lips of a dozen people in a crowded room. A sound file does not even have to be used because the controller has a check box to enable a live audio source to be used as the controller. This can be useful for real-time or performance-animation applications.

The Oversampling spinner is critical for smooth operation. A CD-quality audio waveform changes 44,100 times per second, rising and falling constantly. The Audio controller takes the value of the waveform on the given frame and uses that number to calculate the rotation. This can cause jittery behavior because the waveform could coincidentally be at zero, maximum, or somewhere in between when it is sampled.

Oversampling prevents this jittering movement by smoothing out the waveform MAX sees. The procedure averages the waveform over a large number of samples (maximum 1,000), giving the effect of a much smoother motion.

Tip

If your audio sample rate is high (44,100KHz), you might still see some unwanted jitter, even though the Oversampling spinner is cranked up to 1,000. To eliminate this, load the audio file into a sound editing program and convert it to a lower sample rate as described in the previous Tip (11,025KHz, for example). Fewer samples force the controller to oversample over a wider range of time, effectively doubling or quadrupling the oversampling effect.

Along the bottom of the dialog box are the limits for the Rotation controller. These limits enable you to set a Base angle (which is the Rotation value used when the sound is silent) and a Target angle (which is the Rotation value used when the waveform is at 100 percent).

Eyes and Other Facial Features

Creating animatable eyes is another important part of facial animation. How the eyes are built determines how they are animated and also how they look to the audience. Eyes fall into two broad categories: internal eyes, which include the lid as part of the surface of the face, and external eyes, which have their own self-contained lids.

Internal Eyes

Internal eyes appear more realistic. The eyelids are part of the facial surface, and the eyeball is inside of the skull. If your character design dictates internal eyes, you need to model eye sockets either by modeling the eyelids as part of the entire head mesh or by modeling geometry that is fleshy and separate or attached to the head mesh. The character used for this tutorial has internal eyes.

The eyeball itself can be either a sphere or a hemisphere because only the front part of the eye ever shows through the skin. The pupil can be made with a simple texture map, or it can be a second hemisphere sitting on the first like a contact lens.

Tutorial: Creating Internal Eyes

The following series of exercises explains how to create an internal eye setup. To create this setup, refer to the head, neck, and jaw tutorial in Chapter 2, "Basic Character and Creature Setup." You will use the setup and a space warp to create the elongated cartoonish eyes that the character requires. You will also create a Look At controller to streamline the animation of the eyes.

Because the Space Warp always lies on top of any modifier stack, you will not have to worry so much about the order of these steps and their relation to the modifier stack.

Link the Eyes and Apply a Space Warp

The eyes on the cartoony character need to be oblong to fit in its elongated eye sockets. The best way to create this effect is to use a space warp to stretch the eyes. Then you can rotate them, and the rotate will always happen procedurally under the elongation. In turn, the oblong eye will penetrate the head when rotated.

1. Open the file on the accompanying CD called Facial_EYES_WORK.max.

2. Using the Select by Name tool, select the right and left eyeballs (EyeL and EyeR). Hold down the Ctrl key to make a multiple selection.

3. Click Select and Link, and then press the H key to get the Select by Name list. Click on the bone named Bone_Head to link the eye structure (cornea and eyeball) to the head bone so they will follow the head as it moves.

4. Select the right cornea and link it to the right eyeball. Do the same for the left. Your tree should look like Figure 5.38.

Figure 5.38   If you link the eyes to the head, they will follow the head when it rotates and moves. If you link the corneas to the eyeballs, they will follow the eyeballs' motion.

5. Deselect the Select and Link mode by clicking on the Select button on the Main toolbar.

6. Unhide the head of this character and observe the eye placement within the eye socket. The problem here is that the character's eye socket is oblong and the round eyes do not fit inside the socket correctly (see Figure 5.39).

7. Under the Create/Space Warp panel, select an FFD box Space Warp. Click-drag it around the right eye.

8. Set its length, width, and height to 100 each and set the number of control points to be 2×2×2.

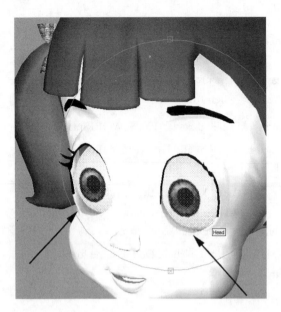

Figure 5.39   Round eyeballs do not work for this cartoony character's oblong eye sockets.

9. With the FFD Space Warp still selected, click on the Align button and align the Space Warp to the eyeball's center, as shown in Figure 5.40. (See Chapter 2 for more information on using the Align tool.)

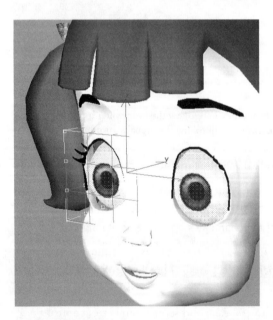

Figure 5.40   Placement of the space warp over eye.

10. Select the right eye and cornea, and then click on the Bind to Space Warp tool and link both the eye and cornea to the FFD box Space Warp. It will be easier to do this if you use Select by Name instead of trying to click in the viewport.

11. Deselect the Bind to Space Warp mode by clicking on the Select button on the Main toolbar.

12. Select the FFD01 and rename it FFD_Cartoon_Eye_R.

13. Change the Sub-Object level of the FFD to be control points, and then select the top corner control points and pull up 20 units (one grid unit = 10).

14. Select the bottom corner control points and pull down 20 units (one grid unit = 10).

15. To reposition the eye, select the cornea and eye and translate it 4 units on the local z-axis so the eyeball is centered in the socket.

16. Repeat steps 3–11 for the left eye.

Using the Look At Controller for Pupil Aiming

A very simple way to create synchronized motion with eyes is by using the Look At controller. By assigning the controller in the Track View or under the Motion panel, you can choose any object to be the target of the eyes' motion.

This technique offers many advantages, including the capability to animate the Look At target with an object that the character's eyes are supposed to be following, such as an insect. Making the eyes move with the motion of another object can be difficult sometimes. However, the Look At controller gives you timing that is right on the money. Another great advantage to using the Look At controller is that when you use a hierarchy in which the eyelids are the children of the eyeballs, the eyelids follow the eye motion up as the eye looks up, producing a subtle and more natural motion.

1. Continuing on in the Facial_EYES_WORK.max file from the previous exercise, go to the Top view and create three dummies. Make two the same size and one a little larger.

2. Select one of the smaller dummies and align it to the right eye. Do the same for the left.

3. Name the dummy over the right eye EyeR_lookAT, name the dummy over the left eye EyeL_lookAT, and name the largest dummy C_LOOKAT.

Tip

This setup will give you the flexibility to move the eyes together in a natural motion using one Look At controller, as well as allowing you to use local Look At controllers to create a cross-eyed or rolling-eye motion, as if your character was hit on the head.

4. Select the largest dummy (C_LOOKAT) and align it to the head mesh. Then drag it out on the local y-axis 500 units. This dummy should now be in front of the face.

5. Drag the two other smaller dummies for the eyes on the local y-axis 400 units so they are approximately centered in the larger LOOKAT controller.

6. Select the right eye, go to the Motion panel, and assign a Look At controller to the Transform controller. This tells the eyeball to follow whatever Look At object you tell it to.

7. To orient the eye to follow the dummy, click on Pick Target and click on the dummy called EyeR_lookAT.

8. The eye still is not oriented correctly. Select the y-axis so the Look At knows how to orient the mesh. Then repeat steps 6–8 for the left eye.

9. Link the two smaller dummies to the bigger dummy (C_LOOKAT).

You now have an operational eye setup. Move either of the smaller independent eye controllers or the larger one. The eyes follow the Look At object and will do so no matter what the orientation of the head. If you use Physique or Skin on your characters, this will still work. If your character is moving great distances, you might want to link the Look At controllers to the head bone also, so that they follow the body around. How you link your constraints and bones totally depends on the scene, and this is where you use the flexibility of your setup to conform to the demands of the scene.

To see a completed version of this eye setup, open the file Facial_EYES_OK.max on the accompanying CD.

Texture-Mapped Pupils

You can also assign a texture map to the eyeballs to create a pupil. You can do this now with MAX R3's new map channels. The map channels enable many maps with many different UVW mappings to be applied to the same object. The eye on the chapter's little girl character has a black map with an opacity map applied to it to create the pupil. This map lies on top of the iris map, which is solid. The opacity map for the pupil lets the iris appear wherever the pupil is not.

To dilate this pupil, you simply adjust an Xform gizmo placed on the eye. To see how this is done, you can open the file FACIAL_PUPILS_OK.max. This file has an Xform modifier applied on top of the bottom Edit Mesh in the stack. The Xform acts on the pupil selection in the Edit Mesh. By scaling this Xform, you can dilate the pupil. Remember to place another Edit Mesh on top of the Xform, or the Space Warp that elongates the whole eye shape will elongate only the selected pupil faces.

Making the Lids Move Smoothly

Another issue you must consider when designing natural-looking internal eyes is the movement of the eyelids. They must move on an arc that is the same radius as the eye. The best method for animating an internal eyelid is to use morphing. Morphing is the cleanest and most streamlined choice because it involves only one track in the Track View. Keep in mind that the arc of the motion begins with the center and front part of the lid leading the motion; the corners of the lid follow this motion at a slower rate.

As discussed earlier, two main muscles move the eyelids: The orbicularis oculi squint and compress both lids, and the levator palpebrea pulls the upper lid up from its relaxed pose of being closed. The lightest way to animate the eyelids is to create morph targets that resemble these poses. You can do this using the NURMS control mesh techniques described earlier (in the tutorial on creating the zygomatic major pose). Remember that morph targets are linear and will move in the most direct line from one pose to another, so you will have to pull control points out as well as down in order to puff out the lid as it closes over the arc of the eyeball.

External Eyes

Eyes for which the lids are not attached to the surface of the face are termed *external eyes*. Using external eyes can simplify things considerably when it comes to animation, because separate lids are typically a hemisphere that can be fitted quite easily to the lid. Rotating the lid allows it to move across the surface of the eyeball quite easily.

The best way to model a set of external eyes is to create a hierarchy structure. The first part of this structure is the actual eyeball. To follow along with this description, load the file called 05max01.max and explore the stack of each object to study the settings (see Figure 5.41).

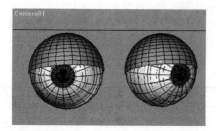

Figure 5.41   External eyes.

Tutorial: Modeling External Eyes

The eyes you will create in the following tutorial are simply constructed eyes that can be used in a variety of situations. The lids of these eyes are not directly attached to the surface of the face; rather, they are separate objects linked to the eyeballs themselves. This allows for simple construction and gives the lids the capability to change shape along with the eyes so the lids follow the surface exactly, even when the eyes are scaled to an oblong shape.

1. From the Geometry Creation panel, create a standard sphere that is 30 units in diameter and has 32 radial subdivisions. Name this sphere R-Eye.

2. Select the sphere and then Shift-click the sphere to clone it as a copy. Name this object R-Eyelid.

3. Select the copy, being careful not to move it. (If you accidentally jog it, you might want to use Grid Snap to align the two pivots exactly.) Within the Modify panel, increase the diameter to 31 units.

4. Remaining in the Modify panel, set the Hemisphere spinner to 0.5. This makes the eyelid half a sphere.

5. Clone the object R-Eye again to make the pupil. Name this object R-EyePupil.

6. Set the diameter of this object to 30.5 units and the hemisphere to 0.9.

7. Select R-Eyelid and R-EyePupil and link them to R-Eye.

8. Duplicate these three objects to make the left eye.

9. Save the file for later use.

Because the objects all rotate around the same center, eye rotation is as simple as rotating the pupil, and blinking is as simple as rotating the lid.

Attaching Pupils via SurfDeform and Conform

Although creating the pupil as a hemisphere (as you did in the previous exercise) can work quite well, there are other methods for attaching a pupil to an eye. Two of these methods use new features of MAX to create a pupil that moves along the surface of the eyeball, regardless of the eyeball's shape.

SurfDeform is a powerful World Space modifier that comes with MAX. It works well with a NURBS surface to create a pupil that moves across the eyeball's surface as an Animation option. Conform does the same thing with polygonal meshes and is a Space Warp (see Figure 5.42).

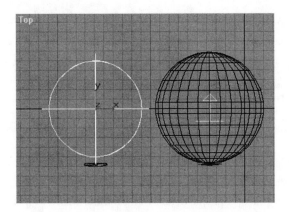

Figure 5.42   SurfDeform helps you attach a pupil to an eyeball.

1. From the Front viewport, create a sphere with a radius of 50. Place this at the origin (X,Y,Z coordinates 0,0,0).

2. From the Modify panel, turn the sphere into a NURBS sphere by right-clicking the Edit Stack icon and selecting NURBS Surface.

3. At the origin, create a cylinder with a radius of 15 and height of 1.

4. With the cylinder still selected, add a SurfDeform modifier to the stack.

5. From within the SurfDeform rollout, toggle Pick Surface and select the sphere.

6. The cylinder is now deformed to the surface of the sphere. Moving the cylinder in x and y, move the cylinder along the sphere. You can "dilate" the pupil by adjusting the U and V Stretch values within the rollout.

The second technique uses the Conform space warp to link the pupil to the eyeball sphere and make it rotate on the eyeball's axis. Although SurfDeform requires that the eyeball be a NURBS surface, Conform also works on any deformable surface, including polygonal surfaces.

1. From the Front viewport, create a sphere with a radius of 50. Place this at the origin (X,Y,Z coordinates 0,0,0).

2. At the origin, create a cylinder with a radius of 15 and height of 1.

3. From the Create/Space Warps panel, create a Conform Space Warp, also at the origin.

4. From the Top viewport, select the Conform Space Warp and orient it so that the arrow points toward the back of the sphere (points upward in the Top viewport).

5. With the Conform Space Warp still selected, activate the Modify panel. From the Conform Parameters rollout, toggle Pick Object and select the sphere.

6. Select the cylinder and bind it to the Conform Space Warp.

7. Translate the cylinder toward the front of the sphere. When it hits the surface, it conforms. As you move the cylinder, it stays on the surface of the sphere, but only through a 180-degree range of motion.

Not only can these two tools be applied to pupils, but they can be used to stick any object to a face. Because they both take into account the deformation of that surface, they work much better than a simple hierarchy. Some other facial details that can be attached in this manner are eyebrows, the nose, facial blemishes such as a wart, or perhaps a mustache. For reference, examples of both of these exercises are located in the file 05max02.max.

Animating with the UVW Gizmo

Another method for animating eyes is to use the Texture mapped method. An animation can be controlled by the UVW coordinates if desired. This way you can create a texture map and move it on both eyes in sync with one another as long as the same texture map and the same mapping coordinates are applied. Referring to the 05max03.max file in the Materials Editor, click the material called Iris. Under the Materials/Maps/Map /Coordinates rollout, you will see spinners for the UV Offset. By moving these spinners, you move the texture map left and right and up and down on the surface of the eyeball. It doesn't take much to move the map. A span of −0.05 to 0.05 with the U Offset spinner moves the texture map up and down on the eyeballs. Likewise, a span of −0.08 to 0.08 with the V Offset spinner moves the texture map right and left on the eyeballs. These controls are animatable and create editable keys in the Track View. This UVW Coordinate motion can be modified in the UVW modifier to create separate motion from right and left eyes as well.

Forehead and Facial Wrinkles

Another great option for additional facial animation is to use Texture Bump maps to create wrinkles on the skin. If you need to make the forehead crinkle when the brow takes on an angry pose, connect the height of the Wrinkle Bump map to the height of a Forehead spinner in the Morpher modifier via an expression or scripting. You can also try to animate the Bump map with a Morpher modifier material and create the Bump from 0.0 to 1.0 as the forehead needs to crease.

Keys to Successful Facial Animation

Four basic factors affect animating the face. If you use these four approaches to facial animation, your character's face will come alive quickly and with more ease than ever before. The four techniques are:

- Layering
- Individual muscles
- Asymmetry
- Weighting

These will help you create the most effective and solid facial animation possible. Layering helps you divide the tasks ahead of you into smaller jobs, making it easier to keep the motion intact and keep it from becoming mushy. You character will have more snap if you approach the animation in layers just like you do when you animate the walk. Isolation of the individual muscle groups helps you create facial animation that mimics life and does not paint you into a corner by limiting the kinds of poses you can create. Asymmetry is important to mimicking real life because no face rests or moves at the same rate all over. Your facial animation will look very mechanical if you do not implement asymmetry into your rig. Finally, weighting the values of each muscle target in both the negative and positive is important to maximizing your targets and their potential.

Layering

Layering facial movement is an extremely useful addition to an animator's bag of tricks. Layering enables you to infuse your character with the many subtle movements—psychological flutters, if you will—that occur in a real person's face. These subtleties provide the viewer with visual cues about what the character is really thinking.

When you base all facial movement on the appropriate muscles independent of one another and the phonemes the character will "speak," you can truly infuse emotion into the dialogue. In other words, you can animate the same dialogue as angry, happy, disgusted, or surprised, without affecting the lip sync. Also, using muscles independently enables you to concentrate more on layering. If you create and perfect the lip sync first and then evoke the character's personality through facial expressions (starting with the lower face and then working with the upper face), you can *layer* the personality on top of the mechanics and timing of the dialogue. This layering process eliminates the "mushiness" that occurs when the face is animated all at once.

Individual Muscles

A facial design based on individual muscles instead of complete expressions provides you with unlimited use and power. Breaking the face into individual muscles will enable you to create the many different levels of a single emotion.

For instance, a face frozen into a final "happy" pose looks mechanical and makes it impossible for you to infuse the subtleties of real emotions that change over time. By animating the effects of muscles individually, you can create deeper levels of the happy emotion, such as false happiness, sly smiling, or utter joy.

MAX's tools offer even more power. Through scripting, you can generate many starting point poses, such as joy or sadness. MAX's Morpher tool then enables manipulation of those starting poses so you can mix in the effects of other simulated muscles to create such expressions as a bittersweet smile or surprise that is dazzled or amazed instead of fearful.

Asymmetry

An asymmetrical facial setup creates a much more realistically emotive character. Each muscle has a left and right counterpart in this setup, which enables you to produce more "cock-eyed" poses. The expressions for contempt, cynicism, haughtiness, impatience, jealousy, mistrust, questioning, skepticism, and suspicion all use at least one half of the face. In other words, with asymmetry, you can get that Jack Nicholson-esque pose you always wanted: that contemptuous, one-eyebrow-cocked, sneering, look with a debauched smile.

Weighting

The ability to weight each value of a target in the negative and positive is a huge leap for animation controls. The negative and positive extremes of each weight can extend the amount of poses you can create to an infinite amount. This function can also make an entire setup light because a negative value of one target might provide for the positive of another, eliminating extra targets.

In addition, the Morpher tool in MAX enables you to weight the many targets and mix their responses. This makes for a really interactive and unlimited tool for facial demands. By using this new tool with individual muscle-based targets, you should be able to create anything the animation demands.

In Practice: Facial Animation

- **Facial anatomy.** Understanding the skeletal and muscular structures of the face is pertinent to creating a solid facial rig.

- **Morpher.** Using the Morpher modifier will create a streamlined, light, and flexible facial setup.

- **Muscle targets.** By creating strong targets for the Morpher modifier that isolate the muscles, you will provide yourself with power and flexibility to create any facial pose your scene demands.

- **Phonemes.** Understanding phonemes and which ones to use with the established muscle target setup will take you to the next level in facial animation.

- **Jaw bone.** Opening the jaw for an "AH" using an actual bone and a dummy constraint controller will give you more control for sliding and slight rotations on the jaw, as well as the usual opening of the jaw. This setup enables the to character scream or whisper a line of dialogue.

- **Tongue.** Use morph targets for the tongue to get the "LA" and "TH" sounds.

- **Breaking down the track.** Track reading and using the Audio controller to quickly break down a sound file will help you nail the dialogue and its inflections, as well as keep track of what is going on in the line for both the facial and body motion.

Chapter 6

Animating with Biped

By Sean Miller

Character Studio's Biped module gives you

the freedom to easily create and animate

"smart" two-legged skeletons. Skeletons typ-

ically use either Forward Kinematics, explic-

itly rotating each joint in a skeleton, or Inverse

Kinematics, which calculates the position

of the limbs, based on the placement of

their extremities. The position of the arm, therefore, is controlled by the position of the hand. To approach life-like motion of the limbs, you must configure the constraints on each skeleton joint to restrict the rotation to the appropriate axis (knees bend but do not twist) and set the appropriate limits for each axis (knees bend backward but not forward). Even with these constraints properly configured, achieving life-like animation can still be difficult, simply because when it's animated, a skeleton still needs to retain qualities such as balance and weight.

Inverse Kinematics knows nothing about the skeleton other than that it is a collection of joints. As such, it is easy to put the skeleton in a pose that is quite out of balance. An example of this is the forward rotation of the spine. Unless the hips move backward as the spine is rotated, a bipedal animal quickly becomes out of balance, and the resulting pose looks unnatural.

Biped not only enables automatic construction of "smart" humanoid skeletons with a built-in IK system, it also allows you to customize the skeleton's structural details (such as the number of fingers and toes) and whether the biped has a tail or even ponytails. Biped is an easy-to-use system that separates animation from character, so you can animate a dance and apply it to an ape or a dinosaur, a giant or a baby, and it will still work.

Two types of animation are available using Biped. You can create a bipedal skeleton and animate in a freeform way using Forward and Inverse Kinematics to position the skeleton any way you want. There is also an automatic animation system based on footsteps, which novice animators can use to create instant walking, running, or jumping animation. Advanced professional animators can also use this as a starting point for creating expressive motion sequences. In addition, professionals will appreciate the ability to work with motion capture files using the Motion Flow Editor to sequence, blend, and transition any motion file.

Tip

Applying Biped's Footsteps to motion capture data is a great way to lock down the character's feet and prevent the sliding that is common to many Motion Capture data files. For more information on this topic, see "Working with Motion Capture Data" later in this chapter.

The IK system used in Biped is designed specifically for animating bipeds and takes into account the mechanics and restrictions of how bipedal animals move. Integral to Biped is the handling of gravity and the biped's center of mass. This enables Biped to interpolate the position of the biped properly when both feet are off the ground and to dynamically balance the biped about the center of mass to achieve life-like motions.

This chapter covers the following topics:

- Creating a biped

- Manipulating a biped

- Animating a biped with footsteps

- Performing freeform animation of a biped

- Converting Biped animations

- Using animatable IK attachments

- Using libraries of biped animation

- Working with motion capture data

- Animating with layers

Creating a Biped

The Biped Creation button is located under the Systems button in the Create panel. To create a biped, click the Biped button to activate the Biped Creation tool. Then in the active viewport, press the left mouse button and drag. A box appears, indicating the size of the biped. Release the mouse button to generate the Biped skeleton.

The Create Biped panel (see Figure 6.1) enables you to configure the skeleton exactly to your needs. This includes details such as how many segments are in the spine and neck, how many fingers and toes, whether the character has a tail and the number of links in that tail, and whether the character has arms. (A bird, for example, has no arms.) These same options are also available after creation in the Structure rollout of the Motion panel. Another important parameter to consider is the Leg Links spinner, which determines how the legs are configured. This has two settings: 3 and 4. A human has a setting of 3 (thigh, shin, and foot), and some birds or dinosaurs have a setting of 4 because the foot bone is extended into their legs and they actually walk on their toes (thigh, shin, tarsal, and foot).

Once it's created, the biped can be controlled through the Motion panel (see Figure 6.2). Select any part of the biped, and all the controls for manipulating and animating the biped appear. Because

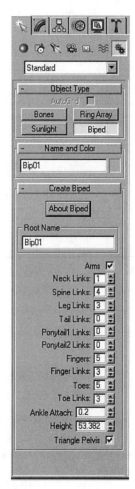

Figure 6.1
From within the Create Biped panel, you can change the structure of the biped.

Biped is essentially a very sophisticated Animation controller, its controls appear on the Motion panel instead of on the Modify panel.

Manipulating a Biped

Bipeds have their own built-in IK, completely separate from MAX's native IK. This system has been configured to give smooth, controllable, predictable motion. Biped's IK always works in real time, and there is no need to apply IK as you might within MAX's native IK. The joints of a biped can be manipulated through translation, rotation, and by using footsteps.

With Biped's IK, if you adjust a biped's arm by moving the hand, the position of the arm and hand returns to the exact starting position if you return the hand to its original position. An additional feature of Biped is the use of IK Blend to blend between Forward and Inverse Kinematics. This feature enables you to link a hand or foot to another object so that hand or foot will follow the object. The amount of IK blending is animatable, so the hand or foot can effectively be attached and detached from the object over time. This enables you to easily animate the biped catching and throwing a ball, dancing with a partner, or performing other actions where the biped interacts with other objects in the scene. The section "Attaching the Hands and Feet to MAX Objects" (later in this chapter) describes IK Blend further.

Translating a biped's joints is straightforward: Grab the joint and move it. The joints moved need not be constrained with end effects or terminators for the joint to move properly. All that intelligence is built into the biped. You can just as easily move the biceps as the pinky and still retain a single, predictable solution for the limb, no matter how many joints the move affects.

Before you can move the biped itself, the Center of Mass object must be selected and moved (see Figure 6.3). Rather than a hip-centric model, Biped uses the center of mass as the top of the hierarchy. As such, the pelvis itself is not translatable. The

Figure 6.2
Selecting the Motion tab brings up the Biped Control panel.

tetrahedral-shaped object found near the center of the pelvis represents the biped's center of mass. Translating this object accomplishes the same effect as moving the pelvis on a hip-centric skeleton.

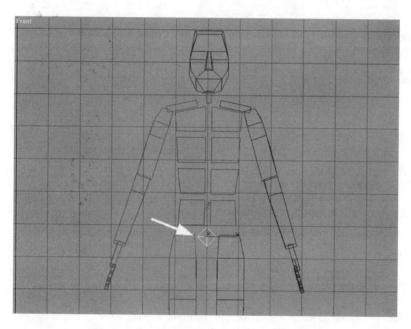

Figure 6.3   To move the biped's body, the Center of Mass object (arrow) must be moved (not the pelvis). The Center of Mass object is represented by a tetrahedron.

Rotating joints is also possible, giving you the flexibility of positioning a skeleton by using any combination of Forward or Inverse Kinematics. Translating joints on the fingers, for example, normally causes a translation of the entire arm. For motions such as hand gestures, rotations are required.

Another thing to be aware of is that not all biped joints can be translated, and not every joint can rotate around every axis. The restrictions on translating joints are that only the Center of Mass object and the leg and arm joints (except for the clavicles) can be translated. The restrictions on rotating joints are more involved. In general, if you cannot rotate a joint in your body about an axis, you cannot rotate the same joint in the biped about that axis. The following are special rotations or restrictions:

- **Elbows and knees.** The elbow and knee joints can be rotated both on their local z-axis (like a hinge) and along their local x-axis (along their length). When they're rotated along their local x-axis, the rotation does not occur at that joint.

Instead the upper and lower leg/arm are rotated together along an axis formed by the hip/shoulder and ankle/wrist.

- **Feet.** If the foot is planted on a footstep, the foot can be rotated on its local y- and z-axes. The foot remains in contact with the footstep, and the leg joints are rotated to maintain the position of the pelvis. A foot cannot be rotated on its local x-axis if the foot is planted.

- **Legs.** If a foot is planted and a leg is rotated, the rotation may be limited to ensure that the foot remains in contact with the footstep.

When a joint is selected, the disallowed motions are grayed out on the menu bar, which can prove a bit frustrating for the novice. When you understand the restrictions, however, nearly any pose can be effectively attained.

Other Biped Selection and Manipulation Tools

In addition to the standard MAX translation and rotation tools, the Biped Motion panel contains the following Biped-specific tools to assist in manipulating your skeletons:

- **Center of Mass.** Found under the Track Selection rollout, these three buttons select the biped's Center of Mass object and enable the Horizontal, Vertical, and Rotational tracks separately. Sometimes, it's difficult to locate the Center of Mass object in a complex scene; this button speeds the process.

- **Symmetrical Tracks.** Found under the Track Selection rollout, this button mirrors the current selection on the opposite side of the body. For example, if the left leg is selected, clicking Symmetrical Tracks adds the right leg to the selection.

- **Opposite Tracks.** Found under the Track Selection rollout, this button selects the identical limbs on the opposite side of the body. For example, if the right arm is selected, clicking the Opposite Tracks button selects the left arm and deselects the right.

- **Copy Posture.** Found on the Keyframing rollout, this handy tool enables you to copy the position of any joint or group of joints.

- **Paste Posture.** Found on the Keyframing rollout, this tool enables you to paste copied postures to another point in the animation or to another biped. Copy and Paste posture are also handy for saving the state of a biped if you want to experiment with a pose. If the new pose does not work out, you can paste the original pose to return the biped to normal.

- **Paste Posture Opposite.** Found on the Keyframing rollout, this tool is almost identical to Paste Posture, except that it mirrors the pose to the opposite side of the body, enabling you to paste a pose from the right leg, for example, onto the left.

- **Bend Links.** Found on the Keyframing rollout, this tool evenly bends linked joints, such as the spine, the tail, or a multi-jointed neck (see Figure 6.4). Activating the Bend Links button causes all the joints in the section (the joints in the spine, for example) to be evenly adjusted when you adjust a single joint.

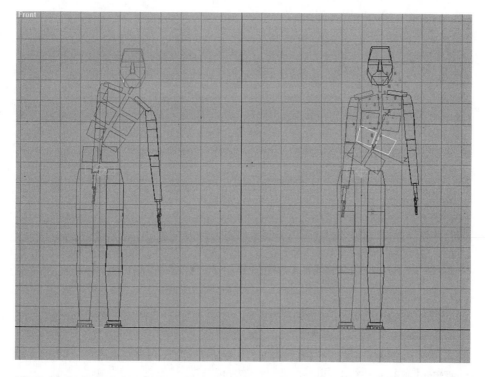

Figure 6.4   In these bipeds, a single spine joint is rotated without (left) and with (right) Bend Links enabled. Bend Links mode makes even rotations of the spine possible.

Animating a Biped

There are many ways to animate a biped. Creating and adjusting footsteps is the obvious method; however, you can also freeform animate bipeds without footsteps. This, however, is a one-way street: After you add keys to a freeform animation, you cannot add footsteps to that biped's animation at a later point. If you are in doubt as to whether footsteps should be used in an animation, it is best to assume they should and to create a freeform area between footsteps. This section takes you through the process of animating with footsteps and freeform animation.

> **Tip**
>
> With Character Studio 2.2, you can now move freely between footsteps and freeform animation using the Convert tool in the Motion panel's General rollout. See "Converting Biped Animations" for more details.

Animating with Footsteps

Footsteps enable you to take advantage of Biped's built-in dynamics to create quasi-realistic motion. The walks, runs, and jumps created by Biped are purposely generic because Biped is a tool that tries not to force a specific style on the animator. The keys automatically generated from footsteps are the minimum required to achieve the motion. This enables you to add the desired characteristics without having to delete the many keys that would have to be generated to achieve a realistic default motion. Instead, these keys should be thought of as a motion "sketch" that can be easily modified.

To create footsteps, activate the Footstep Creation rollouts by clicking the Footstep Track button within the Track Selection. This enables the Footsteps Sub-Object for the selected biped. This means that only footsteps may be selected, created, or manipulated while the Footstep Track button is toggled. After this button has been toggled on, you are free to create footsteps.

Creating Footsteps

There are two methods of creation (footstep creation and adjustment) along with three types of footsteps: walk, run, and jump. The different types of footsteps represent the different timings for the footsteps. Again, you should think of the footstep timing and placement as an easily modified motion "sketch."

- **Walk.** One foot always remains planted, while the other swings forward. At least one foot is always on the ground. There can also be a section in the walk motion—called Double Support—when both feet are on the ground. Both the number of frames in which each footstep remains on the ground (Walk Footstep) and the number of frames in a double support period (Double Support) are defined by spinners that are activated when the Footstep Track button is toggled on.

- **Run.** One foot is on the ground at a time with no double support. There is also a point in the cycle when both feet are airborne. Both the number of frames that each footstep remains on the ground (Run Footstep) and the number of frames that the biped is airborne (Airborne) are defined by spinners that are activated when the Footstep Track button is toggled on.

- **Jump.** Both feet are on the ground equally and are airborne equally. The number of frames that both feet are on the ground (2 Feet Down) and the number of frames that the biped is airborne (Airborne) are defined by spinners that are activated when Footstep Track is toggled on.

Biped footsteps can be created singly or in multiples. When creating a set of single footsteps, you can append the footstep in time to the current footsteps, or you can create it starting at the current frame. Each method has its own button, as described here:

- **Create Footsteps (append).** This button enables you to lay down footsteps by clicking a viewport—a good method for creating footsteps over tricky terrain or for complex motions such as dance steps. Footsteps are appended to any current footsteps.

- **Create Footsteps (at current frame).** Same as Create Footsteps (append), except that footsteps are added starting at the current frame. If the footstep being added overlaps in time with an existing footstep, an alert appears, and the footstep is not created.

- **Create Multiple Footsteps.** This button creates a user-defined number of footsteps with user-specified spacing and timing. Footsteps created in this manner run along a straight line and are best for walking a character through a scene.

Tip

Using the Interpolate option in the Create Multiple Footsteps dialog box, you can change the stride length, stride height, and timing of the footsteps over the footsteps being created.

Activating Footsteps

After a series of footsteps has been laid down, the footsteps must be activated. To activate footsteps, click the Create Keys for Inactive Footsteps button in the Footstep Operations rollout. Activation computes dynamics for the biped for any footsteps that have been created but not yet activated, adding a Footstep track and creating keys within Track View for the biped. After you activate footsteps, you can still modify the walk by manipulating the footsteps or keys. If new footsteps are added after activation, those footsteps must also be activated.

Creating a Simple Walk

You can always get instant gratification from Biped by creating a few footsteps and activating them. The following simple task makes a biped walk and gives you a supply of footsteps with which to work.

1. Load 06max01.max from the accompanying CD-ROM. This file contains a biped and a ground plane.

2. Select any portion of the biped. Then, select the Motion tab to bring up the Biped Motion panel.

3. Footsteps are created and modified from within Footstep mode. Click the Footstep mode button under the General rollout. When this button is toggled on, it enables Sub-Object Footsteps selection on the biped. While you're in Footstep mode, only footsteps can be selected and modified.

4. There are two ways to create footsteps: single footsteps manually placed with the mouse, or multiple footsteps automatically placed. Footsteps can be one of three types: walk, run, or jump. Click the Walk button in the Footstep Creation rollout.

5. The fastest way to create footsteps is with the Create Multiple Footsteps button. This creates a number of footsteps with user-specified spacing and timing that can be modified and manipulated later. Click this button to display the Create Multiple Footsteps dialog box. Enter 10 for the number of footsteps, make certain that the Start Left option is chosen in the General section, and click OK.

6. Ten numbered footsteps appear, which need to be activated for the biped to follow them. To do this, click the Create Keys for Inactive Footsteps button in the Footstep Operations rollout (see Figure 6.5).

7. Right-click to activate the Left viewport and play the animation. The biped now follows these footsteps. Instant gratification!

Appending to an Animation

You can append to Biped-created animations quite easily. It is simply a matter of creating additional footsteps and activating them.

1. Click the Run button and then the Create Multiple Footsteps button. Enter 4 for the number of footsteps (if it isn't already there), choose the Start after Last Footstep option in the Timing section, and click OK. This appends four footsteps to the end of the animation. Activate the new footsteps.

2. Zoom extents the Left viewport and plays back the animation. As you might notice, the biped changes from a walking to a running gait for the new footsteps.

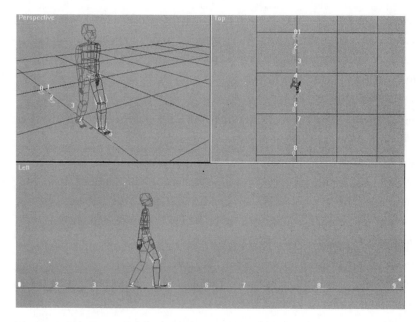

Figure 6.5   When you activate the footsteps, the biped walks.

3. Click the Jump button and then the Create Multiple Footsteps button. For the number of footsteps, enter 2. Then activate the footsteps.

4. Zoom extents the Left viewport and plays back the animation. The biped now ends the run with a small jump.

An example of this animation is stored on the accompanying CD-ROM in the file named 06max02.max. Choose Edit/Hold to put a copy of your work into the Hold buffer, and then you can look at the other file if you want.

Modifying Footsteps

Once activated, the footsteps can be moved and modified on-the-fly, and Biped will adjust the biped to match the footsteps automatically.

1. Using the animation you just created, go to the Display panel and click Unhide All. A small platform with a staircase appears. Play back the animation. The biped should walk right through the stairs because Biped just follows the footsteps, which are laid in a straight line across the ground. Biped does not perform collision detection with other objects in the scene.

2. This obstacle can be overcome quite easily by adjusting the footsteps. Zoom in the platform in the Left viewport. Select any part of the biped and, in the Motion

panel, toggle the Footstep Track button on. Using the standard MAX selection tools, select footsteps 3 through 15. Move these up so that footstep 3 resides on the first step of the platform. Select footsteps 4 through 15 and move these up so that footstep 4 lies on the second step. Repeat until all the footsteps are properly positioned on the stairs.

3. Play the animation. The biped now walks up the stairs and then runs off the edge of the platform. This can also be adjusted quite easily.

4. Select the biped, go to the Motion panel, and enter Footstep mode. Select footsteps 6 through 8. In the Footstep Operations rollout, adjust the Bend spinner to 30. The selected footsteps automatically bend. Footsteps before footstep 6 are not affected, and footsteps after footstep 8 are rotated to maintain their alignment with footstep 8.

5. Play the animation. Notice how the biped automatically banks as it goes through the turn. A problem still exists, however. The biped still runs off the end of the platform and jumps from and lands in midair.

6. In the Front viewport, select footsteps 9 through 13. In the Footstep Operations rollout, turn off the Width option and adjust the Scale spinner so that footstep 13 resides precisely on the edge of the platform. When you clear the check box for the Width option, the width between footsteps remains the same as the footsteps are scaled downward.

7. Now select footsteps 14 and 15, which are still in midair off the edge of the platform. Move these down so they lie level with the ground plane (see Figure 6.6).

Play the animation. The biped now walks up the stairs, rounds a corner, runs, and jumps off the edge. Not bad for a few minutes worth of work.

What has this demonstrated? First, by moving the footsteps up the stairs, you saw that footsteps are sub-objects that can be manipulated either individually or in groups. The footsteps can be moved and rotated anywhere in the scene to account for uneven terrain. Also, groups of footsteps can be scaled and bent quite easily by using the Bend and Scale spinners in the Footstep Operations rollout. The final animation is on the accompanying CD-ROM in a file called 06max03.max.

Individual footsteps or a selected set of footsteps can also be rotated using Select and Rotate. Rotating the footsteps this way is different than using the Bend spinner in that the unselected footsteps are not moved or rotated. When a selected set of footsteps is rotated in this way, the rotation pivot point is the pivot point of the footstep that the mouse cursor is over when you click and drag. If you change the Transform Coordinate Center from Use Pivot Point Center to Use Selection Center and you choose Local Reference coordinate system, each footstep is rotated about its local pivot point. Go figure.

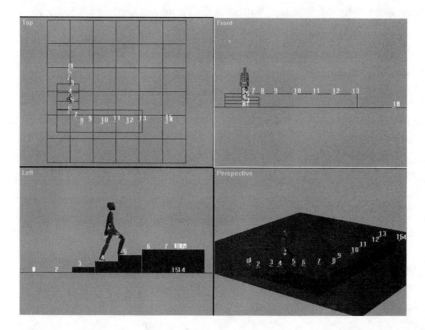

Figure 6.6 Obstacles such as stairs can be overcome quite easily by repositioning the footsteps.

Copying and Pasting Footsteps

Biped enables you to select a set of footsteps, copy those footsteps to a buffer, and splice the footsteps into either the middle or end of the footstep sequence. You can even copy and splice a set of footsteps from one biped to another. The section "Saving and Loading Canned Motions," later in this chapter, provides an example of this.

In this example, you copy and splice footsteps on a single biped.

1. Load 06max04.max from the accompanying CD-ROM. This file contains a biped that walks forward, turns left, and walks a bit farther. For this exercise, you want the biped to turn left again near the end of the animation.

2. Select any portion of the biped, and then select the Motion tab to access the Biped Motion panel. Click the Footstep mode button in the General Selection rollout.

3. Maximize the Top viewport and select footsteps 4 through 8. To be able to splice a set of footsteps into the middle of a sequence, the first and last footsteps selected need to be for the same leg.

4. Click the Copy Selected Footsteps button in the Footstep Operations rollout to place the selected footsteps into the Footstep buffer.

5. Click the Paste Footsteps button in the Footstep Operations rollout. A copy of the footsteps in the buffer appears in the viewport.

6. Rotate the footsteps 90° about the z-axis.

7. Using the Move tool, click and drag the footsteps so that the first footstep is over the biped's footstep number 12. This target footstep turns red to signify that a splice is possible (see Figure 6.7). Release the mouse button.

   The first buffer footstep replaces the target footstep, and the remaining buffer footsteps follow. The original footsteps after the target footstep are automatically copied into the footstep buffer and are now available to paste.

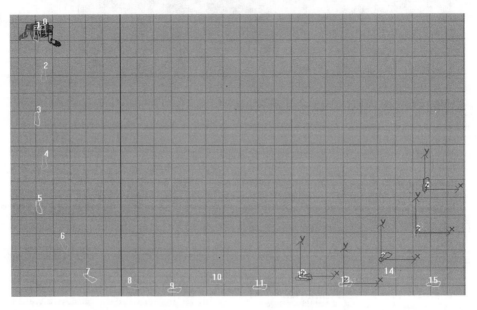

Figure 6.7   When you move the first pasted footstep over a valid target footstep, the target footstep turns red.

8. Rotate the footsteps 90° about the z-axis.

9. Using the Move tool, click and drag the footsteps so that the first footstep is over the biped's footstep 16. Release the mouse button. The buffer footsteps are now spliced on to the end of the animation.

10. Minimize the Top viewport. Click the Perspective viewport to activate it and play back the animation.

After you copy the footsteps into the Footstep buffer and before you paste them into the scene, you can edit the footsteps and associated keys that are in the buffer. To do this, click the Buffer Mode button in the General rollout to toggle on the Buffer mode. The footsteps in the buffer appear in the viewport, applied to the biped. In Track View, the footsteps are shown as the footsteps for the biped, and the associated keys are shown for the biped. You can edit these footsteps and keys just as you would the normal biped footsteps and keys. To return to the actual footsteps and keys for the biped, toggle off the Buffer Mode button.

Dynamics of Motion

As a biped walks, runs, or jumps, several factors affect the biped's motion: Gravitational Acceleration, Dynamics Blend, Ballistic Tension, and Balance Factor. Each of these factors affects the motion of the biped between key frames.

Note

In the Samples directory of the Character Studio CD-ROM, you can find examples of different settings for the parameters described in this section. You can experiment with the set of AVI and MAX files provided.

A walk cycle is the act of falling forward and then catching yourself. To start walking, you extend one leg forward, which shifts your center of mass forward. As your center of mass moves forward past your planted foot, you start to fall forward. The back of your planted foot lifts off the ground, whereas the ball and toes of the foot remain planted. You continue to fall forward until the heel of the moving foot hits the ground. At that point, the momentum of your body starts to pull the back leg forward, and as the back foot leaves the ground, it also pushes you forward. This back leg continues forward until it passes the front leg, and you begin to fall forward again. While one of your feet is off the ground, the other foot supports your entire weight. To maintain balance, the body arcs over the moving foot (the hip shifts toward the planted foot). Biped properly animates the hip to provide this motion (see Figure 6.8).

As you walk, the height of your pelvis (and center of mass) from the ground varies. It is at a minimum right after the front foot hits the ground, and at a maximum as the back leg passes the front leg.

A run cycle is similar to a walk cycle, except that instead of falling forward, you throw yourself forward. In a walk cycle, at least one foot is always on the ground. During a run cycle, however, there are periods in which both feet are off the ground. During these periods, you are airborne or ballistic. You move forward at a constant velocity during this airborne period, and the vertical height of your center of mass is based on how hard you "push off" and also on gravity. Leading up to this push off, your legs are typically bent more than during a walk cycle to generate more power with which to push. As the legs are bent, the center of mass also is lowered.

A jump cycle, in turn, is similar to a run cycle. The only difference is that both feet are in the air at the same time, and both hit the ground at the same time. Again, you move forward at a constant velocity during this airborne period, and the vertical height of your center of mass is based on how hard you push off and also on gravity.

When you land in a run or jump cycle, your center of mass continues downward and forward due to momentum. Your legs act like springs, absorbing this momentum.

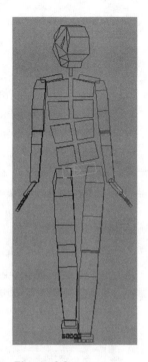

Figure 6.8
When the body is supported by only one foot, the hip swings over the planted foot to maintain proper balance.

Dynamics Blend

Biped stores both Vertical and Horizontal keys for the biped's Center of Mass object. The Horizontal keys are generated at the middle of each footstep's support period, and they provide the forward motion of the biped. The Vertical keys are generated at the start, middle, and end of each footstep. The Vertical keys store the extension of the legs and the actual vertical height of the Center of Mass object.

During walking motions, the height is interpolated based on the extension of the legs recorded at each vertical key. This ensures that the supporting leg's knee angle does not change direction between two vertical keys. In effect, when a person walks, the leg extensions (and the rising and falling foot pivots on the ground) control the height of the body in a natural way.

You can defeat this approach (or selectively blend it) with an interpolation of the actual vertical height by setting Dynamics Blend at each vertical key. At a Dynamics Blend setting of 0, Biped performs a spline interpolation of the vertical heights and ignores the leg extension information at each key. At a Dynamics Blend setting of 1, Biped interpolates the leg extension distances and ignores the vertical heights at each key. You can change the Dynamics Blend value only while the Center of Mass object is selected, Move is active, and Restrict to Z is active.

During running and jumping motions, or transitions between them, the height is always determined by the vertical heights at each key because running and jumping are governed by the requirements of gravity, the heights of the body at liftoff and touchdown, and the duration of each airborne period. For running and jumping vertical keys, therefore, Dynamics Blend is grayed-out because it is not applicable.

Gravitational Acceleration

While the biped is airborne during a run or jump cycle, the vertical dynamics are controlled by Gravitational Acceleration (GravAccel in the Animation Properties rollout of the Biped Motion panel) and the length of time between the lift and landing footsteps. If the length of time between these footsteps is shortened or the Gravitational Acceleration value is decreased, the maximum height during the airborne period is decreased (on the moon, you don't need to jump very high to cover a lot of ground). The Gravitational Acceleration value is not animatable.

Ballistic Tension

The Ballistic Tension value, found in the Body Dynamics section of the Key Info rollout, controls how "springy" the legs are before liftoff and after touchdown in run and jump cycles (see Figure 6.9). The higher the value, the stiffer the legs are, resulting in less leg bending. You can change the Ballistic Tension value only while the Body Vertical track is selected from the Track Selection rollout. This value can be set only at the touchdown key frame, unless three or more Vertical keys are set during the footprint support cycle. In this case, a Ballistic Tension value can also be set at the liftoff key frame.

Balance Factor

The Balance Factor value specifies the biped's weight distribution by positioning the biped weight anywhere along a line extending from the center of mass to the head. You can set this only when Body Horizontal is selected from the Track Selection rollout. A

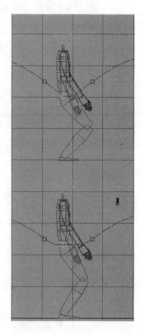

Figure 6.9
The follow-through of a landing for bipeds with a low (top biped) and high (bottom biped) Ballistic Tension.

value of 0 places the biped's weight in the feet. A value of 1 places the biped's weight over the center of mass. A value of 2 places the biped's weight in the head. The Balance Factor value has no effect on the walk, run, and jump cycle motions; however, it can be used to your advantage when you're adjusting the rotation of the spine.

Assume, for example, that a biped is sitting on a chair, and you are animating it so that it leans over a table. With the default value for Balance Factor (1.0), as you rotate the spine forward, the pelvis moves backward to maintain a constant position for the Center of Mass object. If you set the Balance Factor to 0, as you rotate the spine forward, the pelvis remains at the same location. If you attempt to do this while the biped is standing, however, the biped looks very unnatural—like it should be falling over but isn't (see Figure 6.10). The Balance Factor value is set in the Structure rollout while in Figure mode. The Balance Factor value is not animatable.

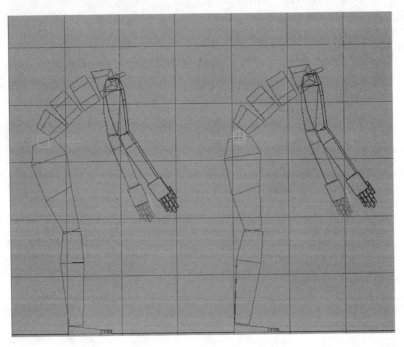

Figure 6.10   The pelvis moves back from the center of mass when the spine is bent forward for bipeds with a normal balance factor (left) and a low Balance Factor (right).

Bipeds in Track View

Although manipulating the footsteps themselves can change the walk quite a bit, the timing of a walk is also very important. A biped's timing can be changed quite radically from within Track View. When viewed as keys within Track View (see Figure 6.11), a Biped animation looks slightly different than ordinary MAX animation. When viewing a Biped animation, notice that the legs, arms, and spine do not have separate keys for each joint; Biped keys span all joints in the limbs (arms, legs, spine, and tail). A leg does not have separate keys for the thigh and shin, for example; instead, it has only one key that comprises the position of all the limb's joints. This enables Biped to transfer animation between disparate skeletons quite easily.

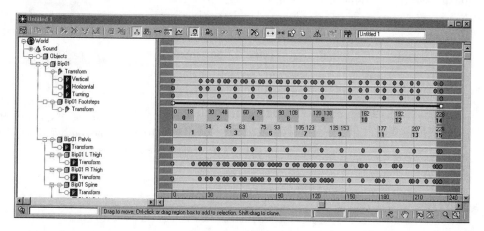

Figure 6.11   Biped tracks in Track View. The footstep keys are represented as blocks rather than dots, and locked Biped keys are highlighted in red.

Footstep Tracks

One of the more important tracks is the Footsteps track, which has a distinct appearance of alternating green and blue blocks (green blocks represent right footsteps; blue blocks represent left). The colored blocks indicate exactly when the feet are on the ground. Space between the footsteps indicates that the foot is airborne. If neither foot has a footstep at a given frame, both feet are airborne, such as in a run or a jump. Walks, by definition, always keep at least one foot on the ground, and if the blocks overlap, both feet are on the ground. Displaying the footsteps this way enables you to know exactly what the feet are doing.

A footstep key actually spans several frames and has a number of components. By default, each footstep is labeled in its center with the footstep number, and each footstep indicates the start and stop frame in the top corners.

To modify a footstep, click the center of the footstep near the footstep number and drag. Clicking the start or stop frame in the corners of the footstep enables you to modify these positions as well, affecting the duration of the footstep. As you can with any other key, you can also select, move, and resize groups of keys.

Right-clicking a footstep key brings up the Footstep Mode dialog box (see Figure 6.12), which gives you control over how the footsteps are displayed, as well as some additional selection tools. The top portion of this dialog box allows you to turn off vertical dynamics in freeform areas; it is discussed in the section "Freeform Animation," later in this chapter. The Footstep Number Display section provides options on the frame information shown for each footstep. The Footstep Edge Selection section enables you to change which portion of the previously selected footsteps remain chosen. If you have chosen three footsteps and click the Left button, for example, only the left edges of these three footsteps remain selected. You can then move these edges to increase or decrease the duration for the footsteps.

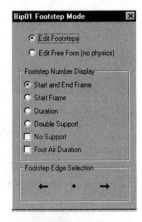

Figure 6.12
Right-clicking the Footstep track displays the Footstep Mode dialog box.

Note

Release 2.2 of Character Studio allows you to select any combination of left and right edges and generally improves footstep editing in Track View.

Other Tracks

In addition to the Footstep tracks, Biped also has another class of keys not normally found within MAX. These are keys for skeletal objects, such as the legs, and are calculated by Biped and shown in red. Called *locked keys*, these are keys that Biped requires to perform its calculations. The locked keys cannot be moved or deleted except by changing the footsteps themselves. If you edit a Footstep track, the locked keys appear and disappear as the track changes. Finally, Biped also creates normal MAX keys (shown in gray). These are for skeletal elements, such as the arms, spine, and head. These keys can be edited, moved, or deleted like any other MAX keys.

To access the Biped Multiple Keys dialog box (shown in Figure 6.13), use the Set Multiple Keys tool in the Keyframing rollout. This dialog box allows you to use a set of filters to select keys within the Track View. It also lets you apply the last transform performed on a portion of the biped to a selected set of keys.

The Tracks section in Select Multiple Keys defines which Biped tracks in the animation are marked for selection. Use this to select the keys for the Biped's Left Leg, Right Leg,

Body Horizontal, and Body Vertical tracks, in any combination. If you want a character's walking body to bounce up and down more, for example, check the Body Vertical box.

Figure 6.13 The Biped Multiple Keys dialog box enables you to quickly select and change the values of multiple keys.

State filters define which portion of the step is selected. Biped divides keys created by footsteps into four states defined by the major movement of the leg. These are not to be confused with the major poses of a walk described in the previous chapters—planted, passing, and lifted. States define where the foot contacts and leaves the ground, not the pose of the body. The states are described here:

- **Touch.** The point in the step where the forward foot first touches the ground.
- **Plant.** Any key where the leg is planted on the ground. These will always be between the touch and lift keys.
- **Lift.** Where the planted leg lifts off the ground.
- **Move.** Any key where the leg is completely off the ground and between Footsteps.

By using a combination of Tracks and State selections, you can select and modify multiple keys. You can change the character of an entire walk quite easily yet keep the walk consistent.

Biped records the last mouse movement and moved body part whenever you do anything with a biped. When you click Apply Increment, Biped applies that mouse move and updates each selected key in Track View that matches the same moved body part type. If you have keys selected on both arms and legs and you move or rotate an arm and perform an Apply Increment, only the selected keys on the arms are modified.

In general, you should never be in Animate mode or use Set Key if you are attempting to just modify a selected set of keys in a uniform way. If you actually set a key when performing the move that is going to be applied to the entire set, the increment of that key happens twice: once for the Set Key and again for the Apply Increment. Select a set of keys, perform some interactive transform on the body part in question, and click Apply Increment. If you do set a key when the interactive move is performed (either via Set Key or if Animate is turned on), the key for that frame should not be selected in Track View when you perform the Apply Increment.

The frame number or key frame for this "last recorded mouse move + body part" makes no difference because Biped is really just recording the "increment," not the actual posture. It is usually convenient, however, to adjust the increment relative to a particular key frame.

Note

In release 2.2 of Character Studio, if you have keys selected for opposing body limbs (such as both legs) and you perform more than one Apply Increment, the first key on the limb opposing the one transformed is not properly modified. If you perform the transform with Animate turned on (and you deselect the modified key in Track View), Apply Increment properly updates the keys.

You may have noticed in the last example that the biped's feet were passing through the steps as the biped walked up the stairs. In the following exercise, you use the Change Multiple Keys dialog box to correct this.

1. Load the file 06max03.max, which is the platform animation created previously.

2. Maximize the Left viewport and zoom in to the area of footsteps 2 through 6. Advance to frame 40.

3. Open Track View and right-click the Filters button. Choose Animated Tracks Only. Right-click Objects and choose Expand All. Scroll the Track View windows to display the Footsteps track and the left and right thigh Transform tracks.

4. Select the right foot in the viewport. Note that in Track View, there is already a key for the left at this frame. Because the foot is off the ground, this is a Move state key.

5. Select a limb of the biped, and, in the Select Multiple Keys section, check Left Leg and Right Leg under Tracks and select Move under State Filters. Click the Select button. All the Move state keys on the right and left legs are selected in Track View.

6. The set of selected keys contains more keys than you want to adjust. Deselect the keys at and before frame 40. Deselect the keys after frame 108 (the right edge of footstep 6 is at frame 108). Deselect the last key currently selected on the right leg (see Figure 6.14).

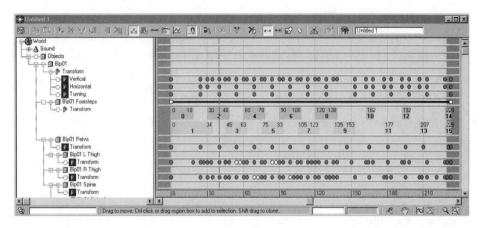

Figure 6.14 The keys on the left and right legs that are selected when you perform the first Apply Increment.

7. Click the Animate button to turn on Animate mode. Move the right foot up two units on the World Z axis.

8. Click Apply Increment in the Change Multiple Keys dialog box.

9. Advance to frame 54 and select the left foot. Move the left foot 10 units on the World Y axis and up one unit on the World Z axis.

10. In Track View, deselect the second key in each pair of keys currently selected. Deselect the left leg key at frame 54 (see Figure 6.15).

11. Click Apply Increment in the Change Multiple Keys dialog box.

12. Play the animation. It's better, but it still needs some refinement.

13. Move to frame 57 and select left leg in the Change Multiple Keys dialog box. Set the State Filter to Move.

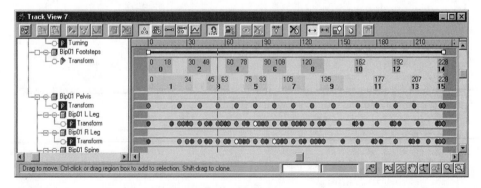

Figure 6.15 The keys on the left and right legs that are selected when you perform the second Apply Increment.

14. Deselect the first of each pair of currently selected keys, as well as the key at 57 and all keys after 108. Move the left foot up 5 units on the z-axis and click Apply Increment in the Change Multiple Keys dialog box.

15. Go to frame 72 and select the right foot. In the Change Multiple Key dialog box, select the right leg and set the State filter to Move.

16. Deselect the key at frame 72, move the right foot −2 on the y-axis and up 4 on the z-axis, and then click on Apply Increment.

17. Play the animation. As the biped walks up the stairs, his feet should no longer pass through the stairs.

The final animation is on the accompanying CD-ROM in the file 06max05.max.

Manipulating Biped Animation Within Track View

Manipulating a biped within Track View is an easy way to change the character of an animation quickly. The timing of the footsteps can be affected just by moving or resizing the footstep blocks.

Walks can also be made into runs or jumps and vice versa. If the footstep keys are placed so that they overlap, the footsteps are walk footsteps (see Figure 6.16). If the footstep keys are moved so that they don't overlap, the double support is eliminated, and the walk footstep becomes a run footstep (see Figure 6.17). If the run footstep is then moved so that both the left and right feet are airborne at the same time and both are in contact with the ground at the same time, it becomes a jump (see Figure 6.18).

Figure 6.16 Footstep 9 is a walk because it overlaps footstep 8 by three frames, giving it double support.

Figure 6.17 Moving the edge of footstep 9 so that it doesn't overlap footstep 8 turns the step into a run, because double support is eliminated.

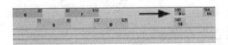

Figure 6.18 Moving footstep 9 so that it overlaps footstep 10 turns it into a jump footstep because both feet are airborne before the step.

Directly Animating a Biped

Besides animating with footsteps, a biped can also be keyframed directly. The only limits are for a walking biped because footsteps introduce calculated keys that cannot be deleted or moved except by changing the footsteps. Outside of this handful of keys, the biped can be keyframed to give a walk more character and life. This animation can be as simple as bobbing the body up and down by animating the center of mass, or as involved as introducing complex leg and arm motions—for a dance sequence or gymnastics perhaps.

Animating a Flip

In this exercise, a gymnastic flip is added to an existing biped animation.

1. Load the file 06max05.max, which is the platform animation created previously. You are going to make the biped do a flip as it jumps off the platform between frames 213 and 233.

2. To make viewing this action easier, maximize the Front viewport and zoom in to the area of the jump.

3. The biped himself can be flipped 360 degrees by rotating his Center of Mass object. Select any portion of the biped and open the Motion panel. Select the Center of Mass object by clicking the Body Rotation button in the Track Selection rollout.

4. Move the slider to frame 219. Click Angle Snap and rotate the Center of Mass object 140 degrees about the y-axis (see Figure 6.19). Press the Set Key button on the Biped panel.

Tip

The Set Key button sets a key for the selected limbs. If a limb is transformed while the Animate button is toggled on, a key is automatically generated.

5. Move the slider to frame 225. As you may notice, the biped tries to reverse his rotation to complete the animation because this is the shortest way to interpolate between the rotation key at frame 219 and the key at 233. This can be fixed by further rotating the body back in the desired direction and setting another key. With Angle Snap still toggled on, rotate the biped's Center of Mass object an additional 200 degrees. Then set a key.

   Note that the biped automatically extends his legs because the plug-in automatically computes the dynamics of the biped. As you will see later, dynamics can be turned off. For this animation, however, it is perfectly acceptable.

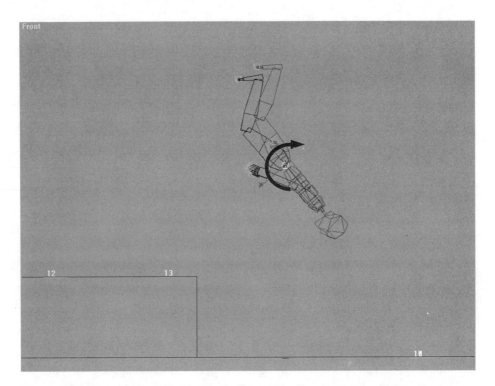

Figure 6.19   Rotating the body is a simple matter of rotating the Center of Mass object.

Play the animation, and the biped does the flip. Still, the animation looks rather stiff. You can give this animation a bit more liveliness in many ways. These methods also employ the various Biped tools.

6. The takeoff step (step 13) is six frames long. To make the takeoff slightly quicker, shorten the step to four frames. From Track View, locate the footstep block for step 13, click its right edge, and drag the edge to shorten the step so it runs from frame 207 to 211.

7. The biped also seems a little light when it takes off. To give the illusion of weight, the body needs to move lower before taking off because the legs need to absorb the shock of the body and also anticipate the leap. On frame 207, when the foot makes contact, select the Body Vertical track and move it down approximately five units in Z. Then set a key.

8. During the flip, the left leg moves forward and kicks backward to make the body flip. Anticipate the kick motion by bringing the left foot forward at frame 207 (see Figure 6.20). Set a key.

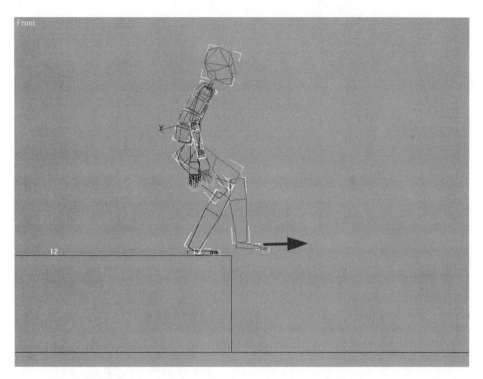

Figure 6.20   Move the right leg forward by dragging the foot. This helps to anticipate the flip.

9. Animate the kick of the left foot. Go to frame 200 and drag the left foot back behind the right leg. Set a key there.

10. The body should bend forward a bit more before it takes off. This can be done by rotating the spine around the z-axis. The easiest way to do this is by using the Bend Links mode. Toggle the Bend Links button on, and then select a spine segment. Go to frame 207 and rotate the segment about 40 degrees around the z-axis. Set a key.

11. Scrub the animation. Notice that the spine motion pops at frame 209. When Biped creates the original jump, it places a key for the spine at frame 209. With the key you just set at frame 207, this key is now extraneous. Either delete this key in Track View, or advance to frame 209 and click the Delete Key button in the Keyframing rollout with a spine segment selected.

12. Scrub the animation. At the end of the jump, the spine straightens out—which is fine for a standing pose—but the spine straightens out too early. Go to frame 207 where the spine key was set. Select the spinal segments. Click Copy Posture.

Move to frame 223, slightly before the landing, and press Paste Posture. The spine bends. Set a key.

13. To anticipate the jump, the arms swing forward quite a bit. Go to frame 205. Select the right hand and move it forward and up so that it is even with the chest and the arm is slightly bent (see Figure 6.21). Set a key. Do the same with the left arm.

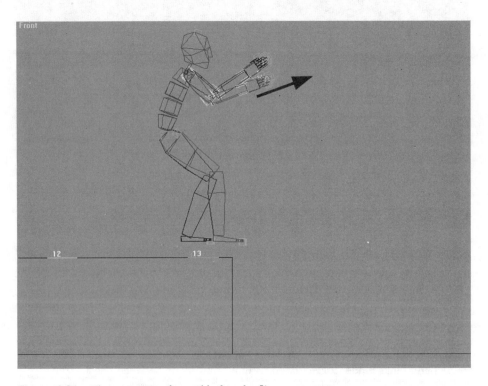

Figure 6.21   The arms swing forward before the flip.

14. When the flip begins, the arms pull in toward the body to help give it rotation. On frame 213, move both the right and left hands so they are roughly even with the hips and the arms are slightly bent. Set keys for both limbs.

15. The head needs to be tucked toward the chest as the body rotates. Go to frame 223 and rotate the head in to the chest. Set a key.

16. Finally, the biped should absorb the impact of the landing a bit more. Go to frame 230 and move the Center of Mass object down about six or seven units (see Figure 6.22). Set a key.

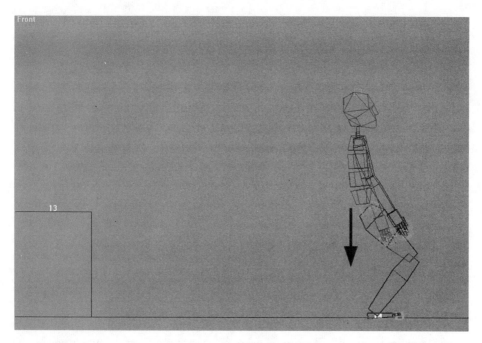

Figure 6.22 Upon impact, the body continues moving down to absorb the shock before the character stands.

Play the animation. These little tweaks go a long way toward making the flip more realistic and natural. The lesson here is that Biped gives you basic motion only; it is the animator who makes the skeleton come alive. Biped is a very nice tool, but it still needs to be driven by an animator.

This animation is stored on the accompanying CD-ROM as 06max06.max.

Freeform Animation

Not every action in every animation requires footsteps. People also stand still, sit, swim, and sometimes fly. As stated previously, as of version 2.2, footsteps were no longer a requirement to animating a biped—making the previously mentioned actions easier to animate. If footsteps are in the scene, the freeform animation must be set up in an area between footsteps. Freeform keys cannot be set before the first footstep, nor after the last.

Freeform Animation Without Footsteps

Since release 2.2, freeform animation without footsteps is no longer an all-or-nothing proposition. After keys have been set, footsteps can be added to the shot by converting your biped into footstep animation. If footsteps are required in addition to freeform animation, you can accomplish this by suspending dynamics. This is discussed in the next section.

Animating a biped in Freeform mode without footsteps gives you many advantages, most important of which is that the biped's IK remains active, making it very easy to pose the character. Biped keys are still calculated in the same way, with the keys being assigned to limbs rather than individual joints. The only exception is that vertical dynamics is suspended while in Freeform mode without footsteps. The vertical and horizontal position of the biped's Center of Mass object between key frames is based on a spline interpolation of the key frames. Because there are no footsteps, there are also no calculated or restricted keys.

Freeform Animation with Footsteps

Freeform animation with footsteps is very similar to animating a biped without them, but the task requires a few extra keystrokes. The Free section must be free of any footsteps. Normally, Biped's dynamics want to control the trajectory of the biped, as in a jump. To animate the character completely unencumbered, these dynamics need to be suspended.

1. Load 06max06.max from the accompanying CD. Open Track View and right-click the Footsteps track to open the Footstep Mode dialog box.

2. In the Footstep Mode dialog box, choose the Edit Free Form (No Physics) option.

3. The areas between footsteps are highlighted with a yellow box. These are areas where vertical dynamics are being calculated. Clicking a box turns it solid yellow, which means vertical dynamics are suspended (see Figure 6.23).

After vertical dynamics are suspended, the biped can be animated in any manner desired: It can fly around the world, for instance, or mount and ride a bicycle.

Note

With release 2.2 of Character Studio, you no longer need any footsteps in a freeform animation. If you later decide you need footsteps, just convert your animation to a footstep file (see the section "Converting Biped Animations").

You can also insert freeform animations between footsteps. Be careful, though, if the character is to resume walking because the freeform animation needs to match up to the footprints at the end of the freeform section; otherwise, the biped seems to pop into place.

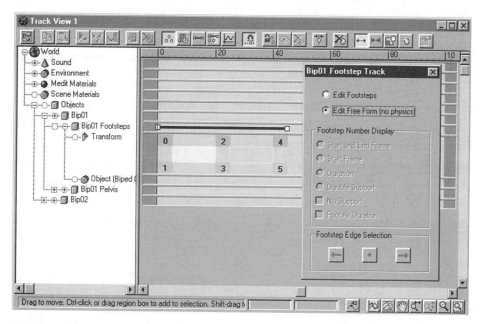

Figure 6.23   Freeform areas with vertical dynamics turned off are shown as solid yellow boxes in the Footstep track in Track View.

Standing Still

If your character's feet are firmly planted throughout the animation, you can place only two footsteps in the scene and extend their lengths from within Track View to match the length of the scene. This locks the feet down and gives you the freedom to animate the upper body as desired.

Attaching the Hands and Feet to MAX Objects

Biped has the capability to attach or lock a biped's hands and feet to any object in the scene, which enables Biped skeletons to grip and hold onto things, as well as to keep their feet firmly locked to moving objects (an escalator perhaps). The object attached may be a point in the World space or a point relative to another object (such as the Object Space object).

These attachments can be animated through the use of the IK Blend spinner in the Key Info rollout (see Figure 6.24). This spinner is the heart of Biped's animatable IK attachments. With it, you can make a biped's hand or foot gradually release its lock. When the IK Blend is set to 1.0, the hand or foot is firmly locked relative to the object space object or at a point in space. If the rest of the biped is moved, the hand or foot remains at the same location. At an IK Blend of 0.0, the motion of the hand or foot is based on the motion of the biped. If the rest of the biped is moved, the hand or foot moves along with it.

Each key for a hand or foot can be set in the Body or Object Coordinate space. If two consecutive keys are set in Body space and the IK Blend value for each is set to 1.0, the location of the hand or foot is interpolated between these keys based on the motion of the object space object. If the Object Space object is moving, therefore, the hand or foot moves along with that object. To attach a hand or foot to an object or a point in space, use the following steps. For this exercise, you can either create a biped and an object to link the hand to on your own, or you can use 06max21.max, provided on the accompanying CD.

1. Select the hand or foot.

2. Position the hand or foot in its desired position relative to the object to follow. If you are using the provided file, it is object1.

3. Click the Select Object Space Object button.

4. Click the object to follow. Not selecting an object binds the hand or foot to a fixed position in World space.

5. In the Kinematics section, choose the Object option.

6. Set the IK Blend spinner at 1.0

7. Click Set Key.

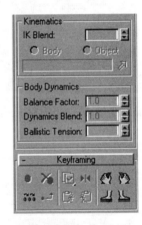

To release an object, spin IK Blend to 0.0 and set another key. As the spinner animates to 0, the lock is gradually broken. If you want to keep a hand or foot locked for a period of time and then release the lock, a second IK Blend key of 1.0 is needed to keep it locked until the release begins. To maintain the position of the hand or foot relative to the Object Space object, toggle on the appropriate Anchor button now found in the Keyframing rollout. This action holds the hand or foot in place regardless of the keys set for the hand or foot. Anchors are not permanent; rather, they are interactive tools that enable you to set keys with the hand or foot in a fixed position relative to the Object Space object (or fixed in World space if no Object Space object has been chosen).

Figure 6.24
The controls for animating a lock are split between the Key Info and the Keyframing rollouts. IK Blend is found under Key Info, and the Limb Anchors are located in the Keyframing rollout.

Tip

Another use for the leg anchors is the ability to change the foot's pivot from the heel to the toe, so you can simulate the roll of the foot during a step. Turn on the Anchor for the appropriate leg, rotate the foot to the desired angle, and click Set Key. Then you can turn off the anchor, but the pivot for that key remains at the toe.

One powerful feature of Biped is the capability to attach portions of a biped to himself using the IK Blend function. This enables you to work with closed loops of biped linkages and objects. A sword can be linked to a biped's left hand, for example, and the right hand can be linked via IK Blend to the sword, creating a closed loop of links that can be animated together. As a result, movement of the left hand controls both the sword and the movement of the entire right arm. In addition, you can animate the IK Blend spinner for the right hand to release its grip on the sword during motion.

Using IK Attachments to Dribble a Ball

In this exercise, you experiment with IK attachments and see how changing the IK Attachment parameters affects the biped's motion.

1. From the accompanying CD-ROM, load 06max07.max, which contains a biped and a ball. Activate the Left viewport and play the animation.

   The left hand has been positioned to be on top of the ball at frame 0. It then moves down to the biped's side at frame 16. The ball moves up and then down to hit the ground, and then it bounces back up. We want the biped's hand to appear to bounce the ball like a basketball player does, so we'll use Biped's animatable IK attatchments.

2. Select the biped's left hand and open the Motion panel.

3. Go to frame 0. In the Kinematics group of the Key Info rollout, click the Select Object Space Object button, and then click the ball. Object Ball appears as the object space object. Toggle Object Space to on. This takes the hand out of Body space so that the hand can follow the ball instead of the body. Set the IK Blend value to 1.0 and click Set Key.

   Based on the height of the ball, you want the hand to remain locked to the ball until frame 12. If you just advance to frame 10 though, the hand is no longer in its proper position relative to the ball.

4. At frame 0, click the Anchor Left Arm button in the Keyframing rollout to toggle it on and click Set Key. This "anchors" the hand to the ball. Advance to frame 10, and click Set Key. Then in the Kinematics section of the Key Info rollout, set the

IK Blend value to 1.0, click Object again, and then click Set Key in the Keyframing rollout to animate the IK Blend. Click the Anchor Left Hand button to toggle it off and play the animation.

Note

Any new Biped keys set will have the default values for the Kinematics section of the Key Info rollout. The defaults are IK Blend 0 and Body space. To edit these values, you must first set a key and then edit the values and set another key. If you have Animate turned on, it will automatically set keys when you change the values.

The hand now remains in a fixed position relative to the ball on frames 0 to 10, and then it drops away from the ball and moves to the side of the biped. Now you want to catch the ball on its rise.

5. At frame 0, with the left hand selected, click the Anchor Left Hand button to toggle it on. Advance to frame 33 and click Set Key. Select Object in the Kinematics section of the Keyframing rollout, set the IK Blend value to 1.0, and click Set Key again. Click the Anchor Left Hand button to toggle it off, and then play the animation. The hand now meets the ball as it is rising.

6. Select Edit, Hold to save the file and start playing with the IK attachment parameters, particularly on frames 0 and 12. Note that if Body space is selected or the IK Blend value is 0, the motion of the ball has no effect on the motion of the hand.

The final animation is stored on the accompanying CD-ROM as 06max08.max.

Using IK Attachments to Ride a Bicycle

In this exercise, you see how Biped's animatable attachments can help with difficult animation tasks. Locking objects to a bicycle, such as both hands to the handlebars, can easily cause dependency loops in MAX's native IK. Biped provides a very elegant solution and enables you to lock different parts of the biped's hierarchy to any object or combination of objects.

1. From the accompanying CD-ROM, load 06max09.max, which contains a biped and a simple bicycle (see Figure 6.25).

2. Select the biped's Center of Mass object (Bip01) and open the Motion panel. Drag the biped so that his pelvis is over the seat. Go to frame 0 and set a key for both the Vertical and Horizontal tracks. This can be done by selecting Body Horizontal in the Track Selection rollout, clicking Set Key, clicking the Body Vertical button, and clicking Set Key again. Alternatively, you can select the

Restrict to XZ or Restrict to YZ button and click Set Key. This creates keys on both the Vertical and Horizontal tracks. When you set the first key, a warning appears, stating that you are about to create a Biped animation without footsteps. This is fine, so click OK.

Figure 6.25   The biped and his bicycle.

3. Link the biped to the bicycle. Click the Select and Link button on the toolbar. Drag a line from the Center of Mass object to the bicycle seat to make the biped a child of the bicycle, enabling him to move wherever the bicycle moves.

4. Bend the biped over a bit so that the arms can reach the handlebars. Select one spine segment and, using Bend Links, rotate the spine approximately 32 degrees about his z-axis so that the chest is over the pedals (see Figure 6.26). Set a key.

5. Select the biped's right foot. Drag this up and forward so that it rests directly over the right pedal. Select the left foot and drag it to the left pedal in the same manner (see Figure 6.27).

6. To link the right foot to the right pedal, select the right foot and click Set Key in the Keyframing rollout. In the Kinematics section of the Key Info rollout, click

the Select Object Space Object button. Click the right pedal to select this as the Object Space object. Set the IK Blend spinner to 1.0 and select Object space. With the Time Slider on frame 0, set a key for the foot.

Figure 6.26   The biped is properly positioned before the feet are linked to the pedals. The spine is bent forward.

Figure 6.27   The biped's legs are anchored to the pedals.

7. Repeat this procedure for the left foot and left pedal.

   Both feet are now locked to the pedals. They will move wherever the pedals move. The pedals have already been linked to the crank, so they rotate as the crank rotates.

   Scrub the animation. The feet now follow the pedals. Next, you need to attach the hands to the handlebars.

8. Select the hands and position them over the handlebars. To get a more natural pose, you should also rotate the arms so that the elbows are slightly out from the body. At frame 0, set a key for each arm to lock in the angle of the elbows.

9. Using the same procedure you did in step 6, lock each hand to the Bike-Handle object and set a key for each hand's IK Blend at frame 0.

10. Rotate the handlebars. The hands and arms should follow.

11. Adjust the biped's Center of Mass object so the pelvis rests firmly on the seat. Set a key at frame 0. Figure 6.28 shows the final position of the biped.

Figure 6.28   With the hands and feet anchored to the bike, the biped's animation is driven by the animation of the bike.

Experiment with the animation. Because the links are bound on frame 0, any motion of the bike past that point is reflected in the biped. You can extend the animation by copying the cycle of the pedals, and you can make the bicycle move by translating it. Rotations to the handlebars are reflected, and if you want to make the biped stand up on the pedals, translate the Center of Mass object up so the biped stands.

This final animation is on the accompanying CD-ROM in a file called 06max10.max.

Saving and Loading Canned Motions

Biped enables you to save motions from one biped and apply them to another. The motions are applied regardless of the differences in size and structure of the two bipeds. This is very powerful in that it enables you to create canned libraries of motions that can be applied anywhere. Biped has two types of motion files: Biped (.BIP) files, which store the footsteps and associated key frames of a biped character, and step files (.STP), which store only the footsteps.

The STP file format is rarely used because it merely generates the default Biped motions when loaded. This file format is mainly provided for programmers who might want to write software that parametrically creates STP footstep patterns (crowds of bipeds walking in a building, for example).

A major feature of Biped is its capability to adapt any BIP file to your character without changing its kinematic structure, dimensions, distribution of weight, and so on. Furthermore, any Physique mapping is also completely independent from the motions. You can load any BIP file onto a biped without changing his Physiqued skin, his pose, kinematic structure, or his center-of-gravity in Biped's Figure mode. The only animation-type data not stored in a BIP file are IK attachments to scene-specific objects—because they are, by nature, scene specific. This data is best stored in scenes in the normal MAX file format.

To save an STP or BIP file, select any portion of the biped and, in the Biped Motion panel, click the Save File button in the General rollout. Select the type of file to save, as well as its path and filename, and click OK. All footsteps (and keys for BIP files) associated with the biped are saved.

To replace the entire animation currently applied to a biped with that defined in a BIP file, select any portion of the biped and, in the Biped Motion panel, click the Load File button. Select the BIP file to load and click OK.

A BIP file can also be read into the Footstep buffer and spliced into the current animation. To do this, you need to be in Buffer mode and then load the BIP file. For you to enter Buffer mode, however, footsteps must be present in the Footstep buffer. To do this, you need to go into Footstep mode, select one or more footsteps, and click Copy Footsteps in the Footstep Operations rollout. This action copies the selected footsteps into the Footstep buffer and enables the Buffer Mode button.

Splicing Biped Animation

Frequently, you will not want to apply the entire animation defined in a BIP file, but only a section of it. At the current time, there is not a way to directly do this. Although you can load the animation defined by the BIP file into the Footstep buffer and delete the undesired footsteps, this causes the animation keys to be regenerated. This can also cause a loss of the very animation data you are trying to splice in. The easiest way to get around this is to place another biped in the scene, apply the animation in the BIP to that biped, and copy and paste motions from this biped to the desired one. In the following exercise, you do precisely that.

1. Load 06max04.max from the accompanying CD-ROM. This file contains a biped that walks forward, turns left, and walks a bit farther. You want to splice in a motion where the biped walks on tiptoes.

2. Create another biped in the Perspective viewport. This biped will be used as an intermediary, holding the animation imported from the BIP file for application to the original biped.

   Because Biped can properly adjust the animation data while moving between dissimilar bipeds, the details of the second biped do not need to match those of the original biped. To prevent the loss of data, however, if the original biped has arms or a tail, the new biped should also. As a practical matter, this biped should be roughly the same height as the original biped.

3. With this new biped selected, go to the Biped motion panel and click the Load File button in the General rollout. Load creep.bip from the accompanying CD-ROM. This is a classic "sneak" walkcycle.

4. Activate Footstep mode for bip02. Select all the new footsteps and move them away from the footsteps for bip01 to make it easier to see both bipeds.

   Play the animation. As the original biped walks along, the new biped creeps along.

5. With the new biped selected, select footsteps 3 through 5, and then click the Copy Footsteps button in the Footstep Operations rollout. Click the Footstep Mode button to exit Footstep mode.

6. Select any portion of the original biped and click the Footstep Mode button. Click the Paste Footsteps button to display the footsteps in the Footstep buffer.

7. Drag the first buffer footstep over the biped's footstep number 10 and release the mouse. The remaining original footsteps are now shown in their saturated colors. Drag these footsteps so the first one is over the new footstep 12, and then release the mouse.

8. Click the Footstep Mode button to exit Footstep mode, activate the Perspective viewport, and play the animation. At this point, you can delete or hide the biped you added to the scene.

    When you splice in a set of footsteps, sometimes the leg rotation near the end of the splice is noticeably incorrect—the upper leg points toward the biped's head. A single key has been improperly set in these cases. To correct this, perform the remaining steps.

9. Select the leg with the incorrect rotation.

10. Toggle the Key Mode Toggle button on (the Key Mode Toggle button is located at the bottom on the MAX window with the Time controls).

11. Click the Select and Move or Select and Rotate button.

12. Click the Next Frame or Previous Frame button to advance to the key frame where the leg rotation is incorrect. Note the frame number and the pose of the biped.

13. Click the Next Frame or Previous Frame button to advance to a key frame where the biped is in a similar pose.

14. Click the Copy Posture button to copy the leg's rotation to a buffer.

15. Return to the key frame where the leg rotation is incorrect. Click the Paste Posture button to set the leg's rotation from the buffer. Then click Set Key.

By using BIP files, you can set up libraries of motion that you can easily apply to any biped. The capability to share animations between bipeds, regardless of their size or structure, is not found in any other application.

Converting Biped Animations

With previous versions of Character Studio, after you created a purely freeform animation, you could not add footsteps. If you even thought you might want to use footsteps, you had to have them in from the start. With release 2.2, you can now easily convert Freeform and Footstep animations. This allows you the freedom of working in the way you are most comfortable, while giving you access to all the tools you need. It is also useful for sharing animation within a database, which helps when you're working with a team during production. You can now use a footstep walk-cycle created by another animator, add it to your database, and convert it to a freeform animation of your character dancing.

When you select the Convert button from the Motion panel's General rollout, the appropriate dialog box for converting from footsteps to freeform, or vice versa, will appear.

Converting to Freeform

Converting an animation to freeform from a footstep animation removes all the dynamics and gravity and sets keys so that you are working with a purely freeform animation. This allows you to use the dynamic functions of Biped's Footsteps and still customize freely to create exactly the animation you want. The process for converting from footsteps to freeform is very simple. You have only one decision to make, and the rest of the process is automated. The one decision you must make is whether to use the following option:

- **Generate a key frame per frame.** Places a key for every limb on every frame.

This might give you more key data than you need, but it will preserve your motion 100 percent. If you don't toggle this option on, Biped will attempt to create the fewest possible keys, which may result in some data loss.

Note

Biped will create keys for each foot with an IK Blend of 1 for the duration of each footstep to prevent sliding and allow the file to be converted back to footsteps easily.

Converting to Footsteps

Converting a freeform animation into footsteps requires a little more preparation. Biped uses the IK Blend values to extract footsteps, placing a footstep wherever the feet have an IK Blend of 1.0. To ensure a clean Footstep file and to prevent sliding in general, set the IK Blend for the feet to 1.0 wherever you want the feet planted, and set it to 0 anywhere the feet are moving.

Tip

When setting keys for the feet in Freeform mode, set the IK Blend for the feet to 1 and select Object Space from the Kinematics section of the Key Info rollout whenever you want to lock the character's feet to the floor. This is a good habit to get into, whether or not you plan to convert between Footsteps and Freeform, but especially when you're working with a team because it allows other animators who may use your animation the option of manipulating the animation in their own ways.

When you have a Freeform animated biped selected and you click the Convert button, a dialog box appears with Generate a Key per Frame and one additional option (described next). You can toggle either option on or off depending on what you want the resulting Footsteps animation to look like.

- **Flatten Footsteps to Z = 0.** Forces the generated footsteps to lie directly on the z-axis, assuming that is your ground plane. This vertically locks the biped's feet to the floor.

Customizing Bipeds

When you become accustomed to working with the default biped structures, you will want to be able to customize them to fit your needs. Whether you want to adapt a default biped to match a model for Physique, or to create a less human character, you can adjust your biped both before and after you create it.

You can edit any of a biped's parameters by entering Figure mode, located in the Motion panel under the General rollout.

Tip

You can enter Figure mode to edit your biped at any time during the animation process. Biped will make the necessary adjustments for you. This is especially useful for making global changes to the posture of a character for the duration of an animation.

Using Figure mode to define a default pose is handy for preparing your biped for Physique (see "Applying Physique to a Biped" in Chapter 7). You can edit the numbers links and their position, rotation, and scale, and then save out the parameters for that biped as a .FIG file to be reloaded whenever you need to restore your biped to that default pose. The figure file contains all the parameters that define your biped, from the position and scale of its links to its pose. This is also great for saving variations of a pose or anatomy. You can save or load .FIG files only when you're in Figure mode.

Mapping Biped Files

The ability to freely transfer animations between bipeds is one of Character Studio's most powerful tools. You can transfer a canned animation from a generic human to a creature with a four-link leg and a tail. Biped will make the necessary adjustments to get it to work, and you can refine it to make it unique for that model.

1. Load 06max01.max from the accompanying CD-ROM. You will be loading a custom figure file onto an existing biped and then mapping a canned motion onto it.

2. Select any link of the biped and open the Motion panel.

3. Click on the Figure Mode button, select Load File, and load hosenose.fig from the accompanying CD.

4. Click on the Footsteps track to activate Footstep mode. Make sure that Scale Stride mode is on (it is by default).

Tip

Scale Stride mode enables bipeds to automatically adjust footsteps to match changes to the biped's leg length, pelvis width, and height. When loading a .BIP or .STP file, it will also allow the gravity to be adjusted in relation to the file. It is a good idea to leave this toggled on for most situations.

5. Select Load File and load the ballet.bip file on the accompanying CD.

6. Click Play and watch the biped dance.

Figure 6.29 Biped intelligently maps animations between differing skeletal hierarchies, even adding dynamics for limbs missing from the original motion file, such as a tail.

Compare that with file 06max13, which contains the traditional human biped ballet dance. Notice the changes that automatically occurred when the action was mapped onto the weirdo biped, which has more leg joints, a different center of gravity, and extra

appendages. It obviously still needs adjustment, but it demonstrates how well a database of motion files can work with diverse
models.

Animating with Layers

Another powerful feature available only in Biped is the use of animation layers. These controls are found in the Layers rollout of the
Motion module when a Biped is selected. This feature allows you
to easily refine or customize biped animations by simply creating
additional layers on top of the existing motion. This is perfect for
refining motion capture data or even customizing a canned walk-
cycle to create a unique animation over a longer range of frames.

Figure 6.30
The Layers rollout.

Animation with the Layers rollout (shown in Figure 6.30) is similar to freeform animation. You can establish a full range of movement on any of the limbs, yet leave the original animation unchanged until you collapse the layers. You can move between layers,
adjusting where necessary, and then collapse into one layer of adjustable tracks when you
are happy with the results. When you finish, you have a unique animation.

When you create a new layer, you gain access to the tools in the Layers rollout. Each new
layer is created on top of the previous one in numerical order and can be given its own
unique name. Navigate throughout your layer stack using the Next and Previous Layer
tools. You control which layers are active by turning layers on and off as needed. When
you delete a layer, all layers above it shift downward one place in the stack, but the custom names remain the same.

To set new keys, use the standard tools in the Keyframing and Key Info rollouts. For special cases in which you want to return the biped limp to its layer 0 position, use the Snap
Set Key tool from the Layers rollout. This is great for blending your adjusted frames
seamlessly into your animations, as you will see in the next exercise.

You also have control over which layers are being played using the Activate All and
Activate Only Me buttons, and you can control the number of layers that are ghosted.
This can come in handy for cross-referencing your layers and being able to see how different any two layers may be. You can also set Key Highlight to highlight limbs at key
frames from layers above and below based on those settings.

Tip

You can deactivate any layer except for the base while editing your animation, but you must either
activate or delete that layer before you can collapse the stack.

Certain functions of Biped are unavailable when you're editing any layer above 0. For example, you cannot set an IK Blend or use the Limb Anchors under the Keyframing rollout. The Animation Properties rollout is also disabled, as is most of the Structure rollout. This doesn't mean you can't manipulate these while working in layers, but you make those changes in layer 0.

1. Load 06max14.max from the accompanying CD. This file contains a biped walking. You will use layers to make the character crouch while walking and then stand back up.

2. Select a portion of the biped and open the Motion panel.

3. Open the Layer rollout and select the Create Layer button. This creates a new layer. Type **Crouch** in the Name field. Naming layers is a good practice because it helps organize your scene.

4. Click Play. Notice that the original biped animation appears as an orange stick figure. This helps you compare the difference between your original frames and the adjusted ones. If you find this distracting, you can toggle this off by setting the Visible Before field of the Layers Rollout to 0. The default is 1.

5. Turn on the Animate button to automatically set keys. Select both feet.

6. Advance to frame 35 and translate the feet 8 units on the z-axis and –6 on the y-axis. Rotate them 15 units on the x-axis. Note that they rotate in opposite directions.

7. Select the left and right calves and rotate them 18 units on the x-axis.

8. Select the Center of Mass by clicking the Body Vertical button in the Track Selection rollout to constrain the vertical translation, and then translate it –7 on the z-axis. This plants your biped back on the ground.

9. Turn on the Bend Links mode in the General rollout and select a spine link. Rotate –10 units in x, 10 units in y, and 43 units on the z-axis.

10. Select the Upper Right arm and rotate 36 units on the x-axis.

11. Select the R Hand and translate it –1 unit in x, –17 in y, and 6 units in z. Then, rotate –22 units in x and z.

12. Adjust the R Clavicle by rotating it approximately –9 units on the y-axis.

13. Rotate the L UpperArm –16 units in x. Then, translate the L Hand 3 units on the x-axis, 9 units on the y-axis, and 6 units on the z-axis.

14. Rotate the biped's Neck –30 units in z, and then rotate the Head 16 units in z to relax the uncomfortable angle between the head and torso.

15. Now that you have a decent pose, play the animation and see how it reads through the course of animation. Watch it in all four views. Not bad, but it could use some finesse.

16. Return to frame 34 and select the L UpperArm. Rotate 15 units in x and y, and then translate the L Hand 4 units in y to give the arm a more natural pose.

17. You're ready to blend it with the original walk frames (see Figure 6.31). Open the Track View, right-click on Filters and select Animated Tracks Only, and then right-click on Objects and select Expand All. Then maximize the window.

Figure 6.31   The final pose for your crouch layer is ready to be blended smoothly into your original animation.

18. Drag to select all keys. Then, press and hold down the Shift key and click and drag to frame 213. This will hold the pose, while blending it with the original animation.

19. Right-click on the box next to Bip01, collapse tracks, and then repeat and choose Select Children. Minimize the Track View, go to frame 0, and press the Snap Set Key button from the Layers rollout. This returns the biped in the current layer to its position in the Original and sets a key for all selected links.

20. Go to the last frame of the animation and click on Snap Set Key again to return to the normal walk. Click Play.

21. The biped's feet go through the floor at the beginning and end. Select Body
    Vertical from the Track Selection rollout and translate the biped 8 units in z.
    Return to frame 0 and repeat. Now play the animation.

You can make any other refinements you want, even adding other layers on top and then collapsing all layers into the original using the Collapse Layer button in the Layers rollout. After the layer is collapsed, you can return to the mode of animation used in the original file, but Biped blends the layer animation into the original tracks. The completed tutorial animation can be found in 06max15.max on the accompanying CD.

Motion Capture

Motion capture files are as notorious for being difficult to clean up and manipulate as they are famous for the realistic movement they can provide. As a result, motion capture is being used more and more by today's professionals to meet the tough deadlines and budgets of today's productions. Motion capture is becoming common not only in games and television, but in feature films, where computer-generated characters have to match up seamlessly with a real character or scene. Biped's ability to share and customize animation files makes it the ideal tool for massaging motion capture files.

Character Studio 2.2 provides a wide array of powerful but easy-to-use tools designed to let the digital artist focus on the creative rather than the technical. Special motion capture tools such as Key Reduction, Footstep Extraction, and clip looping, coupled with the tools such as Layering and Motion Flow mode, along with biped's ability to map animations onto different skeletal structures make it a formidable asset in motion capture animation production.

Biped and Motion Capture Data

Character Studio 2.2 supports both positional marker files and joint rotation files, which you can import onto biped skeletons and save as individual .BIP files to be used separately or put together with the Motion Flow Mode.

- **Biovision (*.bvh).** Contains the skeleton and the motion data in the form of joint rotation values.

- **Character Studio Marker files (*.csm).** This format takes its name from the positional data recorded from markers on the actor's body.

- **Biped (*.bip).** Uses the motion capture tools to easily loop or clean up your Biped animations.

In some cases, the joint names in the marker files may not match those found in standard Biped. Character Studio provides a special file format called the Marker Name (*.mnm) file to map the joint names for you. The Marker Name file is most frequently used when loading .CSM files, but it can be used for .BVH in the event that the joint names don't match.

When loading a Motion Capture file, the raw unfiltered data is stored in a buffer, and then the conversion process runs through the conversion process using the set of parameters defined in the Motion Capture Conversion dialog box. The buffer stores the last loaded raw data, which can be used to compare and replace data loss from key reduction. The parameters are described here:

- **Convert from Buffer.** Use this as an easy way to reconvert the last loaded raw data file, making it easy to experiment and find the right filter settings.

- **Paste from Buffer.** Allows you to paste a key frame from the raw data stored in the buffer onto the selected joint to replace data lost through Key Reduction.

- **Show Buffer.** Displays the buffered raw motion file as a red stick figure. Use this to compare differences between the raw and optimized data.

- **Show Buffer Trajectory.** Supplies another way to reference the buffered animation. Use with Display Trajectories from the motion layout to compare the raw and filtered trajectories.

Converting Motion Capture Data

In their raw form, these files will have a key per frame for each joint for the duration of the animation, making it difficult to edit the motions. The filters in the Motion Capture Conversion dialog box provide an excellent method for controlling the amount and quality of data being imported (see Figure 6.32). To access the Conversion dialog box, create or load a biped, select a limb, and click on the Motion tab to enter Motion mode. Open the Motion Capture rollout and click Load Motion Capture File. Then, select any motion capture or biped file.

The dialog box is divided up by functionality. The main filters for Footstep Extraction and Key Reduction are listed at the top, and their many parameters each have their own section. There are also separate sections for defining the frame range of the selected clip and for talent definition to correct the physical makeup and position of the target biped. The following sections provide details about the sections of this dialog box.

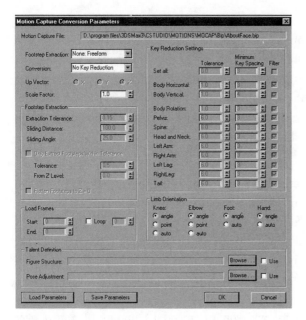

Figure 6.32   The Motion Capture Conversion dialog box contains a comprehensive set of motion capture filters designed to take advantage of Biped's features.

Footstep Extraction

Motion Capture files frequently suffer from sliding feet, among other things. The Footstep Extraction option allows you to bring your animation in as freeform, footstep, or fit to existing footsteps.

Choosing None:Freeform brings in the motion capture without applying Biped's dynamics, creating a freeform animation file. This is great for animations in which the character is not in contact with the ground plane. For animations in which the character is on the ground, it is best to use the On option. This creates footsteps wherever the feet touch the ground within the parameters set in the Footstep Extraction section and applies the footstep dynamics.

Tip

Turn on Set Extract Footsteps to lock down the feet and prevent the foot sliding that is common to Motion Capture data.

You can also use Fit to Existing to fit your motion capture data to the biped's existing footsteps. This is good for importing files containing both footstep- and freeform-type movement.

The parameters in the Footstep Extraction dialog box determine when a biped should create a footstep from the motion capture data. Extraction Tolerance determines how close the motion capture data's foot has to be to the ground to create a footstep. The smaller the number, the more footsteps that are created. Use Sliding Distance to generate sliding footsteps whenever the foot slides more than that percentage of the foot length. The default is 100. You can also use Sliding Angle to create sliding keys based on the angle of the foot's rotation. This is very useful for dance moves or turning animations.

To prevent footsteps from being created on more than one plane, use the Only Extract Footsteps Within Tolerance option. It is often used in conjunction with From Z Level to define the ground plane for the footsteps. Flatten Footsteps to Z = 0 is very important for locking the footsteps to a value of Z = 0. This ensures that the feet of your biped stay planted on the ground and don't hover.

Conversion

The options found under Conversion give you a tremendous amount of control over how your data is going to be imported. You can choose to bring in the raw data, simplify the keys with key reduction, or simply load the animation into a buffer to compare and repair your biped file after the keys have been reduced.

- **Use Key Reduction.** Simplifies keys based on parameters set in the Key Reduction Settings. This is excellent for cleaning up the animations, because too many key frames can lead to more jagged animation.

- **No Key Reduction.** Creates one key per frame for every joint. Use this the first time you import a new .CSM file. This is the only option that will allow you to calibrate your biped to fit the marker data.

Note

This step is usually unnecessary when working with .BVH files because they are already designed to work with bipeds' structure and pass only rotational data.

- **Load Buffer Only.** This loads your motion capture data into the buffer but does not affect the biped.

Tip

Load Buffer Only can be used to replace important details possibly lost during key reduction. To use it, select the limb and click Paste Posture from Buffer.

The Key Reduction Settings section offers a powerful way to explicitly control how much your data is optimized. Character Studio offers you the ability to determine the key reduction parameters per track. You can choose to filter only certain tracks, and you can define by what values those tracks will be reduced.

Setting the Tolerance gives Biped the maximum difference in degrees or units before a key will be set. Lower values will preserve more keys. Minimum Key Spacing reduces keys based on distance in frames. With the default of 3, there will be no more than 1 key every 4 frames.

Note

Tolerance is calculated first, and then Minimum Key Spacing is used for additional savings.

Set All changes all parameters below it to that value, regardless of whether you check the filter radio button.

Tip

You can experiment to find the right Key Reduction settings by using the Load from Buffer button in the Motion Capture rollout. Because the buffer holds the raw data of the last loaded file, this allows you to re-filter without having to browse and find the file again.

Load Frames

Very often, you will want to use only a portion of a motion capture file. For instance, you might want to isolate a karate kick from a sequence of moves within one data file. You can determine the starting and ending frames to crop your import data during the import process, but the default values will be set to include the entire clip. You can also set how many times you want the clip to loop.

Note

Loop does not "create" a loop from a non-looping animation. If the motion does not loop, it might pop or slide. To create clean loops from non-looping frames, use the Motion Flow mode.

Limb Orientation

Limb Orientation parameters are important for controlling rotations that exceed Biped's joint limits.

- **Angle.** Moves the joint to compensate for the out-of-range key.
- **Point.** Rotates the offending joint to create the key.

- **Auto.** The best option for fixing out-of-range rotation keys for the knees and elbows, this will explicitly translate the hand or foot and then adjust the hinge joint to a natural angle.

Talent Definition

Talent Definition allows you to load a custom figure and pose onto which to load your file, as well as to save and load a custom set of conversion parameters.

Figure Structure allows you to load a custom .FIG file to replace the default biped that's needed to open the biped controls in the Motion panel. Use Pose Adjustment to define a calibration file to globally correct any difference between default biped pose and the one expected by the marker file.

The Save/Load parameters define a set of custom filter settings that can be applied to other files. This is particularly useful for converting a series of similar moves from a single motion model.

Calibration for Marker Files

When you're converting motion capture from marker files, such as Character Studio Marker files (*.csm), it may be necessary to adjust the biped to match initial marker positions because the marker files are based on positional data and not rotation of a given limb. This means proportions can make a big difference in the quality of the motion capture conversion.

Tip

You should not have to use this feature because normally, Biped extracts the proper scale and position from the marker file. To see if you need to make any calibration changes, load the raw data as is. Do not reduce keys or extract footsteps. Calibration controls will be disabled if you load anything except the raw marker file.

Calibration controls work much the same as Biped's Figure mode controls. After entering Talent Figure mode, you make modifications to your biped with the Rubber Band option from the General rollout and the Non-uniform scale, and then you save the .FIG file. If you need to make adjustments to the pose to match your motion file, you can use Adjust Talent Pose and then save those changes into a calibration file (*.cal). These can be loaded during the Conversion process using the Figure Structure and Pose Adjustment settings in the Talent Definition Area of the Motion Capture Conversion dialog box.

- **Load Marker Name File.** If the joint names in your motion capture file don't match the biped skeletal names, you can load an .MNM file to map joints between the marker file and the biped.

Note

The Marker Name files are ASCII files that you can edit to customize to your needs. Examples for both marker and Biovision marker name files can be found in your 3dsmax3\cstudio\docs directory, in csm.doc and bvh.doc, respectively.

- **Show Markers.** This will display markers and their names so that you can make the necessary calibration adjustments.

Motion Flow Mode

One of the most interesting features in Character Studio 2.2 is the Motion Flow mode, located in the General Layout. This tool allows you to edit together, in 3D space, by splicing and blending individual .BIP files from your library of animations to create longer animation sequences that can be saved as Motion Flow Editor_(*.mfe) files. These files are attached to the selected biped while in the Motion panel. It is possible to have several bipeds in a scene and have each access a Motion Flow Script. They could even share the same script, which would make it easy to animate multiple characters in a scene.

Note

As of Character Studio 2.2, the Motion Flow mode is available for use only with Biped. Because it relies heavily on Biped's dynamics to create transitions, it cannot be applied to regular MAX bone hierarchies.

Two new rollouts become available when you click on the Motion Flow Mode button in the General rollout of the Motion panel (see Figure 6.33).

- **Motion Flow.** This rollout contains controls for loading, saving, and viewing the Motion Flow files (*.mfe), with the Motion Control Graph.

- **Motion Flow Script.** These tools are for editing and blending biped files, using Biped's physics to easily create transitions between the clips in the Motion Control Graph.

Figure 6.33
The Motion Flow rollouts.

Working with the Motion Flow Graph

The Motion Flow Graph is a graphical representation of the clips available for Motion Flow Scripting. You create the clips first, by selecting the Create Clip tool. This creates a Clip icon, which points to a specific biped animation. After selecting this button, click in the Motion Graph window to create as many clips as you need. Clips are empty when they're first created. Right-click on the clip and select a biped file using the Load Clip browser. You can load the .BIP file as it is, or you can crop it by setting a start and end frame. If you keep Auto Clip Names toggled on, the clip will be given the same name as the biped file it is associated with.

Note

Motion Flow Clips are pointers to biped files, in much the same way that Xrefs point to an object rather than actually loading an object. Changes made to the original clip will affect the Motion Flow Clip.

Reposition clips within the Motion Flow Graph to organize the viewport using the Move Clip tool. You can also delete a clip or transition by using the Delete tool in the Motion Flow Graph window. A warning appears if an active script depends upon the selected clip. This will delete the selected clip and any script attached to it.

If you decide at any time during the Motion Flow editing process that you want to change the animation in a clip, you don't have to go back to the original clip. Simply enter Clip mode by using the Clip Mode tool. You can then use any of the traditional Biped tools to edit and customize the animation. It is important to note that changes made in Motion Flow do not affect the original animation. To keep the changes you've made, you have to use Save File from the General rollout while in Clip mode.

Note

If you rename the biped file that you are saving while in Clip mode, you must manually reload that file into the clip by right-clicking and selecting the new filename. Otherwise, when you save the .MFE file, you will get an error saying you have not saved the changes to that clip.

Motion Flow Scripting

The name Motion Flow Script might be a little misleading. You are not writing a script in code; rather, you are controlling a script that MAX will create to blend your animations together. You provide a list of the clips and the order in which you want them to be played, and you define the transitions between them. Character Studio does the rest for you. This makes it even easier to make use of a motion library as long as it is in Biped (.bip) format.

Tip

Use the Motion Flow Script to create a seamless loop from a single walk cycle by looping the animation upon itself.

You can create any number of scripts within an .MFE file by using the same set of clips to create a series of seemingly unique animations out of the same animation database. This rollout offers the usual Copy, Paste, and Delete functions, as well as a Clip mode that works exactly the same as the Clip mode in the Motion Graph. In addition to these, you also have new functions that make up the heart of the Motion Flow mode.

The Define Script function allows you to create a new script or edit an existing one. If no scripts exist, it will automatically create an empty script and give it the default name of script1. You can change this by clicking in the Script Name field and typing a new name for the clip. You then define the script by clicking on the clips in the Motion Graph in the order you want to add them to your list. The script runs from top to bottom, so the clip you click on first plays first, and so on. You can reorder the clips within a script using the Copy, Cut, and Paste commands.

By default, when you link animations in a script, Motion Flow creates a transition based on each clip's velocity and optimizes for the minimum motion loss. This may not always be the best solution, so you have the option of manually editing and creating your transitions, adjusting the parameters for the source and destination biped frames and the length of the transition. To adjust the default transition, select the source clip in the Motion Flow Script rollout, and then click the Edit Transition tool.

Tip

You can create and store multiple transitions for a clip in the Transition Editor. Once they're associated with a clip, the transitions can be saved to an .MFE file even if the scripts have been deleted.

Creating Transitions

The Auto Transition option, found in the Transition Editor, creates a 25-frame transition between animations, trying to find the best possible place in both the source and destination animations using the minimum motion loss. When you click on Auto Transition, you are given a number of different options for finding the right transition keys. Try these first. Sometimes they work fine as is, and they are also a great starting point for creating your own custom transitions.

In this exercise, you will learn to work with the Transition Editor to create both automatic and custom transitions.

1. Load 06max01.max from the accompanying CD. This file contains a biped with no animation. You will use this to load .BIP files from the motion library and create a custom sequence.

2. Select a portion of the biped, click on the Motion panel, and select Motion Flow Mode from the General rollout.

3. Open the Motion Flow rollout and click on Show Graph. Click on Create Clip and click three times in the Motion Flow Graph window. Three clicks creates clips 1 through 3. Use the Move Clip tool to reposition them next to one another.

4. With Auto Clip Name toggled on, click on the Select Clip/Transition tool and right-click on clip1. Load SkateLoop.bip from the accompanying CD. Leave the default settings for the start and end frames.

5. Notice that the clip name for clip1 has changed to SkateLoop. Now repeat these steps for clips 2 and 3, loading SkateStart.bip and SkateUp.bip (see Figure 6.34).

Figure 6.34   Auto Clip Name keeps the naming consistent with the biped files you load.

6. Open the Motion Flow Script rollout and click Define Script. A new script called script1 is created. Then click on SkateLoop twice. Rename the script by clicking in the Script Name field and renaming it SkateLoop.

7. Click Play and watch your animation. Notice that the second time the skate loop runs, it seems too short. You can fix that by editing the length of the transition. Because the original biped animation was designed as a loop, you just need it to loop back to frame 0. You can adjust that in the Transition Editor (see Figure 6.35).

8. Select SkateLoop in the Motion Flow Script rollout and notice that the other icons in the rollout are now active. Click on Edit Transition.

Tip

You can open the Edit Transition dialog box by right-clicking the transition arrow in the Motion Flow Graph.

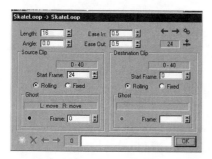

Figure 6.35 The Transition Editor allows you to create smooth, seamless transitions between two clips.

9. Change the Length to 1. In the Source Clip section, set the start frame of the transition to 40 (the last frame of the clip). The length of the source and destination clips is listed at the top of each section. Set the start frame for the destination file to 0 and click OK.

10. Click Play. The transition is much smoother now. If you define the transition as a loop first, whenever you use this clip in another script, it will default as a repeating loop instead of the automatic transition.

11. Select Define Script and use the Create New Script option.

    The first time you create a script, Character Studio automatically creates a new script. Once a script exists, you have the option of editing the existing script by inserting more clips, creating a new script, or redefining the existing one. Redefining a script keeps the script name but deletes the associated clips.

12. Rename the script to skating1. In the Motion Graph, click on SkateStart, and then click four times on SkateLoop. Click Play.

13. The timing is off on the transition from the start to the loop. Right-click on the transition arrow in the Motion Flow Graph window and adjust the transition until it looks right. When you're in the Transition Editor, the Source biped is shown as a yellow stick figure called a ghost, and the destination clip is shown in red. This will help you find an appropriate frame.

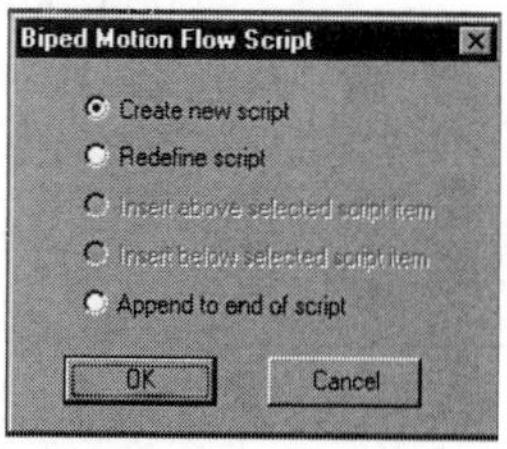

Figure 6.36
After you create a script, clicking on the Define Script tool displays the Biped Motion Flow Script dialog box.

14. Insert the SkateStop clip by clicking on Define Script and selecting the Append to End of Script option. Then, select the SkateStop clip in the Motion Flow Graph.

You can view the finished tutorial by opening 06max18.max on the accompanying CD.

Offsetting an Animation Sequence

You can also offset your sequence of animations as a whole within a scene by editing the start frame, the position, or the rotation in x, y, and z. This can further create the illusion of uniqueness, even if several bipeds in the same scene share the same clip.

For instance, if you are animating two characters in a race, they will both start and run to the finish line. You could create a script that uses a starting animation and that's linked to a run animation. Load the .MFE file onto two bipeds in the same scene, offset them in space and time using the offset controls, and you have a winner and a loser in no time at all. Follow this exercise:

1. Load 06max19.max from the accompanying CD. This file contains two bipeds, one on top of the other, with no animation. You will load the same .MFE file onto both and use that to create a unique animation for each one.

2. Enter Motion Flow mode by selecting a portion of the Bip01 file and clicking on the Motion Flow Mode button in the General rollout of the Motion panel.

3. Select Load File from the Motion Flow rollout, and then load skating1.mfe from the accompanying CD.

4. Select Bip02, enter Motion Flow Mode, and load the same .MFE file. In the Motion Flow Script rollout, change the Start Frame to 10, the StartPositon X to 60, and the Start Position Z to 5.

5. Click Play. The offset gives the illusion that they are unique. Then, you can edit each script independently to create unique animations.

6. Select Bip01 and, in the Motion Flow Graph, create a clip. Right-click on the clip and load SkateUp.bip from the accompanying CD.

7. Add this to Bip01's skating1 script by selecting the second SkateLoop in the Motion Flow Script and clicking Define Script. Choose Insert Below Selected Clip, and then click OK. This adds the SkateUp clip between the last SkateLoop and SkateStop.

8. Click Play. You could edit the scripts further, creating new scripts and loading new clips. Save them as new .MFE files for use in other animations.

The finished file is stored as 06max20.max on the accompanying CD.

Character Studio 2.2 provides a vast array of tools for both the novice and the professional digital artist. Biped gives you speed and ease of use combined with sophisticated control to allow you to create your own unique vision, from scratch or using a shared database of pre-animated material or motion capture data.

In Practice: Biped

- **Manipulating bipeds.** Using Biped's manipulation tools (such as Select Opposite) can help streamline your work. It is also possible to freeze or hide some parts of a biped while working on others.

- **Footstep-driven animation.** Although footsteps certainly take a lot of the drudgery out of creating locomotive sequences, they are only the first step. To truly bring your characters to life, you need to go back over the Biped-generated motions and bring them to life by adding animation. Remember, you can easily convert to Freeform animation or disable Biped's Footstep dynamics to add more life to a footstep animation.

- **Bipeds in hierarchies.** If your biped is a child of another object, the biped and his footsteps move in relation to the parent. This makes scenes that require moving footsteps—such as ice-skating or walking up a moving escalator—possible by parenting the escalator's stairs to the biped.

- **Freeform animation.** Freeform animation between footsteps defaults to having dynamics turned on, which causes the biped to simulate a jump motion. Typically, it is best to turn dynamics off when you start a freeform animation.

- **Animatable locks.** This is a very powerful feature, so make sure you're familiar with the steps for using it. In addition to locking hands and feet to objects or World space, you can lock them in relation to the body itself.

- **Splicing motions.** This is a feature unique to Biped that enables you to apply animation data to bipeds with dissimilar structures. By building and using libraries of canned motions, you can quickly build complex animations for your characters.

- **Converting animations.** You can now convert freely between footsteps and freeform, so you can use the best of both tools with only a little preparation.

- **Motion capture.** The new tools for handling motion capture data make it much easier to work with. Extracting footsteps during the import process prevents the problem of sliding feet. The animation buffer makes it easier to experiment with filter settings and find the right settings for each file.

- **Motion Flow scripts.** Create and customize sequences of pre-animated biped files using Motion Flow scripts. The Transition Editor allows for smooth transitions from one clip to the next. Apply the same script to different bipeds in the same scene, offsetting them individually in space and time, to create larger scenes quickly.

Chapter 7

Animating with Physique

by Sean Miller

Physique is the second half of Character Studio. It's simple interface gives you easy access to very sophisticated and powerful tools for controlling surface deformation—bulging, creasing, sliding, and twisting.

Physique simulates the flow of flesh over muscle and bone using a system of customizable envelopes and cross sections. Combined with Biped, Physique gives MAX users a complete character animation environment. Although Biped is Character Studio's preferred method for creating skeletons, Physique can be used with any type of MAX skeleton, including custom-built skeletons and simple chains of bones. Physique provides more control than the Skin modifier, which is new to R3.

Note

You must have an authorized copy of Character Studio 2.0 or better installed on your computer to do the exercises in this chapter.

This chapter covers the following topics:

- Physique overview
- Using Physique
- Physique and Biped
- Creating realistic bulges
- Using tendons
- Transferring Physique files

Overview

Whether you are creating abstract, cartoony, or photo-realistic characters, you have to control how your surface deforms. One of the more difficult challenges for the CG artist is the believable simulation of flesh and bone. In real life, bones are driven by muscles and tendons beneath the surface of the skin. As the muscles relax and contract, they pull the bones in the skeleton, causing them to rotate. Physique gives you the tools to easily define and manipulate the skin as it follows your bones and to mimic actual skin.

With Physique, your mesh is deformed by assigning each vertex to a hierarchy of MAX objects using spherical *envelopes* based on either the joint scale or user-defined bounding boxes (see "Applying Physique"). You can control the size and shape of these envelopes by editing their cross sections and control points. Anywhere that envelopes overlap, the deformation can be blended, depending on the vertices' locations within the envelope and the envelope's relative strength.

Anyone who has seen a Mr. Universe contest knows how drastically flexing muscles can alter the shape of the skin. Although not every character animated in MAX needs to be a Mr. Universe contestant, the capability to effectively control and manipulate the shape and appearance of the skin is very important to all characters. Physique also gives you the ability to redefine the outline of a mesh to simulate the flexing and twisting of the muscles underneath.

Note

Character Studio and Physique use a few terms that may be new to even experienced MAX users. Many of these are defined further throughout the chapter, but to help you get started, here are some common terms you should become familiar with:

Deformation. The way a MAX surface or mesh bends and moves in relation to the joints of a hierarchy of MAX objects.

Link. A spline segment that passes through the joints of a hierarchy. The network of orange splines allows smooth and organic deformation of the MAX surface.

Weight. Defines the relationship between a vertex or CV and the links in a hierarchy. A vertex with a weight of 1 or more will attempt to follow the movement of its associated link. A vertex can be weighted to multiple links, in which case MAX will interpolate the vertex's position based on its various weights.

Rigid. A type of vertex. Rigid deformation causes vertices to follow a joint's movement without bending or sliding. A rigid vertex influenced by more than one link will be interpolated based on its proximity and weight to the link.

Deformable. These types of vertices follow a joint's movement more organically, bending or sliding to simulate the movement of skin.

Envelopes. At the heart of Physique's control are spherical boundaries attached to each link that can be used to define the weight assignments for a MAX object's CVs and vertices.

Bounds. Bounds are the spherical boundaries that make up an envelope. The *Inner* and *Outer* bounds determine the weight of a link's influence on vertices that fall inside them.

Cross sections. These editable hulls define the shape and form of Physique's envelopes, bulges, and tendons.

Control points. These are the points that define your cross sections. Manipulate them with the standard MAX transformation tools to translate, rotate, and scale them, refining the shape and volume of envelopes and cross sections.

Bulge. Physique's method of simulating the natural bulging and flexing of skin and muscle.

Tendon. Spread surface deformation across multiple joints to simulate the natural movement of skin and bones just as real-life tendons do.

Custom outlines for any portion of a character's geometry can be defined by cross sections and can be applied according to the joint's angle. In theory, it works exactly the opposite of actual motion, in which the bulging muscle pulls on the joint and causes it to bend. In Physique, bending the joint causes the muscle to bulge, and although the procedure works backward, the effect is visually identical. This enables you not only to form bulging muscles, but also to eliminate the nasty crimping and tearing of vertices common in many other 3D packages.

Physique's Tendons feature gives you the capability to spread a joint's effect over many links. This enables you to simulate details such as the small web between the thumb and forefinger or the stretching of the skin around the shoulders as the arm rotates.

Geometry Types and Physique

Physique supports all three of MAX's geometry types: NURBS surfaces, patches, and polygonal meshes. These are supported in their native mode, which simply means that they are not converted to polygonal meshes before deformation. NURBS surfaces are deformed at the CV level, whereas patches and meshes are deformed at the vertex level.

Although any class of geometry works with Physique, it is much easier to deform a patch or a NURBS surface simply because patches have fewer vertices. High-resolution polygonal meshes can be difficult to manage because the large number of vertices bogs down the CPU, making real-time interaction difficult. Additionally, the density of the mesh makes vertex assignment hard to manage and can cause unwanted creasing and tearing.

Building a Deformable Mesh

Something that's easily overlooked during the building of a computer-generated character—whether from a sketch, from a sculpture, or from scratch—is how the character will deform with the skeleton, especially if the person modeling isn't the one doing the setup. Physique will work with a mesh in any position, but by following a few simple guidelines, you can save yourself a lot of unnecessary adjustments.

Create your character's mesh in as neutral a position as possible while keeping the joints from being too close together (see Figure 7.1). This will help minimize unwanted overlapping in vertex assignment. The legs should be slightly spread and approximately shoulder-width apart. Arms should be extended at shoulder height and slightly bent at the elbows if possible to make the position more neutral. Hands should be even with the wrist, palm facing down, fingers spread slightly to minimize confusion between vertices on adjacent fingers.

Low-resolution polygonal meshes, however, work quite well with Physique. The limited number of vertices make deformation setup quick and easy, and MeshSmooth can be placed in the stack after the deformation takes place to create a very smooth surface. MeshSmooth should be toggled off while you're animating and then toggled on right before rendering, creating characters that animate fast and render well.

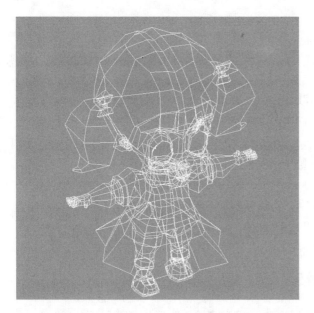

Figure 7.1   You can save yourself a lot of extra work by building your model in the correct pose. A properly positioned mesh gives Physique the room to create envelopes with a minimum of unwanted overlap.

Using Physique

Physique is an object modifier that can be added to an object's stack and then linked to any hierarchy of MAX objects. The hierarchy can be a Character Studio biped, MAX bones, linked dummy objects, or any combination of these.

Once it's linked to a hierarchy, Physique creates a network of splines that are divided into links to control the deformation of the surface. Vertices are assigned to the links using spherical envelopes.

Tip

Because Physique is an object modifier, it should be placed in the stack above any UVW mapping or Sub-Object mapping applied to the object. The texture needs to be applied before the mesh is deformed. Collapse any non-animated modifiers in the stack before applying Physique. This will help speed performance significantly in complex models.

Applying Physique

To apply Physique to a mesh, you have to first add the modifier to its stack. Select More from the Modifier panel and click Physique. This adds Physique to the object's stack and gives you access to the Physique rollout, which appears under the modifier stack. The rollout contains Attach to Node, Reinitialize, and Bulge Editor buttons. You also get controls for saving and loading files in Physique's native .PHY format (see "Saving and Loading Physique Files"). There is also a check box for linking to Root Attach Node. If you want the skin to follow the skeleton, you need to select this option before attaching Physique. Otherwise, the skin will follow the joint rotation, independent of the skeleton's translation in space. This can be handy for simulating Biped's In Place mode.

The Physique Level of Detail rollout controls which components update on your model. By default, Deformable and all its attributes are toggled On. Use these settings to optimize your performance, turning on only those elements you need to see. Often you can turn most of these off after you have set them up and tested them for the model. Turn them back on only when it is time to render.

> **Tip**
>
> With release 2.2, Physique now lets you define separate levels of detail for the viewports and the renderer by toggling the radio button in the Physique Level of Detail rollout. It is important to make sure that any elements you may have turned off while interactively working on your scene are activated in the Level of Detail rollout when you are ready to render. Otherwise, they will not update during the render.

Adding the modifier by itself does not have any effect on the mesh. To be activated, it must be initialized. Click the Attach to Node button in the Physique rollout and select a skeleton node.

In most cases, you will attach Physique to the root node of the skeleton, except in the case of the Biped, where you will select the pelvis. If you want to apply it to only a portion of the skeleton, select the top node of the hierarchy you want to assign it to and turn off Attach to Root Node. This brings up the Initialization panel (see Figure 7.2).

The first time you apply Physique, you will be able to set only a few parameters, which are found in the Vertex-Link Assignment rollout. When initializing, you can select only one envelope type (Deformable or Rigid) to be applied globally. By default, Vertex-Link Assignment is set to Deformable, but you can toggle Rigid on by clicking on the radio button next to it (more on envelope types shortly). You can edit the envelope of any given link on a link-by-link basis at any time after Physique has been applied.

Blending Between Links is used to set the number of links that can affect a vertex. The options are listed here:

- **Nlinks.** The default setting is usually the best. It allows for the most believable mesh deformation.

- **2, 3, or 4 Links.** As the names imply, these limit the number of links that can affect your vertices at the same time. These are usually used only when a game engine has a specific link deformation limit.

- **No Blending.** Similar to the Character Studio 1.X method, vertices can be affected by only one bone at a time. Used only in extremely low-poly models for real-time game engines, this is recommended only as a last resort or to fix certain problems.

Figure 7.2   The Initialization panel contains parameters for all of Physique's attributes. A limited number of choices are available the first time Physique is applied.

You can also set a default envelope in the Radial Falloff Envelopes section. When Create Envelopes is toggled on, which is the default, MAX creates envelopes using either the Object Bounding Box or Link Length method. Object Bounding Box is the default method for envelope creation. This is the best overall solution for defining envelopes because it uses the link's Scale parameters to define the scale of the envelope. Link Length might work okay, but the Bounding Box gives the most accurate envelopes, especially if you have properly scaled the bounding boxes of the Biped or bones hierarchy you are using. If Physique doesn't find any bounding boxes, it will automatically switch to Link Length. During this initial phase, turn Create Envelopes off only if you want to manually assign all your meshes vertices.

Tip

If you are using a non-Biped hierarchy, use the Box Generator utility, found in the Utilities panel, to automatically create bounding boxes for your links. You may want to add this to your Utility rollout by using the Configure Button Sets option. You can then resize and shape them to fit your mesh as you would the Biped, except you can use only MAX's transformation tools.

Envelope Types

Physique uses two types of envelopes, as shown in Figure 7.3. The two types of envelopes are

- **Rigid.** Vertices follow the bone without deforming, except when they're under the influence of more than one envelope. In that case, the vertices will be smoothly blended between the two links. By default, Rigid envelopes appear dark and light green. The inner and outer envelopes are used to determine how vertices will deform when affected by multiple envelopes.

- **Deformable.** Consisting of an inner and an outer spherical bound, Affected vertices follow a deforming spline rather than the actual joint, creating softer and more organic deformation. By default, inner envelopes appear red, and the outer appear purple.

Note

When more than one type of Vertex-Link Assignment is activated, the second type defaults to black for both inner and outer bounds.

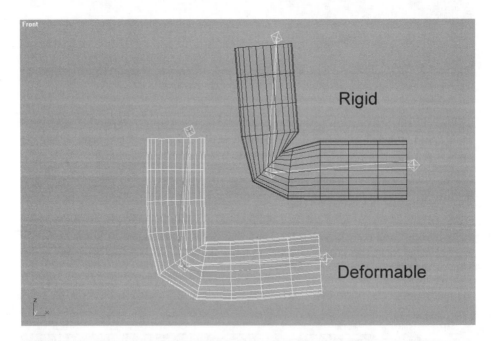

Figure 7.3   Vertices deformed with Rigid envelopes follow the joint's rotation, resulting in a more solid surface. Deformable envelopes stretch and bend the surface for a more organic feel.

Note

Only Deformable envelopes can be used for bulging or Tendon controls.

Although in most cases you will use the default (Deformable), you might want to use Rigid envelopes for areas where the bone is close to the surface of the skin. Changing the envelope for the head will keep it from stretching. You can even have both Rigid and Deformable on the same joint, for areas where the bone is close to the skin. For example, the shin bone is close to the surface, but because the calf is soft, you want to apply bulging. You can use a Deformable envelope to cover the whole lower leg, but scale the Rigid to enclose only the part of the knee and shin you want to keep stiff. They can be used separately or together for different effects. Use Rigid for surfaces such as armor or even a character's head to keep them from sliding or bending. Deformable is better for softer, more organic surfaces that should bend, bulge, or slide over joints.

Envelope Components

An envelope consists of several editable components:

- **Inner bound.** All vertices falling within the inner bound have a base weight of 1.0 (more on weights in a moment) and follow the link exactly. The default color for the Inner bound and its vertices is red.

- **Outer bound.** Defines the outer limit of the envelope's influence. Vertices between the outer and inner bounds fade from 1 to 0 based on the value set in the FallOff parameter. The default color for the Outer bound and the vertices closest to its edge of influence is purple.

- **Cross sections.** The envelope's bounds are shaped by cross sections, which you can translate, rotate, or scale to reposition and shape them to include the vertices you need.

- **Control points.** Each cross section is defined by its control points. You can add, delete, and transform them to reshape an envelope's cross sections.

In order to use Envelopes for deformation, you must turn on the Create Envelopes option in the Radial Falloff Envelopes section of the Physique Initialization dialog box. This gives you access to the controls that define how the envelopes will deform your surface.

- **Object Bounding Box.** Let's you use the link's bounding box to define the envelope scale. This option, toggled on by default, usually gives you the most accurate initial envelope sizes, especially when you're using Biped.

- **Link Length.** If your links don't have bounding boxes or you are not using Biped, this option bases your default envelope scale on the length of each link of the hierarchy.

- **Overlap.** Sets the value by which the Inner bound will overlap the parent and child links. The default of 0.1 keeps them from overlapping in most cases.

- **Smooth.** This determines the size of the outer bounding spheroid. Use Values from 0 to 10, with 0.75 as the default.

- **Falloff.** This sets the vertex weighting falloff between the Inner and Outer bounds of all envelopes in a given Physique.

These values can be changed later for any individual link when Envelope Sub-Object mode is active.

Other settings become available after Physique has been activated, but they are primarily used only for reinitializing.

Tip

If you open a file that was deformed using Physique 1.X, the mesh will still deform, but there are no envelopes. It comes in by default with only vertex weight. To make use of Character Studio's new Envelope system, as well as all the new tools available with release 2.2, you will need to Reinitialize.

Hierarchies and Physique

Physique determines vertex assignments based on the hierarchy of the skeleton, which can be made up of any MAX objects. MAX creates a spline that runs through each joint and is divided by the hierarchy's pivot points. Using the Link Length or Bounding Box scale (if your hierarchy has them), Physique creates a series of spherical envelopes, defining the initial vertex placement. Vertices located within the inner bounding sphere are given a Weight value of 1. This means they will follow the joint exactly. Those vertices between the inner and outer bounding spheres are given values between 0 and 1 based on the degree of falloff defined either in the initialization dialog box or the custom sub-object panel. Vertices under the influence of multiple envelopes are blended based on proximity and envelope strength.

You can make adjustments at any time during the setup process by adjusting the size and shape of the envelopes or manually editing the vertex weight. To see how this works, try adding Physique to a cylinder.

1. Load the file 07max01.max from the accompanying CD-ROM. This contains a simple primitive NURBS cylinder that you will use to learn the principles of envelope vertex assignment.

2. Select the cylinder.

3. From the Modify panel, select the Physique modifier and apply it to the stack.

4. Select Attach to Root Node, press the H key, and select Bone01. The Physique Initialization dialog box appears.

Note

You may have to select More from the Modify panel and scroll through the available Object modifiers to find Physique.

5. Select Bone01, the root node of the bone hierarchy. In the Initialization dialog box, leave all the default settings and click Initialize. This creates Deformable envelopes for the bone, automatically blending the deformation of the envelopes across the two joints. Scrub through the animation to see how the cylinder deforms.

6. Maximize the Front viewport and make sure the display parameters are set to Wireframe.

7. In the Modifier panel, select Envelope from the Sub-Object drop-down menu. Then, select one of the bones to display its envelope (see Figure 7.4).

8. Scrub back and forth to view the animation.

The finished exercise is stored on the CD-ROM in file 07max05.max.

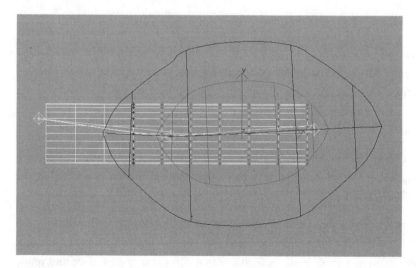

Figure 7.4 Vertices within the bounds of an envelope are colored from red to purple to indicate how much they are being affected by the selected mesh. You can use this as a guide for editing your envelopes or individual vertex weights.

Refining How Physique Affects the Mesh

If a character is being used for a wide variety of shots, the model needs to be tested over a wide range of motion to ensure that the skin behaves the way it should. To test this, it is a good idea to have a test animation that puts the character though its paces. In this animation, the character should move its arms and legs through the extremes of motion.

The file 07max03.max on the accompanying CD-ROM contains a good example of a test animation for putting a biped and its attached mesh through a wide range of motion. The animation is also saved as a Biped file (07bip03.bip) so that you can easily apply it to other models.

Conversely, if a character is being used only for a very specific set of actions, those actions are the only ones that need to be tested. In this case, it might be faster to animate a rough version of the action and then correct any deficiencies in the vertex assignment for those actions only.

Regardless of how you test the motion, if the joint placement of the biped is correct, most of the vertices in the mesh follow along with the biped's joints. Unfortunately, nothing is perfect, and usually stray vertices will cause unwanted pulling and tearing.

Editing Envelopes

When you play back your animation after applying Physique, you may notice that some vertices are left behind or are being deformed by the wrong limbs. You may find that some vertices are deforming too much, while others are not deforming enough. Because Physique relies primarily on envelopes to determine vertex weighting, being able to control their sizes and shapes becomes very important. Using MAX's familiar transformation tools along with the Envelope Parameters dialog box, you can refine and adjust your mesh's deformation quickly, accurately, and efficiently. Often, you will find that you can achieve terrific results using only the Envelope Sub-Object mode.

As you remember, envelopes have an Inner bound and an Outer bound. Each bound is made up of a series of editable cross sections defined by control points, either of which can be edited using MAX's standard transformation tools at the Cross Section or the Control Point selection level.

To view and edit an envelope, select the mesh and choose Envelope from the Sub-Object drop-down menu. Select a joint from the hierarchy. This not only displays the envelope, but gives you access to a set of tools and settings that allow you to customize and refine each envelope in your character's physique in groups or individually.

Blending Envelopes

Each level of Physique editing has specific controls for helping you fine-tune your mesh deformation. Under Blending Envelopes, you have the option to edit your envelopes by Link, Cross Section, or Control Point. Usually, you will start by adjusting the envelope's overall size and position at the Link Selection level.

When editing by Link, you can choose whether the link's Deformable or Rigid envelopes are active under the Active Blending section. You can even use both by checking the boxes next to each. Deformable is on by default, but you can click Inner, Outer, or Both to work with each bound separately or with both.

By default, all vertices are normalized to a weight of 1 to ensure that they will follow the nearest bone as long as they are within an envelope. Enabling Partial Blending will let vertices toward the outer bound of an envelope have values between 0 and 1, such as 0.2, so that it will only partially follow the joint.

The Strength parameter adjusts the influence of an envelope over vertices shared with another link. Setting the value of one envelope higher than another will allow it to exert more control over a vertex that lies partially in two or more envelopes. Falloff affects the rate at which weights change between inner and outer bounds.

Many deformation problems can be solved simply by adjusting an envelope's scale or how much it overlaps its parent or child using these controls:

- **Radial Scale.** Changes the radial scale of an envelope or its bounds. One of the easiest ways to fix unassigned vertex problems is by adjusting the Radial Scale of the envelope's inner or outer bounds to capture the stray vertices.

- **Parent/Child Overlap.** Adjusts how an envelope overlaps its parent or child links to ensure smooth deformation around joints.

You can also use the standard MAX transformation tools to resize and reposition the envelope for the selected link. Working at the Link selection level puts you in the object space of the selected link. Translation moves the selection along the length of the joint, whereas rotation works around the link's z-axis. Scale behaves the same as Radial scale.

While in Link mode, you can also use the Copy and Paste tools to transfer any link's envelope onto another joint, regardless of size. Because envelope parameters are based on joint length, if the joints are radically different, they may require some tweaking, but it is perfect for quickly fixing symmetrical limbs. Adjust the envelope for one link, and then copy and paste onto the opposite. Refine placement on the new limb by mirroring and rotating the envelope into its proper place. For areas where joints are too close together and vertices are being miss-assigned to adjacent links, you can use the Exclude option. This will exclude any vertices in one envelope from any other specified in the Exclude dialog box (see Figure 7.5).

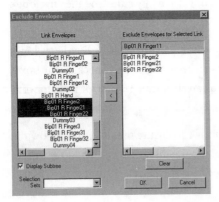

Figure 7.5   Use the Exclude dialog box to keep envelopes from joints that are too close together from crossing over. This makes areas like the fingers much easier to deal with, allowing you to be less accurate in envelope placement.

Editing by Cross Section or Control Point

If editing the scale and overlap isn't enough, you can reshape the envelopes by editing their cross sections and control points. The Inner and Outer bound of each envelope is made up of an oblong sphere defined by four cross sections with control points at each end. By entering their selection level, you can edit them with the same transformation tools you have been using all along.

When you edit in Cross Section mode, you are in the link's object space. For translation, you are restricted to sliding your cross section along the length of the joint to reshape the bound. You can also rotate around the z-axis and scale the cross sections radially.

By editing the control points, you can even change the shape of each individual cross section, as well as reposition the end-points for the envelope's bounds.

> **Tip**
>
> Control points for the cross sections have cylindrical coordinates. When repositioning them, you should use Scale and Rotate. When you scale a control point, it moves perpendicular to the joint. The Rotate tool will rotate the control point around the link's z-axis, maintaining a fixed distance from the joint. The Translate tool scales and rotates simultaneously, making accurate placement more difficult.

When you need more cross sections or control points, just use the options in the Edit Commands section.

- **Insert.** Inserts a cross section or control point as needed. This option is available only in the Cross Section and Control Point selection levels.

- **Delete.** Deletes the selected cross section or control point. You cannot delete an envelope this way.

Tip

You cannot delete envelopes from individual links. If you need to get rid of an envelope's influence, you can set the envelope's Radial Scale to 0.

- **Copy/Paste.** You can copy and paste envelopes or cross sections depending on which mode you are in. You can apply these commands to only whole envelopes and selected cross sections; they are not available while editing control points.

- **Mirror.** Apply this to the selected envelopes or cross sections to flip them along the Mirror axis.

Adjusting Envelopes

With an understanding of the basics, you're ready to test drive the envelope editing commands. In this exercise, you will apply Physique to the mesh and biped from Chapter 6's "Fitting a Biped to a Mesh" tutorial.

1. From the accompanying CD-ROM, load 07max04.max.

2. Select the Meshman mesh and open the Modify panel. Apply Physique to the modifier stack from the Modifier rollout.

3. To assign Physique to the Biped, click on Attach to Node in the Physique rollout. Make sure Link to Root Attach Node is toggled on, and then select the biped's pelvis. The Physique Initialization dialog box appears. Click Initialize.

4. This biped was adjusted in Figure mode; now you can remove it from Figure mode by clicking on the Figure Mode icon in the Motion panel. The shape shifts slightly, but that's okay.

5. The biped has the deformation testing animation from 07max03.bip already loaded. Scrub through the animation to test the deformation.

   It's not bad for the default settings. There are a few problems, though. The shoes deform abnormally, the feet appear to be sharing vertex weights, and the armpits look a little odd. But all of this can be easily fixed by adjusting the envelopes.

6. First, fix the feet. Select the mesh and choose Envelope from the Physique Sub-Object drop-down.

7. Select the joint for the right foot. The envelope appears to be too large. You can see that it includes part of the other foot, as well as the trouser leg.

8. Using the Non-Uniform Scale tool, scale the foot's envelope on the z-axis until the envelope no longer touches the other foot. Scale in x as well to make the envelope fit the foot more. Do the same to the toes. Scrub through the problem frames whenever you make a change so you can see the errors. Be careful, though. If you scale the envelopes too much, vertices will remain behind when you scrub the animation.

9. Now the left foot is no longer being stretched, but the right foot still is. Select the right foot link and, in the Blending Envelopes rollout, click Copy in the Edit Commands group. Select the opposite foot and click Paste. Repeat for the toes. Then scrub frames 40 through 90. There is still a little pulling by the thighs.

10. Select the right calf link and change the Parent Overlap to 0.2. The envelope still includes a piece of the left thigh. You'll change that using the Control Point tools.

Note

To make it easier to know which link you are editing, the selected link's name appears in the Physique Selection Status rollout. Heed this word of caution when you're working with Biped. Physique's links are named for the link's child, so when you are editing the envelope deforming Meshman's thigh, the name reads Bip01 R calf.

11. Select the Control Point tool and notice that the control points for each of the envelope's cross sections are now available. Select the two Outer bound control points that are in the opposite leg (see Figure 7.6) and scale them in x until they no longer touch the other leg. Scrub the animation to see the improvements.

12. When it is adjusted to your taste, return to Link mode by clicking the Link button. Then, select Copy and Paste from the Edit Commands section to transfer the corrected envelope onto the opposite leg. Click Mirror and then rotate 180 degrees in y.

13. Advance to frame 27. The arms flatten when the arms are brought to the side. To fix the armpits, you'll need a good view of them. Zoom in to the upper torso in the front panel and select what appears to be the top spine link (Bip01 Neck). The envelope appears much too large, encompassing too much of the arms and causing them to flatten when the arms come in to the side.

14. Check Initial Skeletal Pose in the Display section of the Blending Envelopes panel; the mesh snaps to the pose it was in when Physique was applied.

15. Make sure Both is toggled On in the Envelope parameters so you can edit both inner and outer envelopes at the same time (see Figures 7.7a and b).

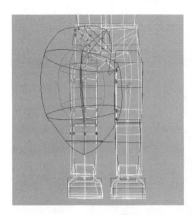

Figure 7.6   The envelopes still overlap the opposite leg. When in envelope mode, it is easy to see potential problems. The envelopes give you a clear idea of exactly which points are being affected by which links.

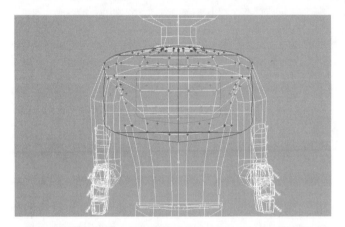

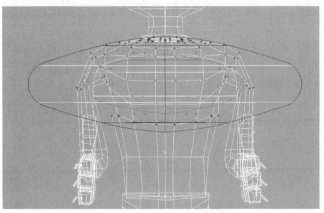

Figures 7.7a and b   By scaling the middle cross sections of the neck link together, you can quickly exclude unwanted vertices.

16. Set the Selection Level to Cross Section and select the center two cross sections of both the inner and outer bounds. Use the Scale transformation tool to shrink the envelope until the Outer bound is just big enough to fit the vertices on the arms. Clear the check box for Initial Skeletal Pose, and your arms should deform properly (see Figure 7.8).

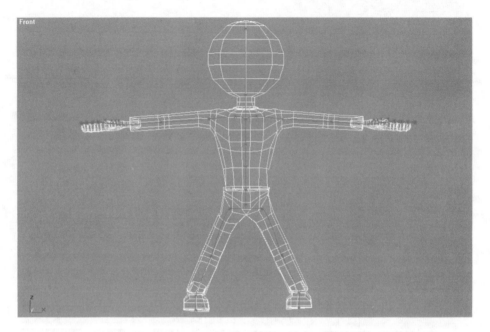

Figure 7.8   When Meshman's envelopes are adjusted properly, the mesh deforms smoothly with the Biped skeleton.

The completed tutorial is stored on the accompanying CD in 07max08.max.

Physique Link Parameters

When you activate Physique, a continuous spline is threaded throughout each joint of the hierarchy. The joints form the subdivisions known in Character Studio 2.2 as *links*. Whereas envelopes are responsible for the majority of the vertex weight assignments (see "Vertex Control" for alternate methods of assigning weights), the links, which now appear as a network of orange lines, control the actual deformation of the skin. The spline bends with the joints to maintain a smooth curve for the weighted vertices to follow.

The bulge can be even further modified by using the Physique Link parameters in the Link Sub-Object panel (see Figure 7.9). These parameters give you additional control over how the skin stretches and compresses as the joint bends, twists, and scales. Use the cylinder file 07max01.max to experiment with the effects of the different link settings.

Bend

Bend parameters control the flow of skin over a bending joint, such as a knee or elbow. They apply to hinge-like movement perpendicular to the axis of the bend.

The Tension setting determines the tightness of the crimp at the bend. A higher number produces a more arc-shaped bend, and a lower number causes the joint to crimp more.

The Bias value determines the angle of the crimp. At 0.5, it is evenly centered between the joints. When the value moves higher, the crimp is angled toward the link's child; when the value is lower, the crimp is angled toward the link (see Figures 7.10 and 7.11).

Figure 7.9
Because the links are essentially a single spline, each of the Link Parameters has Tension and Bias controls similar to those found in the Motion panel.

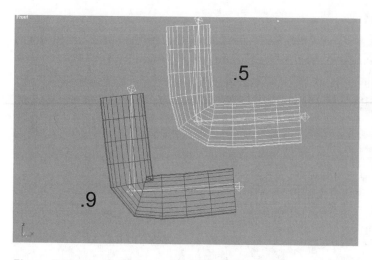

Figure 7.10   A cylinder bent with different Bias settings.

Twist

Twist parameters determine how the mesh is affected when the joint is twisted along its length. This helps to simulate the deformation of the arm when a hand turns a screwdriver.

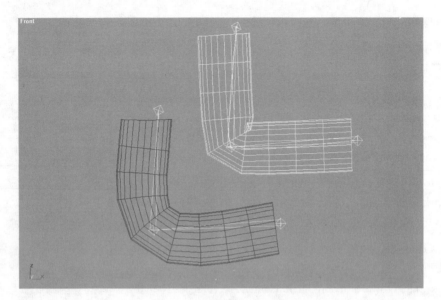

Figure 7.11   The figure on the bottom has a high Bend Tension; the one on the top has a low Bend Tension.

Tension determines how much the skin rotates around the length of the joint. A value of 1.0 causes all skin along the length of the joint to rotate evenly. Lower values emphasize the twist closer to the rotating link, and higher values add extra twisting to the skin farther away from the point of rotation. The effects of Twist are shown in Figure 7.12.

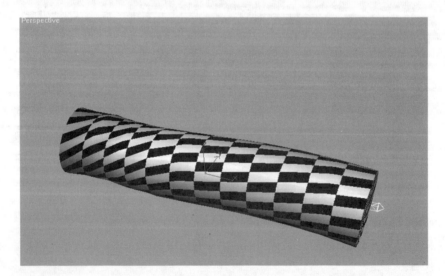

Figure 7.12   The Twist parameter allows you to simulate the twisting of the arm as the hand turns a screwdriver.

Bias shifts the Twist effect toward or away from the link. A value lower than 0.5 puts more of the twist on the skin covering the child link, and a higher value puts more of the twist on the selected link.

Sliding

The Sliding parameter relaxes and tightens the mesh to prevent unwanted bunching and stretching at the joints. Skin on the outside shifts toward the rotating joint, whereas the vertices on the inside shift away. Because this parameter affects the mesh behavior more than the link, you have a different set of controls. Instead of Tension and Bias, you can use values from 0 to 1 for Inside, Outside, and FallOff.

For Inside, the higher the value, the more the skin will shift away from the joint as the angle decreases. The default is 0. For Outside, it is the opposite; higher values cause the skin to slide toward the joint as the angle increases.

FallOff fades the effect along the length of the joint. A value of 1 affects the whole joint, a value of 0 affects none. The default is 0.5 (see Figure 7.13).

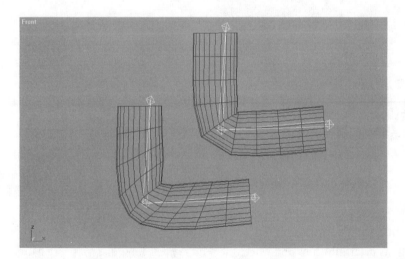

Figure 7.13   Sliding helps you maintain your geometry's overall shape around hinge joints. The upper cylinder has no adjustment, the bottom has both the Inside and Outside slide parameters set to 0.5.

Radial Scale

Radial Scale parameters define how the skin and any underlying cross sections are affected by the scaling of the links. Because Physique looks at the hierarchy and not the physical bones themselves, the links can be scaled by turning off IK and translating the bones to increase or decrease the distance between the links.

Tension controls focus the effect around the joint with lower values and spread out with values larger than 1.

Bias tilts the effect to the parent or child, depending on the values entered. The default of 0.5 affects both equally.

CS Amplitude is a new parameter designed specifically to work with bulges. The values run from 0 to 10, where a value of 0 disables the cross section. A value of 1 is normal. Larger values exaggerate the bulge's effect.

Activating the Stretch and Breathe buttons is one easy way to get squash-and-stretch effects when using Physique. Stretch and Breathe enable you to create this effect automatically by moving or scaling the bone. Stretch pulls out the mesh along the length of the link, whereas Breathe expands the mesh radially (see Figure 7.14). You cannot use this technique with Biped bones, however, because they cannot scale over time.

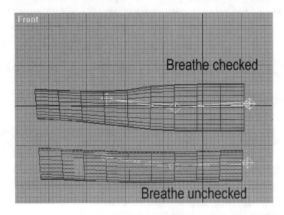

Figure 7.14   Bone scaled with and without the Breathe option.

Physique Joint Intersections

Joint intersections determine how and where the joint creases. Physique tries very hard not to have skin vertices cross over each other because this causes one part of the skin to penetrate another—something that would not happen in real life.

To effect this, Physique places an imaginary plane between the joints and restricts vertices on either side from crossing over. This keeps the skin seamless and can cause a natural crease. A good example is the skin around the fingers. It tends to crease along a nice, flat plane. Sometimes, however, you might want the joint intersections to be less planar, to create a dimple, perhaps.

Typically, the Default Planar joint intersections are fine, but they can sometimes "go flat" before the skin actually touches, particularly when the skin bulges dramatically. This can be tweaked by using the Joint Intersections dialog box. This determines how the plane affects the crease. A Bias value of 1.0 means that the plane is fully active, causing a Planar crease; a lower value reduces the planarity of the effect. The From and To spinners determine how much of the skin around the joint is affected by the plane.

Vertex Control

Occasionally, it can be difficult to get the precise deformation you need from a particular vertex using the envelope sub-object, or you may like assigning vertices the old fashioned way—manually. If a joint affects an unwanted area of the mesh, the vertices in those areas can be reassigned manually to another joint. To do this, select the Vertex Sub-Object rollout from the Physique panel and reassign the vertices or change their behavior. In Physique, vertices are assigned colors—red, green, or blue. The specific color of the vertex defines the way the individual vertex behaves. The Vertex Sub-Object rollout is shown in Figure 7.15.

There are three different types of vertex assignments:

- **Red vertices.** These vertices are Deformable. They flex, bend, and move with the joint to which they have been assigned.

- **Green vertices.** These vertices are rigid. They move along with the joint, but they do not flex or change shape. This is good for areas such as the head and skull, which remain relatively rigid.

- **Blue vertices.** These vertices are not assigned to any specific joint and are known as *root vertices*. They do not move with the skeleton.

By default, each vertex is assigned as Deformable, so every vertex in the body should be red. If a vertex is defaulted as root (blue), it means that the vertex did not lie within the bounding spheres of any joint within the skeleton and could not be assigned. This is

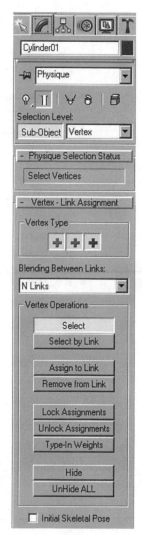

Figure 7.15
The Vertex Sub-Object controls

often caused by joints at the end of the chain, such as the top of the head or the ends of the fingers, which did not protrude through the ends of the mesh when Physique was applied.

The Physique Vertex Assignment rollout contains the tools for selecting and assigning (or reassigning) vertices to the correct links.

- **Vertex Type.** This set of three buttons enables you to control which vertices are selected and assigned. These buttons affect the selection set that you create with the Select, Select by Link, and Assign to Link buttons (described next). For example, if the red button is pressed, only Deformable (red) vertices are selected or assigned.

- **Blending Between Links.** This works exactly the same as the Blending Between Links option in the Physique Initialization dialog box. Set the number of links that you want to be able to affect a given vertex (see "Using Physique" for more details).

- **Select.** Enabling this button lets you use the standard MAX selection tools, such as the box or fence, to select groups of vertices.

- **Select by Link.** This button enables you to select all the vertices currently assigned to a single joint. The type of vertices selected depends on the settings of the Vertex Type buttons.

- **Assign to Link.** This button assigns the currently selected vertices to the selected link. The setting of the Vertex Type button determines how these are assigned. If the button is red, the vertices are Deformable; green assigns them as rigid, and blue assigns them as root.

- **Remove from Link.** Removes active vertices from a link by selecting this option and clicking on a link from the hierarchy. If shared by multiple envelopes, the vertices will remain under the influence of any unselected envelopes. If this removes them from all links, they turn blue, for root.

Tip

Character Studio Release 2.2 provides a check box labeled Initial Skeletal Pose in the Vertex Assignment rollout. This check box enables you to toggle between the initial pose (typically with arms outstretched) and whatever pose the figure happens to be in when you enter Physique's Sub-Object level.

If you manually reassign vertices and override the envelopes, you will have to use Lock Assignments to remove them from envelope influence and prevent them from being reassigned. Unlock Assignments releases them back to envelope control.

In certain cases, especially when you're dealing with low-poly models, you may want to manually adjust a vertex's weight. Using the Type-In-Weights dialog box, you change a weight's value, reassign it to another joint by selecting the joint name you want from the drop-down menu, or scale the weight of an already assigned vertex. The vertices you wish to edit have to be locked, so they aren't accidentally reassigned back to an envelope after you have made your adjustment.

Physique and Biped

Although Physique can be used with MAX's native bones or any hierarchy of objects, marrying the two halves of Character Studio enables Physique to be affected by a Biped skeleton, making full use of the power of Character Studio.

Fitting a Biped to a Mesh

For Physique to work correctly, the biped must be properly fitted to the mesh. The joints of the biped have to line up with the mesh's joints, and links must be positioned to ensure the envelopes will include the proper geometry.

Tip

Because Biped can use the joint's bounding box to determine the initial scale of its envelope, it is helpful to scale the biped's boxes to match the contour of your mesh. This helps ensure that the default envelope sizes are more accurate and require less tweaking.

Physique's Figure mode is identical to Biped's Figure mode. Placing the biped in Figure mode sets an initial pose, which Biped remembers, so you can return the biped to that pose at any time by selecting the Figure mode button. Figure mode also enables resizing and positioning of a biped, allowing you to properly position it within your surface so Physique can apply accurate deformations.

Now it's time for some practice.

1. Load 07max02.max from the accompanying CD-ROM.

2. Create a biped roughly the same height as the mesh. In the biped's Structure roll-out, set the number of fingers and toes to match the character. If your character is wearing shoes, one toe will suffice.

3. Select the mesh, go to the Display panel, and select Freeze Selected or press 6 on the keyboard. This way, the mesh won't accidentally be selected while the biped is being manipulated.

4. Select the biped. Go to the Motion panel and place the biped in Figure mode. In Figure mode, you are free to rotate and scale every joint of the biped.

5. Select the Center of Mass object and position the biped over the body so the hips rest inside the pelvis area. One thing to remember is that manipulating a biped in Figure mode puts the navigation tools in World Space. This means that, from the front, the biped moves along the xz-axis (see Figure 7.16).

Figure 7.16   Proper placement of a biped inside a mesh (note that xz is the front plane).

6. Non-uniform scale the pelvis in z so that the joint between the hips and thighs rests along the V-shaped area, which defines the crease between the tops of the thighs and the crotch (refer to Figure 7.16).

7. Scale the spinal segments so that the shoulders are slightly beneath the shoulders of the mesh and the joint between the shoulder and the upper arm resides above the mesh's armpit.

8. Select the feet and move them up to fit inside Meshman's feet. Then, enter Rubber Band mode to easily position the knees and elbows inside your mesh. The Symmetrical Tracks button can be used to easily select both legs for manipulation. Translate the knees so that they are properly aligned within the joint area of the mesh. Rotate the legs to align them with the mesh.

Tip

Instead of using Symmetrical Tracks, you can adjust one side of a biped and mirror it to the other side using Copy Posture Opposite.

9. Using Rubber Band mode, translate the hands and elbows so the elbows of the biped line up with the elbow area of the mesh. Use the Top viewport to rotate the arms until they fit into the mesh and have a natural bend to them.

10. If your character has fingers that move, adjust the bones in the hand to match the fingers. A biped's fingers can not only be resized and rotated but also moved along the edge of the palm bone to achieve an exact fit.

The completed figure file is stored on the accompanying CD-ROM as meshman_ok.fig.

Tip

Resize the biped's boxes by scaling them to closely match the outline of your mesh. This helps Physique define the initial envelope sizes, making sure the envelopes contain all the right vertices. In Figure 7.17, the head is too small, so when it tilts forward, the top of the skull remains stationary.

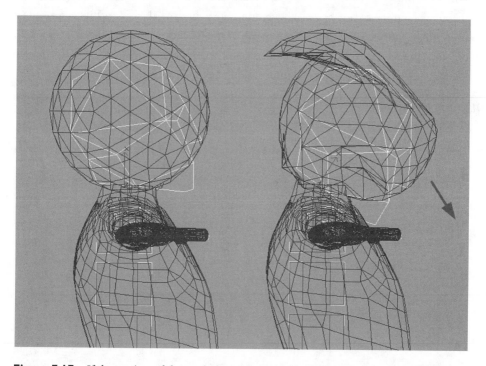

Figure 7.17   If the vertices of the mesh do not lie inside the link envelope's bounding spheres, the vertices will be left behind.

Applying Physique to a Biped

After the mesh has been fitted, you can link the skin to the biped. To deform the entire mesh with a biped, the Physique modifier should be attached to the pelvis. With release 2.2, you can no longer accidentally select the Center of Mass object. The Center of Mass object moves on every frame to reflect the changing mass distribution of the biped. This means that the joint between the Center of Mass and the rest of the biped stretches and changes shape, causing all sorts of problems. Instead, if you try to select the Center of Mass when applying Physique, Character Studio automatically assigns it to the biped's pelvis.

If parts of the body or clothing are modeled as separate objects, such as eyeballs or a hat, select all the objects and apply a single Physique modifier to all of them. Later, you'll be able to make some of the vertices rigid so they do not deform (see the next section for a description of how to do this).

Creating Realistic Bulges

When the muscles in the body flex and relax, they not only move our bones, they also change the outline of our body. When you rotate your arm, the biceps bulge, forming a shape that changes depending on the angle of the forearm's rotation (see Figure 7.18). Physique's Bulge controls simulate that complex relationship by allowing you to animate the shape of your geometry based on rotation angles, as opposed to actual key frames.

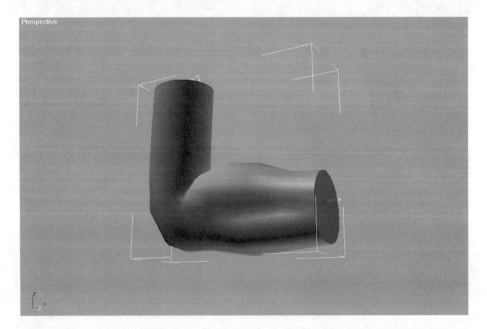

Figure 7.18   A cylinder bulges according to the angle of the joint.

The Bulge Sub-Object level gives you access to the Bulge rollout and all the tools you will need to manipulate the selected link's cross section. Bulge Angles define the angle that has the maximum deformation. You can give this a custom name to make it easier to track. Then, by adding and reshaping bulge cross sections, you can deform for the geometry.

Bulge Angle parameters allow you to set, create, and delete bulge angles. To make it more intuitive and easier to learn, the bulge angles settings offer basically the same editing tools you had for editing envelopes. You can edit the cross sections interactively right in your MAX viewports using the standard MAX transformation tools, or you can work in the Bulge Editor, formerly known as the Cross Section Editor. You also have access to additional controls for how a particular bulge angle affects your mesh (see Figure 7.19).

The Bulge Angle parameters are listed here:

- **Influence.** Determines how far from the current angle the bulge begins to take effect.

- **Power.** Acts as an ease value that is applied to the Influence to control how fast the bulge begins to affect your mesh.

Tip

Influence and Power allow you to use Bulge as a modeling tool, maintaining your bulges across all angles. For instance, if you started with a simple cylinder, using cross sections, you can model a bicep that will remain constant but still deform as the joint rotates, by simply adjusting the Influence angle to 180 degrees. Because the joint can rotate only 180 degrees from whatever the Bulge Angle is, this becomes the new default shape of the cylinder. Because Physique interpolates multiple Bulge Angles, you can define as many other Bulge shapes and angles on top of this as you like.

Figure 7.19
The Bulge rollout has tools to help you shape and define your meshes, bulge angles, and cross sections, and their relative effects.

- **Weight.** Acting as a multiplier, Weight defines how much your bulge angle affects the mesh. With the default value of 1, your mesh will conform 100 percent to the cross sections at the current bulge angle.

The three Cross Section parameters give you control of the number of cross sections and how detailed they are.

- **Sections.** Controls the number of cross sections affecting the selected links.

- **Divisions.** Sets the number of control points that defines the cross sections.
- **Resolutions.** Determines the radial resolution of the cross sections by breaking up the cross sections in a radial grid.

The Bulge Editor

Another way to control your bulges is to use the Bulge Editor. Formerly the Cross Section Editor, this is a floating dialog box that enables you to create bulge angles, their cross sections, and (as you will see later) tendons. You can access this dialog box, shown in Figure 7.20, by clicking the Bulge Editor button from within the main Physique rollout or from the Bulge and Tendon Sub-Object levels.

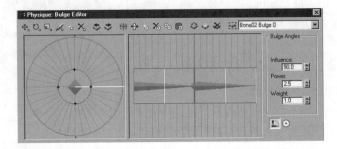

Figure 7.20   The Bulge Editor contains tools for defining and editing Bulge Angles and Bulge Cross Sections.

The Bulge Editor is modeless, which means you can use it along with the standard MAX viewports to select and modify parameters on-the-fly. The window has a toolbar at the top with two windows along the bottom—on the lower left is the Cross Section view, and on the lower right is the Link view. In combination, these can be used to create and manage the bulge of the skin around the joint. You also have the standard Insert, Copy, Paste, Delete, and Mirror tools for copying and pasting cross sections.

The easiest way to visualize exactly how Physique creates and manages bulges is to use a simple, predictable object, such as a cylinder.

1. Open 07max09.max, from the accompanying CD. This contains a cylinder with Physique applied, and the link parameters adjusted to accommodate the bending and twisting the joint will do.

2. In any MAX viewport, select the cylinder, click the Sub-Object button, and set the Sub-Object type as Bulge.

3. From within the Front MAX viewport, select Bone02. The bone's Bulge parameters appear.

4. To create a bulge, you first need to tell Physique at what angle the bulge will be defined. The default angle is the angle at which the bone was positioned when Physique was applied. The second angle should be where the joint is rotated the most. In this animation, the maximum rotation is at frame 30. Move the Time Slider to frame 30.

5. To add a bulge, click the Insert Bulge Angle button. A new bulge angle is created and automatically named Bone2 Bulge 1. Click in the Current Bulge Angle name field and rename it to something more descriptive, such as Bicep1.

6. Next, you need to define the shape you want the Bulge to have. For this you will add and edit cross sections. Enter Cross Section mode by selecting the Cross Section tool under Selection level.

7. In the Cross Section parameters group, click the Insert button and move the cursor over your mesh. A red line appears and follows along the link as you move your cursor to show you where the cross section will be added. Place your cursor close to the bend and click. A thicker red line appears, indicating that the cross section has been added.

8. You can now edit the cross section right in the viewport, or you can use the Bulge Editor to define the bulge for that angle.

Tip

If you choose to edit in the viewport, use only the Scale and Rotate tools in Control Point mode, because Translate actually scales and rotates your points at the same time, making it more difficult to predict the results.

9. For now, use the Bulge Editor. Activate it by clicking on the Bulge Editor icon in the Bulge rollout. Reposition it so that you can see the Perspective viewport. Select the cross section in the middle of the upper arm link and click Select and Scale Ctrl Points from the Bulge Editor toolbar. In the Cross Section view, click the top-most control point and drag it upward. This movement is reflected in both the Link view and within the normal MAX viewports. Notice that this affects the bottom of the mesh in the viewport, forming the triceps (see Figures 7.21a and b.)

10. Now grab the bottom control point and drag it up. The muscle begins to take shape. Select the two control points in the middle and, using the Scale tool, scale them inward to refine the biceps's shape (see Figure 7.22).

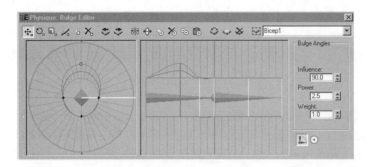

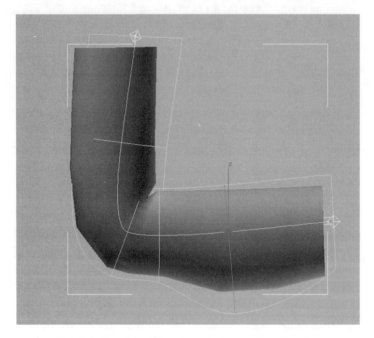

Figures 7.21a and b When you're working in the Bulge Editor, be sure to watch the MAX viewports to see how your model is being deformed. Sometimes the results differ from what you imagined.

11. Scrub the Time Slider. The muscle now bulges. When the joint is flat, there is no bulge, but when the joint is flexed, the bulge appears.

You can find the completed exercise in the file 07max10.max on the accompanying CD-ROM.

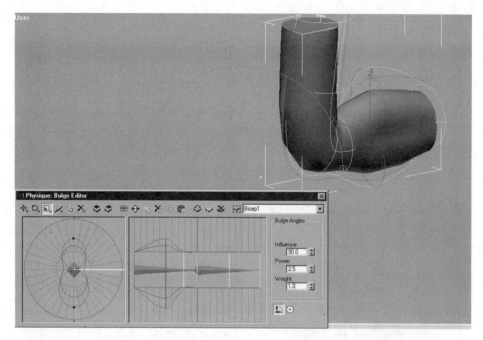

Figure 7.22   Reshaping a bulge cross section changes the shape of your mesh interactively, allowing you to model your bulges accurately and intuitively.

Building Better Bulges

You are not limited to simple bulge shapes, either. Physique lets you add as many bulge cross sections as you need to define the shape you want, and you can edit them in much the same as you would an envelope cross section, except now you are actually deforming the geometry. You can have multiple bulge angles for the same joint, which allows you to simulate the way muscles work in real life. MAX interpolates the shapes based on the angles you set, so if you have two bulge angles, MAX will create a shape based on the Influence, Power, and Weight values you set.

Using the file you created in the previous exercise or 07max10.max from the accompanying CD, try refining the biceps to make them behave more like a life-like muscle. You can further modify the shape of the bulge by adding more cross sections, and you can provide more detail by adding control points to the cross sections. You can also add more bulge angles to further refine how the bulge expands and contracts. Start by editing the cross section you added earlier and then adding some control points.

1. Return to frame 30 and, in the Bulge Editor, select the cross section closest to the elbow joint. Drag the top and bottom control points to bring out the shape of the muscles.

2. Select the middle cross section and use the Insert Control Points tool to add control points to the top, where the cross section defines the triceps area. Using the Scale, Rotate Control Points tool, drag them up and out to give the triceps more definition. Edit the control points for the cross section closest to the elbow so the effect tapers off (see Figure 7.23).

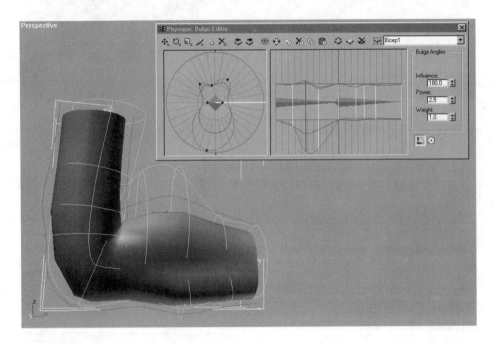

Figure 7.23   Adding control points and reshaping the cross section lets you add as much detail as you need to shape your bulges.

3. Insert another cross section closer to what would be the shoulder using the Insert CS tool from the Bulge Editor toolbar. Notice that it contains the necessary control point to maintain the shape you have set.

4. Next, give your cylinder a more permanent musculature. In the Bulge rollout, set the Influence to 180. Then scrub through your animation. The cylinder now keeps a bit of the bulge shape, but still deforms as the angle increases. You can experiment with the power and weight setting to get the results you need.

When you flex your arm, the shape of the bicep changes based on the rotation of your forearm. You can simulate that by adding another bulge angle. Although it's not perfect, ideally you could create a different set of bulge angles for each muscle group; for a quick and easy demonstration of Physique's power, this works just fine.

5. Go to frame 45 in the animation, where the joint is at maximum rotation in both Z and X. Create a new bulge angle, using the Insert Bulge Angle tool in the Bulge Angle Parameters section of the Bulge rollout. This creates a new bulge angle, based off the previous one, so you can use the same cross sections you just defined to reshape the arm for another angle. Rename it Bicep2.

6. Select the cross section nearest to the elbow and, using the Scale and Rotate Control Points tool, drag the lower control point to flatten out the biceps near the crease of the elbow.

7. Select the cross section closest to what would be the shoulder and edit the lower control point to pull the top of the control point up, shifting the bicep's bulge. Scrub through the animation.

   Oops, the bulge doesn't change much. Because you created your new bulge angle while Bicep1 was active, Physique applied all of Bicep1's parameters to your new angle, including its Influence parameters. This is easily fixed.

8. In the Bulge Angle Parameters section of the Bulge rollout, set Bicep2's Influence to 90. Then scrub the animation—it's much more believable.

You could add another bulge angle to the joint, call it forearm, and actually model your cylinder to look even more like an arm. If you set the Influence angle to 180, it will retain that shape no matter how you animate the arm.

Note

Be sure to change the current bulge angle to Bone02 Bulge 0, or at least return to frame 0 before creating your forearm bulge angle. That way, you won't duplicate all the bulge shapes as the default.

For the final file, with the added forearm and a mesh smooth, see the file 07max11.max on the accompanying CD (see Figure 7.24).

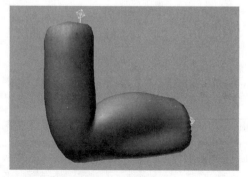

Figure 7.24   With just a few more cross sections and a little tweaking, the cylinder has become a detailed arm.

Tendons

Tendons are used to further refine the way the character's skin behaves across many joints when cross sections and bulge angles aren't enough. They enable you to make one joint affect the outline of another joint's vertices over many links. They can be best used in areas such as the shoulder and pelvic areas, where T-shaped branching exists. They can also be used in skinning hands, particularly the fleshy webbing between the thumb and forefinger. A tendon has three main components:

- **Base.** The base is where one or more tendon cross sections originate. A base can be applied to any link in the skeleton. Usually, the base resides in the torso.

- **Cross sections.** These are much like the cross sections used to create bulges; attach points are located at radial subdivisions of the outline of the cross section.

- **Attach points.** These are the points on the cross sections that can be tied to other links. The attached link is usually a shoulder or pelvic bone. Each attach point can be tied to a different link.

How Tendons Work

For a good example of how tendons affect the skin across multiple joints, use a simple T-shaped mesh and attach a few tendons between the joints as it flexes.

1. Load the file 07max07.max. This file contains a T-shaped mesh and a set of tendons attached to it. The tendons run from the middle joint of the vertical branch to the middle joint of the right horizontal branch (see Figure 7.25).

2. Move the Time Slider to frame 25. Notice how the middle joint on the right limb affects the vertical joint. This is due to the action of a tendon (see Figure 7.26).

3. Move the Time Slider to frame 50. As the middle-right joint flexes down, it affects the skin on the vertical joint.

4. Move the Time Slider to frame 75. Again, the skin on the middle joint bulges, even though many other joints are active.

This shows that tendons can give a more globalized effect than just bulge angles, enabling skin to flow across many joints. The T-shaped branch is very similar to the branches that occur in the human body (between the spine, shoulders, and arms; between the spine, pelvis, and legs; and even between the thumb and forefinger). Tendons can be used to the same effect with a biped or with other types of skeletons, such as 3DS MAX bones.

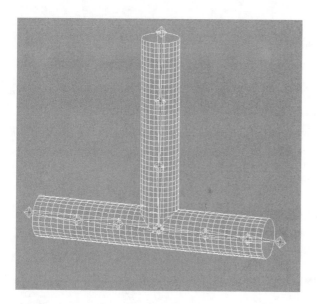

Figure 7.25   This T-shaped object can be used to demonstrate how tendons affect the skin across multiple joints.

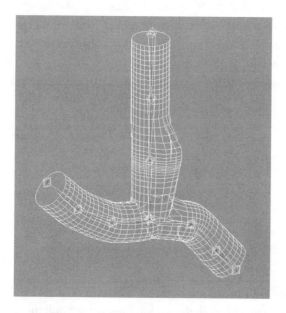

Figure 7.26   As the far joints rotate, the skin on the vertical shaft is affected, even though the two joints are not adjacent.

Creating Tendons

Tendons are created in Tendon Sub-Object mode from the Physique panel. You just need to select the link that will become the base and then click the Create button on the Physique Tendons rollout. This panel has a number of parameters.

- **Sections.** The number of cross section bases created for the link.
- **Attach points.** The number of radial attach points around each of the cross sections.
- **Resolution.** The radial resolution of the cross sections.

A pair of tendons can be used to help maintain the outline of the belly where it meets the pelvic area. Many times, creasing occurs in this area. Tendons can help maintain the shape of the character. Give them a try.

1. Open the file 07max08.max. This file has an animation you can use to test the flexibility of the character.

2. Select the mesh, go to the Physique Modifier panel, and select Tendon Sub-Object mode.

3. Select the central spinal joint (Bip01 Spine 2), scroll down to the Tendons rollout in the Modify panel, and set the default Sections parameter to 1. These must be set before the tendon's base is created.

4. Click the Insert button and move the cursor over the selected link. The purple line that follows the cursor's movement along the link shows where the base will be created. Click in the middle of the link. This creates a base for tendons originating from this joint.

5. Set the Selection Level to Control Point and select the Attach point along the front right of the torso. Use the Top or Perspective viewport, as shown in Figure 7.27.

6. Attach this point to the right clavicle joint. To do this, click the Attach button in the Edit Commands section of the Tendons rollout and click the right clavicle joint from within the Front viewport.

7. Repeat the same procedure for the front-left attach point and the left clavicle joint. The tendons are now attached. However, the tendon does not yet pull the mesh correctly (see Figure 7.28).

8. Save the file as 07max08a.max. You'll modify the tendons in the last exercise.

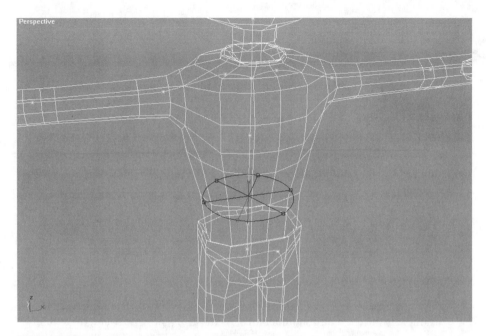

Figure 7.27   The tendon is in place on the spine link and is ready for attachment.

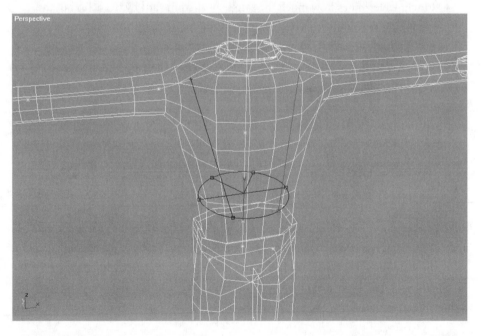

Figure 7.28   After the tendons are properly attached, they look like this, but you will probably need to adjust the parameters before they will behave properly.

Note

To select another attach point, you must deselect the Attach button in the Edit Command section of the Tendon Control panel, select your new attach point, and then toggle the Attach command back on.

Modifying Tendons

After being attached, the tendons may need to be modified so that they affect the way the skin behaves across the joints. The Tendon parameters in the Tendon rollout enable you to modify the way the tendons deform the mesh across multiple links. These parameters are described here:

- **Radius.** Specifies how far out the attach points lie from the body. If you look at the tendons from within a MAX viewport, you see a purple outline that roughly matches that of the character's skin. Increasing or decreasing this amount affects the size of the outline.

- **Pull.** Determines how much the skin is pulled by the attached joint. A good example is the chest and shoulder area. As the arms move outward, the skin of the chest is pulled outward along the surface of the skin as well.

- **Pinch.** Determines how much the skin is pushed inward by the action of the tendon-attached joint. A good example is the crease that forms in the web of the hand, as the thumb moves next to the forefinger.

- **Stretch.** Determines how much the skin is stretched by the tendon-attached joint. This gives the skin more or less pliability.

Normally, the values for all these joints are set at 1.0 to give a good skin behavior when the tendons are attached to a nearby link. If the tendons span multiple links, these numbers should probably be reduced somewhat because the effect of a change on a link normally decreases the further you are from the link. For example, the clavicle should have more of an effect on the upper spine than on the lower spine.

The Tendon Boundary Conditions are also important for tendons that span multiple links. These determine exactly how far the skin is affected. If these are off, only the joint with the tendon is affected. When the Upper Bound value is high, the skin on the spanned joints is also affected by the tendon. This is very important for getting a smooth behavior across the skin.

Note

If a tendon spans multiple joints, it is a good idea to turn off the Joint Intersection parameters for each of the spanned joints. This action prevents the two features from trying to create different outlines at the joint intersections and causing unpredictable results.

1. Continue with 07max08a.max. Unhide all, and then select the mesh. Set the Sub-Object level to Tendons to access the Tendon parameters.

2. Select the Bip01 Spine2 link and, in the Tendons rollout, set your Selection Level to Control Point. Select the two front attach points and change the Radius to 40. This puts the Attach points close to the skin's surface. Set Pull to 2, Pinch to −0.25, and Stretch to 0.25.

3. In the Upper Boundary Conditions, make sure that the Upper Bound is set to 4.0 and Pull Bias is set to 0. Change Lower Bound to −1.

Tip

Higher values in the upper bounds spread the tendon deformation along more joints. The Upper Bound value defines the number of joints you want the tendon to span. You should set this value to 1 unit per link between the base and the attached link.

4. Unhide the Biped skeleton and turn on Animate. At frame 10, rotate the clavicles up 30 degrees in the y-axis. These modifications lift the skin evenly over the front of the chest as the clavicles rise.

5. Make a preview of frames 0 through 20 to see the effect.

Transferring and Storing Physique Data

Physique definitely makes deformation, which used to be one of the most difficult and time-consuming tasks, easier. And the .PHY format makes it easy to transfer that data from one skeleton to another. The .PHY format is a unique file that stores all the information from your character's physique, including envelopes, custom vertex weight, even bulges and tendons, making it possible to store and transfer your custom physiques between models. In a production environment, this is invaluable, making it arguably one of the most important features in the package. The implications are astounding.

In a production environment, revisions and changes are made constantly, often up to the last minute, and every change impacts the schedule. In the past, you couldn't deform the model until it was absolutely final, and you didn't want to have to go back and redo a week's worth of work in the middle of a project. Doing animations without a finished model is always risky, so you would wait until the model was done, textured, and ready to go.

Now, imagine you have a modeler making the model. Working in low-res, all the major attributes and proportions are worked out. The model is pretty much done. It can now be set up with a skeleton and deformed with Physique, complete with bulges and tendons, while someone is working on finishing the model. You could even start animating, making sure to leave a default pose at, say frame 0. Then when the mesh is final, you apply Physique and load the deformation file, and voila. It's ready to go. If significant changes must be made to the model, you might also need to make some minor adjustments, but most of the deformation will probably transfer just fine.

Saving Physique

Saving a .PHY file is easy. Simply apply your deformation as always, adjusting and tweaking. Even vertex weights are saved in this format. With your mesh selected and the Physique modifier active in the Modifier Stack, select Save Physique (*.PHY) File from the Physique rollout.

Loading Physique

To load a .PHY file, you should have a similar skeleton. If there are changes in the skeleton, that can be handled as well, but it is ideal to have a similar hierarchy sharing the same names as the .PHY file. Apply Physique to the model and skeleton into which you want to load your .PHY file. Settings are not important because .PHY will overwrite anything that you tell it to. With Physique active in the modifier stack, select Load Physique File from the Physique rollout. You are given a number of options defining how much of the Physique file that you are loading will be transferred:

- **Link Settings.** If selected, this loads the Link parameters.
- **Bulges.** Loads any associated bulge angles and cross sections if checked.
- **Tendons.** Loads Tendons if selected.
- **Envelopes.** Loads Envelope parameters for selected joints if checked.
- **Locked Vertices.** When necessary, the Locked Vertices option will be available to load data from Locked Vertices in a .PHY file onto the corresponding vertices in the target Physique.

Note

For the Locked Vertices option to work, the meshes have to be identical.

Select the joints you want to transfer to and from, using All Links or by manually selecting the links you need. All Links is available only if both skeletons have equal hierarchies of links. If the two vary at all, you will have to manually select all the links you want to transfer. You may have to load Physique two or more times if the hierarchy is too different, in which case, it is often better to adjust the deformation on the links that didn't transfer. Click OK, and your Physique file is updated with the .PHY data.

> **Tip**
>
> If you have to delete Physique from a skeleton, you must unlink the mesh from the skeleton using the Unlink Selection tool, especially if you plan to reapply Physique.

In Practice: Physique

- **Envelopes.** Envelopes allow you to intuitively and interactively control the vertex assignment of any type of mesh available in 3D Studio MAX today.

- **Vertex reassignment.** Vertices can now be assigned to multiple joints, allowing you the flexibility to adjust and build upon envelope assignment.

- **Bulge angles.** Multiple cross sections and bulge angles make it easy to apply complex skin deformations to simulate muscles and even add surface detail.

- **Using Biped.** Biped automatically creates bounding boxes for its joints, and Physique can use those to generate more accurate envelopes.

- **Tendons.** Tendons affect the skin across multiple joints and are very helpful in branching areas of the body, such as the shoulder and pelvis areas.

- **.PHY format.** The .PHY format now stores all the Physique data, making it incredibly easy to transfer model deformation between skeletons.

Chapter 8

Mesh Deformation

By Shane Olson

You've gone through the process of modeling a character, and now you're excited about animating it. Not so fast: Before you jump in, you must prepare your character for animation. This is where deformation comes in.

If your character is made from several segments (for example, the forearm is separate from the upper arm), deformation is not necessary. If your character is made up of a solid seamless mesh or a variation of it, however, you will need deformation tools to get your character to move and bend realistically.

There are many ways to deform a mesh. In this chapter, we will cover several deformation methods, including how to get your character set up for animation. Most of these tools apply specifically to character animation, but you can use them any way you want.

This chapter explores the following topics:

- Deforming using an FFD lattice
- Deforming using the Xform modifier
- Deforming using the new Flex modifier
- Preparing meshes for bones
- Fitting the skeleton to the mesh
- Character animation using the new Skin modifier

Types of Meshes

A good place to start is to look at the different types of meshes available for creating your character. This brief overview is designed to give you a better idea of which modeling method to use (if you haven't already begun).

3D Studio MAX R3 provides a number of ways to create a mesh. Geometry can be created as polygons, patches, and NURBS surfaces. Additionally, third-party plug-ins (such as Clay Studio and Metareyes) can be used to create meshes by using metaballs. The type of geometry you decide to use in the creation of your characters depends on a number of factors, particularly the demands of the project at hand. Video game developers might need to use polygons instead of patches, for example, simply because most game engines accept only these formats. Regardless of type, any kind of mesh can be deformed in one way or another.

Polygonal Meshes

Polygonal meshes have been the standard for creating objects in 3D Studio MAX since day one. Today, MAX R3's polygonal modeling tools are more powerful than ever, and that makes polygons an attractive choice. Deforming a polygonal mesh, however, can become increasingly difficult as the resolution of the mesh increases.

High-Resolution Meshes

High-resolution polygonal meshes can look fantastic when rendered. Unfortunately, polygons are the hardest geometry type to deform. This is because in high-resolution meshes, the vertex information is so closely packed that the possibility of tearing or creasing the mesh increases geometrically. Additionally, the large number of vertices bogs down the system at animation time. Figure 8.1 shows polygonal meshes of varying resolutions.

Figure 8.1   Low, medium, and high levels of resolution.

To help with the problem of deforming a high-resolution mesh, NURMS technology was added to MAX R3. NURMS (Non-Uniform Rational MeshSmooth) is a new way of calculating within the classic MeshSmooth modifier. NURMS allows you to deform your mesh at a much lower resolution and then add higher resolution at any time. (Deforming a NURMS mesh will be covered more extensively later in this chapter.)

Also helpful with the deformation of high-resolution meshes are FFD lattices, which enable a more subtle deformation that lessens the possibility of tearing.

Low-Resolution Meshes

Low-resolution polygonal meshes are typically used to create characters for the gaming community. The restrictions of gaming systems demand that the geometry of any scene not exceed a certain polygon count. This constrains the resolution of a mesh to limits that most people working in film or video would find inadequate.

Still, with clever texture mapping, a low-resolution character can come across as looking quite nice. Most details, such as wrinkles in clothing, hair, and accessories, are simply created as highly rendered texture maps. But be prepared for changes. With the next generation systems coming out, the polygon count is getting higher and higher, which is good news for those of us in the gaming industry.

From an animation standpoint, the advantage of using low-resolution characters (like that shown in Figure 8.2) is increased performance. Low-resolution meshes can animate quickly, and on a fast system can even be manipulated in real time.

Figure 8.2   Low-resolution meshes animate very quickly, but they can look blocky and don't render well.

Polygonal Meshes and MeshSmooth with NURMS

One significant area of improvement with version 3 of 3D Studio MAX is the MeshSmooth modifier. The most obvious change is the new NURMS capability.

MeshSmooth, an object modifier that adds more detail to a polygonal mesh and smoothes it out, also includes an improved capability to output quadratic polygons for all faces. Plus, it still enables you to retain mapping coordinates and everything else you add below it on the modifier stack.

The biggest benefit of NURMS is the ability to model and animate with a low-resolution mesh and render a high-resolution character. The cool thing about it is that you can view the high-resolution version at any time. You can even view both at the same time for real-time feed back. Just as you can with NURBS, you can weight vertices with NURMS, which is why they're called "non-uniform rational."

The MeshSmooth/NURMS output option converts the entire mesh to four-sided polygons, creating a much smoother mesh. The NURMS improvements are a very welcome addition to those who are animating characters, simply because they enable you to animate a low-resolution version of a character and render a high-resolution version of the character, effectively giving you the best of both worlds.

This technique works simply by adding MeshSmooth to the stack after the Deformation modifier. This interpolates the low-resolution mesh into a high-resolution mesh (see Figures 8.3 and 8.4).

Because this interpolation happens after the deformation, it creates a very smooth-looking surface that is reminiscent of a patch-based model. This is because MeshSmooth calculates the interpolated polygons in much the same way as a Bezier patch, essentially turning your polygonal model into a patch-based model. You can see the results of the MeshSmooth modifier while working on the low-resolution version in real-time by clicking the Show End Result icon at any point below the MeshSmooth modifier in the stack.

To get you started, open MAX R3 and try out this quick tutorial on using MeshSmooth and NURMS.

1. Create a box of any size in the Top viewport.

2. Right-click on the box, scroll down to Convert to Editable Mesh, and select it.

3. Now, to add the MeshSmooth modifier, click on the Modeling tab and click the MeshSmooth icon.

4. To get a slightly higher resolution model, turn the Iterations up to 2.

5. Open the modifier stack and select Editable Mesh. Now click the Show End Result icon.

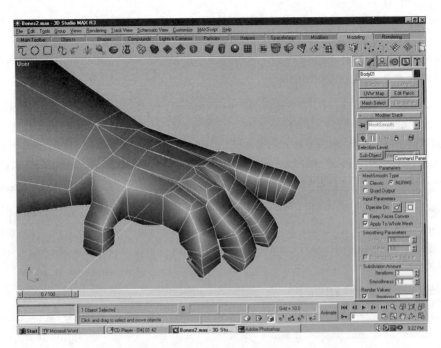

Figure 8.3   Dorothy's very low-resolution hand is deformed.

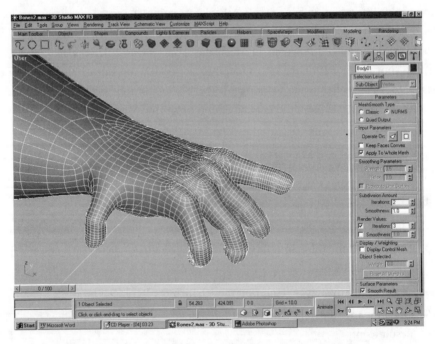

Figure 8.4   When MeshSmooth is added after the deformation, the hand smoothes out into a seamless, organic surface.

6. To be able to see the low-resolution control mesh and manipulate it, select any of the Sub-Object groups, such as Vertices. Figure 8.5 shows an example of a box at this stage.

With your newly created box, you can start to add, extrude, and bevel faces. You can also move the individual vertices and edges. Everything you do affects the underlying mesh. Play around and see what tools are available.

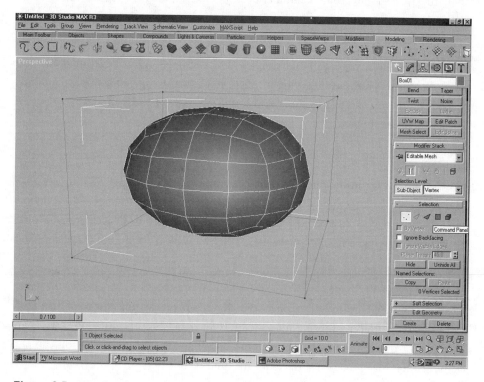

Figure 8.5   Viewing the control mesh on a MeshSmooth modifier.

Tip

You can separate the effects of MeshSmoothing to get hard edges. All you have to do is choose Separate by Material ID or Separate by Smoothing Group within the MeshSmooth modifier.

Patches and Surface Tools

Because they are a bit more complex to manage than polygons, patches have been over-looked to some degree as an effective modeling tool. They are, however, extremely flex-ible both from a modeling and an animation standpoint. From a modeling standpoint, patches are very organic because they can be either three- or four-sided. From an animation standpoint, patches are almost as fast as polygons, especially with the use of Surface Tools, a popular plug-in developed by Digimation. Surface Tools, which is now included in MAX R3, provides an intuitive approach to building patches from spline networks.

One key point regarding patches and Surface Tools is that you can dial up or down the resolution of the patch by using the Steps spinner in the Topology rollout. While you're animating, you should keep the number of steps low for the sake of speed. You can then dial the spinner up to a higher number for rendering. This is similar to the Iterations setting in MeshSmoothing.

With Surface Tools, you can build patches with a simpler spline cage for even more speed. If your machine is still crying for help, you can also toggle the Surface modifier on and off, or you can toggle Show End Result on and off while modeling to see the Surface modifier applied.

NURBS

NURBS provide a third option for character animators. With 3D Studio MAX R3, NURBS are much faster and more fluid. NURBS can be used to create extremely smooth and organic surfaces. Most NURBS modeling happens at the Sub-Object level. Advances in performance and efficiency make Relational NURBS a valid choice for animated characters.

Also new to NURBS with MAX R3 is Surface Approximation. Much like the Patch Topology spinner, Surface Approximation includes separate settings for basic, trimmed, and displaced surfaces, allowing for just the right detail for any situation. Presets are included for quickly setting low-, medium-, and high-resolution results. You can also define settings for individual surfaces for maximum control.

Mapping and Mesh Deformation

One problem many beginning animators face is getting textures to stick to the surface of the character as it deforms (see Figure 8.6). To prevent this, mapping needs to be placed in the stack before the object is deformed. This is the case regardless of the deformation method—whether you use a simple taper, bend, FFD, Flex, Skin, or Physique.

Adding the mapping coordinates can be as simple as generating mapping coordinates when the object is created to selecting multiple groups of faces and adding multiple UVW Mapping modifiers to the stack for each group. The key is that if the mapping occurs after the deformation, the texture floats across the object (see Figure 8.6).

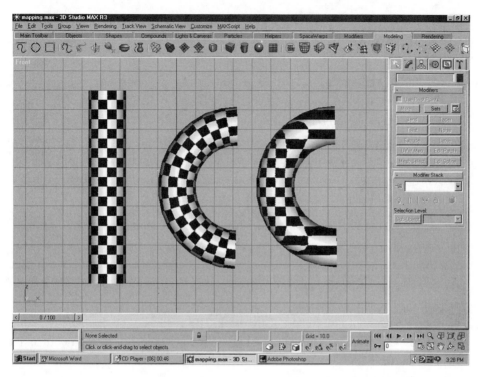

Figure 8.6   If mapping happens before deformation, the texture sticks to the surface of the object and moves appropriately. If the mapping happens after the deformation, the texture stays put and doesn't move with the object, as illustrated on the model to the far right.

Deformations Using FFD Lattices

FFD lattices can be rectangular or cylindrical and can have any number of control points in any direction. This gives you a lot of control when using lattices as an Object or Sub-Object modifier.

Another important set of tools are lattice space warps. These can provide whole new ways of animating. One lattice can be used to deform more than one object at a time. This is great for deforming entire hierarchies of objects.

Object Modifier Lattices

Object modifier lattices are good overall tools for modeling, and their control points can be animated. This makes them a good option for performing mesh deformations. The best way to use Object modifier lattices is for local deformations, such as creating bulging biceps, making morph targets, or making fat bellies jiggle. To accomplish these sorts of effects, the FFD is best applied as a Sub-Object modifier, usually in conjunction with Edit Mesh before the MeshSmooth modifier if there is one.

Space Warp Lattices

Space warp FFDs deform geometry much like Object modifier FFDs. However, space warps can affect many objects, unlike the Object modifier FFDs that affect only one object or sub-object at a time. You can also animate your objects moving "through" the FFD so you can create special effects, such as making a car and its occupants fit though a keyhole, for example. (Chapter 12 contains a tutorial on squishing a teapot through a hole if you would like to see an example of how it's done.)

In addition, space warp FFDs behave much like regular objects and have their own stack. The fact that it can have its own stack makes the FFD space warp an attractive option for some character animation tasks because many of the standard MAX modifiers can affect a lattice. Linked Xform, Physique, and even other lattices can be used to deform the space warp lattice. The one limitation of space warp lattices is that, because they are space warps, they always float to the top of the stack. This might not be desirable for some applications—for example, when you want to add a modifier such as MeshSmooth to the top of the stack.

Deforming a Jaw with an FFD Lattice

One of the most common ways to use an FFD Lattice is to set up morph targets for facial animation. They are especially useful on high-resolution meshes for which you don't have the opportunity to dial the resolution up and down. With a high-resolution mesh, an FFD lattice allows you to get much more natural looking, arced facial poses, rather than tediously going in and moving all those vertices one-by-one.

In the following exercise, you will put an FFD lattice to practical use. You will apply an FFD $4 \times 4 \times 4$ modifier to the vertices surrounding the mouth and then move the points into an asymmetrical cute little smile.

Tip

In a production situation using the new NURMS MeshSmooth along with the Morpher modifier, you would be able to copy Dorothy's head several times to make several morph targets. You could use any deformation method you choose (including FFDs). Then, you could delete the Mapping coordinates and MeshSmoothing modifiers from all your copied heads (morph targets) but leave them on the original mesh. This makes for a very small, manageable, morph target file.

1. Open the file named 08max01.max on the CD-ROM. It contains a high-resolution version of Dorothy's Editable Mesh head.

2. Select Dorothy's head.

3. Right-click on Dorothy's head, scroll down to the Sub-Object/Vertex submenu, and select the vertices that surround the mouth, including the inside of the mouth (see Figure 8.7). You don't have to be too precise, this is just practice.

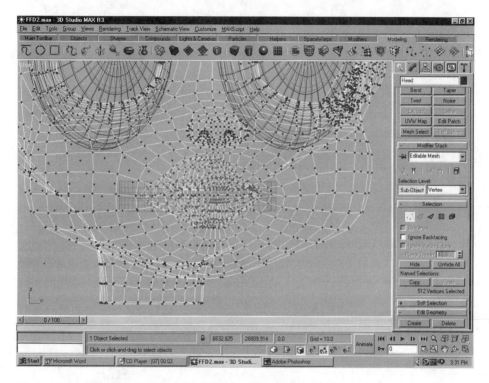

Figure 8.7   Select the vertices that make up Dorothy's mouth.

4. With the vertices selected, add an FFD 4 × 4 × 4 modifier to the stack by selecting More/FFD 4 × 4 × 4. Figure 8.8 shows the result.

5. On the FFD Modify menu, select the Sub-Object/Control Points submenu. You are now free to move the control points any way you want. Notice how doing so deforms the mesh smoothly and evenly.

6. For the quirky smile pose, move and scale the center points outward and upward.

7. To get the twist, select all the points and rotate them all around the viewport z-axis a little bit—just enough to make it asymmetrical. Your final result should look like Figure 8.9.

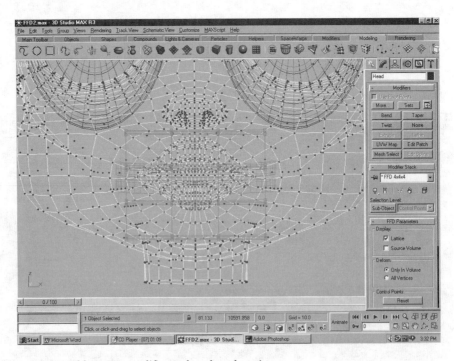

Figure 8.8   Add an FFD modifier to the selected vertices.

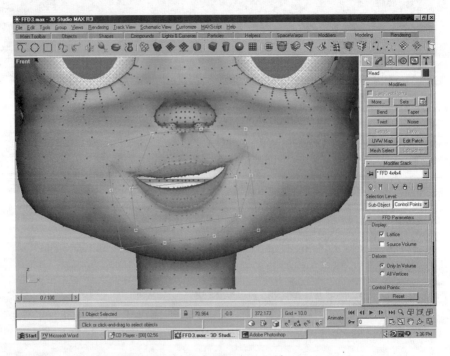

Figure 8.9   Move the FFD vertices to reposition the mouth.

Now, you can see how an FFD modifier is very useful for creating morph targets and other mesh deformations. Play around with the different FFDs to get a better feel for how they work. FFDs are a great option for many modeling and animating tasks. Next, you will explore the new Flex modifier.

Flex

New to MAX R3 is a cool modifier called Flex. The Flex modifier simulates soft-body dynamics. This spring-based system causes vertices to lag behind an object as it moves. Flex works with NURBS, patches, meshes, shapes, and FFD space warps. You can also combine Flex with such space warps as Gravity, Wind, PBomb, Push, and Motor to add realistic surface animation to an object.

Flex is very good at creating secondary motions and overlapping action for character animation. For example, a dog character has really floppy ears, and when the head moves, the ears follow and drag behind. When the head stops, the ears pass the head but keep flopping until they finally come to rest. Adding that extra flopping is where Flex comes in. It's not very precise, but it works for small, quick, secondary animation that is sometimes too tedious to animate by hand.

The Flex modifier affects surfaces in different ways, depending on the surface type:

- **Mesh surface.** Influences every vertex.
- **Patch surface.** Influences both control points and tangent handles. Tangent handles are unlocked and moved independently by the Flex modifier.
- **NURBS surface.** Influences control points.
- **Spline (shape).** Influences control points and tangent handles.
- **FFD space warp.** Influences control points.

Weights

Three Flex modifier sub-objects set which points the modifier affects:

- Center
- Edge Vertices
- Weights

All three of the above weight assignment types have to do with assigning weights to vertices. Assigning weights lets Flex know which vertices you want to be active and how much you want them to be affected. The weight values are shown by color. Yellow points are completely unaffected (rigid), green points are moderately affected, and blue points are affected the most.

Center Sub-Object

The Center sub-object works like the center of most modifiers. As you move the center point around, it changes which vertices the modifier affects. The vertices closest to the center are more rigid, and the vertices fade out in rigidity the farther away from the center they are. You can change the falloff value by adjusting the Feather slider.

Adjusting and using the Center Gizmo is a quick and easy method for getting loose results. The main problem with just using the Center is that it radiates outward in a circle. For a character such as Dorothy, you need more precise control than a basic circular pattern. Otherwise, parts that you don't want to move will wobble. That's where the Edge Vertices sub-object comes in.

Edge Vertices Sub-Object

The Edge Vertices sub-object allows you to manually select the vertices you want to be absolutely rigid and unaffected by the modifier. You can assign Edge Vertices by selecting Sub-Object/Edge Vertices and then selecting any vertices on the mesh. The vertices will become yellow with a pink box around them.

After you have the edge vertices assigned, they act like the center of the effect. The effect falloff radiates from these vertices instead of the default Center Gizmo. This allows you much more precise control over the effect. If you want even more control, you can actually "paint" the weight assignments.

Weights Sub-Object

To "paint" on weights, turn on Sub-Object/Weights, turn on Paint, and then brush the cursor over the object in the viewports. It takes a few strokes to get it working. It's not all that intuitive, and it takes up a lot of memory, but it's fun to use.

Tip

The most precise way to assign weights it to give the individual vertices absolute weights. You do this by selecting the Absolute Weight box, selecting some vertices, and then rolling the Vertex Weight slider or typing in a number. A value of 100 is very rigid; a value of 0 is the least rigid.

Flex Rollout Parameters

Because Flex is brand new to 3D Studio MAX R3, take a moment to become familiar with all its rollout parameters in detail (see Figure 8.10).

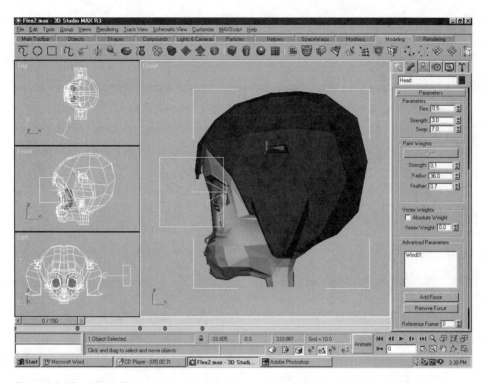

Figure 8.10 Flex rollout parameters.

The three main parameters are:

- **Flex.** Sets the amount of flex and bend. The larger the number, the more the effect increases. The range is from 0 to 1000. This value represents the maximum number of frames a vertex will lag behind.

- **Strength.** Sets the spring strength. The range is from 0 to 100, with 100 being rigid.

- **Sway.** Sets the time for the object to come to rest. The lower the value, the longer it takes the object to come to rest. The range is from 0 to 100.

Paint Weights Group

As described before, Paint paints vertex weights in the viewports to control the amount of lag. Other parameters in the Paint Weights group control the paintbrush itself.

- **Paint.** To begin painting, turn on Sub-Object and click Paint. Click and drag the cursor over the mesh in the viewports to "paint" vertex weights. (It may take a few strokes before you see results.) The vertex color will then change to show the vertex weight. The more you paint, the more rigid they become. You can use Paint in any Sub-Object level.

- **Strength.** Strength refers to the amount of weight the brush leaves on the mesh. Higher values leave more weight, making them more rigid. The range is from –1 to 1. Negative values allow you to remove weight.

- **Radius.** Radius sets the size of the brush, which is represented by a yellow sphere that appears when you roll over any available vertices. The size of the brush is set up in world units. It ranges from 0.001 to 99999.

- **Feather.** Feather sets the hardness of the brush. It ranges from –1 (hard) to 1 (soft).

Vertex Weights Group

The Vertex Weights group of options sets vertex weight manually, which is the preferred method. To manually set weights, turn on Sub-Object Weights, select vertices in the viewports, and then change the value of the Vertex Weight parameter.

- **Absolute Weight.** When selected, this changes the value of the Vertex Weight parameter when you want to assign absolute weights to the selected vertices. Deselect Absolute Weight to add or remove weight based on the vertices' current weight.

- **Vertex Weight**. Allows you to add or remove weight from the selected vertices. Depending on the state of the Absolute Weight parameter, weight assignment is either absolute or relative.

Using Flex for Character Animation

Now let's see Flex in action. This tutorial simulates soft-body dynamics on Dorothy's ponytails. When Dorothy moves her head to the left and right, you want the ponytails to drag behind and flop around after her head stops. Time to get started.

1. Open the file named 08max02.max on the CD-ROM. It contains a mesh of Dorothy's head (see Figure 8.11). The MeshSmooth modifier has already been applied but has been turned off for speed. If you would like to view the results of the MeshSmooth modifier, simply turn it back on again. Also, for your convenience, Dorothy's head has been animated for you with simple rotations. If you click the Play button, Dorothy's head rotates left and right.

2. Select Dorothy's head mesh.

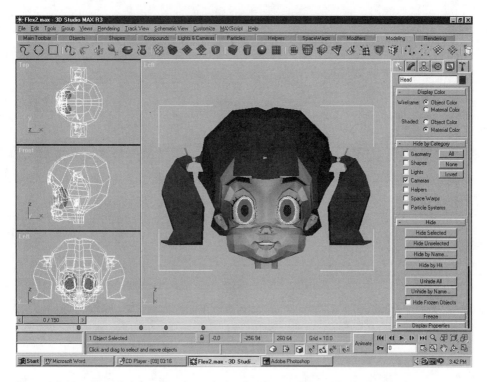

Figure 8.11   Dorothy's head mesh, ready for the Flex modifier to be applied.

3. In the modifier stack, select the line in-between the Editable Mesh and MeshSmooth modifiers, and add a Flex modifier by choosing More/Flex under the Modify panel.

4. To set the weight using Edge Vertices, choose Edge Vertices from the Sub-Object menu.

5. You want Dorothy's head to be rigid, so select all the vertices that make up Dorothy's head (see Figure 8.12). All the selected vertices should turn to yellow with pink boxes around them. Leave the ponytails unselected because you want to flex them.

6. In the Flex parameters drop-down, set the Flex value to 0.5, set the Strength to 3, and the Sway to 7.

7. Move the animation slider bar to see Flex working on the ponytails (see Figure 8.13). For a fully rendered animation, look at the file included on the CD-ROM called 08max02.mov.

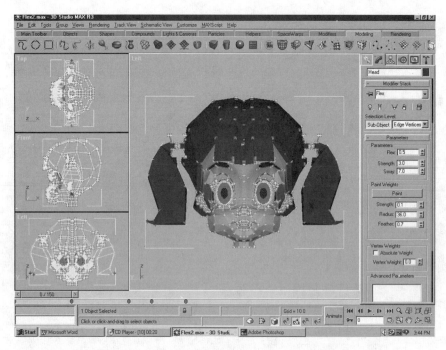

Figure 8.12   Assign Edge Vertices to Dorothy's head.

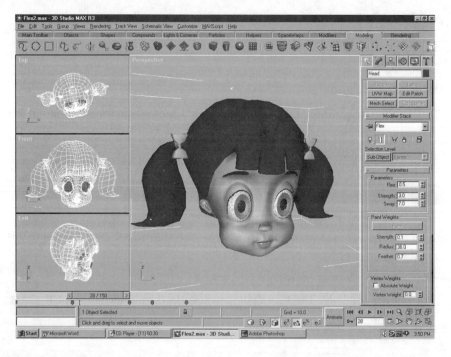

Figure 8.13   Flex in action.

Now that you have a general understanding of how Flex works, go ahead and play around with the different values to see what they do.

Adding a Space Warp Force to Flex

You can even apply space warps to the Flex modifier for added motion in your animations. For example, you can add Wind to animate plants and trees. In such cases, you don't need to create key frames to see the effects; the space warp alone can animate the surface. In the next tutorial, you will learn how to use a space warp as a force, adding a breeze to blow Dorothy's ponytails.

1. From the CD-ROM, open the file called 08max03.max, which contains another mesh of Dorothy's head. Once again, the MeshSmooth Modifier has been turned off. You can turn it back on to view the results of the MeshSmooth modifier at any time.

2. In the Create panel, click Space Warps, and then choose Particles & Dynamics from the drop-down list.

3. Click Wind, and then click and drag in the Front viewport to create a wind gizmo (see Figure 8.14). The arrow indicates which way the wind is blowing. To adjust the gizmo's wind direction, turn on Sub-Object, and then rotate and move the Wind Gizmo to your desired location.

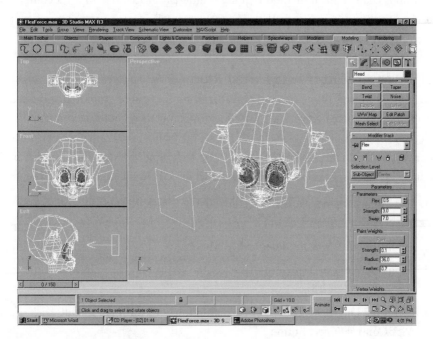

Figure 8.14   Adding a Wind space warp as a force.

4. In the Wind Parameters rollout, set Strength and Turbulence to 10.

5. As in the previous exercise, Dorothy's head should be rigid while her ponytails blow. Select all the vertices that make up Dorothy's head, but leave the ponytails unselected. Add a Flex modifier to the stack between Editable Mesh and MeshSmooth by selecting More/Flex.

6. In the Flex modifier, click Add Force, and then select the Wind Gizmo in one of the viewports.

7. Click Play. The tips of the ponytails undulate in the wind. The Reference Frame value sets the frame where the forces in the list take effect.

Feel free to play around with the Wind parameters and weights to see what kinds of results you get. For best results, combine both object movement and a force.

Basic Skeletal Deformation

Although lattices and Flex are good for some character animation tasks, most characters need to be deformed through the use of some form of skeleton. Several methods can be employed to accomplish this. The most popular methods are Linked Xforms, FFDs, and Physique. Also, new to MAX R3, is a modifier called Skin, which will be covered in depth later in this chapter. Each method requires a different procedure. To get a comparative overview, therefore, it is best to show the fundamentals of each procedure on a simple object such as a cylinder, which is very similar to an arm or leg joint.

Deforming a Cylinder with Linked Xforms

Using Linked Xforms is one method of deformation that can be employed without additional plug-ins. Linked Xform is a very direct manipulation tool that you can use in a variety of situations. It allows you to link a set of vertices to a control object, such as a dummy, a box, or in this case, a MAX bone. This technique leverages the flexibility of this modifier to attach specific vertices of the model directly to the skeleton.

1. Load 08max04.max from the accompanying CD-ROM. This file contains a simple cylinder with a set of MAX bones inside.

2. Apply an Edit Mesh modifier to the cylinder.

3. From the Front or Top viewport, select the vertices on the right side of the cylinder (see Figure 8.15).

4. Select the Linked Xform modifier. Within the Linked Xform rollout, click the Pick Control Object button.

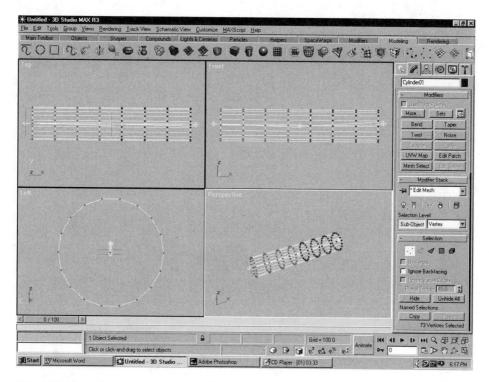

Figure 8.15   Select the vertices on the right side of the cylinder and apply a Linked Xform modifier to them.

5. Select Bone01 as the Control object. Select by name to avoid mistakes.

6. Select the cylinder once again. Then add another Edit Mesh modifier to the stack.

7. Select the vertices on the left side of the cylinder.

8. Add another Linked Xform modifier. Within the Linked Xform rollout, click the Pick Control Object button. Select Bone03 as the control object.

The bones now deform the mesh of the cylinder. Turn on IK and experiment by rotating the bones in the chain or by translating the bones with IK turned on to see the effects. Because the vertices of the mesh are directly connected to the bones, they move along with them. The one problem with this method is that you can get flat spots in the area between the neighboring Linked Xform modifiers (see Figure 8.16).

If the cylinder object was created with spline patches, the flat spots would smooth themselves out automatically. Not all characters are made of splines, however. One way to sneak around this is to introduce a MeshSmooth modifier in the stack after the Linked Xforms. MeshSmooth actually adds vertices and smoothes out the flat spots in the mesh.

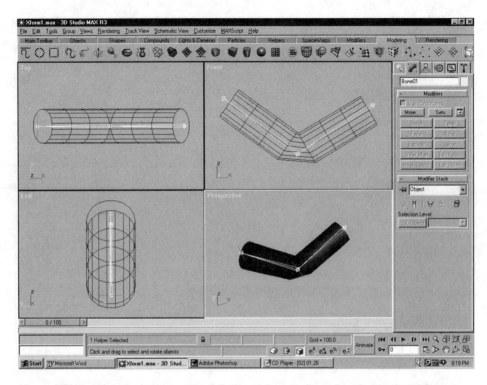

Figure 8.16 Select the vertices on the left side of the cylinder and apply a Linked Xform modifier to them.

Deforming a Cylinder with Space Warp FFDs

FFDs can be used with bones and Linked Xform in much the same manner as in the previous exercise. In this case, however, the bones deform the lattice, which, in turn, deforms the mesh. For denser meshes, this might be a better method because the deformation will prove to be smoother (see Figure 8.17).

1. Load the file 08max05.max from the accompanying CD-ROM. This file contains a simple cylinder with a set of MAX bones inside and an FFD fitted around it.

2. Select the cylinder and bind it to the FFD space warp.

3. Select the FFD and toggle the Sub-Object button to enable control points.

4. From the Front or Top viewport, select the control points on the right side of the FFD.

5. Add a Linked Xform modifier. Within the Linked Xform rollout, click the Pick Control Object button.

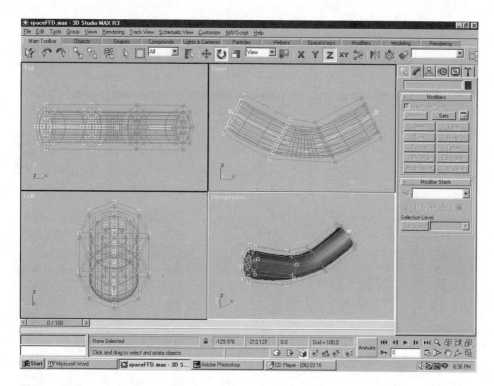

Figure 8.17   An FFD used with Linked Xform provides a much smoother deformation with a denser mesh.

6. Select Bone01 as the control object. Select it by name to avoid mistakes.

7. Select the FFD once again. Add an FFD Select modifier to the stack.

8. Select the control points on the left side of the cylinder.

9. Add a new Linked Xform modifier to the stack. Within the Linked Xform roll-out, click the Pick Control Object button. Select Bone03 as the Control object.

The setup is now complete, and translating the end effector should deform the cylinder. Theoretically, this method can also work for complex characters, because multiple space warp FFDs can be applied to one object.

Deforming a Cylinder with Skin

Skin is a brand new feature added to MAX R3. Like a light version of Physique, Skin will deform any type of mesh using just about any type of reference object from MAX bones to splines. It enables much more discrete control over the mesh than do Linked Xforms, FFDs, or anything else that ships with MAX R3. As you will see later in this chapter, Skin enables vertex-by-vertex control over the deformation of a mesh, along with weighting of vertices between bones. The next tutorial shows you the effects on all four types of meshes (see Figure 8.18). Follow the same steps for each cylinder.

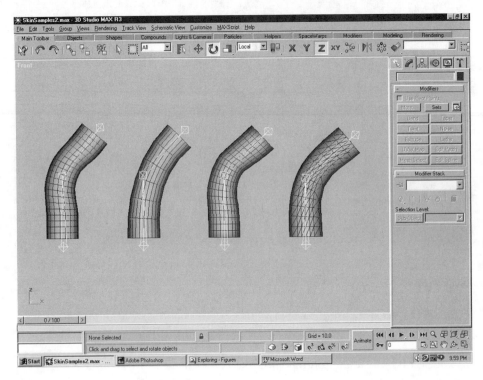

Figure 8.18   Skin applied to four different mesh types, which are deformed using MAX bones.

1. Load 08max06.max. This file contains four cylinders with bones already in them.

2. Select one of the four cylinders.

3. Add Skin to the modifier stack of each individual cylinder.

4. In the Parameters rollout, select Add Bone. For the first cylinder (created with polygons), add bones 02 and 03. For the second cylinder (created with patches), add bones 05 and 06. For the third cylinder (created with Surface Tools), select bones 08 and 09. For the fourth cylinder (created with NURBS), add bones 11 and 12.

5. Rotate the center bones to see how each cylinder reacts.

Feel free to experiment with the different mesh types. We will cover the Skin modifier in depth later in this chapter.

Getting Meshes Ready for Bones

Although deforming a character by using bones might look easy, getting your mesh to deform smoothly can sometimes be a real problem. No matter which plug-in you decide to use, your joints find ways to crimp, bulge, tear, or flatten at the wrong places, making your character look worse than when you started. Every animator runs into these problems, but you can use techniques to help your meshes behave:

- Build the mesh with the character's arms outstretched.
- Add extra detail at the bends.

Arms Outstretched

The best argument for building a character with its arms outstretched is that the arms are exactly halfway between the extremes the arm can take. It is tempting to build a character with its arms at its side. This is one of the more common poses a human takes. Unfortunately, if a character built that way needs to put his arms above his head for any reason, the skin around the underarms has to stretch twice as much as if it were built with the arms outstretched. Centering the arms helps prevent crimping, tearing, and unwanted bulging later on when the character is deformed (see Figure 8.19).

Figure 8.19   Building a character with the arms outstretched allows for a much wider range of motion.

Because the legs don't have nearly the range of motion the arms do, keeping them out-stretched is not as critical, particularly for characters that only walk and sit. If the characters are supposed to perform gymnastics, it might give you a bit more control if the legs are slightly apart when built.

Extra Detail at the Bends

Adding detail only where it is needed keeps your models light and easy to control. Many places on the body don't flex as much as others. The elbow and the skin around it flex quite a bit, for example, but the forearm itself remains fairly rigid. Therefore, the forearm does not need nearly as much detail to retain its shape as the area around the elbow joint. Extra detail also needs to be placed at the knees, the shoulder, the crotch area, and the areas around the wrists and the many joints of the hand. Some good references are the Viewpoint models supplied with MAX and Character Studio, which are built with detail in the proper places.

Eliminating the detail from rigid areas such as the forearm significantly reduces the number of vertices in the model and also reduces the total weight of the model. A lighter model animates easier, deforms more quickly, and renders faster (see Figure 8.20).

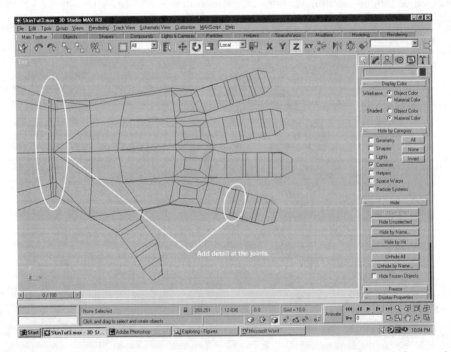

Figure 8.20   Add detail only where it is needed—at the joint areas where the mesh flexes and bends.

Localized Detail for Polygon Meshes

To add detail to a polygonal mesh, MAX R3 has several options: Cut, Slice Plane, and a Slice modifier. To use Cut, select the Edge Sub-Object level, click Cut, and then click-and-drag lines across the surface. Make sure you weld the loose vertices together as you go. To use Slice Plane, select it in the Edge Sub-Object menu, transform the gizmo into place, and then click Slice. To use the Slice modifier with your polygonal mesh selected, choose More/Slice from the modifier list. Click Sub-Object, and then transform the gizmo into place. The slice automatically happens in real time.

The advantage of Slice versus Slice Plane is that you can move or trash Slice at any time. But the disadvantage is that Slice remains on top of the modifier stack unless you choose to collapse it. Slice Plane is permanent, and you don't have to go back and forth from the stack.

Localized Detail for a Patch Surface

Adding detail to a patch mesh is simple. Select an edge that runs perpendicular to the area to which you want to add detail, and then click Subdivide. Subdivide splits each patch into two, all the way around the circumference of the object.

Localized Detail for a Surface Tools Mesh

To add detail to a Surface Tools mesh, simply add more splines in the area where you want the detail.

Localized Detail for a NURBS Surface

To add detail to a NURBS surface, you can do one of two things. You can choose to insert a row, a column, or both. Alternately, you can refine a row, column, or both. Refine adjusts the surrounding UVs to be spread evenly, whereas Insert simply inserts a UV anywhere you choose.

Fitting a Skeleton to a Mesh

After the solid mesh model is built, a skeleton of bones needs to be fit into it for the solid mesh to be deformed. Construction of skeletons was discussed in detail in the previous three chapters. The skeleton can be a biped, a skeleton of MAX bones, or made from geometry such as boxes. The skeleton is usually tied together in a hierarchy and set up for animation using Forward or Inverse Kinematics.

If you are not using Biped and are building a custom skeleton from scratch, it is best to construct the skeleton with the mesh in mind—even going to the point where you are actually loading the mesh model, freezing it, and then building the skeleton within it, and finally linking the skeleton in a hierarchy and setting up IK.

However it is done, the key to fitting a skeleton to a mesh is lining up the joints correctly. Typically, the extra detail modeled in the joints serves as a guide. Line up the joints of the skeleton so they match up with the joints of the mesh. Focus in on the following key areas:

- Elbow and knee
- Hip and pelvis
- Shoulders

The Elbow and Knee Areas

Placement of bones in the elbow and knee areas is fairly straightforward: Center the joint of the bones within the area defined by the joint (see Figure 8.21). If it is modeled properly, the mesh should have a bit of extra detail in this area to help guide the positioning of the bones.

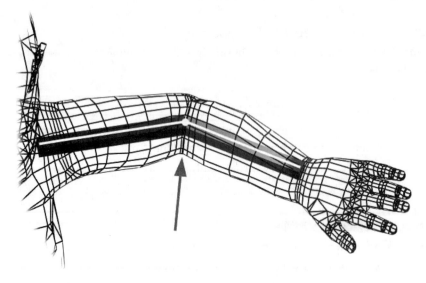

Figure 8.21   Placement of bones in an elbow or knee joint.

The Hip and Pelvis Area

The hips and pelvis can prove a bit problematic. The hip bone needs to be centered within the hip area, with the leg bones proceeding down through the center of the leg. The detail in the crotch usually flows along an approximately 45-degree angle along the so-called bikini line. Place the joint of the hips and the legs along this line, resizing the hips if necessary (see Figure 8.22).

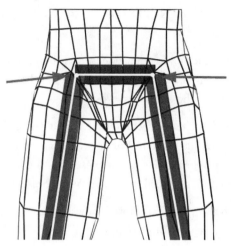

Figure 8.22   Placement of bones in the pelvis area.

The Shoulder Areas

The shoulders, too, can be problematic. A flexible shoulder joint will aid in placement, particularly if the character is normally stoop-shouldered. If this is the case, the shoulder can be rotated downward to match the stoop of the shoulders. The joint between the shoulder and the upper arm should be placed immediately above the armpit (see Figure 8.23).

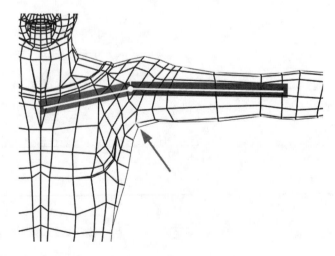

Figure 8.23   Placement of joints in the shoulder area.

Skin

The Skin modifier is a new skeletal deformation tool. It allows you to deform one object with another object. Mesh, patch, and NURBS objects can be deformed by MAX bones, splines, or even another object.

After you apply the Skin modifier and assign bones, each bone has a capsule-shaped *envelope.* Vertices within these envelopes move with the bones. Where envelopes overlap, vertex motion is a blend between the envelopes.

The initial envelope shape and position depend on the type of bone object. MAX bones create a linear envelope that extends from the bone's pivot point to the first child's pivot point. Spline objects create envelopes that follow the curve of the spline. A standard object creates an envelope that follows the longest axis of the object.

To help you get familiar with Skin, the next tutorial shows you how to use the Skin modifier to attach a mesh to a hierarchy of MAX bones.

1. Load 08max07.max. This file contains half of Dorothy's body mesh, along with a set of arm and hand bones already in place (see Figure 8.24).

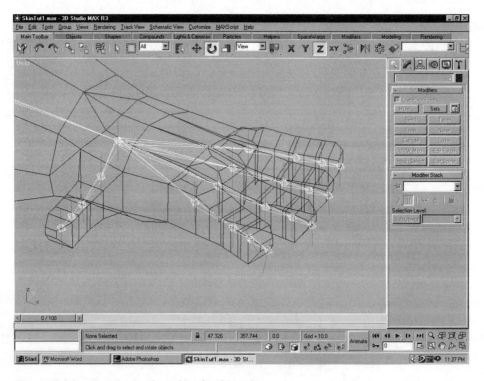

Figure 8.24   Getting a mesh ready to be skinned.

2. Select the body mesh and add a Skin modifier to the stack.

3. Under the Parameters rollout, select Add Bone, and then add all the bones to the list. Selecting and assigning them all by name is the easiest.

That's all there is to assigning the bones! Now comes the fun part, assigning weights.

There are three basic ways to assign weights. You can adjust the envelopes and leave it at that, or you can paint the weights on. The third and most precise way is to manually assign each vertex an absolute or relative value.

In the next few exercises, you will explore all three methods so you can make a better decision as to which method will work best for you. Start by adjusting the default envelopes.

Assigning Weights with Envelopes

By default, Skin assigns an envelope to each bone. Usually it does a pretty good job, but most likely, you will have to go in and adjust them to perfection. Load the file 08max07.max.

1. Select Sub-Object/Envelope and choose Bone07 (the tip of the pinky finger). Notice that the envelope does not engulf the entire area (see Figure 8.25). You will need to adjust the envelope rings to fit.

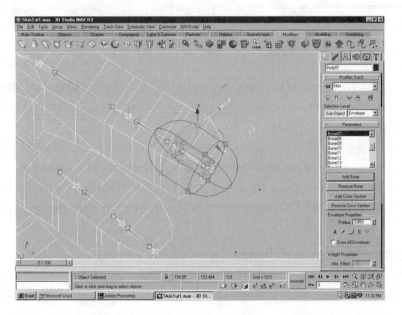

Figure 8.25   The envelope does not engulf the entire area.

2. Select one of the control points on the envelope control ring and pull it outward until you see the color of the vertices change to green or yellow (see Figure 8.26). Or, another option is to use the Radius roller in the Envelope Properties dialog box.

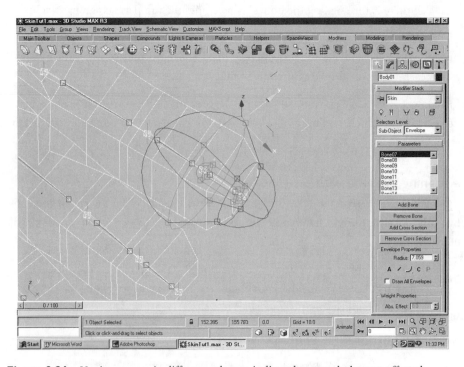

Figure 8.26   Vertices appear in different colors to indicate how much they are affected.

3. Adjust the other ring to match. The vertices should turn red to indicate they are assigned to this bone alone without any falloff. Green or yellow vertices signify influence by other bones.

4. A great feature with envelope assignment is the Cut and Paste option. To use it, copy the newly adjusted envelope setting and paste it onto the surrounding fingertips by clicking the C icon to copy and then the P icon to paste it onto another fingertip. Cut and Paste saves a lot of time when you can find a use for it.

Assigning Weights by Painting

Although it's not too practical for precision, another unique method of assigning weights is by painting them on. This feature is the same as painting on weights with the Flex modifier. The basic steps follow:

1. With a bone selected, click the Paint Weights button, and then start painting on the surface of your mesh. It may take a few strokes to get going.

2. You may find that the Brush Gizmo is entirely too big. To adjust it, simply lower the value in the Radius field.

Assigning Vertex Weights an Absolute Value

The final way to adjust weights is to assign the vertices absolute values. This is the preferred method because it gives you absolute control over your weight assignments. The drawback is how long it takes. It's very tedious if you have a high-resolution mesh, but the well-defined results will save you from pulling out your hair at animation time.

1. To assign an absolute value to vertices, click the Vertices button under the Filters submenu. This allows you to select vertices.

2. Select the vertices to which you want to assign a value.

3. In the Abs. Effect box, enter a value; a value of 0 has no effect, and a value of 1 assigns a rigid single-bone effect.

In Practice: Mesh Deformation

- **Building the mesh.** Try to use the new MeshSmoothing and polygonal tools when you can. Patch modeling is the next best solution. Add extra detail at the joints, and model the character with its arms outstretched.

- **Flex.** This is a great tool for simple, quick secondary animation. Flex works best on things that dangle, wobble, or jiggle. Don't be afraid to experiment.

- **Linked Xforms.** These offer a handy way to perform skeletal deformations right out of the box. Although they don't give you as much control as the new Skin modifier, Linked Xforms can work perfectly well on simple objects needing deformation.

- **Skin.** This is a great skinning tool that's new in MAX R3. It's the next best thing to Character Studio's Physique, but it comes without the price tag. It works nicely with MAX bones—and just about anything else you can think of.

Part III

Animating
the Environment

Chapter 9

Animating Cameras

By Sean Bonney

To most effectively use cameras in your animation, you need to understand the techniques that have evolved over the last century to communicate ideas with moving pictures. The first movies were little more than moving snapshots. Stationary set shots were prevalent in pre-1940's American film. Film cameras were being used in much the same way still cameras had been.

After World War II, an influx of European directors, such as Hitchcock, von Stroheim, Dassin, brothers Siodmak, Wilder, and Tourneur, brought expressionistic ideologies and aesthetics to the art of film. Simultaneously, Orson Welles and his Mercury Theatre arrived from radio, and Welles enthusiastically broke the rules of movie making with his experimental fervor. Additionally, the proliferation of low-budget genre films, also known as "B-movies," allowed an underground movement of talented directors with minuscule budgets the chance to break new ground, with both their stories and their techniques. This inventive period set the stage for the next two decades, when directors such as John Frankenheimer (*Manchurian Candidate*), Sam Peckinpah (*The Wild Bunch*), and Stanley Kubrick (*2001 A Space Odyssey*) established the concept of "Name" directors (later to include Scorcese, Coppola, Spielberg, and Lucas), and acceptance of the director's over-riding control over camera use.

These creative influences, along with the greatly expanded possibilities afforded by moving images and public demand for increasingly complex films, spurred the development of a vocabulary of film techniques. This language of film transformed the camera from a passive recorder of whatever happened to transpire before it, into an active and creative partner in the composition of ideas.

This chapter explores the following topics:

- Traditional film cameras
- Animating camera moves
- Using digital cameras to communicate ideas
- Expressive use of digital cameras
- Combining shots from multiple cameras

Understanding Traditional Film Cameras

Virtually all films and television shows are produced using film language. One of the primary and integral persons involved in film production is the cinematographer. Fluent in the camera vocabulary of film language, the cinematographer is responsible for setting the camera shot and deciding what camera movement is necessary to tell the story. Cinematographers are typically trained in film school and need many years of experience to be able to capture the film sequences that you take for granted.

As a CG animator you are given the same responsibility as the cinematographer: to involve the audience in the scene through the use of a camera. Camera placement and movement is an art that is not easily mastered and should be studied and practiced. All the methods of cinematography that are taught in film school are also valid in CG animation. If possible, take some classes in filmmaking, read books about it, and study the vocabulary of film language. I recommend the following titles:

- *Digital Cinematography* by Ben De Leeuw. 1997. Academic Press/Morgan Kaufmann; ISBN: 0122088751.

- *The Five C's of Cinematography: Motion Picture Filming Techniques* by Joseph V. Mascelli. 1998. Silman-James Press; ISBN: 187950541X.

- *Film Directing Shot by Shot: Visualizing from Concept to Screen* by Steven D. Katz. 1991. Focal Pr; ISBN: 0941188108.

Comic books are also good resources for learning dramatic camera angles. The scene framing used in comics is typically inventive and highly expressive, and it can be a source of inspiration for planning your camera framing. High-quality comic art is also adept at conveying a clear image of the action in simplified outline. This is also called *Action in Profile*. Studying the silhouettes used to convey action in comics can improve your understanding of how careful camera placement with a scene can affect visual and emotional impact.

Some recommended comics and books about comics include the following:

- *Understanding Comics; The Invisible Art* by Scott McCloud. 1994. Harper Perennial; ISBN: 006097625X.

- *The Dark Knight Returns* by Frank Miller. 1986. DC Comics.

- Any of the *Sin City* books by Frank Miller. Dark Horse.

In computer animation, you are freed from the constraints a real-world camera operator faces. This can be both a blessing and a curse. It is very easy to get carried away by the freedom of using a virtual camera. When you push the envelope of what the viewer is accustomed to seeing on the screen—by moving through a scene at supernatural speed or by flying above, below, and through anything—you risk the audience noticing the camera work instead of the idea behind the animation.

You can avoid this by using the camera in ways that people understand. Keep in mind that the viewer of your animation has probably viewed thousands, if not millions, of hours of moving images and should be considered an expert in deciphering those images. The language of film can be a useful shortcut to the successful communication of your ideas.

> **Note**
>
> In film, the viewer identifies with the camera. When the camera moves, the viewer experiences the sensation of movement and frequently finds the onscreen images more real than the space around him. This illusion is called *transference*. Motion rides, for instance, use this illusion to create a successful simulation of physical sensations experienced during a ride through virtual space. Therefore, the viewer can not only watch the action onscreen but also experience it.
>
> If the camera behaves within the strictures of normal human movement, from approximate human height, a sense of realism is created. The viewer becomes a human participant in the onscreen experience. If, however, the camera use exceeds the commonly accepted bounds of human movement, the viewer's transference will be to a more abstract level of involvement.

Try watching a movie or television program with an objective eye. Notice the composition, angles, and movement of each shot. A skilled cinematographer must consider many technical aspects when recording moving images:

- Zoom lenses
- Camera angles
- Field of view
- Camera moves
- Depth of field

Zoom Lenses

The invention of zoom (variable focal length) lenses made it possible for camera "moves" to be made without actually moving the camera. Orthodox cinematographers use the zoom lens only to change the angle of view between shots, preferring to move the camera itself when a move is called for. Changing from a wide-angle shot to a close-up, for example, can be done either by increasing focal length or by moving the camera toward the subject (a dolly move.) Even less orthodox filmmakers, home videographers, love to zoom in and out while making fast pans and tilts to enhance the nauseating effect.

In computer animation, the zoom can be a very effective tool. Because people are accustomed to seeing zoom effects in films and on television, you can use it to accomplish the same effects in computer space. On the surface, zooming appears to move the camera closer to or farther from objects in the scene. In reality, the angle of view is changing, so perceived spatial relationships also change.

The zoom is an aggressive, revelatory camera technique that's used to introduce an element quickly, as well as to suggest an emotional reaction (usually shock or surprise) to the revelation. In Franklin Schaffner's *The Planet of the Apes*, this technique is used to excellent effect in the "human-hunt" scene. In this dramatic scene, brutal militant thugs on horseback corral and capture subintelligent men and women, among them the astronaut protagonist of the film. The viewer is first introduced to the shocking fact that the horse-riding hunters are, in fact, gorillas in uniform, with a quick zoom from the human astronaut's point-of-view (see Figure 9.1).

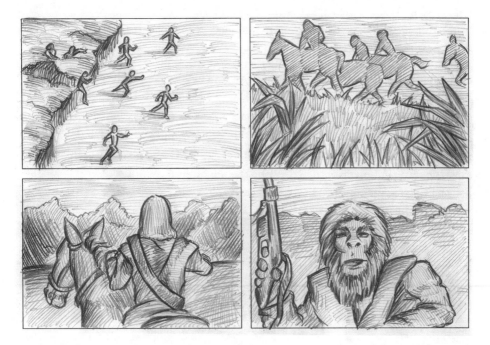

Figure 9.1 In *The Planet of the Apes*, a dramatic camera zoom is used to make a startling revelation: The hunters in this scene are gorillas!

Camera Angle

Varying the viewing angle in a film is done for many reasons, such as to accomplish the following tasks:

- Follow the subject
- Reveal or withhold information
- Change the point of view
- Establish a location
- Develop a mood

A low-angle view usually places the subject in a dominant position, whereas a high-angle view places it in a diminutive position. This rule is not iron-clad, of course, because other aspects of cinematography discussed in this chapter can completely change the context of a shot.

Field of View

Field of view (FOV) is the angle described by an imaginary cone, the vertex of which is at the camera's location. This angle is determined by the focal length of the lens being used.

Close-up camera shots with a wide field of view demand viewer identification with the subject. In Sergio Leone's *The Good, The Bad, and The Ugly,* three gunfighters face one another in the climatic showdown. The camera cuts from one man's face to the next, showing the rising tension of impending death, while simultaneously mythologizing the men through the sheer force of viewer identification (see Figure 9.2). Without dialogue, camera movement, or exposition, the images of those faces and the impact of their internal states are transcribed into the viewer's mind.

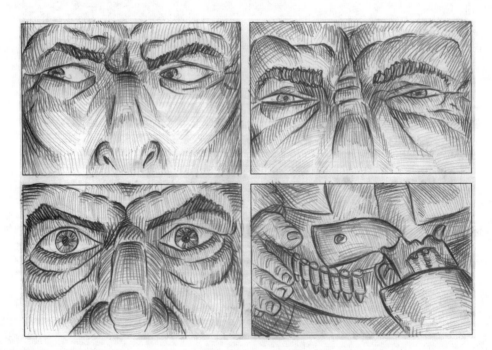

Figure 9.2   In *The Good, The Bad, and The Ugly,* rapid cuts between extreme close-up shots create a powerful impression of the rising tension between three characters at odds.

Short focal length lenses (28mm or 35mm on a 35mm SLR) give a very wide angle of view. Objects in the scene tend to appear far apart from one another. Something appearing on the horizon is nearly invisible, and an object near the camera looks huge. (Figure 9.3 shows an example of how one object looks when viewed through different size lenses.) Wide angles of view are useful for showing many objects in a scene simultaneously, establishing shots of buildings and other large subjects, building interiors, and creating emphasis by exaggerating perspective.

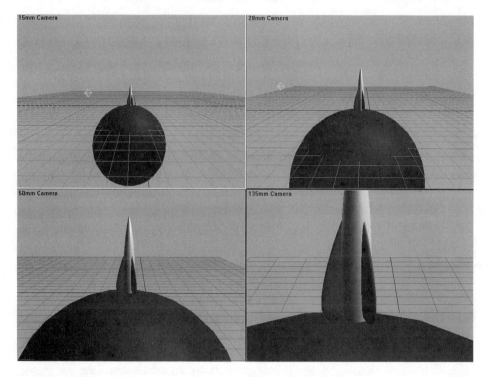

Figure 9.3   The same scene shot with 15, 28, 50, and 135mm lenses.

Medium focal length lenses ("normal" or 50mm on a 35mm SLR) cover a moderate angle of view. The perspective in the resulting display seems to be about what people "normally" perceive with their own vision. The spatial relationships of objects in the scene look normal.

Long focal length, or telephoto, lenses (135mm to 500mm on a 35mm SLR) cover narrow angles of view. Because objects only at the very center of a scene fill the frame, they appear to be very close to the camera. Spacing of objects in the scene appears to be compressed. Such narrow angles of view are useful when you want to show objects both near to and far from the camera in the same shot, or when you just cannot get close enough to the object to view it with a normal or wide-angle lens.

When you're composing cameras for animation, consider restricting yourself to a few lenses. This will lend a consistent feel to your CG cinematography and reduce camera intrusiveness. Refer to Table 9.1 for standard lens lengths.

Table 9.1   Standard Lens Lengths, FOV, and Names

Lens	Field of View	Type of Lens
10mm	132.01°	Fisheye
15mm	112.62°	Extra Wide-Angle
28mm	77.57°	Wide-Angle
35mm	65.47°	Medium Wide-Angle
50mm	48.45°	Standard/Normal
135mm	18.93°	Long/Telephoto
500mm	5.15°	Extra Long/Supertelephoto

Note

In MAX R3, as well as with real-world lenses, the FOV is measured diagonally across the frame. This eliminates the discrepancy between the CG lenses and real-world lenses concerning FOV. In MAX R3, you can also change the FOV degree, measuring to vertical and horizontal.

You have the ability to toggle any camera to orthographic projection, which is necessary if you want to animate text, game tiles, or something that you do not want to have a perspective projection. It is easily done by just clicking the Orthographic Projection check box in the Modify panel under Parameters.

Additionally, you can select from a list of predefined, rendered output sizes and resolutions by using the Output Size list in the Render Scene dialog box. Many industry-standard formats are listed there, including NTSC, HDTV, Panavision, and IMAX.

Table 9.2 outlines the basic types of shots and their uses. Figure 9.4 shows the shots listed in the table.

Table 9.2   Standard Camera Shots and Their Traditional Uses

Shot Name	Visual Composition	Use
Long shot	Characters are small in frame, and all or major parts of buildings appear.	Establishes physical context of action. Shows landscape or architectural exteriors.
Full shot	All or nearly all of a standing person shows. Large parts, but not all, of a building show.	Shows large-scale action (athletics, and so on). Shows whole groups of people. Displays large architectural details.
Medium shot	Character shown from waist up. Medium size architectural details show.	Face plays an important role. Two or three people are shown in conversation. Moderate size architectural detail shows.

Shot Name	Visual Composition	Use
Full close-up	Head and neck of character show. Small architectural details show. An object about the size of a desktop computer fills the frame.	Focuses on one character. Facial expression very important. Displays small architectural details.
Extreme close-up	Frame filled with just part of a character's face. Very small objects fill the frame.	Shows small objects entirely. Very small architectural details show. Emphasizes facial features in character.

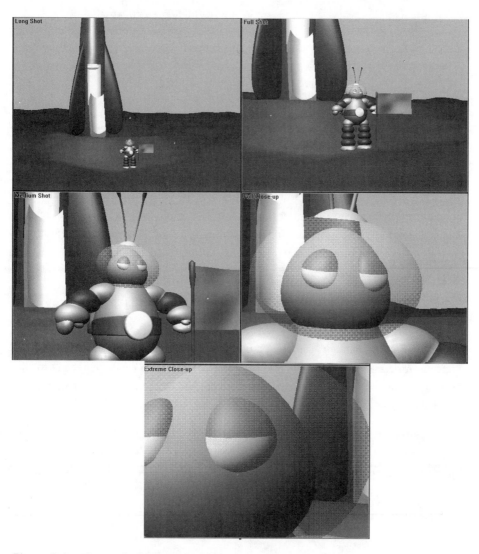

Figure 9.4   The standard camera shots.

Camera Moves

Not long after the invention of motion picture cameras, several basic moves evolved, forming the backbone of today's camera movement techniques. The same techniques apply to the use of virtual cameras in computer animation. You are by no means restricted to these basic moves because virtual cameras are not constrained by time and space. Knowing "real-world" camera techniques, however, is essential because audiences have learned to read moving images through these basic moves.

The fundamental moves (see Figures 9.7 and 9.10) include the following:

- Pan
- Tilt
- Roll
- Dolly
- Track
- Boom

All these moves create motion either by translating the camera's location in space or by changing the rotations around the camera's axis. Another category of moves involves changing the focal length of the camera lens during a shot. These effects are not really moves, however, because the camera remains stationary. Instead the effect simulates a move because the changing angle of view makes objects appear to move closer to or farther away from the screen.

Panning, Tilting, and Rolling

In Oliver Stone's *Platoon*, camera pans are used extensively during the climactic Vietcong/American G.I. firefight. The camera pans from the main characters to their firing guns and back and across, showing the complete frenzy within the characters and the explosions around them (see Figure 9.5).

Tilting and rolling are used to open Steven Spielberg's *Indiana Jones and the Last Crusade* (see Figure 9.6). In the initial fight scene onboard a storm-lashed freighter, wild camera tilts and rolls create a disorienting effect as the battling men are thrown by fists and towering ocean waves (see Figure 9.7). The viewer is as unbalanced by the camera moves as the crew in this scene are.

Figure 9.5 In *Platoon*, pans are used extensively to capture the personal terror and large-scale mayhem of the climactic battle.

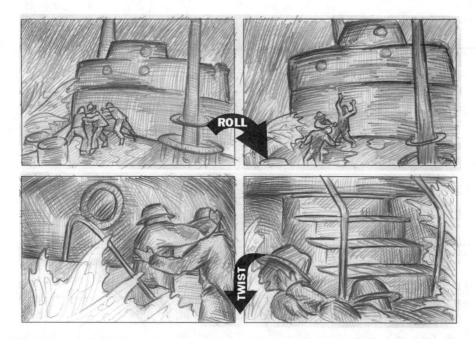

Figure 9.6 The wild motion of the freighter in the opening scenes of *Indiana Jones and the Last Crusade* is enhanced with camera tilts and rolls.

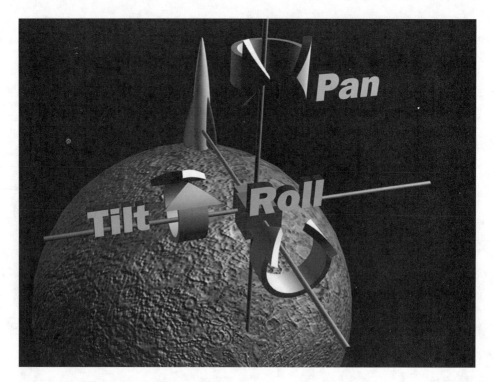

Figure 9.7   The pan, tilt, and roll shots change the orientation of the camera.

In a horizontal panoramic shot, the camera rotates on its vertical axis as much as 360 degrees, taking in the entire visible horizon. The difference between the pan and any other type of camera movement is that the camera rotates on one axis in one location rather than being displaced. Usually, a pan is used to create the following effects:

- Include more space that can be viewed through a fixed frame.
- Follow an action as it moves.
- Connect two or more points of interest.
- Connect or imply a logical connection between two or more subjects.

The most familiar use of a pan is the panoramic shot, a slow horizontal or vertical move. A vertical pan up or down a skyscraper gives a feeling of height, and a horizontal pan over a landscape can show the immensity of a location, such as a valley or mountains. A pan does not always have to be a slow movement in one direction; it can change direction completely. For example, the camera follows a subject and then changes into the opposite direction to follow another subject without a pause. In an airport, for example, this panning from subject to subject could go on forever. Inexperienced camera operators often make the mistake of panning too fast. You have probably seen home videos that cause motion sickness. When you look from one thing to another, you are panning with your eyes. You can do this fairly quickly because you are able to anticipate where your gaze will fall and direct your focus accordingly. When watching a camera pan, the viewer does not have the benefit of this anticipation and can quickly become disoriented.

Differences in playback rate can necessitate a change in pan speed as well. While NTSC-format video is played at 30 frames per second, computer animation is often played back at slower speeds, such as 15 or even 8 frames per second. Panning too quickly causes the difference between one frame and the next to be so great that the illusion of motion is broken. In cinematography, that effect is called *strobing*. In computer animation, it is also referred to as *tearing*.

Controlling Strobing

There are two ways of dealing with strobing in computer animation. One is to make certain that pans are not too fast. The following table gives some safe pan speeds for various conditions. Again, observe film and television footage to see just how slow most pan moves are. Refer to Table 9.3 for recommended pan speeds.

Table 9.3   Number of Frames Needed for a 45° Pan

Type	15 fps	24 fps	30 fps
Quick turn	11	18	22
Comfortable turn	15	24	30
Casual turn	33	54	66

Note

You have to visualize your shot first and then find out the time spent for your turn. Calculate the number of frames you need depending on how many frames you want to use in your animation (NTSC, PAL, and so on). If you still want a very fast pan, consider inserting a straight cut during the movement.

Another way to correct for strobing is to use one of the Motion Blur options when rendering. When you record fast moving objects in real-space with video or film cameras, they often appear blurred. This occurs when the shutter speed of the camera is too slow to freeze that object in motion. This phenomenon is called *motion blur*.

Because virtual cameras do not have a shutter to open and close, this blurring does not occur automatically in computer animation. Instead, you must explicitly tell the camera to add motion blur. This small extra step can be invaluable in simulating the realism of real-world cameras. Three kinds of motion blur are available in MAX R3: Object, Image, and Scene.

- **Object Motion Blur.** This produces motion blur for individual objects in a scene, not the entire scene. This technique creates several samples of the moving object during the rendering process that are slightly shifted in time. In the final image, these samples are dithered together to accomplish the motion blur effect. It can be very effective in reducing the "strobing" of fast moving objects in an animation.

- **Image Motion Blur.** This technique is based on pixel speed and is applied after the frame has been rendered. Because it takes the speed of all pixels of an object into account, it can be used to blur objects and even spherical or cylindrical environment mappings.

- **Scene Motion Blur.** This shares information between frames. It applies its effect at scene level and takes camera movement into account, which Object Motion Blur does not. Most of the information comes from the current frame, but some is from the previous and following frames. The effect is less difference between frames, expanding the acceptable limits of camera motion. It is used mostly when creating blurred "trails" behind moving objects.

Note

One of the other ways to simulate real-world optics in a computer-generated scene is using depth of field (focus). Exercises later in this chapter will cover depth of field and motion blur.

Using Motion Blur

Motion blur is an effective way to reduce strobing, eliminate visual artifacts, and improve the realism in your animations. In the following exercise, you will examine the effects of different types of motion blur when applied to objects and environments seen in a camera pan.

1. Load the file 09max01.max from the CD-ROM (refer to Figure 9.8). Go to the Camera viewport and click the Play button to play the animation in the viewport. In this animation, your camera pans past a small moon where a rocket waits to launch. The camera pans 75 degrees over 60 frames (2 seconds), which, according to Table 9.3, is a comfortable speed.

2. First, examine the rendered animation without any motion blur applied. View the AVI file 09avi01.avi on the accompanying CD-ROM.

Figure 9.8   The camera's subject: a rocket resting on a small moon.

3. Note that the rocket seems to wobble or tear slightly as the camera pans past. Also, the brighter stars leave a strobing effect as they move across the frame.

Vertical lines create a worst-case scenario for strobing because the camera movement is perpendicular to the visual edge. In a similar way, camera tilts are more susceptible to strobing when they are moving past a strong horizontal line.

Note

This scene uses Displacement mapping and Lens Effects, two resource-demanding processes. If you want to speed up the rendering process, you can turn off these functions with the settings under Options in the Render Scene dialog box.

If the rocket no longer seems to rest properly on the moon's surface, it's because it loses volume without Displacement mapping. A simple solution would be to move the moon up on the z-axis until it once again intersects the rocket.

4. Go to frame 30, where the rocket is centered in the camera's view. Select the "rocket" group, right-click on it, and select Properties to open the Object Property panel. In the Motion Blur area, confirm that Enable is not checked.

5. Render a still image of this frame. Note that the rocket is rendered crisply against the background.

6. Bring up the rocket's Object Property panel again and check Enable. Turn on the radio button next to Object and click OK.

7. In the Render Scene dialog box, scroll down to the Object Motion Blur area. Under Object Motion Blur, select Apply. Use the default setting of Duration at 0.5 frames, and set Samples and Duration Subdivisions to 12. This will leave the virtual shutter open from halfway between frames 29 and 30 to halfway between frames 30 and 31.

Note

The Duration Subdivisions setting determines how many samples are possible within the given duration. The Samples setting controls the actual number of samples. Using a Sample value less than Duration Subdivisions causes the samples to be randomly selected.

Higher subdivision settings will increase rendering time. If you can see the individual samples in your rendered image, try increasing Samples. Otherwise, to reduce rendering time, you should use the lowest settings that give the desired degree of smoothness.

8. Render a still image. The vertical edges of the rocket are blurred. To see this effect applied to the entire animation, view the AVI file 09avi02.avi.

9. Now you will apply Image Motion Blur to the rocket. Go back into the Object Property panel for the rocket.

10. Select the Image Motion Blur radio button and click OK.

11. In the Render menu, make sure that the Apply box for Image Motion blur is checked. Set Duration to 0.5.

12. Click on the Clone button on the rendered Camera01 window to copy the frame you just rendered. Render a still image.

13. Compare the two versions closely. You will note that in the Image Motion Blur version, the rocket does not maintain its shape as well, particularly near the tip. This is because Image Motion Blur applies the effect on a pixel-by-pixel basis *after* the frame has been rendered, whereas Object Motion Blur samples each blurred object separately *before* it is rendered.

Note

For adding blur to individual objects in a scene, Object Motion Blur will usually give the best results. For background objects and environment maps, use Image Motion Blur.

14. Return the Motion Blur setting for the rocket to Object.

15. A better use for Image Motion Blur is smoothing backgrounds and environment maps. In the Render Scene dialog box, confirm that Image Motion blur is still checked and check the Apply to Environment Map box.

16. Render a still image. The background of your scene should be nicely blurred in the direction of the camera pan. To increase this effect, set the Image Blur Duration to a higher value.

To see the entire animation with the environment map with Image Motion Blur and the rocket with Object Motion Blur applied, view the AVI file 09avi03.avi.

> **Note**
>
> If you pause on the first frame of the AVI file 09avi04.avi, you will notice that the background is not blurred. Because the camera does not pan before the first frame, there are fewer frames of movement to combine than there are in latter frames. A solution for this would be to start the camera's motion before the first rendered frame.

By using motion blur, you have reduced strobing and improved the realistic appearance of this animation. Other camera moves, such as tilting and rolling, require the same precautions as panning. Motion blur may be called for whenever strongly contrasting visual elements will be traveling rapidly across the frame.

Dolly and Tracking Shots

Orson Welles' *Touch of Evil* opens with the camera following a slow-moving car through the serpentine streets and swift lives of a small border town, establishing the film's noir world and its various characters in a continuous shot that ends when the film's main protagonists witness the explosion of the aforementioned car. This extended dolly shot introduces the audience to the atmosphere and style of the film and provides an important event to begin the story. Figure 9.9 outlines the sequence of that shot. Figure 9.10 shows the changes in the position of the camera.

A *dolly* is a small-wheeled vehicle used to move a motion picture camera and its operators about in a scene. It is piloted by a *dolly grip*, whose job is to smoothly start and stop the dolly and synchronize its motion with the pans and tilts of the camera operator. When you design camera paths, you take on the role of dolly grip. The most challenging part of the job is achieving smooth, subtle starts and stops. As a virtual dolly grip, you need to re-create the human touch in your camera paths.

When the camera moves in and out of a scene (generally on the same axis as the lens), it is referred to as a *dolly move*. When the move is perpendicular to the lens axis, it is called a *tracking shot*. The same precautions must be observed when tracking as when panning.

Figure 9.9   An extended dolly shot opens *Touch of Evil*, introducing the film's moody and dangerous setting.

Figure 9.10   The dolly, track, and boom shots change the position of the camera.

Usually the tracking shot is used to follow a subject or to explore a certain space. It can inspect and focus on details of the overall scene. For example, the camera moves slowly away from a door revealing the rest of the house. In addition, the tracking shot is not restricted to a straight line. It can also turn corners, move forward and backward, come to a halt and start to move again, change speeds, and cross its own path.

Tracking is used very effectively in Francis Coppola's *The Godfather Part II*. The young Vito Corleone, played by Robert De Niro, pursues a vicious crime figure through Little Italy. The criminal is shown moving through the street, oblivious to the fact that he's being followed, while the tracking shot picks up the shadowy form of Vito on the rooftops above, moving parallel. The tracking shot follows them both, contrasting the small and insignificant hood with the successful mafioso (see Figure 9.11).

Figure 9.11   In *The Godfather Part II*, a tracking shot is used to follow Robert De Niro's character as he shadows his target.

The following basic methods can be used to track a subject:

- **Tracking at the same speed as the subject.** The most familiar use of this method is to follow two or more persons in conversation. The camera could track them on a parallel path in line or slightly behind or ahead of them. This type of shot is also often used when following a conversation in cars or on any other subject that is moving.

- **Tracking faster or slower than the subject.** A variation of the previous technique, this method enables you to show a subject enter or leave the center of the action. In order to show that somebody is winning in a race, the camera would track the subject slightly slower. If you want to show that he is losing, you would track him slightly faster, maybe passing him during the course of the shot.

- **Moving toward or away from the subject.** The camera can also move directly forward or backward. A dolly move toward a subject's face can be used to show a moment of realization. It could also be used as an introductory shot. For instance, the camera pulls back from a picture of a little forest to reveal that you are not on earth but on a spaceship.

Zoom Versus Dolly

Some people object to the Zoom effect because the viewer is brought closer to (or farther from) the subject without changing perspective. In a zoom shot, the entire image is magnified equally. In a dolly shot, the camera moves toward the subject, and the perspective changes. Objects also pass by the side of the frame, suggesting to the viewer that he is physically moving. The moving camera creates a feeling of depth, whereas the zoom tends to flatten space, which is better for filming because a moving camera draws too much attention to the move itself.

The speed of dolly and tracking moves is often based upon how fast a person moves. Refer to Tables 9.4 and 9.5 for recommended speeds.

Table 9.4   Pedestrian Gaits

Movement	Miles per Hour	Feet per Second	Inches per Second
Casual stroll	1.5–2.0	2.2–3.0	26–36
Average walk	2.5–3.5	3.6–5.0	43–60
Brisk walk	4–5	6–8	72–96
Average jog	6–8	9–12	108–144
Average run	8–10	12–15	144–180
All out sprint	12–16	18–24	216–288

Table 9.5   Number of Frames Needed to Move 10 Feet

Movement	15 fps	24 fps	30 fps
Casual stroll	50–68	80–109	100–136
Average walk	30–42	48–67	60–83
Brisk walk	19–25	30–40	38–50
Average jog	12–17	20–27	25–33

Movement	15 fps	24 fps	30 fps
Average run	10–12	16–20	20–25
All out sprint	6–8	10–13	13–17

Boom or Crane Shot

Perhaps the greatest boom shot in film history occurs in *Gone With the Wind*. As Scarlet O'Hara steps forward into the midst of hundreds of wounded soldiers, the camera pulls back from her distraught expression, elevates higher and pulls back to show the dying and dead spread everywhere, and up and back to a Confederate flag whipping in the wind. This camera move gives context to Scarlet's emotions and allows the viewer an over-reaching perspective on the scene (see Figure 9.12).

Figure 9.12 An elaborate boom shot in *Gone With the Wind* places Scarlet O'Hara's misery in the context of the larger devastation surrounding her.

When the camera moves up or down, the shot is traditionally called a *crane shot*, but actually the crane is capable of moving in many directions. It is the least natural move to be made with a camera because you rarely see the world from the high position of a crane. A crane shot draws attention to itself because of the exotic viewing angle and the change of perspective when it moves. Because there is no restriction on camera moves in a virtual environment, CG animators tend to employ crane shots without considering the attention this move calls to the camera itself. Observe the same timing and rendering practices with a crane shot as you would with a tilt.

Depth of Field

One of the problems faced by users of real-life camera optics is that depth of field is limited. When an object in the foreground of a shot is in focus, the background is out of focus. This characteristic is a problem in some circumstances, but it can also be very useful for emphasizing a particular element of the visual composition. Virtual cameras have unlimited depth of field. This leads to computer-generated images that are sharply focused from foreground to background.

You might want to introduce limited depth of field to re-create the "realism" people are used to seeing in film and television. Shallow depth of field enables you to isolate specific objects in a scene. You can also shift the plane of focus during a shot to move emphasis from one object to another. This effect was used to great advantage in *Jurassic Park*, when the game warden was surprised by a velociraptor emerging from the undergrowth (see Figure 9.13).

Figure 9.13   Depth of field is used to draw the audience's attention to an emerging threat in *Jurassic Park*.

Throughout Orson Welles' work in particular, deep focus provides clear, precise focus to all objects in the screen. An example of this occurs in *Citizen Kane*, when Charles Kane addresses his wife while she is assembling a jigsaw puzzle. Mrs. Kane dominates the foreground, dwarfing her husband in the background, which symbolizes a man overwhelmed by the massiveness of his towering house, Xanadu (see Figure 9.14).

Note

Depth of field can add realism to your imagery in much the same way motion blur does—by mimicking the visual style viewers have come to expect.

Figure 9.14 In *Citizen Kane*, deep focus makes all screen elements clear, providing an unusual juxtaposition.

With MAX R3, it is easier than ever to apply such effects to your animations. An Effects option has been added under Rendering. With this option, you can add lens effects, color balance, and depth of field effects to your scene in much the same way you add atmospheric effects.

Depth of Field (DOF) effects are linked to a particular camera and get focal parameters from either the selected camera or the Rendering Effects dialog box. The focal point for DOF effects can be determined either from the Target Distance of the camera or within the DOF Parameters.

Using Depth of Field

Depth of field can be used to emphasize a certain part of your scene, to draw the viewer's attention to the next storytelling element or to create a particular mood. In this exercise, you will test various depth of field settings.

1. Load the file 09max02.max from the accompanying CD-ROM. The subject for your camera is a series of rockets lined up on the surface of a moon.

2. Go to the Camera viewport and render a still image. All the elements of this scene are in focus, as you can see in Figure 9.15. This is a visual style that has come to be associated with computer graphics.

Figure 9.15   Without any depth of field effects, all the elements in this scene are in focus.

3. Go to Rendering and Effects to open the Rendering Effects dialog box.

4. Click on the Add button and add a Depth of Field effect. A set of Depth of Field parameters will appear when this effect is selected in the Effects list.

5. In the Cameras area, click on the Pick Cam button, and then select Camera01 either by clicking on it in one of the viewports or by using the Select Objects dialog box.

6. In the Focal Point area, click on the Pick Node button and select Camera01, Target. Any MAX object can be selected as a focal point.

7. In the Focal Parameters area, leave Custom turned on. This will allow you to modify the focal length settings used for depth of field within this dialog box, instead of using the settings for the selected camera.

8. Set Focal Range to 50 and Focal Limit to 75. Leave Horiz and Vertical Loss at their default settings of 10. This indicates that the image will remain in focus for 50 units, on the camera's z-axis, on either side of the focal point, and will reach the maximum amount of blur with 75 units. The amount of this blur is controlled by the Loss settings.

9. Render a still image. After the image has been rendered, the Depth of Field effect is calculated and applied. The rockets closest to the camera (and closest to the Focal Point) are kept in focus, whereas those farthest away are out of focus (see Figure 9.16).

Figure 9.16 Scene elements closest to the Focal Point remain in focus, while other elements are blurred (Focal Range = 50, Focal Limit = 75).

 Note

When using multiple Rendering Effects, be certain that Depth of Field is the last one listed in the Effects list (and hence the last rendered). Otherwise, some effects may not be included in the Depth of Field effect, resulting in an unnatural appearance.

10. For a more subtle effect, set Focal Range to 100 and Focal Limit to 150. If you have not closed the rendered Camera01 window, you can update the Depth of Field effect without re-rendering the frame. In the Preview area of the Rendering Effects dialog box, click on Update Effect. Figure 9.17 shows the result. If you have a particularly fast computer, you can try checking the Interactive box under Preview, Effects. Then you can watch as your changes to Effects parameters are rendered with each edit.

Figure 9.17   Increasing the depth of field means only scene elements far away from the camera are blurred (Focal Range = 100, Focal Limit = 150).

Note

Using the Update Effect feature in the Rendering Effects dialog box makes tweaking effects much easier.

In this section, we discussed the use of traditional film techniques because it is important not only to be technically able to animate a camera but also to understand the ways and possibilities of expressing yourself when using a camera during the process of film-making.

These techniques will help you to realize your idea of the final outcome, be it a logo animation, a character animation, or an architectural walkthrough. The final film will be what you want it to be and not a randomly achieved result. Compare it to learning a language: The more elaborate a language you can handle, the better you can express yourself. This is also true for film language.

Digital Cameras for Storytelling

Now that you have some grounding in the techniques used with traditional film cameras and translating those techniques into the realm of computer generated film, it is time to put these skills to use. This section covers using digital cameras for storytelling.

Storytelling in this sense can have a broad range of applications. Any use of a camera to capture imagery can be considered a story. Beyond the obvious short movies and cartoons, other content, such as architectural walk/flythroughs or flying logos, can also be broken down into story elements. The most basic story elements are listed here:

- **A plot with a clear beginning and ending.** In some cases, the arc of this plot may be fairly shallow, such as walking through an office building to a spectacular view from the top floor.

- **At least one character.** The subject of a story could be the previously mentioned building, a company logo, or a more conventional personified character.

- **Suspension.** Stories always raise questions, which they sometimes answer immediately, hours later, or never. Questions raised range from the simple (such as what final shape a morphing logo will take) to the complex (such as a character's purpose or motivation).

The way in which you use your cameras in a scene can have a strong impact on how successful you are in telling your story, or even on the content of that story.

When planning your camera shots, keep the following points in mind:

- **Compare your animation to sequences created by professional cinematographers.** Try to recall movie shots that express or capture the kind of motion you are working with. They may prove a good source for ideas on timing, composition, camera motion, and transitions.

- **Check your camera moves for economy.** If a lot of camera time is spent on low-key action, your audience may lose interest. Use transitions to eliminate insignificant material.

- **Avoid moves that draw attention to the camera at the expense of the subject.** If you're using an unusual camera move, consider whether you are enhancing or distracting from the idea behind the shot.

- **Compose and evaluate your camera moves by using the Camera viewport as a viewfinder.** Do not rely on looking at the orthagonal viewports.

- **Give the viewer time to absorb significant objects or actions before you move on.** An extra half-second can ensure that important story elements are not lost on the viewer.

- **Do not move the camera too quickly, even if the action you are covering is very fast-paced.** It is all too easy to overwhelm the viewer with information. Unless that is your goal, move at a comfortable pace.

Tip

Use a stopwatch to time yourself acting out or imagining a camera shot. This will give you a good starting point for timing camera moves. A stopwatch is also useful for examining live-action film sequences and transitions.

When framing your shots, it is important to consider the cropping that will be done to your image. Rarely does the resolution of your viewport match your output resolution. This means the image will probably be cropped either on the vertical or horizontal edges. Displaying your animations on a television monitor can also reduce the amount of image displayed because of the bezel surrounding the screen.

To avoid these problems, you can use the Video Safe Frame to be sure the frame displayed in your viewport matches your output resolution. Safe Frames are activated and configured in the Viewport Configuration dialog box. To display Safe Frames in a particular viewport, right-click on the Viewport Label and check Show Safe Frame.

In the exercises in this chapter, you will explore different camera techniques in conjunction with an animated character animation sequence.

The Camera As Communicator

One of the most basic uses of the camera is to clearly communicate an idea. Even a basic idea, such as that a character is tall and imposing, can be either enhanced or completely contradicted by camera angle, depth of field, and so on. By varying the camera angle and lens length, the identical model can appear either imposing or diminutive (see Figure 9.18).

When focusing on the communicative use of the camera, consider the following aspects of a scene:

- **The emotional relationship or linkage between objects that share a scene.** Using a camera angle that places a monster in a submissive or diminished relationship to its victim contradicts the expected aggressor/victim relationship.

- **The physical juxtaposition of scene elements.** It is not enough to create a model of an enormous structure. Camera use can make an object seem either huge or insignificant, regardless of its virtual dimensions.

- **The two-dimensional "read" of a composed frame.** This aspect is overlooked by many beginning animators. The final result of a shot that makes perfect sense in three dimensions will be a two-dimensional movie or still image. The basic silhouettes or Action in Profile must communicate clearly, or the intended meaning may be lost.

Figure 9.18   The spaceman appears massive when you use a 20mm lens with a low angle, but it's insignificant when you use a 50mm lens with a high angle.

Camera Use for Communication

In this tutorial, you will create and animate a camera to clearly communicate a short animated story. While most animators prefer to use a unique camera for each shot, it is sometimes beneficial (when rendering a preview, for example) to keep all your camera moves within a single camera. Because nearly every aspect of the cameras in MAX is animatable, this is fairly easy to accomplish. A later exercise will demonstrate the use of several cameras within a scene and the compositing of those cameras into a continuous sequence using Video Post.

1. Load the file 09max04.max from the accompanying CD-ROM. Go to the camera_birdseye viewport and play back this animation. This story should be a familiar one: A small rocket lands on a moon-like surface, and a space-suited alien hops out, bounds across the surface, and plants a flag to signal his conquest of this planetoid. This is a 22-second (660-frame) animation. To see this scene rendered, view the AVI file 09avi04.avi on the accompanying CD-ROM.

Note

A "bird's eye view" refers to a 3/4 perspective view, in which most of the scene elements can be viewed from a neutral position.

2. Analyze the use of the camera in this shot. Although the focus of the scene is contained within the camera's composition, and the basic story is evident, many elements of the story are either undone or not fully realized:

- The rocket comes across as weak and toy-like, instead of as a powerful craft capable of crossing interplanetery distances.

- The spaceman's jetpack-enhanced leap does not read very well.

- When viewed from above, the spaceman's effortless low-gravity walk seems flat and not very bouncy.

- The action in the second half of this animation is too small in the frame; a lot of information is being lost simply because this is such a wide field of view.

It is helpful to plan out the camera moves and angles you will be employing. Table 9.6 lists a general outline of shots for this animation. Each shot has been planned to clearly communicate part of the story. Note that several shots are continuations from preceding shots, meaning that there are no hard cuts between those shots. If you want to see how this sequence will turn out using the camera moves listed in Table 9.6, view the AVI file 09avi05.avi on the accompanying CD-ROM.

Table 9.6   Camera Shots Needed to Communicate the Story

Description	Frames	Camera Moves
Establishing shot	0–84	pan
Rocket descends	85–175	tilt
Rocket touchdown	176–250	none (stationary)
Spaceman exits rocket (continuation from previous shot)	251–298	pan, tilt, and track
Lands after jump	299–328	none (stationary)
Spaceman surveys landscape	329–402	none (stationary)
Several bounding steps	403–487	dolly
Plant flag (continuation from previous shot)	488–541	dolly and track
Frame final shot (continuation)	542–599	dolly and track
Final shot	600–659	track (continuation)

Note

When following a particular subject with the camera, you may find subsequent shots with similar beginning and ending points. It is advisable to make these transitions smoothly, as hard cuts between similar camera angles can be visually jarring.

3. Unhide the Camera01 and its target. This camera has been set up in the start position for the first camera shot (see Figure 9.19). Assign the "camera_birdseye" viewport to Camera01, and keep trying to evaluate your camera moves by using this framing mechanism, as opposed to solely aligning your camera and target in the orthogonal viewports.

Note

The establishing shot should provide the viewer with a frame of reference for the action to come. Even though it might last only a few seconds, that will be time enough for your audience to absorb the setting.

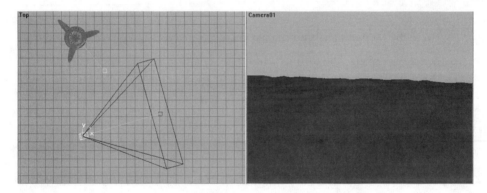

Figure 9.19 The starting position for the establishing shot, as seen from above and from the camera itself.

Tip

To prevent accidental selection of the "ground plane" object, freeze it by going to the Freeze roll-out of the Display panel, clicking on the Freeze by Hit button, and clicking on "ground plane."

Tip

If you find that this scene is updating slowly, consider hiding the "ground plane" object to speed up screen redraws. To free up additional system resources, delete "ground plane" from the scene and merge it back in at render time.

4. Turn the Animate button on and go to frame 84. Select the camera target and move it in the Top viewport until it is aligned with the center of the rocket

(see Figure 9.20). This establishing shot gives the viewer a feel for the setting of this story and introduces the first character with the exhaust from the rocket.

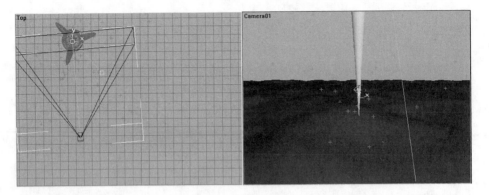

Figure 9.20   The ending position for the establishing shot, which creates a 2.8 second pan across the landscape.

5. Go to the Motion panel and change the camera target's In tangent to Linear.

6. Select the camera, and then set a position key either by right-clicking on the Time Slider bar or by using the Create Key, Position button in the Motion Panel. Change the camera's In tangent to Linear. You should get in the habit of doing this for all the camera and target position keys because it generally leads to smoother camera moves.

Tip

If your camera or camera target uses a Bezier controller, setting key tangents to Linear usually creates more stable camera moves.

7. Go to frame 85 for the introduction of the rocket. Go to a Left viewport, select the camera target, and move it to a position near the bottom of the rocket. The camera itself does not move very far from its last position. It basically just moves a little closer to the rocket (see Figure 9.21).

8. The camera needs to follow the rocket through this shot and up to frame 175. To accomplish this, move the target at frame 175 until it lines up again with the base of the rocket. Moving a camera's target on its z-axis is one way to accomplish a camera tilt.

9. To keep the camera "locked down" for this sequence, set a position key at frame 175.

The introductory shot displays the rocket in a traditional, though effective, angle. The upward angle connotes strength, and the downward movement implies an alien origin while solidifying the viewer's sense of being an observer on the lunar surface. This shot has been cut prior to the rocket's actual landing to preserve the tension of its impending contact and carry some motion into the next shot.

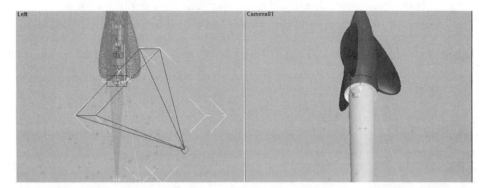

Figure 9.21   The camera's target moves to the base of the rocket as the rocket is introduced to the scene.

10. Go to frame 176 for the beginning of the stationary shot that will finalize the landing of the rocket and introduce the second character. Go to a Top viewport and move the camera in a counter-clockwise direction around the rocket and a little closer to the rocket.

11. Go to a Front viewport and move both the camera and its target along the View Y axis until the Camera viewport matches that shown in Figure 9.22.

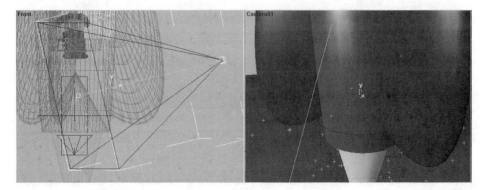

Figure 9.22   The camera lines up a few frames early in a position to frame the opening of the rocket's hatch.

12. The stationary part of this shot ends after frame 250, so go to frame 250 and set position keys for both the camera and its target. By frame 250, the rocket's hatch has opened, and the spaceman stands ready to exit. By moving the camera to this location before the opening of the hatch, you give the viewer a chance to "settle" before the commencement of the next action.

13. This shot continues through 298 as the spaceman leaps out of the rocket, boosted by his own jetpack. Go to frame 298 and move the camera and target as shown in Figure 9.23.

    This camera move is fairly complex, incorporating small movements along and around each axis. The basic intent of the move is a camera track, as the camera moves laterally to follow the flying spaceman.

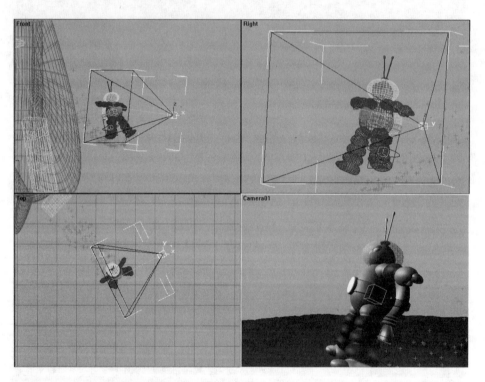

Figure 9.23   The camera follows the leaping spaceman in a complex camera move that most closely resembles a tracking move.

14. Go to frame 299 for the spaceman's landing after his jump. Move the camera and target in front of the spot where the spaceman will land, as shown in Figure 9.24.

15. Go to the end of this stationary shot at frame 328 and lock down both the camera and the target with position keys.

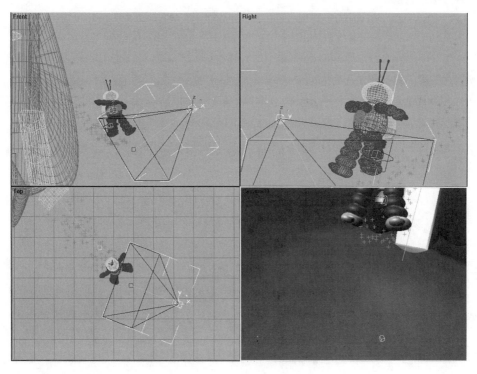

Figure 9.24   The camera is lined up for the spaceman's landing.

The purpose of this shot is to end the spaceman's aerial moves and ground him. Using a camera angle that fills the frame with the ground texture induces a sense of heaviness that is intensified by the down angle on the spaceman after he has landed.

16. At frame 329, the spaceman will begin his look back and forth. Move the camera and target directly in front of the spaceman, level with his head (see Figure 9.25).

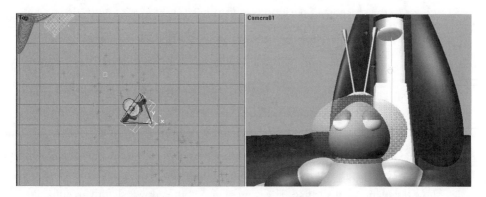

Figure 9.25   A tight camera angle to capture the spaceman's head movements.

17. This stationary shot lasts through frame 402. Go to frame 402 and set position keys for the camera and the target.

   This part of the animation consists of small head movements, the closest thing to facial expression this character is capable of. A very tight camera angle captures this motion and draws the viewer's attention to the spaceman's inner state.

18. The next shot will follow the spaceman as he bounds along. Go to frame 403 and move the camera away from the spaceman and slightly down on the z-axis, as shown in Figure 9.26.

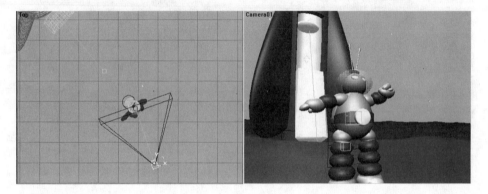

Figure 9.26   Pull the camera back to frame the entire spaceman for his moonwalk.

19. The camera target does not need to move very far to start this shot. Pull it back from the camera and down a bit on the z-axis.

20. Go to frame 487 for the end of this dolly move. Pull the camera back to frame the spaceman a little wider than he was at the beginning of the shot. You can use the Dolly Camera button (available when a camera viewport is active) to do this.

21. The target needs to be moved as well. It stays in the same basic position with respect to the spaceman's position (see Figure 9.27).

   In this dolly shot, the camera moves only slightly faster than its subject. Keeping the camera level with the ground and framing the horizon in the vertical middle of the shot allows the spaceman to visually break free of the ground plane with each step, enhancing the bouncy feel. Also, moving the viewer through the shot increases the sense of distance traveled, even more so because backward movement prevents the audience from anticipating the camera motion.

22. As you saw in Table 9.6, the rest of the camera moves transition smoothly one to another, without any hard cuts. The camera dollys and tracks to frame 541 to show the planting of the flag. The camera also booms down slightly to enhance

the heroic nature of the action. Because the distance between the camera and its target remains roughly the same throughout this move, the best way to accomplish this is to select both objects and move them in Top and Left viewports until they resemble Figure 9.28. This camera move accomplishes two things: It keeps the spaceman squarely in-frame, and it adds a touch of heroic glamour with the slight up-angle.

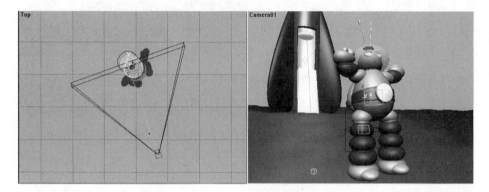

Figure 9.27   The end of the dolly shot, following the spaceman in his bounding steps.

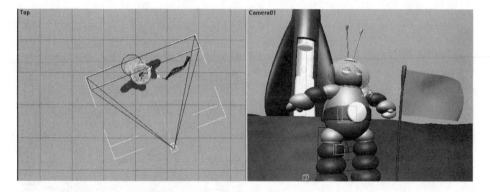

Figure 9.28   The camera dollys and tracks to frame the heroic flag-planting.

23. For the camera move to frame 599, use a dolly and track. Move the target closer to the camera to tighten the field of view (see Figure 9.29).

    The spaceman is turning toward the planted flag, which has ceased its secondary bouncing motion. The focus of the animation is shifting to the flag, and if you mirror the spaceman's turning gaze, the viewer's eyes will be drawn to the flag as well.

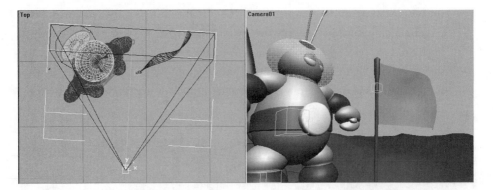

Figure 9.29   The camera moves in and swings to a side angle to set up for the final composition.

24. The final camera move is a small tracking move, which ends up with the flag dominating the frame. Go to the end of the animation (frame 660) and move the camera and target as shown in Figure 9.30.

This is the closing shot—and possibly the one image that will remain most firmly fixed in the viewer's mind. This shot needs to clearly communicate the idea of the piece or make a concluding comment on it. The image displayed on the flag celebrates MAX R3 and explains the motivation behind the preceding animation.

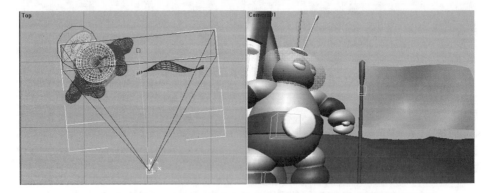

Figure 9.30   The final camera move frames the flag and the spaceman gazing at it.

25. As stated earlier, one of the advantages of using only one camera is the ease of creating previews. Go to Rendering, Make Preview and specify the parameters you desire for this preview. Previews can be a great tool for working out the timing of camera moves and transitions. If you want to see a rendered preview of this sequence, view the AVI file 09avi05.avi on the accompanying CD-ROM.

> **Note**
>
> MAX R3 uses your video card display drivers or the software driver you have selected to create previews, capturing the screen at each frame. This can create some odd video artifacts if you minimize MAX R3 or bring up another window during the creation of a preview animation.

To examine a completed MAX file for this scene, load the file 09max05.max from the accompanying CD-ROM.

To review this animation using the camera moves you have created, view the AVI file 09avi05.avi on the accompanying CD-ROM. The story is a lot clearer than the static perspective you analyzed at the beginning of this exercise. Because you've used the camera to enhance and communicate each story element, the camera has become an active part in this animation.

Camera usage in this animation is fairly unobtrusive, however. Planning camera moves using the techniques of traditional cinematography usually prevents the audience from becoming aware of the camera as an entity separate from the action. With the advent of digital cameras and the freedom they afford, the rules of traditional film are no longer requirements driven by budget and logistics. In the following tutorial, you will explore the use of digital cameras as expressive partners in the creation of unusual visuals.

Experimental Cameras

When you're creating cameras for experimental or unusual animation, the techniques of traditional filmmaking might not suffice. Extreme camera angles, quick zooms, and other unusual camera moves can add excitement and novelty to your animations. This may seem like a contradiction of the guideline mentioned earlier in this chapter—that the camera should not call attention to itself with excessive motion. While it's true that expressive camera use leads to a greater audience awareness of the camera, the goal here is to enhance and exaggerate your animation with the camera.

For good examples of some innovative camera techniques, examine films like John Woo's action-packed *Broken Arrow*, Katsuhiro Ôtomo's surreal animated film *Akira*, and the Wachowski brothers' *The Matrix*.

If you're considering expressive use of the camera, take into account the following aspects of a scene:

- **The camera should advance the concept behind the animation in a creative or even abstract way.** For example, creating a quick widening of the camera angle during a character's moment of panic or surprise may increase the viewer's empathy by mimicking the character's attitude.

- **Special effects such as blur, glow, and depth of field can add to the content of a shot, especially when used in unexpected ways.** A frantically ringing telephone might appear even more desperate if you add a subtle glow around the object and shorten the depth of field, which blurs the rest of the scene.

- **Quick camera moves may be appropriate for action-filled animations.** Although aggressive camera moves, pans, and zooms can be tiring for the viewer (especially over a lengthy amount of time), they may be very useful for a high-energy music video.

- **Be certain not to obscure the underlying meaning of a shot with inappropriate camera moves.** A succession of quick cuts and lightning-fast zooms might not work if you're filming a low-key conversation, for example.

Expressive Camera Use

In this tutorial, you will create and animate several cameras to express and exaggerate a short animated story (see Figure 9.31). You will use the animated story from the previous exercise, but you wind up with a much less conventional result. Analyzing each part of this animation will yield some creative and unusual ways to film it.

Load the file 09max04.max from the accompanying CD-ROM. If you are not familiar with this scene from the preceding tutorial, you can look at two AVI files on the accompanying CD-ROM that will familiarize you with it. The file 09avi04.avi shows the animation from a static viewpoint, which gives you an overview of the action. The file 09avi05.avi shows the animation from the perspective of a moving camera, which gives you a feel for the mood of this story. Table 9.7 shows the camera shots, scene ranges, and shot durations you will use in this animation.

Table 9.7   Camera Shots Planned to Express the Story

Description	Camera	Scene Range	Scene Duration
Rocket descends camera_shot01	0–175	176	
Touches down and hatch opens	camera_shot02	165–275	111
Spaceman exits	camera_shot03	265–285	21
Spaceman leaps	camera_shot04	270–305	72
Lands, looks around, takes steps	camera_shot05	304–502	199
Pulls out flag and plants it	camera_shot06	502–660	159

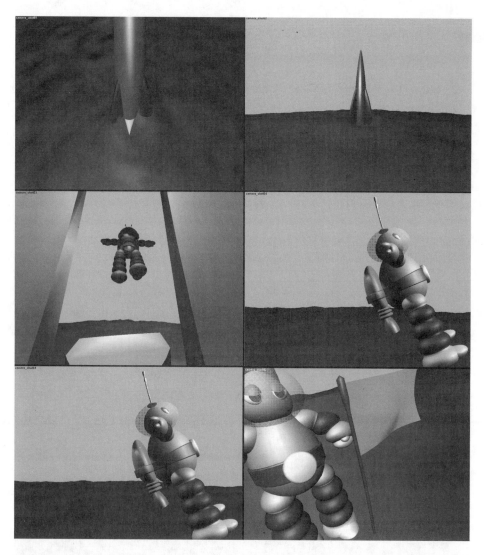

Figure 9.31   The six camera moves you will create in this tutorial.

The first section of this animation concerns the rocket's descent, which is fairly leisurely and emphasizes movement along the World Z axis. You will complement this motion with a spiraling camera shot that's centered on the rocket's base, drawing closer to the rocket as the rocket nears the ground plane.

1. Go to the camera viewport and change it to Perspective by pressing the P key. Zoom to show the rocket and the area around it. Create a Helix spline roughly

centered on the rocket's path. Set the following parameters for the spline: Radius1 = 37, Radius2 = 15, Height = 225, Turns = 3. Name this shape "camera_shot01_path."

2. Mirror the spline around the World Z axis so that the beginning of the path is on top.

3. Go to a Top viewport and move the spline so it is roughly centered on the rocket. Go to a Front viewport and move the spline on the View Y axis until it is roughly centered on the rocket, including the rocket thrust object. This is the path that the camera for the first shot will follow, spiraling down to the rocket's landing (see Figure 9.32).

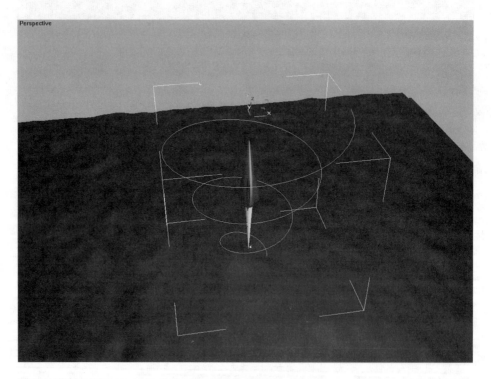

Figure 9.32   The camera path for the rocket's descent.

4. Go to a Top viewport and create a target camera aimed at the rocket. Set the lens length to 20mm. Name this camera "camera_shot01."

5. To bind the camera to the path, go to the Motion panel, select the Position controller, and assign a Path controller. In the Path Parameters rollout, pick camera_shot01_path as the Path Object.

6. Turn the Animate button on, go to frame 175, and set %AlongPath to 100. This enables the camera to reach the end of the path at frame 175.

7. Select the camera's target, go to frame 0, and move the target to the center of the rocket. Go to a Front viewport and move the target to the vertical center of the rocket, just above the fins.

8. Go to frame 174 and move the target down to the bottom edge of the rocket. See Figure 9.33 for the beginning and ending frames for camera_shot01. To view this sequence, go to the "camera_shot01" viewport, set the viewport to Wireframe display, and scrub through frames 265 to 285.

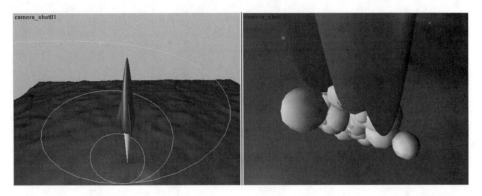

Figure 9.33   The camera for the first shot starts with a high perspective on the rocket and ends with a close-up of the rocket landing.

Tip

To keep your viewport from getting cluttered, hide each camera and target when you finish animating them. You will still be able to view from these cameras while they're hidden.

The next section begins with the actual touchdown of the rocket and introduces the spaceman as the hatch opens. A wide angle opening shot will contrast nicely with the close angle that ends shot 1. The opening of the hatch abruptly reveals the spaceman within. You can enhance that effect and propel this character into the viewer's awareness with a fast zoom.

9. Go to a Top viewport, and create a target camera with the target centered on the rocket and the camera extending at a 45 degree angle in the lower-right corner of the viewport. Set the lens length to 15mm. Place the camera approximately 100 units from the target, as shown in the Target Distance value at the bottom of the camera parameters rollout. Name this camera "camera_shot02."

10. Go to frame 165. This shot will overlap the preceding one by ten frames. Go to the camera viewport and change your view to camera_shot02. Use the Pan tool to drag the viewport down until the bottom of the rocket is centered in the viewport. If you need to precisely place the camera, you can move the camera and target together in an orthogonal viewport (see Figure 9.34).

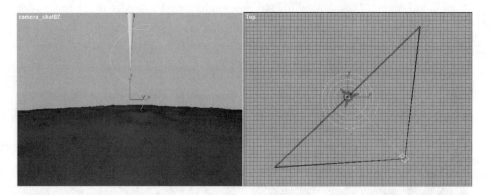

Figure 9.34   A target camera is placed for the second shot.

11. Go to frame 225 and set a key locking the lens length to 15mm. The most straightforward way to do this is to change the Lens value and then change it back to 15mm. At this point in the animation, the rocket hatch has opened, mostly revealing the spaceman within.

12. Go to frame 245 and set Lens to 200mm. This will have the effect of zooming in quickly. This shot will last until frame 275, although the camera angle will not change during the last 30 frames. See Figure 9.35 for the beginning and ending frames for camera_shot02. If necessary, use the Pan tool to frame the zoomed in shot. To view this sequence, go to the camera_shot02 viewport, set the viewport to Wireframe display, and scrub through frames 165 to 275.

The third camera shot is a short one, showing the spaceman's leap from within the rocket. This shot is only 20 frames long, but it will help impart a sense of momentum to the spaceman by having him leap directly away from the camera in a burst of smoke.

13. Go to the Top viewport and go to frame 265. Create a target camera near the center of the rocket, with the target slightly in front of the spaceman. Name this camera "camera_shot03." Set Lens to 15mm. Then go to a Front viewport, move the camera up on the View Y axis until it is a few units below the spaceman's feet, and move the target up on the y-axis until it is just above the feet. This shot

will last through frame 285. See Figure 9.36 for the beginning and ending frames for camera_shot03. To view this sequence, go to the camera_shot03 viewport, set the viewport to Wireframe display, and scrub through frames 165 to 275.

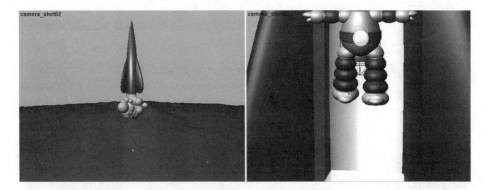

Figure 9.35   The camera for the second shot starts with an extreme pull-back and zooms in quickly to show the spaceman leaping through the rocket hatch.

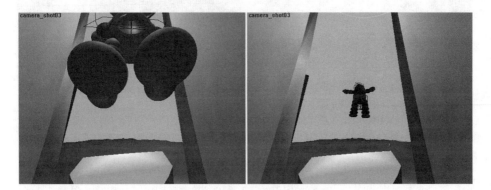

Figure 9.36   This short shot has the spaceman bounding out of the rocket hatch and receding directly away from the camera.

In the fourth shot, the spaceman is leaping across the sky, propelled by his jet-pack. You can enhance this motion by viewing it from a low angle, framing the spaceman against the sky. The spaceman's velocity will also be expressed by his movement, across the camera frame, from left to right throughout this shot.

14. Go to frame 270 and go to a Top viewport. Create a target camera pointing up along the Y View axis, with the target slightly in front of the spaceman. Place your camera so that Target Distance is approximately 25 units. Name this camera "camera_:shot04." Set Lens to 35mm.

15. Go to a Front viewport and move the camera up on the View Y axis until it is even with the bottom of the open doorway. Move the target up on the y-axis until it is vertically aligned with the spaceman's belt. Create a position key for the target.

16. Go to frame 305 and move the target down on the y-axis until it is even once again with the spaceman's belt.

17. Go to a Top viewport and move the target until it is just behind the spaceman. See Figure 9.37 for the beginning and ending frames for camera_shot04. To view this sequence, go to the camera_shot04 viewport, set the viewport to Wireframe display, and scrub through frames 270 to 305.

Figure 9.37   The spaceman leaps across the sky and crosses the viewport.

The fifth shot in this sequence is a special case. You will link a target camera to the spaceman so that its movement will be based on the spaceman's animation. This camera will point toward the character's face for most of this shot. A continuous close-up shot like this implies a strong level of empathy, making the viewer imagine the character's inner state by moving with the character in a face-to-face relationship.

Note

Linking a camera to your character can be very useful in creating detail animation after whole body animation has been applied. If you link a camera to a character's head, for example, you will always have a stable viewport from which to animate facial expressions, no matter what contortions your character may be going through.

18. Go to a Top viewport and go to frame 0. Create a target camera directly at the spaceman's face, with the target at the back of the spaceman's head. Place your camera so that Target Distance is approximately 5 units. Name this camera "camera_shot05" and set Lens to 35mm.

19. Go to the Camera viewport and change your view to camera_shot05. Select the camera, go to a Front viewport, and zoom in on the camera. Right-click on the camera, and choose Select Target to add the target to the selection. Adjust the position of the camera and the target until the spaceman's helmet fills the viewport.

Tip

If you find that the camera is clipping out portions of the spaceman's helmet that get too close, go to the Clipping Planes rollout in the camera's Modifier panel, check Clip Manually, and set Near Clip to 0.

20. Select the camera and target, click Select and Link, and link both these objects to dummy_spaceman. Press the H key to select the dummy. As the spaceman moves throughout the scene, the camera moves with it.

21. Go to frame 304 and create position keys for both the camera and the target.

22. Go to frame 322. At this point, the spaceman is leaning forward, recovering from his landing. So pan the camera down a bit and dolly out, using the camera viewport controls, until his helmet is centered in the viewport once again (see Figure 9.38).

Figure 9.38   The spaceman's head is framed via the "face-cam."

23. Go to frame 341 (where the spaceman is standing up straight) and pan the viewport to center the view on his helmet. Create a position key for the target to keep the next change in position from beginning any earlier than this frame.

24. At frame 355, the spaceman is gazing to his right and gesturing in that direction. To continue mimicking his motions, go to a Top viewport and move the camera close to his body, nearer his left shoulder. Move the target to a position in front of his right arm. This camera angle should have the viewer looking along the spaceman's outstretched arm (see Figure 9.39).

Figure 9.39   The spaceman surveys the landscape he has come to claim.

25. At frame 379, he is looking to his left. Mirror the camera and target moves you created in step 24. When you finish, the camera is looking along the spaceman's outstretched left arm.

26. Go to frame 403, where the spaceman is preparing to start his bounding steps. Move the camera and target back to positions close to those set in step 23 to center the spaceman's helmet in the Camera viewport. For the remaining duration of this shot, through frame 502, the camera can be allowed to follow the action without additional keys.

The sixth and final camera shot shows the spaceman whipping out a flag from some concealed pocket and planting it decisively in the ground. The camera will follow this quick motion with some fast pans and rolls. The animation ends with him nodding in satisfaction at the flag, which waves romantically in the breeze.

27. Go to frame 502 and go to a Top viewport. Create a target camera directly in front of the spaceman, within (virtual) arm's reach. Place the target behind the spaceman. New to MAX R3 is the ability to toggle between target and free cameras in the Modifier panel. Go to the Type list in the Parameters rollout and change to Free. The reason you originally used the Target type is that target cameras are much easier to aim while they are being created.

28. Name this camera "camera_shot06" and set Lens to 24mm. Pan the camera up until the spaceman's torso is framed in the left half of the viewport, adjusting the camera manually in an orthagonal viewport if necessary. Orbit the camera down a bit so the spaceman is framed from a low angle (see Figure 9.40).

Figure 9.40   Viewing the spaceman from a low angle, preparing for an heroic gesture.

29. Go to frame 533, which is the highest point of the spaceman's wave of the flag. Pan up until the spaceman's helmet is vertically centered in the viewport, and then dolly out just a bit so the spaceman's right upper arm is visible. Create a rotation key for the camera.

30. At frame 540, the flag has been planted. Go to a Top viewport, rotate the camera −35 degrees around the Local X axis and −10 degrees around the Local Z axis.

31. Go back to the Camera viewport and pan the camera so the flag fills most of the viewport, with the spaceman to the side (see Figure 9.41). To view this sequence, go to the camera_shot02 viewport, set the viewport to Wireframe display, and scrub through frames 304 to 502.

Figure 9.41   When the spaceman plants his flag, the camera swings into a jaunty angle in response.

32. The ending camera move is much slower-paced, to give the audience plenty of time to absorb the meaning. Go to frame 630, go to a Top viewport, and rotate the camera −10 degrees on the Local Y axis. Go back to the Camera viewport and dolly out just enough to get the entire flag in frame.

33. In order to keep the camera's trajectory from wandering too much between these last two keys, change the Out tangent at frame 540 and the In tangent at frame 630 to Linear. You can do this either by right-clicking on the key in the Track Bar and selecting the Position track, or by using the Key Info rollout in the Motion panel.

34. Finally, just to keep the camera from "dying," go to the last frame (660) and dolly the camera out a tiny bit. You do this to maintain some small camera movement because the sudden freezing of a dynamic camera can be jarring. To view this sequence, go to the camera_shot02 viewport, set the viewport to Wireframe display, and scrub through frames 502 to 660.

To examine a completed MAX file for this scene, load the file 09max06.max from the accompanying CD-ROM. To review this animation using the camera moves you have created, view the AVI file 09avi06.avi on the accompanying CD-ROM. This AVI has been compiled from each camera using Video Post techniques explained in the next section.

In this tutorial, you have learned how to animate a series of cameras to film an animation using expressive and unusual camera angles and moves. The techniques used are fairly unconventional and should prove useful when you're animating cameras for high-energy animation or in cases where you need to call attention to a shot. In the next exercise, you will use Video Post to compose this series of camera shots into one continuous render.

Multiple Cameras and Video Post

Video Post is an essential tool for animating with multiple cameras. This utility allows you to mix sequences of your animation, choose which cameras to render from, apply filters and effects, and even use input from previously rendered stills or animations. In the following exercise, you will set up six cameras, apply effects to some of them, and compose them all in Video Post into one render queue.

The time frame used by Video Post can differ from that of your scene range, or even run at different frame rates. For example, you could begin your Video Post queue with a segment from the end of your animation, or you could render 100 frames of animation in only 50 frames, effectively doubling the speed of that segment.

Sometimes, you might want to use Video Post to overlap sequences. Suppose, for example, that a dramatic explosion occurs at frame 100. You set up two camera angles from which to film this action, and you use Video Post to capture frames 0–105 from the first camera and frames 100–150 from the second. These two shots will overlap by five frames, causing the explosion to repeat quickly when the final animation is viewed. This effect is used often in movies and on television to get more screen time out of special effects, violent collisions, and explosions.

Video Post for Compositing

Load the file 09max06.max from the accompanying CD-ROM or continue with the file you creating in the preceding tutorial. To preview the results of this tutorial, view the AVI file 09avi06.avi on the accompanying CD-ROM.

A series of cameras have been set up to capture this short animation, with some overlapping frame ranges. Table 9.8 shows the camera shots you've already created, along with the Video Post ranges you will use to film this animation.

Table 9.8   Camera Shots and Video Post Settings Needed for Compositing

Description	Camera	Scene Range	Scene Duration	Video Post Range
Rocket descends	camera_shot01	0–175	176	0–175
Touches down and hatch opens	camera_shot02	165–275	111	176–286
Spaceman exits	camera_shot03	265–285	21	287–328
Spaceman leaps	camera_shot04	270–305	72	329–400
Lands, looks around, takes steps	camera_shot05	304–502	199	401–599
Pulls out flag and plants it	camera_shot06	502–660	159	600–758

1. Go to Rendering, Video Post to open the Video Post utility. To preview the queue you will be creating in this tutorial, click on the Open Sequence button on the Video Post toolbar and open the file 09vpx01.vpx on the accompanying CD-ROM. Figure 9.42 shows the Video Post queue. To reset the queue to an empty sequence, click on the New Sequence button.

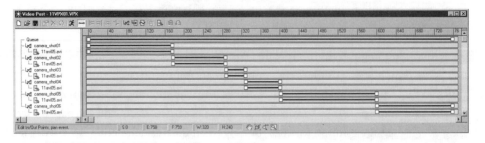

Figure 9.42   The Video Post queue, which will composite six cameras together.

2. To add the rendering sequence for the first camera shot, click on the Add Scene Event button. Under View, select camera_shot01. Set VP Start Time to 0 and VP

End Time to 175. Leave the Lock to Video Post Range button checked to ensure that the scene range rendered is the same as the Video Post range. Click OK to close this dialog box.

3. Select the camera_shot01 Scene Event in the queue, and then click on the Add Image Output Event button. Click on the Files button and set the name to 09avi06.avi and type to AVI. Note that the VP Start and End Times are automatically set to the same values used in the Scene Event. These two VP events will cause frames 0 to 175 of your animation to be rendered from camera_shot01 and saved to an AVI file.

4. Deselect the Scene Event by clicking on a blank area of the queue. Add another Scene Event, selecting camera_shot02 as the View. Set VP Start Time to 176 and VP End Time to 286. The scene range that you want to render for this shot actually begins earlier than frame 176. Clear the Lock to Video Post Range button and set Scene Start to 165. This allows you to start the render at any point in your scene's range.

5. Select the camera_shot02 event and add another Image Output Event. Click on Files and specify the same AVI file you used for the previous shot.

6. Repeat steps 4 and 5 for the four remaining shots in this scene, using the Scene Range and Video Post Ranges from Table 9.8. Note that shots 3 and 4 are special cases, in that the Video Post Range for these shots covers twice as many frames as the Scene Range. These shots will be sub-frame sampled to produce a slow-motion segment. In order to specify a different range length, clear the check box for Lock Range Bar to Scene Range. This will allow you to set a Scene End value that results in fewer or more rendered frames than Video Post frames.

Note

The distinction between Video Post Range and Scene Range is an important one. The order in which VP events are executed is determined by VP Range, whereas Scene Range determines which frames of your animation are rendered. VP Range can be identical to Scene Range, can start at a different frame, or can run at a different frame rate.

7. To render this sequence, click on the Execute Video Post button, and then specify the Range (VP Range, not Scene Range) and Output Size.

Rendering previews is essential to working out camera timing prior to final rendering. Although MAX's Preview function does not currently support multiple cameras, you can get a similar result by editing one of the Scene Events in your queue and choosing Render Options. Turning off Effects, Atmospherics, Mapping, and Shadows will greatly increase rendering time and still give you the visual information necessary to assess camera moves. Changes made to one Scene Event's Render Options will be reflected in the remaining Scene Events. In addition, you can try specifying a small output size when you execute the sequence.

To view this animation with all the camera shots composited together, view the AVI file 09avi06.avi from the accompanying CD-ROM.

In Practice: Animating Cameras

- **Study established camera techniques, and try to learn the basics of film language.** Using the same techniques in computer animation helps the artist communicate effectively.

- **Don't be afraid to bend or break the established rules of film language.** Innovative directors and experimental animation can be a great source of inspiration.

- **Consider the psychological impact of camera effects.** Depth of field, viewer placement, field of view and camera moves all contribute to the degree to which the audience is immersed and its emotional reaction to the subject matter.

- **Make the camera transparent for clarity.** When clear communication of ideas is the goal, maintaining proper framing of the subject, unobtrusive camera moves, and a clear two-dimensional "read" of the frame are crucial.

- **Use flashy moves to add expression.** For more expressive camera styles, quick zooms, unusual camera angles, and a mix of lens lengths can add excitement and energy to your animation.

- **Even after cameras have been animated for a scene, you can further enhance the content of the scene during the compositing stage.** Video Post is an essential tool for compositing multiple cameras, allowing you to freely mix the order and frame rate of animated sequences.

Chapter 10

Animating Lights and Atmospheres

By Sean Bonney

Lighting is an important element in all artwork. Essential in establishing the mood of a scene, it can also focus the viewer's attention on a particular element or area, or help separate background from middleground and foreground, adding more depth to your work. Highlights can reveal details; shadows can hide or suggest mood. The significance of lighting is often overlooked. While careful lighting cannot turn a poorly created scene into good artwork, bad lighting can certainly ruin a well-executed image.

Atmosphere is a closely-related topic. Adding fog, smoke, or clouds to a scene enhances the mood and creates depth. In some cases, an element such as a prominent burning torch that's used to create atmosphere becomes an important scene element.

This chapter discusses lighting and atmospheres from a practical standpoint, putting particular emphasis on the new features available in 3D Studio MAX R3. The tutorials in this chapter show you how to animate the various parameters associated with them.

This chapter explores the following topics:

- Illumination types
- Shadow controls new to MAX R3
- Controlling ambient light
- Attenuating light with distance
- Applying atmospheric effects
- Interaction of atmosphere with shadows and volume light
- Setting up and animating lights and atmospheres
- Simulating a naturalistic outdoor environment
- Simulating an indoor mechanical environment
- Creating special effects with light, atmosphere, and rendering effects

Lighting and the Surface Normal

The surface normal is an important concept to grasp, at least in general terms, because all lighting calculations are based on it. Fortunately, you can gain a basic understanding of it without getting into trigonometry or complicated mathematics.

A *surface normal* is a unit vector perpendicular to and centered on a face, which is the smallest possible Planar surface. Each face has a normal, which you can visualize as a line pointing straight out of the face. Using MAX's Show Normals command, you can display an object's surface normals:

1. Open the file 10max01.max. This scene consists of a simple water tower illuminated by a Target Spotlight (see Figure 10.1).

Figure 10.1   This water tower is being illuminated by a single light source. The high specular level on the tank shows the reflection of that light source.

2. Select the "tank" object.

3. In the Modify panel, go into Sub-Object/Face mode and select all the faces in this object.

4. Turn on Show Normals in the Normals section of the Surface Properties rollout.

In the Camera01 viewport, notice that all the normals are perpendicular to their faces (see Figure 10.2). The line linking the Spotlight to its target illustrates the direction to the light source. The angle created between the surface normal and a vector to the light source determines how much diffuse light the face receives.

Almost all lighting calculations are related to the angle between the light source and the face's normal. They work slightly differently for diffuse and specular light, which are explored next.

Figure 10.2   The surface normals extend perpendicularly from the faces of the water tank.

Surface Normals and Diffuse Light

Roughly speaking, the more directly the normal points at the light source, the more brightly the face is lit. As the normal points farther away from the light (either because of modeling or animation), the face becomes darker.

So think of the normal this way: If the normal is pointing directly at the light source, the face receives maximum diffuse illumination. As the normal starts to point away from the light source and the angle between the normal and the light source increases, the face receives less diffuse light. If the normal is pointing 90 degrees or more away from the light source, the face receives no light at all. To see how diffuse light affects an object, try this simple experiment.

1. Open the file 10max01.max or continue from the preceding tutorial.

2. Select the Spot01 light.

3. In the Modify panel, go to the Affect Surfaces area of the General Parameters rollout. By default, Diffuse and Specular are checked, indicating that this light will affect those types of illumination on objects in its range.

4. Go to the Camera01 viewport and render a frame. Notice that the water tank is well-lit and has a bright highlight.

5. Turn Diffuse off and render another frame. This time the water tower is barely lit at all, except for the highlights. This light has been excluded from affecting the diffuse surface lighting. Figure 10.3 shows how diffuse lighting differs from specular lighting.

Figure 10.3   The water tower illuminated with both diffuse and specular lighting (left) and with only specular lighting (right).

6. Turn Diffuse back on to continue to the next exercise.

Specular Light and Placing Highlights

To determine the amount of specular light that a face receives, MAX uses calculations similar to those for determining diffuse light, but the process is a little more complex. MAX uses the face's normal to calculate whether the specular light can be "seen" by the viewport or camera after it has bounced off the face. A specular highlight moves across the surface of an object if the object, the light, or the point of view moves. The following short exercise demonstrates how changing the position of a light source dramatically alters the appearance of the highlight.

1. Open the file 10max01.max or continue from the preceding tutorial.

2. Go to the Camera01 viewport and render a frame. Note the position of the bright highlight on the water tank.

3. Go to a Top viewport, select the Spot01 light, and move it approximately 400 units on the View X axis.

4. Render another frame from the Camera01 viewport. The highlight has moved to the right because the normals for those faces are now pointing almost directly at the light source. Figure 10.4 shows how the highlight is affected when you move the light source.

Figure 10.4 Moving the light source changes the position of the specular highlight, as well as that of the diffuse lighting.

Moving the light source even a short distance can have a significant impact on the final result. If you need to precisely place highlights on objects, the Place Highlight tool can make it a straightforward task. Follow these steps:

1. Open the file 10max01.max or continue from the preceding tutorial. Go to the Camera01 viewport and select the Spot01 light. Turn on Smooth + Highlights mode if it is not already on.

2. Click and hold the mouse button over the Align icon. Move down to the Place Highlight icon, and then release the mouse button to select it. The icon should become active in the toolbar and have a green wash, which indicates it is in a pick mode.

3. Click on the water tank and drag the icon across the surface. As you move the icon, the Spotlight is moved to place the highlight on the selected faces. Also, the normal for the currently active face is displayed (see Figure 10.5).

Naturally, as the light is moved, the diffuse lighting is also affected. This can produce a new problem: having to place a light where you need it because your highlights might not give you the diffuse illumination you want. This is why highlights are often created with separate lights. Here's how it works.

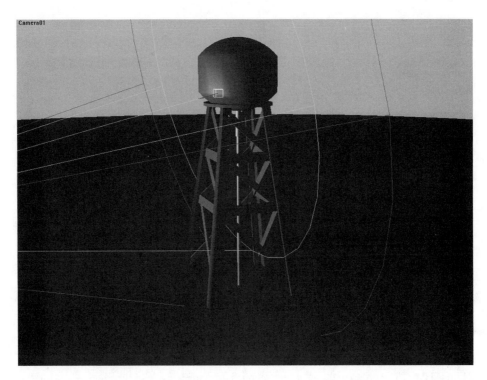

Figure 10.5   The Place Highlight tool allows you to specify which face on a particular object will receive the center of the specular highlight from the selected light source.

Note

When precise positioning of highlights and diffuse illumination is required, you can use several lights that each affect either the specular component or the diffuse component exclusively. Turn off the Affect Diffuse or Affect Specular check box in the Color section of the light's General Parameters rollout to create a specular-only or diffuse-only light.

1. To return the spotlight to it's original position, use Type In-Transform (Ctrl+T) and enter –150 for X, –250 for Y, and 200 for Z.

2. Clone this light as a Copy and name it "Highlight01."

3. Go to the Modifier panel and note that the first entry under General Parameters gives this light's type. Change the Type to Omni. Under Affect Surfaces, turn off Diffuse. This light now affects only highlights.

4. Use the Place Highlights tool to move the highlight across the water tank.

5. Now the water tank has two highlights, as shown in Figure 10.6. To turn off the highlight cast by the original Spotlight, select Spot01 and clear the Specular check box.

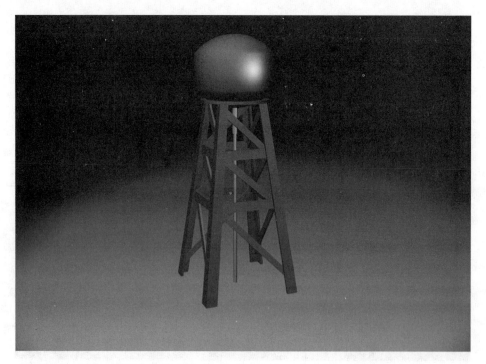

Figure 10.6   The diffuse lighting is being applied from the left side of the water tower, and the specular highlight is being applied from the right.

Shadow Colors and Density

Where there is light, there is shadow, and several new options have been added in MAX R3 to offer greater control of shadows. Shadow color can be assigned, blended with light color, and rendered with variable density. To see how to tweak shadow attributes, follow these steps:

1. Open the file 10max02.max or continue from the preceding tutorial.

2. Select the Spot01 light. Turn on Cast Shadows. The type of shadow that's cast is set in the Shadow Parameters rollout. Set the Type to Ray Traced Shadows. Note that the next rollout changes to Ray Traced Shadow Parameters.

3. Render a frame to see a hard shadow cast by the water tower (see Figure 10.7).

4. In the Shadow Parameters rollout, change the shadow's color to a medium blue (R50, G50, B150). Make a copy of the rendered frame using the Clone button on the Frame window. Then render another frame and compare the two renders. Note that only the shadow color has changed.

Figure 10.7   A ray-traced shadow is being cast by the Spotlight, which is providing the diffuse lighting.

5. To lighten the shadow without changing the color, change the Density setting to 0.5. Render another frame.

Tip

When you're making subtle changes to light settings, use the Clone button on the rendered Frame window to copy the image before you make new test renders. Then you can compare renders side by side.

6. In order to see the effect light color can have on shadow color, first change the light color to bright yellow (R255, G255, B0). Then increase shadow Density to 1.0 to make the shadow's color more obvious. Render a still to see the change in illumination.

7. Turn on Light Affects Shadow Color. Render another still to see the subtle tint added to the shadow.

   Another method for comparing renders is Render Region. In the Render pop-up on the Toolbar, select Region. When you start rendering, a dashed outline box shows what area will be rendered. Resize and reposition as desired, and then click

OK to continue. Only the selected region will be over-written in your render window (see Figure 10.8).

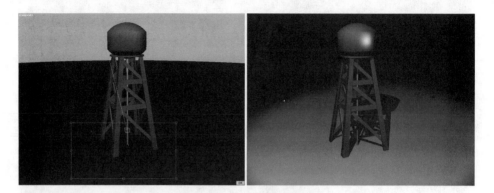

Figure 10.8   Use Render Region to update only a portion of the render window. Here the updated portion shows the effect of turning on Light Affects Shadow Color.

8. Reset the light color to white (R255, G255, B255) to continue to the next exercise.

These new controls for tweaking the appearance of shadows greatly simplify the process of adjusting lights by isolating shadow attributes from the intensity and color of the shadow-casting light. This allows you to change the appearance of a shadow without affecting the illumination of a scene.

Ambient Light

In the real world, ambient lighting is the accumulated low intensity light that is visible on objects not directly illuminated. In MAX R3, ambient lighting sets the darkest value that objects in shadow can achieve. Bright ambient color values can make an image appear washed out. The ambient light setting can be globally set in the Rendering Environment dialog box or can be determined per material in the Material Editor.

New to MAX R3 is the ability to control ambient lighting with specific light sources. Ambient illumination cast from a specific light source is still responsive to the position of objects and their surface normals. Areas on the surface of an object that do not receive direct illumination will be most affected by ambient light. Here's how to create an ambient light source.

1. Open the file 10max03.max or continue from the preceding tutorial.

2. Go to the Camera01 viewport and render a frame for reference.

3. Select the Highlight01 light. Clone this light as a Copy and name it "Ambient01."

4. In the Affect Surfaces Group, check Ambient Only. When a light source is used to control ambient illumination, it cannot affect diffuse or specular lighting or cast shadows.

5. Change the color of the Ambient01 light to a pale yellow (R255, G255, B150). Set Multiplier to 0.2.

6. Make a copy of the rendered frame using the Clone button. Render a new frame.

Compare the two renders, shown in Figure 10.9. The effects of the ambient-only light will be most obvious on the ground plane because this object is not receiving much direct illumination. You should also be able to discern a subtle change in the darker side of the water tank. Ambient lighting decreases the contrast between the directly lit and shadowed areas of a surface. Now delete the Ambient01 light to be ready for the next tutorial.

Figure 10.9   The figure on the right show the changes made to this scene by adding a light that affects ambient illumination.

Attenuation

Attenuation lets you control how a light's illumination grows or fades with distance. The Far Attenuation settings control over what distance the light fades to zero. The Near Attenuation settings specify how the light ramps up to its Multiplier value. Attenuating your lights can make them appear much more realistic, especially when you are simulating a point light source, such as light bulb, which would be expected to fade with distance. To see how attenuation affects lighting, follow these steps:

1. Open the file 10max04.max or continue from the preceding tutorial.

2. Render a still now if you didn't during the preceding exercise. Note that the ambient illumination being cast from the Ambient01 Omni light has decreased

the contrast between lit and shadowed surfaces on all objects in the scene. The effect is especially noticeable on the ground plane because it receives illumination from the ambient light source only.

3. Go to a Left viewport. Click the Zoom Extents button to show all the objects in the scene.

4. Select the Ambient01 light and open the Attenuation Parameters rollout.

5. To activate far attenuation, check the Use box in the Far Attenuation part of the rollout.

6. Set Start to 750 and End to 1000. The Start radius is outlined in yellow, and the End radius is outlined in brown (see Figure 10.10).

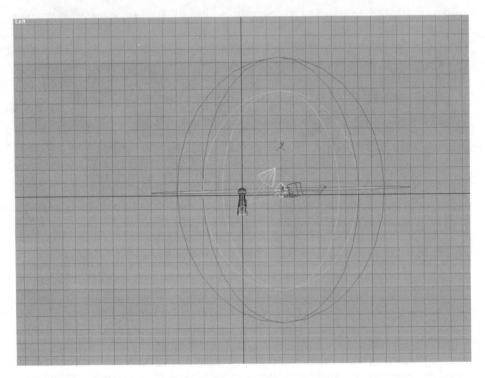

Figure 10.10   Attenuation values are displayed with wire radii to show how attenuated light will intersect with the scene.

7. Render a still to see how attenuating the ambient light causes the ambient illumination to fade to zero as the distance from the light approaches the End of the far attenuation (see Figure 10.11).

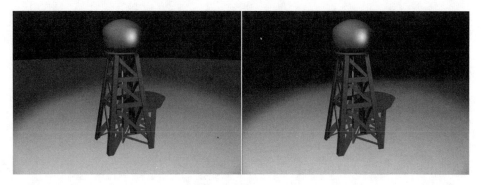

Figure 10.11   The ambient light illuminates the entire ground plane (left) when the light is not attenuated; it fades out with distance (right) when attenuation is applied.

The various lighting types explored in this section enable you to customize the appearance of light in your scenes by tweaking specific controls without affecting other aspects of illumination. Separating specular, diffuse, and ambient lights can make it much easier to get the look you want.

Key and Fill Lights

Key lights provide the primary illumination for a scene and will be the most noticeable source of light. *Bounce* or *fill* lights are used extensively in real-world set lighting for several purposes, such as preventing scenes from becoming washed out from powerful key lights. In computer graphics, fill lights are often used to provide soft illumination to surfaces that aren't being directly illuminated. Using global ambient light (which you control either in the Environment dialog box or on a material basis) can do much the same thing.

Fill lights can also be used to simulate the effect of reflected light, such as what occurs when bright sunlight illuminates a hardwood floor and casts a yellowish tint on the surrounding walls. To examine a scene with a simple key/fill light setup, follow these steps:

1. Open the file 10max09.max. (Do not continue with your file from the preceding exercise.) This scene contains the familiar water tower with three light sources, but only one light is currently turned on. Go to a Top viewport to see the general layout of these lights. These lights are positioned in a basic triangle setup as shown in Figure 10.12. Note that the two fill lights are displayed in black to indicate they are currently deactivated.

2. Go to the Camera viewport and select the key_light. This is a target Spotlight that casts raytraced shadows. This light provides both diffuse and specular illumination, which is appropriate for a main source of direct light. Render a still to see how one strong key light affects this scene (see Figure 10.13).

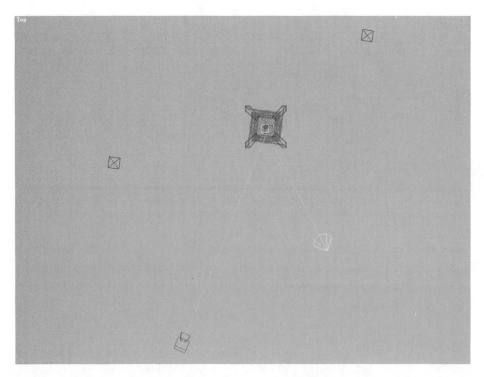

Figure 10.12   A basic three light setup: one key light and two fill lights.

Figure 10.13   A single key light provides a strong sense of direct illumination. The bright specular highlight and dark shadow indicate the direction of the light.

3. Select the fill_light01. This is an Omni light, which affects only diffuse illumina-
    tion. As a general rule, fill lights should not cast specular highlights. This light
    has been given a soft green color to give the appearance of light being reflected
    from the ground plane. The multiplier for this light is only 0.65; in most cases,
    the fill lights will be dimmer than the key lights. Turn this light on and render a
    still to see what a single fill light adds to this scene (see Figure 10.14). Note that
    the ground plane is no longer affected because the light is positioned below it.

Figure 10.14 Adding a fill light to this scene provides some soft illumination to the left side
of the water tower.

4. Select the fill_light02. This light is similar to the first fill light, though it is even
    dimmer. The effect of this light will not be as noticeable as the previous, particu-
    larly from the current camera viewpoint. Primarily, the ground plane will be lit.
    Turn this light on and render a still to see. It should look like the one in
    Figure 10.15.

The proper combination of key and fill lights can give your images a fully lit feel,
helping to avoid excessive direct lighting or dark spots. Placing fill lights to simulate

reflected lighting adds to the realism of a scene by mimicking the action of real-life ambient illumination.

Note

A new feature in MAX R3 allows you to convert the default lighting (the lights used to calculate illumination when no user-created lights are present) to standard MAX lights. The command is Add Default Lights to Scene, and it is found in the Views menu. Note that this tool is available only if you have Default Lighting checked in the Rendering Method tab of the Viewport Configuration dialog box.

Figure 10.15   The second fill light adds subtle illumination to the backside of the water tower and brightens the ground plane.

Atmospherics

Atmospherics typically refer to light effects such as fog, haze, clouds, and smoke. This type of effect also includes volumetric lights, which are atmospheric effects restricted to a light's cone of illumination or attenuation range. In a volumetric light, however, the fog parameters are linked to some of the light's parameters.

Using Atmosphere

Atmosphere can be used in a scene in many ways. In this exercise, you will apply distance fog to the environment range of a camera, create a discrete gizmo to contain an atmospheric effect, and see how the order in which effects are rendered can change the appearance of a scene.

1. Open the file 10max05.max.

2. To access atmospheric effects, go to the Rendering menu and select Environment.

3. In the Atmosphere rollout, click on the Add button and select Fog from the list. Then click OK.

4. Under Fog Parameters, set Fog Color to a light gray-blue (R150, G180, B190).

5. The density of the fog is controlled by the environment ranges for the camera as well as with the Near% and Far% settings in the Fog Parameters area. The Near% refers to the how thick the fog will be at the Near distance of the camera's environment range. The Far% controls the density at the environment range's Far distance. Set the Near% to 10 and the Far% to 50.

6. Go to the Camera01 viewport. Render a still to see the Fog effect applied (see Figure 10.16).

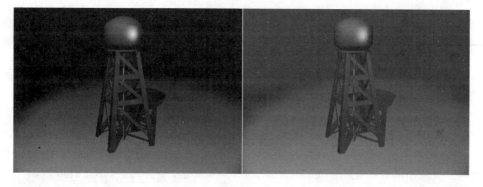

Figure 10.16 Adding a Fog effect diffuses the image according to the Fog Color and Environment Ranges.

Note

Atmospheric effects are rendered in Perspective and Camera viewports only; they are not visible in orthogonal viewports.

7. The Near% and Far% settings refer to the environment ranges for the camera. Select "Camera01" and go to a Top viewport. To display these ranges, check Show in the Environment Ranges area of the camera's General Parameters rollout.

8. In the Top viewport, zoom out to show the entire camera range. Set the Near Range to 405 and the Far Range to 750. Then render a still frame to see how the fog has been pushed back, leaving the water tower clearer, as shown in Figure 10.17.

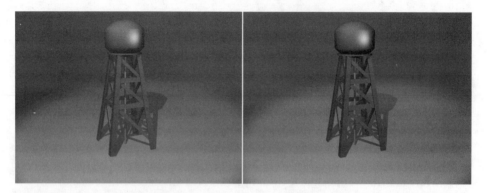

Figure 10.17   Increasing the Near Environment Range clears the fog from objects closest to the camera.

9. Now you will add combustion by using an atmospheric apparatus. Activate a Top viewport. Then go to Create/Helpers and choose Atmospheric Apparatus from the list. Create a CylGizmo centered on the water tower with a radius of 150 and a height of 75.

10. Go to a Left viewport and move the apparatus down on the View Y axis until it rests on the ground plane. Go to the Camera01 viewport, and you should see the image shown in Figure 10.18.

11. New to MAX R3 is a feature that enables you to create and edit atmospheres and effects from within the Modify panel. Note that this functionality is not present in the Create panel. With the CylGizmo selected, go to the Modify panel. Under the Atmospheres rollout, click on the Add button and select Combustion from the list. Click OK to add this effect. (If a combustion effect were already present in this scene, you could apply it to this apparatus by turning on the Existing radio button.)

12. To edit the Combustion effect, select it in the Atmospheres list and click Setup.

13. Set Inner Color to light green (R125, G200, 150) and Outer Color to medium blue (R145, G165, B215). Set Density to 7 in the Characteristics group. Render a still frame to see the result of adding this atmospheric effect. As you can see in Figure 10.19, this effect created a localized cloud at the base of the water tower.

Figure 10.18   The Cylindrical Gizmo, which will be used to create a Combustion effect.

Figure 10.19   The cloud was added to this scene with a Combustion effect.

14. Effects are rendered in the order shown in the Environment dialog box's Effects list. To see this, go to a Top viewport and select the CylGizmo. Clone it and move the clone approximately 1,000 units on the View Y axis. Note that the cloned gizmo automatically retains the atmospheric effect applied to the original. Return to the Camera viewport and render a still to see the added cloud.

15. These clouds contrast rather sharply with the rest of the image because they are being rendered after the fog. To render them before the fog, select the Combustion effect and click the Move Up button. Render another still image to see how the cloud is tinted by the Fog effect (see Figure 10.20). The change will be most evident in the areas of denser fog.

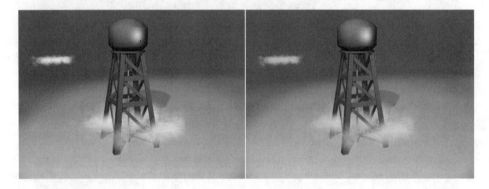

Figure 10.20   The clouds rendered after the fog (left) and before (right.)

To examine a completed MAX file for this scene, load the file 10max06.max from the accompanying CD-ROM.

Fog and clouds can be used to add depth and mystery to a scene. Atmospheric effects can be combined to set a distinct mood, so long as they are rendered in a sensible order. Next, delete the second gizmo, CylGizmo02, to continue to the next exercise.

Atmospheres and Shadows

A new option in MAX R3 allows atmospheric effects to cast shadows, greatly adding to the realism of combustion effects, such as clouds. If you activate the Atmosphere Shadows check box in the Shadow Parameters rollout of shadow-casting lights, shadows are cast by discrete atmospheric effects that the light rays intersect.

1. Open the file 10max06.max or continue from the preceding tutorial.

2. Select the Spot01 light. Go to the Shadow Parameters rollout and under Atmosphere Shadows, check On.

3. The intensity of atmospheric shadows is determined by the Opacity setting. Set Opacity to 50.

4. Set Color Amount to 50 to evenly blend the atmosphere color with the light color. Render a still image to see the shadow cast by the cloud (see Figure 10.21).

Figure 10.21   The shadow is now being affected by the atmospheric effects.

Volumetric Lights

Volumetric lighting refers to atmospheric effects applied to specific lights. This technique is often used to simulate the interaction of light with dust or haze in the air. In this tutorial, you will add a volumetric Spotlight to illuminate the water tower from below.

1. Open the file 10max07.max or continue from the preceding tutorial.

2. Open the Environment dialog box, select the Combustion atmosphere, and turn off Active to deactivate the effect.

3. Unhide the object "light box." This object will serve as an apparent source for the volumetric light.

4. Go to a Top viewport and create a target Spotlight, named "Spot02," that originates behind the light box and points toward the center of the water tower.

5. Go to a Front viewport and move the light source down on the View Y axis to a
   position just below the ground plane (see Figure 10.22).

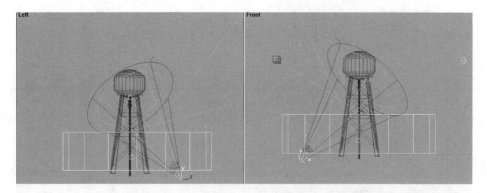

Figure 10.22   The Spot02 light is positioned to cast a tight cone of light onto the water tower.

6. Change the light's color to bright yellow (R255, G255, B100). Reduce the
   intensity of this light by setting Multiplier to 0.5.

7. Turn off Cast Shadows to see the effect of volume light without shadows.

8. Go to the Atmospheres and Effects rollout and add a Volume Light effect. Then
   go into the setup for this effect and set the Density to 3.

9. Render a still frame. Note that the volumetric Spotlight casts a visible cone of
   illumination, as you can see in Figure 10.23.

10. Volumetric shadows can also be cast by lights in MAX. To have the Volume light
    break up around the objects in the scene, turn on Cast Shadows. Leave Shadow
    Type set to the default Shadow Map.

11. Render a still frame. The light casts volumetric shadows around the tower sup-
    ports. If the light seems excessively occluded, the light box might be casting a
    shadow as well. Use the Exclude button to exclude the light box from shadow
    casting.

12. Render another still. The volumetric light should break up around the water
    tank supports, creating streaking shadows within the effect (see Figure 10.24).

To examine a completed MAX file for this scene, load the file 10max07.max from the
accompanying CD-ROM.

Figure 10.23   The Spotlight now casts a volumetric cone of light.

Figure 10.24   The volumetric light is broken up by objects within the cone of light.

This technique can be very useful for search lights, energy discharge effects, and dramatic light sources. When adding volume lights, be certain to turn on Cast Shadows, and use Shadow Mapped shadows if you want the light to be broken up by objects in your scene.

Naturalistic Outdoor Scene

Setting up lights and atmospherics for an outdoor scene requires you to pay special attention to the way in which light travels, refracts, and is diffused in reality. You can often attain good results by considering the volume of air between the viewer and the horizon. Farther air masses will be diffused through increasing amounts of airborn particles. Astronomical objects will be colored by the atmosphere they are viewed through and will be obscured by more haze as they approach the horizon.

In this section, you will create lights and atmospheric effects to correctly depict the appearance of a midmorning scene, and then you will animate those effects to create a sunrise.

Lighting and Atmosphere Setup

The way in which light travels through an outdoor scene can be affected by many factors. Time of day determines intensity and light contrast. The season of the year, as well as the amount of pollution in the air, can have a dramatic effect on the color of the atmosphere. Outdoor light also reflects a great deal. Sunlight bounces from the ground, reflects more strongly from shiny surfaces such as water, and can cast lens flares and other visual artifacts when viewed from certain angles.

Lighting an Outdoor Scene

In this tutorial, you will light a naturalistic outdoor scene, adding fill and key lights to create an overall mood.

1. Open the file 10max11.max. The scene consists of an idyllic farm with mountains in the distance. The mountains are created at render time using displacement mapping, so they will not be visible in the viewport. So far, no lights have been created. Render a still frame to view the scene shown in Figure 10.25 with default lighting. The default lighting gives you a good idea of the structure of this scene, but not the mood or depth.

2. To begin the lighting setup, you will create a couple of low intensity fill lights to give the scene a basic tint. Go to a Left viewport and create a Target Direct light beaming down from behind the camera to the center of the scene. Go to a Top

viewport and move the light approximately 900 units on the View X axis. This angle will counterbalance the angle of the key light you will create later in this exercise. Name the light "sky_fill." (See Figure 10.26.)

Figure 10.25   An idyllic farm scene, with mountains in the distance. Only default lighting is used.

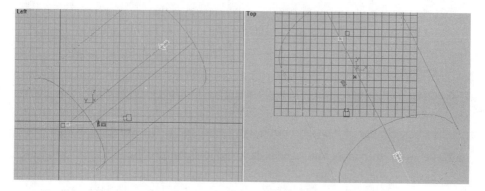

Figure 10.26   The sky_fill light will simulate the reflection of light from the atmosphere.

3. Set the sky_fill light's color to a light blue (R165, G200, B225). You want this to be a subtle effect, so set Multiplier to 0.3. Confirm that Cast Shadows is not checked. To make this light affect the entire scene, increase the light's radius by setting both the Hotspot and Falloff settings (found in the Directional Parameters rollout) to approximately 920. This infinite light will cast a low-intensity blue tint on the scene, simulating light rays being refracted through the atmosphere.

4. Go to a Left viewport and create a Target Direct light below the ground plane, pointing up to the center of the scene. Go to a Top viewport and move the light approximately –800 units on the View X axis to align it perpendicular to the other fill light (see Figure 10.27). Name this light "ground_fill."

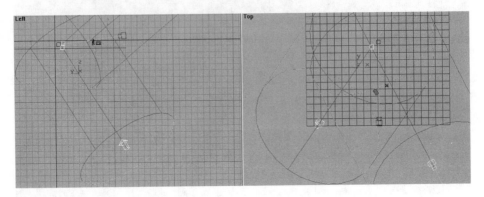

Figure 10.27   The ground_fill light will simulate the reflection of light from the ground.

5. Set the ground_fill light's color to light green (RGB 165, 220, 75). The effect of light bouncing from the ground is usually less than that coming from the sky, so set the Mulitiplier to 0.2. By default, the Hotspot and Falloff values for this light will be set to the same values you used for the last Direct light you created. This will work fine.

6. Open the Exclude/Include dialog box and exclude the ground plane from illumination. Because the light source is beneath the ground plane, this will not affect the appearance of the scene, but it may speed up the rendering calculation.

7. Render a still frame. The scene is dark and low-contrast, but it's starting to look like morning. Note that adding these low-intensity fill lights creates a much dimmer image than the one you rendered in step 1 (see Figure 10.28) because default lighting is deactivated as soon as a light is created. These two lights create a base fill color scheme that will complement the rest of the lighting. Direct

lights are often used to light large scenes because their effect is not limited to a cone of illumination or a point of origin.

Figure 10.28   The two fill lights create an even, diffuse mood.

8. Before continuing with the lighting, consider the background. Clearly, a solid black sky contributes nothing to the mood of the scene. Open the Environment dialog box and click on the button beneath Environment Map. Choose Browse From: Material Editor and select the Diffuse Color: Sky Color map. Choose Instance for Method so that any changes you make to this map will be automatically reflected in the environment map.

9. Render a still frame. As you can see in Figure 10.29, this simple gradient adds quite a bit to the look of this scene. The background will be largely obscured by atmospheres you will add later, but it is very important as a base layer.

10. Naturally, the main, or key, light for this scene will be the sun. Go to a Left viewport and create a Target Direct to the left of the scene objects, pointing toward the camera. Go to a Top viewport and move the light approximately −450 units on the View X axis. When you finish, this light should originate near

the coordinates X: –425, Y: 1445, Z: 445 (confirm this with the Type-In Transform). Name this light "sun_key." (See Figure 10.30.)

Figure 10.29   An appropriate background image can really add to a scene.

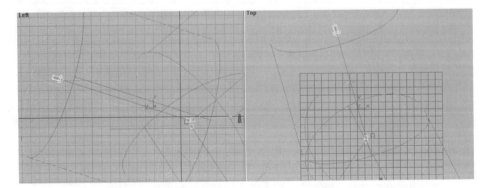

Figure 10.30   The key light, representing the sun, will be the primary source of illumination for this scene.

11. Set the sun_key light's color to a very light yellow (R245, G245, B200). This is going to be the dominant light source, so set the Mulitiplier to 1.5. Go to the Camera01 viewport and confirm that the light is in-frame.

12. Turn on Cast Shadows and set Shadow Type to Ray Traced in Shadow Parameters. To keep the hard shadows cast by this light from conflicting with the bounce lights, set the shadow's color to dark green (R0, G35, B0) and set the Density to 0.8.

13. Render a still frame. Figure 10.31 shows that the scene is much brighter with a key light. The shadows cast across the rolling hills give a good indication of the key light's direction. If something seems odd, it's most likely the absence of a visible sun. That will be added later in this exercise with a Render Effect.

Figure 10.31   This scene's basic light setup is complete: two fill lights and a single key light.

Note

Using shadow-mapped shadows can give nice, soft results. When they're animated, however, shadow maps tend to flicker or crawl. Therefore, ray-traced shadows are recommended when the position of the light source or target is animated.

14. The final light in this setup is a small light originating from the lamp on the front of the barn. Go to a Top viewport and zoom in on the barn. Create an Omni light just in front of the lamp. Go to a Left viewport and zoom in on the

barn. Move the light approximately –45 units on the y-axis until it is level with the lamp (see Figure 10.32).

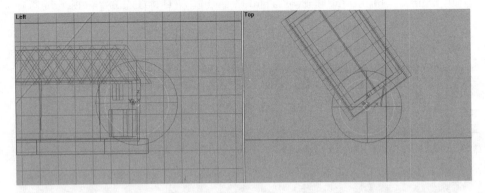

Figure 10.32   An Omni light will be used to create a small lamp for the front of the barn.

15. Name this light "barn_light." Set this light's color to light blue (R185, G255, B245). Set Multiplier to 1.0.

16. This light should illuminate only its immediate surroundings, so go to the Attenuation Parameters rollout. Check Use in the Far Attenuation area and set Start to 18 and End to 23.

Note

When you're creating or editing a complex lighting setup, try to work with only one light at a time to get a feel for the exact contribution each light makes to the scene.

17. The last step is to add a Render Effect to the sun_key light so it will be visible. Select sun_key and in the Modify Panel, go to the Atmospheres and Effects rollout.

18. Add a Lens Effect to this light. Go into the setup for this effect and add a Glow effect. The default size should work, but change the second Radial Color to bright orange (R255, G165, B0).

19. Now you will add a few flares to simulate the side effects of viewing a bright light source through a camera lens. Add an Automatic Secondary effect. Select the effect in the Lens Effects Parameters rollout. Set the Minimum percentage to 10, the Maximum to 50, and the Intensity to 50. This light will now cast a series of circular flares (see Figure 10.33).

To examine a completed MAX file for this scene, load the file 10max12.max from the accompanying CD-ROM.

Figure 10.33   Adding a Lens Effect to the sun_key light creates the visible representation of the sun.

The lighting setup for this scene is now complete. Key and fill lights illuminate the scene from multiple angles and draw the viewer's attention to the key elements: the sun and the barn.

However, for this scene to achieve a high degree of realism, you must perform one more important step. The excessive clarity of the air and the lack of distinct clouds make the scene appear artificial. In the next section, you will remedy this by adding atmospherics to this scene.

Adding Atmosphere to an Outdoor Scene

Creating atmospheres for an outdoor environment is really the process of visualizing the particulate matter, dust, and water vapor suspended in the air. When you are looking at a deep blue sky, you are really seeing a vast depth of water vapor. Likewise, the colors of a brilliant sunrise are the result of airborne pollution, weather fronts, and other atmospheric disturbances.

In the preceding exercise, you created lights to properly illuminate an outdoor scene. Now you will add atmospheric effects to simulate the diffusion of those lights by particles and vapor suspended in the air. Because this is a midmorning scene, some low-lying fog would also be appropriate.

1. Open the file 10max12.max or continue from the preceding tutorial.

2. The Environment Ranges for the camera will determine how fog effects are rendered. Go to a Left viewport and select Camera01.

3. Zoom out to show the camera and its cone. In the Environment Ranges area of the camera's General Parameters rollout, check Show. Set the Near Range to 380 and the Far Range to 2000. This will cause fog effects to begin just in front of the barn and end behind the mountains (see Figure 10.34).

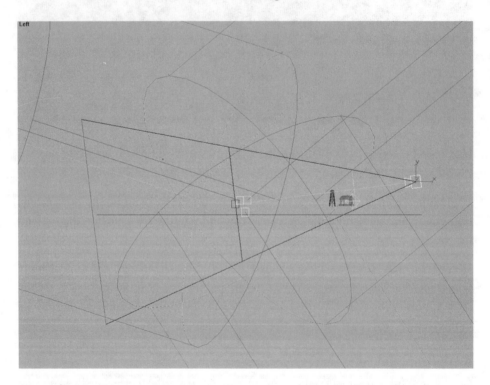

Figure 10.34   The camera's Environment Ranges determine at what distance from the camera fog effects are applied.

4. The first atmospheric effect you will create is an overall distance fogging. Open the Environment dialog box and add a Fog effect. Set the Near% to 10 and the Far% to 40.

5. The default white fog is graying this image out a bit. You can use a map to control fog color or opacity. Open the Material Editor and go to the Fog Map material. Drag the Diffuse Color map to the Environment Color map in the Environment dialog box. Select Instance as the method. This gradient map will be used to determine the fog's color, mapped with the V coordinates along the depth of the camera plane. Render a still to see how the fog changes the mood of the scene (see Figure 10.35).

Figure 10.35 A Fog effect will be used to create the general diffusion of light that accrues with distance.

6. Next you will add some low-lying fog with a more cohesive, wispy appearance. Go to the Display panel and unhide BoxGizmo01. This atmospheric apparatus covers the entire ground plane.

7. Select the gizmo, go to the Modify Panel, and add a Volume Fog effect. Set Density to 3.5, Step to 10, and Max Steps to 20. Under Noise, set Size to 50. This creates large, fluffy wisps of ground fog. To keep the fog from terminating abruptly at the edges of the gizmo, increase Soft Gizmo Edges to 0.5. Render a still to see the addition of low-lying wisps of fog. The image should look like Figure 10.36.

Figure 10.36   Ground fog lying among the hills adds to the sense of a mid-morning scene.

8. Now you will create some varied cloud layers. Go to the Display panel and unhide BoxGizmo02. This apparatus extends beyond the area of sky visible from the camera and provides a pattern of clouds for the entire sky.

9. Select BoxGizmo02, go to the Modify Panel, and add a Combustion effect. Go to the Environment dialog box and rename this effect "Cloud Layer." Set the inner color to a medium teal (R75, G145, B145) and the outer color to a pale green (R200, G210, B180). Set Regularity to 0.75 so that most of the gizmo will be used for the effect. Set Flame Size to 250, Density to 0.5, and Samples to 9. This creates a general field of hazy clouds. Render a still to see how this enhances the appearance of the sky (see Figure 10.37).

10. The final element to be incorporated into the atmosphere of this scene is a group of smaller, coherent clouds. A few denser clouds closer to the camera will add depth and interest to the sky. Unhide SphereGizmo01.

11. Add a Combustion effect to this apparatus. Go to the Environment dialog box and rename this effect "Clouds." It makes sense to use the same colors as in the Cloud Layer effect, so copy those colors using the Color Clipboard.

Figure 10.37   The sky is now filled with hazy clouds, the result of a Combustion effect applied to a Box Gizmo.

Note

The Color Clipboard utility, found in the Tools panel, allows you to copy, paste, and swap colors. This can be very handy when coordinating atmosphere or light colors.

12. Set Flame Size to 60, Density to 2, and Samples to 25. These settings create small fluffy clouds.

13. Go to a Top viewport and make several copies of the Spherical gizmo, moving them around on the View XY plane to create the appearance of scattered clouds. (See Figure 10.38.)

14. Render a still and examine these clouds carefully. You may notice they all have the same shape. To randomize the shape of these clouds, use the New Seed button in the Modify panel. This will generate a random seed to keep the clouds from looking exactly the same (see Figure 10.39).

To examine a completed MAX file for this scene, load the file 10max13.max from the accompanying CD-ROM.

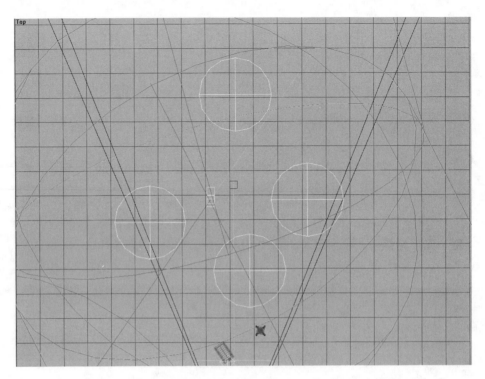

Figure 10.38   Four spherical gizmos distributed on the XY plane create individual clouds.

Figure 10.39   The completed light and atmosphere setup for this scene.

This completes the atmosphere setup for this outdoor scene. Building up layers of atmosphere, starting with the most subtle and distant effects and adding more dramatic and closer effects, is a good technique for keeping your effects organized.

Fog effects are useful whenever you need to introduce subtle atmospheric diffusion or actual fog to a scene. Combustion effects are more appropriate for discrete units of atmosphere, such as clouds and puffs of vapor.

Animating Light and Atmosphere

Once the lighting for a scene has been set up, you can animate almost all the associated parameters to show the passage of time, changes in weather, or more dramatic special effects. Changes in color, contrast, and intensity of light can suggest different moods or even changes of season.

Animating Light in an Outdoor Scene

In this exercise, you will animate the lights created in the preceding tutorials to create a rising sun.

1. Open the file 10max13.max or continue from the preceding tutorial. Open the Time Configuration dialog box and set End Time to 450. Assuming that Frame Rate is set to NTSC (30 frames per second), this will create an animation sequence lasting 15 seconds. The sunrise you create will cover about 3 hours of real time when played back at a rate of 5 seconds per hour. If you want to preview the results of this tutorial, view the AVI file 10avi01.avi.

2. An animated material has been provided for you to use as a background. Open the Material Editor and select the Animated Sky material. Drag the Diffuse color called Sky Color (Mix) to the Environment Map button in the Environment dialog box. Choose Instance as the method.

    This material is a mix between a dark star-filled sky and a rosy morning sky. The sky will be automatically animated over the length of this animation. In order to show this change, you need to keep the overall diffuse Fog effect from affecting the background. Select the Fog effect and turn off Fog Background.

3. You should probably deactivate the other atmospheric effects so you can concentrate on the lights you are animating. Clear the Active check box for all effects except Fog.

4. A path has been set up to control the movement of the sun as it rises. Unhide sun_path. To assign the sun to this path, select the sun_key light, go to the Motion panel, and assign a Path controller to the Position channel.

5. In the Path Parameters rollout, select sun_path as the Current Path Object. At frame 0, set the %Along Path to 100 to place the sun below the horizon. It may appear that the sun is above the horizon, but recall that the ground will be displaced at render time. (See Figure 10.40.)

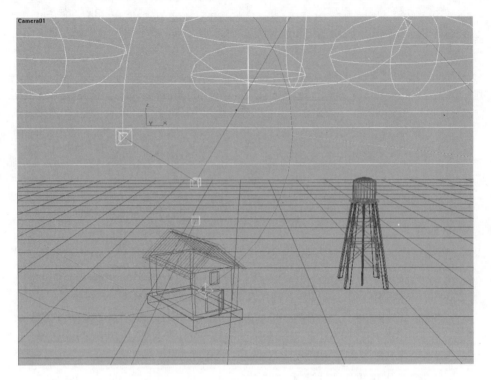

Figure 10.40   The sun is attached to the path that will carry it as it rises.

6. To work with multiple lights from a single dialog box, open the Light Lister, available from the Lights Toolbar tab. Go to the Lights rollup to edit the properties of any of the lights in this scene.

7. This stage of the animation corresponds roughly to 5:30 a.m., so the sun's effect should be diffuse and tinted blue. Set the color for the sun_key light to pale green (R200, G245, B225) and reduce Multiplier to 0.5. Set Shadow Density to 0 to prevent this light from casting visible shadows while it is below the horizon.

Note

The new Light Lister tool can greatly simplify the process of editing lighting setups by allowing you to turn lights on and off, edit light settings, and set global parameters from a single dialog box.

8. The fill lights will be setting the tone at this point, so set the color for the sky_fill light to medium teal (R85, G160, B160) and set Multiplier to 0.3.

9. To keep this light from over-illuminating the distant mountains and achieve a more silhouetted effect, check Use under Far Attenuation, set Start to 2000, and set End to 2600. Note that while you cannot set these values from the Light Lister, you can select any light for editing in the Modify panel by clicking on the first button under each light.

10. Set the color for the ground_fill light to medium blue (R145, G135, B160) and set Multiplier to 0.4. This completes the low-key lighting that will suggest pre-dawn. (See Figure 10.41.)

Figure 10.41   The lighting and background at the beginning of this animation suggests a cool pre-dawn mood.

11. Go to frame 170 and turn on the Animate button. To maintain the lack of shadows from the sun, set another Shadow Density = 0 key. The easiest way to do this is to increment and then decrement the Density value in the Modify Panel.

12. Go to frame 250. This will be the point in your animation where the sun has just risen over the horizon. The sun will be bright and warm, and the fill lights will be fading.

13. Set the sun_key's %Along Path to 75. This will make the sun move more slowly across the sky as compared to the remainder of the animation.

Note

When the sun (or any other large astronomical object) nears the horizon, light rays passing from it to a planetary surface are being viewed through increasing amounts of atmosphere. This increases the refraction of those light rays, meaning that the apparent velocity of the rising sun is slower at sunrise (or sunset) than when it is higher in the sky.

14. Set the color for the sun_key light to pale orange (R245, G220, B170) and increase Multiplier to 1.0. To increase the contrast between the Diffuse and Ambient areas of the illuminated areas, set Contrast to 25. To make the sun's shadows start to show up clearly, increase Shadow Density to 0.4.

15. Set the sky_fill color to light green (R125, G165, B85) and decrease Multiplier to 0.2. Increase the Far Attenuation Start to 2500 and the End to 3000.

16. Set the color for the ground_fill light to pale green-yellow (R170, G190, B75) and decrease Multiplier to 0.3. As the sun becomes more intense and the fill lights fade, the focus of this animation shifts to the rising sun (see Figure 10.42).

Figure 10.42   At this point in the animation, the sun has risen over the horizon and is starting to significantly brighten the scene.

17. Go to frame 450. This animation will end with the sun high in the camera view-port, corresponding roughly to 10:00 a.m. Set the sun_key's %Along Path to 75.

18. Set the color for the sun_key light to bright yellow (R255, G225, B60) and increase Multiplier to 1.75. Decrease Contrast to 15. Increase Shadow Density to 0.6.

19. Set the sky_fill color to light yellow (R200, G215, B90) and increase Multiplier to 0.5. Increase the Far Attenuation Start to 3000 and the End to 3200.

20. Increase the ground_fill Multiplier to 0.4. The sun has now fully risen, and with the help of the fill lights, it illuminates this scene (see Figure 10.43).

Figure 10.43   At the end of this animation, the sun has cleared the horizon and fully illuminates the scene.

To examine a completed MAX file for this scene, load the file 10max14.max from the accompanying CD-ROM. To review this animation using the camera moves you have created, view the AVI file 10avi01.avi on the accompanying CD-ROM.

By carefully balancing the changes in light intensity and color, you have animated the dramatic changes in mood that accompany sunrise. Whenever you animate lights for outdoor scenes, try to imagine how light is reflected and refracted through the atmosphere. Sometimes you may need many more fill or key lights than you used in the preceding tutorial. The Light Lister will become an indispensable tool in those cases, allowing you to effectively manage many of the key properties of all the lights in your animation.

If you render this sequence to AVI, I recommend that you keep all the atmospheric effects except Fog deactivated because they have not been animated to complement the lights.

Animating Atmosphere in an Outdoor Scene

In the next tutorial, you will animate atmospheric effects to add swirling morning fog, dissipating high-level cloud cover, and the motion of individual clouds. In addition, you will animate the diffuse Fog effect to properly maintain the color and intensity of the lighting.

1. Open the file 10max14.max or continue from the preceding tutorial. If you want to preview the results of this tutorial, view the AVI file 10avi02.avi.

2. Go to frame 0 if you are not there already. Bring up the Environment dialog box to tweak the atmospheric effects. Increase the Near% of the Fog effect to 25, thickening the fog closest to the camera.

3. You will need to animate the Fog's Environment Color Map. Go to the Material Editor and select the Animated Fog Color material. Drag the Diffuse Color Animated Fog Color Map (Gradient) to the Fog's Environment Map button. This map has been set up with colors that will work well for the beginning of this animation; you will animate them throughout this tutorial.

4. Increase the Density of the Volume Fog to 5, the Noise Size to 70, and Color to pale blue (R235, G255, B255). This creates large clumps of dense fog.

5. In the upper Cloud Layer effect, you want the appearance of scattered, small clouds. Set the Flame Size to 150 and Density to 0.3. Set Flame Detail to 3.0 to increase the details among the smaller clouds. Render a still to see how this cloud layer, along with the other atmospheric effects, creates a heavy, cloudy mood (see Figure 10.44).

Note

Before you render any stills, be sure to reactivate any atmospheric effects you turned off in the preceding exercise.

Figure 10.44   The atmosphere at the beginning of this animation is cloudy, with heavy ground fog.

6. Go to frame 150 and turn on the Animate button. This is the point just before the sun rises. To cause the Fog effect to clear, choose Fog and set the Near% to 15 and the Far% to 30.

7. Go to the Animated Fog Color Map in the Material Editor and set the following color changes to the gradient material.

   Color #1: R150, G220, B145
   Color #2: R165, G190, B130
   Color #3: R80, G165, B130

   These changes will push the fog color toward warmer and brighter colors as the sun starts to rise.

8. You'll want the Volume Fog to thin out at this point, so choose Volume Fog and reduce Density to 3.

9. This is also a good time to set the Phase velocity of this effect. Phase animates an effect without respect to Wind Speed or any actual movement of the gizmo or camera. Think of it as the churning a stationary cloud goes through over time. Set the Phase for the Volume Fog to 3.

10. For the fog to cycle smoothly over the entire course of this sequence, the phase must continue to increase. So open Track View and expand Environment/Volume Fog/Phase. Select the Phase controller and click on the Parameter Curve Out-of-Range button. Select Relative Repeat as the interpolation type. This will cause the fog to continuously cycle at the same rate. Close Track View and return to the Environment dialog box to continue.

11. To increase the size of the clouds in the upper layer, choose Cloud Layer and increase Flame Size in the Characteristics group to 200.

12. Set the Phase to 50 and the Parameter Curve Out-of-Range type as in step 10. This layer of clouds will cycle much more quickly than the ground fog because it is farther away from the viewer.

13. The individual clouds should warm up in tone and get a little thicker at this point. Increase Density for the Cloud effect to 4. Set Inner Color to pale green (R175, G225, B185) and Outer Color to a similar green (R190, G220, B180).

14. Set the Phase to 75 and the Parameter Curve Out-of-Range type as in step 10. These individual clouds will cycle fairly quickly, which will work well with the movement you will give them across the sky (in a later tutorial). Render a still to see how the scene looks at this point in the animation. It should be similar to Figure 10.45.

Figure 10.45   As the sunrise approaches, the sky clears and the ground fog starts to recede.

15. Go to frame 250. The sun has risen at this point, and the scene should be notice-
    ably warmer in tone and brighter. The Volume Fog should be almost cleared by
    now, so set Density to 0.5.

16. To make the upper clouds get thicker, set Density for the Cloud Layer effect to 0.8.

17. The tones of the individual clouds continue to warm, approaching yellowish
    hues. Set the Inner Color to yellow-green (R190, G215, B125) and Outer Color to
    tan (R220, G215, B180). Warming the tones used in these atmospheric effects
    will complement the brighter sun to enhance the drama of the risen sun. Render
    a still, and you can fully appreciate the effect, as shown in Figure 10.46.

Figure 10.46   The sun has risen, clearing the ground fog away.

18. Go to the end of this animation (frame 450). The sun is high in the morning
    sky, all traces of fog have cleared, and the air is bright and warm. Set the Near%
    to 0 for the Fog effect.

19. In the Material Editor, set the following color changes to the Animated Fog
    Color Map gradient.

Color #1: R230, G220, B140
Color #2: R210, G205, B103
Color #3: R140, G180, B80

20. Set the Density for the Volume Fog to 0 so the ground fog will completely dissipate as the sun rises.

21. By setting warmer tones for the upper cloud layer at the end of the animation, you support the general warming of the sky. Set the Cloud layer's Inner Color to light yellow (R220, G215, B125) and Outer Color to pale tan (R225, G220, B180).

22. Use the Color Clipboard to copy these colors to the Clouds effect. By using the same colors for both the high and low clouds, you join them visually; each level of cloud cover now receives roughly the same amount of light from the sun.

23. To keep the individual clouds from completely disappearing into the upper cloud layer, increase the clouds' Density to 5. By clearing the fog away entirely and warming the colors used in the cloud effects, you have created a bright morning atmosphere. Render a still to see how the scene looks with the sun fully risen (see Figure 10.47).

Figure 10.47   At the end of this animation, the atmosphere is clear and warm.

To examine a completed MAX file for this scene, load the file 10max15.max from the accompanying CD-ROM. To review this animation using the camera moves you have created, view the AVI file 10avi02.avi on the accompanying CD-ROM.

If you render this scene or view the AVI file 10avi02.avi, you will see the sun rise from a foggy dawn sky to brighten the landscape, dispelling fog and casting brilliant shadows across the ground. By animating density, color, and phase parameters for the atmospheric effects in this scene, you have accurately simulated a dramatic sunrise.

A few minor points still need to be addressed in this scene. The ground fog churns and dissipates as it should, but it doesn't seem to move in response to any wind, and it doesn't retreat earlier from the areas of ground cover that receive the first rays of the sun. In addition, the individual clouds are relatively motionless. In the next tutorial, you will animate the movement and scaling of the various gizmos involved to put the finishing touch on this animation.

Transforming Gizmos for Atmospherics

Ground fog is the result of water vapor condensing at low temperatures. Therefore, the viewer will expect the fog to dissipate first from the area closest to the camera and then move toward the distant mountains. The fog should also be affected by prevailing winds throughout this sequence.

1. Open the file 10max15.max or continue from the preceding tutorial. If you want to preview the results of this tutorial, view the AVI file 10avi03.avi.

2. Go to a Top viewport and select the BoxGizmo01 helper. This gizmo fixes the position and scaling of the ground fog.

3. Turn the Animate button on and go to frame 175. Move the gizmo –100 units on the View X axis and 200 units on the View Y axis.

4. Go to frame 450. Move the gizmo 200 units on the View Y axis. The movement will give the effect that the ground fog is clearing from the ground that is being lit by the sun.

5. Go to frame 0. Select all four spherical gizmos. These helpers control the placement of the individual clouds.

6. Move the selection 1000 units on the View X axis and 100 units on the View Y axis. This moves the clouds out of the camera frame.

7. Go to frame 100 and move the gizmos –2000 units on the View X axis and –300 units on the View Y axis. This moves them across the camera frame and out of

view again. If you want to see how these clouds move across the camera frame, go to the Camera viewport and turn on Trajectories in the Motion panel (see Figure 10.48).

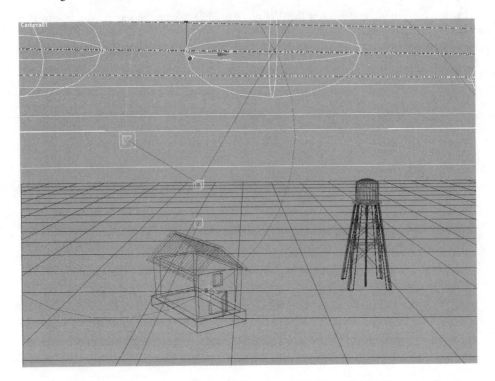

Figure 10.48   The trajectories these four cloud gizmos will follow across the camera frame.

8. To simplify working with the velocity of these gizmos, change their Position controllers to Linear. To do so, either you can select each gizmo in turn and change its controller in the Motion panel, or you can open Track View, select all four Position tracks, and assign the controller once.

9. To make the clouds go across the sky several times, duplicate the Position keys. If all four gizmos are selected, you can copy their keys using the Track Bar. Select the keys at frames 0 and 100 and shift-drag them to copy. You'll want an offset of 101 frames, so that the new keys are at frames 101 and 201, respectively. This will force the gizmos to immediately snap to the next cycle without any in-between frames; otherwise, the clouds might be seen quickly moving backwards across the sky to their start positions.

10. Duplicate the two unique Position keys again to create keys at frames 202 and 302.

11. Once again, copy the two Position keys to frames 303 and 403. You have now created four duplicate motions across the camera frame (see Figure 10.49).

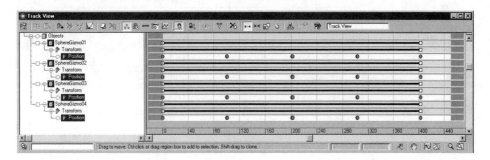

Figure 10.49   The spherical gizmos' motion is repeated four times, as shown in Track View.

12. Play this animation back in the Camera viewport, and you will see the four clouds move across the frame fairly quickly. Each pass moves at the same speed. Although you might expect the clouds to move quickly in the pre-dawn hours, they should slow down and even stop as the sun rises and the atmosphere becomes calmer and warmer.

You slow the clouds toward the end of the animation by gradually increasing the number of frames between keys. Open Track View to edit the keys. You can move keys in Track Bar, but you can't move them beyond the current Time Frame.

13. Select the keys at the following frames and relocate them as specified:

Frame 403 to frame 625

Frame 302 to frame 366

Frame 303 to frame 367

Frame 201 to frame 229

Frame 202 to frame 230

By spreading these keys out—even extending them beyond the current Time Frame—you slow the gizmos as the end of the animation approaches (see Figure 10.50).

14. If you play this animation back in the Camera viewport, you will see the four clouds move across the frame in unison. Clearly this kind of mechanical movement will not work. To break up the synchronicity of the cloud's motion and vary their velocities, go to Edit Ranges mode in Track View. (Make certain all four Position tracks are still visible.)

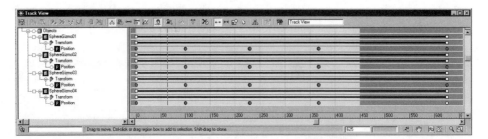

Figure 10.50   The velocity of the spherical gizmos will gradually decrease over time.

15. Click and drag the right end of each Position range to make each gizmo move at a slightly different speed. Avoid scaling any ranges either much longer or shorter than the others because that cloud will then move noticeably slower or quicker.

16. Click and drag the bar of each Position range to change the beginning and ending frames. By changing the length and beginning/ending frames of the Position ranges, you randomize the cloud's movement (see Figure 10.51).

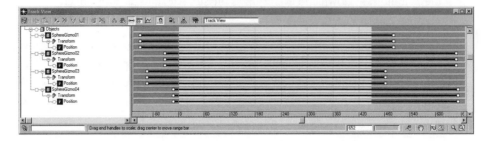

Figure 10.51   The randomized Position ranges of the spherical gizmos.

If you want, you can add more clouds to the scene by copying the spherical gizmos and moving them around in a Top viewport. If you turn on Trajectories in the Motion panel, you can ensure that the copied gizmo won't either begin or end its cycle in the camera frame. Consider re-scaling the copied gizmos and creating a new seed to maintain uniqueness. Additionally, you should randomize the Position ranges of any new gizmos.

Be aware that adding several gizmos in this way can greatly increase render time because each gizmo represents an additional Combustion effect.

To examine a completed MAX file for this scene, load the file 10max16.max from the accompanying CD-ROM. To review this animation using the camera moves you have created, view the AVI file 10avi03.avi on the accompanying CD-ROM.

In this exercise, you added movement to the atmospheric effects in this scene and further integrated them into the overall effect by keying in responses to simulated forces like wind or sun. By setting up looping animations for the cloud movements, you greatly simplified the process of adding consistent, yet randomized, discrete atmospheric effects.

Animating light and atmosphere for naturalistic scenes requires both a scientific eye for the interacting forces found in nature, and an artistic sensibility to the emotional impact of color and volume light. If you combine these skills with the techniques you have learned in this section, you should be well-prepared to create a variety of outdoor lighting and atmospheric moods.

Special Effects

Lighting and atmospheric effects can be especially important for special effects work. When you're animating energy effects, futuristic environments, or explosions, light and atmosphere can easily become the central focus of the shot. In this section, you will add light and atmosphere to a futuristic scene.

When lighting for special effects shots, you can pay less attention to the natural or scientific propagation of light. Instead, light can take on a more expressive quality because it usually has a more specific role in the scene. For example, in the preceding section, the sun was used to cast even and natural lighting across the scene as it rose, so its color and intensity were kept consistent with the behavior of sunlight in a morning sky. In the next exercise, you will animate a series of lights blinking in a ring without much concern for how much of the scene such lights would actually illuminate. Because these lights are used to express a quick mechanical cycling, the bright flaring effect is more important to the scene.

Animating Light for Special Effects

To preview what you'll be working on in the upcoming tutorial, open the AVI file 10avi04.avi. This scene, shown in Figure 10.52, consists of a futuristic energy reactor. Plasma is being fed to the reactor from below through transparent tubes. Gaseous waste is carried off via several flexing hoses. The blinking lights you'll animate are set in a ring bracket around the circumference of the chamber.

1. Open the file 10max17.max. You will first create a pair of specular and diffuse omni lights. Go to a Top viewport and create an Omni light to the left and below the reactor. Then go to a Left viewport and move the light roughly –85 units on the View Y axis until it is below the reactor (see Figure 10.53).

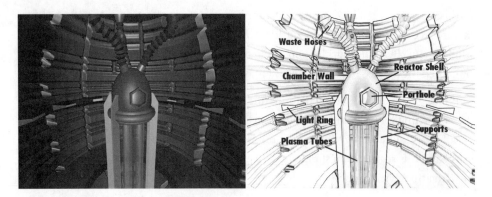

Figure 10.52   The various components of this scene, which you will be augmenting with light and atmosphere.

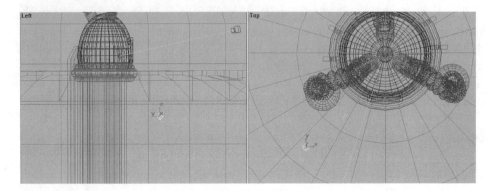

Figure 10.53   This Omni light is positioned to cast a general diffuse light.

2. Name this light "Omni_Diffuse." In the Modify Panel, in the Affect Surfaces group, turn off Specular so that no highlights will be cast by this light. Set Color to medium blue (R135, G145, B220) and set Multiplier to 0.5. Render a still to see the pale blue cast this light creates in the scene. It should look like Figure 10.54.

3. Now you will create a light to cast specular highlights. Clone the Omni_Diffuse light using Copy as the method. Name this light "Omni_Specular." Turn Diffuse off and Specular on so that this light will cast only highlights and will not affect diffuse illumination. Set Color to pale blue (R210, G210, B240) and set Multiplier to 0.65.

4. To place this light, go to the Camera viewport and turn on Smooth + Highlights mode. Select the Place Highlights tool and drag the icon across the surface of the reactor to place the highlight high on the left side of the reactor (as shown in Figure 10.55). Render a still to see the difference this light makes in the scene.

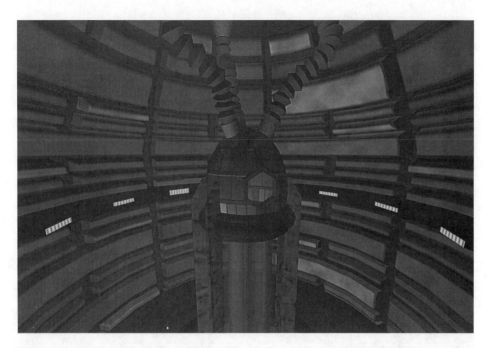

Figure 10.54   The base diffuse lighting of this scene.

Figure 10.55   The Place Highlight tool moves a light to cast a specular highlight on the selected face.

5. Next you will simulate a series of blinking lights by animating a single Target Spotlight on a path around the ring of lights. The extruded faces closest to the reactor have been textured with a bright yellow material and will function as lamps. Go to a Top viewport and create a Target Spotlight that originates from behind the lamp to the left of the reactor. Place the target directly in the center of the reactor. Then go to a Left viewport and move the light and its target roughly –25 units on the View Y axis until both are aligned with the lamps (see Figure 10.56).

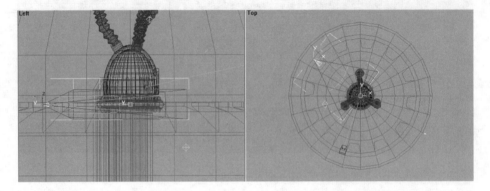

Figure 10.56   This Target Spotlight simulates a small brilliant lamp that points inward from a ring of lights.

6. Name this light "Spot_Ring01." Set Color to medium green-yellow (R200, G245, B100) and set Multiplier to 1.5.

7. Spotlights can cast either circular or rectangular areas of illumination. Go to the Spotlight Parameters rollout and turn on Rectangle. Set Hotspot to 15, Falloff to 25, and Aspect to 5. This creates a beam of light with the same proportions as the lamp faces. To keep the light from illuminating the far side of the chamber, go to Attenuation Parameters and turn on Far Attenuation Use1, set Start to 125, and leave End set to 200. Render a still to see how this brightens and sharpens the look of the scene (see Figure 10.57). Note that the beam of light coming from the spotlight will not be apparent until a volume light effect is applied.

8. This light needs to move from lamp to lamp around the circle. Go to a Top viewport and zoom out to show the entire scene. Confirm that the Spot_Ring01 light is positioned behind a lamp, pointing at the reactor. (See Figure 10.58.)

Figure 10.57   The scene's lighting is enhanced with a specular light and a single spotlight.

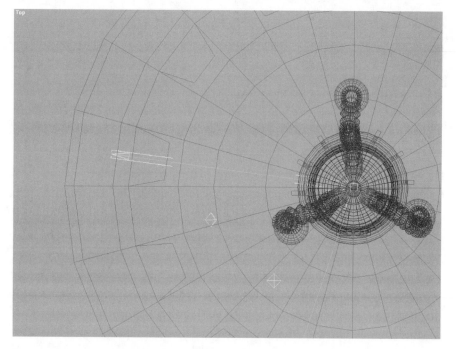

Figure 10.58   A spotlight is positioned to act as a lamp illuminating the reactor.

9. Go to frame 10 and turn the Animate button on. Move the light to the next lamp in the series, moving in a clockwise direction. Use the corners of the Transform gizmo to allow for X and Y unconstrained movement.

10. Go to frame 20 and move the light to the next lamp. If you turn on Trajectories, you will see that a circular path is emerging, as shown in Figure 10.59.

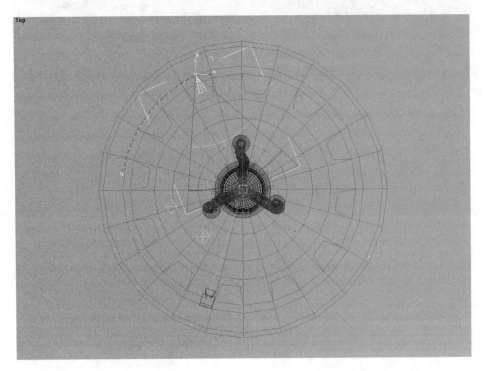

Figure 10.59   This light will follow a circular path to create the effect of a series of lights blinking sequentially.

11. Continue moving the light to each lamp in turn, incrementing the frame count by 10 each time, until the light reaches the final lamp by frame 110. To complete this cycle, copy the key from frame 0 to frame 120. Turn the Animate button off.

12. This light needs to move instantly from lamp to lamp; its position should not be interpolated. Open Track View and expand to the Spot_Ring01 Position track. Select all of the Position keys and change their In tangents to Step. The Out tangents are automatically changed to Step as well. Using the Step tangent causes the value of one key to be maintained until the next key is reached. This means the light will remain motionless until the next key moves it instantaneously to the next position.

13. In case you later need to change the time frame of this animation, select the Position track and change its Parameter Curve Out-Of-Range Types to Loop. This light will now loop around the ring continuously.

14. To create two more lights to fill out this effect, clone the Spot_Ring01 light twice, using Copy as the method.

15. All three of these lights need to be spread evenly around the ring. Open Track View, go into Edit Ranges mode, and show all three lights. Drag the Spot_Ring02 range to begin at frame 40. Drag the Spot_Ring03 range to begin at frame 80 (see Figure 10.60). This will separate the three lights by 120 degrees, or one-third of the circle.

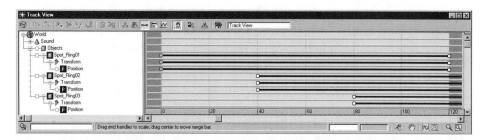

Figure 10.60   Off-setting the ranges of the lights by one-third the length of their animation sequence will evenly space them along the path.

16. To examine the scene up to this point, load the MAX file 10max18.max. Next you will create a light within the reactor to shine out through the porthole. Go to a Top viewport and create a Target Direct light that originates within the reactor. Place the target straight down on the View Y axis, near the light ring. Go to a Front viewport and move the light and its target approximately 10 units on the View Y axis until they are centered in the reactor porthole. (See Figure 10.61.)

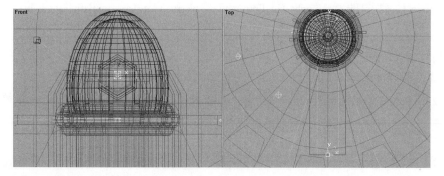

Figure 10.61   This Target Direct light will simulate a coherent beam of light being cast through a porthole in the reactor's surface.

17. Name this light "Direct_Reactor" and set Color to bright red (R250, G20, B20).

18. To cause this light's beam to be shaped by the porthole, confirm that Shadow Casting is turned on. In the Shadow Parameters rollout, set Type to Shadow Map. In the Shadow Map Parameterss rollout, set the shadow map Bias to 0.1.

19. This light's cone of illumination must encompass the entire porthole, so go to the Directional Parameters rollout and set the Cone type to Circle. Increase Hotspot to 20.

20. To cause the light to fade out before it reaches the chamber wall, turn on Use Far Attenuation in the Attenuation Parameters rollout. Set Start to 150 and End to 220.

21. The final light for this setup will illuminate the plasma as it rises in the tubes beneath the reactor. Go to a Top viewport and create an Omni light just below the reactor. Placing it in front of the reactor will make its illumination visible to the camera. Go to a Left viewport and move this light approximately –250 units on the View Y axis until it is aligned with the plasma's starting position, as shown in Figure 10.62.

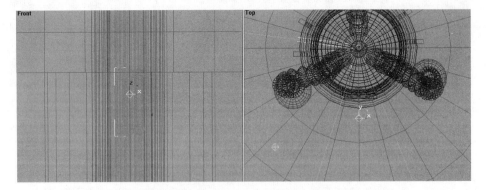

Figure 10.62   This Omni light will illuminate the plasma as it rises, simulating the light-generating properties associated with such exotic material.

22. Name this light "Omni_Plasma." Set Color to bright red (R250, G65, B65) and set Multiplier to 0.5.

23. To restrict this light's illumination to the plasma tubes, go to the Attenuation Parameters rollout, turn on Use in the Far Attenuation group, and then set Start to 70 and End to 100.

24. Go to frame 30. Go to a Front viewport and turn the Animate button on. Move the Omni_Plasma roughly 220 units on the View Y axis until it is just below the reactor.

25. You will need to set this light's Out-Of-Range setting so it will loop through these keys. Instead of opening Track View with a toolbar button, right-click on the viewport label and choose View/Track/Track View. Expand Objects/ Omni_Plasma/Transform/Position. Select the Position track and set the light's Parameter Curve Out-Of-Range Types to Loop so that it will continuously follow the motion of the plasma. You can reset the viewport to its previous configuration by right-clicking the upper-left corner of the Track View frame and selecting the desired view.

To examine a completed MAX file for this scene, load the file 10max19.max from the accompanying CD-ROM. To review this animation using the camera moves you have created, view the AVI file 10avi04.avi on the accompanying CD-ROM.

If you render this animation (or view the AVI file 10avi04.avi), you will see effect of lights moving around the reactor and the plasma being illuminated by its dedicated light. This scene is not yet complete, however. The lighting you have set up must be augmented with Atmospheres and Rendering effects before it will begin to evoke a powerful industrial mood.

Animating Atmosphere for Special Effects

In this tutorial, you will add atmospheric effects to the previously animated lights to create volume light, glow, and smoke. In a high-tech scene, you might expect every Spotlight to cast a visible cone and that the vast energies being contained in the reactor would also give off a visible light effect. Volume light, combined with noise controllers, can serve both these needs. You can create the clouds of plasma gas and steam that is often associated with science-fiction by adding a couple of atmospheric apparati (gizmos) to position combustion effects.

1. Open the file 10max19.max. If you want to preview the results of this tutorial, view the AVI file 10avi05.avi.

2. Play the animation in the Camera viewport. The Spotlights circling the reactor need some volume effects to become more dramatic. Select the Spot_Ring01 light, go to the Atmospheres & Effects rollout, and add a Volume Light atmosphere.

3. Select this atmosphere and click Setup to open the Environment dialog box. Rename this effect "Volume Light: Ring" and set Density to 3.

4. To extend the volume light effect beyond the light's Far Attenuation setting, increase the Volume Light's Attenuation End% to 150.

5. To make this cone of illumination a little less perfect, turn Noise on and set the Amount to 0.4. The speed of the Noise turbulence is set with the Phase value. Go to frame 120, turn the Animate button on, and set Phase to 6. Then turn the Animate button off.

6. This volume effect should be applied to the other two ring lights, so click on the Pick Light button and choose Spot_Ring02 and Spot_Ring03. Render a still, and you see three cones of light being cast from the ring, as shown in Figure 10.63.

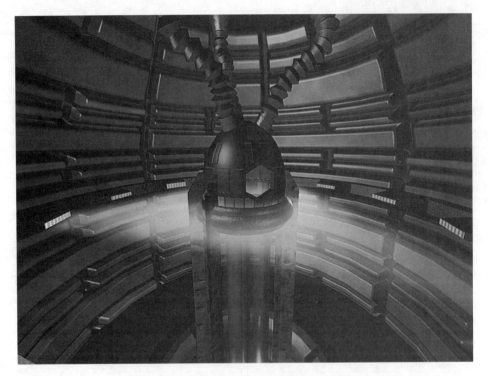

Figure 10.63   Three volume lights illuminate the reactor from the circle of lamps.

7. To make the cone of light emanating from the reactor visible, select the Direct_Reactor light and add a Volume Light effect to it using the Atmospheres & Lights rollout.

8. In the Environment dialog box, change the name of this effect to "Volume Light: Reactor." Set Density to 7.5. To keep this volume light from extending all the way across the chamber, set the Attenuation End% to 90.

9. To break up this cone of light, turn Noise on and set Amount to 0.3. Set type to Turbulence.

10. The Multiplier for the Direct_Reactor light will have the strongest impact on the appearance of this effect. For a truly chaotic look, you will assign a Noise controller. Right-click on the Direct Reactor light and choose Track View Selected. Expand Direct Reactor/Object/Multiplier. Select the Multiplier track and assign a Noise Float controller.

11. Right-click on the Multiplier track to access the Noise Controller Properties dialog box. Set Strength to 1.5 and check the >0 box to generate random values ranging from 0 to 1.5. Render a still to see the cone of light emanating from the reactor (see Figure 10.64).

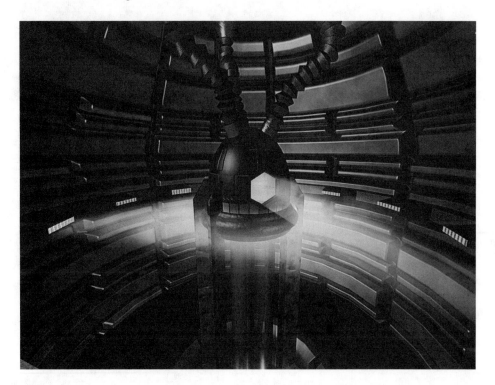

Figure 10.64   A flickering cone of volume light emanates from the reactor.

12. To vary the intensity of this light to coincide with the injection of the plasma, animate the Noise Strength value. Turn the Animate button on and go to frame 30. Increase Noise Strength to 3.

13. Go to frame 60 and set Strength to 1.5. To make this variance continue, select the Noise Strength track and set its Parameter Curve Out-Of-Range Types to Loop. Turn the Animate button off.

14. The next atmosphere to add to this scene is a boiling cloud of vapor at the bottom of the chamber, where the plasma tubes disappear into the floor. Go to a Top viewport and create a helper spherical atmosphere apparatus that's centered on the reactor. Make this gizmo large enough to cover the entire chamber diameter. A radius of 275 units should be sufficient.

15. Go to a Front viewport and move the gizmo approximately –235 units on the View Y axis until the gizmo center is aligned with the chamber floor. Scale the gizmo non-uniformly 50% on the View Y axis (see Figure 10.65).

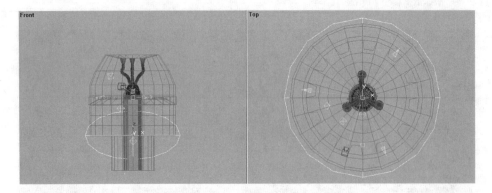

Figure 10.65   This spherical atmosphere apparatus will be used to generate a cloud of plasma fog at the bottom of the reaction chamber.

16. Click the New Seed button on the Modify panel to randomize this gizmo. You should get in the habit of generating unique seeds for all atmospheric apparati, unless you need several gizmos to generate identical results.

17. Add a Combustion atmosphere to this gizmo. Open the Environment dialog box and rename this effect "Combustion: Plasma." Set the Inner Color to pale yellow (R255, G255, B170) and the Outer Color to bright red (R255, G30, B30). Reduce Density to 5. Render it, and you will see a turbulent red-yellow combustion effect like that shown in Figure 10.66.

18. The speed with which the atmosphere will churn is set by the Phase value. Turn the Animate button on, go to frame 120, and set Phase to 240. The combustion will churn visibly, from second to second. Turn the Animate button off.

19. You might expect a reactor like this one to put off a lot of heat and steam. You can simulate that with a hemispherical combustion effect. Go to a Top viewport and create a spherical atmospheric apparatus centered on the reactor, with a radius of 50 units. Go to a Front viewport and move the gizmo roughly –15

units on the View Y axis until its center is aligned with the bottom of the reactor shell. Check Hemisphere in the Sphere Gizmo Parameters rollout and scale the gizmo 500% non-uniformly on the View Y axis. Name this gizmo "SphereGizmo_Steam." If you scale this hemispherical gizmo in this fashion, it will contain a volume appropriate for rising steam or smoke (see Figure 10.67).

Figure 10.66   A turbulent cloud of plasma vapor fills the bottom of the reaction chamber.

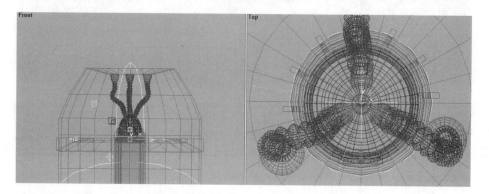

Figure 10.67   This atmospheric apparatus will be used to create a rising cloud of steam.

20. Add a Combustion effect and rename the effect "Combustion: Steam." Set the Inner Color to medium teal (R155, G180, B180) and the Outer Color to dark teal (R70, G80, B80).

21. To make this atmosphere simulate rising smoke, set Flame Type to Tendril. Increase Stretch to 2 to elongate the effect along its Local Z axis. Set Regularity to 0.6 to more evenly fill the apparatus.

22. Decreasing Flame Size to 15 will create thinner tendrils of smoke. Set Density to 5 for a light, hazy appearance.

23. Turn the Animate button on, go to frame 120, and set Phase to 120. This displays a relatively slow internal churning of the steam.

24. Just as Phase controls the internal movement of the combustion, Drift controls the apparent movement of the individual tendrils along the Local Z axis. At frame 120, set Drift to 250. Turn the Animate button off. Render a still to see the tendrils of steam rise from the reactor (see Figure 10.68).

Figure 10.68   Steam rises from the reactor's surface.

To examine a completed MAX file for this scene, load the file 10max20.max from the accompanying CD-ROM. To review this animation using the camera moves you have created, view the AVI file 10avi05.avi on the accompanying CD-ROM.

In this tutorial, you have added several types of atmospheric effects to simulate different aspects of this scene. Atmospherics can be a very useful tool for increasing the depth, realism, and visual complexity of an animation. Subtler applications of fog or combustion than were used in this scene can be very useful in adding vitality and density to light sources.

One final step is needed to complete this animation. As the ring lights revolve around the circle, it is a little difficult to tell which lamp is emitting the light. In the next exercise, you will use Rendering Effects to add a bright flare to these light sources.

Animating Lens Effects for Special Effects

Rendering effects are similar to atmospherics in that they can provide distortion, granularity, and special effects to a scene. Rendering effects, however, are not rendered simultaneously with scene objects. They are rendered and automatically composited after the frame is rendered. The most typical uses are for lens flares, blur, and depth of field effects, but rendering effects can also be used to adjust color balance, brightness, and contrast.

In this tutorial, you will add lens flares to several lights in this scene to make them more dramatic.

1. Open the file 10max14.max or continue from the preceding tutorial. If you want to preview the results of this tutorial, view the AVI file 10avi06.avi.

2. The lamps on the ring should become brighter when they're "turned on." An easy way to do this is to add a lens effect to the light. If you add such an effect to the existing spotlights, however, the center of the effect will be at the origin of the light, not at the front of the lamp. You will need to create a second series of lights solely for Lens Effects. Go to a Top viewport and select the Spot_Ring01 light.

3. Clone this light using Copy as the method and name the clone "Spot_Ring01_FX." Change the type to Omni and turn both Diffuse and Specular lighting off. This light will not affect the illumination of this scene. Note that turning this light off would keep it from emitting lens effects, so it must be left on.

4. Go to the Motion panel and turn on Trajectories mode to display this light's path. The path needs to be scaled and repositioned so the position keys occur

just in front of the ring lamps. Go into SubObject: Keys mode and select all the keys in this path. Scale these keys around the Transform Coordinate Center until the path is just within the circle of lamps, as shown in Figure 10.69.

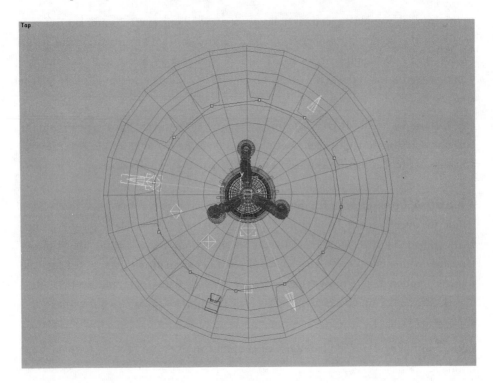

Figure 10.69   This Omni light will be used to create a Lens Effect to accompany the volume light.

5. Before repeating steps 3 And 4 for the other two spotlights, you will need to temporarily extend the time frame. In SubObject: Keys mode, only keys in the current time frame are visible in the viewport. Because the keys set for the two remaining spotlights have been offset beyond the current time frame, they will not be selectable. Open the Time Configuration dialog box and set Animation End Time to 200. Click OK.

6. Repeat steps 3 and 4 for the Spot_Ring02 and Spot_Ring03 lights. Clone each light and scale the new light's path to fit within the ring of lamps.

7. Open the Time Configuration dialog box and set Animation End Time to its previous value of 120. Click OK.

8. Select the Spot_Ring01_FX light. Go into the Atmospheres & Effects rollout and delete the Volume Light: Ring effect. Add a Lens Effect and go into the setup for

the new effect. Under Lens Effects Global Parameters, set Intensity to 60 to make this a more subtle effect.

9. Rename this effect "Lens Effects: Ring01." Add a Glow element, go to the Glow Element rollout, and set Intensity to 75. Set the second Radial Color to bright yellow (R245, G255, B0).

10. Add a Star element, go to the Star Element rollout, and set Size to 15. Set Width to 3 and Intensity to 7. This generates a bright flare at the origin of the volume light being cast by the Spot_Ring01 light.

11. For the two remaining Spotlights (Spot_Ring02 and Spot_Ring03), delete the volume light effect and add a Lens Effect. Figure 10.70 shows the result. You will need to add identical but unique Lens Effects to the lights to avoid an occasional bug with the way MAX R3 applies the same Lens Effect to multiple lights.

Figure 10.70   Lens flares will make the ring of lamps more obvious and dramatic.

12. You can save the parameters you have already set up for the Lens Effects: Ring01 effect and load them into two identical lens effects using the Load and Save buttons in the Lens Effects Globals rollout.

To examine a completed MAX file for this scene, load the file 10max15.max from the accompanying CD-ROM. To review this animation using the camera moves you have created, view the AVI file 10avi06.avi on the accompanying CD-ROM.

Lens effects provide an invaluable way to add dramatic flourishes to an animation and can support a variety of special effects, such as explosions, space effects, and camera effects.

In Practice: Animating Lights

- **Plan your lighting carefully and light progressively.** Start with just one light, set it up, and then add another light, and so on. Remember that lights don't operate in a vacuum; in addition to all their parameters, they also interact with the materials and each other.

- **Break up your lights into specific tasks.** Using different lights to affect diffuse, specular, and ambient illumination can increase your control over the quality of your lighting setup.

- **Take advantage of MAX R3's new features to adjust shadow appearance.** Evaluate shadows to determine whether changing their color and/or density would improve the effect.

- **Attenuation parameters.** Careful use of Attenuation parameters—as well as the Hotspot/Falloff values—in conjunction with shadows can greatly improve your lighting.

  In certain specialized cases, the Place Highlight tool can greatly ease the task of precisely placing specular highlights.

- **Atmospheric effects and volume lights can add greatly to the depth of your scene.** Use volume lights to increase the visual impact of light sources. Use atmospheres to simulate denser air volumes, particle vapor, or weather effects.

- **Lights can be animated to simulate moving light sources, environmental changes, or special effects.** In some cases, lights can be used to create very specific effects without having much of an impact on scene illumination.

- **Animated atmospheric effects can provide subtle mood changes, weather effects, and a great range of discrete vaporous scene elements.** Modulating the Phase variable is often the key to determining the emotional feel of an atmospheric effect.

- **Rendering effects provide a quick method for adding a variety of post-rendering effects and image adjustments.** Lights that do not affect diffuse, specular, or ambient illumination can be used to precisely place rendering effects without affecting scene illumination.

Chapter 11

Particle Systems, Space Warps, and Dynamics Simulations

By Brandon Davis

This chapter focuses on procedural anima-

tion tools in MAX R3, particularly particle

systems, space warps, and dynamic simulations. Specifically, this chapter covers the ollowing topics:

- Using particle systems to create natural phenomena
- Driving animation with particle systems
- Using expressions to control particle systems
- Creating natural motion with dynamics simulations

Particle systems are used to generate the motion of several objects via parameters and not individual key frames. After it's generated, the motion can be applied to a multitude of static and animated objects. This kind of animation is called *procedural animation* because it isn't a brute force approach of pose-to-pose key framing, but instead relies on rules and procedures that are calculated on a frame-by-frame basis. Particle systems are most commonly used to mimic the motion of complex and dynamic natural phenomena such as rain, smoke, splashes, and fire. They can also be used to generate the animation of a large group of objects, such as a school of fish, lemmings, or tumbleweeds.

Given an emission point, direction, and set of parameters, particles will be born, will follow their prescribed rules during their lifetime, and then will die. But often it's necessary to influence particles with external forces that can be used to push, pull, and guide particles around. This is where space warps come in. A Gravity space warp can be applied to particles to create a global force that pulls the particles downward, whereas a Noise space warp can be used to randomly apply turbulence within a specific region.

Particle Systems

Existing as their own class in the Creation panel, particle systems consist of two elements: an emitter and particles. Although they work very similarly, the six particle systems that ship with MAX can be differentiated by how they emit particles. Some emitters are simply non-rendering planes, but others can be animated objects. All particle systems, regardless of parameters, follow a specific sequence of events: birth, motion, and death. After they're emitted, particles move in a specified direction unless they are influenced by an external force, such as a space warp. A particle will die at a certain frame and disappear from the scene or be recycled back to the emitter.

The following list outlines the particle systems that ship with 3D Studio MAX R3 (see Figure 11.1):

- **Spray** and **Snow**. These are very simplistic and offer a limited amount of control. These two particle systems shipped with the first release of MAX and have been included in later versions for compatibility reasons. However, when simplicity is required, they can often suffice. They are useful for quick and simple effects, such as welding sparks and rain.

Figure 11.1   The six particle systems that ship with 3D Studio MAX R3.

- **Super Spray**. An augmented version of the original Spray particle system, this uses the new Super Particle features. It allows more advanced control over how the particles are emitted and what kind of particles can be used. This is most useful when you're creating effects that are emitted from a single point, such as a garden hose spraying water or sparks from a blacksmith's forge.

- **Blizzard**. An enhanced version of the older Snow particle system, this also uses the new Super Particle features. It is almost identical to Super Spray, except that instead of emitting from a point in space, it emits from a plane. Blizzard comes in handy when you need to create such effects as sparks and splashes from a larger surface area.

- **Particle Cloud (PCloud)**. This is a specialized particle system that shares attributes (similar to both Super Spray and Blizzard). The main feature of Particle Cloud is its ability to fill a user-defined volume with particles. This capability to use a volume makes PCloud useful when you're creating stationary particles for starfields or gaseous volume, such as clouds.

- **Particle Array (PArray)**. One of the most useful particle systems in MAX. It too uses the new Super Particle features common to the new particle systems, however, it uses objects as emitters. It gives you specific controls for defining how particles are distributed across the surface of an object. It also has the added advantage of being able to break apart geometry into chunks to use in a particle simulation. This fragmentary capability makes it the perfect tool for "blowing stuff up," more so than the Bomb space warp.

Space Warps for Particle Systems

After a particle is emitted, it is allowed to be influenced by an external force or, in this case, a *space warp*. Space warps are forces that influence the motion of objects in world space instead of object space. When a particle system is bound to a space warp, the space warp binding is applied to the particle system's modifier stack similar to a Mesh modifier. Several different groups of space warps work with particle systems.

Particles and Dynamics

The Particles and Dynamics group of space warps can be used to affect particles or create dynamics simulations. As you can see in Figure 11.2, this group includes the following space warps:

- **Gravity** creates a planar directional or spherical attraction/repulsion force. The Decay value localizes the effect so that it affects only particles within a certain area of influence and not globally.

- **Wind** is similar to gravity, with both planar and spherical fields, except it has controls for creating turbulence in the field. The turbulence can be used regardless of the strength or direction of the field.

Figure 11.2
The Particles and Dynamics space warps as they appear in the Command panel.

- **Push** is a directional point force that has controls for determining when the force is applied and released, as well as strength in Newtons or pounds.

- **Pbomb** is perfect when you want to add an explosive force to a particle system. You can explode or implode particles spherically, cylindrically, or along a plane with randomization controls. You can also specify an area of influence and control how the force falls off over distance.

- **Motor** applies a rotational torque effect to particles. It has parameters very similar to Push, with on/off timing and feedback parameters.

Particles Only

The Particles Only group contains space warps that work with particle systems only. They include the following (see Figure 11.3):

- **Path Follow.** Sends particles along a spline path with plenty of controls for determining how fast particles move and rotate along the path. There are also good timing controls for finessing the frames at which Path Follow events happen.

- **Deflector.** A simple non-rendering plane that will cause bound particles to collide with it. It has one parameter to control the amount of bounce or deflection.

- **Spherical Deflector (SDeflector).** A spherical version of Deflector, but with more advanced controls. It has bounce with variation, chaos, and a percentage of velocity for particles to inherit from its collisions.

- **Universal Deflector (Udeflector)** Another variation of the Deflector space warp. This one, however, uses Mesh objects to determine the deflection field. UDeflector has controls very similar to Sdeflector with the addition of a friction parameter.

- **Planar Omniflector (POmniFlect).** Part of a new breed of deflector space warps included in MAX R3. POmniFlect uses a non-rendering plane to reflect or refract particles. It also includes special spawning controls to determine the amount and velocity of spawning. Like Motor and Push, it has timing controls.

- **Spherical Omniflector (SOmniFlect).** A spherical version of an Omniflector with identical controls.

- **Universal Omniflector (UOmniFlect).** A special version of the Omniflector that uses objects to determine the field. It extends the functionality of the Universal Deflector.

Figure 11.3
The Particles Only space warps as they appear in the Command panel.

Dynamics Interface

Also new to MAX R3 are three space warps that allow particles to participate in a dynamics simulation. These include the following (see Figure 11.4):

- **Planar DynaFlect (PDynaFlect).** A planar dynamics deflector that is attached to objects, causing particles to push the objects around. By using this on one side of a box, you can have a hose of water spray a box off the top of a table.

- **Spherical DynaFlect (SDynaFlect).** A spherical version of the dynamics deflectors.

- **Universal DynaFlect (UDynaFlect).** A version of the dynamics deflectors that uses an object to define the field.

Figure 11.4   The Dynamics Interface space warps as they appear in the Command panel.

Geometric/Deformable

One space warp works with Particles in the Geometric/Deformable category. These are normally reserved for working on mesh objects.

- **Displace.** This works much like the Displace modifier, by moving particles based on the grayscale values of an image or map.

Particles at Work

Now that you're familiar with all the particle systems and relevant space warps in MAX R3, you're ready to start putting them to use. In the exercises that follow, you will create these effects:

- Cigarette smoke
- Underwater bubbles
- A waterfall
- A flock of birds
- Dust trails with expressions

Later, you will also use PArray for object detonation and you will work with particles in a dynamic simulation.

Creating Cigarette Smoke

In the first exercise, you'll use a Super Spray particle system and Wind space warp to add turbulent, natural-looking smoke that's emitted from the tip of a cigarette. Some very simple texturing techniques will make geometry look like wispy smoke particles. In the past, many people (including myself) believed it was impossible to produce the natural curling and clumping particle motion found in nature without third-party tools. As you'll see in this example, the capability has been there for some time. It's just a matter of getting the proper values down.

1. Load the particletut-cigmsoke.max file from the CD-ROM. You'll see a generic cigarette in an ashtray (see Figure 11.5).

2. In the Create panel, choose Particle Systems from the list and click Super Spray. Press and drag to create a Super Spray particle system in the Top viewport directly over the lit tip of the cigarette mesh. This will cause the Super Spray you created to point upward along the World Z axis, which is the direction you want to emit smoke.

3. Open the Super Spray parameters in the Modifier panel. Let's change how MAX displays the particles in the viewports. First, change the Viewport Display parameter to Dots instead of Ticks. This particle system is going to emit lots of particles, and using Dots instead of Ticks will make it easier to see trajectories and clumping. Second, change the Percentage of Particles to 25%. This will basically show every fourth particle in the viewport and should more accurately portray the motion within the system than a value of 10% would (see Figure 11.6).

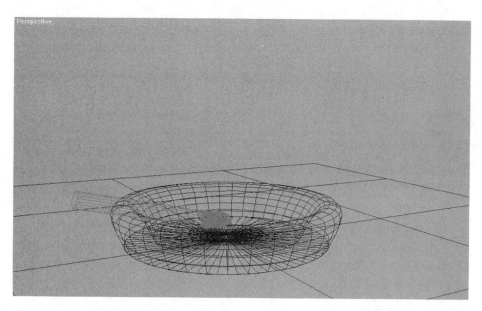

Figure 11.5 The ashtray and cigarette, ready for smoke.

Figure 11.6 Dots and Ticks displayed in a viewport.

4. In the Particle Generation rollout, set the Particle Quantity to Use Rate, and set the Value to 50. This will cause 50 particles to be emitted at every frame. If you run the animation at this point, you'll see the Super Spray emit a very thin stream of particles for about 30 frames and then die off.

5. Next, set the Speed value to 3 so particles will have less initial velocity. Few things in nature are uniform and congruent, so you should add variation where it's available to create a bit of randomness in your work. Here 25% variation should suffice.

Note

In the Software Z-buffer, Dots particles are represented by single pixels. This can be a problem, depending on your resolution. Also, Dots and Ticks are displayed as a constant scale, no matter what the size of the particles or their distance from the camera. For example, a particle directly in front of a camera is going to be displayed the same as one very far away. Only Mesh and Box properly display the scale of particles in the viewports.

6. By default, Super Spray emits particles starting from frame 0 to frame 30. In this case, you want particles to be emitted for the duration of the animation. So in the Particle Timing group of the Particle Generation rollout, change the Emit Stop value to 300.

Tip

If you need for particles to be emitted prior to the start of your animation, you can always set the Emit Start to negative frames. This just causes a bit of extra overhead for the system as it has to "pre-compute" the earlier frames.

7. In the same group, you'll see Display Until and Life. These are related in that they cause particles to die, but they differ in that one affects particles locally and the other affects them globally. Change Display Until to match the length of the animation, in this case 300. If it remains at the default 100 frames, *all* the particles will disappear globally at frame 100. Also, set the Life value to 60 for now. With that, particles will start to die as they reach the age of 60 frames. You can increase the Life value, say to last the duration of your scene, but this often isn't necessary. Whenever a particle is present in a scene, it is taking processing power from your system. If the camera doesn't see particles past age 60 or so, why keep them alive? Adjust this as you go.

Caution

Be careful when adjusting values with spinners. Programmers set step intervals to values, and these values can vary from parameter to parameter. One click of a spinner could raise or lower a value by 0.01 or 1.0 depending on how it's set. For this reason, it can be dangerous to drag spinners on parameters that are computationally expensive, such as Rate or Spawns. You might accidentally assign 50,000 or such a high value that your system bogs down considerably. It's often a good idea to just type in the value you need.

8. Go to the Particle Type rollout. This is where you define what geometry will be used to define particles. Choose Facing for the Particle Type. Facing particles are

2D planar polygons that always orient themselves to the camera, unless set otherwise. In some cases, Special particles are useful for the same types of effects as the rising smoke. Special particles are similar to Facing, except that they consist of three intersecting and perpendicular facing planes.

Now if you play the animation as it's set, you'll get a thin stream of particles rising upward. Now you need to apply an external force to help guide and disturb their motion. A Wind space warp does the trick.

9. Go to the Create panel's Space Warps section and choose Wind from the Particles & Dynamics pull-down. Click-drag anywhere in the Top viewport to create a Wind space warp. You want a planar Wind to point upward along the z-axis. The location of the space warp is irrelevant because you will be using it as a global force, meaning its influence is applied equally anywhere in the scene.

10. Now, let's set up the basic parameters for the Wind space warp. Most of Wind's parameters are relevant to the scale of the scene; because this scene is small, start with low values. Set the Strength to 0.01 and leave the Decay at 0. Decay is used to localize the effect, but you're not going to do that in this scene.

11. To bind the Super Spray to the Wind space warp to activate the effect, use the Bind space warp button or hot key and click-drag from the Super Spray to the Wind space warp. After it is bound, the Wind binding will show up above the Super Spray in the modifier stack, and the Wind space warp immediately starts to influence the particles. Right off, however, you can see that this is just too much velocity. So go back to the Super Spray's Speed parameter and drop the value down to a minute 0.1. This will cause particles to seep from the emitter and be pushed upward by the Wind space warp.

12. Take a look at the animation now. The Wind space warp should be slowly pushing the particles upward. In this case, it's still a bit too fast, so select the Wind in the viewport and then in the Modify panel and drop the Wind's Strength to a minute 0.005. The strength of the Wind isn't your primary goal here, it's the turbulence.

13. Using the Wind rollout's turbulence controls (Turbulence, Frequency, and Scale), you'll create a noise field that will push and pull at the particles causing them to clump and twist along in their motion like real cigarette smoke. A good rule of thumb that I use when setting up turbulence is to set all three parameters at 0.02. Give this a try.

If you play the animation now, you'll see that steady stream of particles start to sway and clump (see Figure 11.7). The Turbulence parameter controls the strength of the disturbance, and Frequency varies the turbulence over time. Scale is probably the most important factor because if it's not set appropriately to your scene, the turbulence will look wild and messy. A lot of people make the simple mistake of setting these parameters too high. It's actually most important to set them according to your scene's scale.

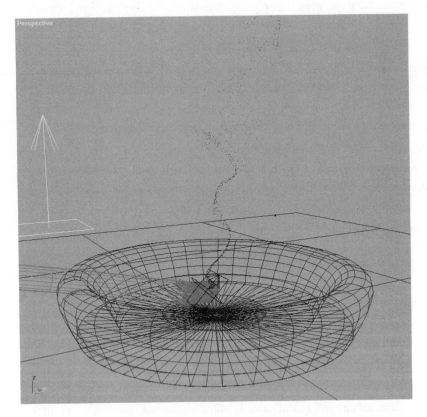

Figure 11.7   Wind space warp with Turbulence bound to particles.

Tip

Particle systems are calculated linearly on a frame-by-frame basis. Each successive frame is dependent on the previous frame. This is why it's always harder to scrub a particle system backward in time. For example, look at particles at frame 10. Assuming the particles were emitted at frame 0, MAX has to compute 10 frames of particle trajectories before it can display frame 10 accurately. Now go to frame 300. Assuming the particles live this long, MAX has to compute 290 frames to display frame 300 properly. But now just go back one frame to 299. You'd think that because it's only one frame this should be a fast update, but it's not. MAX has to start over at frame 0 and compute 299 frames. This is always something to consider when working with particles. Be aware of how far along you are in particle age when working with the Time Slider.

14. To make long, elegant smoke curls and turbulence, try playing with the three turbulence settings. If you get lost, you can always go back to 0.02 as a starting over point. For this scene, I preferred the best settings: Turbulence at 0.02, Frequency at 0.15, and Scale at 0.24.

    Render the scene now, and you should see thousands of squares that grow to scale from the emitter. Before you make a smokey map for the particles, adjust their size. You could have set the size earlier, but it's one of those things that you rarely know until you do a test render.

15. Go back to the Super Spray's Particle Generation rollout. At the bottom, you'll see a particle size group. Set the Size to 1.5 and add about 25% Variation so they aren't all the same size. The Grow For and Fade For parameters are useful for making particles grow from nothing to full scale and then shrink down to nothing over a set number of frames. In this case, set the Grow For to 60 and the Fade For to 0. This way, the particles will gradually reach their size in 60 frames.

16. To make a material for the smoke particles, select the upper-left sample slot in the Material Editor and drag this material onto the Super Spray. Start with a Standard material and assign it to the Super Spray particle system. Set the Diffuse color to pure white and bring the Ambient up to about medium gray. Smoke doesn't shine, so turn all the Specular controls down to 0. If you re-render the scene now, you'll see gray-white facings.

17. The challenge is to make each facing particle look like a soft round disk with an opacity mask. Go down to the Maps rollout and assign a Mask map to the Opacity channel. For the Map slot, assign a Noise Map. You'll use this to make some variation in the opacity of each particle. The only thing you need to change here is the Tiling in the X axis. Set it to 0.1, which will cause the noise to stretch a bit.

Tip

If you can't see what you're working on in your material slot, try toggling off the Show End Result button at the top.

18. Go back to the Mask Map rollout by clicking the Go to Parent button. Assign a Gradient map to the Mask slot. In the Gradient parameters, change V Tiling to 1.5 and Gradient Type to Radial to create a slightly elliptical gradient. The reason for all the stretching is that you want to create long wisps of smoke and not uniformly round puffs (see Figure 11.8).

Figure 11.8   Noise Map masked by a radial Gradient map for the smoke's opacity channel.

If you render the scene now you'll see that things are starting to come together.

However you'll notice that the radial gradient doesn't seem to be working. This is because particles in MAX treat opacity differently. In fact, one entire section of the Particle Type rollout is dedicated to handling mapping control. In this case, the particles will apply the gradient map over the lifetime of the particle, which is not what you want. Instead, you have to face map the particles. The smoke is also too dark and thick. You need to make it much more transparent and lighten it up a bit.

19. In the Shader Basic Parameters rollout at the top of the Material Editor, check the Face Map check box and set the colored Self-Illumination to a medium gray. You can just drag the Ambient color if you want to. This will lighten up the smoke more without changing the scene's lights.

20. Finally, bring the Opacity Channel's value down from 100 to 5. This is *not* the value in the Maps rollout, but the value at the top of your material to the right of the color swatches and directly below the self-illumination value. This will lessen the effect of the Mask map in the opacity of the material. Look at the top of the Material rollout: The overall Opacity is still set at 100, even though a material is present in the Opacity channel. If you render the scene, the gradient will mask the opacity of the particles, but because the main opacity is still set at 100, you'll also be able to see the edges and corners of the facings. To remedy this, drop Opacity to 0. It's a good idea to do this whenever you apply an Opacity map to a material.

Note

You really have to think of each material as having two Opacity channels when an opacity map is assigned. When there is no Opacity map, only a value, that value is a percentage of "transparency" for the whole material. However, when you assign a map to the Opacity slot, unless the map value is 100%, the original opacity will still be included. For example, if you add a Noise map to the Opacity slot of a material and leave both values at 100%, the Noise map is 100% responsible for the opacity of the material. But if you turn the value on the Noise mapped Opacity channel down to 10% (for example), the other 90% is collected from the initial opacity at the top of the material. This is why if you want to completely mask something, you should turn your main Opacity to 0.

So there you have it, quick and easy cigarette smoke created with the standard MAX R3 tools (see Figure 11.9).

Figure 11.9   The completed and rendered scene.

Here are a few simple things you need to remember when making smoke particles:

- Start with low turbulence parameters and work your way upward in scale. If you start too high, it's harder to find the right scale.

- Wind Strength isn't always necessary. In fact, if all you're trying to do is add turbulence, leave Wind Strength at 0.

- Be sure to turn on the Face Map option in your smoke material; if you don't, the map will be applied over particle age. If you use a gradient opacity map without Face Map activated, the smoke will fade away over time.

Creating Underwater Bubbles

This time we're going to make use of the Bubble Motion parameters and instanced geometry with a PArray to make underwater bubbles.

1. Start by loading the particletut-bubbles.max file. This is a very simple scene with an object that will emit bubbles.

2. Create a PArray particle system anywhere in the scene. The location of the icon is irrelevant because PArray always uses an object as an emitter. Open up the PArray rollout in the Modifier panel. Click the Pick Object button and select the emitter object. This will tell PArray to use the object as an emitter.

3. In the Particle Formation group, make sure Over Entire Surface is selected.

Note

The Particle Formation group in the Parray rollout offers several different ways to emit particles from an object. Most are self-explanatory. Over Entire Surface causes particles to be randomly emitted from the surface of the object, and Along Visible Edges will constrain particle emission to the visible edges of the polygons of the object. At All Vertices causes particles to be emitted from only the vertices of the object, and At Distinct Points limits emission to a set number of points on the surface of the object (which is good for hair). Finally, At Face Centers forces particles to be emitted from the center of all faces on the object.

4. For now, set the Viewport Display options to Ticks and Percentage of Particles to 100%. You're not going to be emitting a large amount of bubbles, so 100% will be fine.

5. In the Particle Generation rollout, set the motion parameters. For Rate, specify 3 particles per frame. Set the Speed to a slow 0.5 to keep the initial velocity down, but add 25% Variation to break up the uniformity of emission velocity. Spread the emission out a bit by setting Divergence to 20 degrees.

6. You want some particles to already be emitted before frame 0, so set Emit Start to –30 and Emit Stop to 100. You should immediately start seeing particles emitted at frame 0. Also, set the Display Until and Life to match your scene duration (100 in this example). This way bubbles will be visible throughout the animation.

7. As before, leave the particle size alone for now and instead jump all the way down to Bubble Motion. Each main parameter, Amplitude, Period, and Phase, has a Variation parameter to randomize the values. Amplitude controls the strength of the bubble motion, Period is the number of frames it takes to complete one cycle of bubble oscillation, and Phase is the initial position of the oscillation pattern. Set Amplitude to 1.5, Period to 10, and Phase to 180 degrees, and then put in 25% Variation to all three parameters.

8. By default, particles will be emitted along the surface normals of the object. In this case, though, you want to mimic bubbles floating to the surface, so use a Wind space warp to blow the bubbles upward. This time it's much simpler because you're not dealing with turbulence. Create a Wind space warp in the scene and point it upward along the World Z axis. Keep the strength low (about 0.02) so the bubbles don't race upward. Be sure to bind the particles to the space warp.

Now if you look at the animation, you should get particles with bubble-like motion floating upward and away from the emitter (see Figure 11.10). The next thing you have to do is make some geometry to represent the bubbles. You'll notice that one of the standard available particles in PArray is spheres. These are fine in most cases, but these bubbles should be semi-amorphous blobby particles. To make them look like that, you will use the Instanced Geometry option and apply your own geometry to the particles.

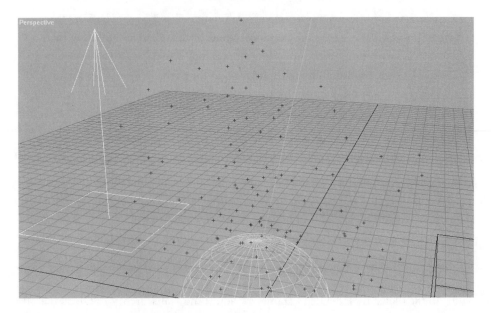

Figure 11.10   Particles with bubble motion.

9. Go to the Create panel and create a geosphere with default parameters. Don't make it too big; a Radius around 6 should be fine. Also jump to the Material Editor and assign a Standard Material to the geosphere.

10. To wobble and distort the geosphere over time, add a Noise modifier. Change the Strength parameters all to 5 (X,Y,Z) and check the Animate Noise check box to

distort the geosphere over the course of the animation. The noise will be too large for this situation, so bring the Scale value down to an acceptable level, say 10 to 20. This should make the distortions more noticeable but not out of control.

11. Now go back to the PArray and the Particle Type rollout. Change the Type from Standard Particles to Instanced Geometry. This will gray out the other parameters in the rollout but open up the instanced geometry parameters. Click the Pick Object button and assign the geosphere as your instanced geometry.

    You won't see your particle system change at all unless you do one of two things: render or, in the basic parameters rollout, change the Viewport Display option from Ticks to Mesh (see Figure 11.11). Go ahead and change the display options at the top of the PArray rollout. Notice that wobbly spheres have replaced particles. If you play the animation, you'll see that they all wobble similarly in unison. This is because the Noise modifier and its animation are applied globally to all particles. You need to change this to make it look more realistic.

12. The Instanced Geometry parameter's Animation Offset Keying option's three choices are None, Birth, and Random. None, by default, does not offset the object's animation. Birth applies the animation to particles as they are birthed. Random randomly applies the animation to the particles given a set Frame Offset. Set the Offset Keying to Birth.

13. You want to derive the material of the bubbles from the instanced geometry, so in the Material Mapping and Source group, set the radio button to Instanced Geometry and click the Get Material From button.

14. Now go back to the Material Editor and the bubble material. Bring the Specular controls up to say, a Specular Level of around 90 and Glossiness of 70, to make sharp highlights like on real bubbles. Next, change the Opacity to 25 so the bubbles are more transparent. Start changing the colors a bit by making the Ambient color a medium shade of blue-green and the Diffuse a lighter shade of the same blue-green.

15. In the Material's Extended Parameters, adjust the Transparency Falloff so the opacity isn't uniform. If you look at a bubble in the real world, the edges are less transparent than the sides facing toward or away from you. To mimic this, set the Falloff to In and the Amount to 100.

16. If you look at the material icon now, you'll notice there's less transparency at the edges. The next thing to do is to add some faked reflections at these edges. Add a Falloff Map to the Reflection channel. In the white channel, add a Bitmap Map.

For the bitmap, choose a reflection map of some kind—in this case, it's the standard Chromic.jpg that ships with MAX. Now in the Falloff Type drop-down parameter, use the Perpendicular/Parallel method. This will cause the reflection map to appear only at the edges of the bubble. Lastly, because you don't want 100% reflection, drop the value in the Reflection channel to about 25.

Now if you render your scene, you should see nice blobby bubbles floating upward from your emitter object. If you ran into any problems with this exercise, try loading the finished file particlestut-bubbles-complete.max and take a look at the settings to see where things went wrong. You need to keep two things in mind when using animated instanced geometry:

- Be sure to adjust your Animation Offset Keying. When this is set to None, your animations will all occur in unison, destroying any realism in the scene.

- Don't forget to hide your instanced geometry source. It's very easy to forget about it and leave it in your scene.

Creating a Waterfall

Using particles, spawning, and MAX R3's new deflector space warps, you can create a waterfall that splashes down on rocks. In the next exercise, you'll produce a stream of particles raining down from above and splashing dynamically on the rocks and water below.

1. Load up the particletut-waterfall.max file. This is a simple scene with a water plane and several rocks.

2. Looking in the Front viewport, you'll notice a little gap at the top of the two main rocks. Place a Super Spray particle system there or in any other logical place where you can create a decent waterfall onto the rocks and water below (see Figure 11.11). You're going to use a Gravity space warp to pull the particles downward realistically, so don't worry about pointing the emitter down, just point it outward.

3. In the Particle Generation rollout, set Speed of 1.0, add a little Variation, and set Emit Start, Emit Stop, and Display Until to match your scene (0, 150, and 150 respectively, in this case). Because you don't want the particles to stay around during the entire duration of the scene, make Life 90, which is about 75% of the animation's total length.

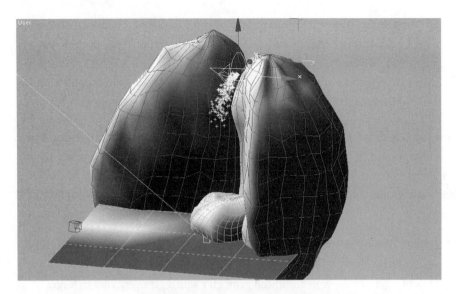

Figure 11.11   Place the Super Spray between the two main rocks.

4. Now you need to put some gravity in the scene. Create a Gravity space warp anywhere in the scene and set it to Planar so that the force is in a downward direction through the water plane and not spherical. The default Gravity Strength of 1.0 is pretty strong, so try setting it to 0.1.

5. Now bind the Super Spray to the Gravity space warp; otherwise, it will have no effect on the particle motion.

   Play the animation. You should see a nice steady stream of particles falling to the water plane. The problem here is that the particles are too tightly packed. This was fine for thin wispy cigarette smoke, but in this case, the stream should spread out a bit. This is where you use Super Spray's Off Axis/Spread and Off Plane/Spread parameters to control more than just the emission direction.

 Note

At the top of the Super Spray rollout are four parameters that control the direction and spread of particle emission. You might wonder why this is necessary if the Super Spray icon has directional capabilities. Off Axis and Off Plane allow you to fine-tune the direction of emission, although this is often not necessary because it's more intuitive to just point the emitter in the direction needed. However, the two Spread parameters are very useful. Off Axis/Spread controls the spread angle of emission. A 45-degree spread will create a wide but paper-thin, fanlike particle stream. Off Plane/Spread allows you to create a more conical emission, with a limitation of 180 degrees.

6. Try spreading the emission out a bit, at least 20 degrees. Whether you use the Off Plane/Spread is up to you, but I think it makes for more realistic flows even when you need a nice sheet of particles.

Now you've got to set up collisions for the particles. You have three items to deal with: the water and the two large rocks at the water level.

7. The water is a planar object, so all you need is a simple Deflector space warp. From the Particles Only section of Space Warps, click-drag a Deflector into a place near the large rocks in the water. Make it big enough to catch any particles that will eventually bounce off of the rocks. The Deflector's Bounce value simply tells the particles with how much force to deflect from the plane. Higher numbers cause particles to bounce farther, whereas the lowest numbers cause particles to practically stick. For the water plane and waterfall, you don't want the particles to bounce around, so a value of 0.1 should be fine.

Tip

Deflectors don't care about geometry, so it's a good rule of thumb to place them fairly level to the surface from which you're supposed to be deflecting particles.

At this point, go ahead and bind the Super Spray to the Deflector. Sometimes you can miss the binding or think you did and wonder why things aren't working. If things do seem to move oddly or your system chugs hard, double-check the bindings on your particle system. It's easy to bind space warps redundantly if you're not careful, and that can be a CPU hog. Now when you play the animation, you should see particles falling to the water and not passing through the geometry.

Tip

An alternative way to bind space warps is to select the particle system, click the Bind to Space Warp button, and then press H or the hot key that brings up the Selection dialog box. This will let you choose the space warp you want to bind to from a list instead of dragging around in a cluttered scene. Be sure to click the Select button when you're finished, or the next time you go to select, you'll still be in Bind mode.

8. The next step is to make the two rocks at the water level deflect particles as well. You will use a special spherical deflector called SOmniFlect. It works similarly to Deflectors, but it deflects particles from a spherical force. Go ahead and create one by click-dragging over one of the rocks near the water plane. Make sure the icon is relatively the same size as the rock geometry.

Before we go farther, let's talk about the different deflectors available in MAX R3. In the Space Warps, Particles Only rollout, you'll see several deflectors. We've already talked about the simple Deflector. SDeflector is similar, but it uses a spherical force to deflect particles instead of a planar force. SDeflector also adds Variation to the Bounce parameter, Chaos to randomize deflection even further, and Inherit Velocity to control how much velocity a particle is passed on from a moving SDeflector.

Next is the UDeflector, which, again is very much related to the two previous deflectors. UDeflector is unique in that, it derives its deflection source from a mesh object in the scene instead of from a planar or spherical force. You'd tend to want to use these more often than not, but the truth is that UDeflectors are much more CPU-intensive depending on the density of the source mesh. Often a planar or spherical deflector is enough to make the deflection convincing and can save you a lot of processing speed.

The next generation deflectors are the OmniFlectors: POmniFlect, SomniFlect, and UOmniFlect. These originally came from Eric and Audrey Peterson's Aegis plug-ins, adding many new controls to reflection and refraction of particles. Reflection is basically the same as deflection, but refraction is quite the opposite effect, causing particle trajectories to be skewed inward in the force's area of influence. OmniFlectors also allow you to have an On/Off time for activation, something that was previously controlled awkwardly by animating Bounce parameters. They also add controls over the percentage of colliding particles that reflect, refract, or spawn (more on spawning later).

9. Okay, let's get back to that SOmniFlect you placed around the first rock. You want it on throughout the duration of the animation, so set the Time On to 0 and Time Off to 150. You want all particles to reflect off the space warp, so set Reflects at 100%. Anything less than this will cause some or all particles to pass through the space warp, letting the Refraction controls take over. So in other words, if your Reflects setting is at 100%, Refraction is completely overridden because nothing can pass through to be refracted in the first place. Now move on to Bounce. You want the water particles in this scene to bounce off, but not with the same velocity that they collided with the space warp. So, drop Bounce to about 0.3. As always, add some Variation and Chaos. Finally, bind the Super Spray to this new space warp.

Tip

Now keep in mind when binding one space warp to another that if your Time Slider is past frame 0, the new space warp will immediately come into play and most likely slow your system down a bit. For this reason, it's a good idea to jump back to a non-calculated frame, such as frame 0, and then bind particles to space warps.

10. Instead of creating a second new SOmniFlect space warp for the second rock in the waterfall, you can clone the previous one. This makes sense because you've

already set common parameters between them. Select the first SOmniFlect and clone it over to the next rock by Shift-dragging. Make sure you choose Copy instead of Instance when cloning. An instance would seem to make sense, but these rocks are of different sizes, and you have to adjust accordingly. You can adjust the icon size in the Radius parameter at the bottom of the SOmniFlect rollout. Do as you did before: Scale it up so that it is close to the size of the rock and don't forget to bind the Super Spray to the new space warp.

Take a look at your animation so far. You should see the particles falling to the water, bouncing off the rocks, and coming to rest on the water before they die away (see Figure 11.12). This is pretty cool, but you can make it more realistic. First off, if you have ever watched a waterfall, you might have noticed that the volume and speed of the water varies slightly. This can be mimicked by alternating the Rate and Speed of particle emission. Another thing you should do is cause the particles to splash on the rocks when they collide. This is accomplished through Spawning, an option in the Super Particle systems for MAX R3. Spawning causes particles to emit more particles upon certain events, in this case collisions.

Figure 11.12   Particles colliding with space warps.

11. Select your Super Spray particle system and go to the Particle Generation rollout. The Use Rate option should already be set by default, and your Speed

should be fairly low. Now right-click on the Super Spray to bring up the
RCMenu. At the bottom of this popup menu, you'll find a handy Track View
Selected option. Select this to open Track View to your selected object and its
parameters. Expand the Super Spray entry by clicking the plus sign next to the
object name. There should be an entry with a blue circle called Object
(SuperSpray). When you expand that entry, it exposes all the parameters within
the Super Spray rollouts. The two parameters you want to work on are Speed
and Birth Rate.

12. First select Speed. By default, it uses a Bezier Float controller to define the value.
You're going to modify this a bit by causing it to use a random value between 0
and 3. To do this, click the Assign Controller button and choose Noise Float from
the list. Then right-click on Speed and choose Properties from the popup menu.
This will bring up the controls for the Noise Float controller. First set the
Strength to 3 and check the >0 check box. This prevents the random value that's
generated from ever dropping below zero. Next, change the Frequency value to a
lower amount, say 0.05. Notice that the spline in the Characteristic graph
changes accordingly. You can also see the changes by viewing the Speed track
with function curves in Track View.

Tip

MAX offers a very handy tool pair called Hold/Fetch. They work together to allow you to temporarily back up or restore your scene without actually saving the files. Whenever you activate
Hold from the Edit menu at the top of the MAX interface, a copy of your current scene and settings is copied to the AutoBack directory. From then on, you can continue to work, but if you want
to restore your scene, you can use the Fetch command. This will return your scene to the state it
was in when Hold was last activated. This comes in handy in situations when you're experimenting a
bit and you might want to return to the original state of the scene. It's often a good idea to do a
Hold on a scene before you perform a risky task in MAX. You need to be careful of one thing
though: Hold is instantaneous. You are not prompted with "Are you sure you want to hold?" and
you can't "Un-Hold" your scene.

13. A similar effect needs to be applied to the Rate parameter. The idea is to take a
set value and add some randomness to it. If Rated had a Variation value, that
would suffice. However, it doesn't, so you need to make one with a Float List.
Start by selecting the Super Spray's Birth Rate track in Track View and assigning
a new controller with the Assign Controller button. By default, it uses a Bezier
Float controller. Now change this to a Float List controller. Doing so removes the
Bezier controller and adds an Available slot. List controllers are incredibly powerful because they allow you to combine several controllers to determine a value.

14. Now select the Available slot and assign a Bezier controller. This essentially puts you back to square one with a Bezier controller in the Birth Rate track and a non-keyframed value of 0. But notice that the Available slot is still there, just beneath the Bezier controller (see Figure 11.13). This means you can add another controller to the Float List.

Figure 11.13
A Float List controller lets you stack several controllers together to define one value.

15. Before you go adding new controllers, you need to set the value of the Bezier controller with a key. Use the Create Key button to create a key at frame 0 in the Bezier controller's track. Set the value to 100. This defines the initial Birth Rate of the particle system to 100 particles per frame.

16. In the Available slot, assign a Noise Float just like you did before in the Speed track. Then right-click on the Noise Float to open the Properties dialog box. First, change the Seed value to anything other than the Seed value in the Speed track. This will keep the randomness random among the two tracks; otherwise, they will use the same patterns. You can still set the Frequency to 0.05 just like Speed, but change the Strength to a high setting like 300, leaving the >0 option unchecked (see Figure 11.14). You do this because you want the randomness to both add and possibly take away from the initial base value of 100 in the Bezier Float.

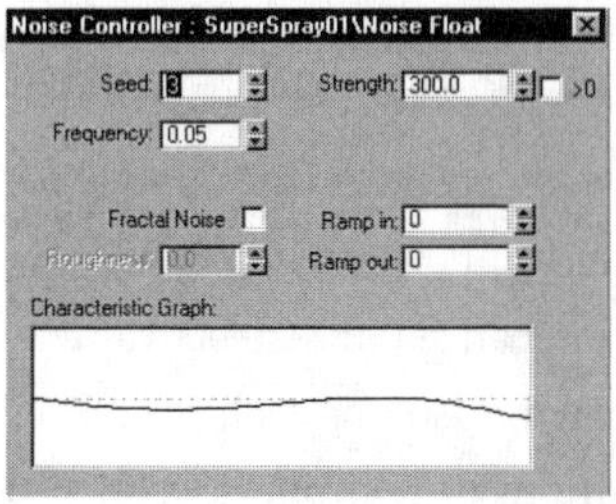

Figure 11.14   Noise controller properties.

Having done that, take a look at your animation. You may have to lower the Percentage of Particles in the Viewport display so your system doesn't bog down too much. The result of this latest step should be a pulsing waterfall with a more realistic velocity and volume. Next you'll set up particle spawning.

There are several different ways to spawn particles. First there's None, which will not spawn any particles. Die After Collision causes particles, regardless of their age, to die after colliding with a deflector (a persist value is optional). Spawn on

Death will cause particles to spawn or emit other particles when the initial particle dies. Spawn Trails causes particles to leave trails of spawned particles (this is good for fireworks). Spawn on Collision causes the particles that collide with the space warps to spawn more particles, like splashes in the real world.

17. Go to the Particle Spawn rollout near the bottom of the Super Spray parameters. Choose Spawn on Collision from the list. Set the Spawns to 3. This will cause three particles to be spawned for every particle that collides with a bound space warp. Where you see Variation, add a little. Direction, Speed Chaos, and Scale Chaos should be treated the same way. Direction Chaos adds randomness to the direction at which particles are spawned; Speed and Scale Chaos do the same for spawned speed and scale, respectively. Finally, set these spawned particles to have a shorter lifetime than the original waterfall particles. Basically, they can splash all they want, but you don't want an uncontrollable amount of leftover particles in the scene just waiting to die. You do this by choosing a life value in the Lifespan parameter of the Lifespan Value Queue. A number between 15 and 30 should be fine. After you enter a number, click the Add button to add it to the queue. You can add several values in the queue, and as particles are spawned over and over, the lifespans will cycle through the queue.

Note

Below the Lifespan Value Queue is an Object Mutation Queue that works almost identically. However, it causes the particles to mutate from one object to another. This allows you to do things like have snowflakes spawn teapots and spheres.

If you decide that your spawns are getting a bit out of control but you don't want to change the amount of particles in your scene, you have two options. First, in the Particle Spawn rollout for Super Spray, you can set an Affects value. This is a percentage of particles available that will spawn. Also, for each of the OmniFlectors, a Spawns parameter appears at the bottom of the rollout. This too is a percentage. This is often preferred because it gives you more control, such as causing one tiny round rock to spawn fewer particles than a large jagged one.

Now the animation of the waterfall is complete. The last couple things you'll have to take care of are the size and type of particles used and a texture for them. This, of course, was all completely irrelevant during the animation creation process. These are things that you have to render your scene to evaluate, so go ahead and render once.

What type of particles should you use? You might think that metaparticles would make sense for mimicking water, but this isn't always the case. First off, they have much higher overhead than standard particles and require many more particles to make the effect look realistic. For the waterfall, you're dealing with highly disturbed water, which tends to look white and foamy. To accomplish this, you'll use a mapping technique that's almost identical to what you did before in the cigarette smoke tutorial.

18. Set the Particle Type to Facing to create 2D polygonal faces. The Size, of course, is going to depend on the scale of your scene. In the Particle Size rollout, set Size to 5 and Variation to 7. You'll also turn the Grow For setting to 0 and the Fade For to somewhere between 10 and 30 frames. This way, particles won't just up and disappear when they die; instead, they'll shrink to nothing.

19. Now for the texture. Start with a Standard Material and set the Ambient color to a medium shade of blue. This will help add a tint of blue to the water. Also set the Diffuse color to white to simulate the whiteness of raging water. There should also be a medium amount of Specularity and Glossiness in the material, although it will be hardly noticeable in this situation. Before you go any farther, make sure Face Map is checked at the top of the Material rollout; otherwise, your maps won't work properly.

20. Now assign a Gradient Map to the Opacity channel. Set the Gradient Type to Radial and change the middle color to a medium shade of blue. It's often a good rule of thumb to bring down the saturation of colors in a nature scene, so try not to make the blue too rich and saturated. We also need to help illuminate this water material, so simply drag the new Gradient map from the Opacity channel to the Self-Illumination channel. Choose Instance from the resulting popup menu. This will force any changes you make in one channel to affect the other.

Now render away or play waterfall.mov to see the results. Everything should really come together now. You've got a variable stream of water particles falling toward the water, splashing on the rocks below. The only thing left is to be sure to motion blur the particles. This is best achieved by enabling and cranking up the Image Motion Blur property from about 3 to 5 on the Super Spray (see Figure 11.15).

Now that you've completed this exercise, here are some things to consider when creating large water flows and interacting with deflectors:

• Sometimes you can get away with using fewer large particles than vast numbers of small particles. This is advantageous because it will save you both calculation and render time. However, when the particles are the center of focus and are easily discernable, it may be necessary to use more small particles to achieve a realistic look in both motion and shading.

Figure 11.15   Completed waterfall scene.

- Remember that all particles in a scene need to be calculated, regardless of the percentage displayed. The main reason for lowering the amount of particles displayed in the viewports is to speed up redraws and reduce clutter in your scene. If your particles are bound to deflector space warps, all particles in the system need to be checked for collisions, even particles that aren't being displayed. The only way to reduce the overhead of space warp collisions is to reduce the amount of particles being checked. A good way to do this is just to temporarily reduce your particle count.

- Be careful not to bind space warps redundantly. This causes the space warp interaction to be calculated multiple times and is basically the same as cloning and binding. Every time you bind a space warp, that binding shows up in a generic modifier stack entry. You can rename these by going into the Stack Editor.

- Although in many cases cleverly mapped 2D facing particles will suffice, sometimes it's necessary to add more 3D detail. In those cases, Sphere particles or Metaparticles can help. Both will generate much more geometry than facings and are slower to calculate and render, but they will catch shadows and highlights much better.

- Noise controllers and Variation are your friends. Use these to break up the uniformity of particle motion in your scene. This will always give you more realistic results when you're mimicking fluid dynamics.

Creating a Flock of Birds

You've seen how particles systems can be used to create natural phenomena such as water and smoke. Now you'll see how particles can be used to define the motion of several objects procedurally. This is much faster and easier than keyframing each object one at a time. The procedural method is also non-destructive, allowing you more freedom for defining entire blocks of motion. In this exercise, you will be using animated instanced geometry and a Path Follow space warp to create a flock of birds.

1. Load the particletut-birds.max file from the CD-ROM. This example file contains a simple bird mesh with animated wings and a Line spline to guide them. What you want to do is create particle motion along the path and then replace each particle with an instance of the animated bird.

2. Create a PArray particle system in the Perspective viewport. PArray always needs a mesh object for an emitter, so you need to create one for it.

3. In the Front viewport, create a rectangle spline. It doesn't need to be very big, 25 Length and 50 Width is sufficient. Now go to the Modifier panel and add a Mesh Select modifier. This will convert the rectangle to a planar mesh. The reason for doing this instead of just converting the rectangle to a mesh is flexibility. You may want to go back to the rectangle's parameters and adjust the Length and Width values.

4. Now look at the Line spline in the scene. This is the path along which you're going to send particles. You can edit this spline if you'd like, or you can even create your own path. The only restriction is that it's got to be an open shape, no closed splines. You need to line up the emitter with the path, so select the rectangle and move it so that it's perpendicular to the start of the path. Basically, it should look like the path is shooting out of the rectangle (see Figure 11.16).

5. One thing you may have noticed, especially in shaded view, is that when you modified the rectangle into a mesh, geometry appeared on only one side. This is important because PArray will emit particles from emitter geometry's normals. You have to orient the rectangle so that the normals face the direction of emission. In doing so, you may notice that as the normals face away from your view,

the shaded geometry disappears. A quick way to correct this is either to set your Viewport Configuration to Force 2-Sided or to use Wireframe.

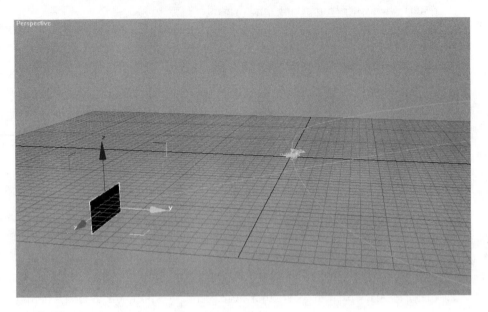

Figure 11.16   Orient the rectangle to the spline.

6. Select the PArray and assign the rectangle as the Object-Based Emitter. It may be difficult to select the rectangle in the Perspective viewport because the Select cursor ignores objects with normals facing away. The workaround here is to select it either from the top view or by using the Selection dialog box's H hot key.

Okay, if you play the animation at this point, you'll just see particles emitted from the rectangle with default PArray settings. Make sure they are at least going in generally the right direction; if they are emitting opposite of the Line spline, you should rotate the rectangle 180 degrees. If you're not seeing particles when you play, another reason may be because your PArray icon isn't visible in the active viewport. This isn't always necessary, but if you have this problem, be sure to move the icon into view by the first frame. Now let's set up the PArray parameters for the scene.

7. At the top of the PArray rollout, the Particle Formation to Over Entire Surface is already set so particles will be emitted from all portions of the rectangle. You are going to be using very few particles, so you can bring the Percentage of Particles up from the default value to 100%.

8. In the Particle Generation rollout, set Particle Quantity to Use Total 10. This will cause PArray to emit a maximum of 10 particles for the duration of emission. Define the duration of emission by setting Emit Start to 0 and Emit Stop to 50. Also set Display Until and Life to 300, the duration of the animation. This way the particles will remain throughout and won't die. You don't want to kill any birds!

    Play the animation. You should have a 50 frame burst of 10 particles that remain alive for the entire animation. Now you need to wrangle them with a Path Follow space warp.

9. You'll find the Path Follow space warp hiding with the deflectors in the Particles Only rollout of Space Warps. Create one anywhere in your scene; location is irrelevant.

10. Take a look at the Path Follow rollout in the Modifier panel. Click the Pick Shape Object button, and then select the Line spline in the perspective viewport to be the path. In the Current Path group, "Object: Line01" appears. Be sure the Unlimited Range check box is checked, otherwise the effect will be localized and not global. Bind the PArray to the Path Follow space warp before going further.

    If you play the animation at this point, you should see that the particles are starting to follow the spline path. At first they are going to be a little crazy because you're using the default settings in Path Follow. Let's make some changes.

11. Scroll down to the bottom of the Path Follow rollout to the Motion Timing group. Start Frame should be left at 0 so the space warp takes immediate effect, and Last Frame should be set to 300, the length of the animation. These parameters can effectively "turn on or off" a Path Follow effect. Travel Time is one of the most important parameters to this space warp because it will override the Speed setting in your particle system. Start adjusting it to a much larger number. You'll notice that it determines how many frames it takes the bound particles to travel the entire length of the spline path. So ultimately, you'll want to set this to the duration of the animation, or 300. As always, it's good to take advantage of Variation to add some randomness when available.

12. Now take a look at the Particle Motion parameters in Path Follow. There are two options for sending particles along a path: Along Offset Splines and Along Parallel Splines. Along Offset Splines will cause the particles to follow the path closely, using any difference in emitter distance to offset the motion, whereas Along Parallel Splines will always follow the exact shape of the spline relative to the location of the emitter. Basically, it makes a copy of the path and starts it

directly at the emitter. It's sometimes confusing, so in this case, try experimenting with both. Switch between the two methods and move the emitter around.

So now that you have the particle motion down, it's time to move on to the
instanced geometry.

13. Go back to the PArray parameters and choose Instanced Geometry from the
    Particle Types group. Scroll down a bit to the Instancing Parameters and use the
    Pick Object Button to select the bird mesh. Press the H key and choose bird-
    body from the list. If you insist on picking in the viewport, be sure to select bird-
    body, not the wings. By default, this will bring in only the selected object,
    regardless of a hierarchy. To instance the hierarchy as well, check the Use Subtree
    Also check box.

14. Now go back to the top of the PArray rollout and set the Viewport Display
    to Mesh. This will let you see animated birds instead of ticks or dots (see
    Figure 11.17).

Figure 11.17   Setting the display type to Mesh allows you to see each instanced geometry.

When you can see the animated birds, you'll notice a couple problems. First, they
all flap their wings in unison. Second, they are all pointing the wrong way. In
addition, they aren't pointing along the path, but are facing one direction
throughout. And they intersect. You can correct the first problem using the
Animation Offset Keying options in the Instancing Parameters dialog box.

None is default, and as you can see, the wing flapping animation is absolute. Birth will shift this animation to start when a particle is born, thereby offsetting the animation more realistically. There is a problem though. What if more than one particle is born on a given frame? Random fixes this by setting a random offset to the animation, based on a given value.

15. Back at the Instancing Parameters, use the Random option for Animation Offset Keying and set the Frame Offset to a value greater than 5.

16. The birds are oriented incorrectly because the particles are oriented to the World coordinates. Also, by default, PArray rotations are set to Random. To resolve this, go down to the Rotation and Collision rollout. Set the Spin Axis Controls to Direction of Travel/Mblur. Ignore the Stretch value unless you want surreal birds.

    That's only the first step. The birds may be turning properly, but they are still oriented wrong. The quickest way to fix this is to rotate the bird model so it points upward as though it is flying through the World Z axis. You can do this in a viewport and see the result on the particles in realtime.

Now your scene is complete. For a final look at the scene rendered, take a look at flock-ofbirds.mov on the CD-ROM.

You need to consider the following things when using particle systems to procedurally animate groups of objects:

- When using particles with Instanced Geometry, keep in mind that particle motion is applied to geometry based on pivot points. Just like copying motion from a box to a sphere, the animation is distributed via pivot points. This is why you have to be sure your pivot points are set correctly, otherwise the motion will not look correct.

- Because particle motion is applied to pivot points, it's important to remember that particle collisions may not translate properly to instanced geometry, or even standard particle geometry for that matter. When a particle collides with a space warp, the collision occurs at the pivot point, not the boundary of the mesh. This is why it's often a good idea to place deflectors slightly above geometry.

- Even though you are using particles for creating the motion of several objects, this doesn't mean you're going with Ticks and Dots for viewport display. Don't forget to use the Mesh option to show your instanced geometry in the viewports. On the flipside, if your scene is really intense and displaying the instanced geometry is overbearing on your system performance, you can always choose to display Ticks, Dots, or (optimally) Bounding Boxes.

Creating Dust Trails with Expressions

You can also use expressions to control the emission of particles. Consider the scene for the next exercise: A UFO object flies in and wobbles over a desert ground plane. You want to add some dust particles that will be kicked up as the UFO gets close to the ground surface. Normally in a situation like this, you'd have to keyframe the position and amount of particles emitted to match the movement of the UFO object, but instead we are going to save some time and add flexibility by using expressions to automate this process.

1. Load the particletut-dust.max file.

2. Create a PArray particle system in your scene. You need to emit particles radially from an object on the ground. Remember, PArray uses object normals to emit particles, so you'll use a cylinder to emit particles from its sides. Go to frame 0 and, in the Top viewport, create a Cylinder primitive that is lined up directly under the UFO object on the ground plane. Make the Radius about half of the UFO's radius (about 8 units). The cylinder doesn't have to be tall either. A Height of 1 is fine. You don't want this object to render with the scene, so right-click on it to open the Properties dialog box and clear the Renderable check box.

3. Select the PArray. In the Basic Parameters rollout in the Object-Based Emitter group, click Pick Object, and then click on the cylinder in the viewport. This assigns the cylinder as the emitter. Notice that when you play the animation, particles are emitted through the top and bottom. You need to delete those vertices as well.

4. Add an Edit Mesh modifier to the cylinder primitive. Go to the Sub-Object/Face level and delete the top and bottom faces. If you are having trouble selecting only those faces, make sure your selection method is set to Window and not Crossing. All that should remain is the outer radial faces for particles to emit from (see Figure 11.18).

    Now if you look at the animation, you'll see a moving UFO and a stationary emitter. There are several ways you can make the emitter move with the UFO but remain on the ground plane. The easiest is linking.

5. Still at frame 0, link the cylinder to the UFO object. In the Hierarchy/Link Info dialog box for the cylinder, turn off Inherit Move Z and Rotate X Y Z. This will cause the cylinder to be linked to the UFO's movement only in the x- and y-axis. As the UFO approaches the ground plane, the emitter won't rotate or disappear along the z-axis.

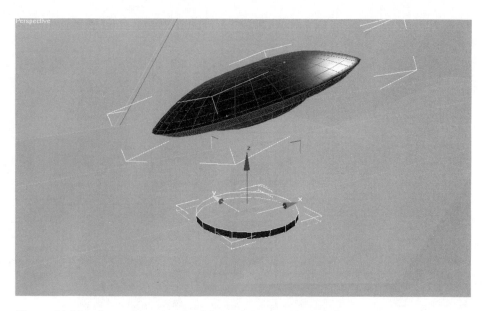

Figure 11.18   Create the emitter by deleting the top and bottom faces of a cylinder.

6. Click the Select icon, and then select the Parrray. In the Modify Panel, in the Particle Generation rollout, go to Particle Motion and set the Speed to 1 for now, and then add some Variation and Divergence to break up the uniformity of the emission. Next, set up the Particle Timing according to the scene. Emit Start should be your first frame (frame 0), and Emit Stop should be your last frame (frame 150). Display Until should be set to the last frame of the animation so the particles don't all disappear suddenly. This should create the appearance of dust being kicked up and fading away quickly, so set the Life to no longer than 30 frames.

Play the animation. A steady stream of particles should be radially emitted from just below the UFO at all times (see Figure 11.19). The trick now is to use a simple expression to control the rate at which particles are emitted. Again, there are several different ways to do this—even several different expression-based ways. But basically, you'll tell MAX to emit more particles as the UFO gets closer to the ground plane and fewer particles as it rises high above it.

7. With the PArray selected, right-click and choose Track View Selected. This will automatically bring up Track View, with PArray already selected and its parameters isolated. Expand the Object track to expose all of PArray's parameters. Select the Birth Rate track and assign a Float expression. Then, right-click on the Birth Rate track and select the expression Properties. This will bring up the Expression

Editor for that track. Simple expressions aren't too difficult—in fact, they are just that: simple. So don't be intimidated.

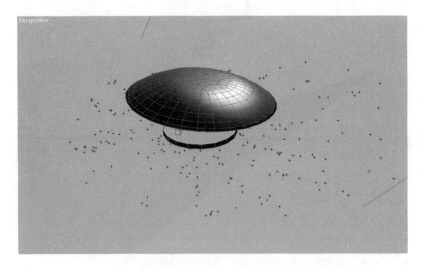

Figure 11.19   Particles radially emitted from the cylinder emitter.

8. First you need to define the UFO's position as a Vector variable. It is a vector variable because you are dealing with an array of three numbers (x, y, and z) and not a single value. Select the Vector radio button and, in the Create Variables/Name field, type **UFO** to define the UFO variable. Click Create, and you'll notice that the new variable is added to a list of vectors (see Figure 11.20). Select that vector variable from the list and click the Assign to Controller button to tell MAX that this variable relates to the position track of the UFO. In the resulting Track View Pick dialog box, select the UFO's Position track (see Figure 11.21).

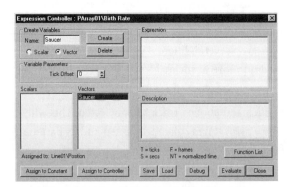

Figure 11.20   Create a vector variable in the Expression Editor.

Figure 11.21   Assign the new variable to the UFO's Position track.

9. Enter 50–UFO1.z in the Expression Editor's Expression window. This expression is for the Birth Rate track and generates a value that is determined by 50 particles per frame minus the UFO's Z position. The Z position will decrease as it approaches the ground plane, which resides at 0 on the z-axis.

10. This expression doesn't take effect immediately. Click the Evaluate button for MAX to process the expression and feed it into your animation.

11. Without leaving the Expression Editor, take a look at the animation up to this point so you can see that this effect is basically starting to work. Change your expression to 100–(UFO.z*10) so that it will reach 0 on the z-axis more quickly. The new expression tells MAX to use a Rate of 100 particles minus the product of the UFO's Z position multiplied by 10.

12. Evaluate the expression and play the animation. You'll see a much more pronounced effect.

13. The last thing you need to do is texture the particles. In the Material Editor, assign the Dust material to the particles.

Now that your scene is complete, try some different ideas with expression controls on particles. It's not too difficult to apply the same ideas to particle velocity or size. In general though, you should consider these things when using expressions to automate particle parameters:

- Expressions aren't as difficult as they may seem. It can be very intimidating to get started with them at times. One of the easiest approaches to using expressions is to just reference and alter tracks from other objects. For example, you can create a variable that references a sphere's radius track and call it "radius." Then divide this value by two and apply it to a different sphere's radius, causing their values to have a dependent relationship.

- You have to be very careful with your variables. If you mis-spell a variable, it will cause an error in the evaluation of the expression.

- If you want to monitor a value generated by an expression, use the Debug button in the Expression Editor. This dialog box will always update, showing you exactly what's going on with the expression.

Object Detonation with PArray

In past versions of MAX, the only way to conceivably "blow up" an object was with the Bomb space warp. This was fine for some situations, but what if you wanted the fragments to interact with your scene by deflecting off other objects or one another? MAX R2 added PArray, a special particle system that uses objects for emitters, but that has the unique ability to fragment the emitter geometry and apply particle motion to them. In this final exercise, you'll use the object fragments controls in PArray to explode an object into chunks that interact with a scene.

Figure 11.22
The Object Fragment parameters.

1. Load the particletut-explode.max file. This is a 150-frame animation of an aircraft crashing into the ground. You're going to use a PArray particle system to fragment the aircraft's geometry and blow it apart, letting the pieces behave dynamically.

2. Create a PArray anywhere in the scene. Assign the aircraft as the object-based emitter. Set the Viewport Display to Mesh so you can see the fragments you're going to generate.

3. Scroll down to the Particle Type rollout and set the Type to Object Fragments (see Figure 11.22). This is a unique feature of PArray. Just below this, you'll see the Object Fragment controls. Leave the Thickness at 1, but set the Number of Chunks to 200. This essentially creates 200 fragments.

Note

Scroll back up and you'll notice that a lot of the PArray parameters have been grayed out. When you use Object Fragments, parameters such as Percentage of Particles, Rate, and Emit Stop become irrelevant.

4. Set the Emit Start to 50 so the particles will start appearing when the aircraft starts to crash. Don't forget to set Display Until to match your scene's length. Also you want to set the Life value to 150 so fragments don't die.

Play the animation. At frame 50, you should see what looks like a second copy of the aircraft geometry form a fragment array (see Figure 11.23). The original geometry remains though. You need to hide this geometry on the same frame where particles are emitted.

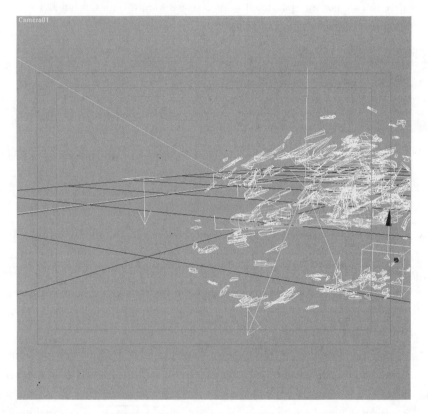

Figure 11.23   PArray breaks up the emitter object into fragments and applies particle motion to them.

5. Select the aircraft object and right-click to get to Track View Selected. Select the Aircraft object track, and you'll notice an eye-shaped button appear on the Track View toolbar. If you don't see this, make sure you're in Edit Keys mode and not Function Curves mode. The eye-shaped button is the Add Visiblity Track button, which lets you create a special track that controls the visibility of an object. Click this button and select the resulting visibility track. By default, it's assigned a

Bezier controller and a value of 1.0 or 100% visible. You can simplify animating this track by assigning an On/Off controller, which you'll find in the Assign Controller dialog box. Notice that when you add this controller, a long blue bar appears in the track. All sections along the Track View timeline that are blue indicate that the object is visible. Whenever you add a key, it switches between visible and invisible. So just add a single key at frame 50. Using an On/Off controller is very advantageous when you need stepped values that change immediately and are not interpolated. In this case, we want the aircraft object to completely disappear at frame 50 with no in-between values.

Note

In 3D Studio MAX R3, the Visibility value has been extended to the Object Properties panel in the Render Controls group. Visibility is displayed here as a value with a spinner. This can be tricky to animate with, often requiring using Track View. In addition, you can't assign controllers from this location. However, it is a very quick and easy way to make adjustments to an existing track.

So you now have an aircraft object that disappears and emits fragments in all directions. What you need to do is set up some space warps to influence the fragments. Remember that, although the fragments are geometry, their motion is still defined by particles.

6. Create a Gravity space warp anywhere in the scene and bind the PArray to it. Make sure it's planar and points downward in the scene. Bring the Strength down a bit, to about 0.3, so the particles don't rush downward. Strength is one of the most important factors to consider when you're setting the scale of a scene. You may be animating a mile-long spaceship, but if the particles move swiftly, it will look like an inch-long model shot at regular speed.

7. As you may have noticed, the fragments are disappearing through the ground plane. You can resolve this by laying a deflector over the ground plane (see Figure 11.24). Instead of using the generic Deflector space warp, try the more powerful POmniFlect. To create that effect, click-drag over a good portion of the ground plane. It doesn't have to completely cover it, but it should cover at least the area in which the aircraft crashes. Don't forget to bind the PArray to this new space warp.

8. In the POmniFlect parameters, set Time On and Time Off to 0 and 150, respectively. This turns on the space warp throughout the duration of the animation. Next, decrease the Bounce value to 0.5 so the fragments don't bounce with full velocity. As usual, be sure to add some Variation to give randomness to the bounce velocity, and add some Chaos to give randomness to the bounce angle.

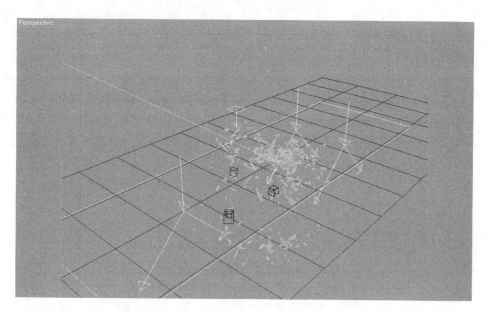

Figure 11.24 A POmniFlect space warp is added to scene.

Now the animation is in good shape. The aircraft geometry disappears at the same time PArray generates fragments. These fragments explode outward, fall to the ground, and bounce when they hit. However, there are still a few problems. First off, the fragments don't rotate. Also, you can see that the fragments' velocity is the same as that of the crashing aircraft. This is caused by the Object Motion Inheritance default setting of 100%; 100% of the emitter object's velocity is passed on to the particles. A simple way to visualize this is to imagine a comet that's trailing particles. With Object Motion Inheritance set to 100%, the particles would never trail behind the emitter because they are essentially going the same speed. Inversely, if the value is set to 0% the particles will trail behind the emitter with only their emission velocity.

9. Go back to the PArray and take a look at the Object Motion Inheritance rollout. You could set the Influence to a lower percentage, thereby limiting the amount of particles that are affected by the motion inheritance, or you could decrease the Multiplier setting and, thereby, the strength of motion inheritance. Try the latter—changing the Multiplier to 0.75 and adding 25% Variation to mix things up a bit.

10. Lastly, set up some rotation. Scroll down to the Rotation and Collision rollout and set the Spin Axis Controls to Random. When using Object Fragments, your

rotation options are limited to Random and User Defined. Set the Spin Time to 60 and add some Variation. This will determine how many frames it takes for a fragment to complete a 360-degree rotation.

The animation is complete now. Here are some things to consider when working with object fragments and space warps:

- Keep in mind that when you fragment an object, the fragments are not separate objects per se, but that they remain PArray geometry with particle motion. This is why you can't use these fragments in a dynamics simulation and have them bounce realistically.
- Fragments collide with space warps using their pivots only, not their actual geometry. This can cause geometry intersection problems.
- Rotating fragments will continue to rotate, regardless of the position velocity.

Third-Party Particle Tools

Several third-party particle plug-ins can correct the problem of continually rotating fragments by dynamically dealing with object fragments or allowing the rotation to be dependent on particle velocity. The following sections describe some of the available plug-ins.

Particle Studio

Written by Oleg Bayborodin (Orbaz Technologies) exclusively for Digimation, Particle Studio is the evolution of the popular SandBlaster plug-in. This next-generation particle system uses a unique approach to manipulating particle motion via targets. You can specify groups of geometry and have particles move to and from them, even disassembling and reassembling the target geometry. Particle Studio takes this paradigm farther by arranging the workflow by events in an Event Map. This gives you complete control over when events such as emission or fragmentation take place, whether it's at absolute time, relative time, or particle age.

Matterwaves

A commercial plug-in from Cebas Computer, Matterwaves gives particles very advanced, map-based controls over emission of particles. You can use textures to define where, how many, and how fast particles are emitted from an object. Some of the unique features in Matterwaves include particle-to-particle collisions, particle instancing, and advanced fragmentary dynamics.

RealFlow

Developed by the Spanish group Next Limit, RealFlow is a full-blown, standalone fluid dynamics simulator with hooks to import particles and procedurally generated geometry into 3D packages such as 3D Studio MAX R3. RealFlow can not only mimic fluids, but very realistically simulate gases, liquids, slimy viscous fluids, and even elastics. It has very precise real-world controls, such as Density, Mass, Elasticity, Damping, and Viscosity, for fluids and the scene objects they interact with. A vast list of powerful forces are available, allowing you to constrain particle motion to simple attractors and vortex fields or even complex gravitational splines.

Particles Plus

Peter Watje, a developer at Discreet, has written a list of freeware plug-ins available to MAX users. The most useful particle plug-in is Particles Plus. This is an extension of the old Spray particle system from MAX R1, but with many enhancements. It includes several different emitter variations, including radial and spherical emitters, as well as particle types beyond the standard facing and tetrahedron. Particles Plus has excellent sampling controls to avoid the pulsing that's common with high-velocity emitters. Peter's also added a looping particle cycle for game developers.

Rigid Body Dynamics Simulations

It is often very difficult and time consuming to animate complex dynamic motion with traditional keyframe techniques. For example, animating a pair of thrown dice spinning and bouncing on a craps table can be a somewhat daunting task with traditional keyframe methods. A quicker, more accurate, and realistic method is to use rigid-body dynamics simulations to "generate" the animation based on physical models. A tool such as MAX's Dynamics Utility can be used to give objects the properties of real-world objects, such as density, mass, and friction. These properties are then used to calculate the physical interaction of the objects. Rigid objects deflect off of other objects with a varying degree of power, depending on their mass and bounce coefficient. Objects can be affected by such forces as gravity and wind, allowing them to realistically fall or blow away.

The drawbacks to this simulation method are speed and lack of control. Dynamics simulations require lots of computer horsepower, often akin to raytracing. Every object goes through a question and answer session with the simulation, which can be very time consuming depending on the complexity of your scene. More often than not, the Q&A session is required to increase the sample rate to avoid simulation errors, which increases overall processing time. You also don't have the same kind of hands-on forced method of animating like you do with keyframing. Instead, you have to set up the properties of the objects in the scene and let nature take its course. That sounds fine, except that technically correct often isn't aesthetically correct. That's why simulation tools are more popular among artists who require absolute accuracy, such as forensic animators. For all others, it's yet another tool to speed up the process of creating realistic motion.

Dynamics Utility Workflow

In 1997, MAX R2 introduced the Dynamics Utility (see Figure 11.25), and since then, it has seen some improvements. The general workflow for using the Dynamics Utility is to set up your scene to be animated, set the properties of your objects, process the simulation, adjust properties, and then repeat if necessary. Try a simple simulation example.

1. Reset your scene so you have a fresh start. Try a cube that collides with a ground object. Create a box and make it sufficiently large, say Length and Width of 200 units each. You don't have to make it very high; in fact, a Height of 10 is fine in this case. Rename this object Ground.

2. Now create a cube using the box primitive and the cube creation method. Move it along the z-axis so that it's above the ground object at least 50 units. Now slightly rotate it on its x-axis so it won't land so evenly below.

3. You now have two objects that will collide. You need to add an essential force to the scene: gravity. Create a Gravity space warp with the planar force pointing downward along the z-axis (see Figure 11.26).

4. To create a dynamics simulation, go to the Utility panel and select Dynamics. First off, you have to define a new simulation by clicking the New button. This lets you store several different simulations in the same scene.

5. In the Objects in Simulation group, click the Edit Object List button. This will bring up a selection dialog box separated into two fields: available objects in the scene on the left and objects assigned to the simulation on the right.

Figure 11.25
The Dynamics utility.

Select both the Ground and Cube objects and click the greater-than arrow (>) to assign them to the simulation.

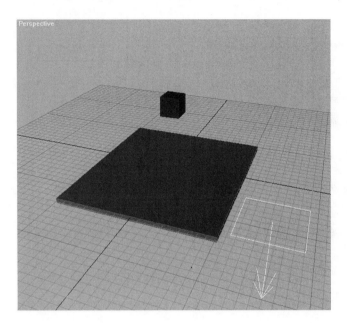

Figure 11.26   Two objects that will collide in a dynamics simulation.

6. In the Effects group, select the Global Effects radio button and click the Assign Global Effects button to bring up a selection dialog box in which you can assign forces that will affect all objects equally. Assign the Gravity space warp to this list.

7. Down further, you'll see the Collisions group. This is just like the Global Effects group, but it allows you to assign objects to global collisions. Assign both objects to this list.

8. Now you can give this simulation a first pass. In the Solve group, check Update Display w/Solve so you can see the simulation in progress. Click the Solve button.

   This will begin the calculation process. What you should notice is that both objects fall because they are both assigned gravity via Global Effects. You need to tell the ground object that it is unyielding to forces and doesn't move at all. Press Escape to stop the simulation.

9. Use the Edit Object button to access the all-important Edit Objects dialog box (see Figure 11.27). In the upper-left corner, you'll notice a drop-down box with a list of all objects assigned to the simulation. Right now, both the ground object and the cube have identical properties. But by selecting an object from this list,

you can update its properties. Select the ground object and, under Dynamic Controls, check This Object Is Unyielding to tell the simulation that the ground object can't move.

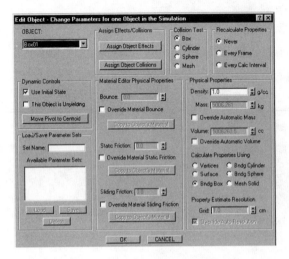

Figure 11.27   The Edit Objects dialog box.

10. The next step is very important: Select the ground object and delete the keys that were generated in the last pass. You can select them in the Track bar and then press Delete. Normally, the Dynamics Utility erases the previous simulation when you run it a second time. However, sometimes the keys remain in the initial state, and the simulation won't run properly.

11. Click the Solve button to run the simulation again. This time the ground object should remain in place, and the cube should bounce and eventually come to a stop.

That's a simple Dynamics exercise. You can vary the rotation and orientation of the cube to get different results when you reprocess the simulation. You can also vastly speed up the simulation if you disable the Update Display w/Solve setting. Try this, and you should see a marked speed improvement. The only problem with this method is that you can't see the simulation in progress and are left to "wait and see."

Using Constrained Hierarchies

The Dynamics Utility will pay attention to objects linked in hierarchies as long as they are set up properly. To properly simulate a hinged joint, you must lock the move and specific rotation axis. Try using hierarchies in the following simulation.

1. Load the dynamics-link.max scene. It contains a simple hierarchy of boxes that you'll use to simulate a hinged set of objects (see Figure 11.28).

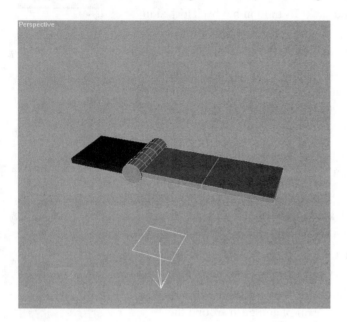

Figure 11.28   Dynamic hierarchies example.

2. Set up the scene in the Dynamics Utility by assigning all the box objects to the simulation. You don't have to worry about the cylinder because it's purely cosmetic and is actually a child of Box01, which will remain still as an anchor. Use the Edit Object button to change the properties of Box01 to an unyielding object.

Note

If an object is going to be motionless, why should it participate in the simulation? All objects in a hierarchy need to be included in the simulation, even if only one object in that hierarchy is going to be participating.

3. Assign Gravity01 to Global Effects. This will apply gravity to all objects in the simulation (not the scene), but Box01 will not be affected because you just set it up as an unyielding object. Go ahead and solve the simulation.

    Something's wrong, isn't it? Box02 and Box03 should have ignored their hierarchies and just fallen into nothingness. This is where you need to constrain their motion and rotation to simulate hinged joints. This is a very simple process that takes only a few moments.

4. First, select Box02, and in the Hierarchy panel's Link Info rollout, check Move X, Y, and Z (see Figure 11.29). Try to move the object. You can't? Its motion has been locked in the space. Now only an outside force such as a collision or parent can move it. You will also notice that this hinge joint should rotate only on a single axis (y-axis). You'll need to lock the x and z rotation to constrain all rotation to the y-axis. Check the X and Z channels in the Rotate group of Link Info. Be sure to do the same for Box03.

5. Run the simulation again. This time, the boxes should swing downward but remain together and constrained like a hinged joint.

   You can simulate all kinds of different joint types by locking motion and rotation channels this way. Now try changing things a bit. Up until now, you've been using global effects, which are very convenient and useful in most cases, but are ultimately limited. Try adding a ball to the simulation and make it bounce off of and push around the hinged objects. In this segment, you'll also experiment with Density and Mass to alter the outcome of a simulation.

Figure 11.29
The Link Info panel.

6. Create a sphere that's no bigger than any of the objects currently in the scene. Move the sphere above Box03 so it will fall and collide with the hinged object. Be sure to add the sphere to the simulation via the Edit Object list.

7. Change Global Effects to Effects by Objects, and then go into the Edit Object dialog box to assign effects. Box01 needs no attention, it's not going anywhere. You will notice that Box02 and Box03 already have Gravity assigned to them in the Assign Object Effects list. This is because you were using the global controls earlier. Remove gravity from their effects list with the arrow buttons.

8. The other thing you need to do with Box02 and Box03 is set up object collisions. This is the button directly below Object Effects, and it works just as it did before. For these two boxes, you need to assign the sphere and the parent box, Box01. You don't need to worry about Box02 and Box03 colliding because they are already linked together and shouldn't collide in the first place.

9. Now choose the Sphere's properties and assign Gravity to its Effects list. All the boxes in the simulation need to be assigned to the Sphere's collision as well.

If you run the simulation, you'll notice that the hinged objects don't move until the sphere collides with them, but when it does, they still move constrained properly. Now what if you want the sphere to be a heavy bowling ball instead of a sponge ball? This is where Density and Mass come into play. The general rule is that in a collision, the object with the highest mass "wins" and stays more on course, whereas the object with a lower mass is pushed off of its trajectory.

10. Back to the Sphere's properties in the Edit Object dialog box. Look at the Physical Properties group on the right. By default, every object is assigned a Density of 1.0, which automatically generates a Mass of 385kg. This can be changed either by adjusting the Density or by using the Override Automatic Mass check box to set the Mass specifically. Try raising the Density to 20g/cc, and then run the simulation again. This time the sphere should push the boxes aside more forcefully.

Other areas to explore here include using the Bounce, Static Friction, and Sliding Friction parameters. By default, these are acquired by properties assigned in the object's materials. However, you can override them in the Physical Properties group. Bounce Coefficient defines how far an object is displaced from its trajectory on collision. For realistic results, you'll want to keep this value below 1.0. Friction is always caused when two objects press against each other, and in the Dynamics Utility, there are two kinds of friction: Static and Sliding Friction. Static Friction defines how easily one object moves along the surface of another. High values make it more difficult for an object at rest to get into motion. Sliding Friction takes over after one object starts moving along the surface of another. Higher numbers cause objects to slide for shorter lengths of time.

Try adjusting these values for the hinged box example by either assigning a material and changing the values there or by overriding them in the Dynamics Utility. Be sure to run the simulation again for the changes to take effect.

Dynamics Objects

New to MAX R3 are dynamics objects. Currently, these include Damper and Spring (see Figure 11.30). Both are parametric objects that can be used in a simulation to affect other objects. Damper applies either a damper or actuator force much like a shock absorber. Spring applies a simple spring force with tension. Both objects can be free floating or can have their extents linked to objects in the scene. In the example of a Damper, you can marry the piston to a tire and the base to the frame of a vehicle, effectively simulating a real shock absorber. Then in a dynamics simulation, when the tire is hit by a force, the damper goes into effect, absorbing a given portion of the force and passing on the rest to the base object.

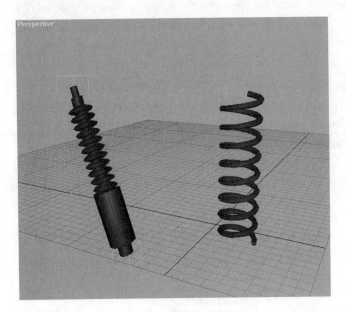

Figure 11.30   Damper and Spring Dynamics Objects. Notice the Damper is bound to the pivot points of two dummy objects and will operate accordingly.

Using Particles in Dynamics Simulations

In the past, it was impossible for particles to participate in a dynamics simulation. For MAX R3, a new set of particle space warps, called DynaFlectors, was added. When these are linked to an object, they can be used to pass the force of particle collision on to the underlying object. With these new space warps, it's possible to use a hose of water to spray boxes around. Give it a try.

1. Load dynamics-particles.max from the CD-ROM. This simple scene has a sphere lying on a flattened box while a Super Spray particle system emits particles all over the box (see Figure 11.31). This scene is partially set up in the Dynamics Utility. If you run the simulation at this point, the particles will have no effect on the simulation.

2. You need to add an SDynaFlect to the sphere. You can find this space warp in the special Dynamics Interface portion of the Space Warps rollout. This is a spherical space warp, but planar and universal versions are also available in the same rollout. Create an SDynaFlect at the sphere's location and make the radius large enough that it envelops the sphere.

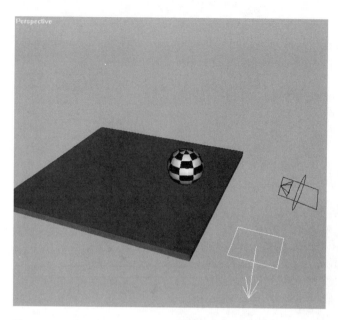

Figure 11.31 Particles can be used in dynamics simulations to push objects.

3. Because the SDynaFlect is a particle space warp and only works with particles, bind the Super Spray to the SDynaFlect. Otherwise, the particles will ignore it.

4. In the SDynaFlect parameters, set the Time Off to match the final frame of the scene, 300 in this case. You want this space warp to be active throughout the animation. Set the Bounce to a more realistic 0.2 so particles will lose velocity on collision. Under Physical Properties, change the Units of Mass to Kg. This will cause the particles to exert more force on the sphere. Although you're dealing with a deflector, think of these parameters as the physical properties of the particles.

5. In the Dynamics Utility, click Edit Object and select Sphere01 from the object list. Then click Assign Object Effects and assign SdynaFlect01 to the included effects list. If you run the simulation at this point, you'll see a big problem. The sphere isn't reacting properly. You need to link the SDynaFlect to the sphere so that any force exerted on the space warp is passed on to the sphere.

Tip

When you link the space warp to the object, make sure they are lined up as closely as possible. It is fast and easy to do this when you use the Snap tool set to pivot point.

If you run the simulation again, you should see the particles push the sphere off the box (see Figure 11.32). For a final tweak, you might want to make adjustments to the space warp's parameters to simulate more powerful water spray.

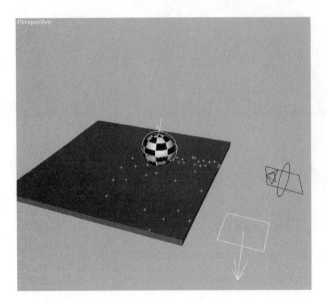

Figure 11.32   Particles bound to a DynaFlect space warp are used to push the sphere off the box in a dynamics simulation.

Some things to think about when running dynamics simulations are

- Global Effects and Collisions can be both a timesaver and a time waster. Don't assign effects or collisions to objects that don't need it. In fact, keep as many objects out of your simulation as possible. Your simulations will process much faster with fewer objects and forces to deal with.

- Don't forget to lock the motion and rotation on object hierarchies when you're simulating rotational constraints such as ball-and-socket joints and hinges.

- When simulating fast moving objects, you might have to increase the Calc Intervals Per Frame. This is essentially a sample rate for the simulation. It will both slow the calculations and allow for more accurate results.

- Sometimes when coplanar surfaces come to rest on one another, they pass through one another (like, for example, a stack of boxes that aren't moving). This is a very difficult problem to solve within the simulation. Because the Dynamics Utility creates a key at every frame, you can delete the keys that aren't needed, such as the keys past the point at which the objects come to rest and stop moving.

In Practice: Particles, Dynamics, and Space Warps

- **Know when to use the correct particle system.** In MAX, not all particle systems are created equal. Each has its particular strengths and weaknesses. The more you recognize this, the easier it gets to employ them correctly.

- **Use the supersampling options to avoid particle pulsing.** The pulsing problem is most common when you have emitters moving very quickly.

- **You don't always have to display every particle in a system.** If your scene starts to bog down, just adjust the Percentage of Particle to a lower amount. MAX will still process the particles, but the display will be much faster because MAX won't have to refresh each particle in the viewports.

- **Wind can be used for more than just a directional force.** Even when the Strength value is set to 0, the Turbulence parameters will still affect particles, assuming these values are greater than 0. This makes it a useful global force field as well.

- **Noise controllers and Variation are the key to making particle motion look more natural.** Most major parameters in MAX particle systems (such as Speed, Rotation, Size, and so on) have a Variation parameter that adds a randomness to the main value. Noise controllers in a Float List can also be used in place of Variation.

- **Several volumetric tools work with particles in MAX.** These volumetric tools are very good for creating dust and gaseous effects. You can, however, cheat and use the facemapping techniques discussed in this chapter to produce similar effects—often with faster results.

- **Dynamics simulations can be processed over a given set of frames, not the entire scene length.** You can always delete any keys you don't need after the simulation is complete.

Chapter 12

Deforming Objects with Space Warps

By Brandon Davis

As you saw in the previous chapter, space warps can be used to alter the motion or behavior of particle systems and add forces to dynamics simulations. They can also distort and deform mesh objects. Just about any object to which you can apply a modifier can be deformed with a space warp. However, you can use only Object Deformation space warps, not Particle/Dynamic or force-specific space warps such as Gravity and Push.

This chapter focuses on deforming objects with space warps, including these particular topics:

- Using space warps to create secondary motion on an object.
- Deforming geometry to conform to target geometry.
- Controlling object deformation within a space warp's area of influence.
- Causing objects to deform other objects without collision detection.

Space Warp Basics

Space warps are different from modifiers in that they work in World space and not Object space. For this reason, space warps affect objects in a scene equally, regardless of their locations. Let's take a quick look at the two different coordinate systems:

- **World space.** This is the universal coordinate system in which all scenes are contained. World space never changes, transforms, nor distorts. It remains constant throughout. The Home grid in your MAX viewports represents World space.
- **Object space.** Every object in your scene has its own unique localized coordinate system centered around the pivot point. Modifiers, mapping, and vertex information are stored in Object space.

A good way to visualize these differences is to look at a Noise map. When a Noise map references Object space, the noise pattern "sticks" to the object as it moves around in World space (see Figure 12.1). However, if the Noise map references World space, it appears to move when the object moves. The reason is that the noise map becomes locked to world space, and the object travels "through" it (see Figure 12.2). Object space-based deformers, such as the Bend Modifier only affect an object relative to its position. No matter where the object is located in the scene, the Bend effect is the same because it references Object space, meaning the object's spatial coordinates. With a World space-based version of Bend, the effect varies depending on the object's location in World space (see Figure 12.3).

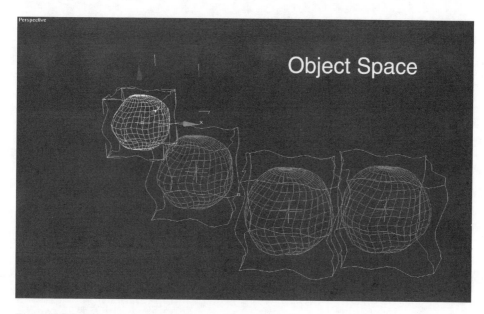

Figure 12.1 Object space-based Noise modifier applied to animated sphere. Notice how the noise deformation is uniform regardless of location.

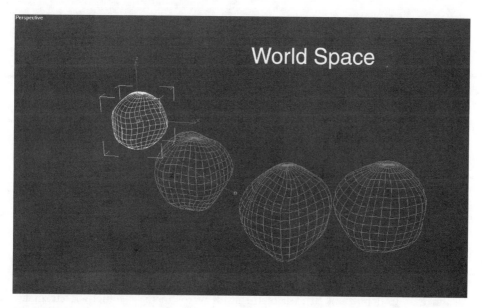

Figure 12.2 A World space-based Noise space warp applied to an animated sphere. Notice this time that the noise deformation changes as the sphere moves through World space.

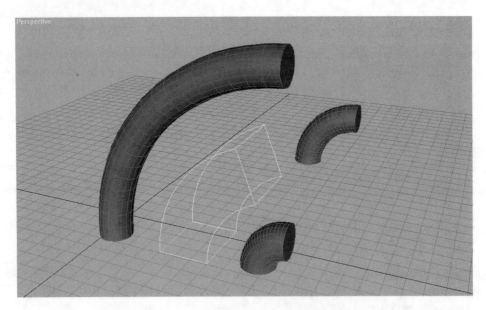

Figure 12.3   Three identical cylinders bound to the same Bend space warp. Because it works in World space, the Bend space warp affects each cylinder differently depending on its location.

Three groups of space warps work with objects: Geometric/Deformable, Modifier-Based, and World Space Modifier. They are described in more detail here.

- **Geometric/Deformable.** These are non-rendering geometric objects that are used to deform mesh objects. Often, these objects have an area of influence and will affect mesh objects only when they enter this boundary.

- **Modifier-based.** These space warps duplicate certain modifiers in MAX such as Bend and Skew. What's different about these is that they work in World space, allowing you to apply their effects across a multitude of bound objects or to move objects through their area of influence.

- **World space modifier.** This is a special object-based space warp. They are linked to the object, but their effects reference World space.

Geometric/Deformable Space Warps

Lets take an in-depth look at each of the space warps in the Geometric/Deformable category.

- **FFD Box.** A free-form deformation lattice based on a box shape, much like the FFD Box modifier. It has a user-defined scale and number of control points. By pushing and pulling control points on the lattice, you can deform a mesh object without touching a single vertex. Because it works off of a volume, you don't have to worry about changing vertex order or surface topology (see Figure 12.4). And because it's a space warp that references World space, you can move objects through the lattice. For example, by setting up the lattice around a keyhole, you can squish a character through the hole.

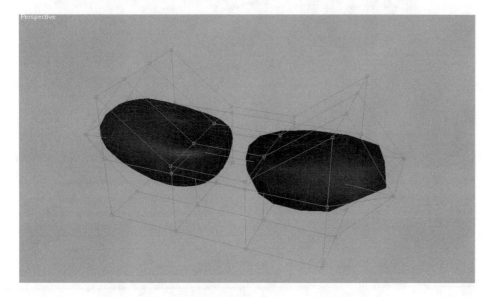

Figure 12.4 Two spheres of differing segments affected by an FFD Box.

- **FFD Cylinder.** Another free-form deformation lattice very much like FFD Box, except that it works off a cylindrical volume with a Radius, Height, and variable number of control points. These FFD space warps are some of the most useful space warps in MAX.

- **Wave.** Generates a sine wave in World space based on a planar object (see Figure 12.5). Often, this space warp is used to create ocean waves and wavy motion of objects, such as fish. By default, the effect is spread across objects uniformly, but this can be localized by adjusting the Decay value in the space warp. Decay causes the effect to taper off over a specified distance.

- **Ripple.** Creates a sine wave in concentric circular patterns instead of the linear patterns of Wave. This is the same ripple pattern you see when you drop a rock into a body of water. The Ripple space warp is nearly identical to the ripple modifier except that it references World space. Its area of influence can be altered with the Decay parameter (see Figure 12.6).

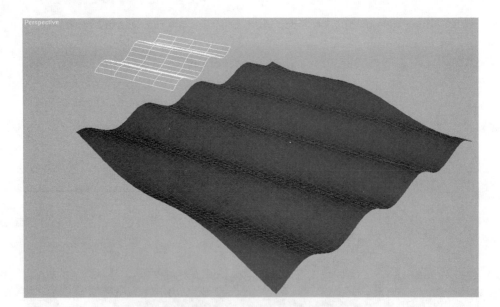

Figure 12.5   A plane primitive bound to Wave space warp.

Figure 12.6   Ripple space warp's amplitude lessened over distance with the Decay parameter.

- **Displace.** Causes mesh object's vertices to be forced in a direction based on a mapping gizmo. The amount of displacement can be controlled with Strength and Decay parameters. What makes this space warp so powerful is that the force can be controlled with an image or map. Areas on the map with lighter colors apply more force, and areas with darker colors apply less force (see Figure 12.7). The Ability to use a map instead of a set bitmap is a very powerful feature that frees you from the burden of adjusting a bitmap in a paint program by letting you use the power of the Materials Editor to mix, mask, and use procedural textures.

Figure 12.7   Two masked maps used to displace a Plane primitive.

- **Conform.** Similar to Displace with the exception that it forces vertices in a planar direction a set distance or until they cover a specified object. This allows you to animate objects moving over the surface of other objects (see Figure 12.8).

- **Bomb.** Applies a spherical explosive force to object faces based on an area of influence with falloff. The faces can be exploded individually or in groups much like the object fragments feature in PArray. Bomb also contains its own gravity controls. When you need to explode objects quickly and easily, Bomb is very handy (see Figure 12.9). However, it doesn't actually change the composition of the mesh object, so you can't have the fragments interact with your scene. When you need the fragments to interact with your scene, use PArray.

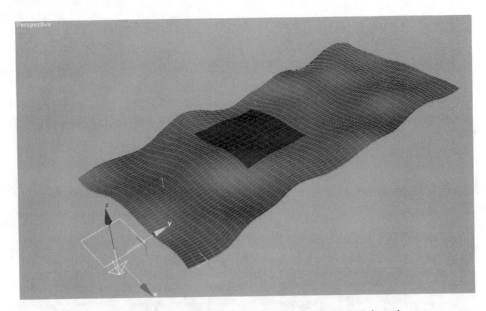

Figure 12.8   A Conform space warp used to project one object on top of another.

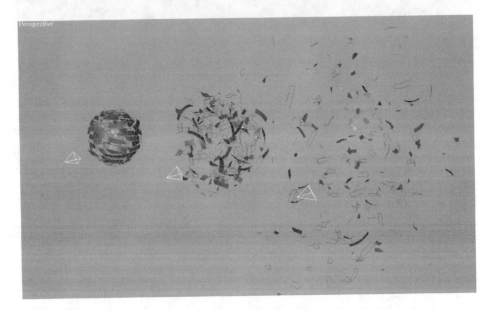

Figure 12.9   Bomb space warps with different detonation times applied to spheres.

Modifier-Based Space Warps

Dozens of modifiers are available in MAX, but only a small handful also exist as Modifier-based space warps. In many ways, these space warps work exactly the same as the modifiers, except that they operate in World space of course. These space warps also add a Decay parameter to localize their effects on objects.

- **Bend.** Bends objects 360 degrees on one axis with directional control. The effect can be limited to specific regions of the object with the Limits parameters. Be sure your object has enough tesselation detail to deform properly (see Figure 12.10).

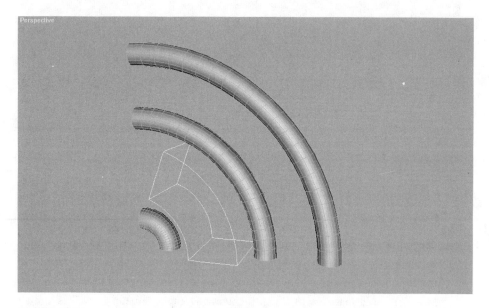

Figure 12.10   Bend space warp applied to three cylinders in different locations.

- **Skew.** Applies a uniform offset to an object's vertices along one axis. Skew gives you parameters to control the amount and direction of the effect. It too has Decay and Limit controls.

- **Twist.** Applies a single-axis rotational or twisting force to an object's vertices. Use the Angle parameter to control the degree of twisting force that is applied. The Bias parameter allows you to compress the twisting effect relative to the gizmo's center/pivot point. You can limit the effect of Twist with the Limits and Decay parameters.

- **Noise.** A very useful space warp that creates a box volume of random noise to displace an object's vertices. The scale and strength of the noise can be non-uniform, allowing you to apply more force in certain directions (see Figure 12.11).

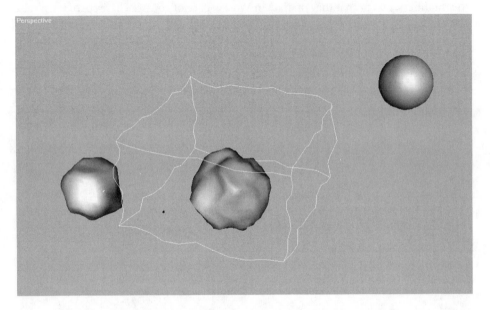

Figure 12.11   Three spheres bound to a Noise space warp. Notice how the effect can be localized to the gizmo by setting the Decay parameter.

- **Taper.** Inversely scales both ends of a mesh object. Its effect is similar to creating a cone from a cylinder by scaling one end down and the other up. You can control the amount of curve between the gizmo's extents along two axes. As with all Modifier-based space warps, Taper includes a Decay parameter, as well as Limit controls for localizing the effect to the extents of the gizmo.

- **Stretch.** Useful for non-uniformly scaling objects while retaining their original volume. This is achieved by scaling along one axis and applying the inverse effect in the other axes. Use this space warp in specific locations in a scene to cause rubbery objects to squash and stretch as they reach the space warp gizmos.

World Space Modifiers

A few new World Space modifiers (WSMs) were added in 3D Studio MAX R3. World Space modifiers are space warps that are carried by the object they are bound to. For this reason, they are added to an object via the modifier stack and not traditional space warp binding. However, they show up in the modifier stack above all modifiers as a space warp binding. The following list provides brief descriptions of the World Space modifiers included in 3D Studio MAX R3:

- **Camera Map.** Applies mapping coordinates to the bound object based on a specified target camera. When the same map is applied as a Screen Environment map, the camera-mapped object "disappears" into the image and becomes invisible. The difference between the Camera Map WSM and the Camera Map modifier is that the WSM uses World coordinates. This allows you to move the camera and not reveal the object, whereas the normal modifier version reveals the object if it moves or the camera moves.

- **Displace Mesh.** Allows you to view geometric displacement on an object that has a displaced material applied. Without this WSM, the material-based displacement is applied at render time and is viewable in that fashion only. New to 3D Studio MAX R3, this WSM only works correctly with Editable Mesh objects and objects to which a Disp Approx modifier has been applied. This is not a modifier that you'd often keep in an object's modifier stack. It should be used temporarily to view an object's displacement in the viewports (see Figure 12.12).

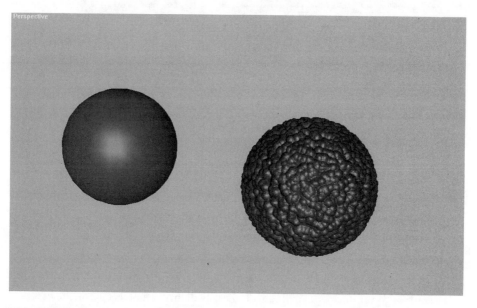

Figure 12.12 Two spheres with identical displacement materials assigned. The sphere on the right uses a Displace Mesh WSM to show the result of the displacement at the material level.

- **Displace NURBS.** Originated in MAX R2.5 as the NURBS Mesher modifier, this is similar to the Displace Mesh WSM, allowing you to view a NURBS object's displacement in the viewports. To do this properly, the Displace Mesh WSM converts the NURBS surfaces into a single mesh object.

- **MapScaler.** Maintains the scale of a map regardless of how the object is scaled. This is most useful for scaling flat surfaces, such as walls, so the applied mapping is retained across the transformation (see Figure 12.13).

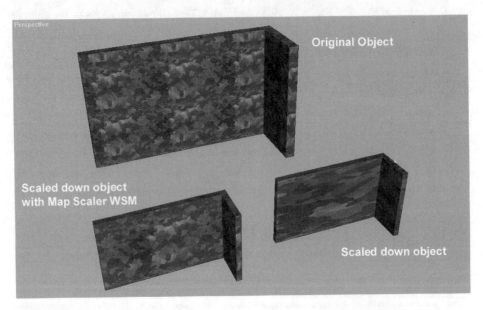

Figure 12.13   An object scaled down both with and without Map Scaler WSM. Notice how Map Scaler WSM maintains the original mapping coordinates, even after an object has been scaled.

- **PatchDeform.** Nearly identical to the PatchDeform modifier, this allows you to deform an object based on a specified patch object in the scene. The main difference is that the WSM version adds a Move to Patch function that causes the bound object to snap to the reference patch (see Figure 12.14).

- **PathDeform.** This is similar to the PathDeform modifier except that it doesn't deform an object relative to the specified object's location. Instead, it works off of World coordinates, allowing you to easily deform an object along the exact location of a spline in your scene. This tool is very useful for creating growing spline shapes, such as vines and tentacles, as well as for deforming objects, such as coaxial cables, along a path to form a spline shape (see Figure 12.15).

Figure 12.14   Three box objects all deformed to a patch surface via PatchDeform WSM.

Figure 12.15   Beveled text deformed along a spline path with PathDeform WSM.

- **SurfDeform.** Almost identical to PatchDeform, except that this uses a NURBS surface as a reference for the deformation.

- **SurfaceMapper.** Lets you create your own mapping coordinates based on a NURBS surface. You can use this unique tool, which is new to 3D Studio MAX R3, to apply mapping to several objects based on the normals of a single NURBS surface.

Using Wave and Conform to Animate a Magic Carpet

The best way to understand object deformation space warps is to try them. In this first exercise, you will animate a magic carpet moving above a landscape object's surface. You will use the Conform space warp to deform the carpet relative to the landscape below and the Wave space warp to create a secondary wavy motion.

1. Start by loading the magic-carpet.max file from the CD-ROM. You should have a patch grid landscape and a plane primitive for the magic carpet. Conform applies its force to vertices, so it works best with the vertices of mesh objects and not the control points of patch objects.

2. Create a Conform space warp in either the Top view or the Perspective view by click-dragging. It's important to choose the correct viewport when creating a Conform space warp because Conform is directional and derives its vector from the z-axis of the viewport you create it in. So if you were to create it from one of the side viewports, the Conform arrow would point sideways instead of projecting downward like you want it to (see Figure 12.16).

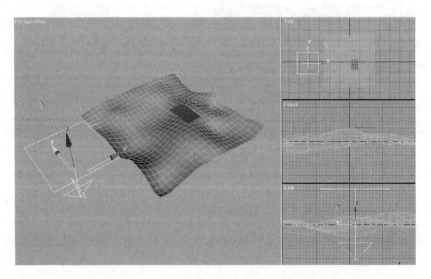

Figure 12.16   Create the Conform space warp in the Top viewport so it projects downward through the z-axis.

3. In the Conform parameters, choose the landscape for Wrap to Object (see Figure 12.17).

4. The next set of Conform parameters control the force on the vertices. Set the Standoff Distance to 10. Next, bind the carpet to the Conform space warp. Notice how the carpet snaps to the shape of the surface directly beneath it. Select the carpet and move it around your scene. Notice that it retains this conformity. Conform causes the carpet's vertices to be projected downward to the landscape object and then to be backed off to a standoff distance of 15. As you see, you can't move the carpet upward or downward; only the pivot point moves. To animate the carpet in either direction, you have to animate the Standoff Distance Value.

5. Move the carpet off the edge of the landscape. Notice how it deforms uniformly when the landscape is not directly under it. This uniform deformation is controlled with the other Conform value, Default Projection Distance (see Figure 12.18).

Figure 12.17
Default Conform parameters.

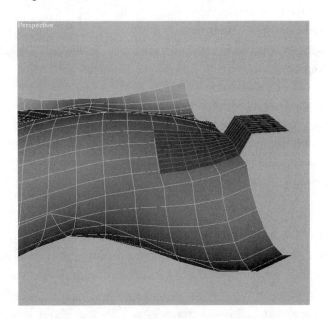

Figure 12.18   The Projection Distance parameter controls how the object deforms when it's not directly over the Wrap To object.

6. Go ahead and create some animation for the carpet. For example, try animating it from one corner of the landscape to the other. The carpet mesh should automatically deform properly. Turn off the Animate button when you're finished.

7. To add some wavy motion to the carpet, start by creating a Wave space warp in the Top or Perspective viewport. This is a two-stage click-drag creation process. When you click-drag, you are defining the center of the Wave space warp, as well as the size. Don't make it too small, but also don't make it dwarf the landscape. Now when you release the mouse button, you need to perform a second drag operation. This determines the initial amplitude of the waveform. It doesn't matter what you set here because you're going to change it in the next step.

8. Bind the carpet to the Wave space warp. The carpet should immediately start deforming again. Set both the amplitudes on the Wave to 5. A Wavelength of 77 creates enough space between the wave peaks and troughs. Now go to the last frame, turn on the Animate button, and animate the Phase to 5. If you play the animation now, you'll see the waveform animating along.

Figure 12.19
Wave space warp binding's Flexibility parameter.

If you look at the carpet object's modifier stack, you'll see the Conform Binding and the Wave Binding. Something special that the wave binding has is a flexibility value (see Figure 12.19) that allows you to apply a multiplier to the Wave's amplitude from within the carpet's stack. This is a very useful feature when you want one Wave to affect several objects with differing amounts of amplitude.

Using FFD to Squish a Teapot Through a Hole

Whether you're trying to thread a camel through the eye of a needle or push a ship into a bottle, the FFD space warp is great for pushing objects through small spaces. You can localize an FFD space warp to a location in space, such as a hole, so the space warp will not be carried along with an object. In the next exercise, you will use an FFD space warp to deform and squish a teapot through a tiny hole in a wall.

1. Load the squishing-teapot.max file. It shows a wall object with a hole cut in it and a teapot on one side. Notice that when you view through a Shaded viewport, the wall is translucent. This is a useful property called See-Thru that allows you to see the teapot deformation on both sides of the wall.

2. In the Front viewport, zoom into the area near the hole in the wall. Create an FFD Cylinder space warp centered around the hole (see Figure 12.20). Set the Radius to 30 and the Height to 63. This should make it quite a bit larger than the hole, but not much larger than the teapot. Set the number of points to Side 6, Radial 2, and Height 6 so that you have a little extra on the height of the space warp.

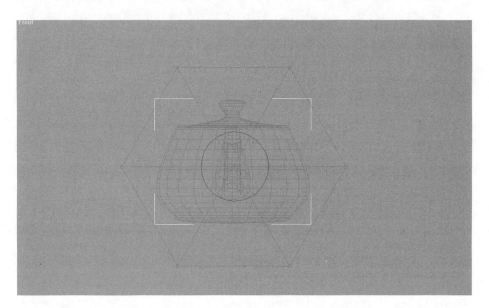

Figure 12.20   An FFD Cylinder space warp centered around the hole in the wall.

3. Move the space warp so that it's centered on the hole. You should have three sets of control points on either side of the wall. Bind the teapot to the FFD space warp. Then play the animation to see that the teapot passes right through the wall and space warp without any affect.

4. Next, squish the teapot by scaling some control points. You can select control points either by using the Sub-Object button in the FFD rollout or by right-clicking and choosing Control Points (Alt+Shift+C). Select the two innermost sets of control points. They should turn yellow to show they are selected.

5. The next step is a non-uniform scale along the x- and y-axes in the Front view-port. You don't want to scale the control points along the z-axis because you don't want to warp the teapot in its direction of travel, only perpendicularly. Scale the selected control points inward so they are just a tiny bit smaller than the diameter of the hole. You may find it difficult to scale along multiple axes with the manipulator gizmo. MAX R3 now has those L-shaped objects to the edges of the manipulator (see Figure 12.21). These dual axis constraints allow you to lock the transformation to two axes at once.

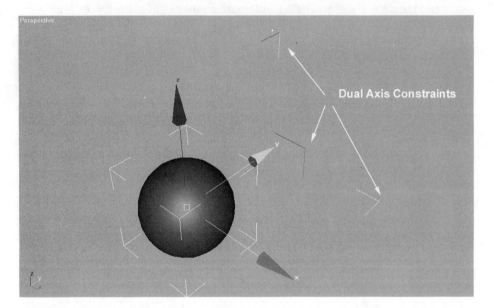

Figure 12.21   Manipulator dual axis constraints.

6. If you look from the Top viewport, the FFD space warp should have an hour-glass appearance, with the innermost control points scaled in. Select the next set of control points that lay between the innermost and outermost control points. Scale these similarly to the previous set, but only go half the distance (see Figure 12.22). In the Front viewport this should be about the diameter of the teapot.

Now play the animation. Notice that as the teapot reaches the extents of the FFD, it starts to deform inward on itself until it squishes down to fit through the hole. Finally, it expands to its full size as it exits the space warp (see Figure 12.23).

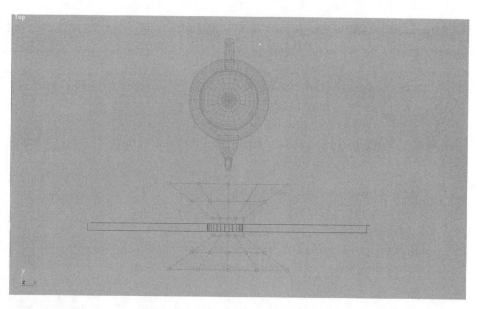

Figure 12.22   Top view of FFD space warp shows that the control points are scaled inward properly.

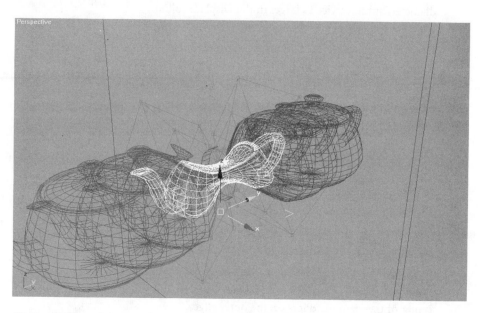

Figure 12.23   The teapot now squishes through the hole with the help of the deformation from the FFD space warp.

Using Displace to Create a Large Bedbug

In this exercise, you'll link a Displace space warp to an object to deform a bed cover as "something" moves below it. This is a technique that is much faster than actually using a type of collision detection. Think of it as a force field for geometry instead of particles. When the bound object comes into the area of influence of the force field, its vertices are pushed outward or in the direction of the field.

1. Load the bedbug.max file. This has a large plane primitive and an animated sphere that moves around under it. If you play the animation, you'll notice that the sphere pokes through the surface of the plane. You want to use a Displace space warp to deform the plane where the sphere is under it.

2. In the Top viewport, create a Displace space warp directly over the sphere. Make sure it's larger than the sphere's diameter, but not twice as large. In the Displace rollout, you'll notice parameters similar to the UVW Mapping modifier (see Figure 12.24). This is because Displace gets its force direction from mapping coordinates projected by the Displace gizmo. In this case, you want to displace the plane in one direction, so make sure the Map gizmo is set to Planar.

3. With the Displace space warp created, bind it to the plane object.

   In the Image group, you'll notice slots for Bitmap and Map. You could make a map for displacement in a paint program, such as Paint or Adobe PhotoShop, but why not just use a map from the Materials Editor instead? All you need to do is create a radial black-and-white gradient so the space warp displaces the plane's vertices strongest at the center of the gizmo and less on the outer edges.

4. To do this, click the slot next to Map on the Displace rollout. Choose a Gradient map in the Materials/Map Browser

Figure 12.24
Displace space warp parameters.

dialog box. You can't adjust any of the Gradient's parameters from within the Modifier panel, so drag this new map into a sample slot in the Materials Editor. Choose Instance from the popup dialog box so any changes you make to the Gradient in the Materials Editor will immediately be applied to the displacement.

5. The default Gradient settings are almost perfect for what you need to do, just change the Gradient Type from Linear to Radial.

6. Before you go further, you must link the Displace space warp to the Sphere. Then when the sphere moves along its path, the Displace space warp will follow. Do this by selecting the space warp and choosing the Sphere as the parent.

7. Play the animation, and you'll see that nothing has happened. You need to define the strength of the displacement. In the Displace rollout, set Strength to 10. Try the animation again and notice how the plane's vertices near the Sphere get displaced upward. You can control the amount of displacement by changing the Strength setting (see Figure 12.25).

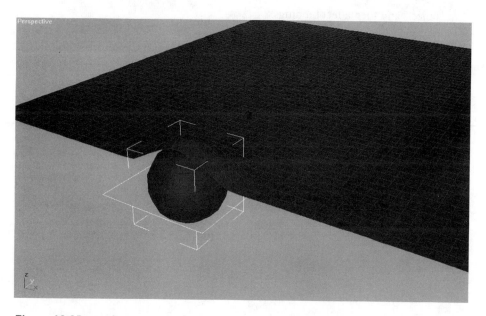

Figure 12.25   With a Displace space warp linked to the animated sphere, it appears as though the sphere is deforming the plane.

In Practice: Deforming Objects with Space Warps

- **The effects of Space Warps are global to bound objects.** For example, if a Ripple space warp is bound to several objects, it affects them equally regardless of the location of the Space Warp icon. The only way to localize the effect is to use the Decay value. Any Decay value above 0 will start to attenuate the effects of the space warp on objects.

- **The Ripple and Wave space warps add a special Flexibility value each time they are bound to an object.** This appears in the modifier stack with the space warp and allows you to adjust its influence on objects individually. With this powerful feature, you can slowly ramp up or down the effect without changing any of the space warp's parameters. This also lets you moderate the influence of one space warp on several objects.

- **Space Warp bindings always appear at the top of the modifier stack.** The modifier stack's operations on an object are completely linear; modifiers first affect objects and then affect bindings.

- **Space Warps don't have the same overhead as soft-body dynamics simulations.** They don't do any kind of collision detection, but rather they work off fields or approximations. As a result, space warps are much faster at deforming objects. This is something to remember when you need one colliding object to deform another. With clever use of space warps, you can get fast collision-based deformations.

Recommended Readings

Cyclopedia Anatomicae: More Than 1,500 Illustrations of the Human and Animal Figure for the Artist
by Gyorgy Feher, Andras Szunyoghy (Illustrator), Andras Szuriyoghy (Illustrator)
Hardcover (November 1996) Black Dog & Leventhal Pub; ISBN: 1884822878;
Dimensions (in inches): 1.76 × 12.67 × 10.82
`http://www.amazon.com/exec/obidos/ASIN/1884822878/qid%3D943998540/`
`102-7492836-1302406`

The Artist's Complete Guide to Facial Expression
by Gary Faigin
Hardcover—1 page (November 1990) Watson-Guptill Pubns; ISBN: 0823016285;
Dimensions (in inches): 1.11 × 11.31 × 8.67
`http://www.amazon.com/exec/obidos/ASIN/0823016285/qid%3D943998612/`
`102-7492836-1302406`

Cartooning the Head and Figure
by Jack Hamm
Reading level: Young Adult Paperback Reissue edition (June 1982) Perigee; ISBN:
0399508031; Dimensions (in inches): 0.56 × 10.73 × 8.32
`http://www.amazon.com/exec/obidos/ASIN/0399508031/qid=943998672/sr=1-1/`
`102-7492836-1302406`

Anatomy Coloring Book
by Wynn Kapit, Lawrence M. Elson (Contributor)
Paperback—161 pages, 2nd edition (July 1993) Addison-Wesley Pub Co; ISBN:
0064550168; Dimensions (in inches): 1.12 × 8.74 × 11.10
`http://www.amazon.com/exec/obidos/ASIN/0064550168/qid=943998769/sr=1-1/`
`102-7492836-1302406`

The Animation Foundation Web site
Page on ARM SWINGS—THE FIGURE EIGHT
`http://www.animfound.com/tips/figure8.html`

Index

Colophon

MAX Professional Animation was layed out and produced with the help of Microsoft Word, Adobe Acrobat, Adobe Photoshop, Collage Complete, and QuarkXPress on a variety of systems, including a Macintosh G3. With the exception of the pages that were printed out for proofreading, all files—both text and images—were transferred via email or ftp and editied on-screen.

All the body text was set in the Minion family. All headings, figure captions, and cover text were set in the Gill Sans family. The Seans Symbols and Zapf Dingbat typfaces were used throughout for special symbols and bullets.

MAX Professional Animation was printed on 50# Husky Offset Smooth at RR Donnelley & Sons in Crawfordsville, Indiana. Prepress consisted of PostrScript computer-to-plate technology (filmless-process). The cover was printed on 12pt C1S with coatings of Matte layflat film with spot gloss UV.

New Riders Professional Library

Internet Explorer 5
by Microsoft

Internet Explorer 5 delivers the most rewarding Web experience ever by bringing you the best browser, complete communication and collaboration, True Web Integration, and webcasting including Active Channels™. Find what you want quickly with Explorer Bars. View the coolest, most entertaining Active Channels, and surf safely, thanks to Internet Explorer's Security Zones. Browse the Web and your PC with a Single Explorer.

To order, visit the Web site at http://www.microsoft.com.

To install Internet Explorer 5, go to the 3rdParty\Microsoft\ folder.

3.   Chapter Project Files

On this CD, you will find project files, provided by the authors, for every chapter of the book. You can install these to your system from the CD-ROM interface. To install the Example files, just click the SOURCE.EXE. If you are not using the CD-ROM interface, you can find the Examples in the \EXAMPLES folder.

Please note that the MOV files may require special versions of QuickTime and specific compressors. Versions of QuickTime and compressors are shipped with 3D Studio Max 3, so you shouldn't have any problems if you have it installed. If you do not have 3D Studio Max 3, you may not be able to view those files.

4.   User Services Information

Sometimes you will need help. We are here for you; however, our help can only assist with information about the book, help with the CD-ROM, things that may be missing, and so on. We, unfortunately, are not authorized to assist with computer malfunction, system errors, or third-party applications.

If you need help or are unsure where to go for help, you can contact us through our website. You should get a response within 24 to 48 hours. Go to www.mcp.com/support to submit an email. You will need to provide the following information:

- Full Title of the Book (*3D Studio MAX 3 Professional Animation*)
- ISBN of the Book (0735709459)
- Your Name
- Your Email Address
- Your Problem or Question
- System Information

Sometimes we will have already resolved problems, such as file updates or errata. You can find this information and more at www.mcp.com/info.

You can also call 1-317-581-3833, from 10:00 a.m. to 3 p.m. US EST.

What You'll Find on the MAX 3 Professional Animation CD
(continued)

If you have AutoPlay turned on, your computer will automatically run the CD-ROM interface. If AutoPlay is off, please follow these instructions:

1. Insert the CD-ROM in your CD-ROM Drive.
2. From the Windows Desktop, double-click the My Computer icon.
3. Double-click the icon representing your CD-ROM drive.
4. Double-click the icon titled START or START.EXE to begin.

3.   Third-Party Evaluation Software

We have compiled programs that we think will help you get going. If you are not using the CD-ROM interface you can find these products in the \3RDPARTY folder.

Although we have tried our best to provide the most recent versions, newer ones may have been released between the time this book was released and the date you purchased it. Please check with each manufacturer to insure that your products are up to date.

You will find three programs—The Ultimate MAX/VIS Internet Guide, Communicator 4.7, and Internet Explorer 5—on this CD-ROM.

The Ultimate MAX/VIZ Internet Guide
by Applied IDEAS, Inc

This CD contains a full version of The Ultimate MAX/VIZ Internet Guide. The first and only, complete database of Internet sites for MAX/VIZ users! Wondering where all the cool sites are? Where to download free stuff? Where to buy everything from books to plug-ins to hardware? Perhaps you need a job! Instead of scouring the web for days or weeks, just query the Ultimate Internet Guide by topic with a click of a button. It's all here at your fingertips, fast and simple!

To order, visit the Web site at http://www.applied-ideas.com.

To install The Ultimate MAX/VIZ Internet Guide go to the 3rdParty\AppliedIDEAS\ folder.

Communicator 4.7
by Netscape

The latest and greatest! Just as the web is constantly evolving, so too is Netscape Communicator. To meet the needs of its customers,
Netscape Communicator provides next-generation browsing, email, calendar, and information management features.

To order, visit the Web site at http://www.netscape.com.

To install Communicator 4.7, go to the 3rdParty\Netscape\ folder.

What You'll Find on the MAX 3 Professional Animation CD

CD-ROM CONTENTS

1. Licensing Agreement
2. Browsing the CD-ROM via the CD-ROM Interface
3. Third-Party Evaluation Software
4. Chapter Project Files
5. User Services Information

I.   Licensing Agreement

By opening the CD package, you are agreeing to be bound by the following agreement:

All of the software included with this product is copyrighted, in which case all rights are reserved by the respective copyright holder. You are licensed to use software copyrighted by the publisher and its licensors on a single computer. You may copy and/or modify the software as needed to facilitate your use of it on a single computer. Making copies of the software for any other purpose is a violation of the United States copyright laws. COPYRIGHT© 2000, New Riders Publishing.

This software is sold as is, without warranty of any kind, either express or implied, including but not limited to the implied warranties of merchantability and fitness for a particular purpose. Neither the publisher nor its dealers or distributors assumes any liability for any alleged or actual damages arising from the use of this program. (Some states do not allow for the exclusion of implied warranties, so the exclusion might not apply to you.)

This CD-ROM includes documents in an electronic format. These documents are licensed to you for your individual use on one csomputer. You may make a single second copy of this electronic version for use by you on a second computer for which you are the primary user (e.g. a laptop). You may not copy this to any network, intranet, the Internet, or any other form of distribution for use by anyone other than yourself. Any other use of this electronic version is a violation of U.S. and international copyright laws. If you would like to purchase a site license to use this material with more than one user, please contact New Riders at license@mcp.com.

2.   Browsing the CD-ROM via the CD-ROM Interface

Following are the system requirements for this New Riders Publishing CD-ROM:

Processor:	486DX or higher
OS:	Microsoft Windows 95/98/NT
Memory (RAM):	24 MB
Monitor:	VGA, 640x480 or higher with 256 color or higher
Storage Space:	10 MB Minimum (will vary, depending on the type of installation)
Other:	Mouse or compatible pointing device
Optional:	Internet connection and web browser. For your convenience, you will find some web browsers on this disk. See "3. Third-Party Evaluation Software" for more information.